尾田栄一郎

When I was a kid I raised a rhinoceros beetle. But I fiddled with the beetle's horn too much while it was growing, and it ended up twisted at a strange angle. They say to strike while the iron is hot, but I feel like I did a bad thing there. I wonder if the rhinoceros beetle would have grown into a bazooka beetle if I'd attached a bazooka to its back while it was a pupa. Maybe if I had equipped it with armor and a katana, I could have gotten a fully armed rhinoceros beetle. Except that's sort of unethical—I guess the rhinoceros beetle is best the way it is! Now let's get started on volume 63!

–Eiichiro Oda, 2011

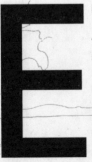iichiro Oda began his manga career at the age of 17, when his one-shot cowboy manga **Wanted!** won second place in the coveted Tezuka manga awards. Oda went on to work as an assistant to some of the biggest manga artists in the industry, including Nobuhiro Watsuki, before winning the Hop Step Award for new artists. His pirate adventure **One Piece**, which debuted in **Weekly Shonen Jump** in 1997, quickly became one of the most popular manga in Japan.

ONE PIECE VOL. 63
NEW WORLD PART 3

SHONEN JUMP Manga Edition

STORY AND ART BY EIICHIRO ODA

English Adaptation/Lance Caselman
Translation/Laabaman, HC Language Solutions, Inc.
Touch-up Art & Lettering/Vanessa Satone
Design/Fawn Lau
Editor/Alexis Kirsch

Published by VIZ Media, LLC
P.O. Box 77010
San Francisco, CA 94107

11
First printing, July 2012
Eleventh printing, March 2022

viz.com

SHONEN JUMP MANGA

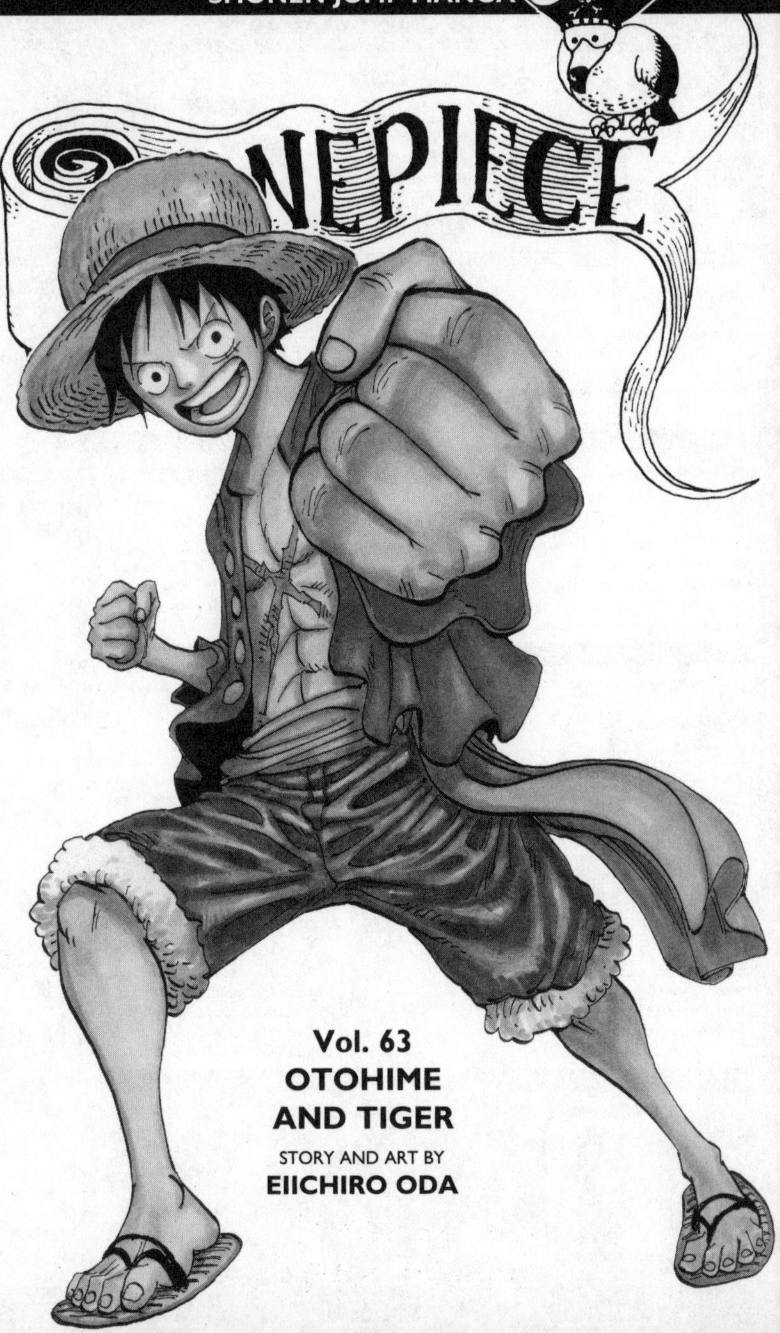

Vol. 63

OTOHIME AND TIGER

STORY AND ART BY

EIICHIRO ODA

The Straw Hat Crew

Monkey D. Luffy

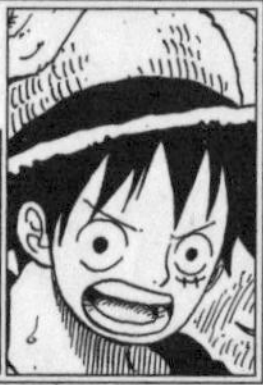

A young man who dreams of becoming the Pirate King. After training with Rayleigh, he and his crew head for the New World!

Captain, Bounty: 400 million berries

Roronoa Zolo

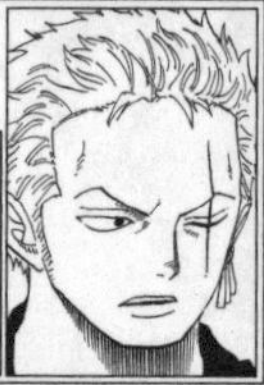

He swallowed his pride and asked to be trained by Mihawk on Gloom Island before reuniting with the rest of the crew.

Fighter, Bounty: 120 million berries

Tony Tony Chopper

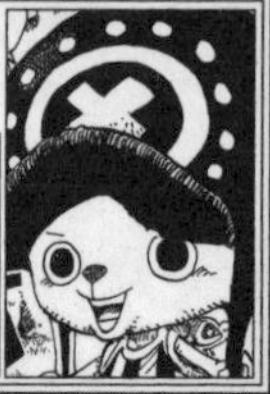

After researching powerful medicine in Birdie Kingdom, he reunites with the rest of the crew.

Ship's Doctor, Bounty: 50 berries

Nami

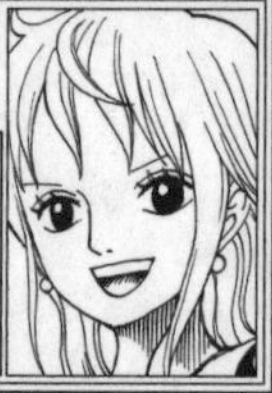

She studied the weather of the New World on the small Sky Island Weatheria, a place where weather is studied as a science.

Navigator, Bounty: 16 million berries

Nico Robin

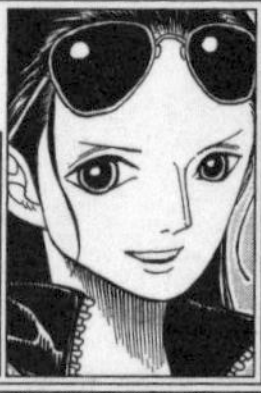

She spent her time in Baltigo with the leader of the Revolutionary Army: Luffy's father, Dragon.

Archeologist, Bounty: 80 million berries

Usopp

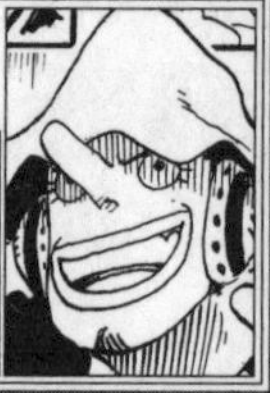

He trained under Heracles at the Bowin Islands to become the King of Snipers.

Sniper, Bounty: 30 million berries

Franky

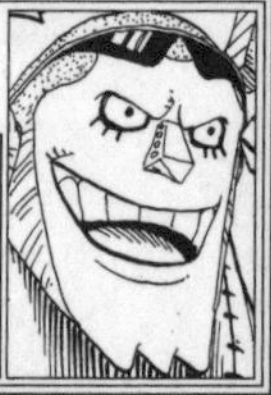

He modified himself in Future Land Baldimore and turned himself into Armored Franky before reuniting with the rest of the crew.

Shipwright, Bounty: 44 million berries

Sanji

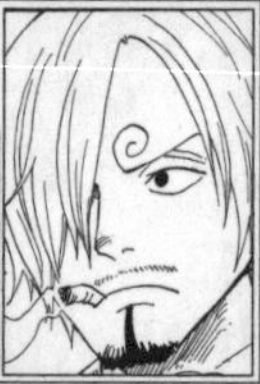

After fighting the New Kama Karate masters in the Kamabakka Kingdom, he returned to the crew.

Cook, Bounty: 77 million berries

Brook

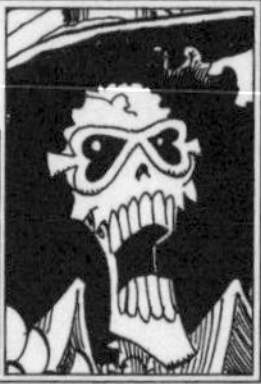

After being captured and used as a freak show by the Longarm Tribe, he became a famous rock star called "Soul King" Brook.

Musician, Bounty: 33 million berries

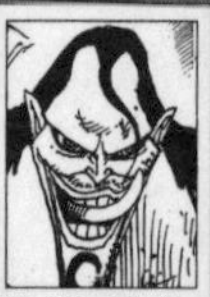

Wet-Haired Caribou

Captain of the Caribou Pirates

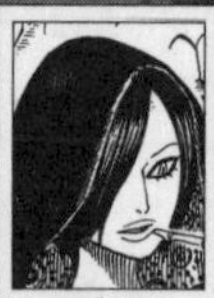

Madame Sharley

Owner of the Mermaid Café

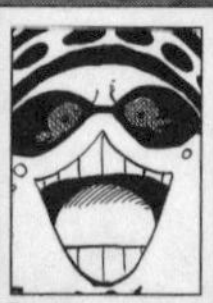

Pappagu

The Designer/President of the Criminal brand

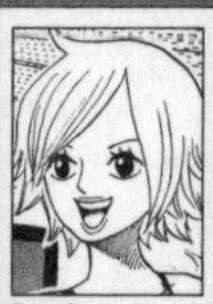

Camie

Works at the Mermaid Café

The story of ONE PIECE 1»63

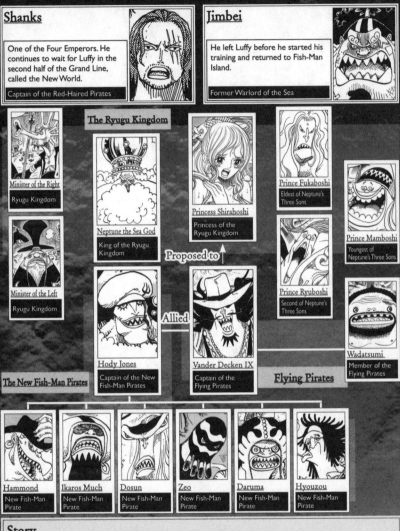

Shanks

One of the Four Emperors. He continues to wait for Luffy in the second half of the Grand Line, called the New World.

Captain of the Red-Haired Pirates

Jimbei

He left Luffy before he started his training and returned to Fish-Man Island.

Former Warlord of the Sea

The Ryugu Kingdom

Minister of the Right

Ryugu Kingdom

Minister of the Left

Ryugu Kingdom

Neptune the Sea God

King of the Ryugu Kingdom

Princess Shirahoshi

Princess of the Ryugu Kingdom

Prince Fukaboshi

Eldest of Neptune's Three Sons

Prince Ryuboshi

Second of Neptune's Three Sons

Prince Mamboshi

Youngest of Neptune's Three Sons

Proposed to

Allied

The New Fish-Man Pirates

Hody Jones

Captain of the New Fish-Man Pirates

Flying Pirates

Vander Decken IX

Captain of the Flying Pirates

Wadatsumi

Member of the Flying Pirates

Hammond

New Fish-Man Pirate

Ikaros Much

New Fish-Man Pirate

Dosun

New Fish-Man Pirate

Zeo

New Fish-Man Pirate

Daruma

New Fish-Man Pirate

Hyouzou

New Fish-Man Pirate

Story

Having finished their two years of training, the Straw Hat crew reunites on the Sabaody Archipelago. They set sail more determined than ever to reach The New World!

The Straw Hats finally reach Fish-Man Island, said to be 30,000 thousand feet below the sea. But with the New Fish-Man Pirates attacking, it seems like they may be in for a rough time! While they search the island, Neptune appears and invites them to Ryugu Palace to thank them for rescuing a shark. Inside the palace, Luffy meets the mermaid princess, Shirahoshi. But because of Vander Decken, Shirahoshi is unable to leave her room. In order to help grant her wish to leave the palace, Luffy takes her outside for the first time in years...

Vol. 63
Otohime and Tiger

CONTENTS

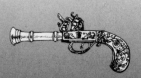

Chapter 615:
MARK-MARK CURSE

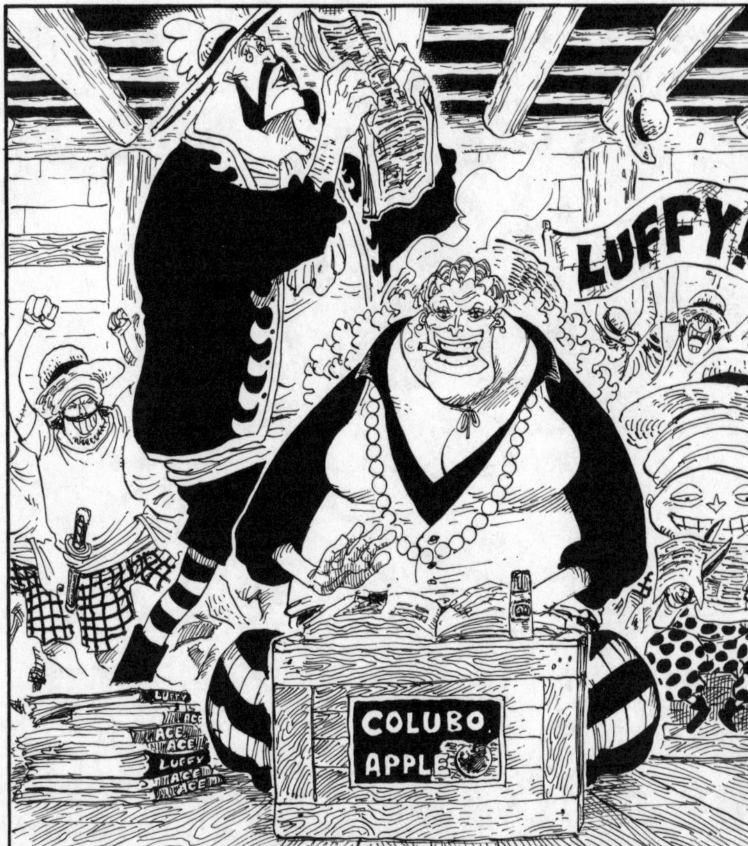
LUFFY!!
LUFFY
ACE
ACE
ACE
LUFFY
ACE
ACE
COLUBO
APPLE

DECKS OF THE WORLD, VOL. 3: "MT. CORVO"

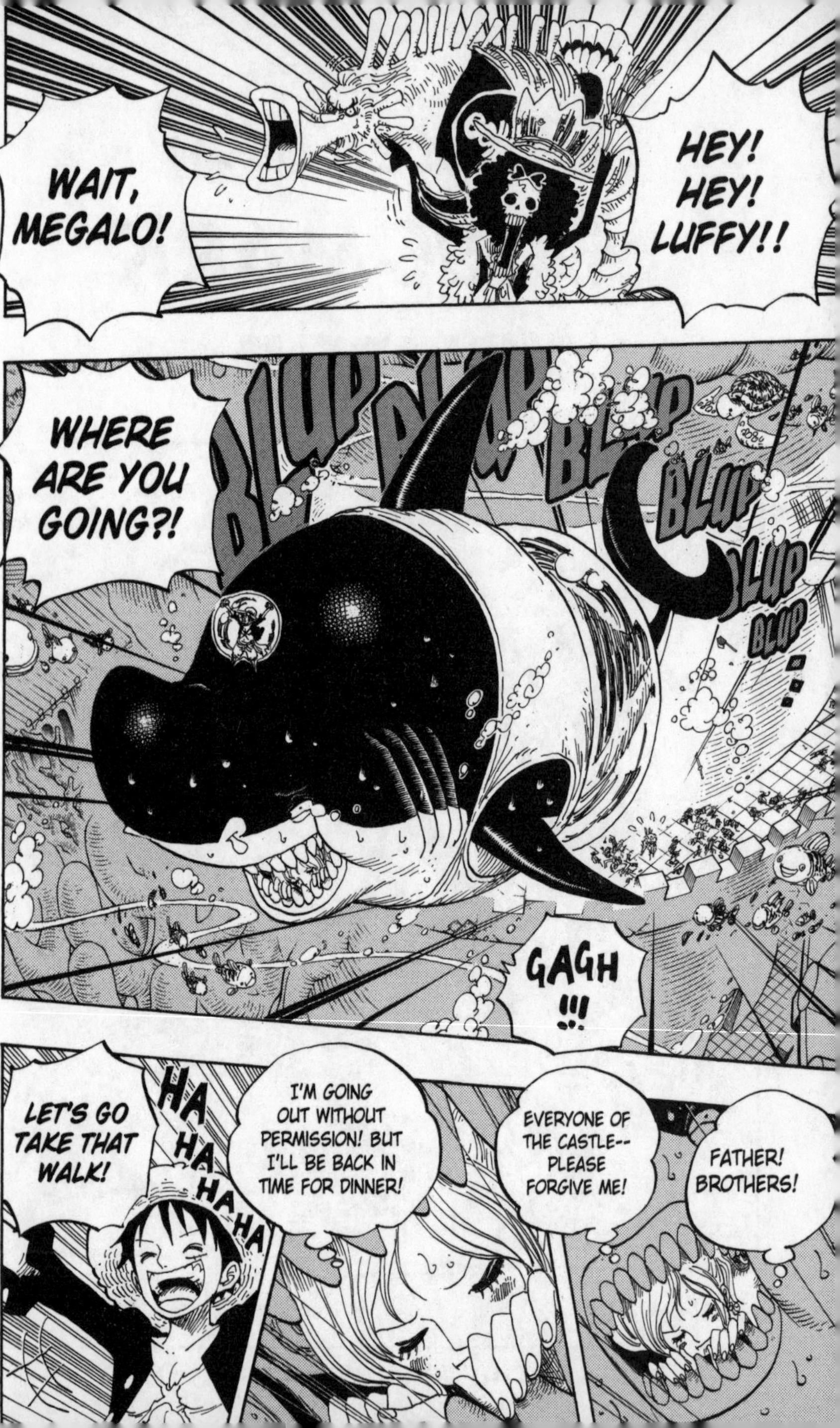
HEY! HEY! LUFFY!!
WAIT, MEGALO!
BLUP BLUP BLUP
BLUP
BLUP
BLUP
BLUP
WHERE ARE YOU GOING?!
GAGH !!!
FATHER! BROTHERS!
EVERYONE OF THE CASTLE-- PLEASE FORGIVE ME!
I'M GOING OUT WITHOUT PERMISSION! BUT I'LL BE BACK IN TIME FOR DINNER!
HA HA HA HA
LET'S GO TAKE THAT WALK!

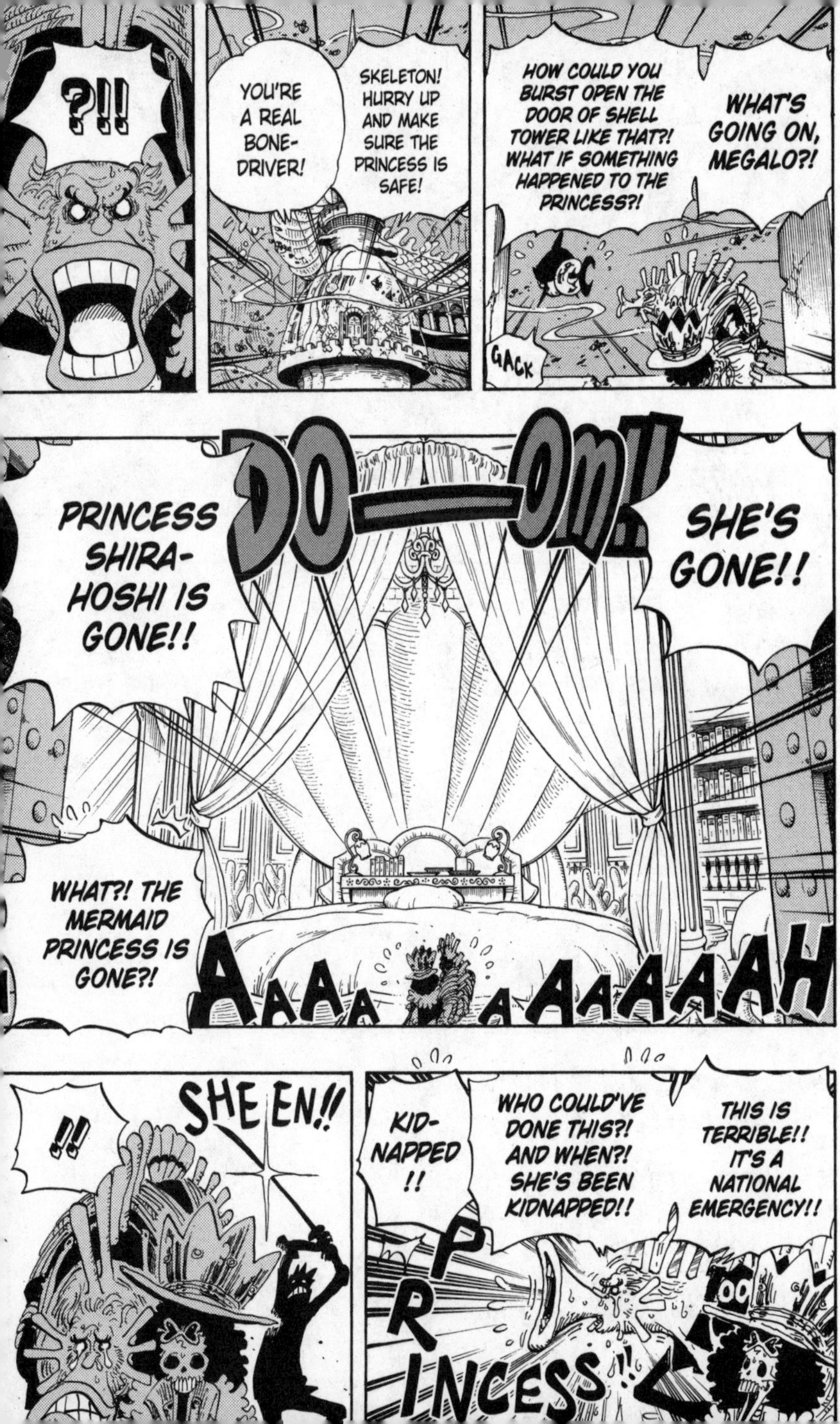
WHAT'S GOING ON, MEGALO?!
HOW COULD YOU BURST OPEN THE DOOR OF SHELL TOWER LIKE THAT?! WHAT IF SOMETHING HAPPENED TO THE PRINCESS?!
GACK
SKELETON! HURRY UP AND MAKE SURE THE PRINCESS IS SAFE!
YOU'RE A REAL BONE-DRIVER!
?!!
SHE'S GONE!!
DO—OM!!
PRINCESS SHIRA-HOSHI IS GONE!!
AAAAAAAAAAH
WHAT?! THE MERMAID PRINCESS IS GONE?!
THIS IS TERRIBLE!! IT'S A NATIONAL EMERGENCY!!
WHO COULD'VE DONE THIS?! AND WHEN?! SHE'S BEEN KIDNAPPED!!
KID-NAPPED!!
PRINCESS!!
SHE EN!!
!!

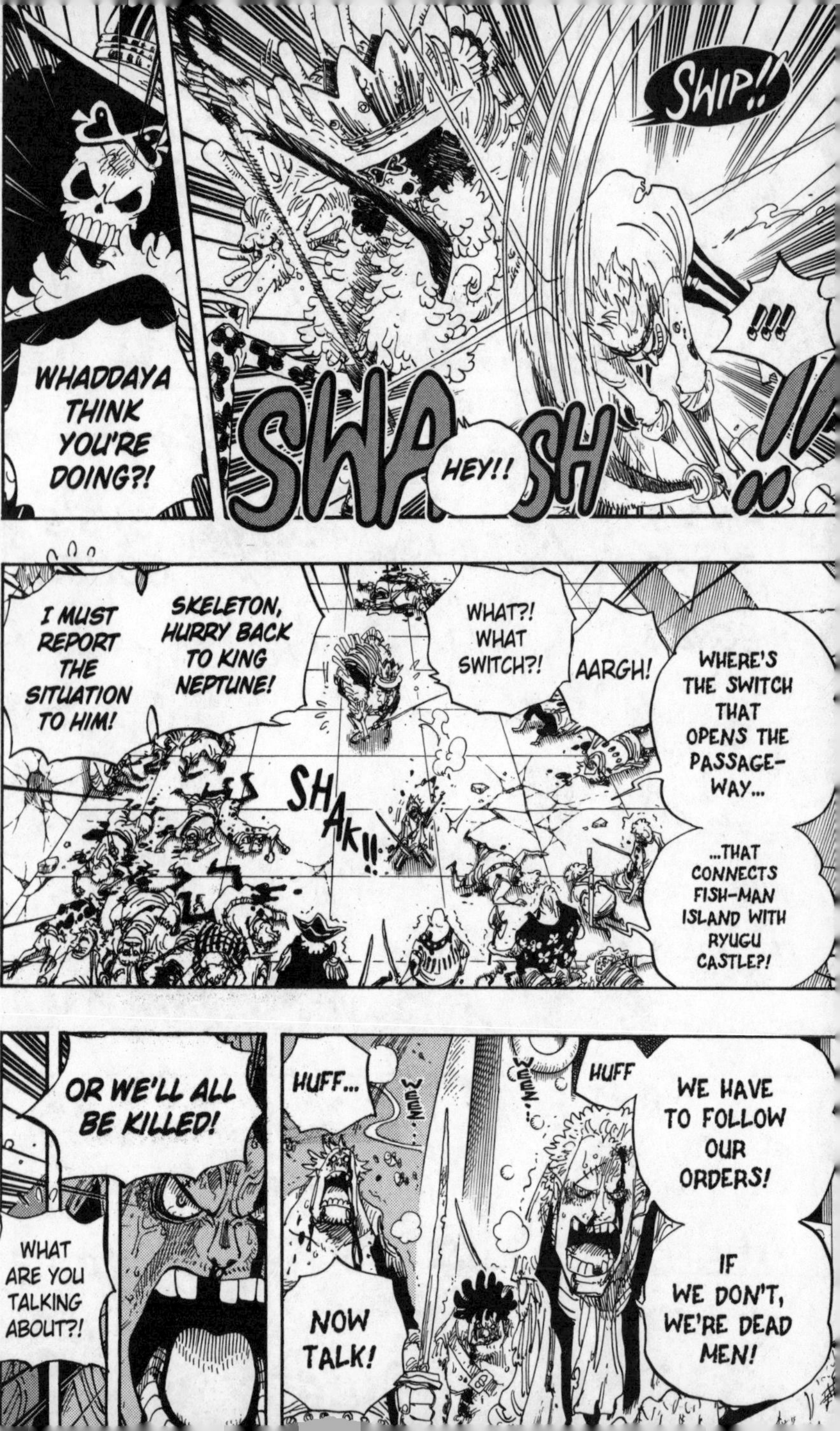
SWIP!!
!!!
SWA SH
HEY!!
WHADDAYA THINK YOU'RE DOING?!
WHERE'S THE SWITCH THAT OPENS THE PASSAGE-WAY...
...THAT CONNECTS FISH-MAN ISLAND WITH RYUGU CASTLE?!
AARGH!
WHAT?! WHAT SWITCH?!
SHAK!!
SKELETON, HURRY BACK TO KING NEPTUNE!
I MUST REPORT THE SITUATION TO HIM!
WE HAVE TO FOLLOW OUR ORDERS!
HUFF
HUFF...
IF WE DON'T, WE'RE DEAD MEN!
NOW TALK!
OR WE'LL ALL BE KILLED!
WHAT ARE YOU TALKING ABOUT?!

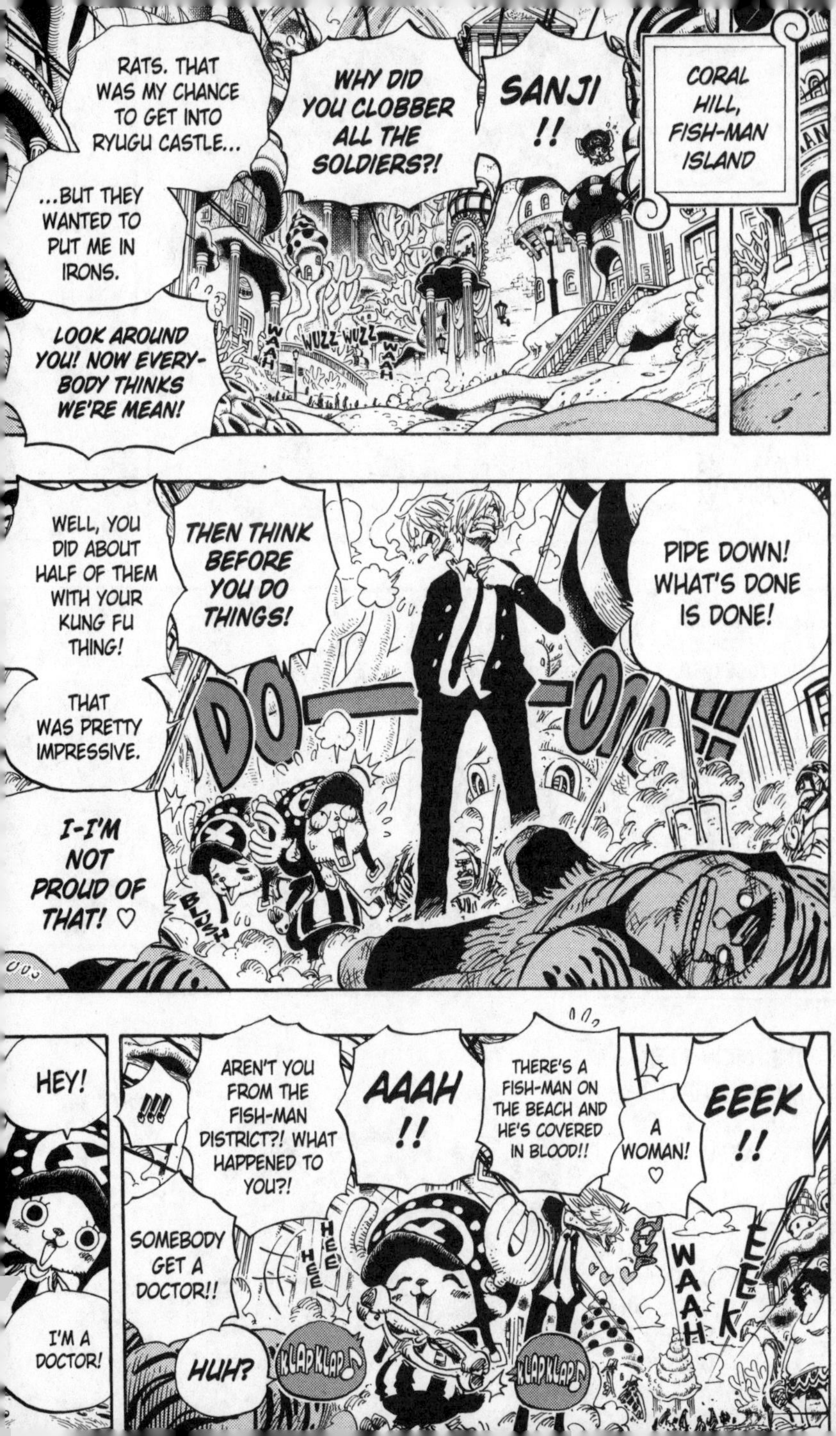
CORAL HILL, FISH-MAN ISLAND
SANJI!!
WHY DID YOU CLOBBER ALL THE SOLDIERS?!
RATS. THAT WAS MY CHANCE TO GET INTO RYUGU CASTLE...
...BUT THEY WANTED TO PUT ME IN IRONS.
LOOK AROUND YOU! NOW EVERYBODY THINKS WE'RE MEAN!
WAAH
WUZZ WUZZ
WAAH
PIPE DOWN! WHAT'S DONE IS DONE!
DO—OM
THEN THINK BEFORE YOU DO THINGS!
WELL, YOU DID ABOUT HALF OF THEM WITH YOUR KUNG FU THING!
THAT WAS PRETTY IMPRESSIVE.
I-I'M NOT PROUD OF THAT! ♡
BLUSH
EEEK!!
A WOMAN! ♡
EEEK
WAAH
THERE'S A FISH-MAN ON THE BEACH AND HE'S COVERED IN BLOOD!!
AAAH!!
AREN'T YOU FROM THE FISH-MAN DISTRICT?! WHAT HAPPENED TO YOU?!
!!!
SOMEBODY GET A DOCTOR!!
HEE HEE
KLAP KLAP
KLAP KLAP
HUH?
HEY!
I'M A DOCTOR!

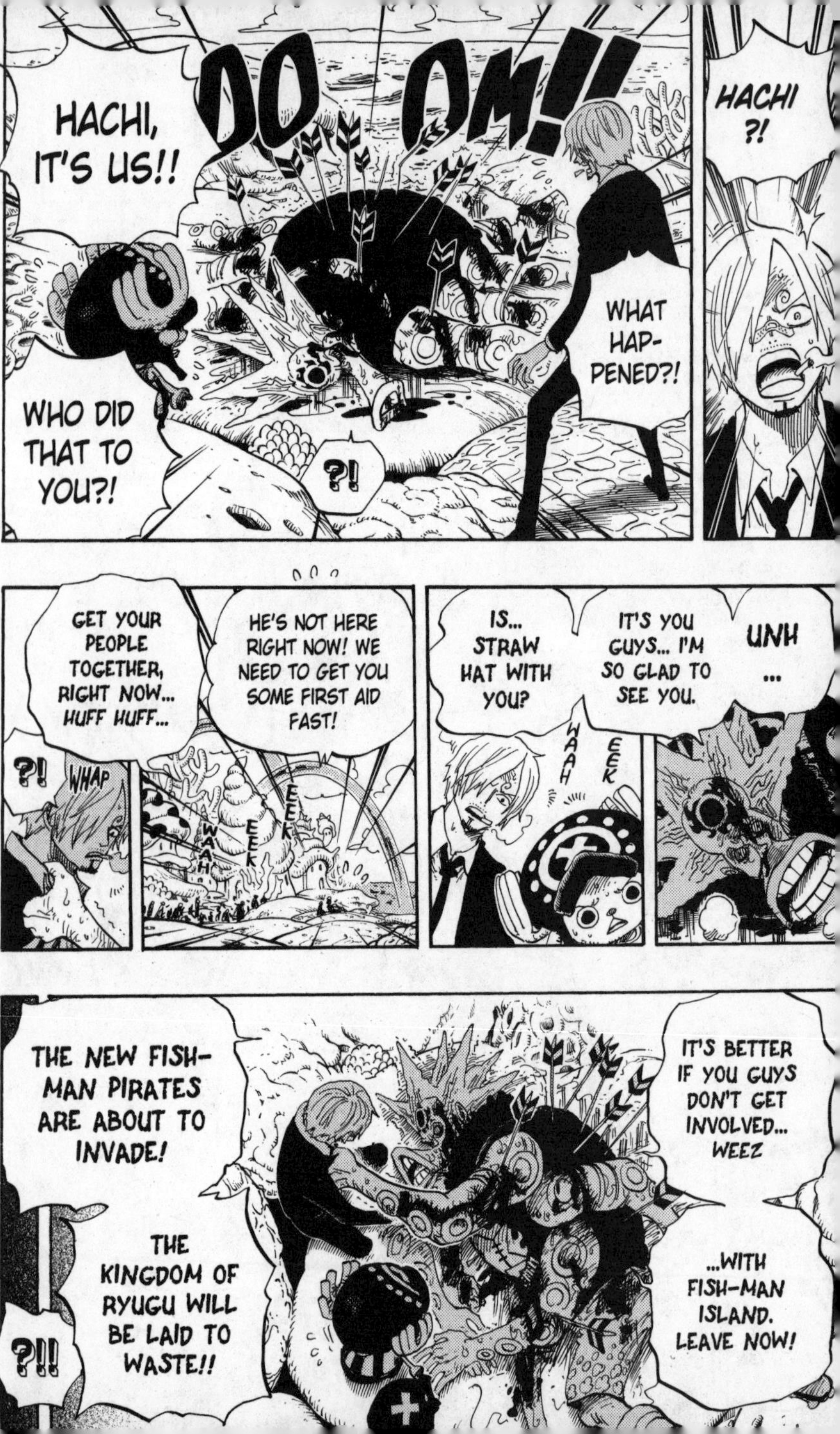
HACHI ?!
DO-OM!!
HACHI, IT'S US!!
WHAT HAP-PENED?!
WHO DID THAT TO YOU?!
?!
UNH ...
IT'S YOU GUYS... I'M SO GLAD TO SEE YOU.
IS... STRAW HAT WITH YOU?
EEK
WAAH
HE'S NOT HERE RIGHT NOW! WE NEED TO GET YOU SOME FIRST AID FAST!
EEK
EEK
WAAH
GET YOUR PEOPLE TOGETHER, RIGHT NOW... HUFF HUFF...
?!
WHAP
IT'S BETTER IF YOU GUYS DON'T GET INVOLVED... WEEZ
...WITH FISH-MAN ISLAND. LEAVE NOW!
THE NEW FISH-MAN PIRATES ARE ABOUT TO INVADE!
THE KINGDOM OF RYUGU WILL BE LAID TO WASTE!!
?!!

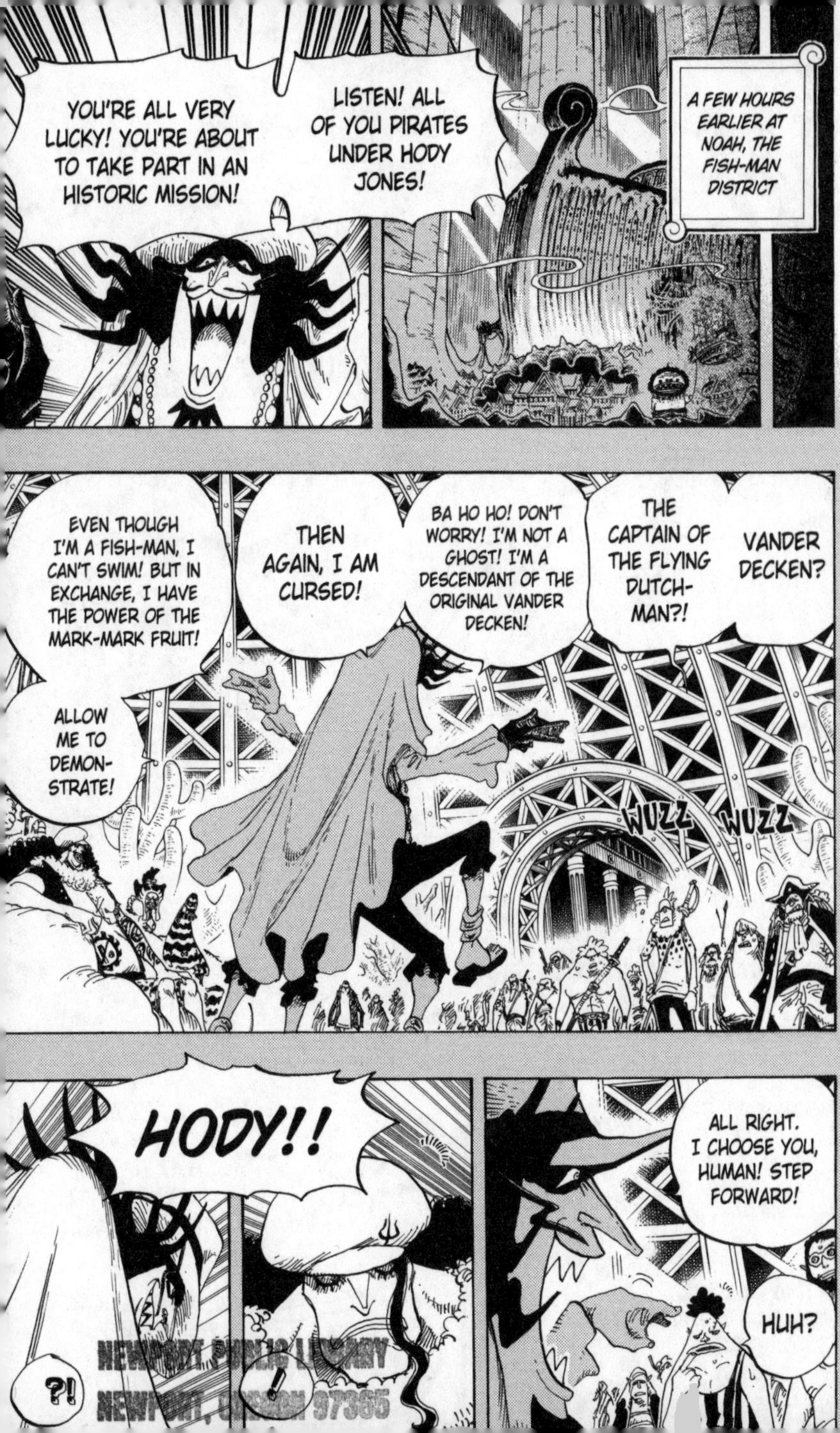
A FEW HOURS EARLIER AT NOAH, THE FISH-MAN DISTRICT
LISTEN! ALL OF YOU PIRATES UNDER HODY JONES!
YOU'RE ALL VERY LUCKY! YOU'RE ABOUT TO TAKE PART IN AN HISTORIC MISSION!
VANDER DECKEN?
THE CAPTAIN OF THE FLYING DUTCH-MAN?!
BA HO HO! DON'T WORRY! I'M NOT A GHOST! I'M A DESCENDANT OF THE ORIGINAL VANDER DECKEN!
THEN AGAIN, I AM CURSED!
EVEN THOUGH I'M A FISH-MAN, I CAN'T SWIM! BUT IN EXCHANGE, I HAVE THE POWER OF THE MARK-MARK FRUIT!
ALLOW ME TO DEMON-STRATE!
WUZZ
WUZZ
ALL RIGHT. I CHOOSE YOU, HUMAN! STEP FORWARD!
HUH?
HODY!!
?!
!

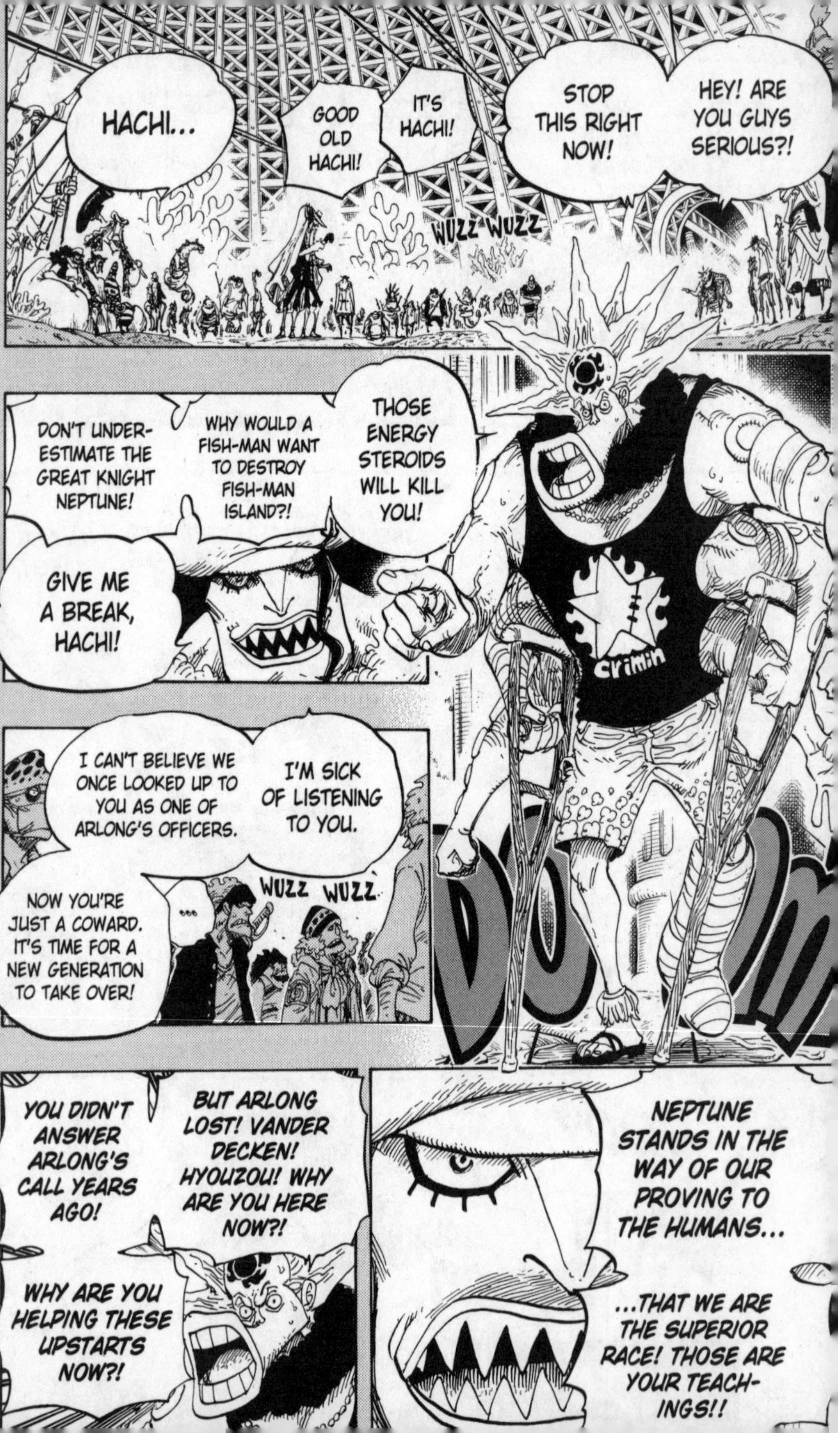
HEY! ARE YOU GUYS SERIOUS?!
STOP THIS RIGHT NOW!
IT'S HACHI!
GOOD OLD HACHI!
HACHI...
WUZZ WUZZ
THOSE ENERGY STEROIDS WILL KILL YOU!
WHY WOULD A FISH-MAN WANT TO DESTROY FISH-MAN ISLAND?!
DON'T UNDER-ESTIMATE THE GREAT KNIGHT NEPTUNE!
GIVE ME A BREAK, HACHI!
I'M SICK OF LISTENING TO YOU.
I CAN'T BELIEVE WE ONCE LOOKED UP TO YOU AS ONE OF ARLONG'S OFFICERS.
...
WUZZ WUZZ
NOW YOU'RE JUST A COWARD. IT'S TIME FOR A NEW GENERATION TO TAKE OVER!
NEPTUNE STANDS IN THE WAY OF OUR PROVING TO THE HUMANS...
...THAT WE ARE THE SUPERIOR RACE! THOSE ARE YOUR TEACH-INGS!!
BUT ARLONG LOST! VANDER DECKEN! HYOUZOU! WHY ARE YOU HERE NOW?!
YOU DIDN'T ANSWER ARLONG'S CALL YEARS AGO!
WHY ARE YOU HELPING THESE UPSTARTS NOW?!

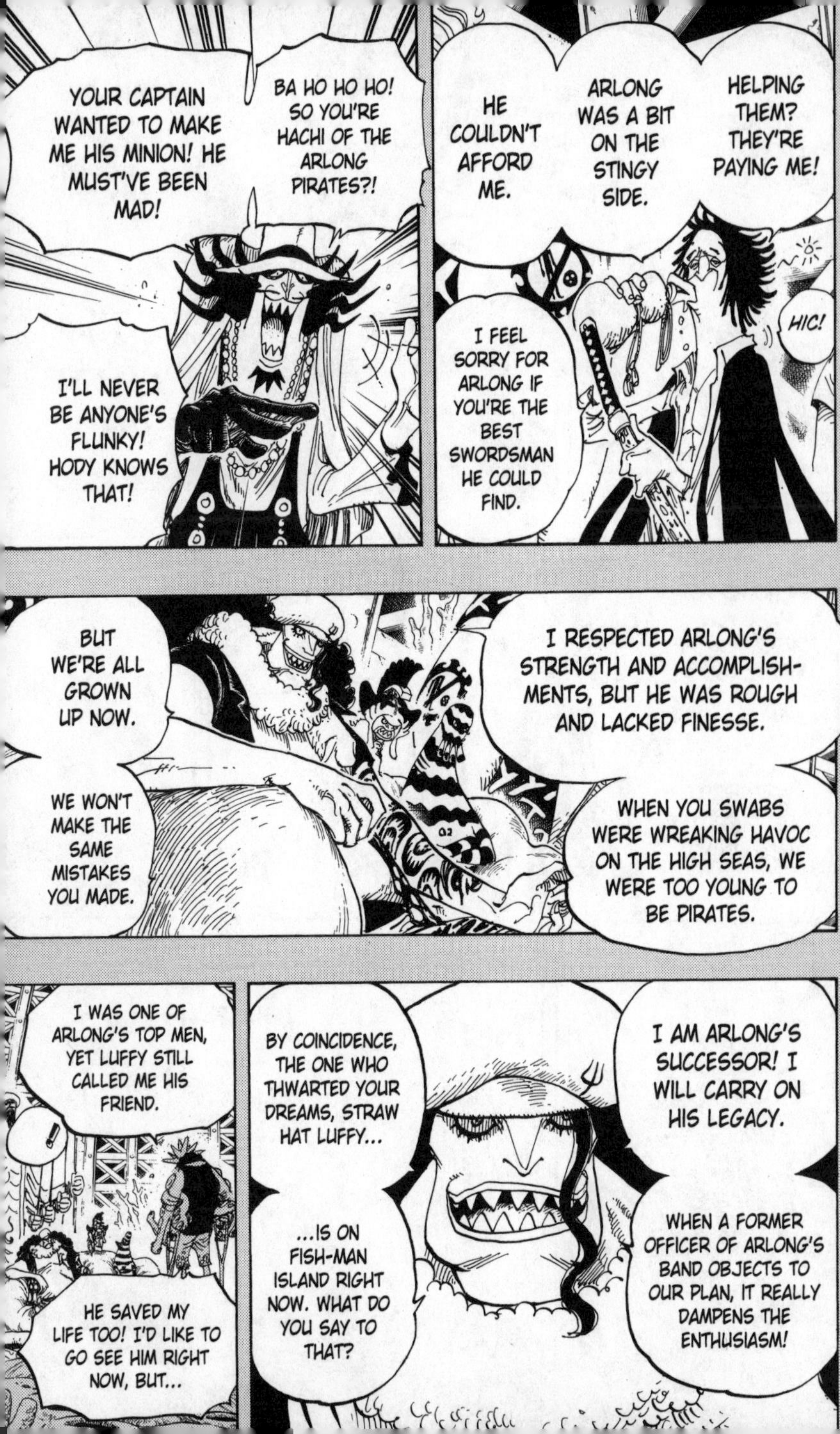
HELPING THEM? THEY'RE PAYING ME!
ARLONG WAS A BIT ON THE STINGY SIDE.
HE COULDN'T AFFORD ME.
HIC!
I FEEL SORRY FOR ARLONG IF YOU'RE THE BEST SWORDSMAN HE COULD FIND.
BA HO HO HO! SO YOU'RE HACHI OF THE ARLONG PIRATES?!
YOUR CAPTAIN WANTED TO MAKE ME HIS MINION! HE MUST'VE BEEN MAD!
I'LL NEVER BE ANYONE'S FLUNKY! HODY KNOWS THAT!
I RESPECTED ARLONG'S STRENGTH AND ACCOMPLISHMENTS, BUT HE WAS ROUGH AND LACKED FINESSE.
WHEN YOU SWABS WERE WREAKING HAVOC ON THE HIGH SEAS, WE WERE TOO YOUNG TO BE PIRATES.
BUT WE'RE ALL GROWN UP NOW.
WE WON'T MAKE THE SAME MISTAKES YOU MADE.
I AM ARLONG'S SUCCESSOR! I WILL CARRY ON HIS LEGACY.
WHEN A FORMER OFFICER OF ARLONG'S BAND OBJECTS TO OUR PLAN, IT REALLY DAMPENS THE ENTHUSIASM!
BY COINCIDENCE, THE ONE WHO THWARTED YOUR DREAMS, STRAW HAT LUFFY...
...IS ON FISH-MAN ISLAND RIGHT NOW. WHAT DO YOU SAY TO THAT?
!
I WAS ONE OF ARLONG'S TOP MEN, YET LUFFY STILL CALLED ME HIS FRIEND.
HE SAVED MY LIFE TOO! I'D LIKE TO GO SEE HIM RIGHT NOW, BUT...

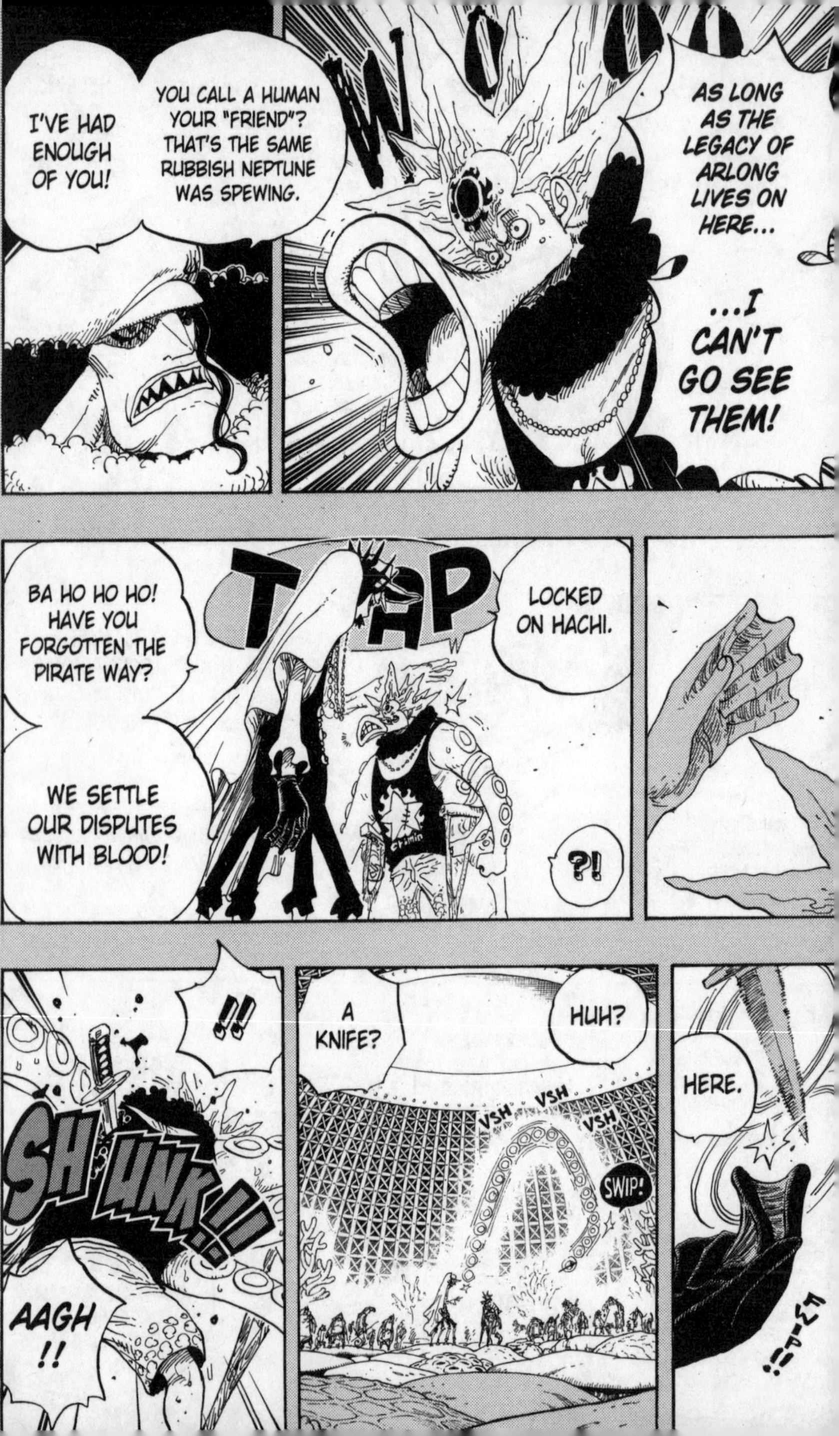
AS LONG AS THE LEGACY OF ARLONG LIVES ON HERE...
...I CAN'T GO SEE THEM!
WOO
YOU CALL A HUMAN YOUR "FRIEND"? THAT'S THE SAME RUBBISH NEPTUNE WAS SPEWING.
I'VE HAD ENOUGH OF YOU!
LOCKED ON HACHI.
TAP
BA HO HO HO! HAVE YOU FORGOTTEN THE PIRATE WAY?
WE SETTLE OUR DISPUTES WITH BLOOD!
?!
HERE.
HUH?
A KNIFE?
VSH
VSH
VSH
VSH
SWIP!
!!
SHUNK!!
AAGH!!

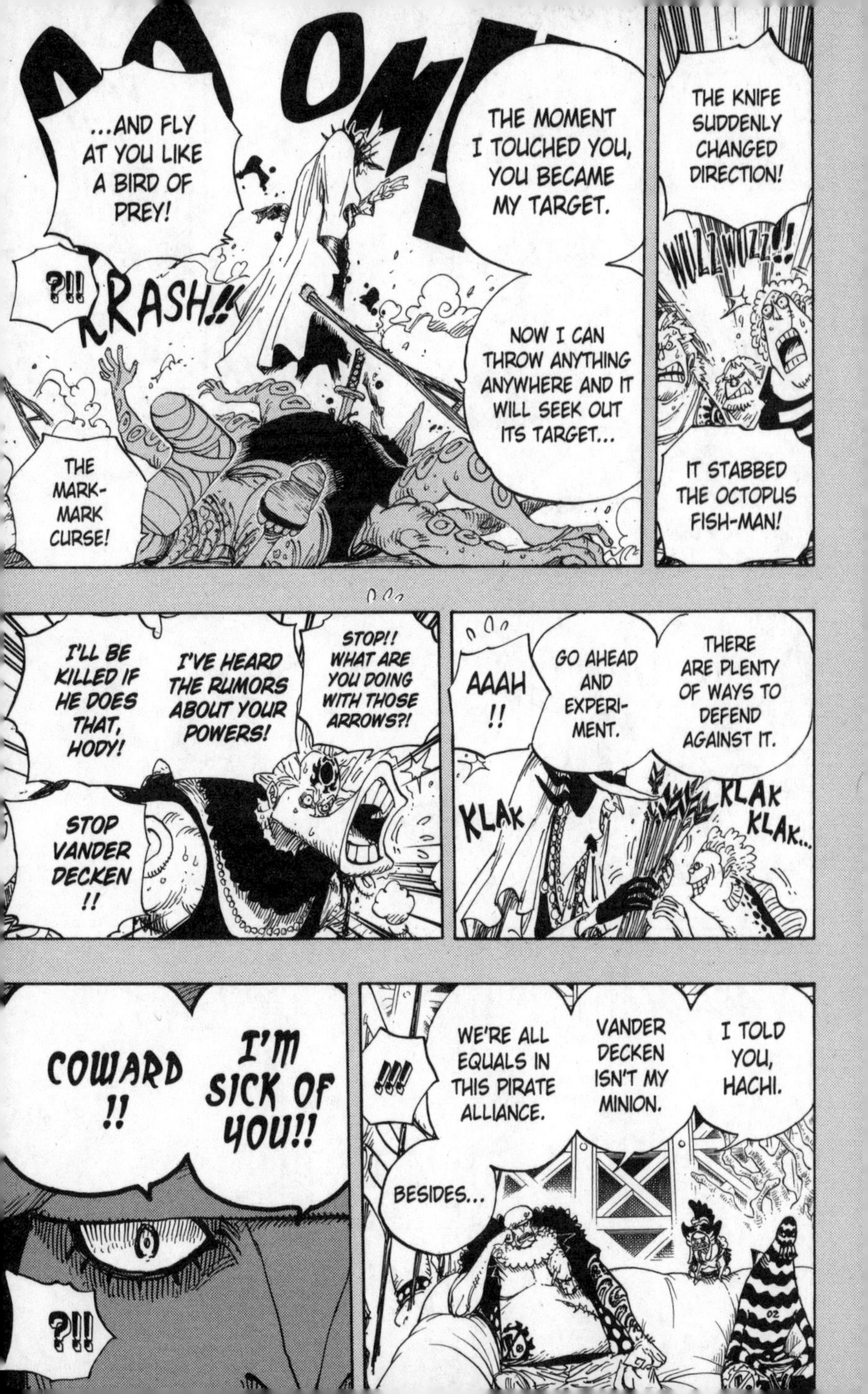
THE KNIFE SUDDENLY CHANGED DIRECTION!
WUZZ WUZZ!!
IT STABBED THE OCTOPUS FISH-MAN!
THE MOMENT I TOUCHED YOU, YOU BECAME MY TARGET.
NOW I CAN THROW ANYTHING ANYWHERE AND IT WILL SEEK OUT ITS TARGET...
...AND FLY AT YOU LIKE A BIRD OF PREY!
?!!
CRASH!!
THE MARK-MARK CURSE!
THERE ARE PLENTY OF WAYS TO DEFEND AGAINST IT.
GO AHEAD AND EXPERIMENT.
AAAH!!
KLAK KLAK...
KLAK
STOP!! WHAT ARE YOU DOING WITH THOSE ARROWS?!
I'VE HEARD THE RUMORS ABOUT YOUR POWERS!
I'LL BE KILLED IF HE DOES THAT, HODY!
STOP VANDER DECKEN!!
I TOLD YOU, HACHI.
VANDER DECKEN ISN'T MY MINION.
WE'RE ALL EQUALS IN THIS PIRATE ALLIANCE.
!!!
BESIDES...
I'M SICK OF YOU!!
COWARD!!
?!!

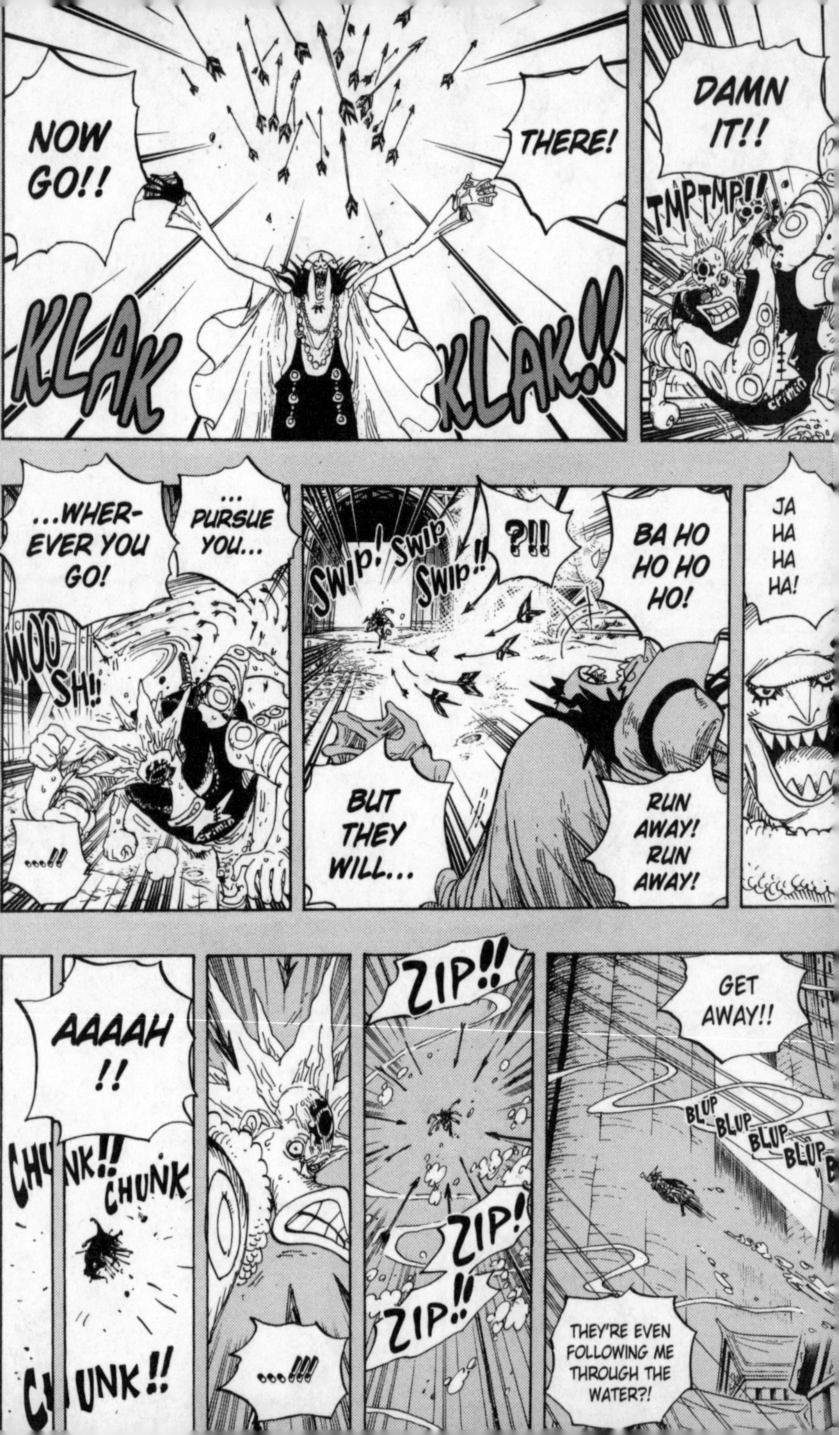
DAMN IT!!
TMPTMP!!
THERE!
NOW GO!!
KLAK!!
KLAK
JA HA HA HA!
BA HO HO HO HO!
?!!
SWIP! SWIP SWIP!!
RUN AWAY! RUN AWAY!
BUT THEY WILL...
... PURSUE YOU...
...WHER-EVER YOU GO!
WOOSH!!
...!!
GET AWAY!!
BLUP BLUP BLUP BLUP
THEY'RE EVEN FOLLOWING ME THROUGH THE WATER?!
ZIP!!
ZIP!
ZIP!!
...!!!
AAAAH!!
CHUNK!! CHUNK
CHUNK!!

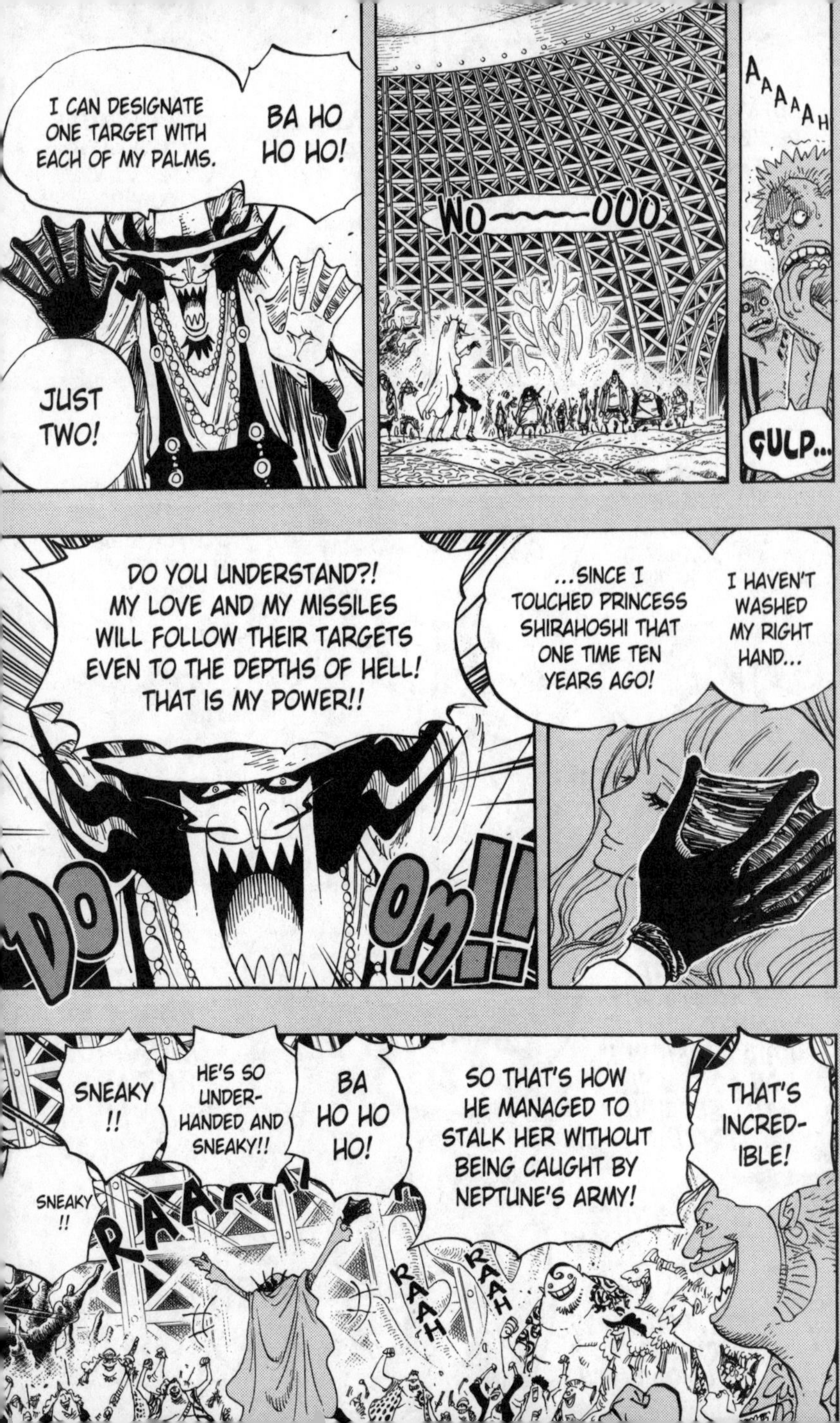
AAAAAH
GULP...
WO———OOO
BA HO HO HO!
I CAN DESIGNATE ONE TARGET WITH EACH OF MY PALMS.
JUST TWO!
I HAVEN'T WASHED MY RIGHT HAND...
...SINCE I TOUCHED PRINCESS SHIRAHOSHI THAT ONE TIME TEN YEARS AGO!
DO YOU UNDERSTAND?! MY LOVE AND MY MISSILES WILL FOLLOW THEIR TARGETS EVEN TO THE DEPTHS OF HELL! THAT IS MY POWER!!
DOOM!!
THAT'S INCREDIBLE!
SO THAT'S HOW HE MANAGED TO STALK HER WITHOUT BEING CAUGHT BY NEPTUNE'S ARMY!
RAAH
RAAH
BA HO HO HO!
HE'S SO UNDERHANDED AND SNEAKY!!
SNEAKY!!
RAAAH
SNEAKY!!

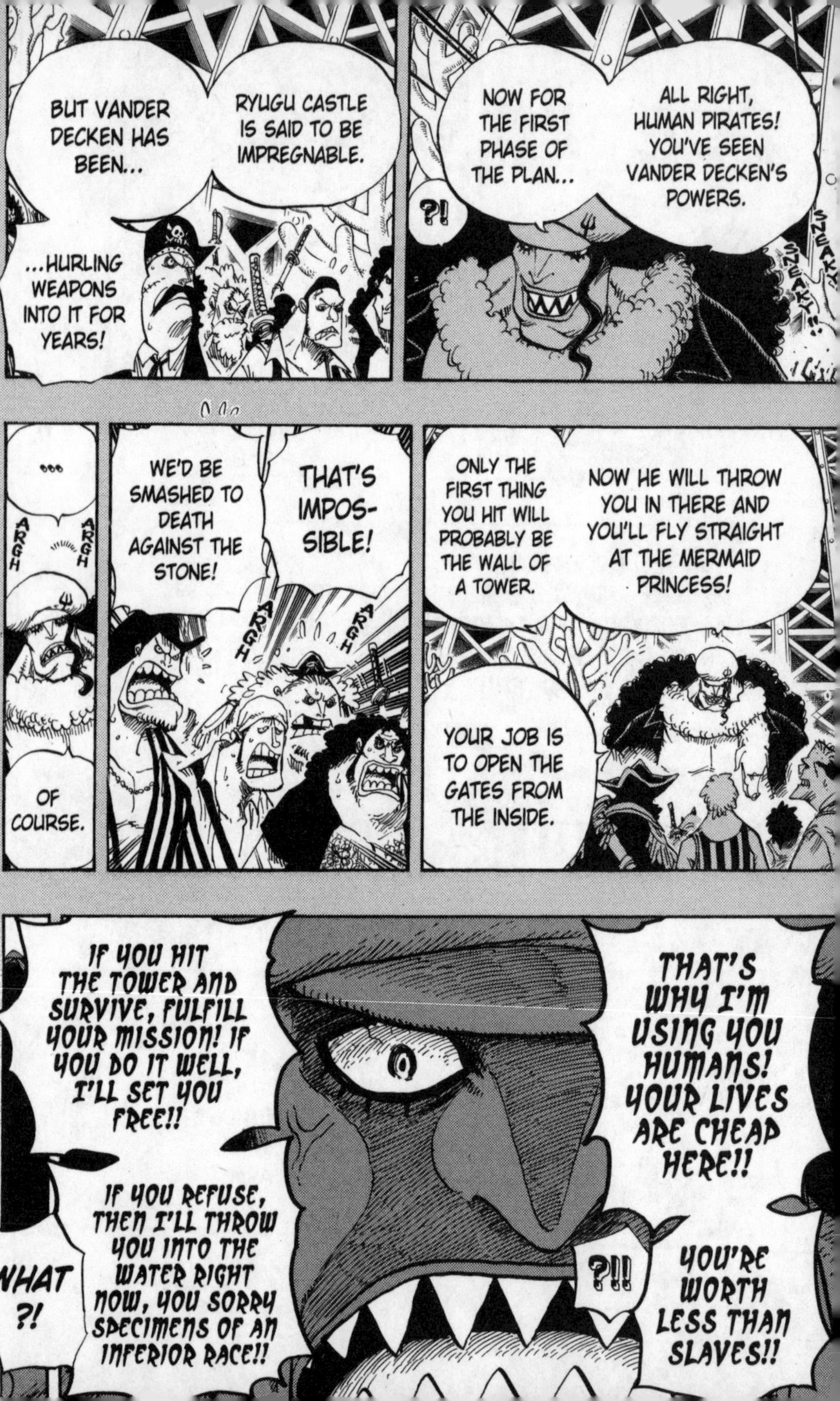
ALL RIGHT, HUMAN PIRATES! YOU'VE SEEN VANDER DECKEN'S POWERS.
NOW FOR THE FIRST PHASE OF THE PLAN...
?!
SNEAKY SNEAKY!!
RYUGU CASTLE IS SAID TO BE IMPREGNABLE.
BUT VANDER DECKEN HAS BEEN...
...HURLING WEAPONS INTO IT FOR YEARS!
NOW HE WILL THROW YOU IN THERE AND YOU'LL FLY STRAIGHT AT THE MERMAID PRINCESS!
ONLY THE FIRST THING YOU HIT WILL PROBABLY BE THE WALL OF A TOWER.
YOUR JOB IS TO OPEN THE GATES FROM THE INSIDE.
THAT'S IMPOSSIBLE!
WE'D BE SMASHED TO DEATH AGAINST THE STONE!
ARGH
ARGH
...
ARGH
ARGH
OF COURSE.
THAT'S WHY I'M USING YOU HUMANS! YOUR LIVES ARE CHEAP HERE!!
IF YOU HIT THE TOWER AND SURVIVE, FULFILL YOUR MISSION! IF YOU DO IT WELL, I'LL SET YOU FREE!!
?!!
YOU'RE WORTH LESS THAN SLAVES!!
IF YOU REFUSE, THEN I'LL THROW YOU INTO THE WATER RIGHT NOW, YOU SORRY SPECIMENS OF AN INFERIOR RACE!!
WHAT?!

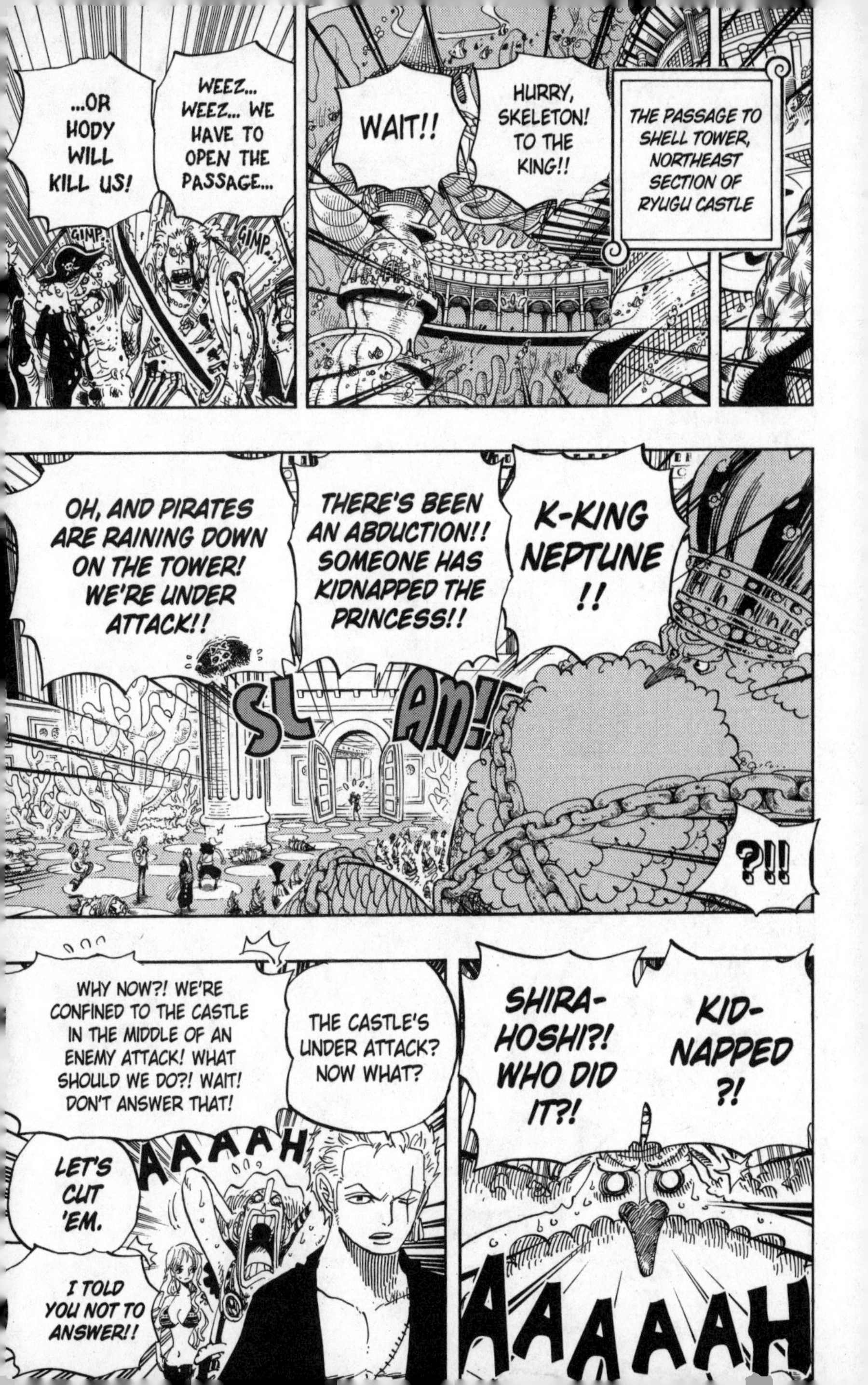
THE PASSAGE TO SHELL TOWER, NORTHEAST SECTION OF RYUGU CASTLE
HURRY, SKELETON! TO THE KING!!
WAIT!!
WEEZ... WEEZ... WE HAVE TO OPEN THE PASSAGE...
...OR HODY WILL KILL US!
GIMP...
GIMP.
K-KING NEPTUNE !!
THERE'S BEEN AN ABDUCTION!! SOMEONE HAS KIDNAPPED THE PRINCESS!!
OH, AND PIRATES ARE RAINING DOWN ON THE TOWER! WE'RE UNDER ATTACK!!
SLAM!!
?!!
KID-NAPPED ?!
SHIRA-HOSHI?! WHO DID IT?!
AAAAAH
THE CASTLE'S UNDER ATTACK? NOW WHAT?
WHY NOW?! WE'RE CONFINED TO THE CASTLE IN THE MIDDLE OF AN ENEMY ATTACK! WHAT SHOULD WE DO?! WAIT! DON'T ANSWER THAT!
AAAAH
LET'S CUT 'EM.
I TOLD YOU NOT TO ANSWER!!

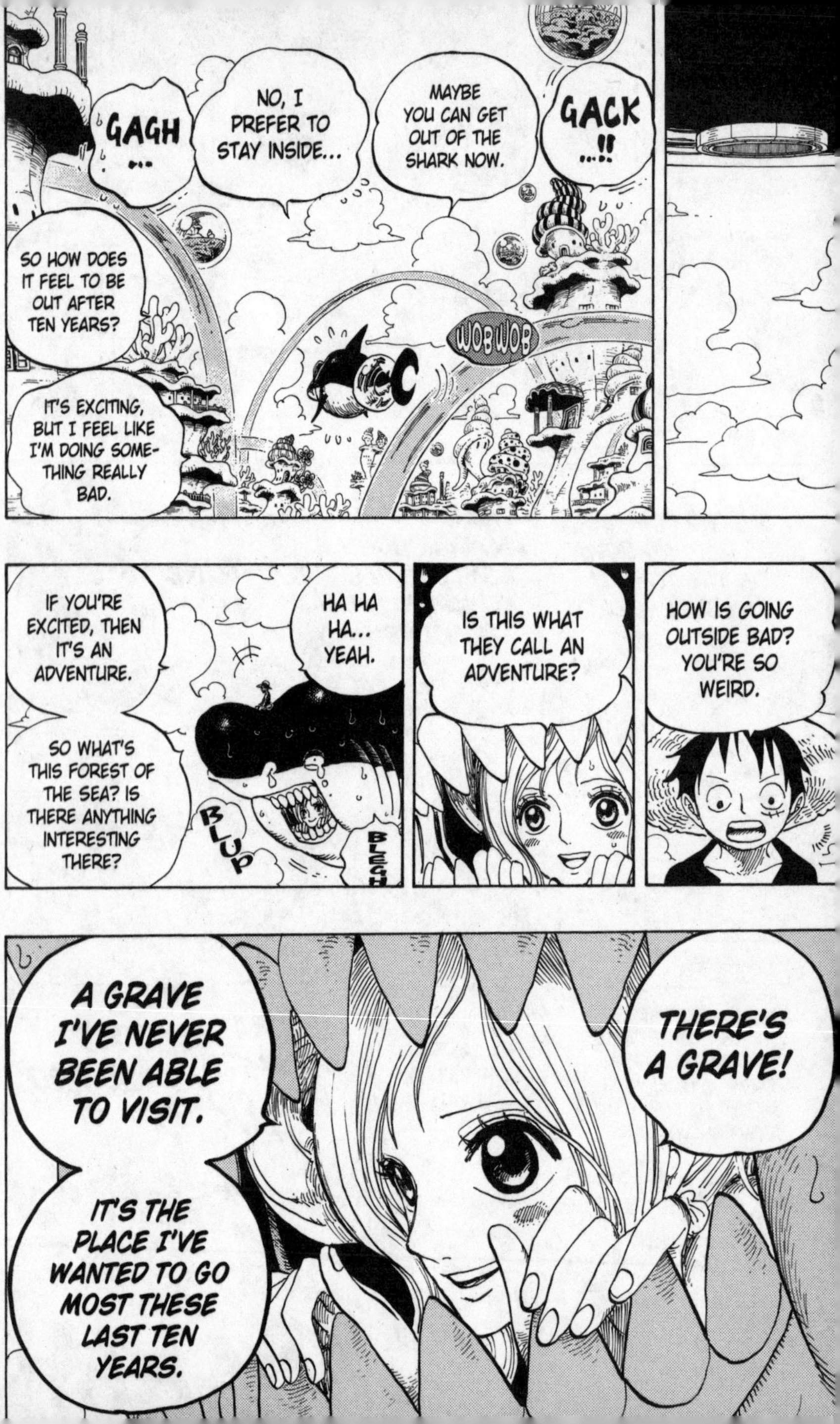
GACK ...!!
MAYBE YOU CAN GET OUT OF THE SHARK NOW.
NO, I PREFER TO STAY INSIDE...
GAGH ...
WOBWOB
SO HOW DOES IT FEEL TO BE OUT AFTER TEN YEARS?
IT'S EXCITING, BUT I FEEL LIKE I'M DOING SOMETHING REALLY BAD.
HOW IS GOING OUTSIDE BAD? YOU'RE SO WEIRD.
IS THIS WHAT THEY CALL AN ADVENTURE?
HA HA HA... YEAH.
IF YOU'RE EXCITED, THEN IT'S AN ADVENTURE.
SO WHAT'S THIS FOREST OF THE SEA? IS THERE ANYTHING INTERESTING THERE?
BLEGH
BLUP
THERE'S A GRAVE!
A GRAVE I'VE NEVER BEEN ABLE TO VISIT.
IT'S THE PLACE I'VE WANTED TO GO MOST THESE LAST TEN YEARS.

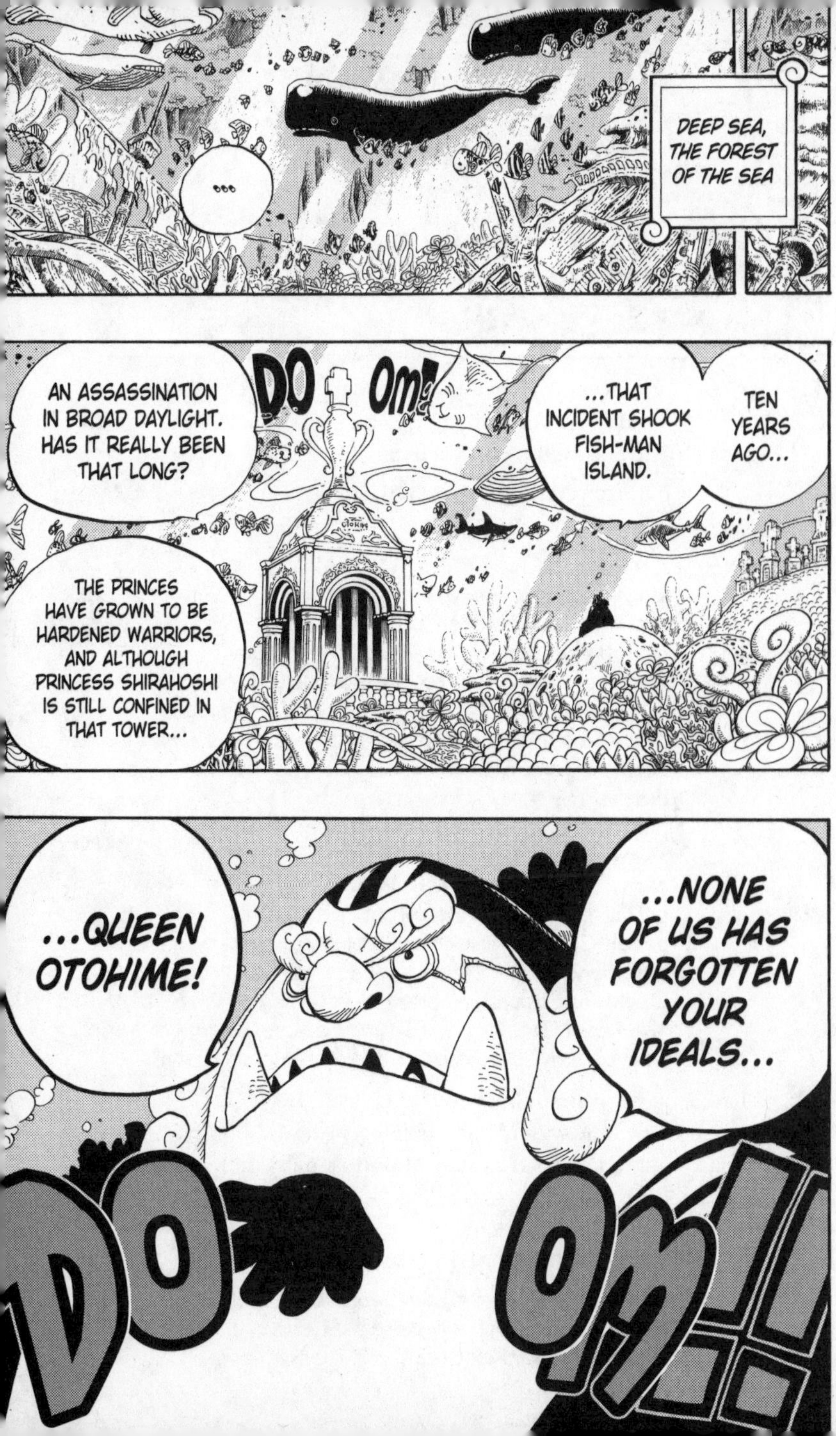

DEEP SEA, THE FOREST OF THE SEA
...
TEN YEARS AGO...
...THAT INCIDENT SHOOK FISH-MAN ISLAND.
DO OM!
AN ASSASSINATION IN BROAD DAYLIGHT. HAS IT REALLY BEEN THAT LONG?
THE PRINCES HAVE GROWN TO BE HARDENED WARRIORS, AND ALTHOUGH PRINCESS SHIRAHOSHI IS STILL CONFINED IN THAT TOWER...
...NONE OF US HAS FORGOTTEN YOUR IDEALS...
...QUEEN OTOHIME!
DO OM!!

SBS Question Corner

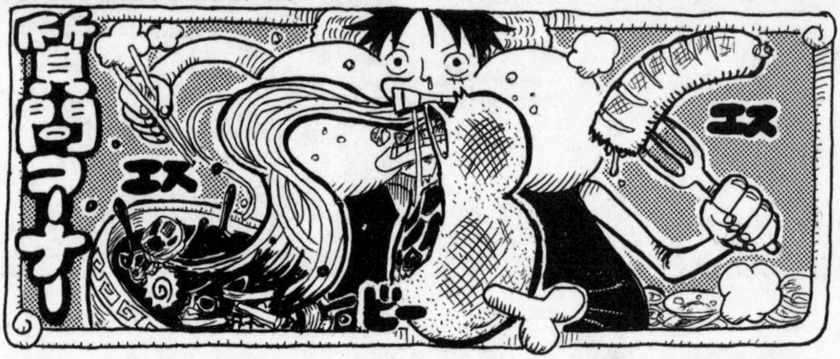

質問コーナー
エス
エス
ビー

(Ponio, Aichi)

Reader (Q): We recently learned how to use the Color of Observation Haki.☆ So I'm going to try and guess what you're about to do, Odacchi.

You're…**Starting SBS!**

--Yoyogi Parks

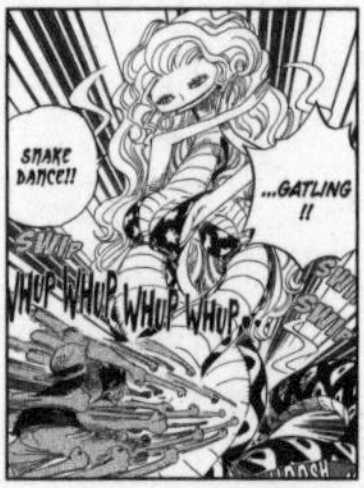

SNAKE DANCE!!
...GATLING !!
WHUP WHUP WHUP WHUP

Oda (A): Ahh! You read my mind!

Darn you, you Haki user! So I guess we just got started, but first I've got three things I need to say to you all. Once again, due to the selfishness of yours truly, volume 63 is a special volume containing 12 chapters. But the price is the same as always! That means that I couldn't take a single page for the end of volume extras! I'm really sorry.

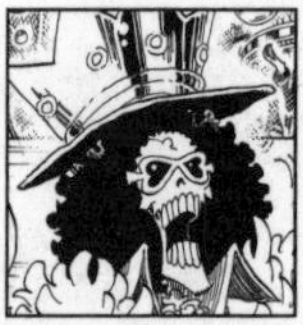

Number two, because there aren't as many extras, the Voice Actor SBS will carry over to next volume! Oh man, I'm so sorry for keeping Brook's voice actor Cho waiting! Next volume, I swear! And number three! Okay. Recently I love canned food! Ouch! Hey, could you stop throwing things?! What the heck?! Do you not want to hear what I've been up to recently? But canned mackerel is so good!

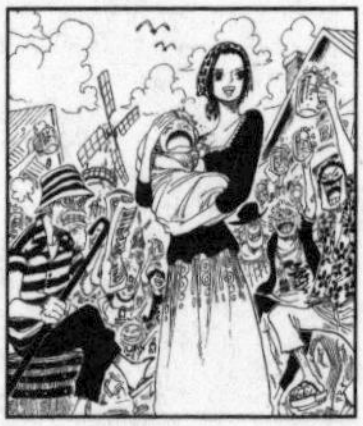

Q: I have a question about the cover of chapter 614. You know, the one with Makino holding a baby? What I want to know is…**is that Makino's baby?!** And **am I the father?!**

--Tanpopo

A: OF COURSE YOU'RE NOT!!

Sorry, I got a little worked up there. But well, it does mean that Makino has become a mother. She looks very happy. I bet that guy's the father. Yeah, it's gotta be that guy…

Chapter 616:

ANNIVERSARY FOR REVENGE

*RIKA'S RICEBALL

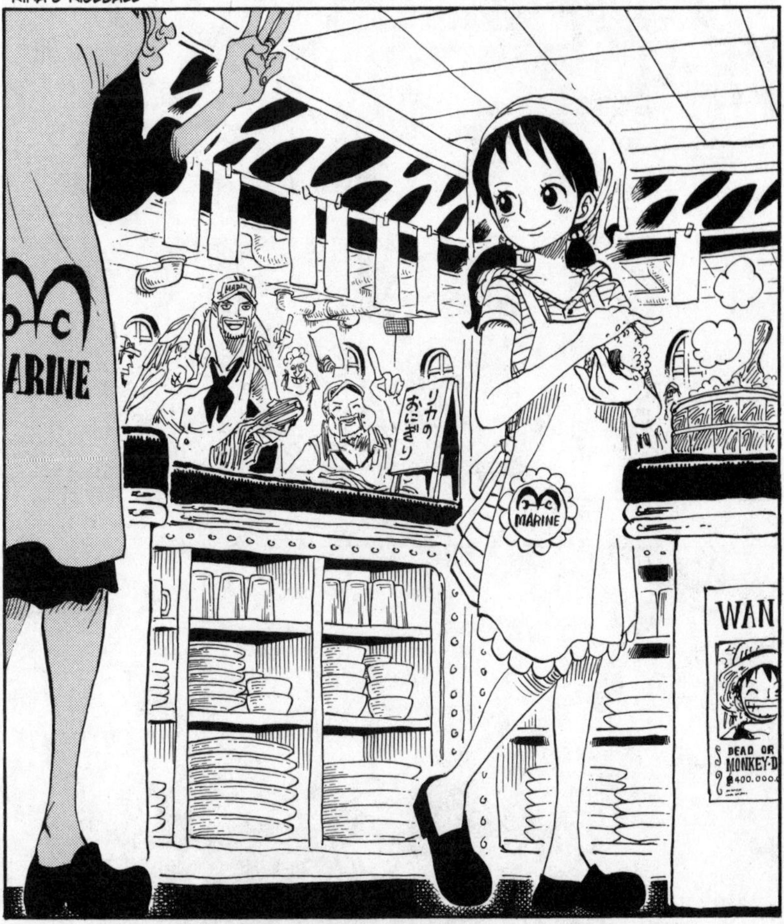
MARINE
リカのおにぎり
MARINE
WAN
DEAD OR
MONKEY·D

DECKS OF THE WORLD, VOL. 4:
"SHELLS TOWN'S SERVER IN TRAINING, RIKA"

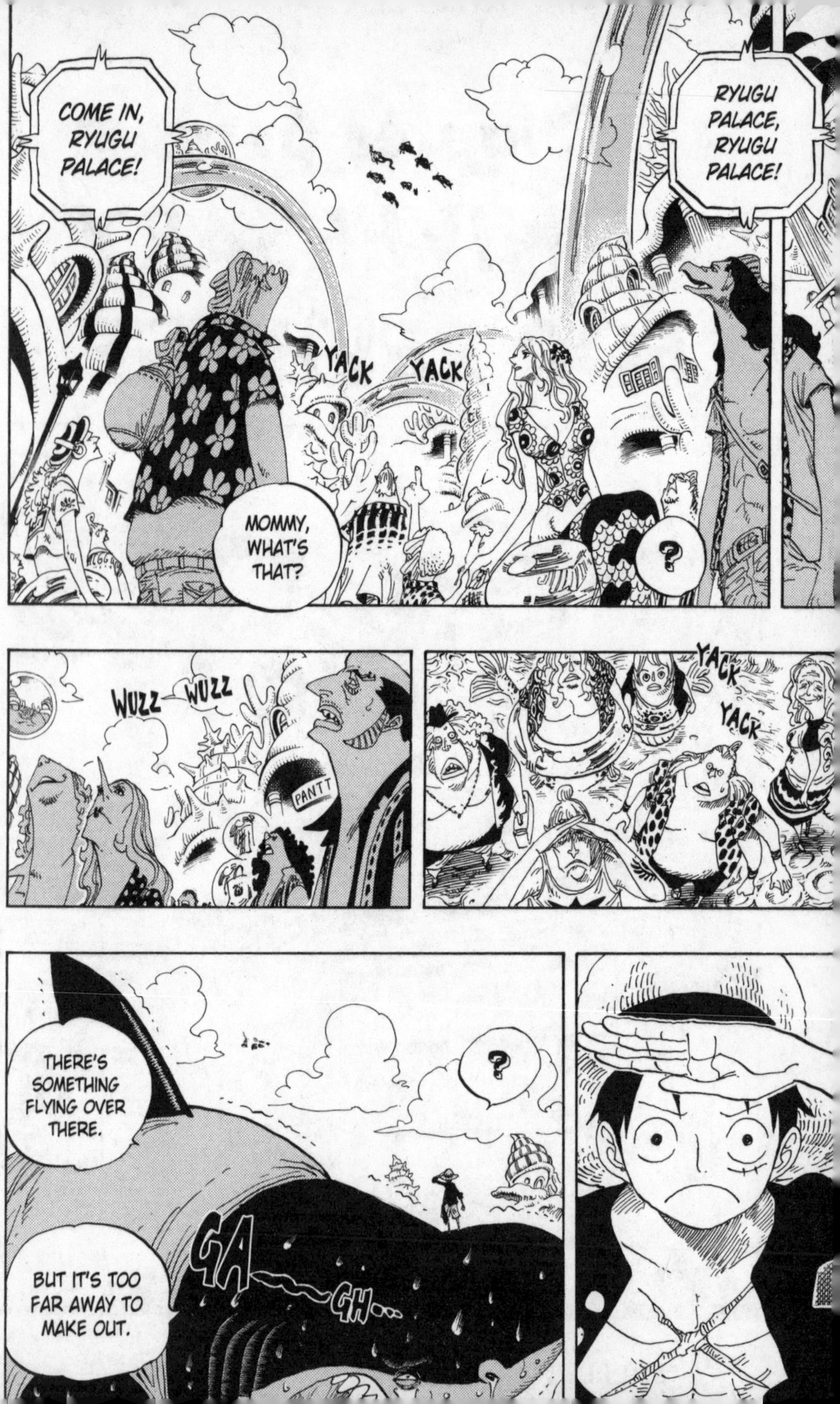
RYUGU PALACE, RYUGU PALACE!
COME IN, RYUGU PALACE!
YACK
YACK
?
MOMMY, WHAT'S THAT?
YACK
YACK
WUZZ WUZZ
PANTT
?
THERE'S SOMETHING FLYING OVER THERE.
GA~~GH...
BUT IT'S TOO FAR AWAY TO MAKE OUT.

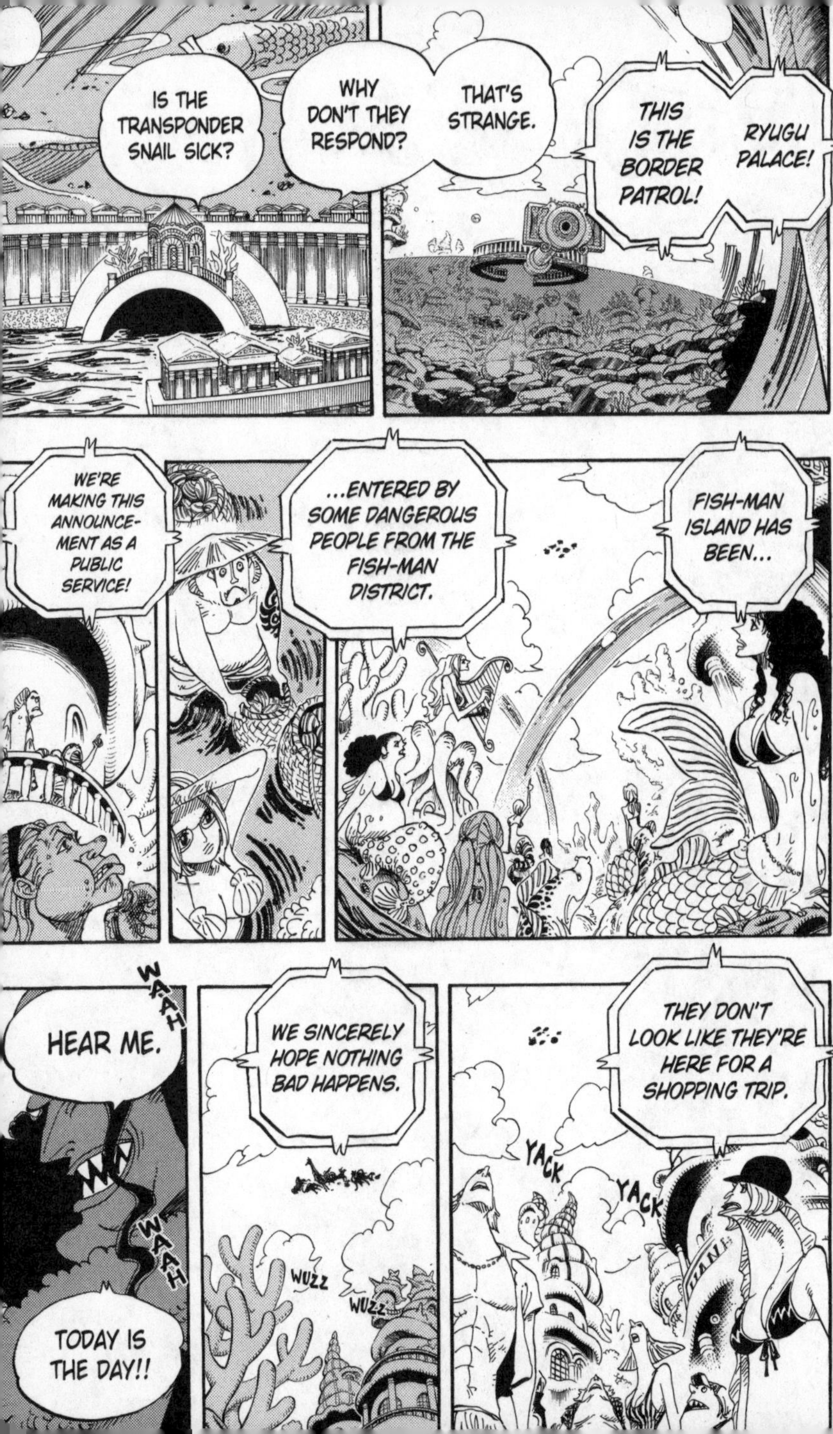
RYUGU PALACE!
THIS IS THE BORDER PATROL!
THAT'S STRANGE.
WHY DON'T THEY RESPOND?
IS THE TRANSPONDER SNAIL SICK?
FISH-MAN ISLAND HAS BEEN...
...ENTERED BY SOME DANGEROUS PEOPLE FROM THE FISH-MAN DISTRICT.
WE'RE MAKING THIS ANNOUNCE-MENT AS A PUBLIC SERVICE!
THEY DON'T LOOK LIKE THEY'RE HERE FOR A SHOPPING TRIP.
YACK
YACK
WE SINCERELY HOPE NOTHING BAD HAPPENS.
WUZZ
WUZZ
WAAH
HEAR ME.
WAAH
TODAY IS THE DAY!!

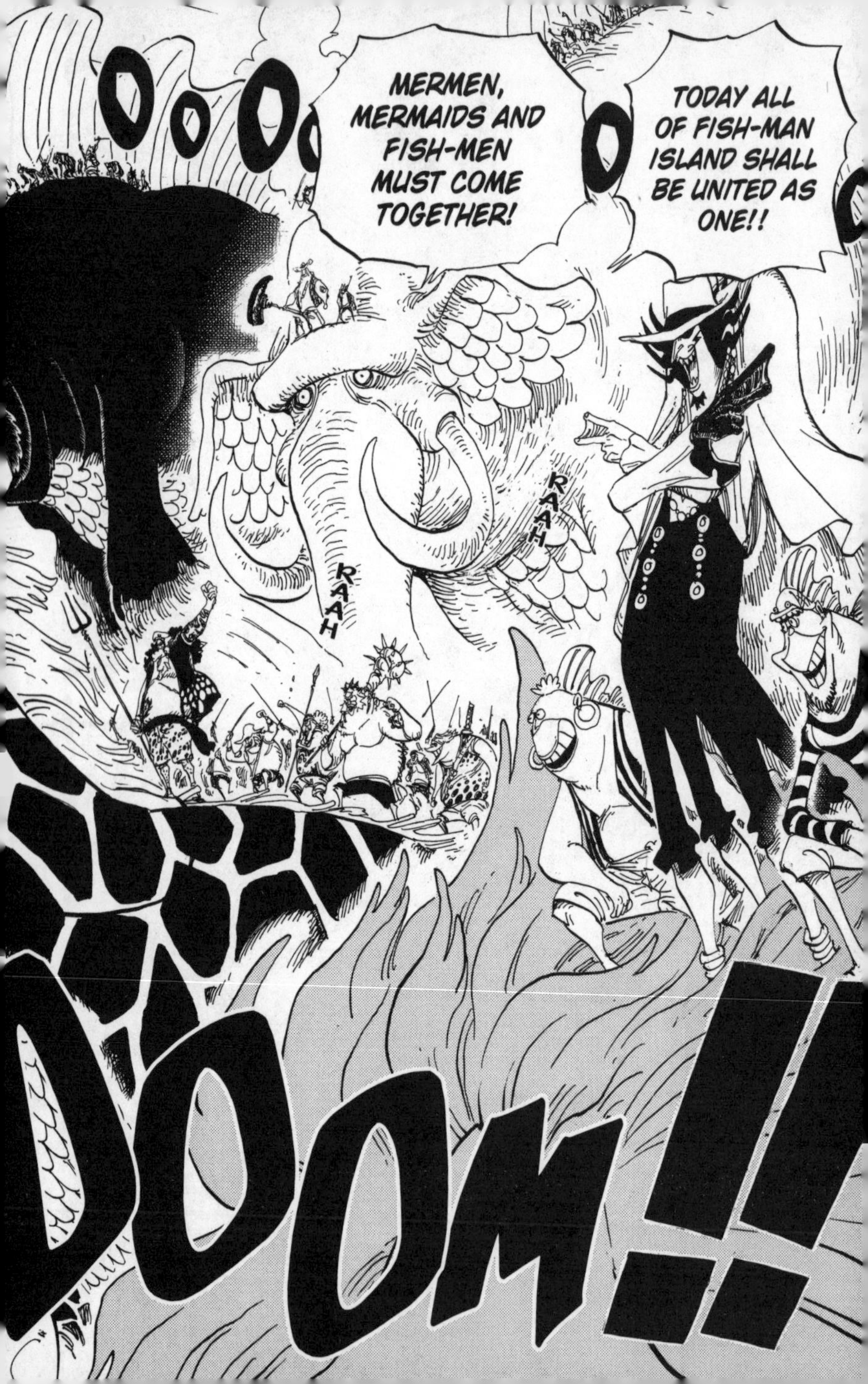
TODAY ALL OF FISH-MAN ISLAND SHALL BE UNITED AS ONE!!
MERMEN, MERMAIDS AND FISH-MEN MUST COME TOGETHER!
OOOOO
RAAH
RAAH
DOOM!!

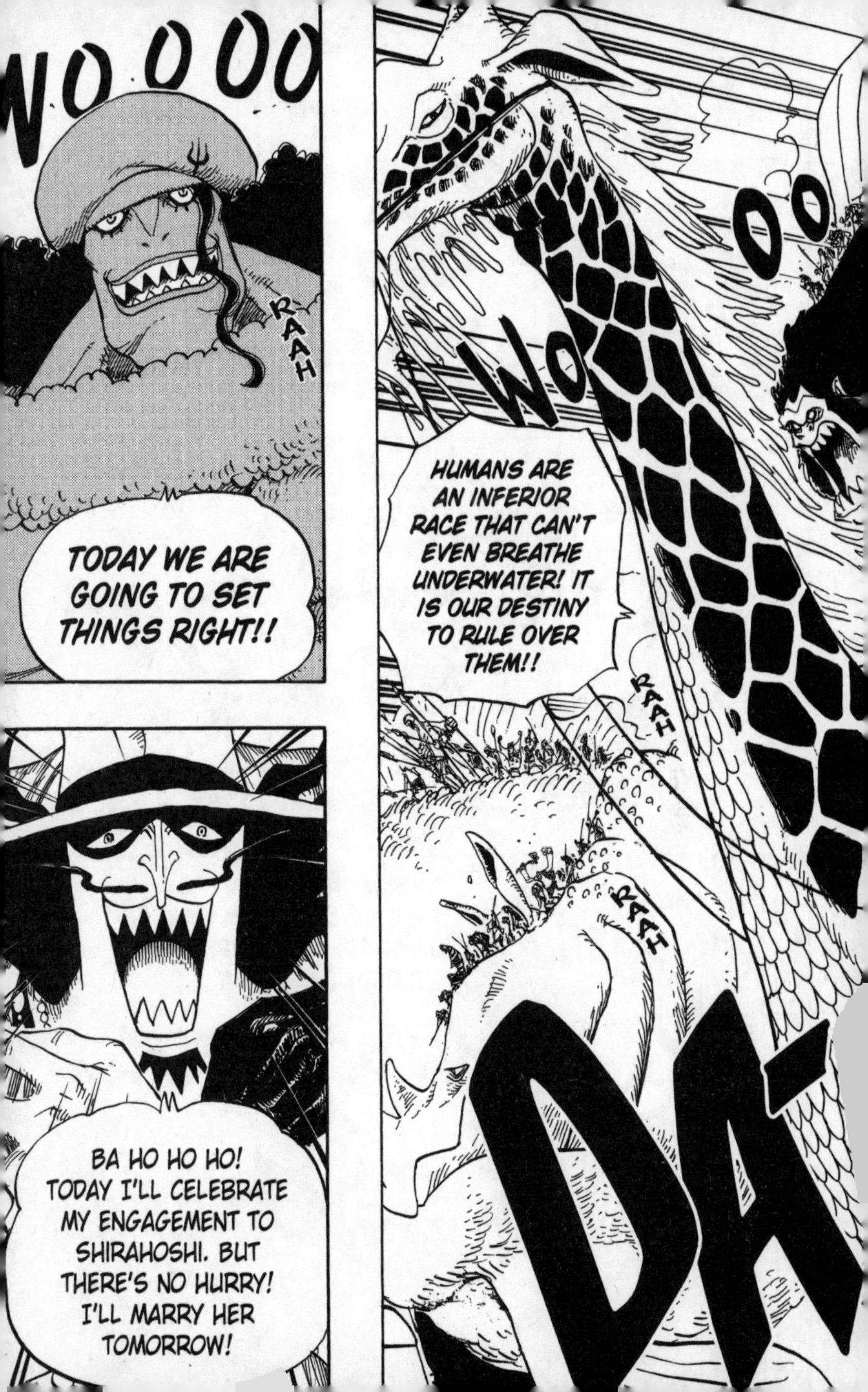
WO OO
HUMANS ARE AN INFERIOR RACE THAT CAN'T EVEN BREATHE UNDERWATER! IT IS OUR DESTINY TO RULE OVER THEM!!
RAAH
RAAH
DA-
WO O OO
RAAH
TODAY WE ARE GOING TO SET THINGS RIGHT!!
BA HO HO HO! TODAY I'LL CELEBRATE MY ENGAGEMENT TO SHIRAHOSHI. BUT THERE'S NO HURRY! I'LL MARRY HER TOMORROW!

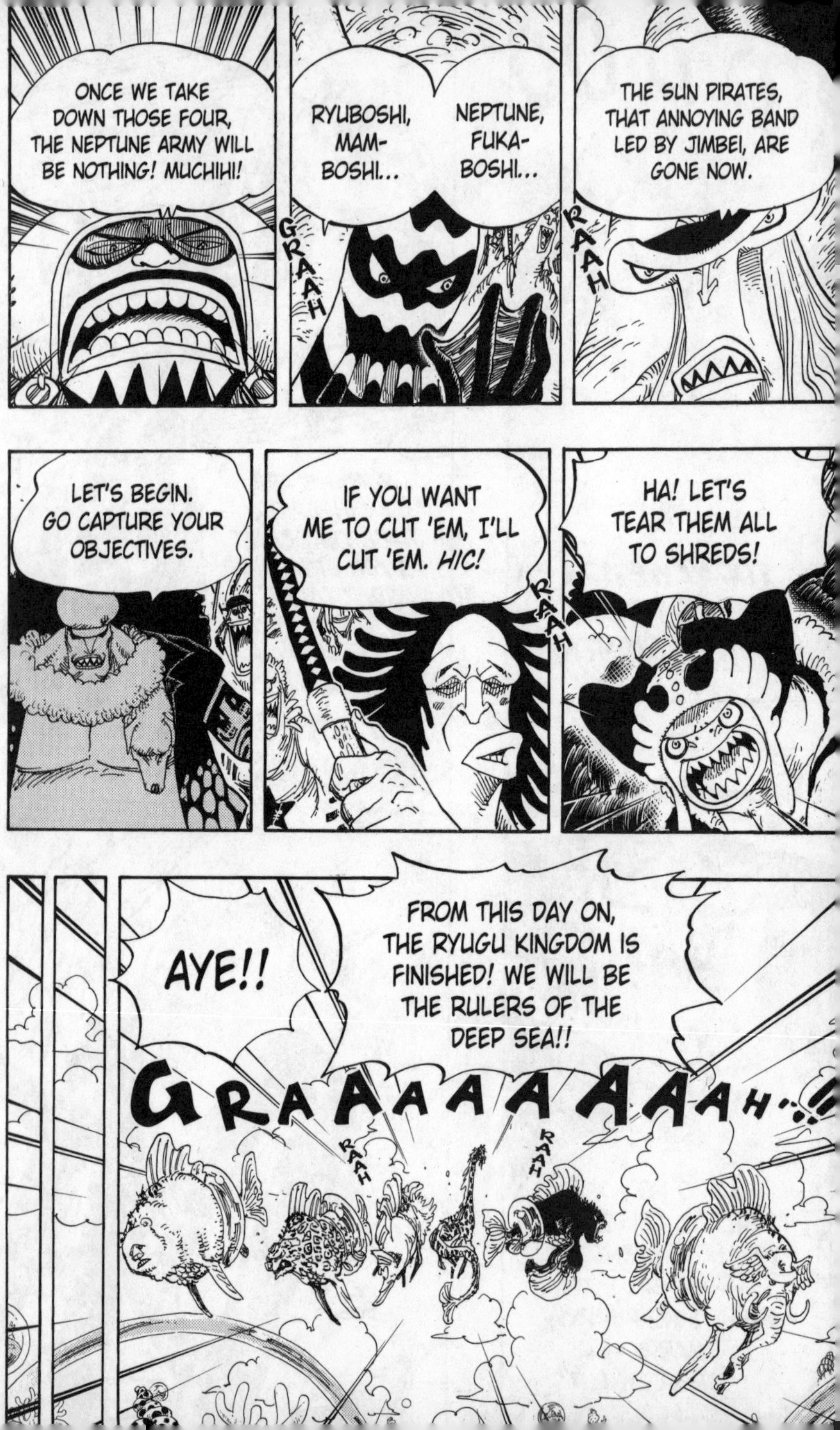

THE SUN PIRATES, THAT ANNOYING BAND LED BY JIMBEI, ARE GONE NOW.
RAAH
NEPTUNE, FUKA-BOSHI...
RYUBOSHI, MAM-BOSHI...
GRAAH
ONCE WE TAKE DOWN THOSE FOUR, THE NEPTUNE ARMY WILL BE NOTHING! MUCHIHI!
HA! LET'S TEAR THEM ALL TO SHREDS!
RAAH
IF YOU WANT ME TO CUT 'EM, I'LL CUT 'EM. *HIC!*
LET'S BEGIN. GO CAPTURE YOUR OBJECTIVES.
FROM THIS DAY ON, THE RYUGU KINGDOM IS FINISHED! WE WILL BE THE RULERS OF THE DEEP SEA!!
AYE!!
GRAAAAAAAAAH!!
RAAH
RAAH

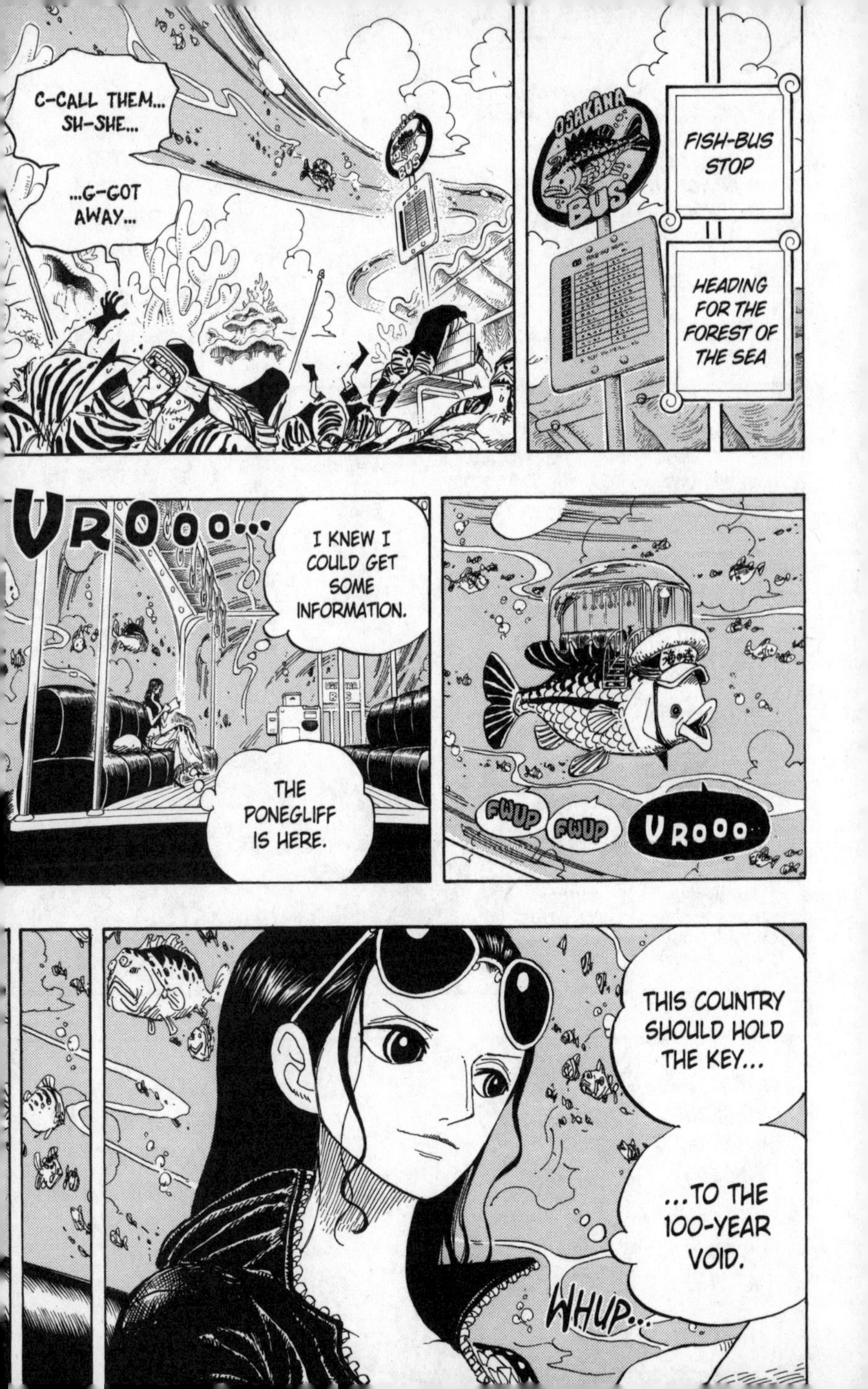
OSAKANA
BUS
FISH-BUS STOP
HEADING FOR THE FOREST OF THE SEA
C-CALL THEM... SH-SHE...
...G-GOT AWAY...
VROOO
FWUP
FWUP
VROOO...
I KNEW I COULD GET SOME INFORMATION.
THE PONEGLIFF IS HERE.
THIS COUNTRY SHOULD HOLD THE KEY...
...TO THE 100-YEAR VOID.
WHUP...

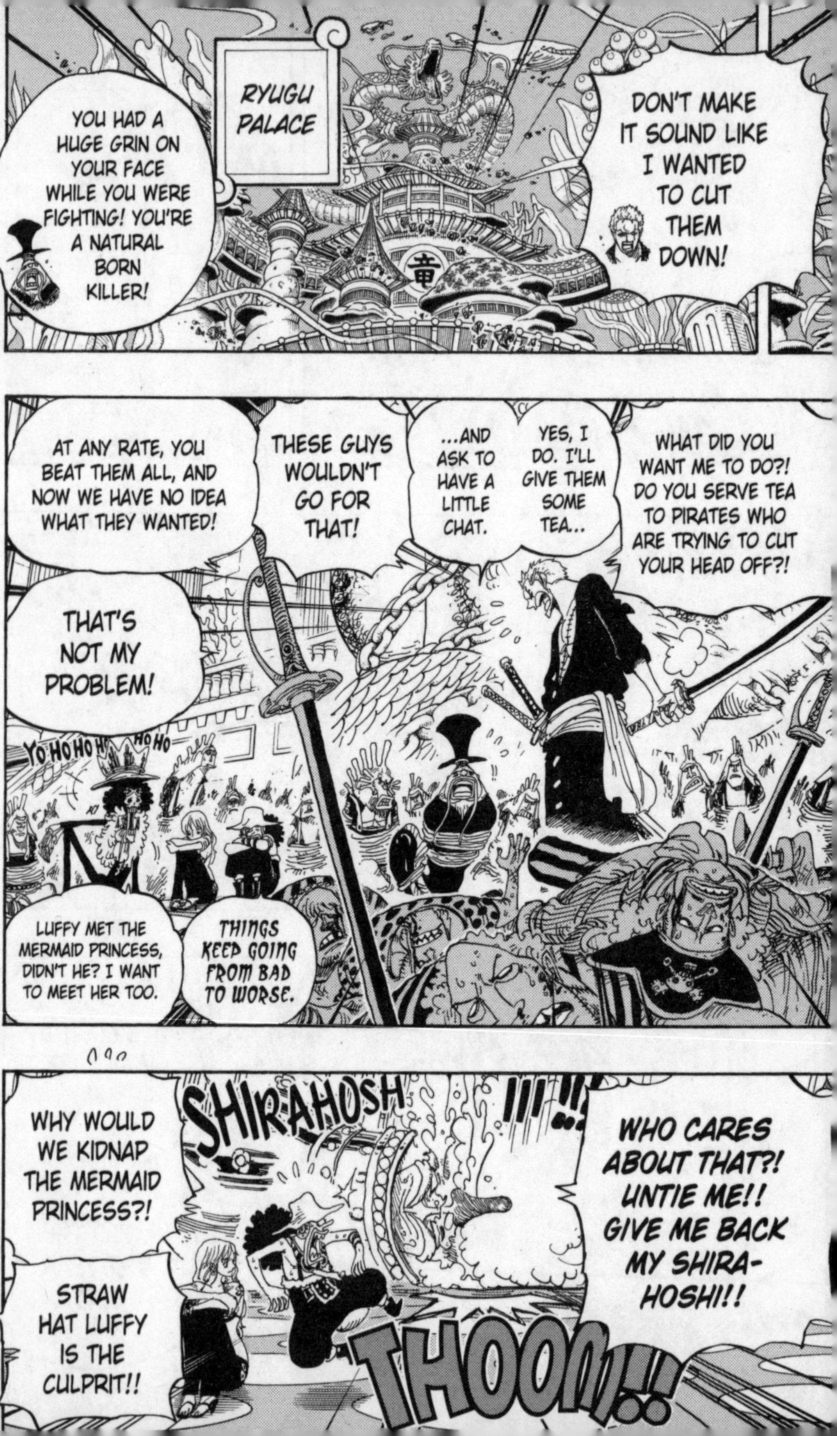
DON'T MAKE IT SOUND LIKE I WANTED TO CUT THEM DOWN!
RYUGU PALACE
YOU HAD A HUGE GRIN ON YOUR FACE WHILE YOU WERE FIGHTING! YOU'RE A NATURAL BORN KILLER!
WHAT DID YOU WANT ME TO DO?! DO YOU SERVE TEA TO PIRATES WHO ARE TRYING TO CUT YOUR HEAD OFF?!
YES, I DO. I'LL GIVE THEM SOME TEA...
...AND ASK TO HAVE A LITTLE CHAT.
THESE GUYS WOULDN'T GO FOR THAT!
AT ANY RATE, YOU BEAT THEM ALL, AND NOW WE HAVE NO IDEA WHAT THEY WANTED!
THAT'S NOT MY PROBLEM!
YO HO HO HO HO
THINGS KEEP GOING FROM BAD TO WORSE.
LUFFY MET THE MERMAID PRINCESS, DIDN'T HE? I WANT TO MEET HER TOO.
WHO CARES ABOUT THAT?! UNTIE ME!! GIVE ME BACK MY SHIRA-HOSHI!!
SHIRAHOSHI!!!
WHY WOULD WE KIDNAP THE MERMAID PRINCESS?!
STRAW HAT LUFFY IS THE CULPRIT!!
THOOM!!

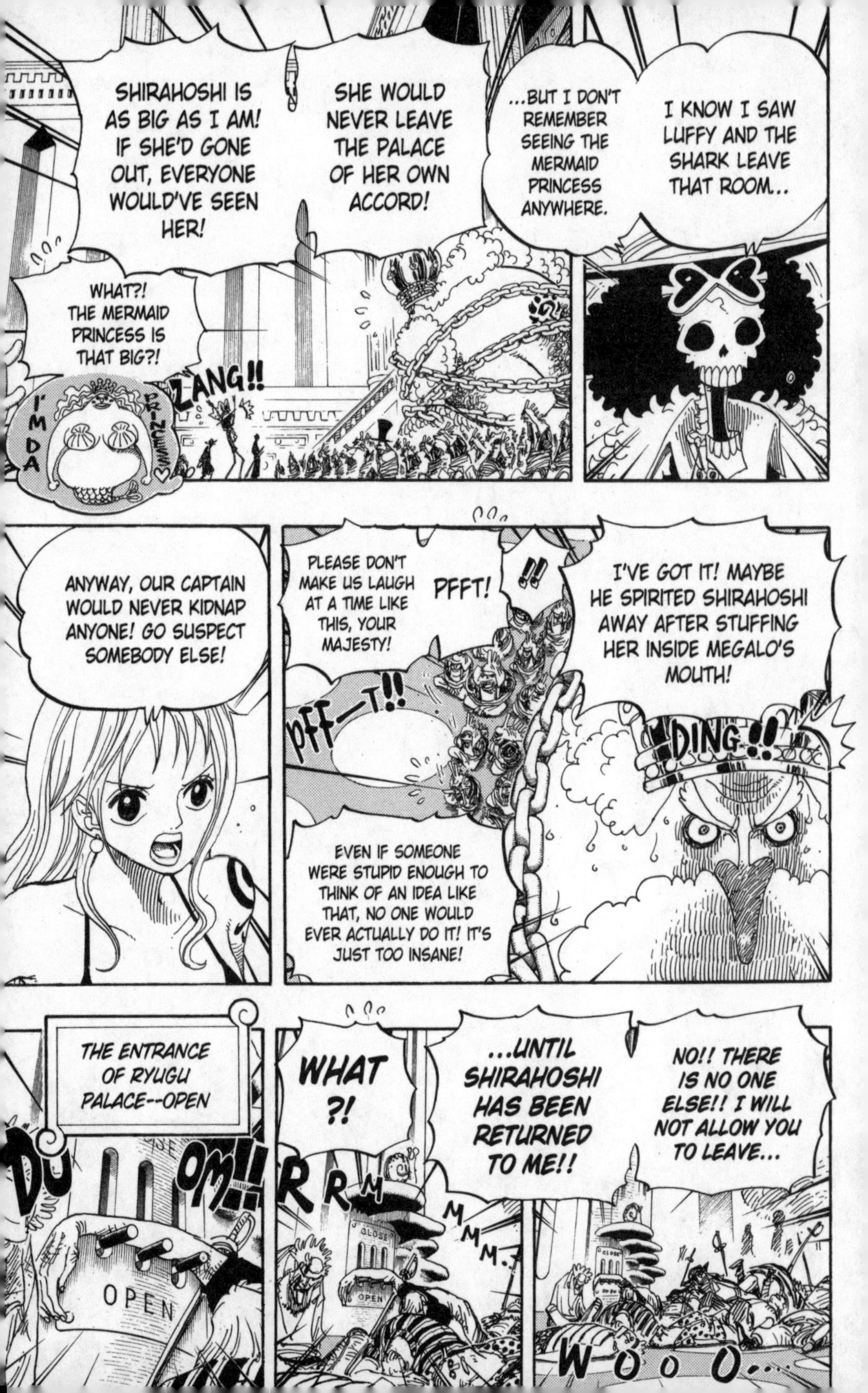
I KNOW I SAW LUFFY AND THE SHARK LEAVE THAT ROOM...
...BUT I DON'T REMEMBER SEEING THE MERMAID PRINCESS ANYWHERE.
SHE WOULD NEVER LEAVE THE PALACE OF HER OWN ACCORD!
SHIRAHOSHI IS AS BIG AS I AM! IF SHE'D GONE OUT, EVERYONE WOULD'VE SEEN HER!
WHAT?! THE MERMAID PRINCESS IS THAT BIG?!
ZANG!!
I'M DA PRINCESS♡
I'VE GOT IT! MAYBE HE SPIRITED SHIRAHOSHI AWAY AFTER STUFFING HER INSIDE MEGALO'S MOUTH!
DING!!
!!
PFFT!
PLEASE DON'T MAKE US LAUGH AT A TIME LIKE THIS, YOUR MAJESTY!
PFF—T!!
EVEN IF SOMEONE WERE STUPID ENOUGH TO THINK OF AN IDEA LIKE THAT, NO ONE WOULD EVER ACTUALLY DO IT! IT'S JUST TOO INSANE!
ANYWAY, OUR CAPTAIN WOULD NEVER KIDNAP ANYONE! GO SUSPECT SOMEBODY ELSE!
NO!! THERE IS NO ONE ELSE!! I WILL NOT ALLOW YOU TO LEAVE...
...UNTIL SHIRAHOSHI HAS BEEN RETURNED TO ME!!
WOOO...
WHAT ?!
RRMMMM...
OPEN
THE ENTRANCE OF RYUGU PALACE--OPEN
DOOM!!
OPEN

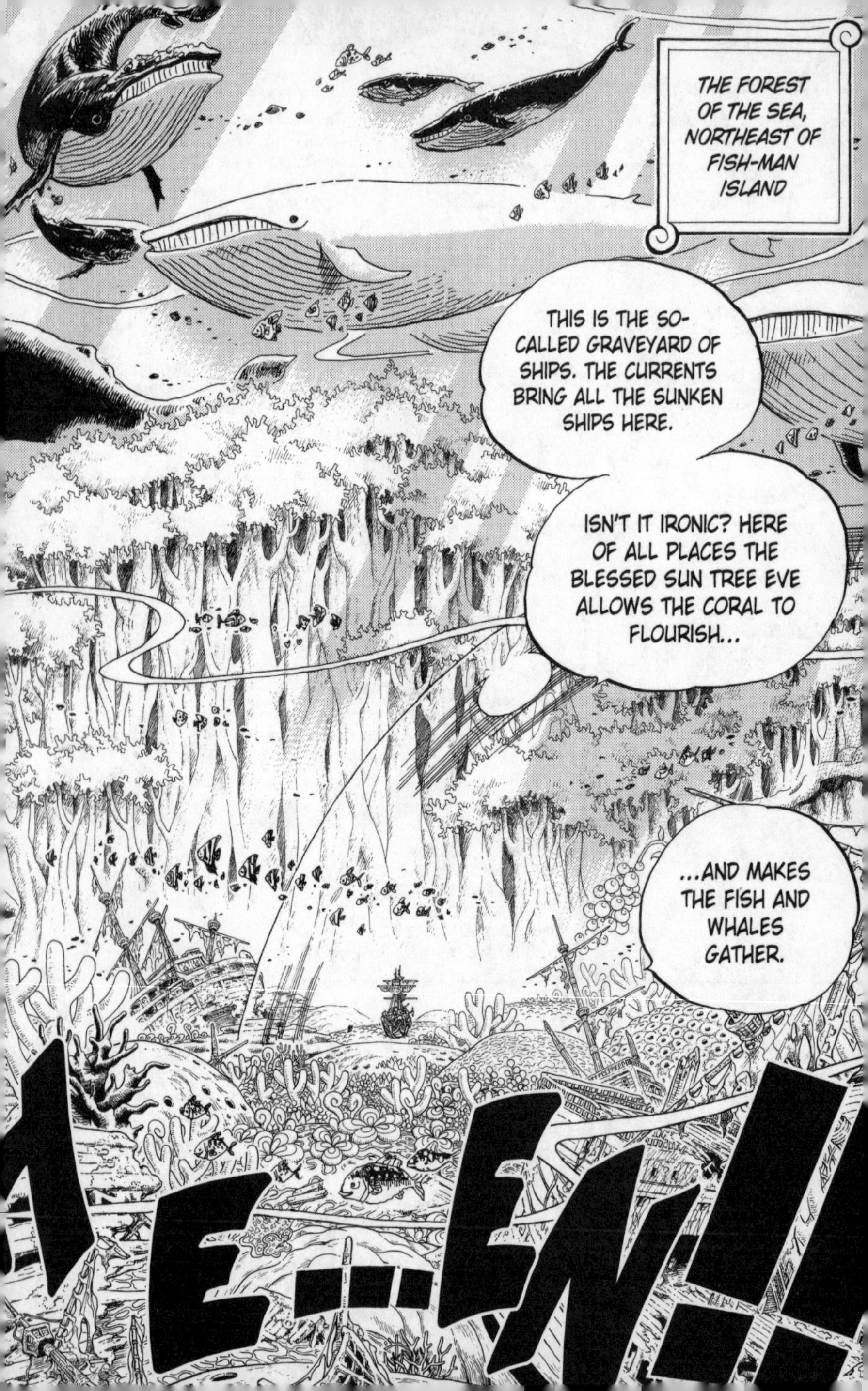
THE FOREST OF THE SEA, NORTHEAST OF FISH-MAN ISLAND
THIS IS THE SO-CALLED GRAVEYARD OF SHIPS. THE CURRENTS BRING ALL THE SUNKEN SHIPS HERE.
ISN'T IT IRONIC? HERE OF ALL PLACES THE BLESSED SUN TREE EVE ALLOWS THE CORAL TO FLOURISH...
...AND MAKES THE FISH AND WHALES GATHER.

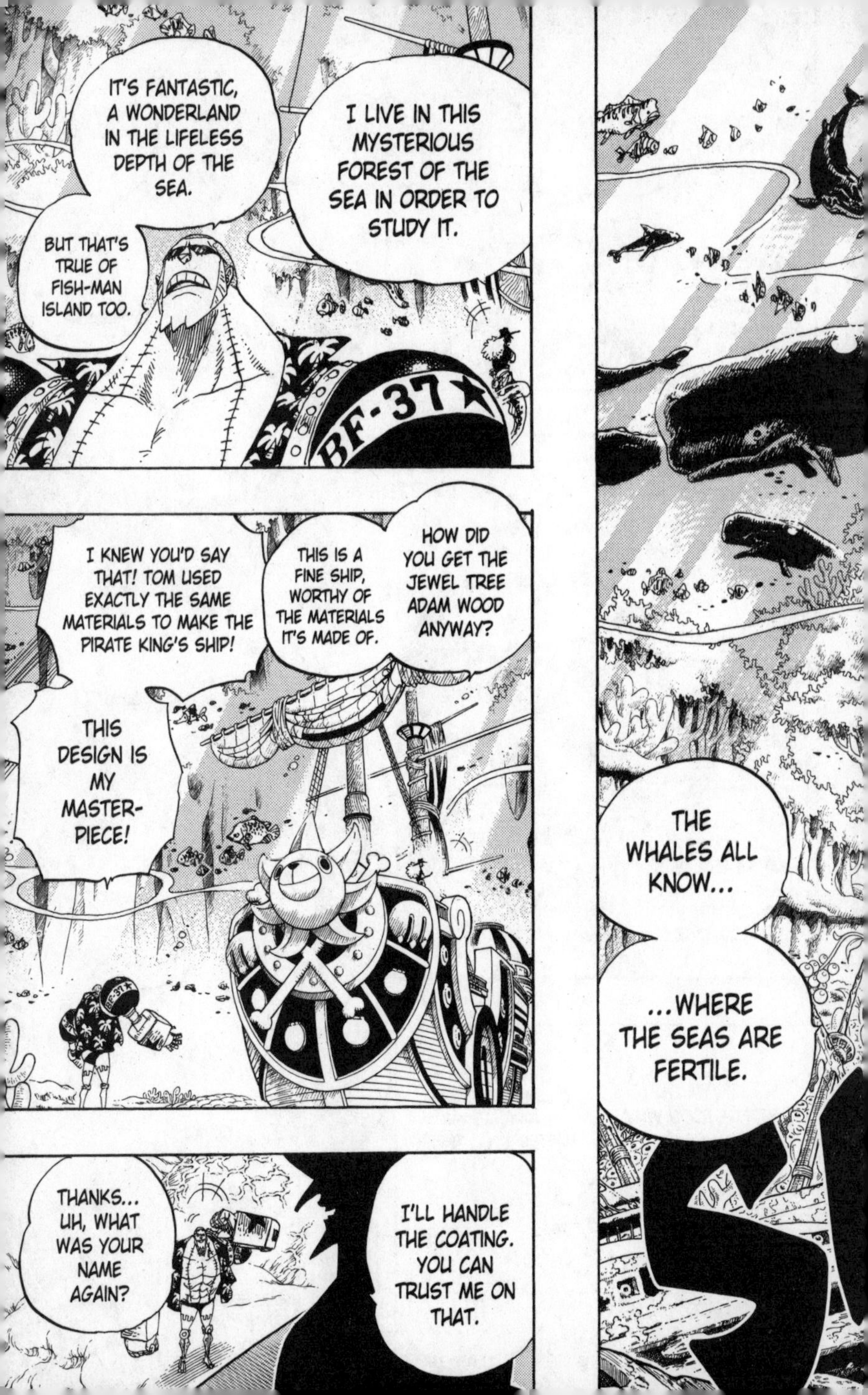
THE WHALES ALL KNOW...
...WHERE THE SEAS ARE FERTILE.
I LIVE IN THIS MYSTERIOUS FOREST OF THE SEA IN ORDER TO STUDY IT.
IT'S FANTASTIC, A WONDERLAND IN THE LIFELESS DEPTH OF THE SEA.
BUT THAT'S TRUE OF FISH-MAN ISLAND TOO.
BF-37
HOW DID YOU GET THE JEWEL TREE ADAM WOOD ANYWAY?
THIS IS A FINE SHIP, WORTHY OF THE MATERIALS IT'S MADE OF.
I KNEW YOU'D SAY THAT! TOM USED EXACTLY THE SAME MATERIALS TO MAKE THE PIRATE KING'S SHIP!
THIS DESIGN IS MY MASTER-PIECE!
I'LL HANDLE THE COATING. YOU CAN TRUST ME ON THAT.
THANKS... UH, WHAT WAS YOUR NAME AGAIN?

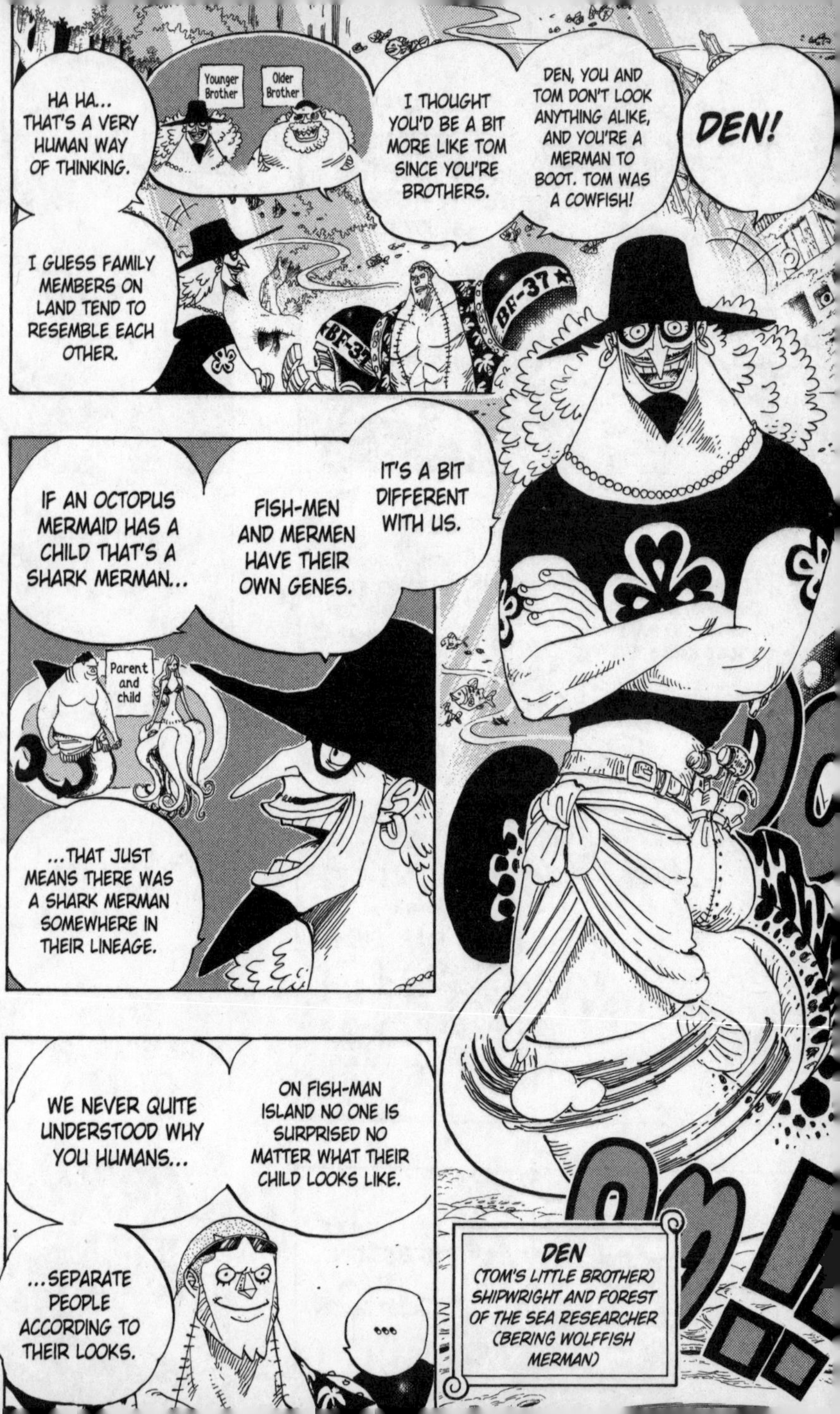
DEN!
DEN, YOU AND TOM DON'T LOOK ANYTHING ALIKE, AND YOU'RE A MERMAN TO BOOT. TOM WAS A COWFISH!
I THOUGHT YOU'D BE A BIT MORE LIKE TOM SINCE YOU'RE BROTHERS.
Older Brother
Younger Brother
HA HA... THAT'S A VERY HUMAN WAY OF THINKING.
I GUESS FAMILY MEMBERS ON LAND TEND TO RESEMBLE EACH OTHER.
BF-37
DEN
(TOM'S LITTLE BROTHER)
SHIPWRIGHT AND FOREST OF THE SEA RESEARCHER
(BERING WOLFFISH MERMAN)
IT'S A BIT DIFFERENT WITH US.
FISH-MEN AND MERMEN HAVE THEIR OWN GENES.
IF AN OCTOPUS MERMAID HAS A CHILD THAT'S A SHARK MERMAN...
Parent and child
...THAT JUST MEANS THERE WAS A SHARK MERMAN SOMEWHERE IN THEIR LINEAGE.
ON FISH-MAN ISLAND NO ONE IS SURPRISED NO MATTER WHAT THEIR CHILD LOOKS LIKE.
WE NEVER QUITE UNDERSTOOD WHY YOU HUMANS...
...SEPARATE PEOPLE ACCORDING TO THEIR LOOKS.
...

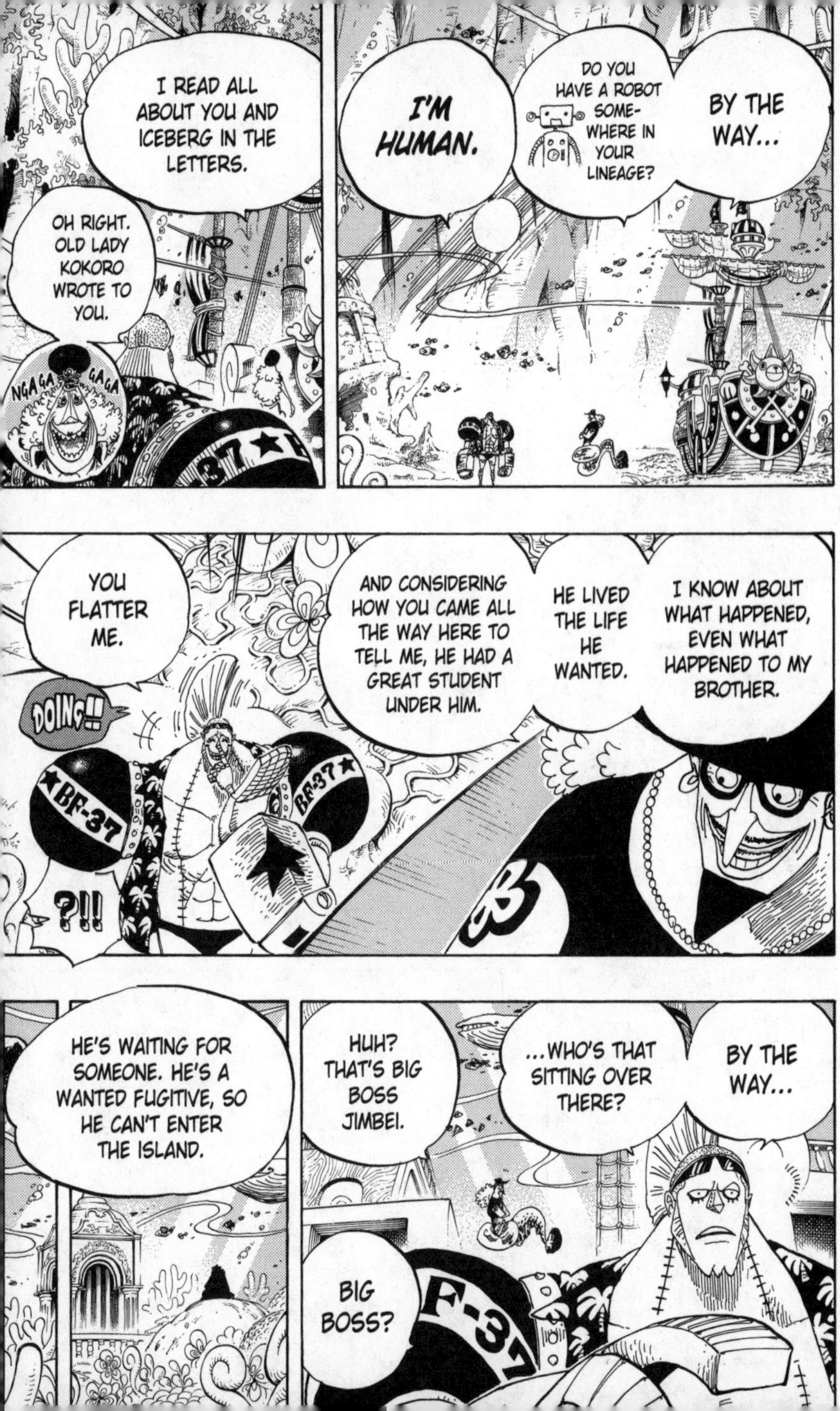
BY THE WAY...
DO YOU HAVE A ROBOT SOME-WHERE IN YOUR LINEAGE?
I'M HUMAN.
I READ ALL ABOUT YOU AND ICEBERG IN THE LETTERS.
OH RIGHT. OLD LADY KOKORO WROTE TO YOU.
NGAGA GAGA
I KNOW ABOUT WHAT HAPPENED, EVEN WHAT HAPPENED TO MY BROTHER.
HE LIVED THE LIFE HE WANTED.
AND CONSIDERING HOW YOU CAME ALL THE WAY HERE TO TELL ME, HE HAD A GREAT STUDENT UNDER HIM.
YOU FLATTER ME.
DOING!!
?!!
BY THE WAY...
...WHO'S THAT SITTING OVER THERE?
HUH? THAT'S BIG BOSS JIMBEI.
BIG BOSS?
HE'S WAITING FOR SOMEONE. HE'S A WANTED FUGITIVE, SO HE CAN'T ENTER THE ISLAND.

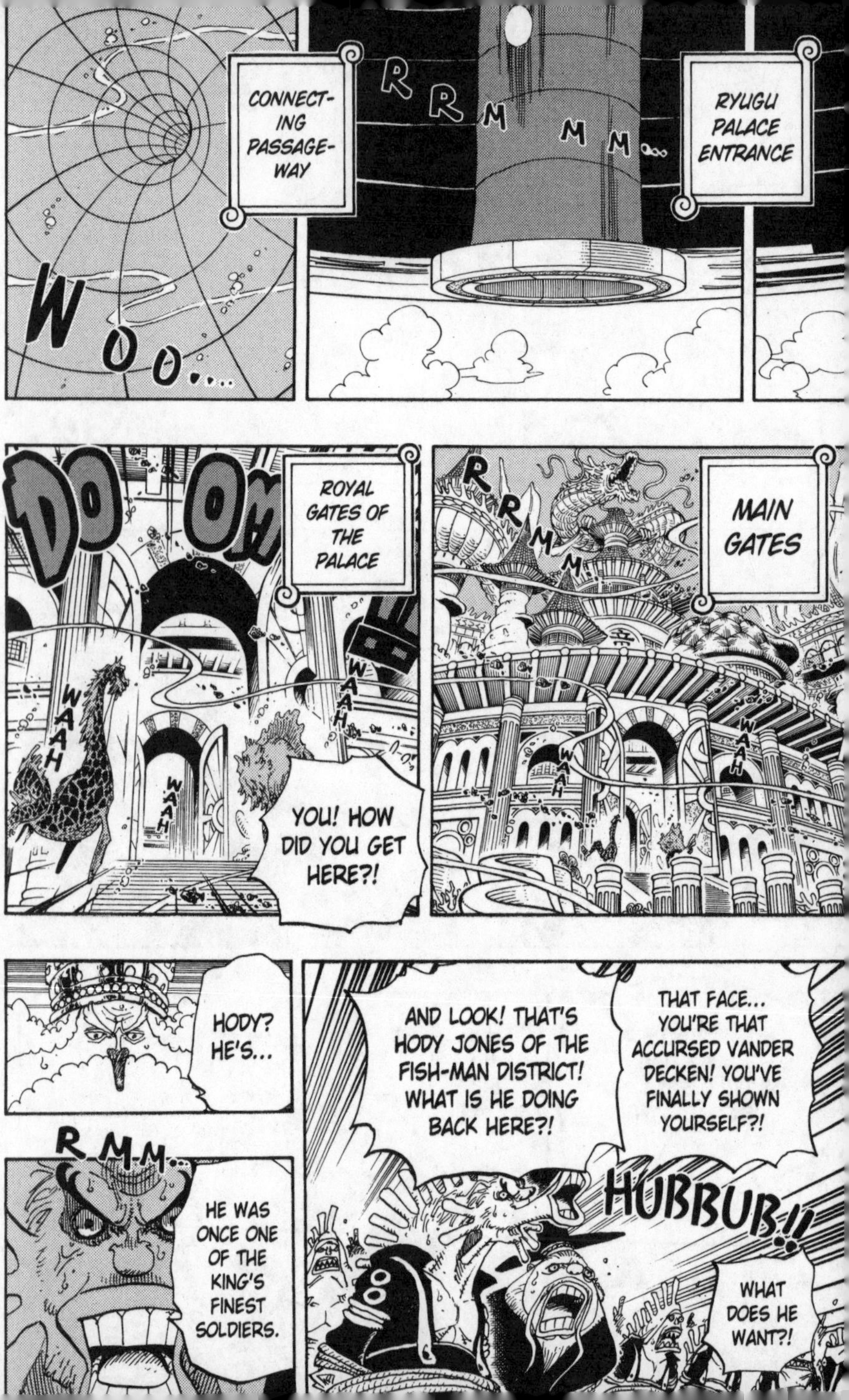
RYUGU PALACE ENTRANCE
RRRMMMM...
CONNECTING PASSAGEWAY
WOO...
MAIN GATES
RRRMM!
WAAH
WAAH
ROYAL GATES OF THE PALACE
DOOM
WAAH
YOU! HOW DID YOU GET HERE?!
WAAH
WAAH
THAT FACE... YOU'RE THAT ACCURSED VANDER DECKEN! YOU'VE FINALLY SHOWN YOURSELF?!
AND LOOK! THAT'S HODY JONES OF THE FISH-MAN DISTRICT! WHAT IS HE DOING BACK HERE?!
HUBBUB!!
WHAT DOES HE WANT?!
HODY? HE'S...
RMM...
HE WAS ONCE ONE OF THE KING'S FINEST SOLDIERS.

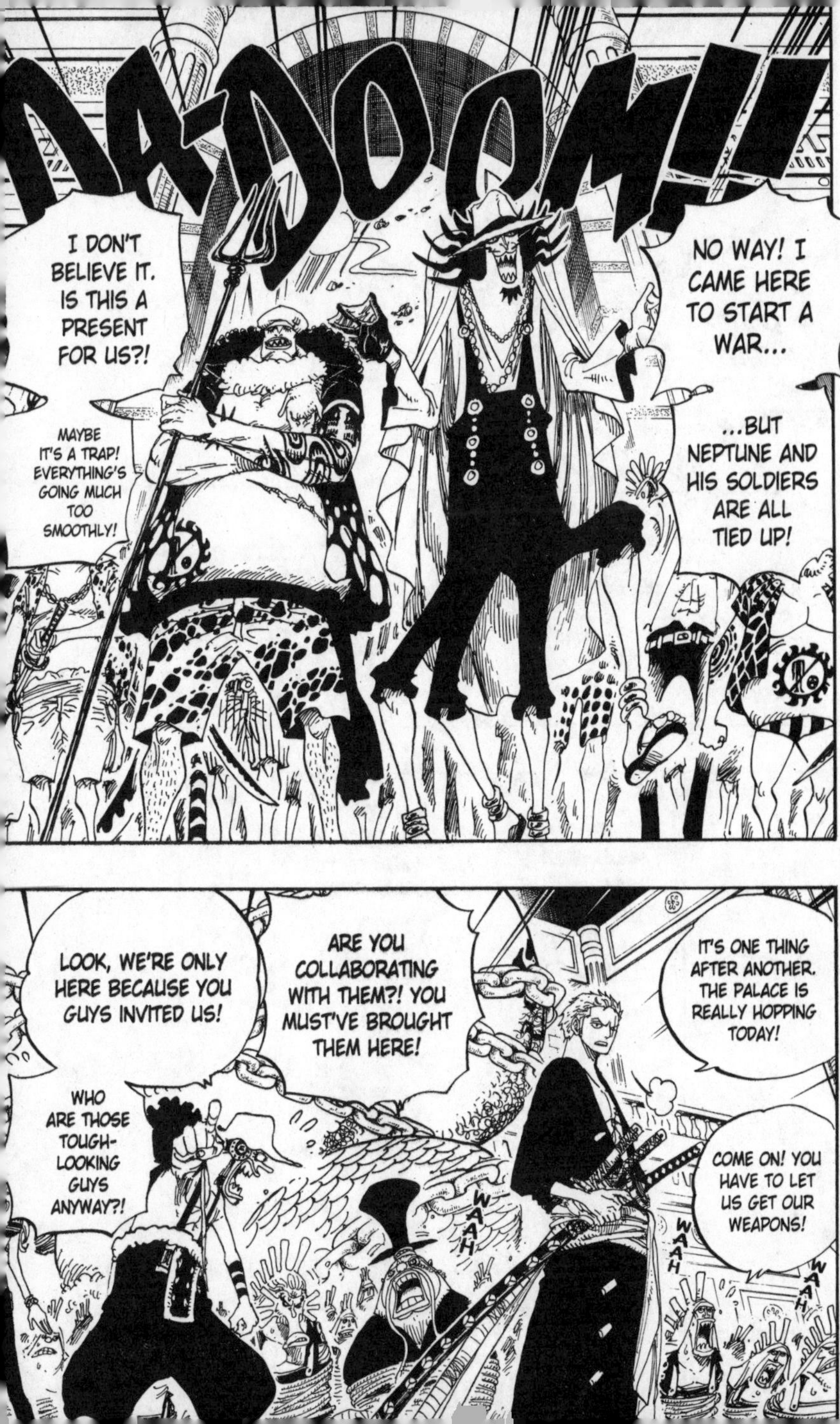
DA-DOOM!!
NO WAY! I CAME HERE TO START A WAR...
...BUT NEPTUNE AND HIS SOLDIERS ARE ALL TIED UP!
I DON'T BELIEVE IT. IS THIS A PRESENT FOR US?!
MAYBE IT'S A TRAP! EVERYTHING'S GOING MUCH TOO SMOOTHLY!
IT'S ONE THING AFTER ANOTHER. THE PALACE IS REALLY HOPPING TODAY!
COME ON! YOU HAVE TO LET US GET OUR WEAPONS!
WAAH
WAAH
WAAH
ARE YOU COLLABORATING WITH THEM?! YOU MUST'VE BROUGHT THEM HERE!
LOOK, WE'RE ONLY HERE BECAUSE YOU GUYS INVITED US!
WHO ARE THOSE TOUGH-LOOKING GUYS ANYWAY?!

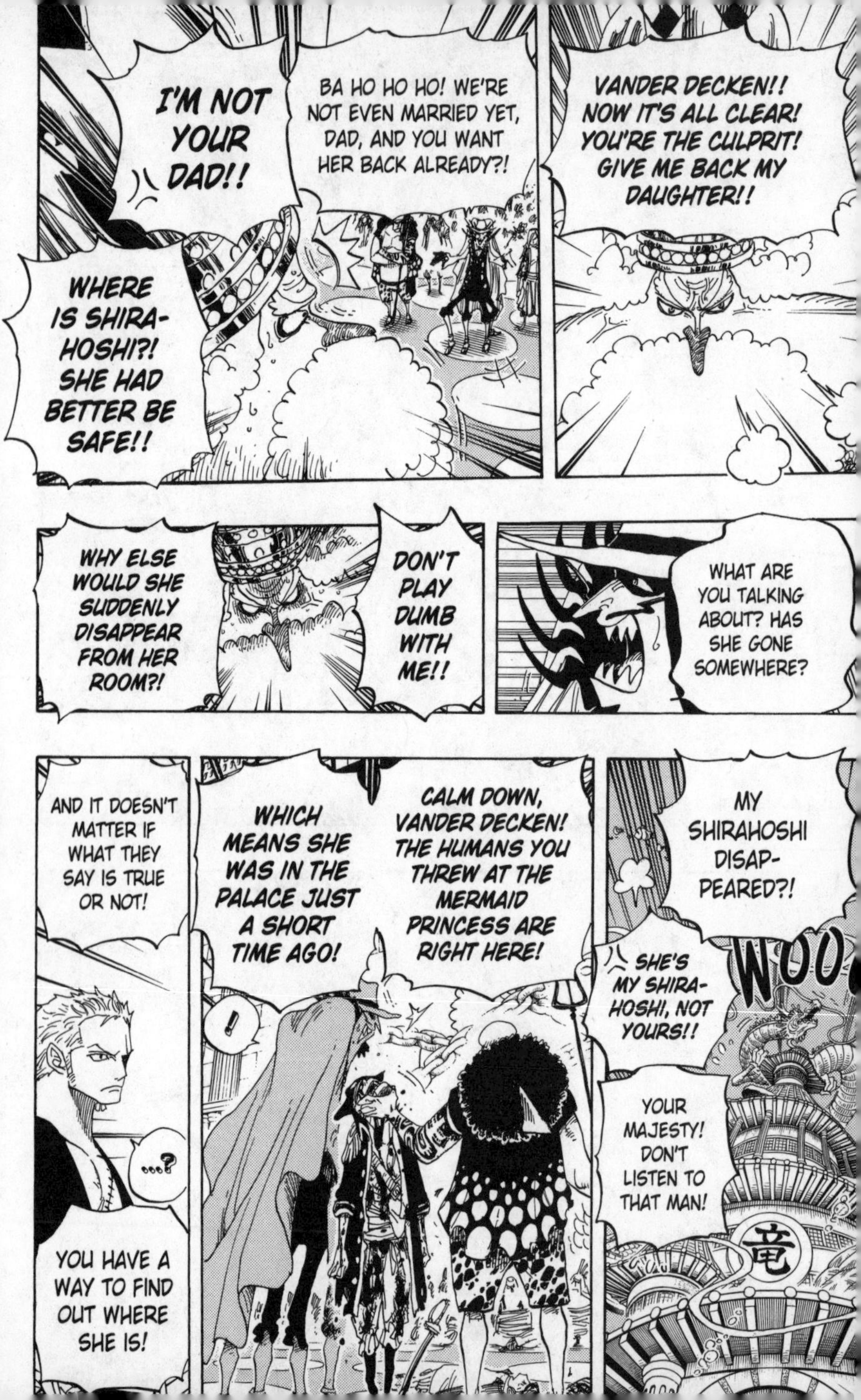
VANDER DECKEN!! NOW IT'S ALL CLEAR! YOU'RE THE CULPRIT! GIVE ME BACK MY DAUGHTER!!
BA HO HO HO! WE'RE NOT EVEN MARRIED YET, DAD, AND YOU WANT HER BACK ALREADY?!
I'M NOT YOUR DAD!!
WHERE IS SHIRAHOSHI?! SHE HAD BETTER BE SAFE!!
WHAT ARE YOU TALKING ABOUT? HAS SHE GONE SOMEWHERE?
DON'T PLAY DUMB WITH ME!!
WHY ELSE WOULD SHE SUDDENLY DISAPPEAR FROM HER ROOM?!
MY SHIRAHOSHI DISAPPEARED?!
WOO
SHE'S MY SHIRAHOSHI, NOT YOURS!!
YOUR MAJESTY! DON'T LISTEN TO THAT MAN!
竜
CALM DOWN, VANDER DECKEN! THE HUMANS YOU THREW AT THE MERMAID PRINCESS ARE RIGHT HERE!
WHICH MEANS SHE WAS IN THE PALACE JUST A SHORT TIME AGO!
!
AND IT DOESN'T MATTER IF WHAT THEY SAY IS TRUE OR NOT!
...?
YOU HAVE A WAY TO FIND OUT WHERE SHE IS!

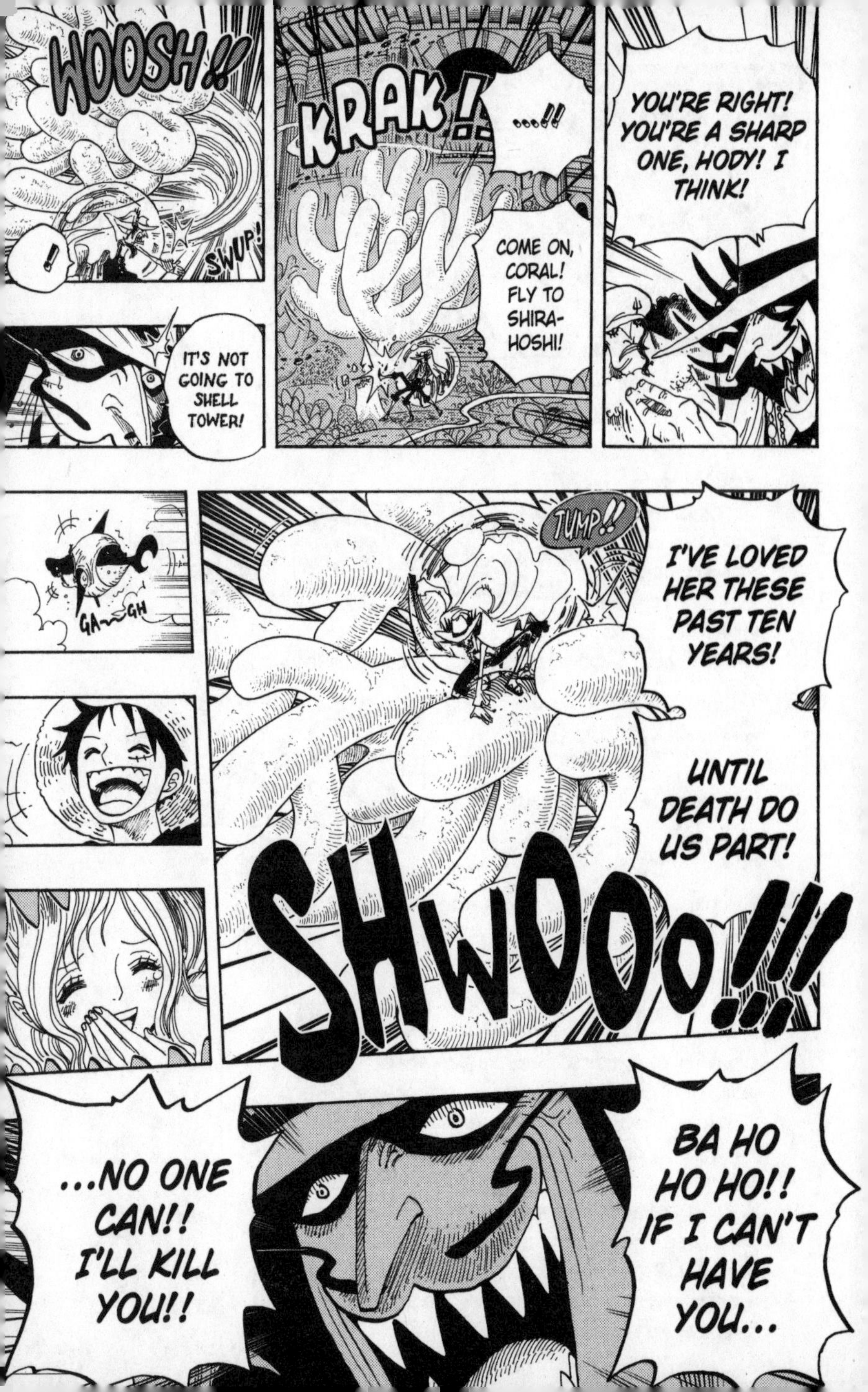
YOU'RE RIGHT! YOU'RE A SHARP ONE, HODY! I THINK!
KRAK!
...!!
COME ON, CORAL! FLY TO SHIRA-HOSHI!
WOOSH!!
!
SWUP!
IT'S NOT GOING TO SHELL TOWER!
TUMP!!
I'VE LOVED HER THESE PAST TEN YEARS!
UNTIL DEATH DO US PART!
SHWOOO!!!
GA~GH
BA HO HO HO!! IF I CAN'T HAVE YOU...
...NO ONE CAN!! I'LL KILL YOU!!

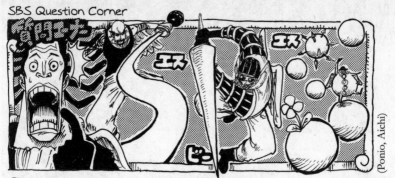

(Ponio, Aichi)

Q: Is Chopper wearing a bonnet over the hat he wore two years ago? If it's not, could you please explain it thoroughly?

--Oonuki=πge

A: You're not wrong. He just put something on top of it. The pink hat is really special to Chopper, so he wouldn't change it.

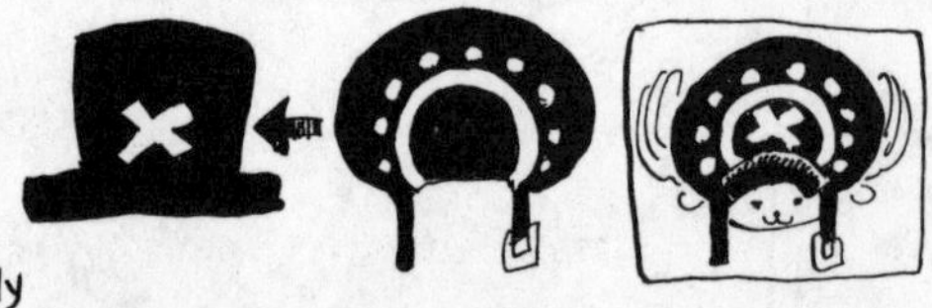

Q: I'd like to see the Kraken picture that Robin drew.

--Ruki

A: Good question. Let's take a look...
...!ξ...!.!

Q: In chapter 612, there was someone (a fish) who looked like Octopako at Fishverly Hills. Why was she so angry?

--Princes Shirasuboshi

A: There is, isn't there?! Octopako is the woman who dumped Hachi, and she appeared on the chapter cover of chapter 203 in volume 22. You've got good eyes! She's actually a socialite who grew up in Fishverly Hills. She dreams of marrying the prince, but of course she's never even been to Ryugu Palace. So she's angry that Camie, who used to work at Hachi's store, and a bunch of pirates from who knows where were invited to Ryugyu Palace. She's like, "I've never even Been!!"

Chapter 617:

INCIDENT AT CORAL HILL

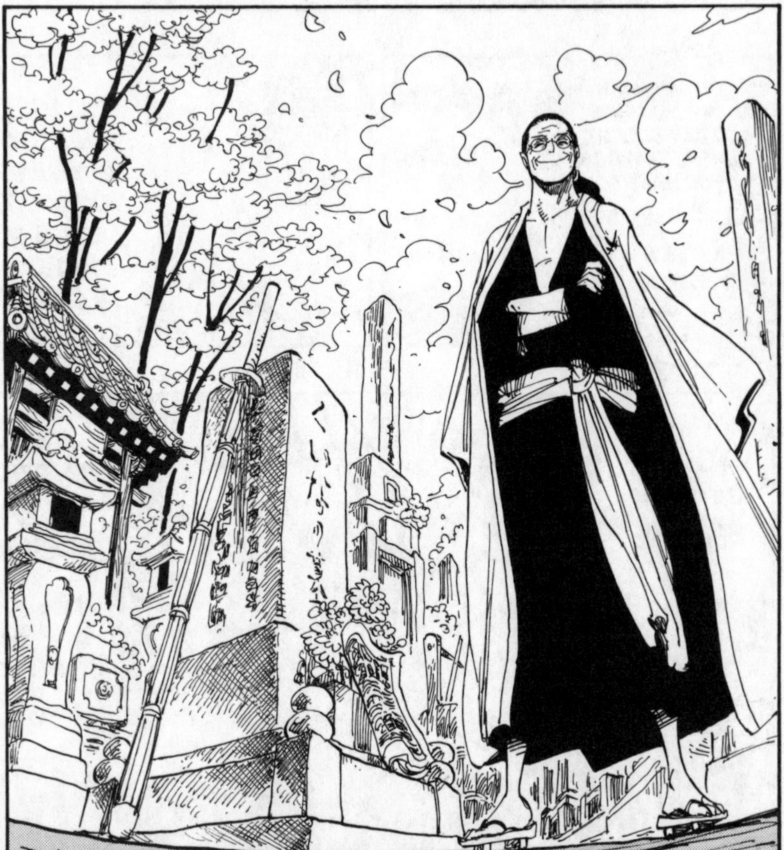

DECKS OF THE WORLD, VOL. 5:
FROST MOON VILLAGE–REPORTING TO KUINA

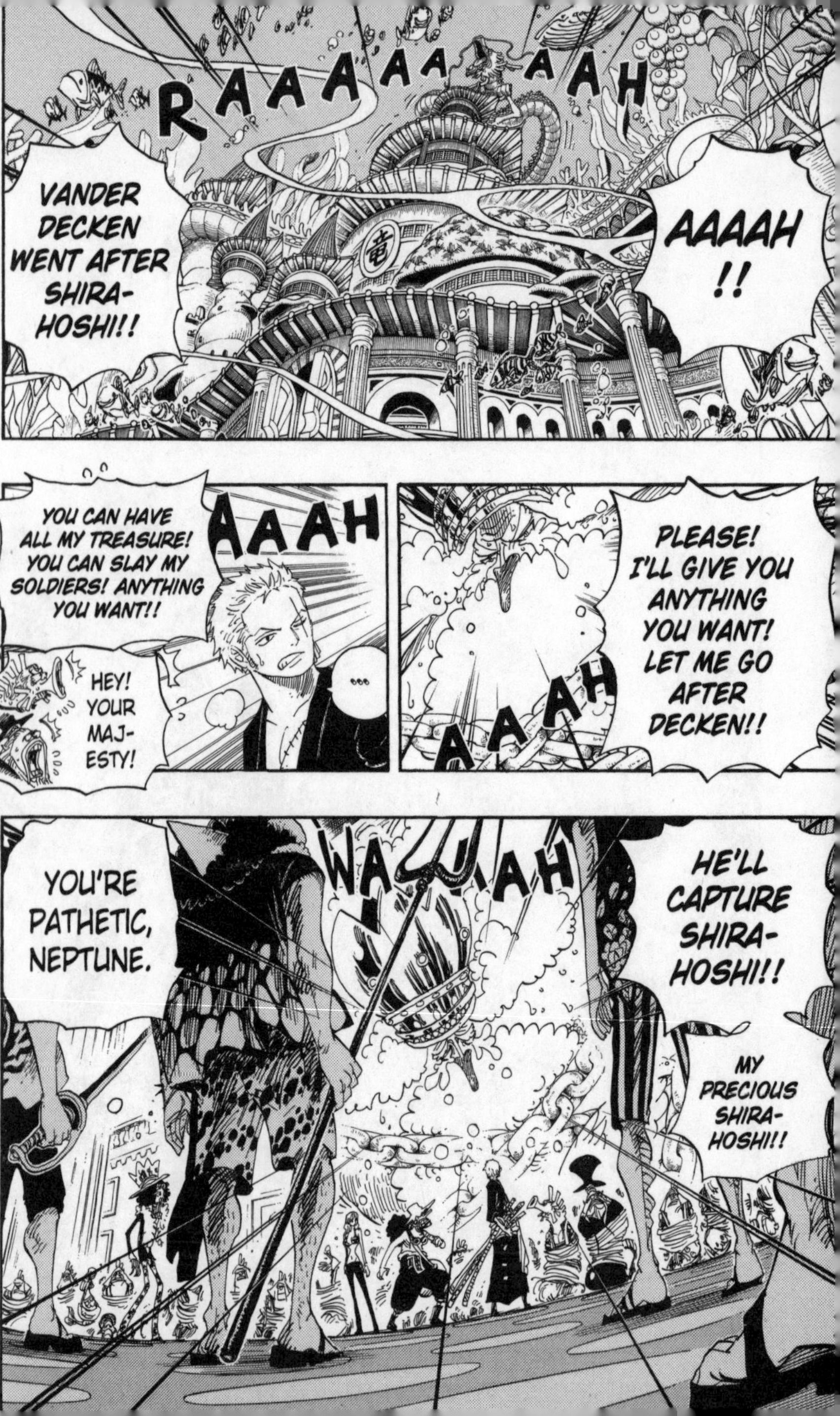
RAAAAAAH
AAAAH!!
VANDER DECKEN WENT AFTER SHIRA-HOSHI!!
PLEASE! I'LL GIVE YOU ANYTHING YOU WANT! LET ME GO AFTER DECKEN!!
AAAAH
AAAH
YOU CAN HAVE ALL MY TREASURE! YOU CAN SLAY MY SOLDIERS! ANYTHING YOU WANT!!
...
HEY! YOUR MAJ-ESTY!
WAAAH
HE'LL CAPTURE SHIRA-HOSHI!!
MY PRECIOUS SHIRA-HOSHI!!
YOU'RE PATHETIC, NEPTUNE.

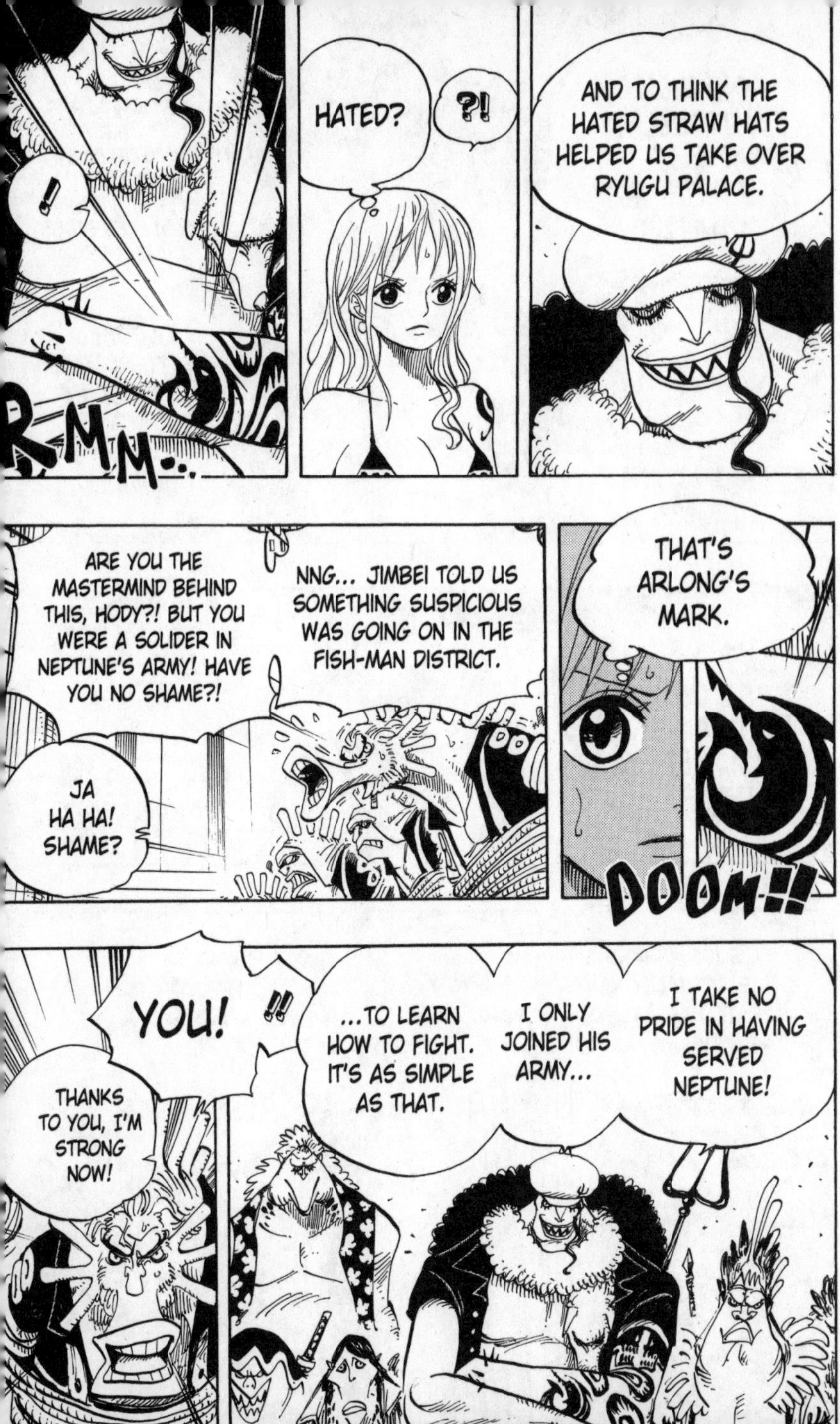
AND TO THINK THE HATED STRAW HATS HELPED US TAKE OVER RYUGU PALACE.
?!
HATED?
!
RMM...
THAT'S ARLONG'S MARK.
DOOM!!
NNG... JIMBEI TOLD US SOMETHING SUSPICIOUS WAS GOING ON IN THE FISH-MAN DISTRICT.
ARE YOU THE MASTERMIND BEHIND THIS, HODY?! BUT YOU WERE A SOLIDER IN NEPTUNE'S ARMY! HAVE YOU NO SHAME?!
JA HA HA! SHAME?
I TAKE NO PRIDE IN HAVING SERVED NEPTUNE!
I ONLY JOINED HIS ARMY...
...TO LEARN HOW TO FIGHT. IT'S AS SIMPLE AS THAT.
YOU!!!
THANKS TO YOU, I'M STRONG NOW!

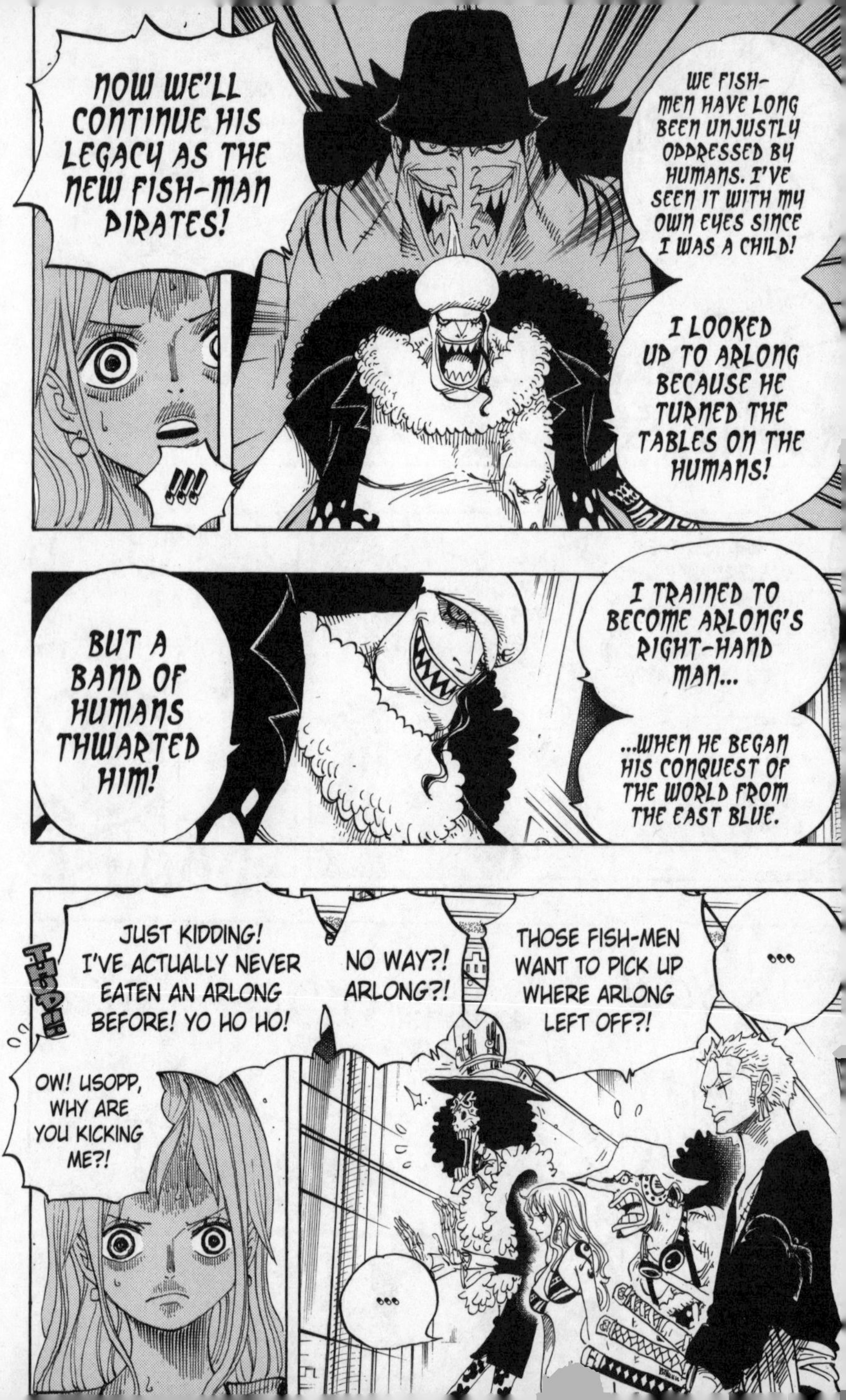

WE FISH-MEN HAVE LONG BEEN UNJUSTLY OPPRESSED BY HUMANS. I'VE SEEN IT WITH MY OWN EYES SINCE I WAS A CHILD!
I LOOKED UP TO ARLONG BECAUSE HE TURNED THE TABLES ON THE HUMANS!
NOW WE'LL CONTINUE HIS LEGACY AS THE NEW FISH-MAN PIRATES!
!!!
I TRAINED TO BECOME ARLONG'S RIGHT-HAND MAN...
...WHEN HE BEGAN HIS CONQUEST OF THE WORLD FROM THE EAST BLUE.
BUT A BAND OF HUMANS THWARTED HIM!
...
THOSE FISH-MEN WANT TO PICK UP WHERE ARLONG LEFT OFF?!
NO WAY?! ARLONG?!
JUST KIDDING! I'VE ACTUALLY NEVER EATEN AN ARLONG BEFORE! YO HO HO!
...
THUD!!
OW! USOPP, WHY ARE YOU KICKING ME?!

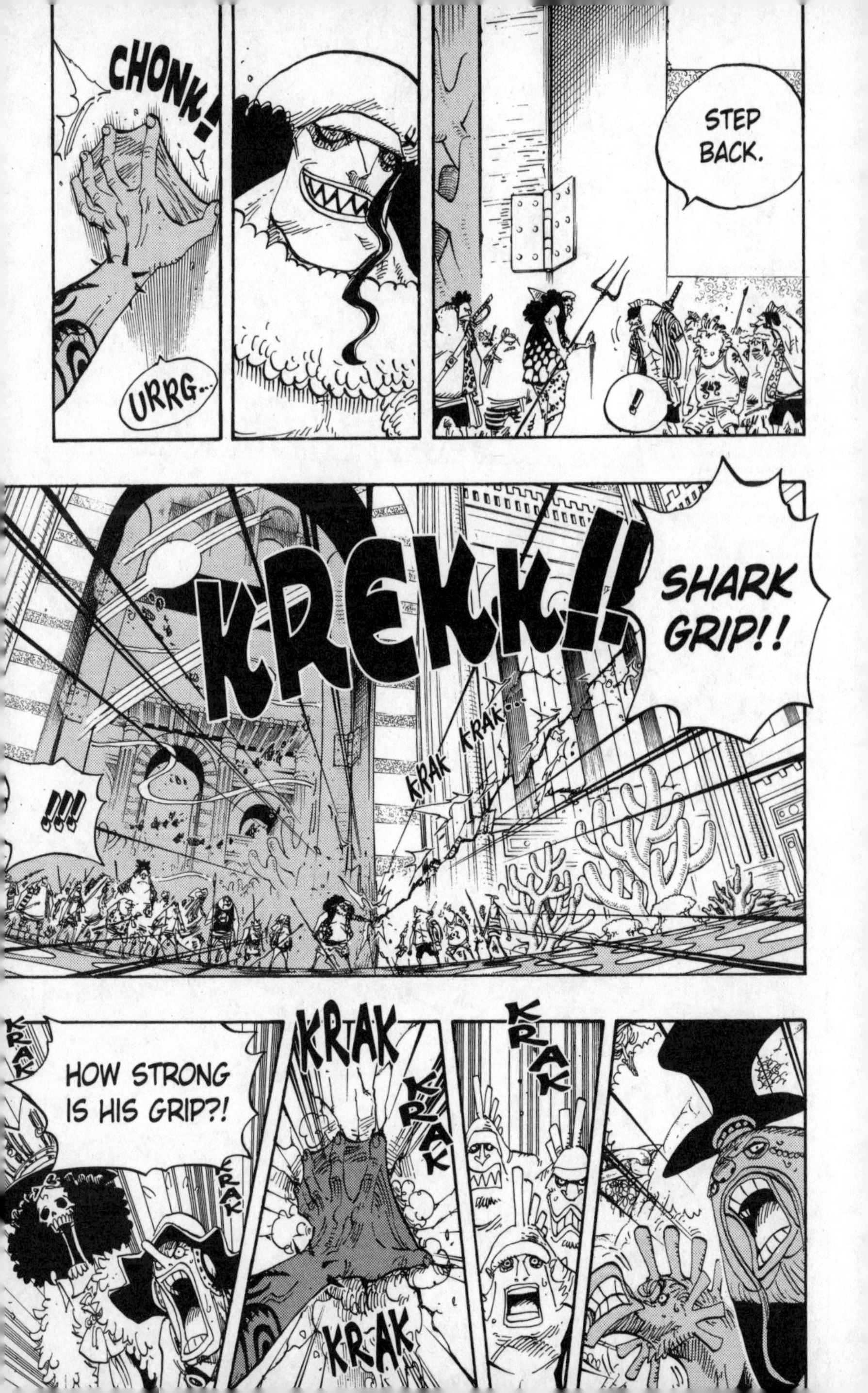
STEP BACK.
!
CHONK!!
URRG...
SHARK GRIP!!
KREKK!!
KRAK KRAK...
KRAK
!!!
KRAK
KRAK
KRAK
KRAK
KRAK
HOW STRONG IS HIS GRIP?!
KRAK
KRAK

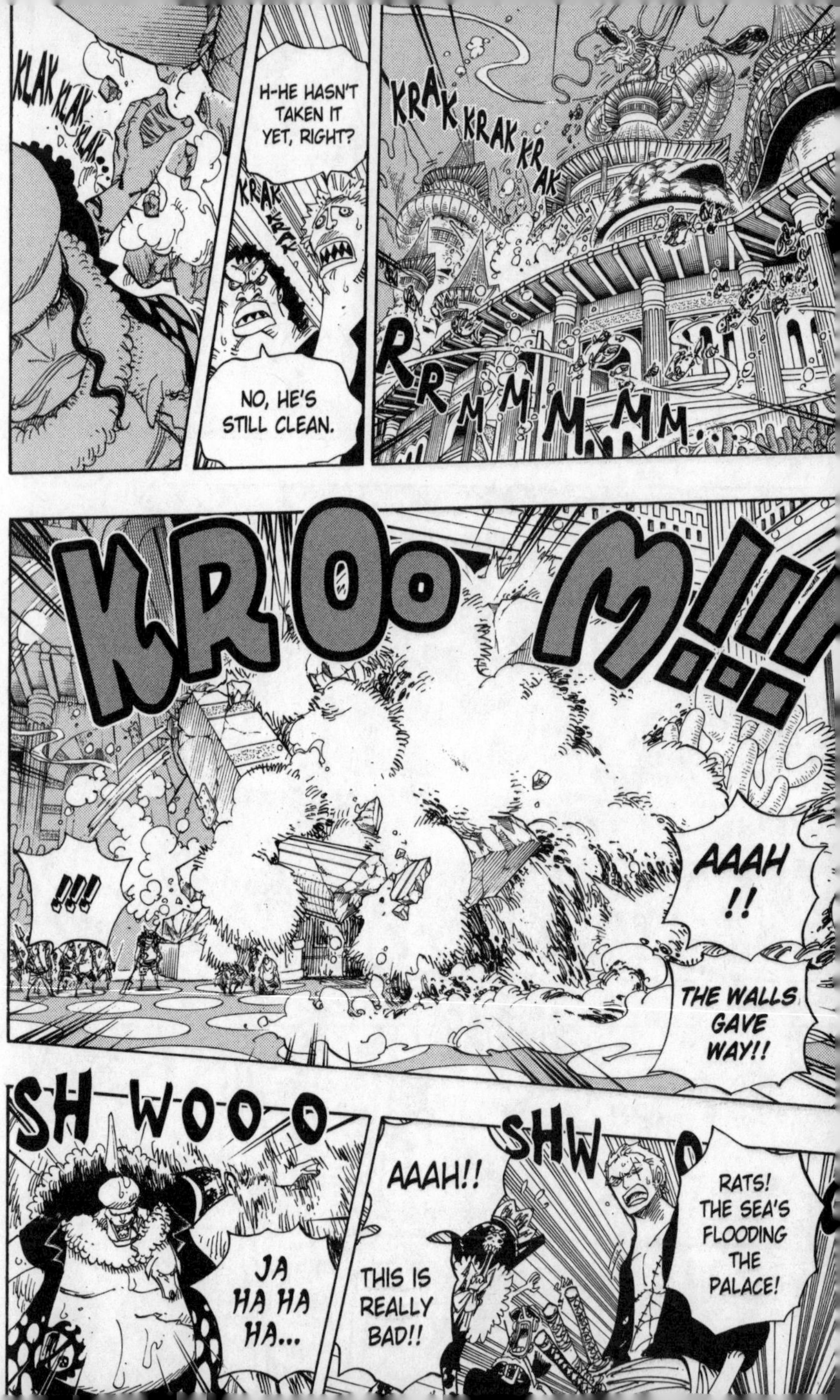
KRAK KRAK KRAK KRAK
RRMMMMMM...!!
H-HE HASN'T TAKEN IT YET, RIGHT?
KRAK
NO, HE'S STILL CLEAN.
KLAK KLAK KLAK
KROOOM!!!
AAAH!!
THE WALLS GAVE WAY!!
!!!
SHW O
AAAH!!
RATS! THE SEA'S FLOODING THE PALACE!
THIS IS REALLY BAD!!
SH WOO O
JA HA HA HA...

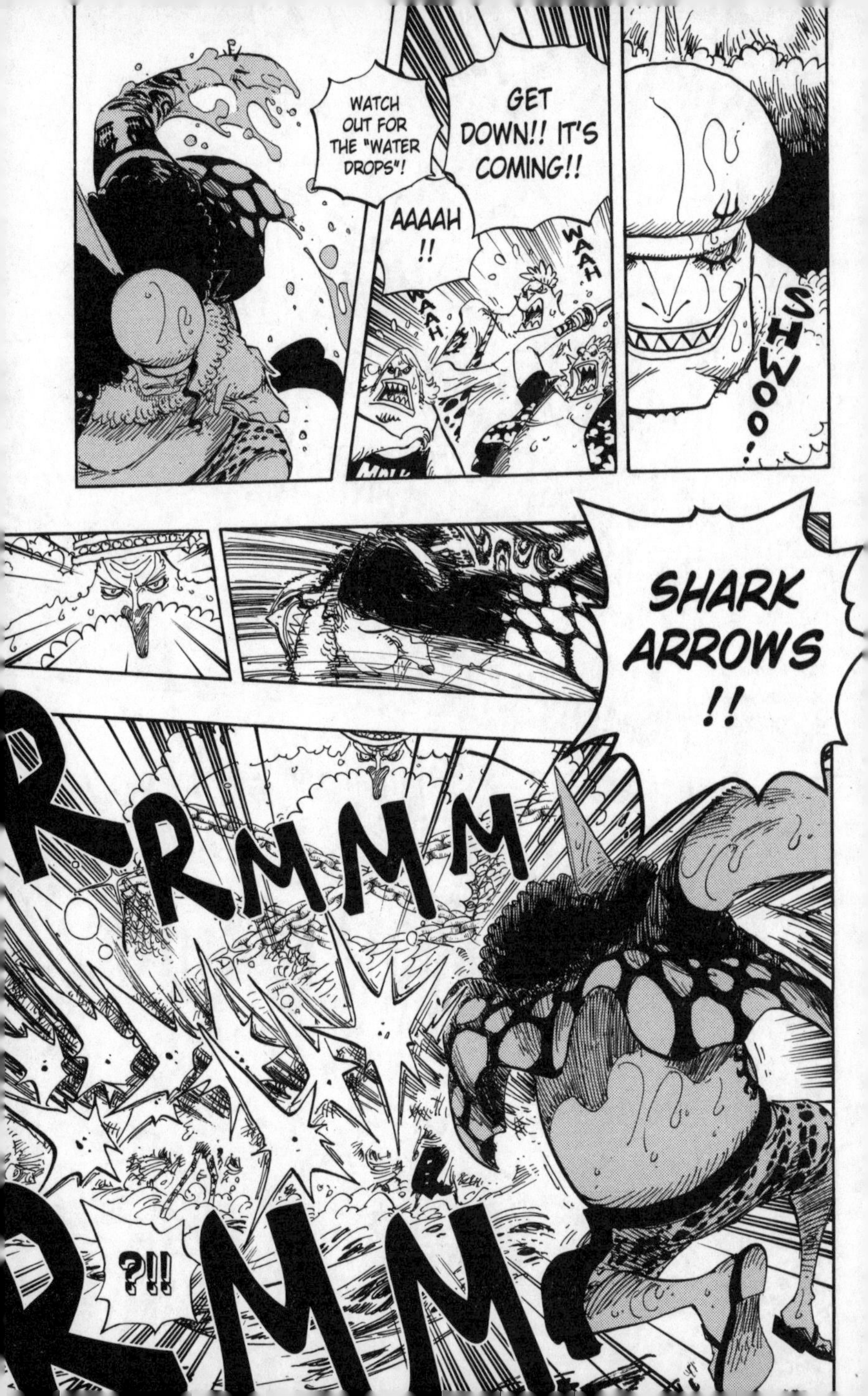
SHWOO...
GET DOWN!! IT'S COMING!!
WATCH OUT FOR THE "WATER DROPS"!
AAAAH !!
WAAH
WAAH
SHARK ARROWS !!
RRMMM
RMMM
?!!

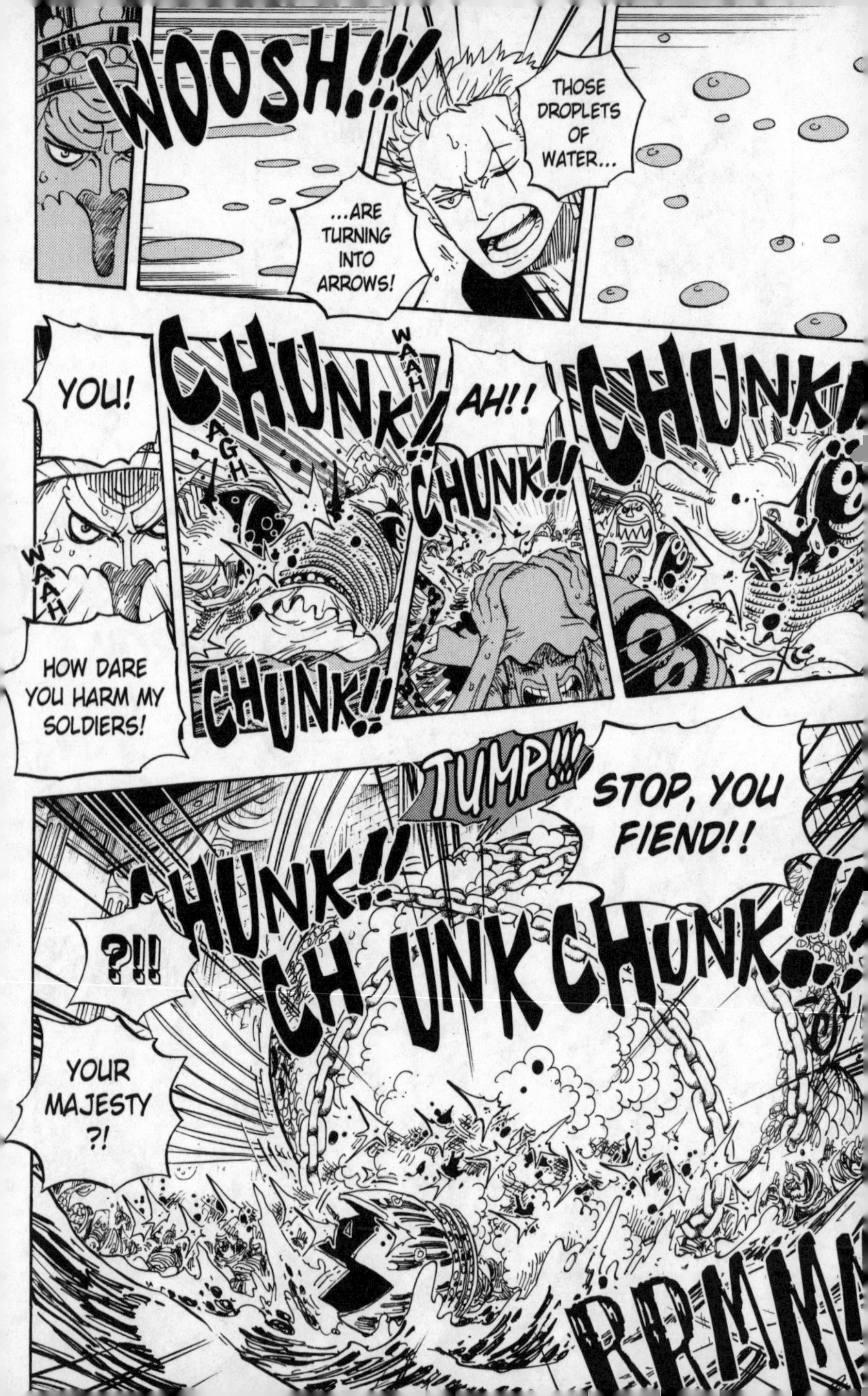
THOSE DROPLETS OF WATER...
...ARE TURNING INTO ARROWS!
WOOSH!!!
CHUNK!!
AH!!
CHUNK!!
WAAH
CHUNK!!
AGH
CHUNK!!
YOU!
WAAH
HOW DARE YOU HARM MY SOLDIERS!
STOP, YOU FIEND!!
TUMP!!!
CHUNK!!
CHUNK
CHUNK!!
?!!
YOUR MAJESTY ?!
RRMM

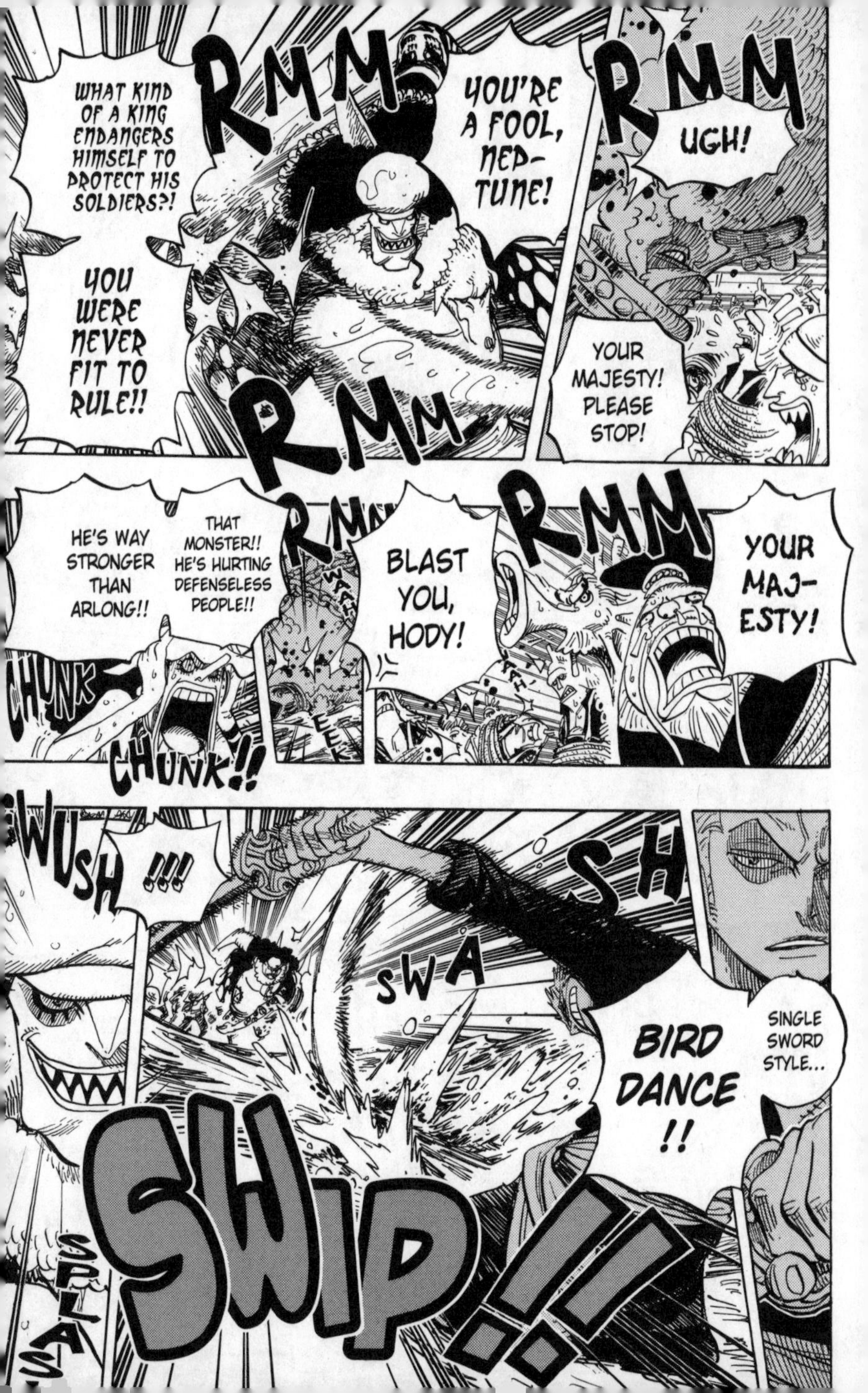
RMM
UGH!
YOUR MAJESTY! PLEASE STOP!
RMM
YOU'RE A FOOL, NEPTUNE!
WHAT KIND OF A KING ENDANGERS HIMSELF TO PROTECT HIS SOLDIERS?!
YOU WERE NEVER FIT TO RULE!!
RMM
RMM
YOUR MAJESTY!
BLAST YOU, HODY!
WAAH
EEEK
HE'S WAY STRONGER THAN ARLONG!!
THAT MONSTER!! HE'S HURTING DEFENSELESS PEOPLE!!
CHUNK
CHUNK!!
SH
SINGLE SWORD STYLE...
BIRD DANCE!!
SWA
WUSH!!!
SWIP!!
SPLAS

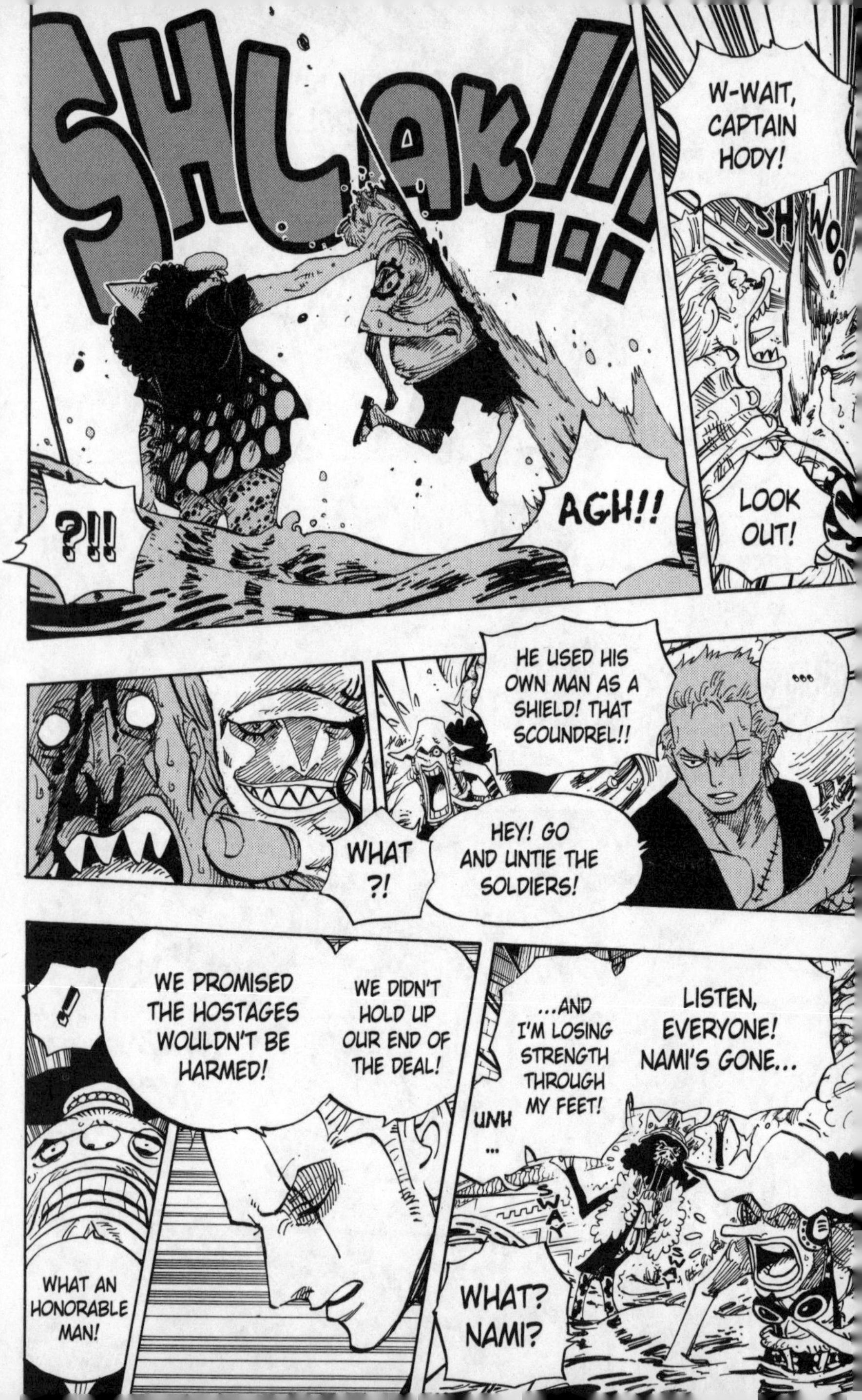
W-WAIT, CAPTAIN HODY!
SHWOO
LOOK OUT!
SHLAK!!
AGH!!
?!!
...
HE USED HIS OWN MAN AS A SHIELD! THAT SCOUNDREL!!
HEY! GO AND UNTIE THE SOLDIERS!
WHAT ?!
LISTEN, EVERYONE! NAMI'S GONE...
...AND I'M LOSING STRENGTH THROUGH MY FEET!
UNH ...
SWAY
SWAY
WHAT? NAMI?
WE PROMISED THE HOSTAGES WOULDN'T BE HARMED!
WE DIDN'T HOLD UP OUR END OF THE DEAL!
!
WHAT AN HONORABLE MAN!

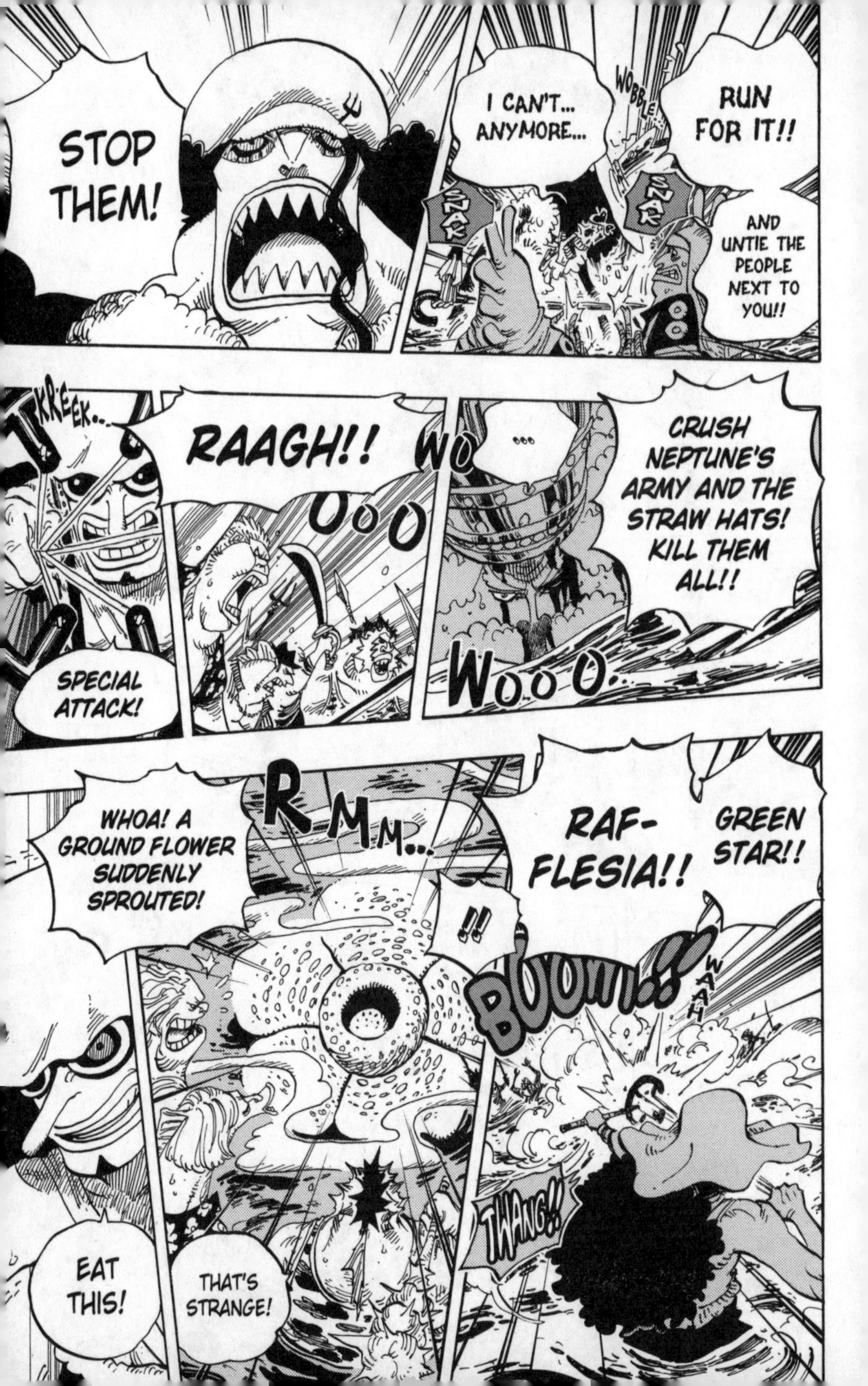
RUN FOR IT!!
AND UNTIE THE PEOPLE NEXT TO YOU!!
WOBBLE
I CAN'T... ANYMORE...
SNAK
SNAK
STOP THEM!
CRUSH NEPTUNE'S ARMY AND THE STRAW HATS! KILL THEM ALL!!
...
WOOO...
RAAGH!!
WOOO
KREEEK...
SPECIAL ATTACK!
GREEN STAR!!
RAF- FLESIA!!
!!
RMM...
WHOA! A GROUND FLOWER SUDDENLY SPROUTED!
WAAH
THWANG!!
THAT'S STRANGE!
EAT THIS!

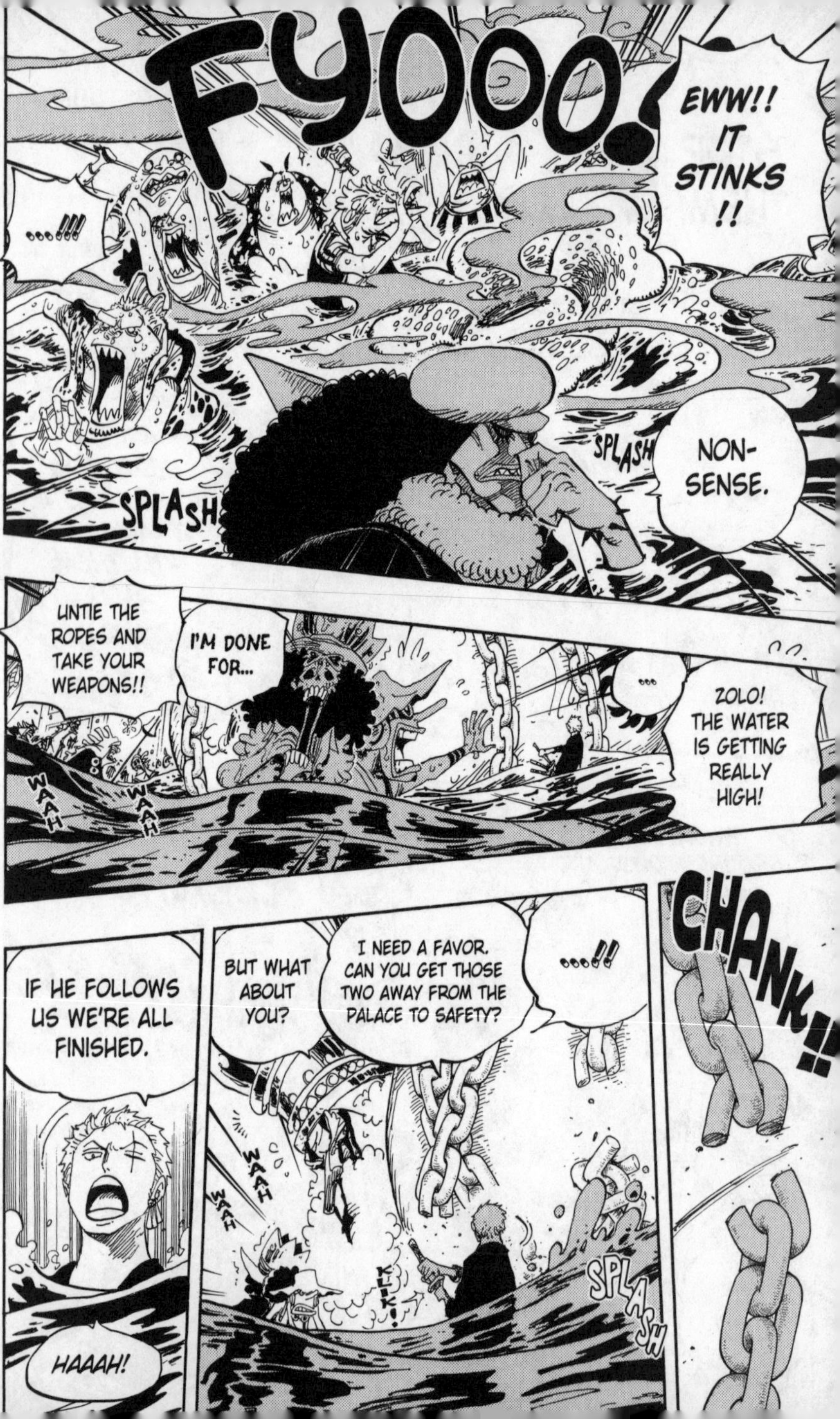
FYOOO!
EWW!! IT STINKS!!
...!!!
SPLASH
NON-SENSE.
SPLASH
ZOLO! THE WATER IS GETTING REALLY HIGH!
...
I'M DONE FOR...
UNTIE THE ROPES AND TAKE YOUR WEAPONS!!
WAAH
WAAH
CHANK!!
...!!
I NEED A FAVOR. CAN YOU GET THOSE TWO AWAY FROM THE PALACE TO SAFETY?
BUT WHAT ABOUT YOU?
WAAH
WAAH
KLIK!
SPLASH
IF HE FOLLOWS US WE'RE ALL FINISHED.
HAAAH!

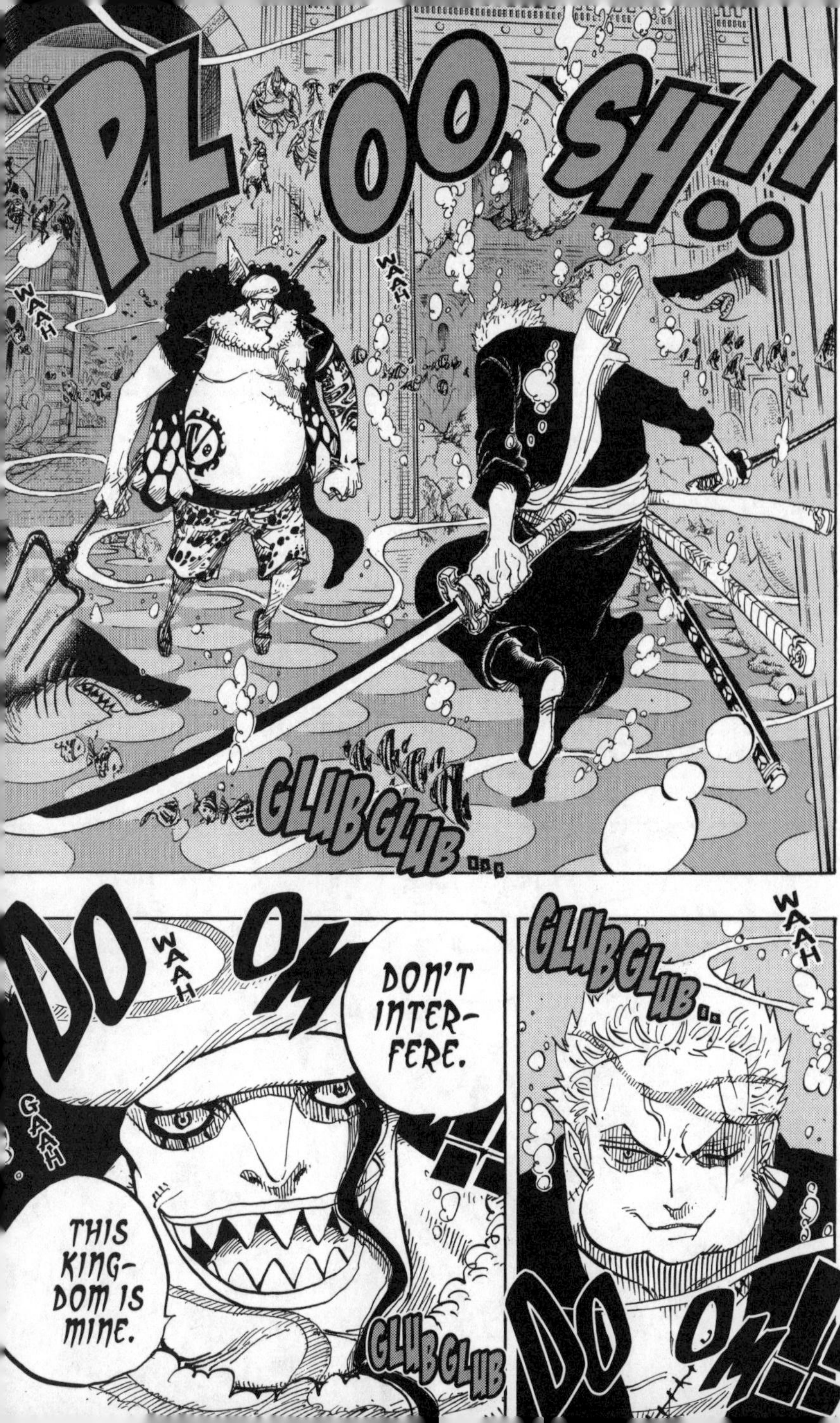
PLOOSH!!
WAAH
WAAH
GLUB GLUB...
WAAH
GLUB GLUB..
DOOM!!
DON'T INTER-FERE.
DOOM
WAAH
GAAH
THIS KING-DOM IS MINE.
GLUB GLUB

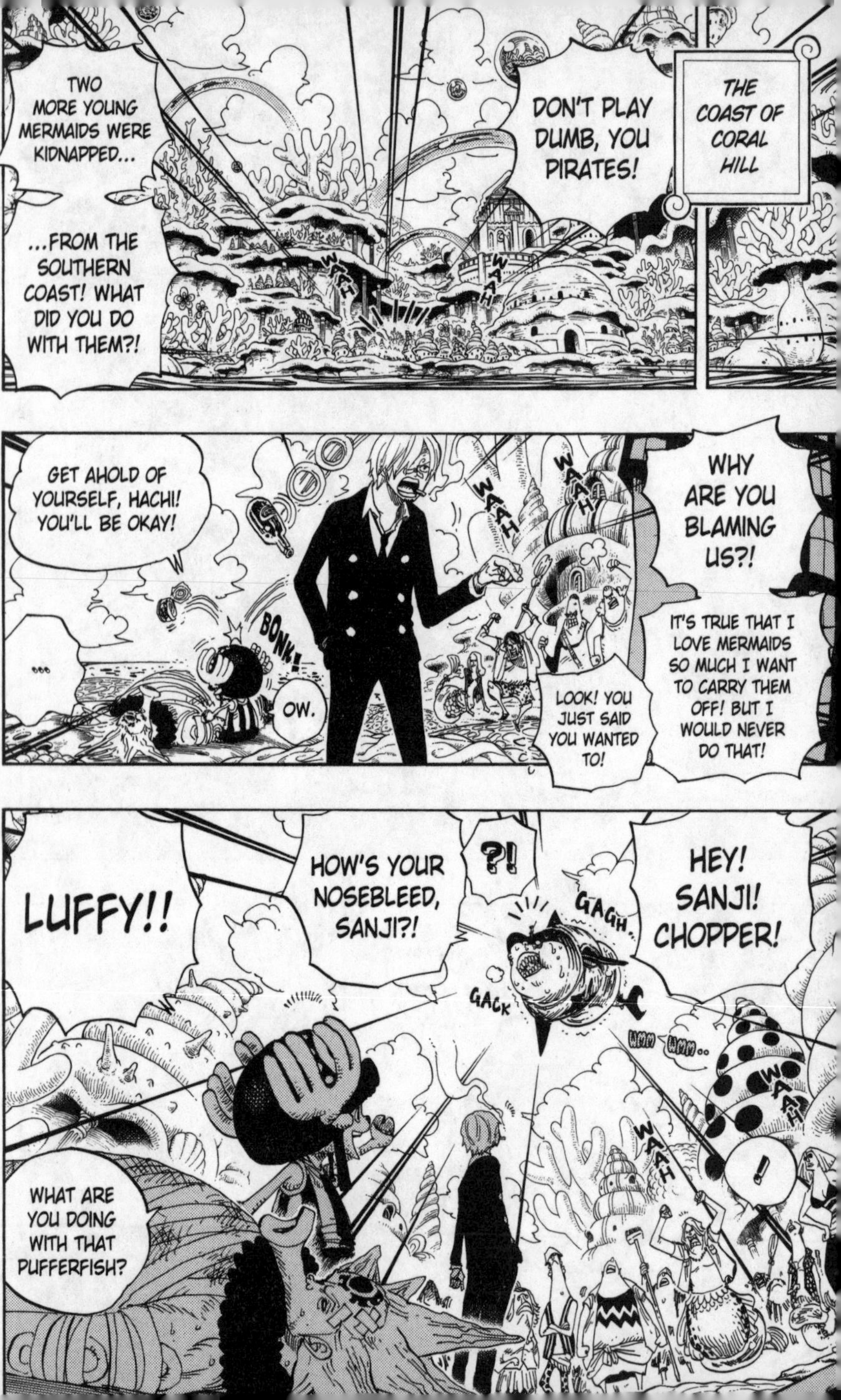
THE COAST OF CORAL HILL
DON'T PLAY DUMB, YOU PIRATES!
TWO MORE YOUNG MERMAIDS WERE KIDNAPPED...
...FROM THE SOUTHERN COAST! WHAT DID YOU DO WITH THEM?!
WAAH
WAAH
WHY ARE YOU BLAMING US?!
IT'S TRUE THAT I LOVE MERMAIDS SO MUCH I WANT TO CARRY THEM OFF! BUT I WOULD NEVER DO THAT!
LOOK! YOU JUST SAID YOU WANTED TO!
WAAH
WAAH
BONK!
OW.
GET AHOLD OF YOURSELF, HACHI! YOU'LL BE OKAY!
...
HEY! SANJI! CHOPPER!
GAGH
?!
HOW'S YOUR NOSEBLEED, SANJI?!
LUFFY!!
GACK
UMM UMM..
WAAH
!
WAAH
WHAT ARE YOU DOING WITH THAT PUFFERFISH?

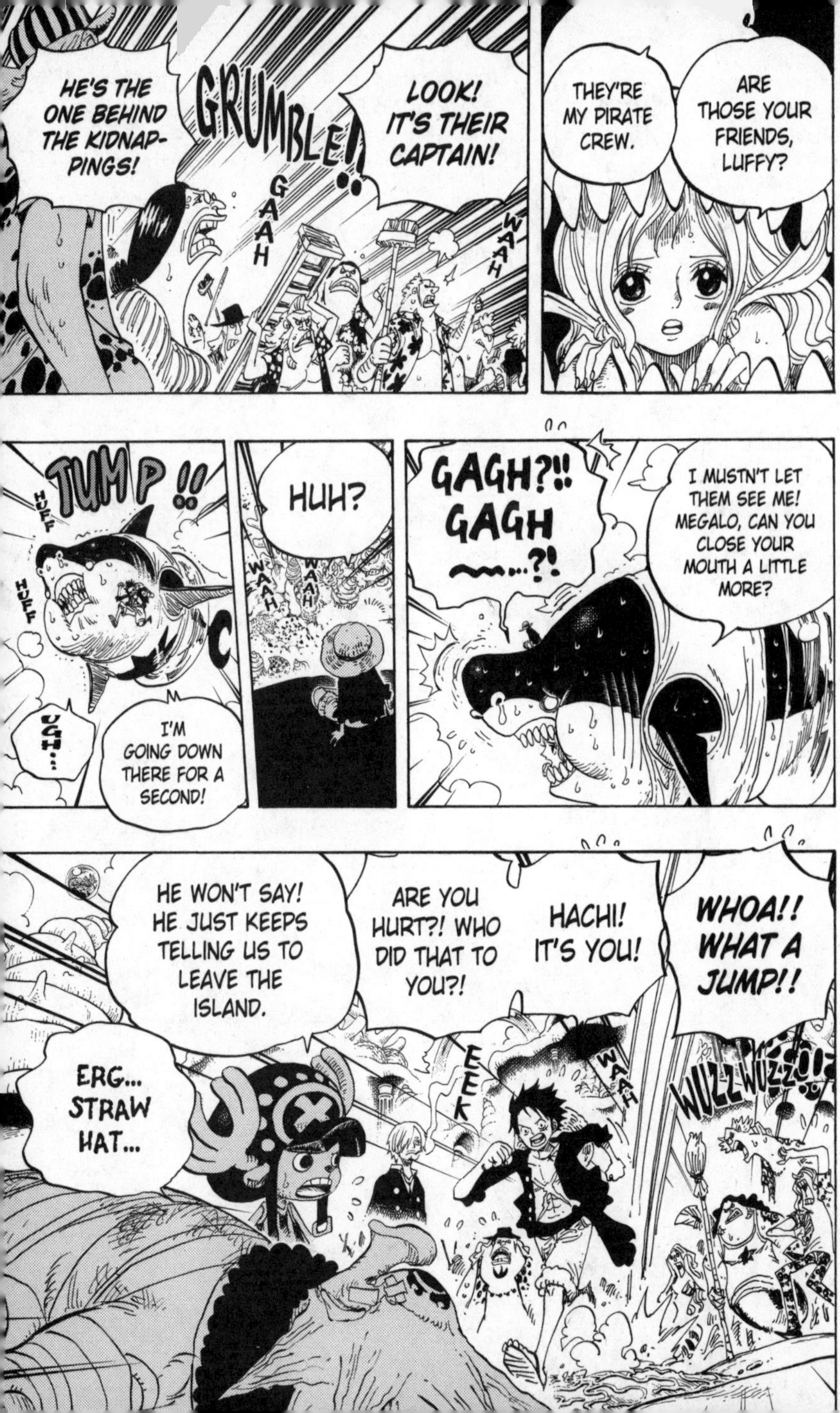
ARE THOSE YOUR FRIENDS, LUFFY?
THEY'RE MY PIRATE CREW.
LOOK! IT'S THEIR CAPTAIN!
GRUMBLE!!
GAAH
WAAH
HE'S THE ONE BEHIND THE KIDNAP-PINGS!
I MUSTN'T LET THEM SEE ME! MEGALO, CAN YOU CLOSE YOUR MOUTH A LITTLE MORE?
GAGH?!! GAGH ~~...?!
HUH?
WAAH
WAAH
TUMP!!
HUFF
HUFF
I'M GOING DOWN THERE FOR A SECOND!
UGH...
WHOA!! WHAT A JUMP!!
WUZZ WUZZ!!
WAAH
HACHI! IT'S YOU!
EEK
ARE YOU HURT?! WHO DID THAT TO YOU?!
HE WON'T SAY! HE JUST KEEPS TELLING US TO LEAVE THE ISLAND.
ERG... STRAW HAT...

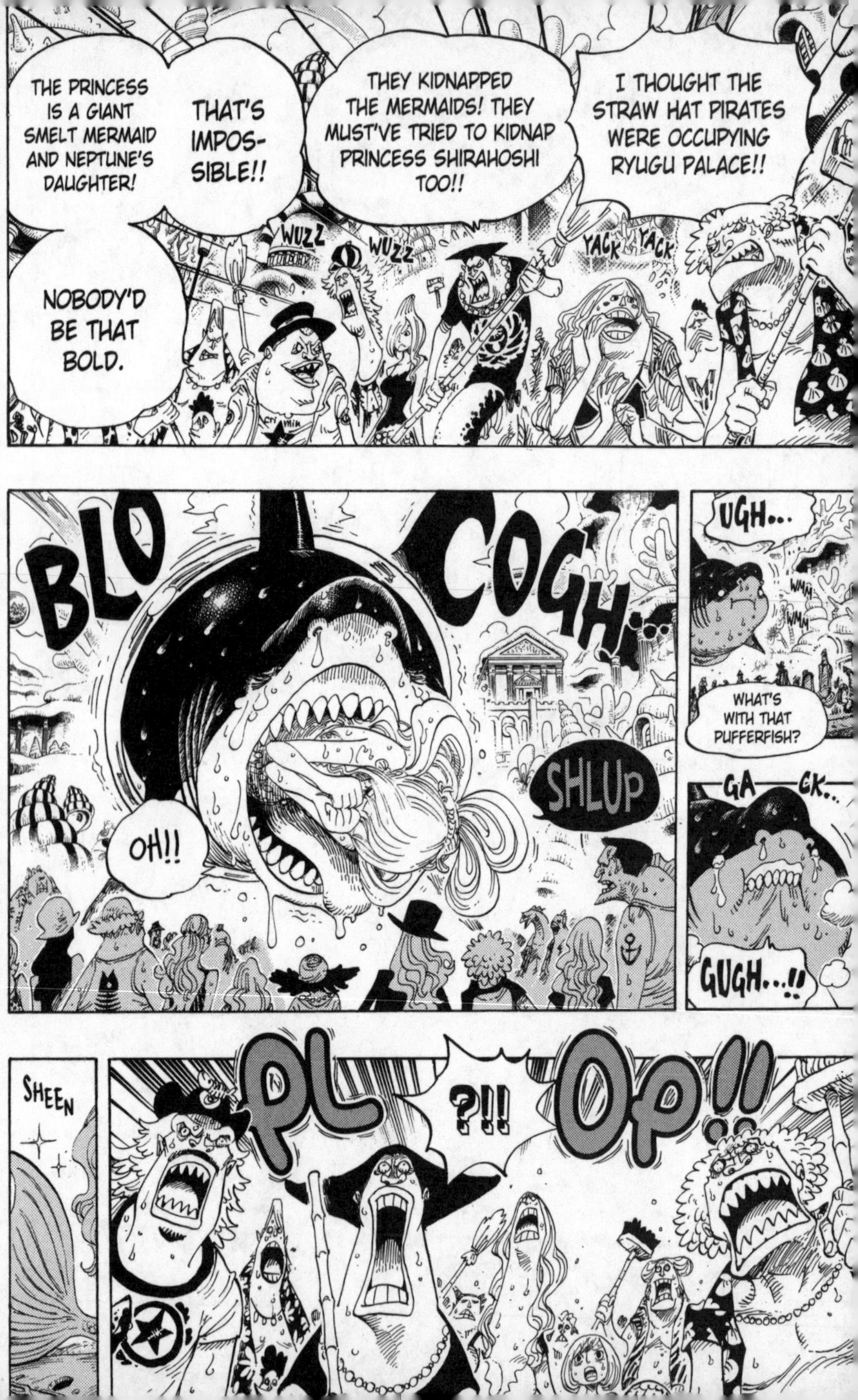
I THOUGHT THE STRAW HAT PIRATES WERE OCCUPYING RYUGU PALACE!!
THEY KIDNAPPED THE MERMAIDS! THEY MUST'VE TRIED TO KIDNAP PRINCESS SHIRAHOSHI TOO!!
THAT'S IMPOS-SIBLE!!
THE PRINCESS IS A GIANT SMELT MERMAID AND NEPTUNE'S DAUGHTER!
NOBODY'D BE THAT BOLD.
YACK YACK
WUZZ WUZZ
UGH...
WMM WMM
WHAT'S WITH THAT PUFFERFISH?
GA-CK...
GUGH...!!
COGH
BLO
SHLUP
OH!!
PL OP!!
?!!
SHEEN

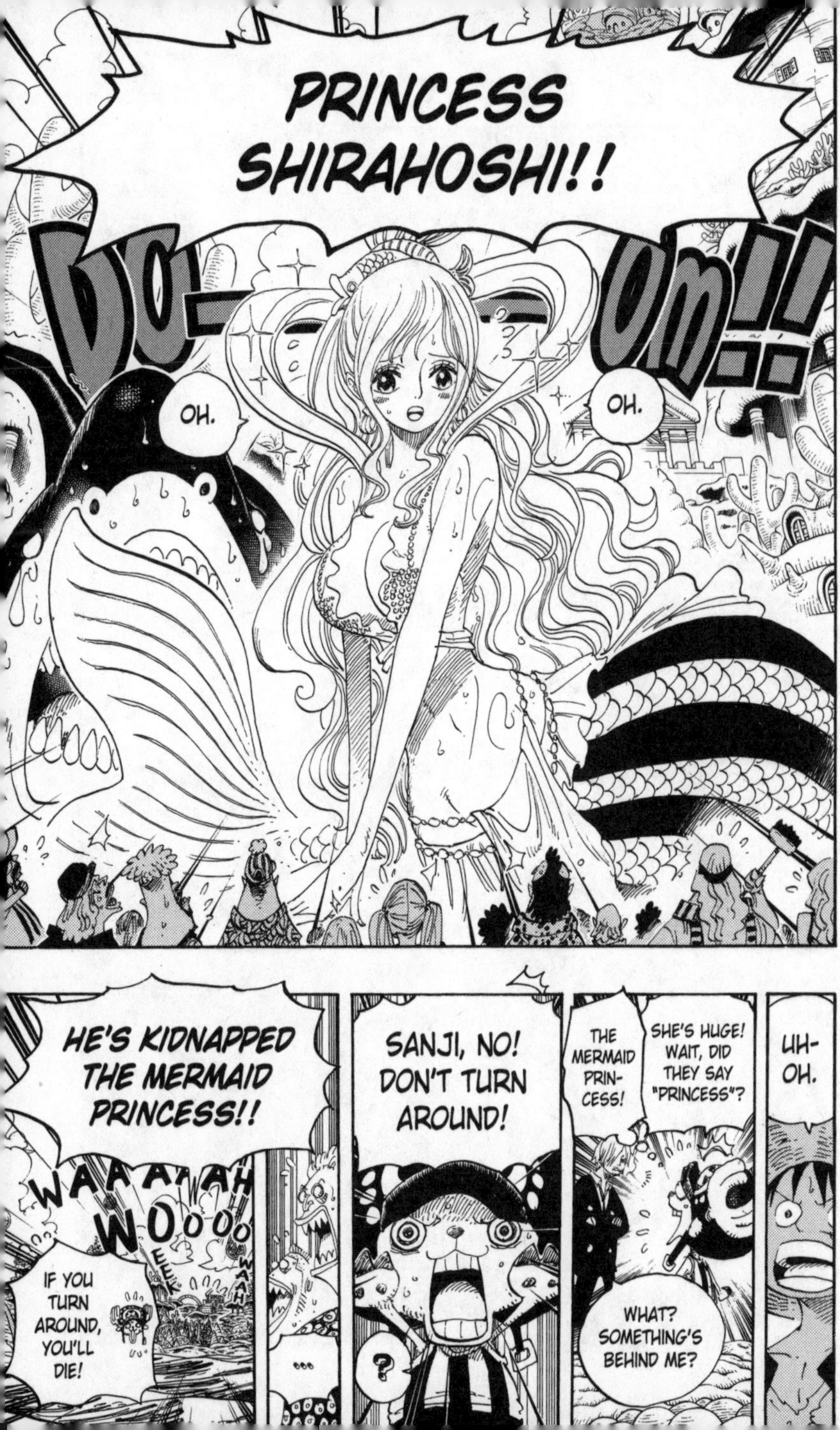
PRINCESS SHIRAHOSHI!!
BOO-OOM!!
OH.
OH.
UH-OH.
SHE'S HUGE! WAIT, DID THEY SAY "PRINCESS"?
THE MERMAID PRIN-CESS!
WHAT? SOMETHING'S BEHIND ME?
SANJI, NO! DON'T TURN AROUND!
?
...
HE'S KIDNAPPED THE MERMAID PRINCESS!!
WAAAAAH
WOOOOO
EEEK
WAAH
IF YOU TURN AROUND, YOU'LL DIE!

Chapter 618: PROPOSAL

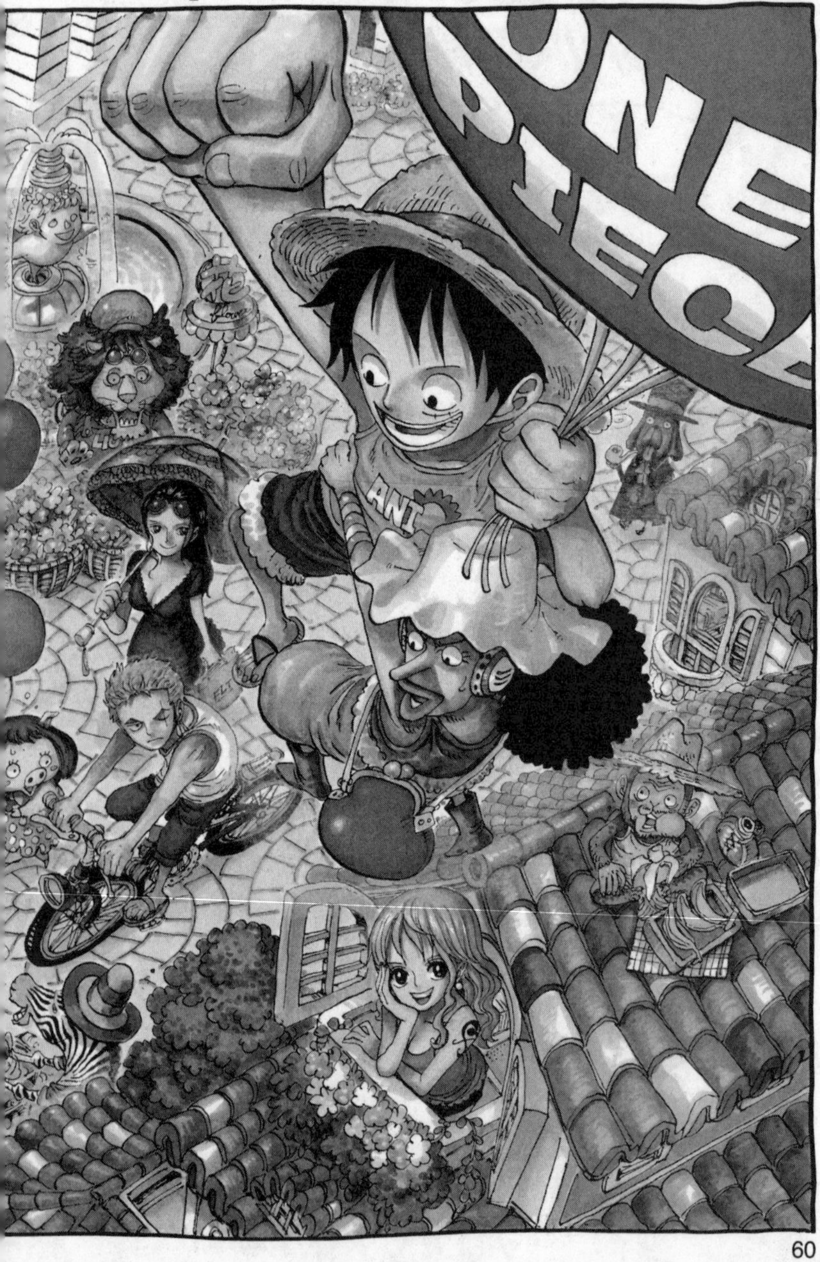
ONE PIECE
ANI

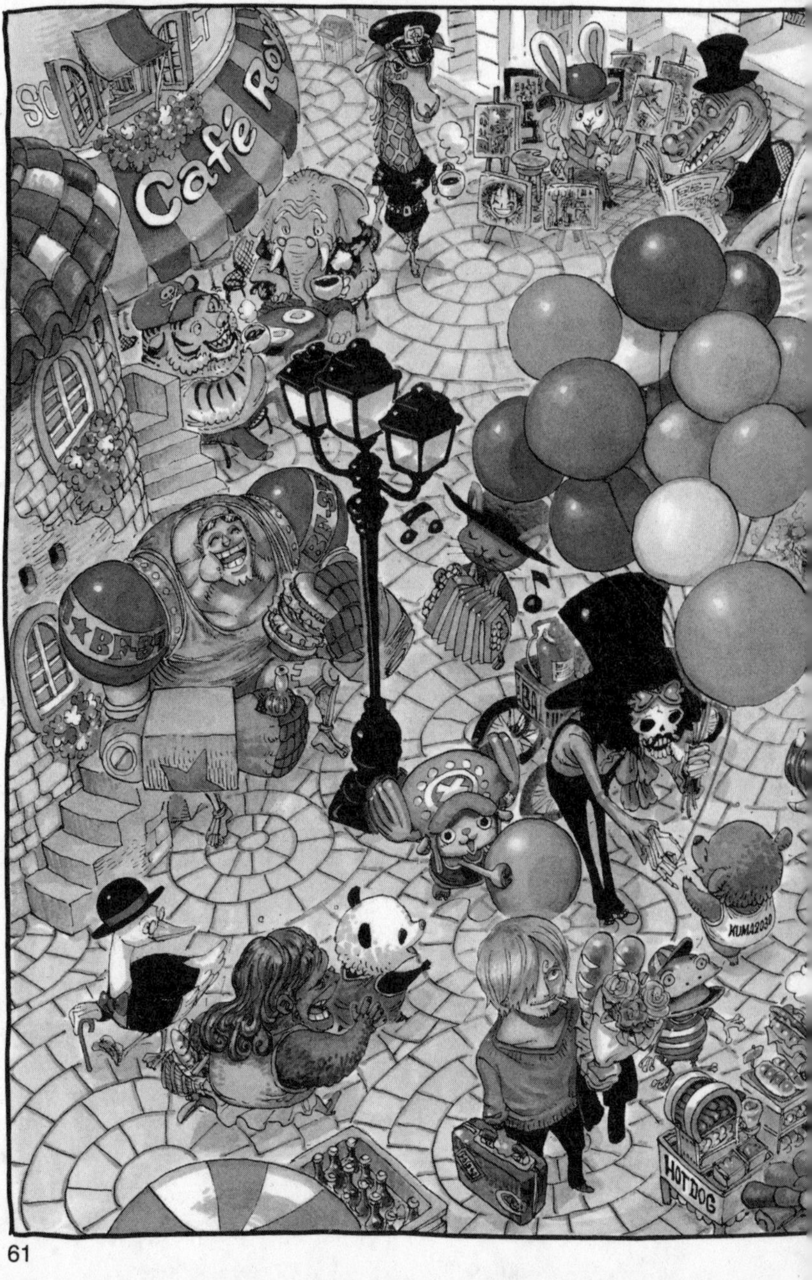
Café Ro
KUMA2030
HOT DOG

vol.63
ONE PIECE

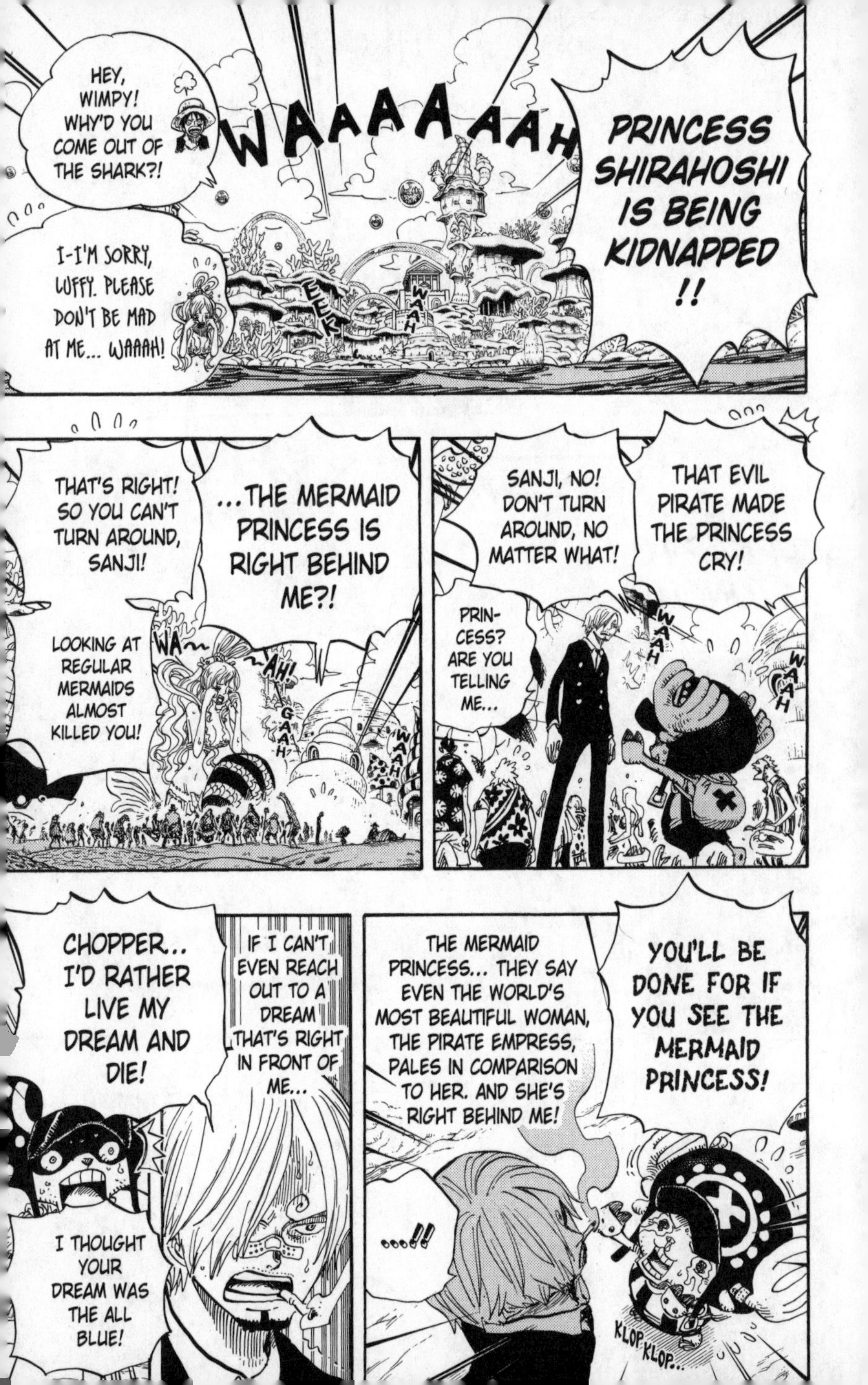
PRINCESS SHIRAHOSHI IS BEING KIDNAPPED!!
WAAAAAAH
WAAH
EEK
HEY, WIMPY! WHY'D YOU COME OUT OF THE SHARK?!
I-I'M SORRY, LUFFY. PLEASE DON'T BE MAD AT ME... WAAAH!
THAT EVIL PIRATE MADE THE PRINCESS CRY!
SANJI, NO! DON'T TURN AROUND, NO MATTER WHAT!
WAAH
WAAH
PRIN-CESS? ARE YOU TELLING ME...
...THE MERMAID PRINCESS IS RIGHT BEHIND ME?!
THAT'S RIGHT! SO YOU CAN'T TURN AROUND, SANJI!
WA~
AH!
GAAAH
WAAAH
LOOKING AT REGULAR MERMAIDS ALMOST KILLED YOU!
YOU'LL BE DONE FOR IF YOU SEE THE MERMAID PRINCESS!
THE MERMAID PRINCESS... THEY SAY EVEN THE WORLD'S MOST BEAUTIFUL WOMAN, THE PIRATE EMPRESS, PALES IN COMPARISON TO HER. AND SHE'S RIGHT BEHIND ME!
...!!
KLOP KLOP...
IF I CAN'T EVEN REACH OUT TO A DREAM THAT'S RIGHT IN FRONT OF ME...
CHOPPER... I'D RATHER LIVE MY DREAM AND DIE!
I THOUGHT YOUR DREAM WAS THE ALL BLUE!

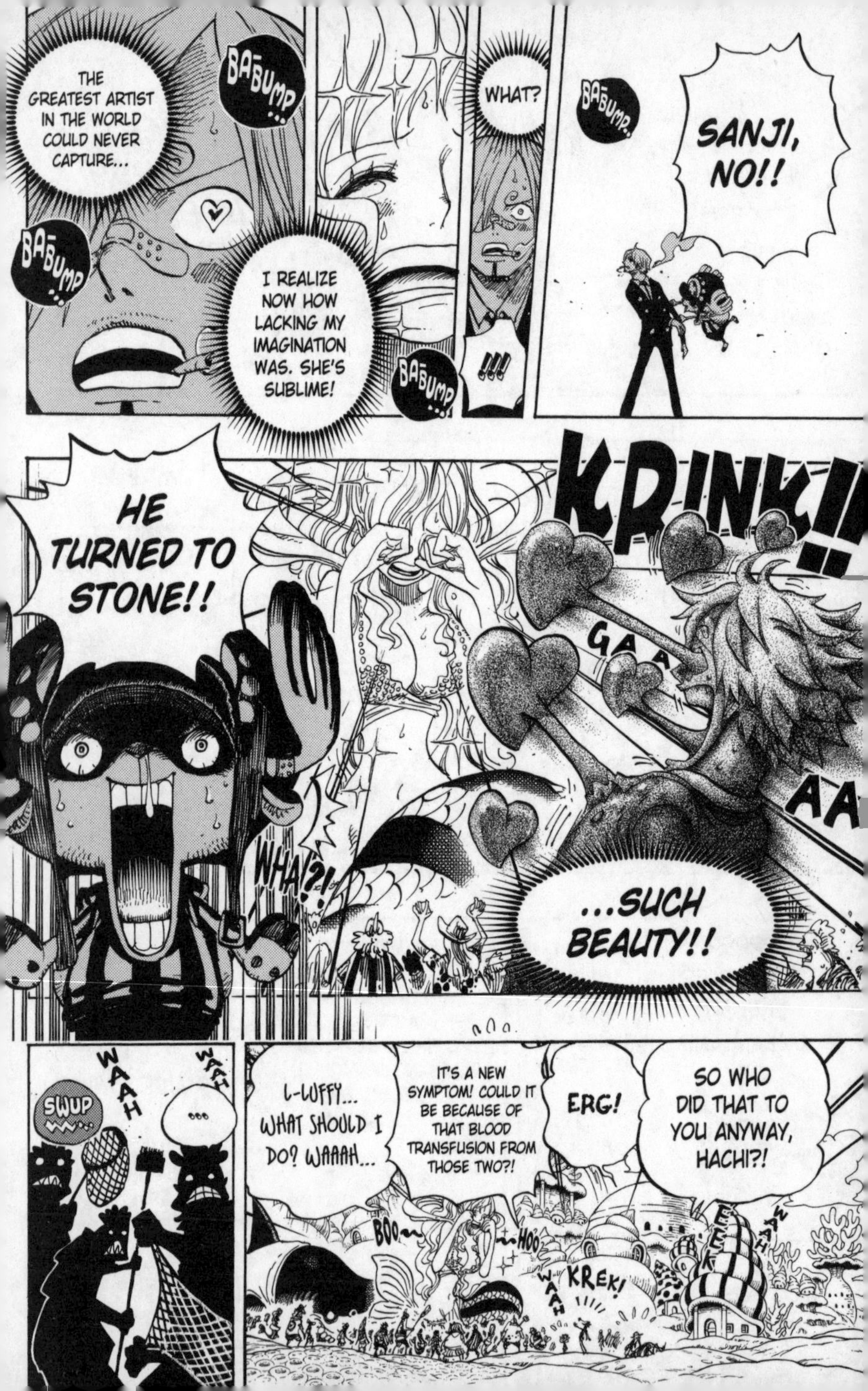
BA-BUMP
SANJI, NO!!
WHAT?
!!!
BA-BUMP
THE GREATEST ARTIST IN THE WORLD COULD NEVER CAPTURE...
BA-BUMP
BA-BUMP
I REALIZE NOW HOW LACKING MY IMAGINATION WAS. SHE'S SUBLIME!
BA-BUMP
KRINK!!
GAAAAA
...SUCH BEAUTY!!
WHA!?!
HE TURNED TO STONE!!
SO WHO DID THAT TO YOU ANYWAY, HACHI?!
ERG!
IT'S A NEW SYMPTOM! COULD IT BE BECAUSE OF THAT BLOOD TRANSFUSION FROM THOSE TWO?!
L-LUFFY... WHAT SHOULD I DO? WAAAH...
WAAH
EEEK
KREK!
WAAH
BOO~
~HOO
WAAH
...
SWUP
WAAH

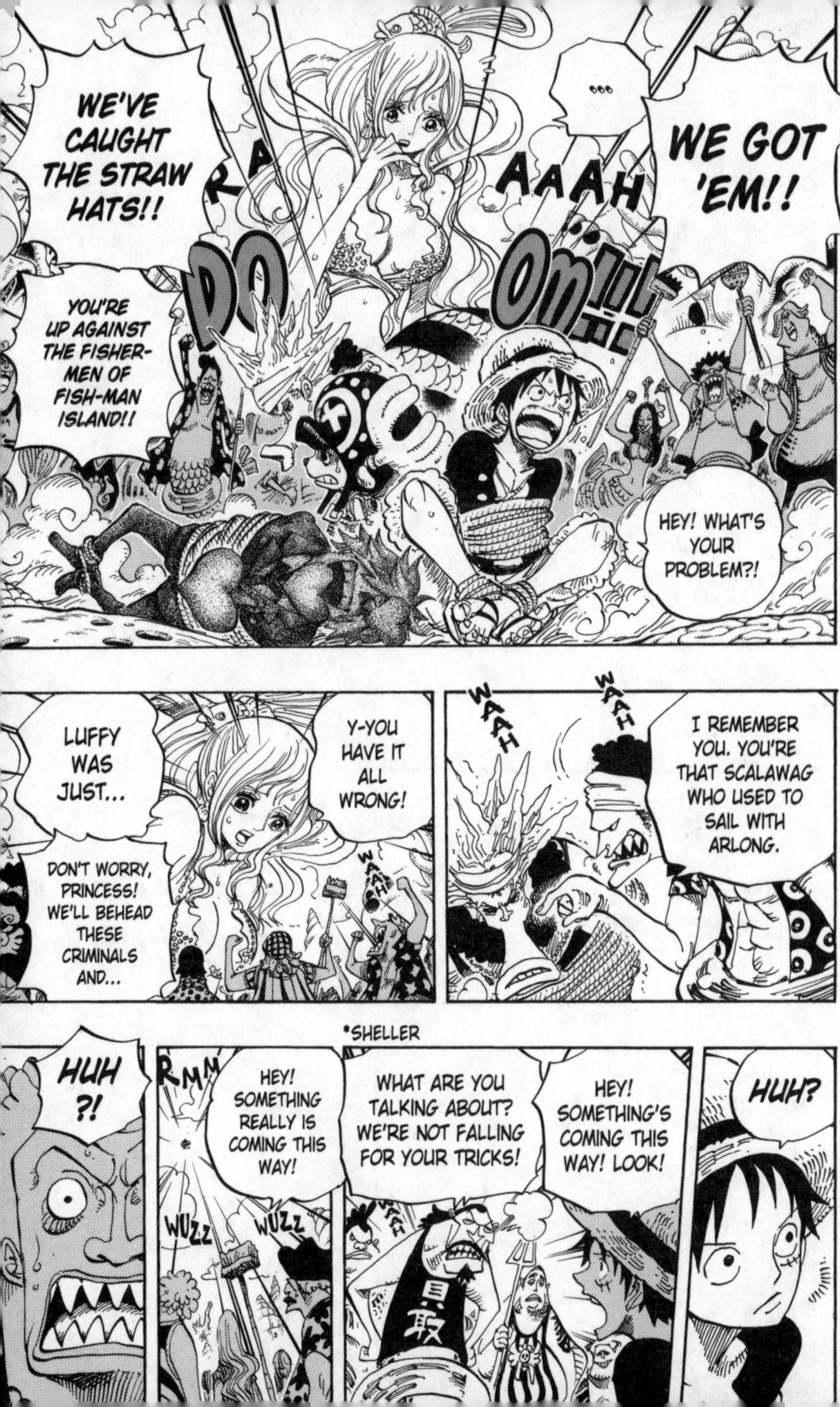
...
WE GOT 'EM!!
AAAH
WE'VE CAUGHT THE STRAW HATS!!
RA
DOOM
HEY! WHAT'S YOUR PROBLEM?!
YOU'RE UP AGAINST THE FISHERMEN OF FISH-MAN ISLAND!!
WAAH
WAAH
I REMEMBER YOU. YOU'RE THAT SCALAWAG WHO USED TO SAIL WITH ARLONG.
Y-YOU HAVE IT ALL WRONG!
LUFFY WAS JUST...
WAAH
DON'T WORRY, PRINCESS! WE'LL BEHEAD THESE CRIMINALS AND...
*SHELLER
HUH?
HEY! SOMETHING'S COMING THIS WAY! LOOK!
WHAT ARE YOU TALKING ABOUT? WE'RE NOT FALLING FOR YOUR TRICKS!
WAAH
HEY! SOMETHING REALLY IS COMING THIS WAY!
RMM
WUZZ
WUZZ
HUH ?!

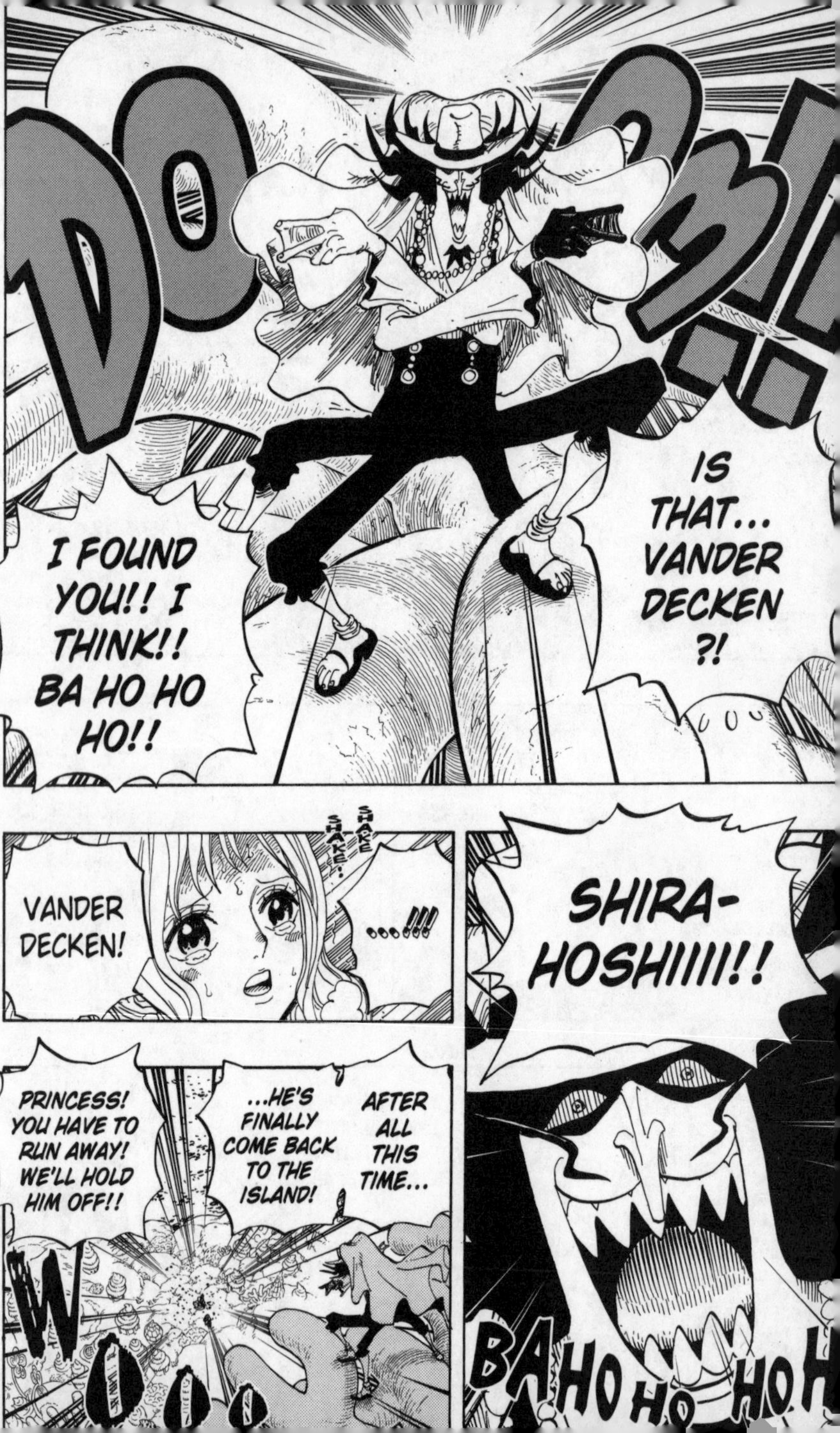
IS THAT... VANDER DECKEN?!
I FOUND YOU!! I THINK!! BA HO HO HO!!
SHIRA-HOSHIIIII!!
BA HO HO HO
SHAKE SHAKE
...!!!
VANDER DECKEN!
AFTER ALL THIS TIME...
...HE'S FINALLY COME BACK TO THE ISLAND!
PRINCESS! YOU HAVE TO RUN AWAY! WE'LL HOLD HIM OFF!!

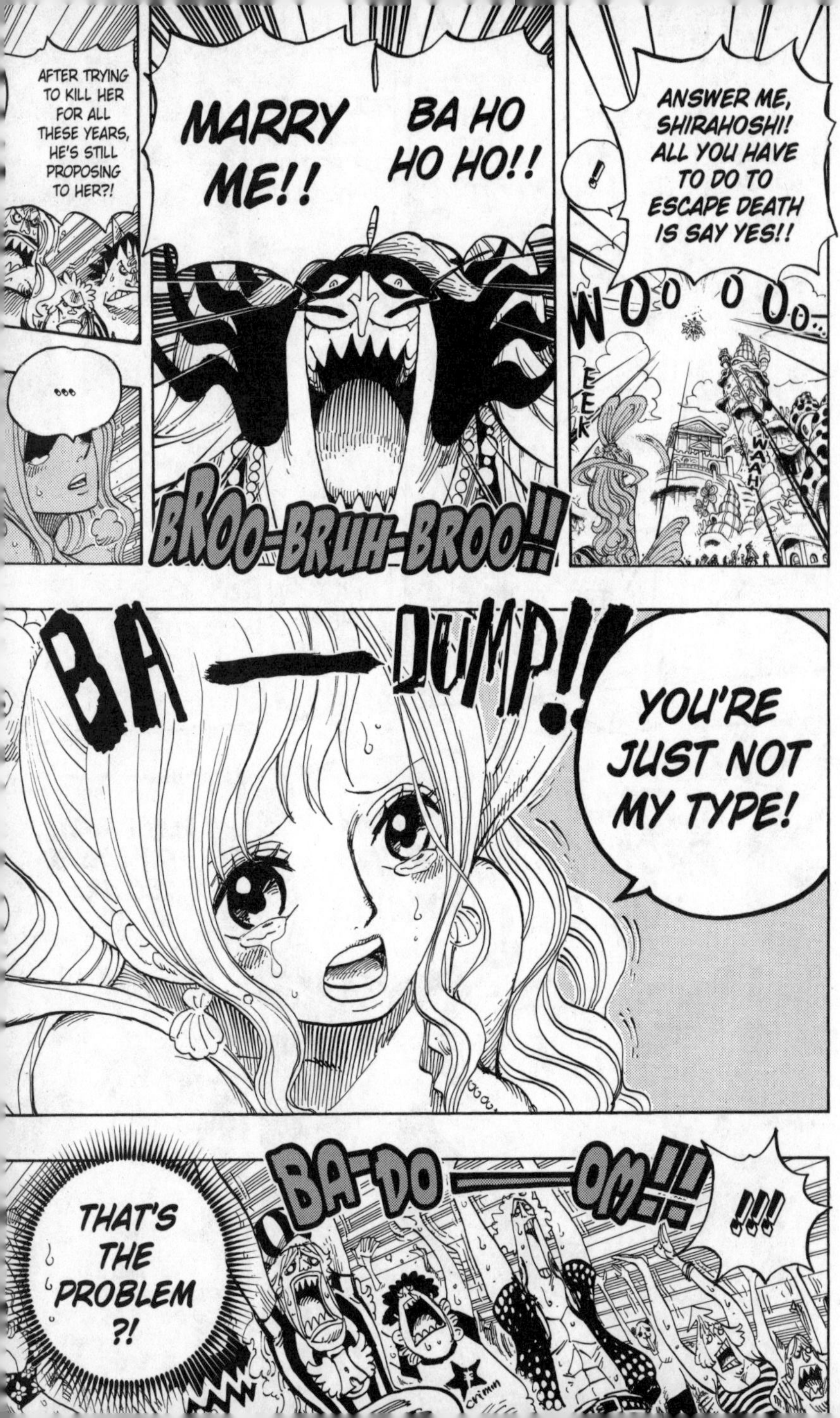
ANSWER ME, SHIRAHOSHI! ALL YOU HAVE TO DO TO ESCAPE DEATH IS SAY YES!!
!
WOO O O O...
BA HO HO HO!!
MARRY ME!!
BROO-BRUH-BROO!!
AFTER TRYING TO KILL HER FOR ALL THESE YEARS, HE'S STILL PROPOSING TO HER?!
...
YOU'RE JUST NOT MY TYPE!
BA—DUMP!!
!!!
BA-DO—OM!!
THAT'S THE PROBLEM ?!

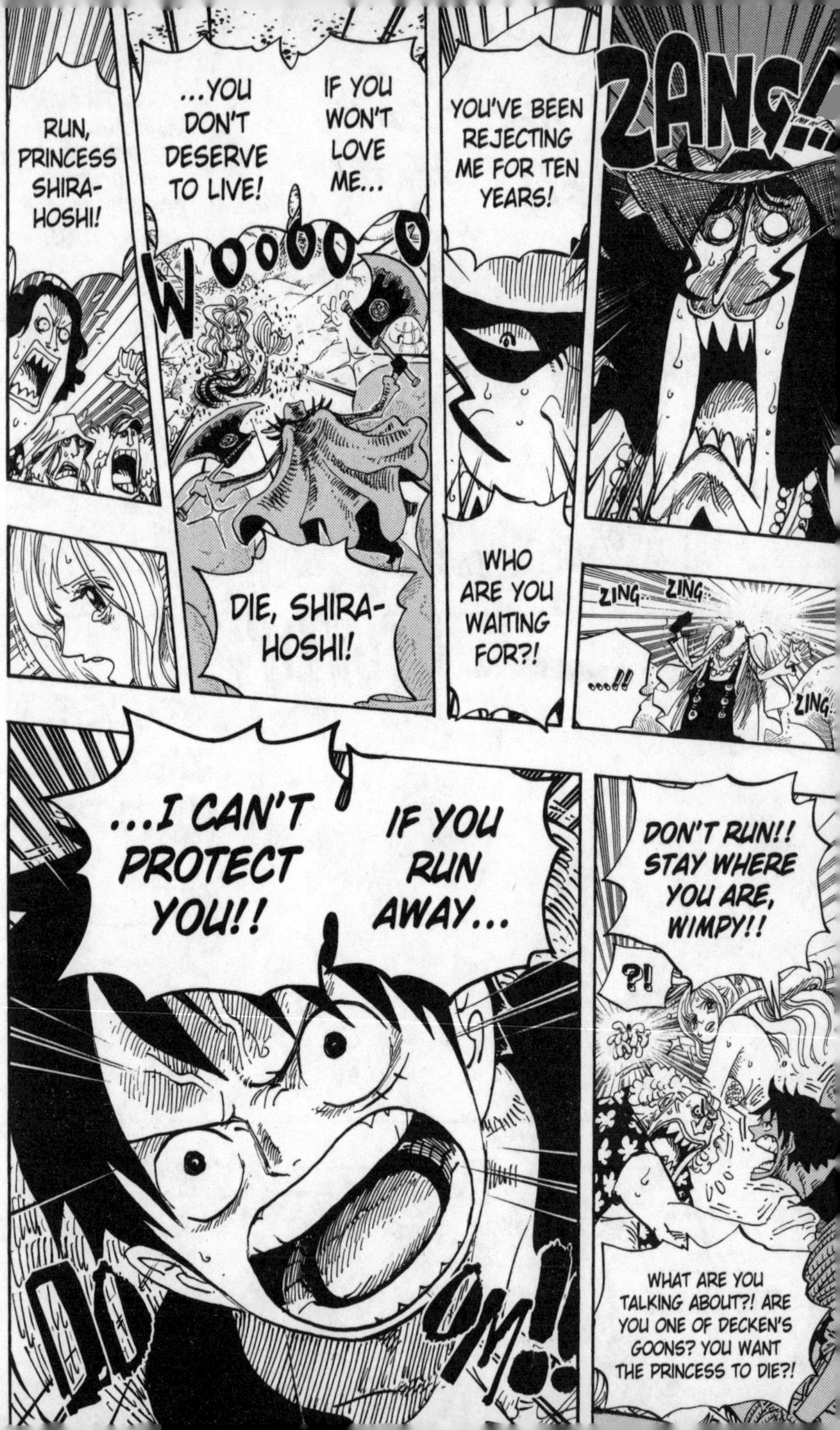
ZANG!!
YOU'VE BEEN REJECTING ME FOR TEN YEARS!
IF YOU WON'T LOVE ME...
...YOU DON'T DESERVE TO LIVE!
WOOOOO
DIE, SHIRA-HOSHI!
RUN, PRINCESS SHIRA-HOSHI!
ZING ZING
...!!
ZING
WHO ARE YOU WAITING FOR?!
DON'T RUN!! STAY WHERE YOU ARE, WIMPY!!
?!
WHAT ARE YOU TALKING ABOUT?! ARE YOU ONE OF DECKEN'S GOONS? YOU WANT THE PRINCESS TO DIE?!
IF YOU RUN AWAY...
...I CAN'T PROTECT YOU!!
DOOM!!

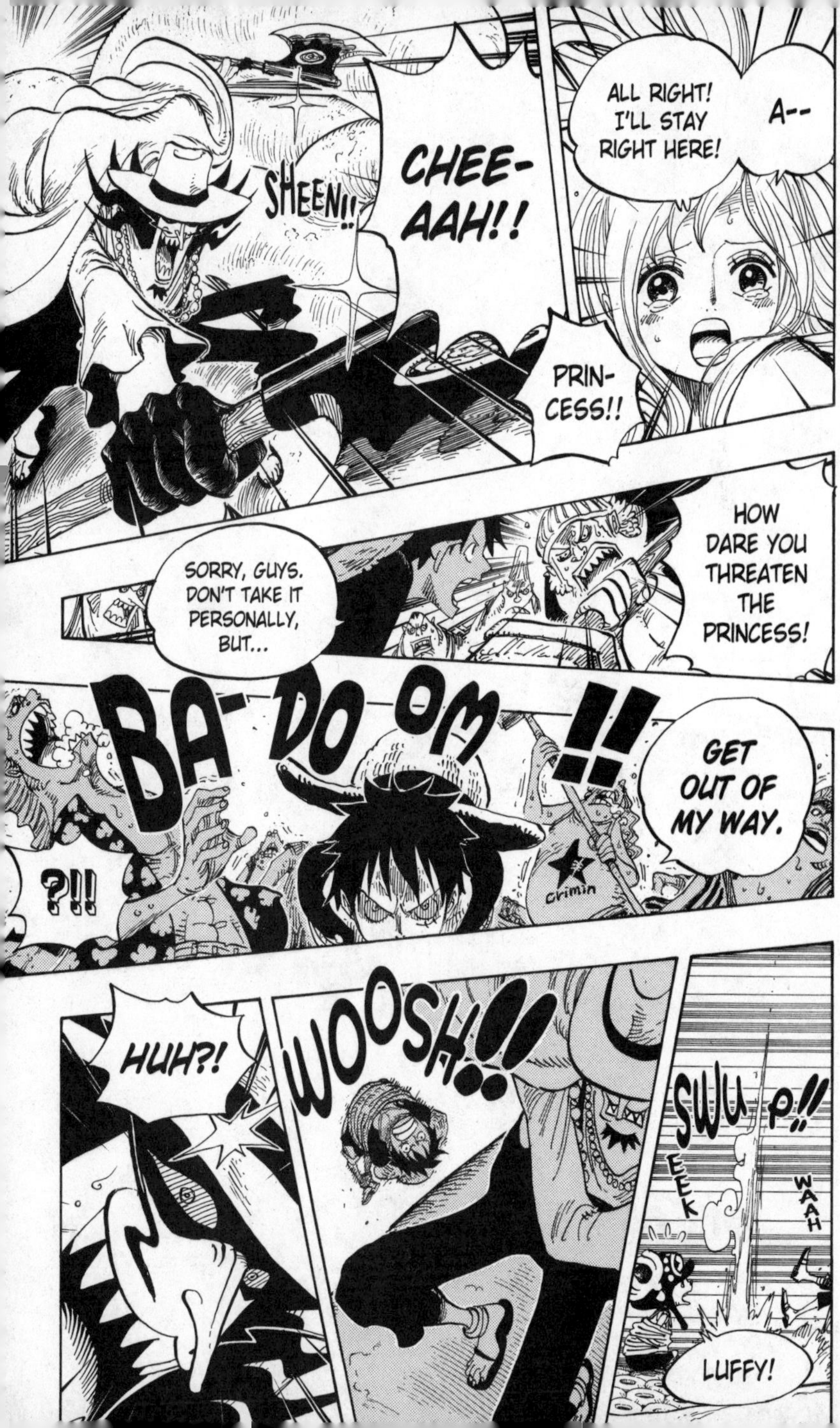
A--
ALL RIGHT! I'LL STAY RIGHT HERE!
PRIN-CESS!!
CHEE-AAH!!
SHEEN!!
HOW DARE YOU THREATEN THE PRINCESS!
SORRY, GUYS. DON'T TAKE IT PERSONALLY, BUT...
GET OUT OF MY WAY.
BA-DO-OM!!
Crimin
?!!
SWUUP!!
WAAH
EEK
LUFFY!
WOOSH!!
HUH?!

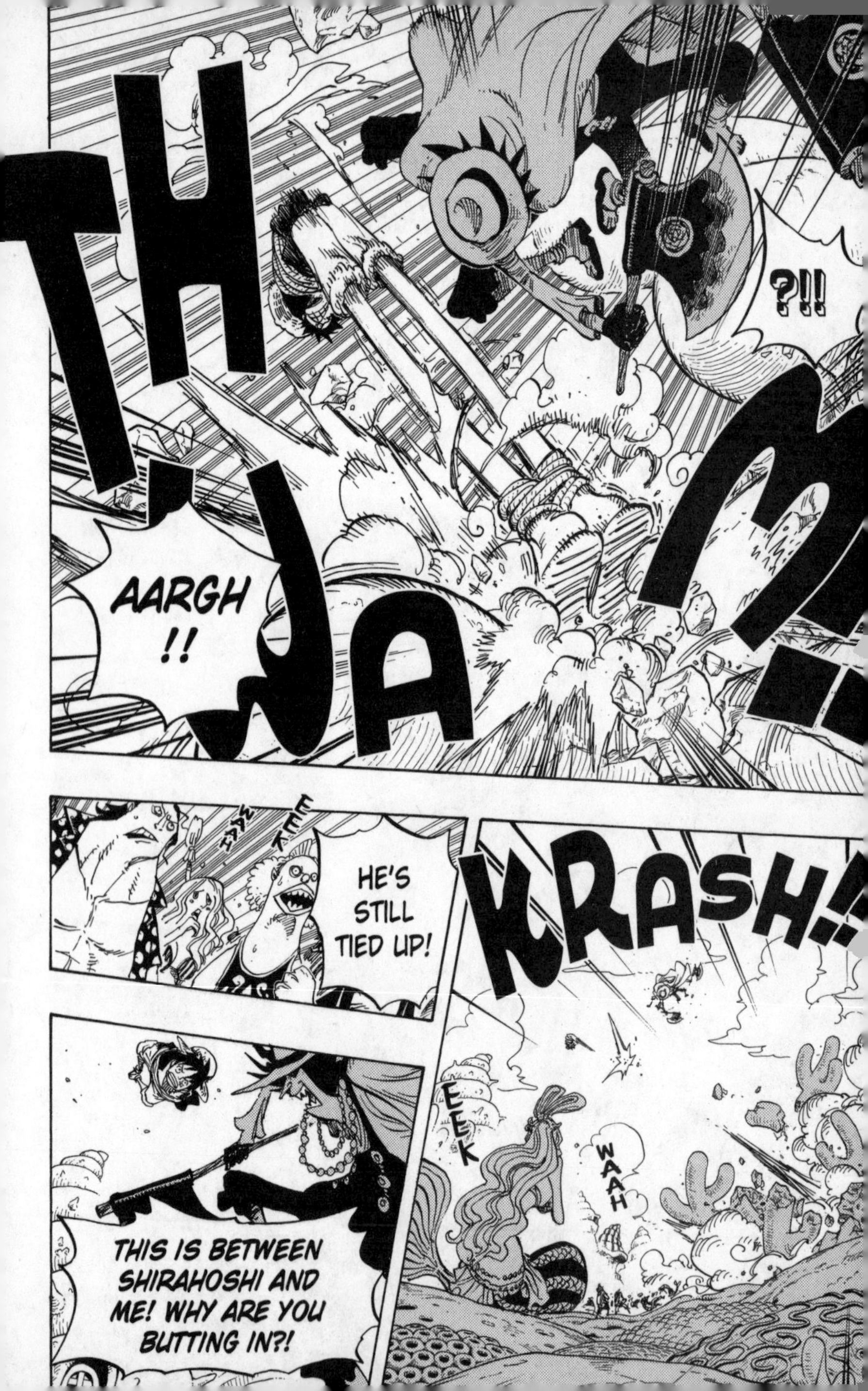
?!!
THWAM!!
AARGH!!
KRASH!!
EEEK
WAAH
EEE
WAAH
HE'S STILL TIED UP!
THIS IS BETWEEN SHIRAHOSHI AND ME! WHY ARE YOU BUTTING IN?!

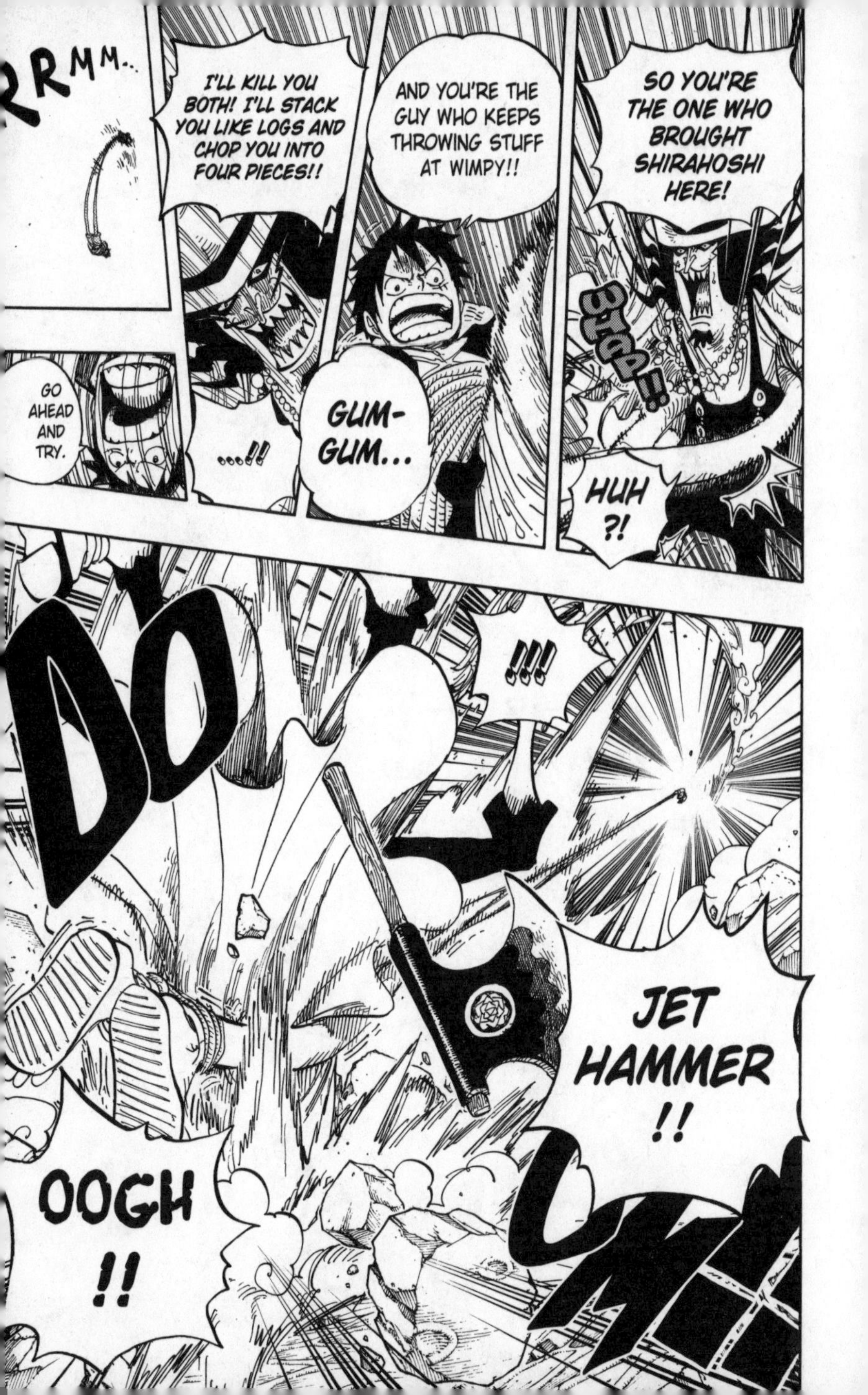
SO YOU'RE THE ONE WHO BROUGHT SHIRAHOSHI HERE!
WHAP!!
HUH ?!
AND YOU'RE THE GUY WHO KEEPS THROWING STUFF AT WIMPY!!
GUM-GUM...
I'LL KILL YOU BOTH! I'LL STACK YOU LIKE LOGS AND CHOP YOU INTO FOUR PIECES!!
...!!
RRMM...
GO AHEAD AND TRY.
!!!
JET HAMMER !!
DO
OOGH !!

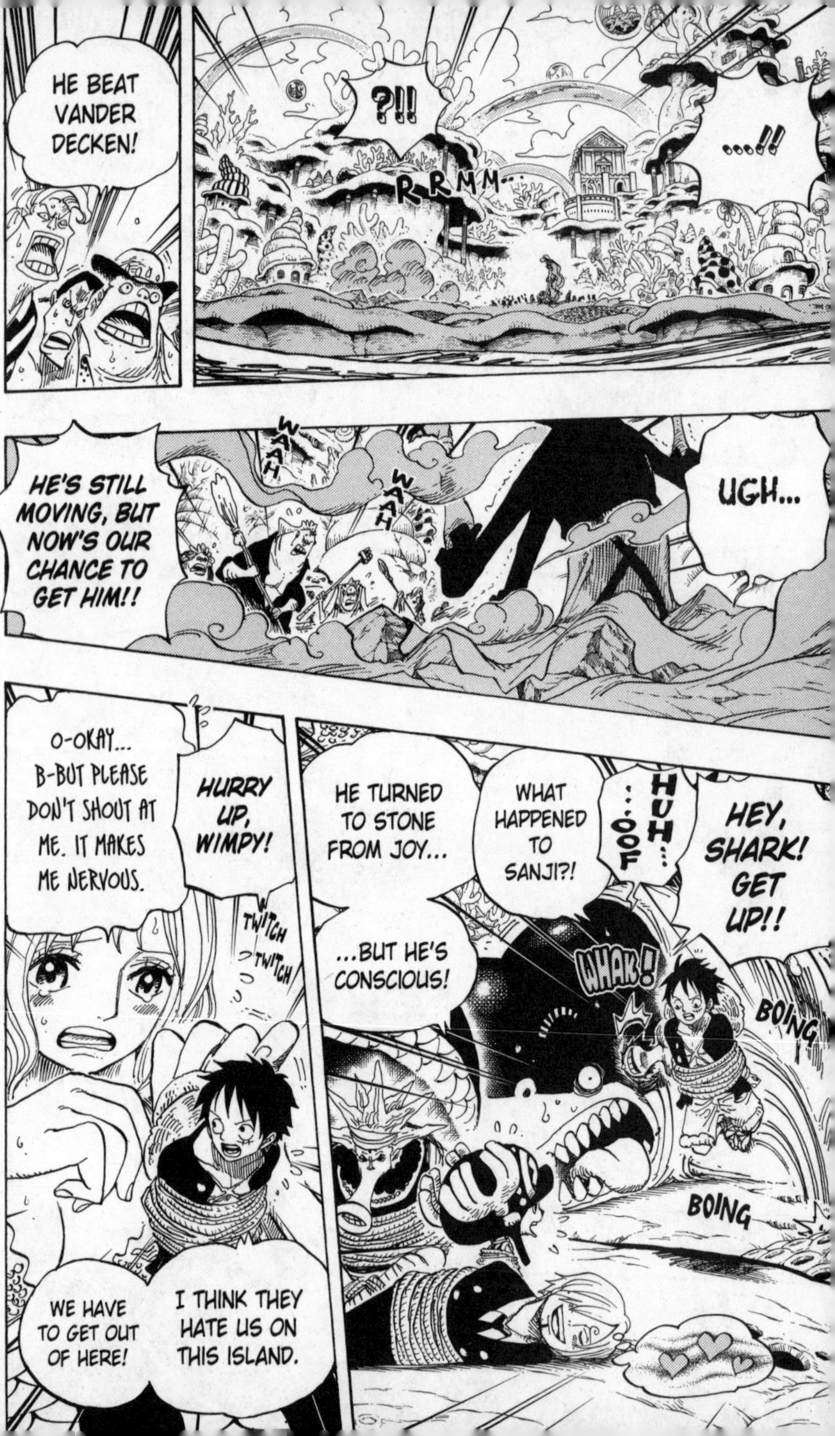
?!!
RRMM...
...!!
HE BEAT VANDER DECKEN!
UGH...
WAAH
WAAH
HE'S STILL MOVING, BUT NOW'S OUR CHANCE TO GET HIM!!
HEY, SHARK! GET UP!!
HUH...
...OOF
WHAT HAPPENED TO SANJI?!
HE TURNED TO STONE FROM JOY...
...BUT HE'S CONSCIOUS!
WHAK!
BOING
BOING
HURRY UP, WIMPY!
O-OKAY... B-BUT PLEASE DON'T SHOUT AT ME. IT MAKES ME NERVOUS.
TWITCH
TWITCH
I THINK THEY HATE US ON THIS ISLAND.
WE HAVE TO GET OUT OF HERE!

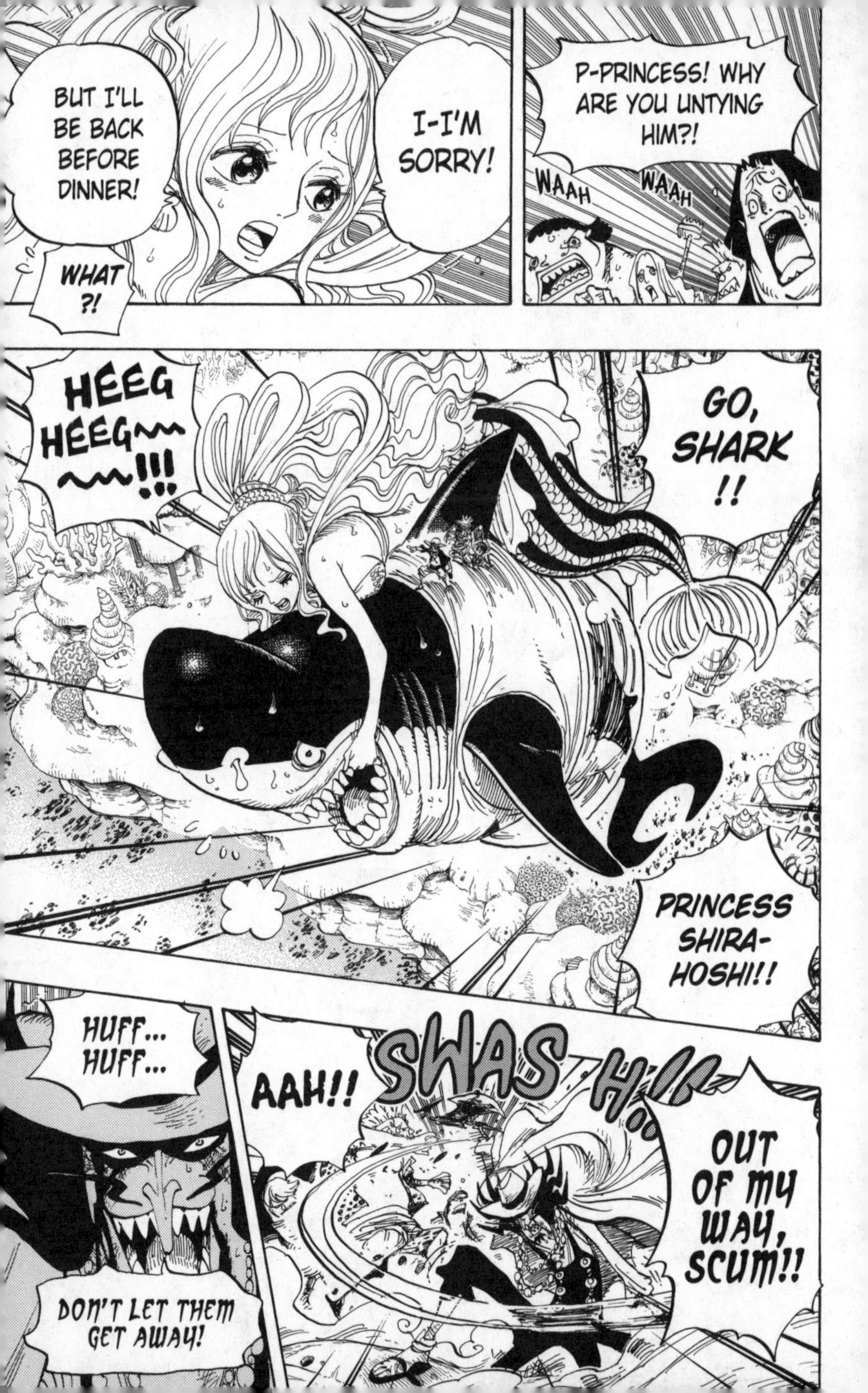
P-PRINCESS! WHY ARE YOU UNTYING HIM?!
WAAH
WAAH
I-I'M SORRY!
BUT I'LL BE BACK BEFORE DINNER!
WHAT ?!
GO, SHARK !!
HEEG HEEG~~~~!!!
PRINCESS SHIRA-HOSHI!!
OUT OF MY WAY, SCUM!!
SWASH
AAH!!
HUFF... HUFF...
DON'T LET THEM GET AWAY!

WADA-TSUMI!!
GRAAAGH !!
SPLASH...
?!!
GUM-GUM...
VROOO...
RRMMM...
RIGHT!! HERE I GO!!
IT'S THE GIANT MONK!
MURMUR!
CRUSH THEM!!

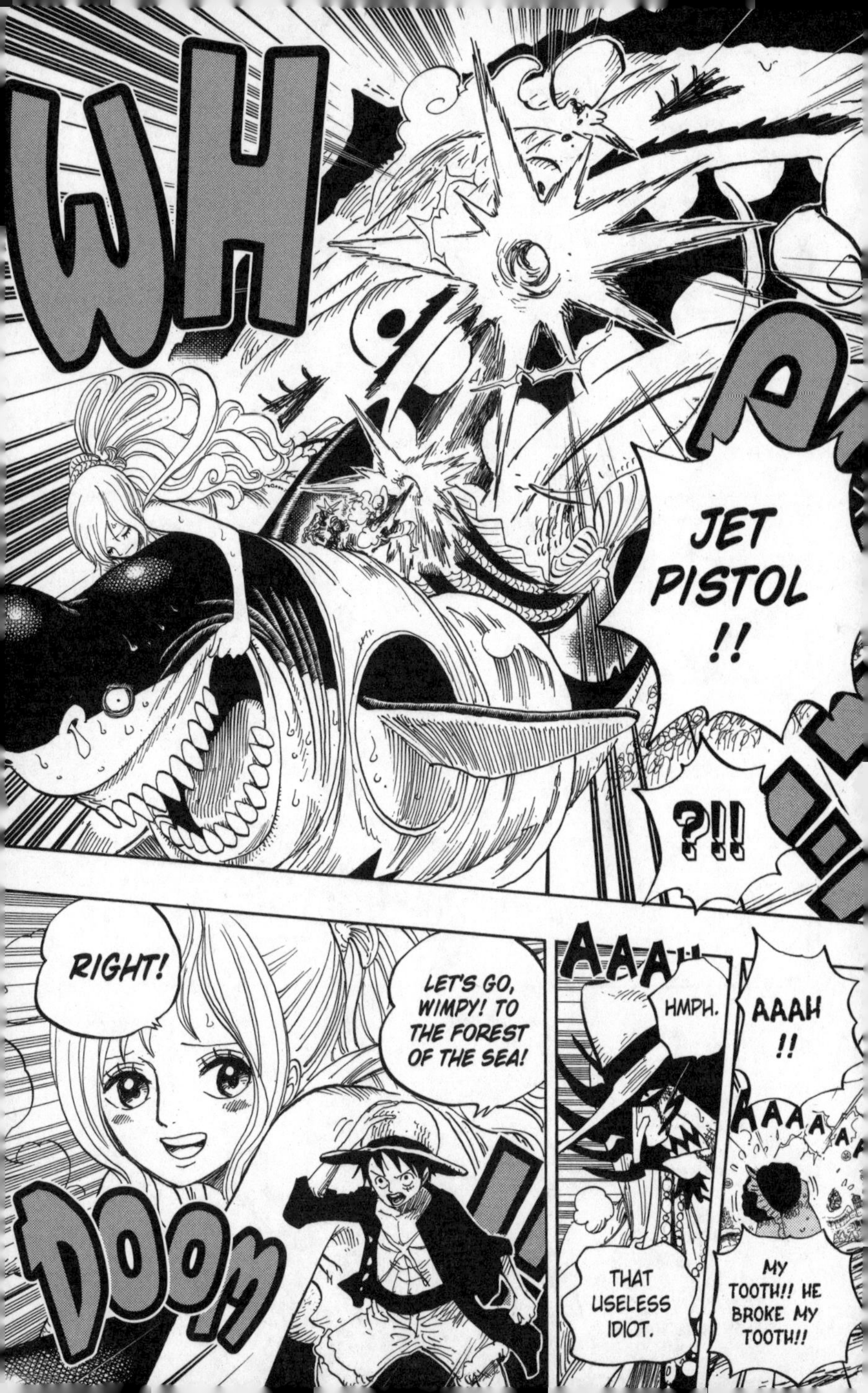
JET PISTOL !!
?!!
WH
AAAH !!
MY TOOTH!! HE BROKE MY TOOTH!!
HMPH.
THAT USELESS IDIOT.
LET'S GO, WIMPY! TO THE FOREST OF THE SEA!
RIGHT!
DOOM

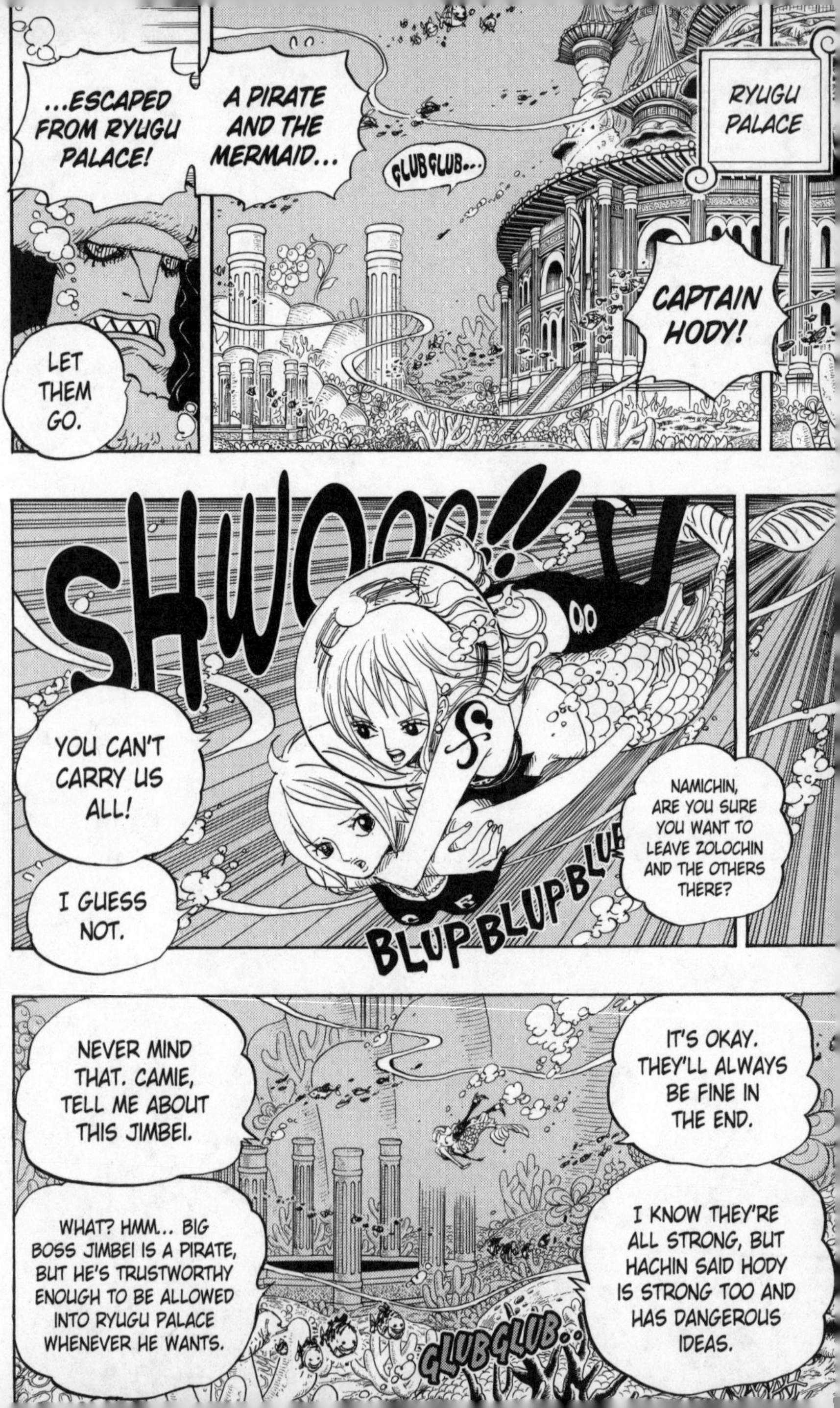
RYUGU PALACE
CAPTAIN HODY!
A PIRATE AND THE MERMAID...
GLUBGLUB...
...ESCAPED FROM RYUGU PALACE!
LET THEM GO.
SHWOOO!!
NAMICHIN, ARE YOU SURE YOU WANT TO LEAVE ZOLOCHIN AND THE OTHERS THERE?
BLUPBLUPBLUP
YOU CAN'T CARRY US ALL!
I GUESS NOT.
IT'S OKAY. THEY'LL ALWAYS BE FINE IN THE END.
I KNOW THEY'RE ALL STRONG, BUT HACHIN SAID HODY IS STRONG TOO AND HAS DANGEROUS IDEAS.
NEVER MIND THAT. CAMIE, TELL ME ABOUT THIS JIMBEI.
WHAT? HMM... BIG BOSS JIMBEI IS A PIRATE, BUT HE'S TRUSTWORTHY ENOUGH TO BE ALLOWED INTO RYUGU PALACE WHENEVER HE WANTS.
GLUBGLUB..

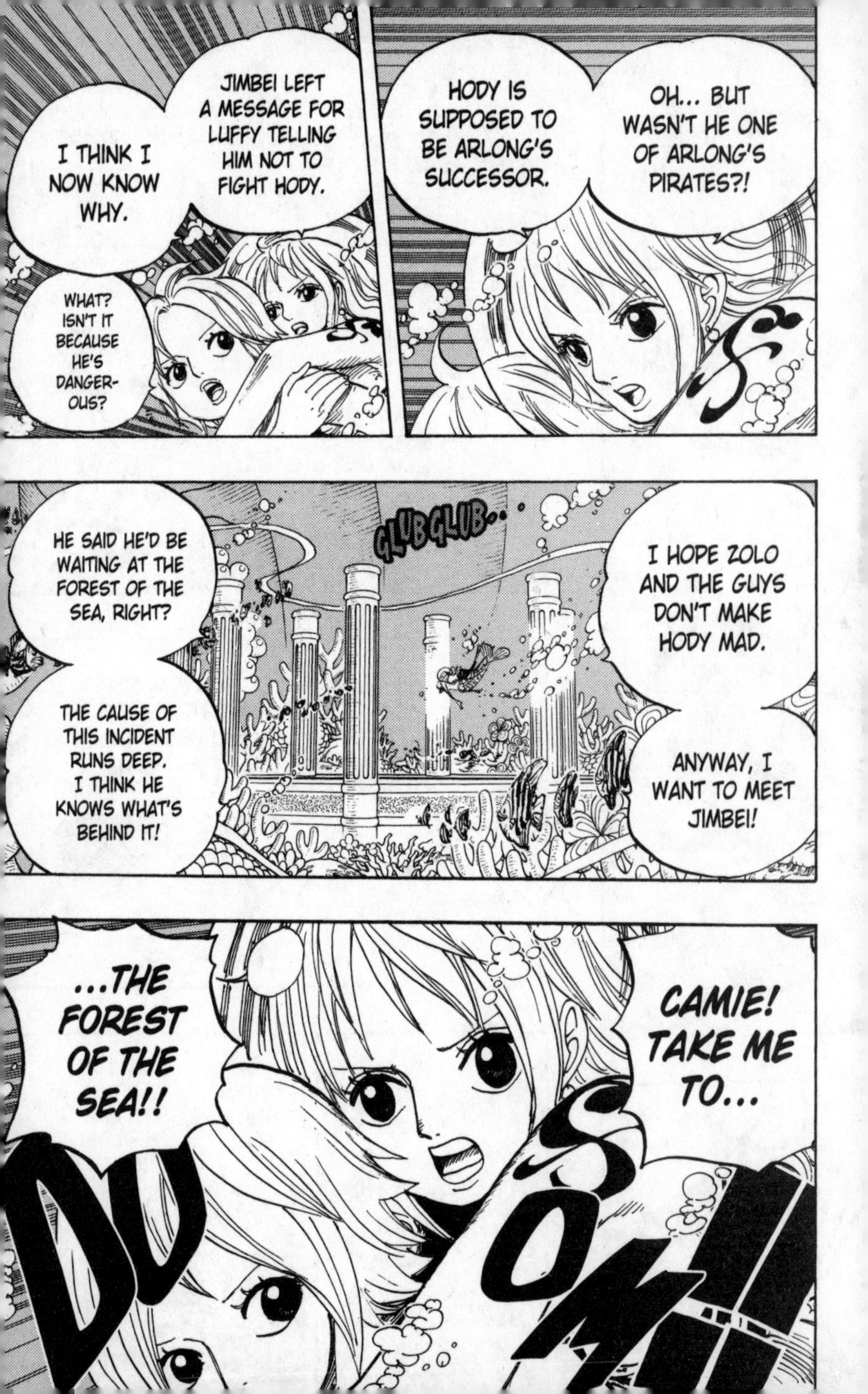
OH... BUT WASN'T HE ONE OF ARLONG'S PIRATES?!
HODY IS SUPPOSED TO BE ARLONG'S SUCCESSOR.
JIMBEI LEFT A MESSAGE FOR LUFFY TELLING HIM NOT TO FIGHT HODY.
I THINK I NOW KNOW WHY.
WHAT? ISN'T IT BECAUSE HE'S DANGEROUS?
I HOPE ZOLO AND THE GUYS DON'T MAKE HODY MAD.
GLUBGLUB..
ANYWAY, I WANT TO MEET JIMBEI!
HE SAID HE'D BE WAITING AT THE FOREST OF THE SEA, RIGHT?
THE CAUSE OF THIS INCIDENT RUNS DEEP. I THINK HE KNOWS WHAT'S BEHIND IT!
CAMIE! TAKE ME TO...
...THE FOREST OF THE SEA!!

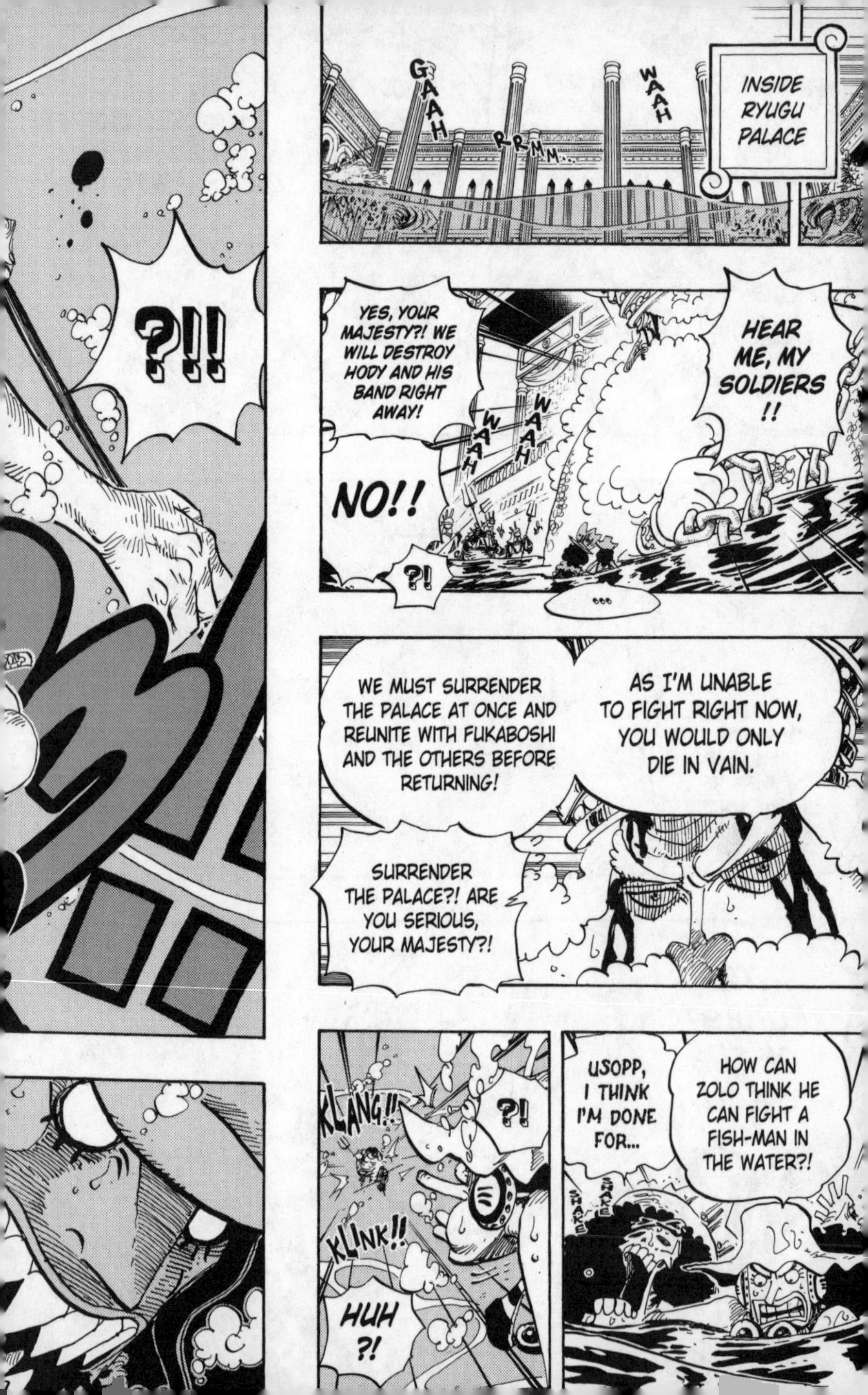

INSIDE RYUGU PALACE
WAAH
GAAH
RRMM...
HEAR ME, MY SOLDIERS!!
YES, YOUR MAJESTY?! WE WILL DESTROY HODY AND HIS BAND RIGHT AWAY!
WAAH
WAAH
NO!!
?!
...
AS I'M UNABLE TO FIGHT RIGHT NOW, YOU WOULD ONLY DIE IN VAIN.
WE MUST SURRENDER THE PALACE AT ONCE AND REUNITE WITH FUKABOSHI AND THE OTHERS BEFORE RETURNING!
SURRENDER THE PALACE?! ARE YOU SERIOUS, YOUR MAJESTY?!
?!!
HOW CAN ZOLO THINK HE CAN FIGHT A FISH-MAN IN THE WATER?!
USOPP, I THINK I'M DONE FOR...
SHAKE
SHAKE
?!
KLANG!!
KLINK!!
HUH?!

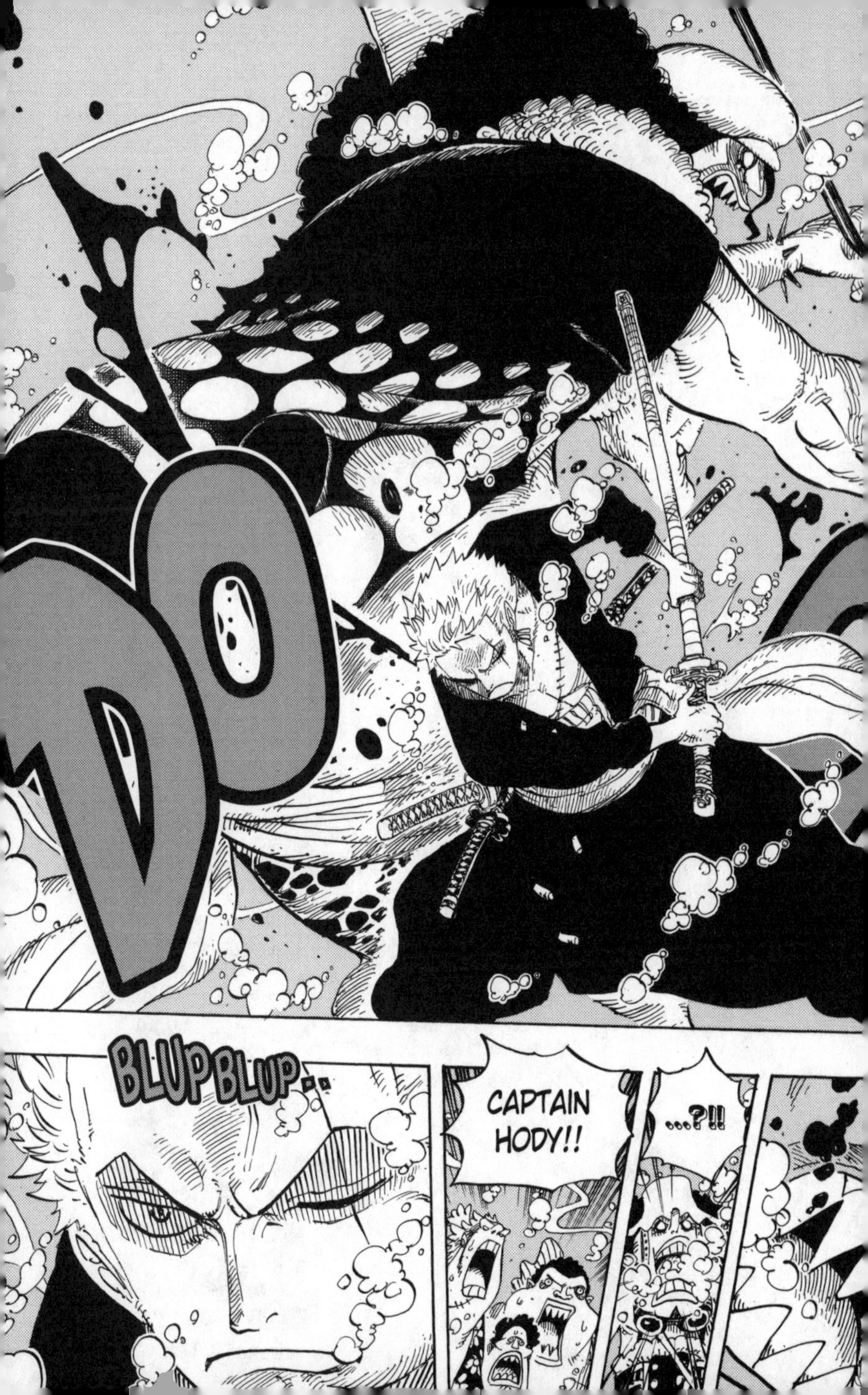
DO
...?!!
CAPTAIN HODY!!
BLUP BLUP..

SBS Question Corner

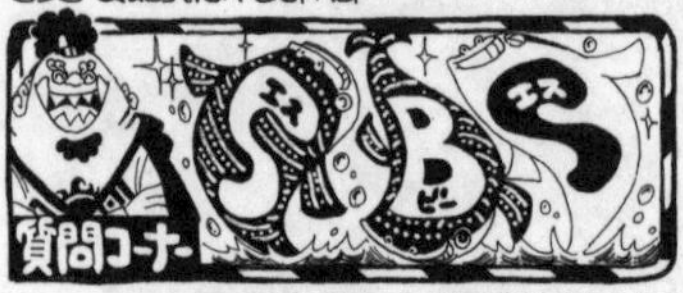
質問コーナー

(Micchii, Fukuoka)

Q: Odacchi!! I have a favor to ask!! Please draw the Seven Warlords of the Sea, who gave Luffy and Whitebeard so much trouble during the Paramount War two years ago, when they were children!! --Yutaka Harada

A: Sure thing! Now what do you suppose they'll be doing in two years? Here are the seven warlords of the sea before the war two years ago.

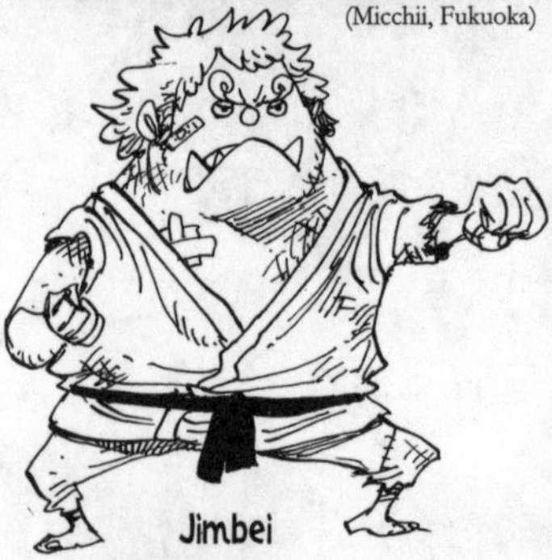

Jimbei

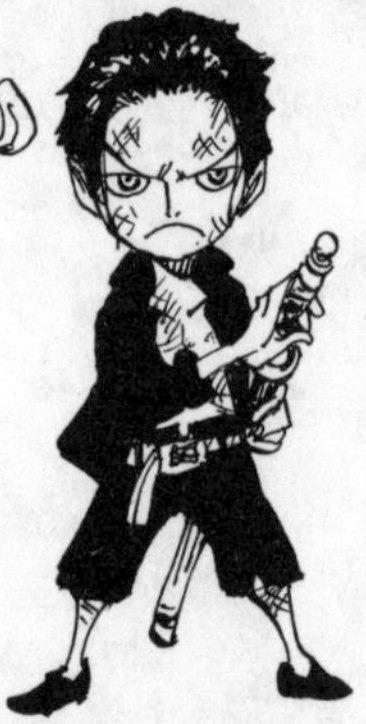

Dracule Mihawk

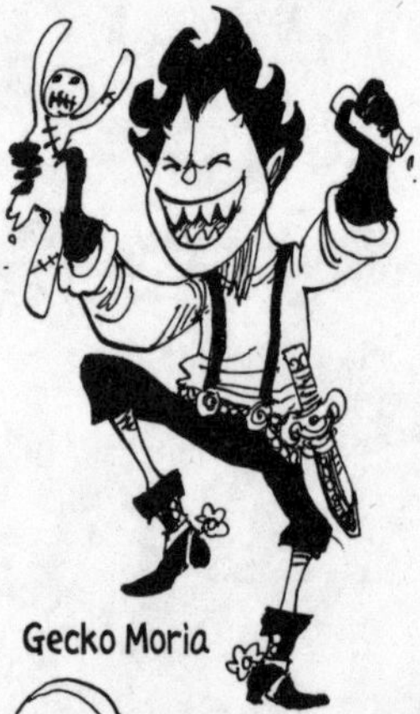

Gecko Moria

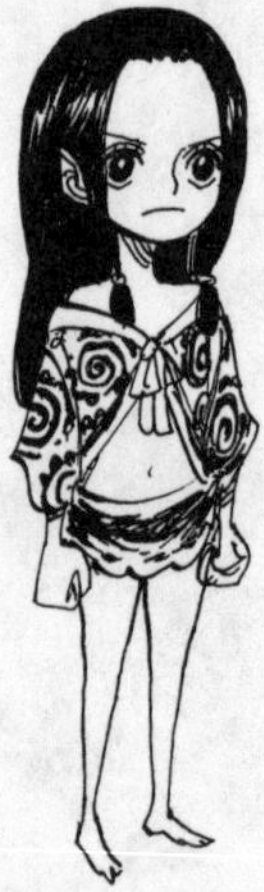

Boa Hancock

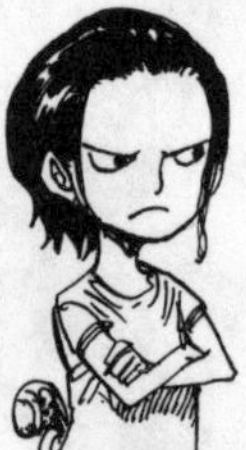

Crocodile (Former Seven Warlord of the Sea)

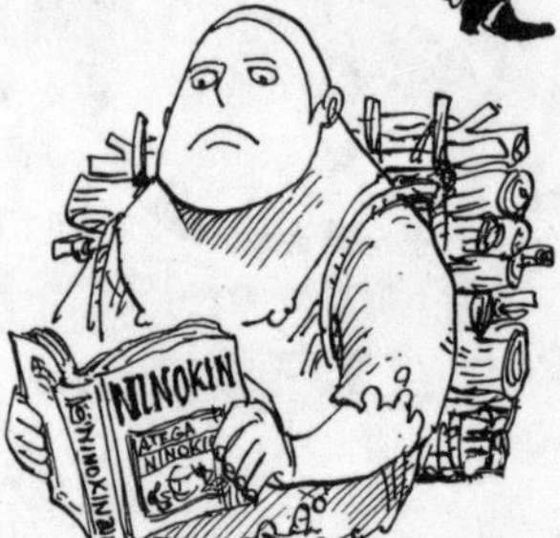
NINOKIN
ATEGA NINOKI

Bartholomew Kuma

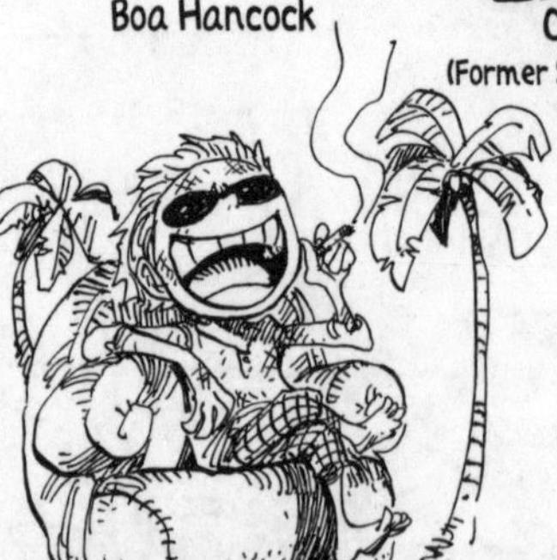

Donquixote Doflamingo

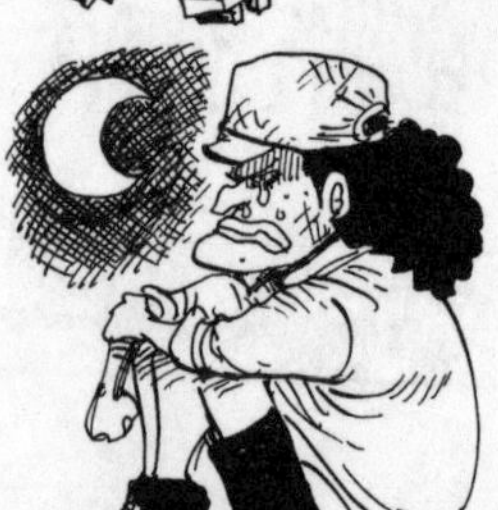

Marshall D. Teech

Chapter 619:
AT THE FOREST OF THE SEA

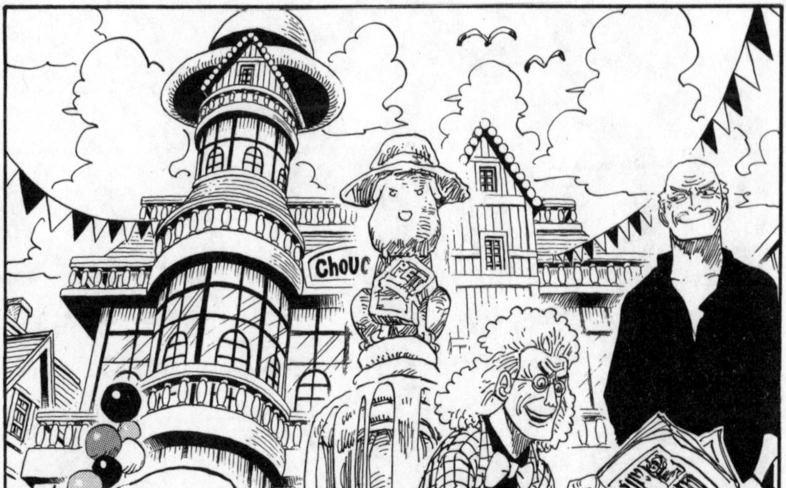
CHOUC

DECKS OF THE WORLD, VOL. 6: "GRAND OPENING IN ORANGE TOWN OF THE GIANT PET FOOD SHOP CHOUCHOU"

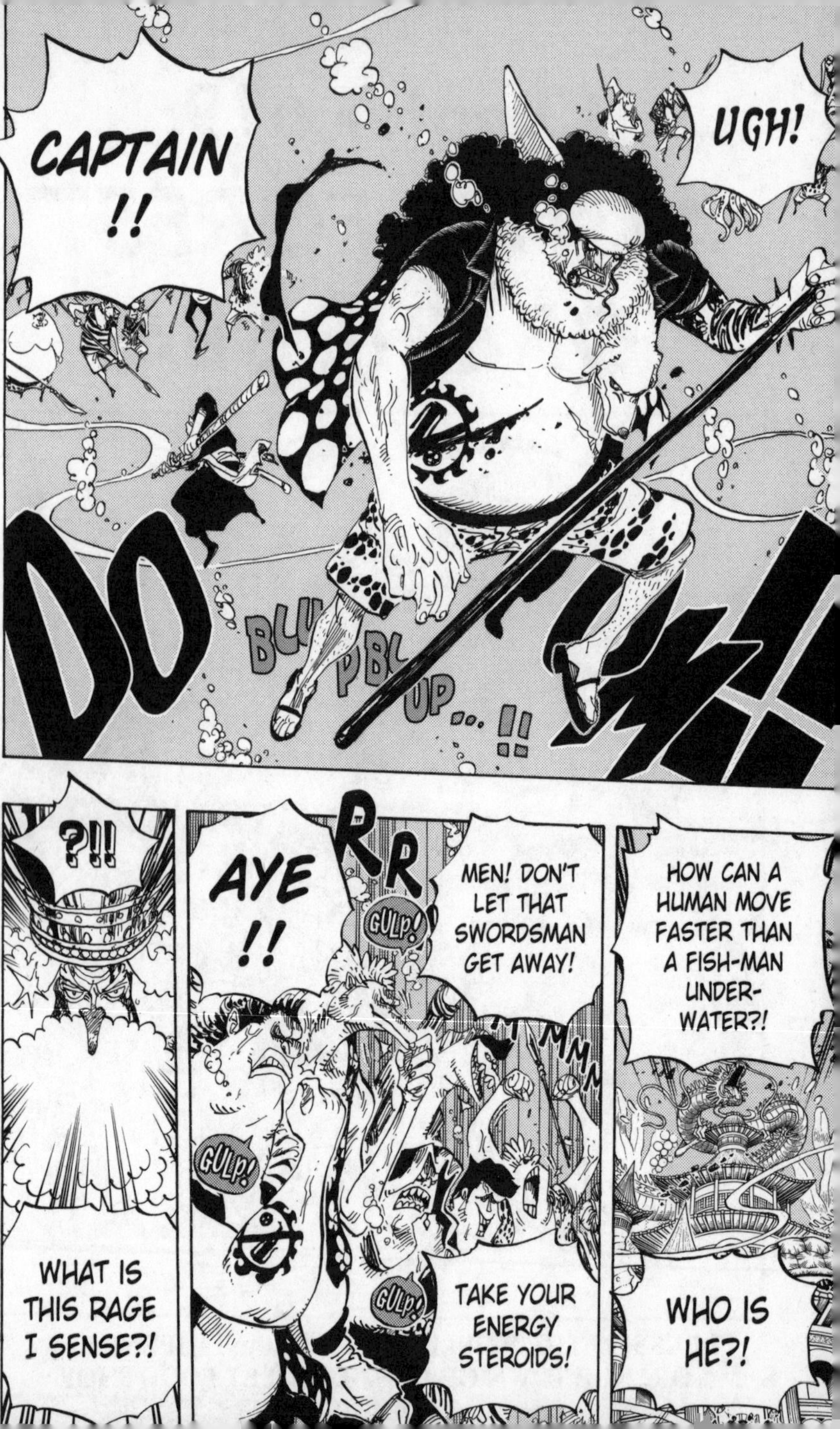

UGH!
CAPTAIN!!
HOW CAN A HUMAN MOVE FASTER THAN A FISH-MAN UNDER-WATER?!
WHO IS HE?!
MEN! DON'T LET THAT SWORDSMAN GET AWAY!
AYE!!
GULP!
GULP!
GULP!
TAKE YOUR ENERGY STEROIDS!
?!!
WHAT IS THIS RAGE I SENSE?!

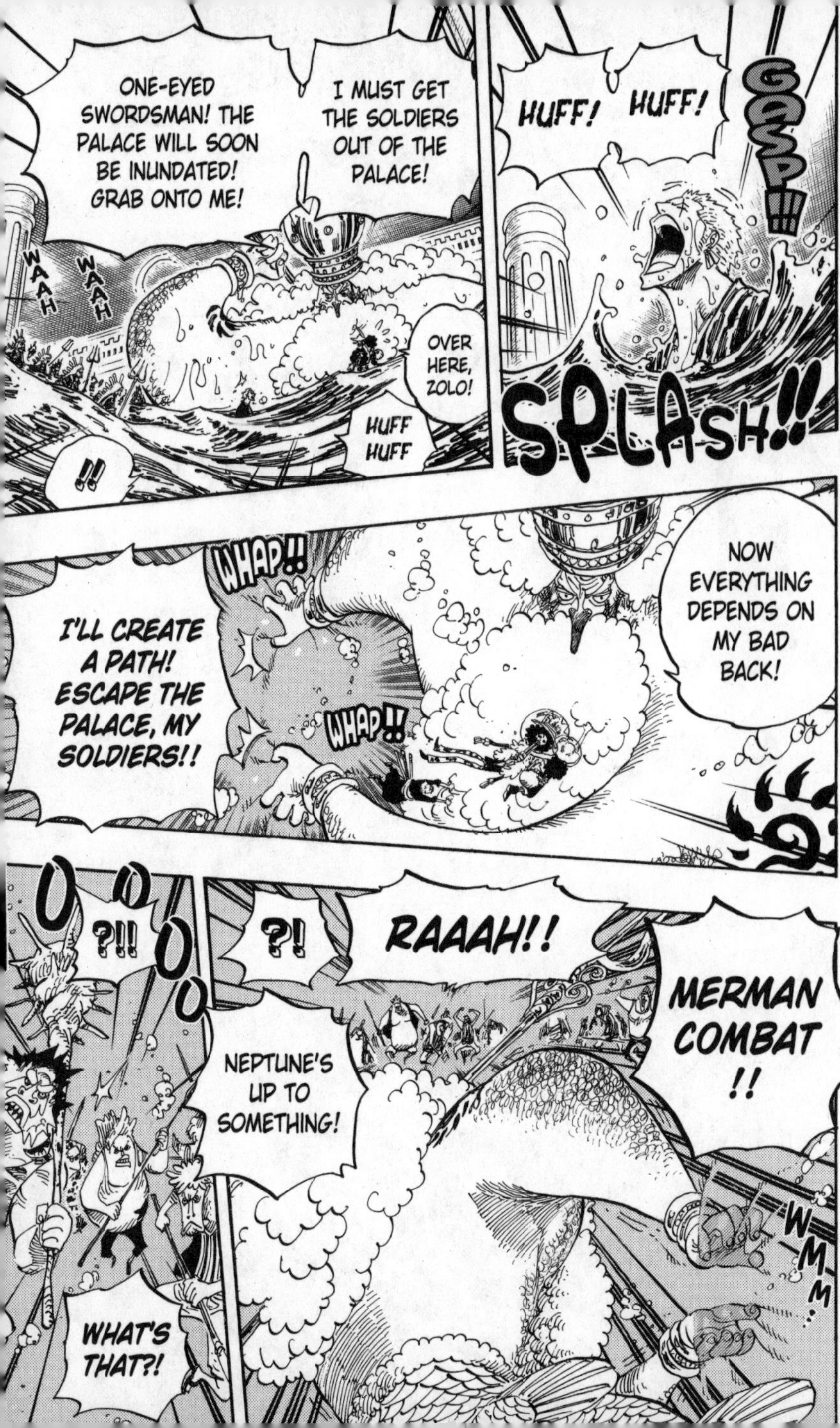
GASP!!!
HUFF! HUFF!
SPLASH!!
I MUST GET THE SOLDIERS OUT OF THE PALACE!
ONE-EYED SWORDSMAN! THE PALACE WILL SOON BE INUNDATED! GRAB ONTO ME!
WAAH
WAAH
OVER HERE, ZOLO!
HUFF HUFF
!!
NOW EVERYTHING DEPENDS ON MY BAD BACK!
WHAP!!
WHAP!!
I'LL CREATE A PATH! ESCAPE THE PALACE, MY SOLDIERS!!
RAAAH!!
MERMAN COMBAT!!
WMMM...
?!
NEPTUNE'S UP TO SOMETHING!
OOOO
?!!
WHAT'S THAT?!

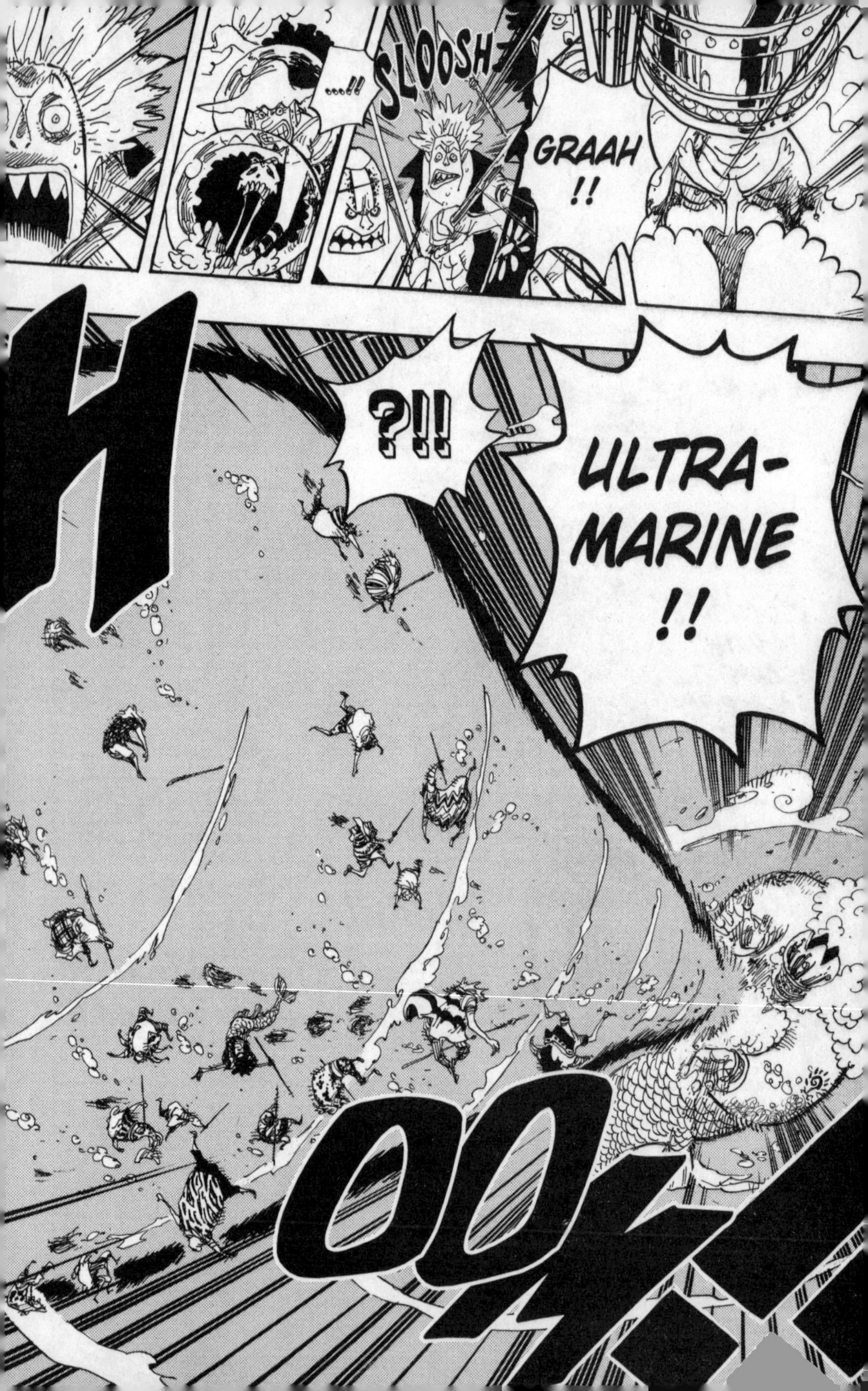
GRAAH!!
SLOOSH
...!!
ULTRA-MARINE!!
?!!

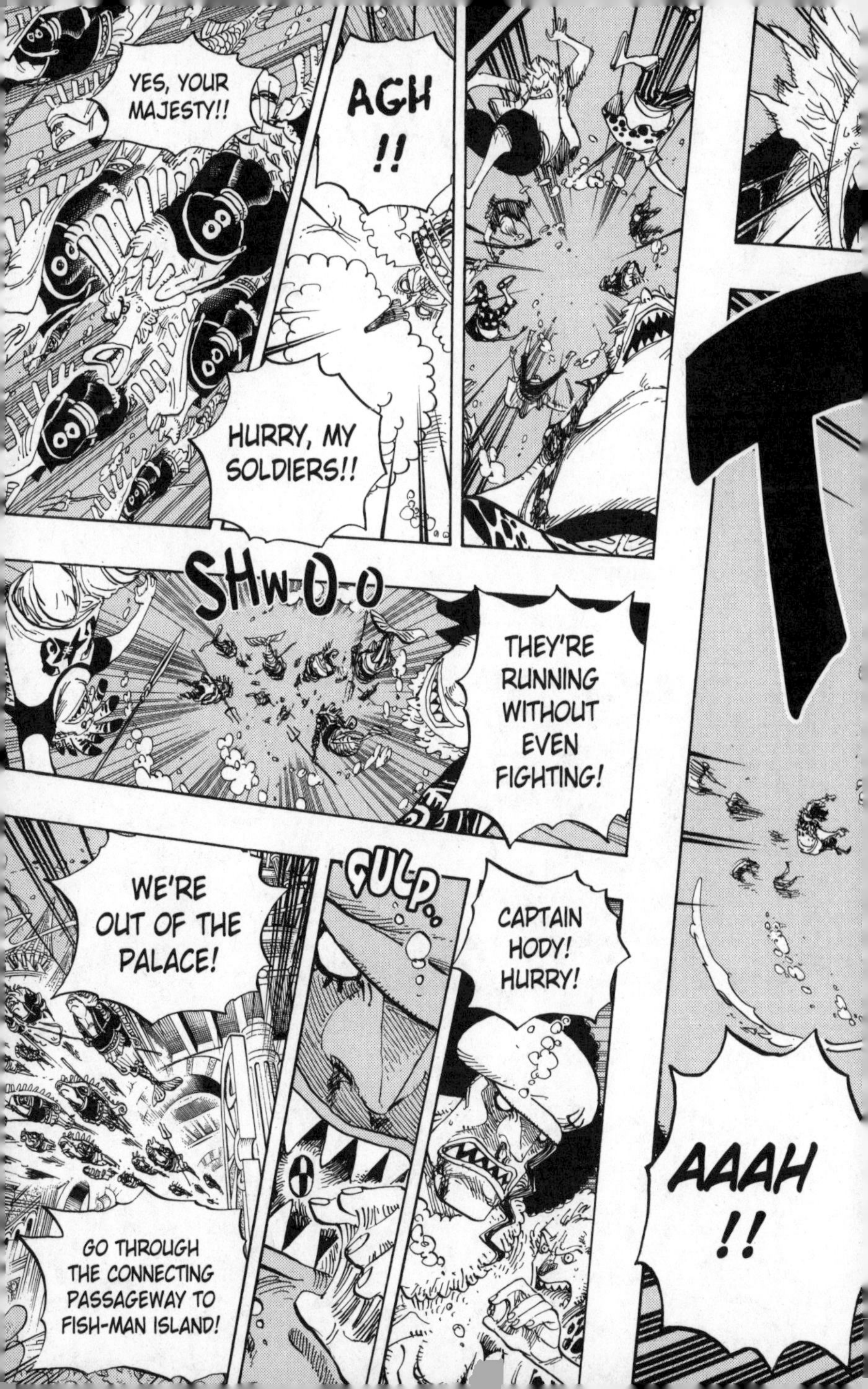
AAAH!!
AGH!!
YES, YOUR MAJESTY!!
HURRY, MY SOLDIERS!!
SHWOOO
THEY'RE RUNNING WITHOUT EVEN FIGHTING!
CAPTAIN HODY! HURRY!
GULP
WE'RE OUT OF THE PALACE!
GO THROUGH THE CONNECTING PASSAGEWAY TO FISH-MAN ISLAND!

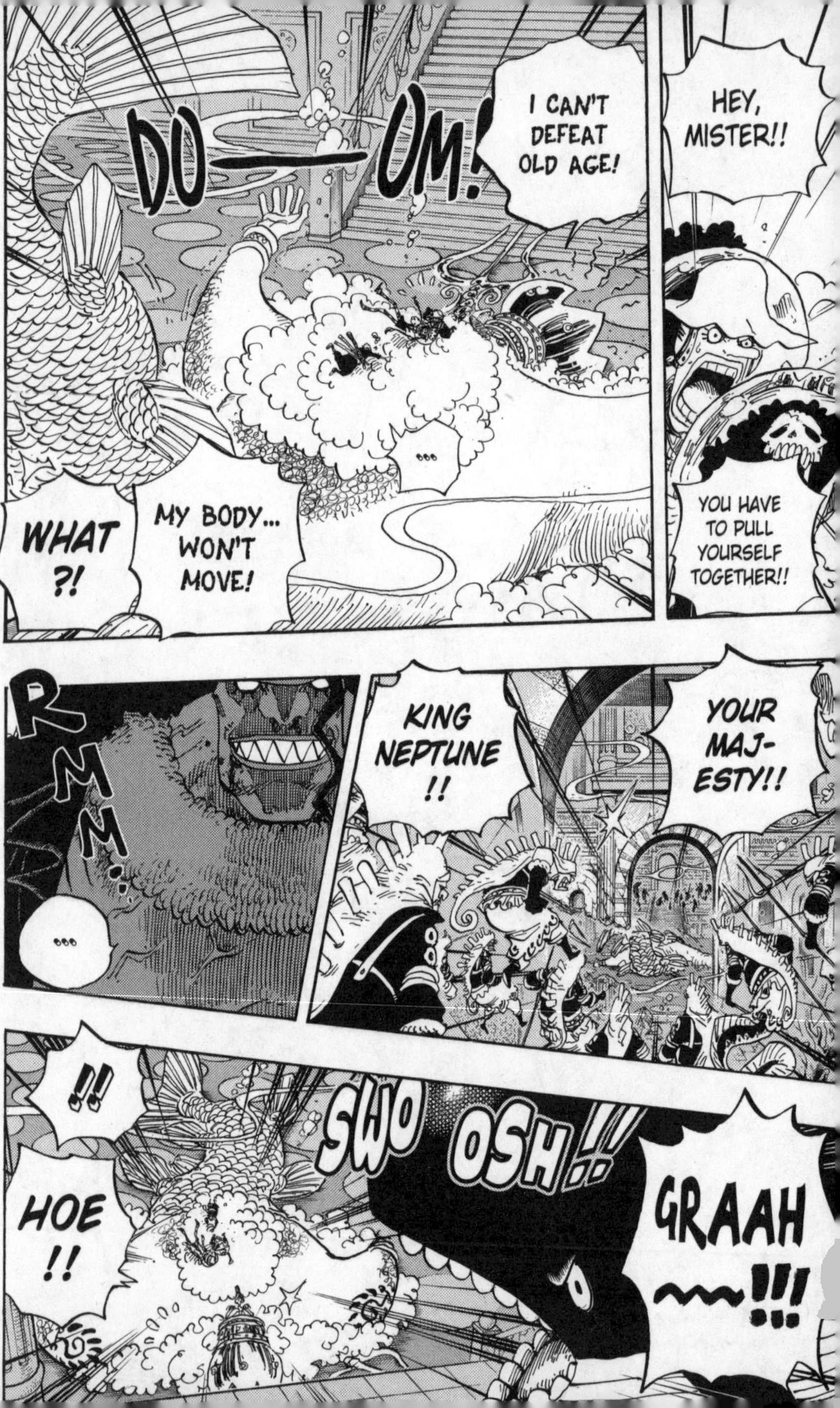
HEY, MISTER!!
YOU HAVE TO PULL YOURSELF TOGETHER!!
I CAN'T DEFEAT OLD AGE!
DO—OM!
...
MY BODY... WON'T MOVE!
WHAT?!
YOUR MAJ-ESTY!!
KING NEPTUNE!!
RMM..
...
GRAAH~~!!!
SWOOSH!!
!!
HOE!!

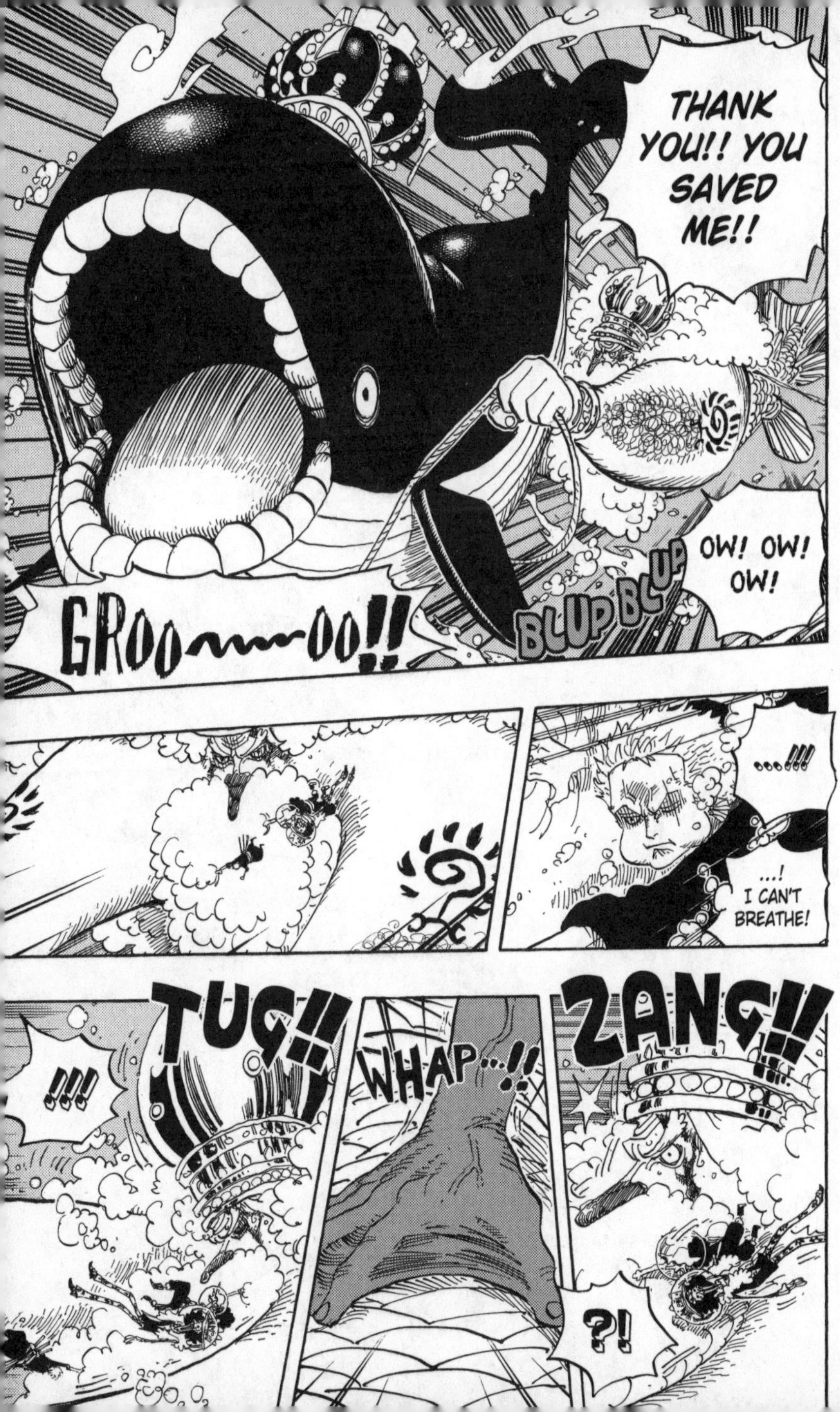
THANK YOU!! YOU SAVED ME!!
OW! OW! OW!
BLUP BLUP
GROO~~~OO!!
...!!!
...! I CAN'T BREATHE!
ZANG!!
WHAP...!!
TUG!!
!!!
?!

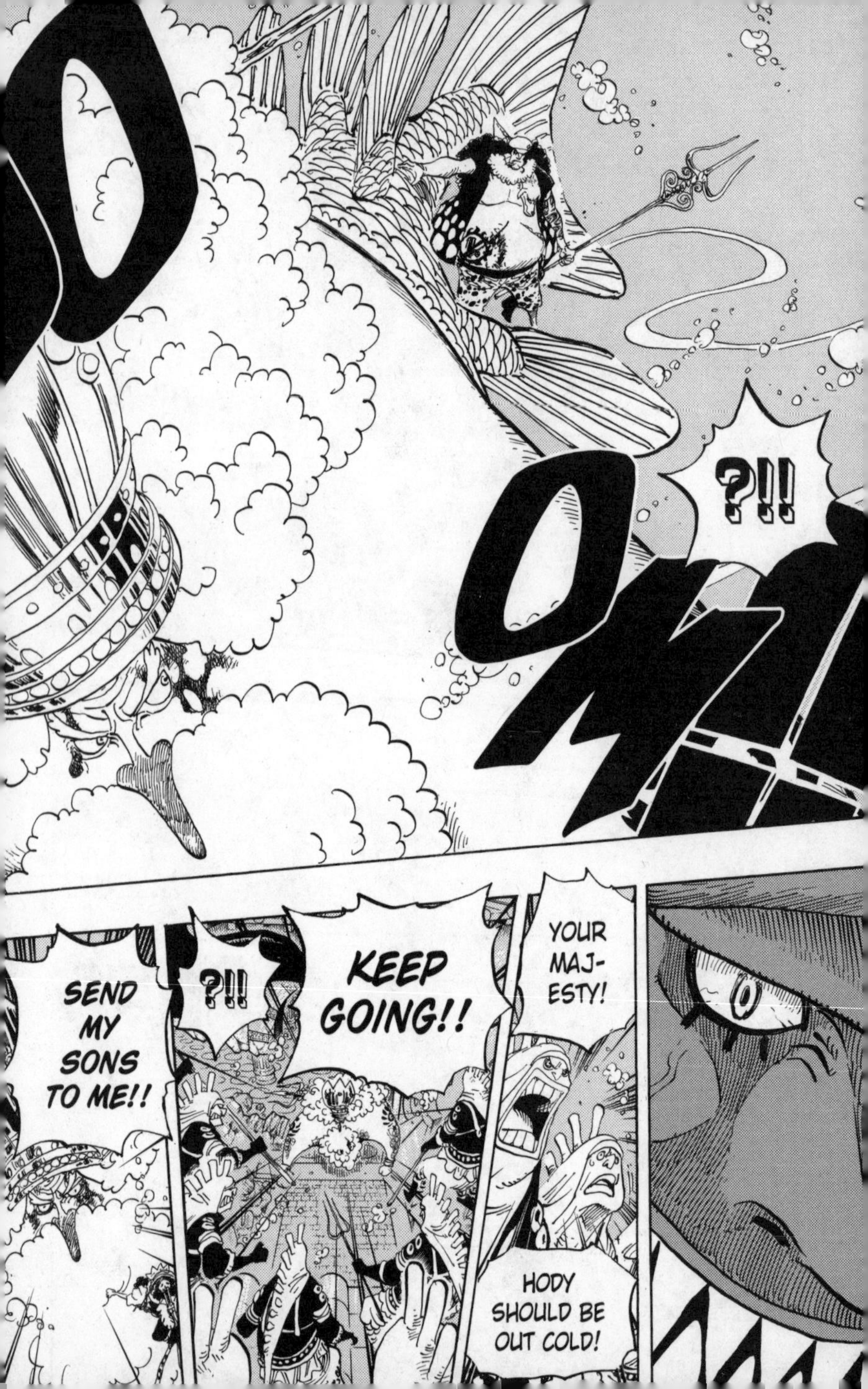
?!!
YOUR MAJ-ESTY!
HODY SHOULD BE OUT COLD!
KEEP GOING!!
?!!
SEND MY SONS TO ME!!

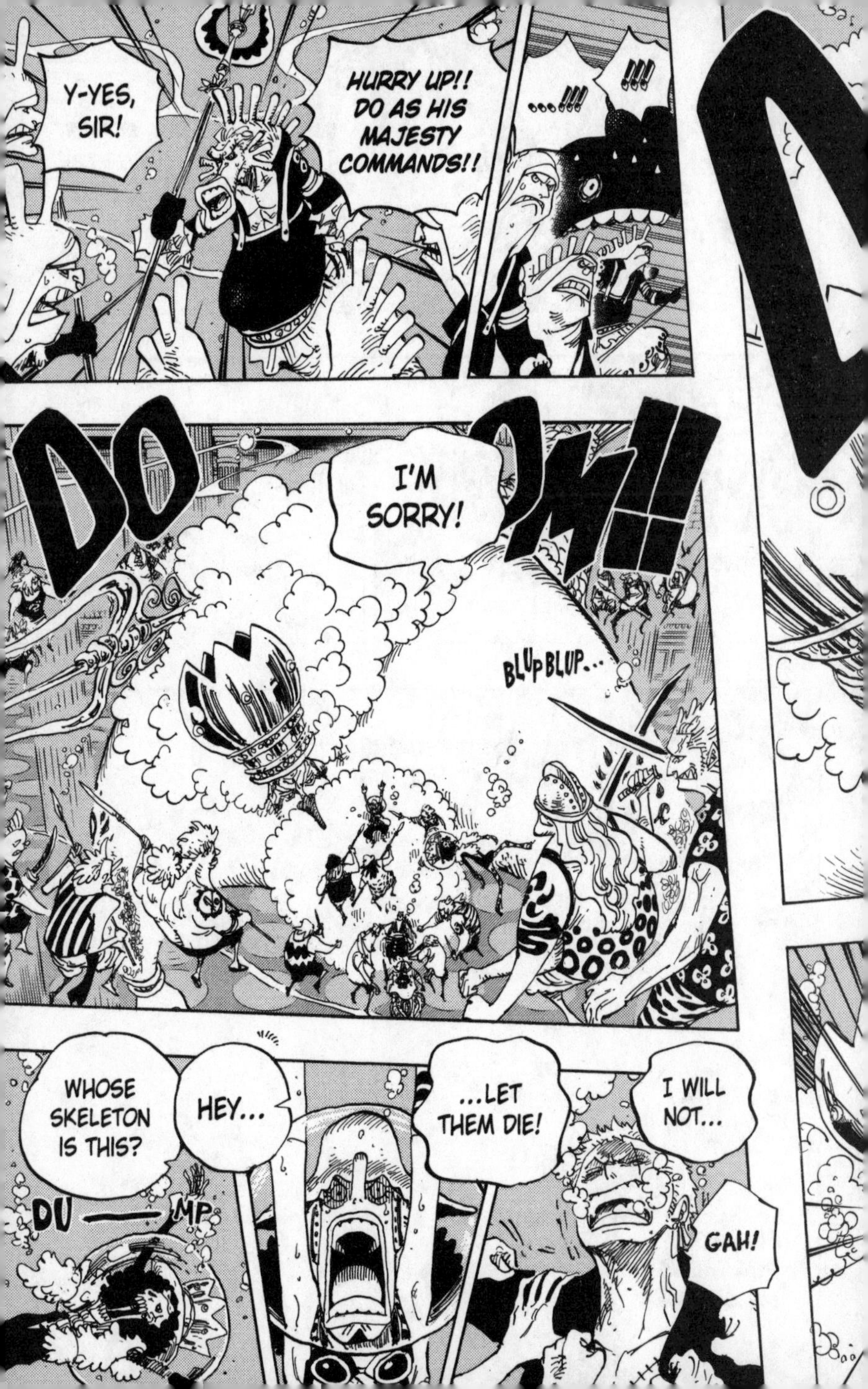
!!!
...!!!
HURRY UP!! DO AS HIS MAJESTY COMMANDS!!
Y-YES, SIR!
DO
OM!!
I'M SORRY!
BLUP BLUP...
I WILL NOT...
GAH!
...LET THEM DIE!
HEY...
WHOSE SKELETON IS THIS?
DU——MP

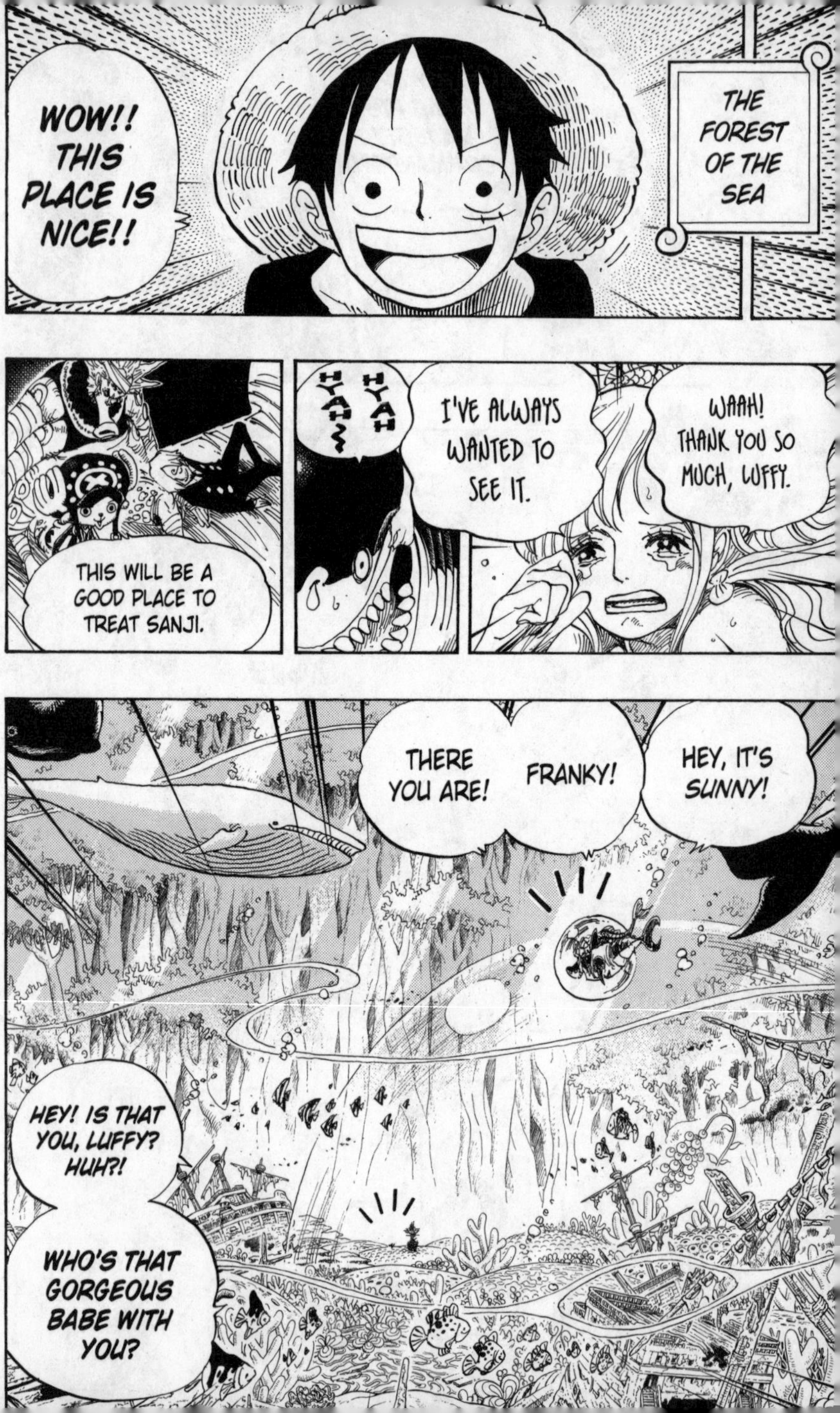
THE FOREST OF THE SEA
WOW!! THIS PLACE IS NICE!!
WAAH! THANK YOU SO MUCH, LUFFY.
I'VE ALWAYS WANTED TO SEE IT.
HYAH HYAH
THIS WILL BE A GOOD PLACE TO TREAT SANJI.
HEY, IT'S SUNNY!
FRANKY!
THERE YOU ARE!
HEY! IS THAT YOU, LUFFY? HUH?!
WHO'S THAT GORGEOUS BABE WITH YOU?

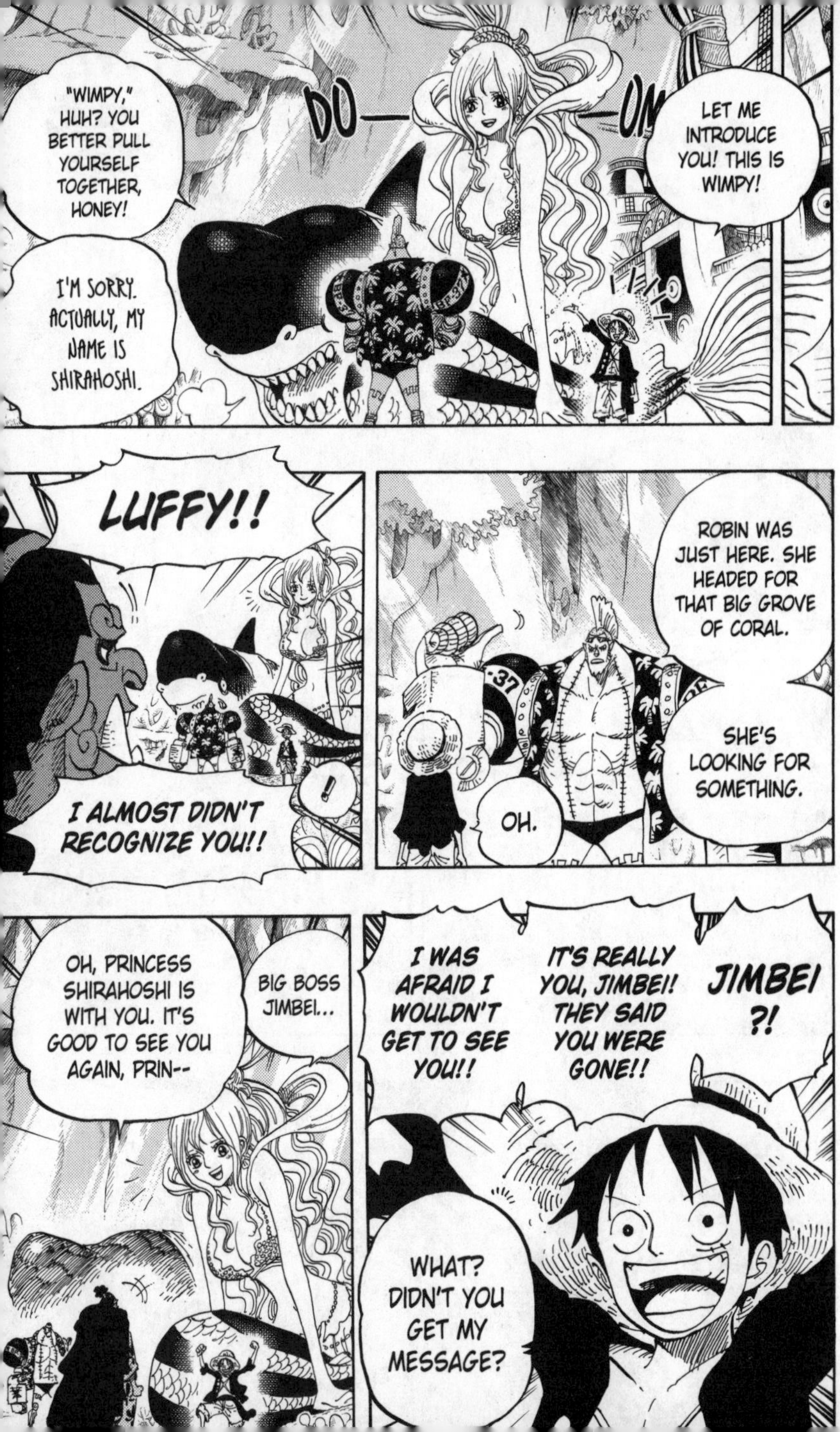
LET ME INTRODUCE YOU! THIS IS WIMPY!
DO—
"WIMPY," HUH? YOU BETTER PULL YOURSELF TOGETHER, HONEY!
I'M SORRY. ACTUALLY, MY NAME IS SHIRAHOSHI.
ROBIN WAS JUST HERE. SHE HEADED FOR THAT BIG GROVE OF CORAL.
SHE'S LOOKING FOR SOMETHING.
OH.
LUFFY!!
I ALMOST DIDN'T RECOGNIZE YOU!!
!
JIMBEI ?!
IT'S REALLY YOU, JIMBEI! THEY SAID YOU WERE GONE!!
I WAS AFRAID I WOULDN'T GET TO SEE YOU!!
WHAT? DIDN'T YOU GET MY MESSAGE?
BIG BOSS JIMBEI...
OH, PRINCESS SHIRAHOSHI IS WITH YOU. IT'S GOOD TO SEE YOU AGAIN, PRIN--

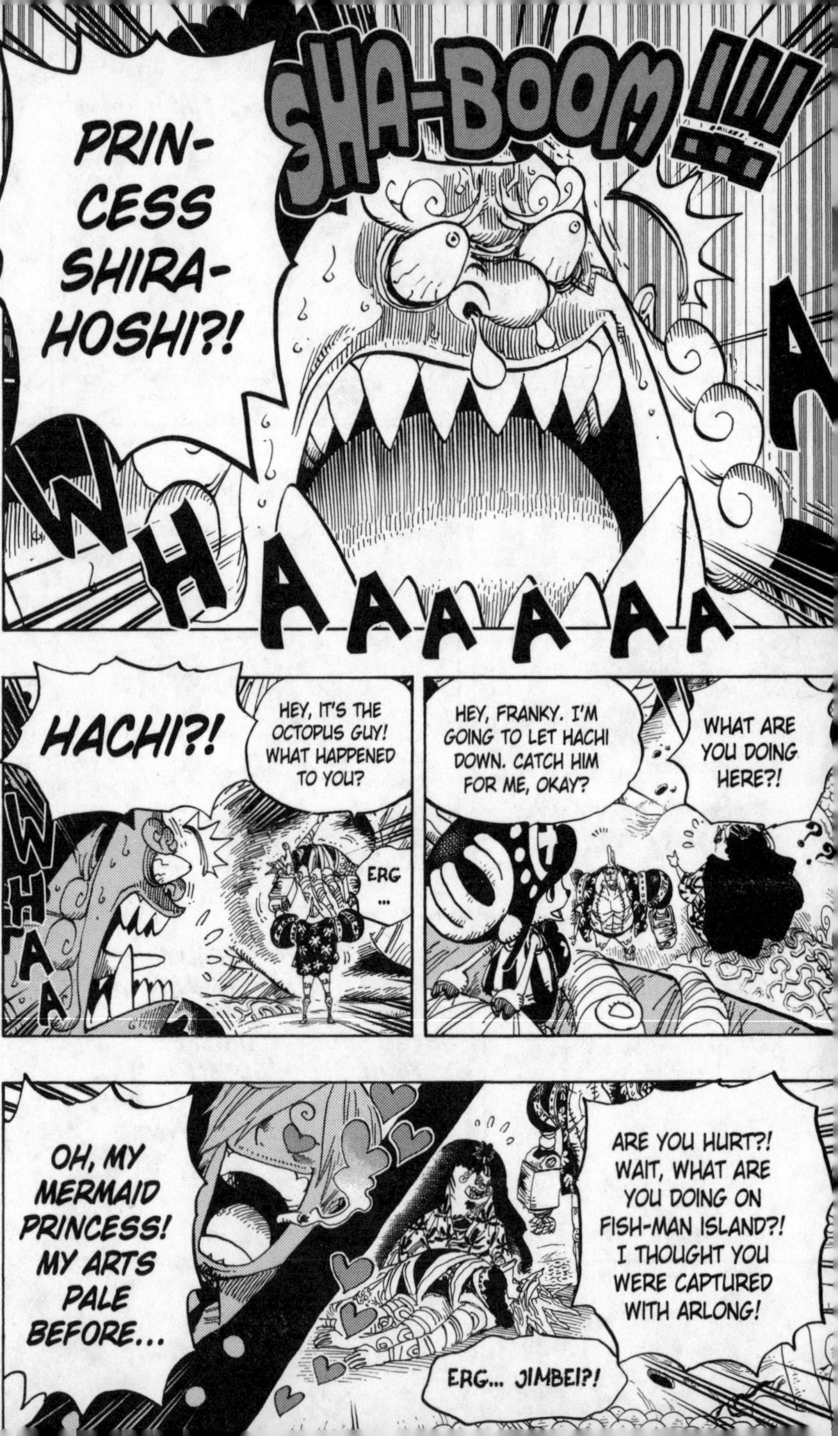
SHA-BOOM!!!
PRIN-CESS SHIRA-HOSHI?!
WHAAAAAAAAA
WHAT ARE YOU DOING HERE?!
HEY, FRANKY. I'M GOING TO LET HACHI DOWN. CATCH HIM FOR ME, OKAY?
HEY, IT'S THE OCTOPUS GUY! WHAT HAPPENED TO YOU?
HACHI?!
ERG ...
WHAA
ARE YOU HURT?! WAIT, WHAT ARE YOU DOING ON FISH-MAN ISLAND?! I THOUGHT YOU WERE CAPTURED WITH ARLONG!
ERG... JIMBEI?!
OH, MY MERMAID PRINCESS! MY ARTS PALE BEFORE...

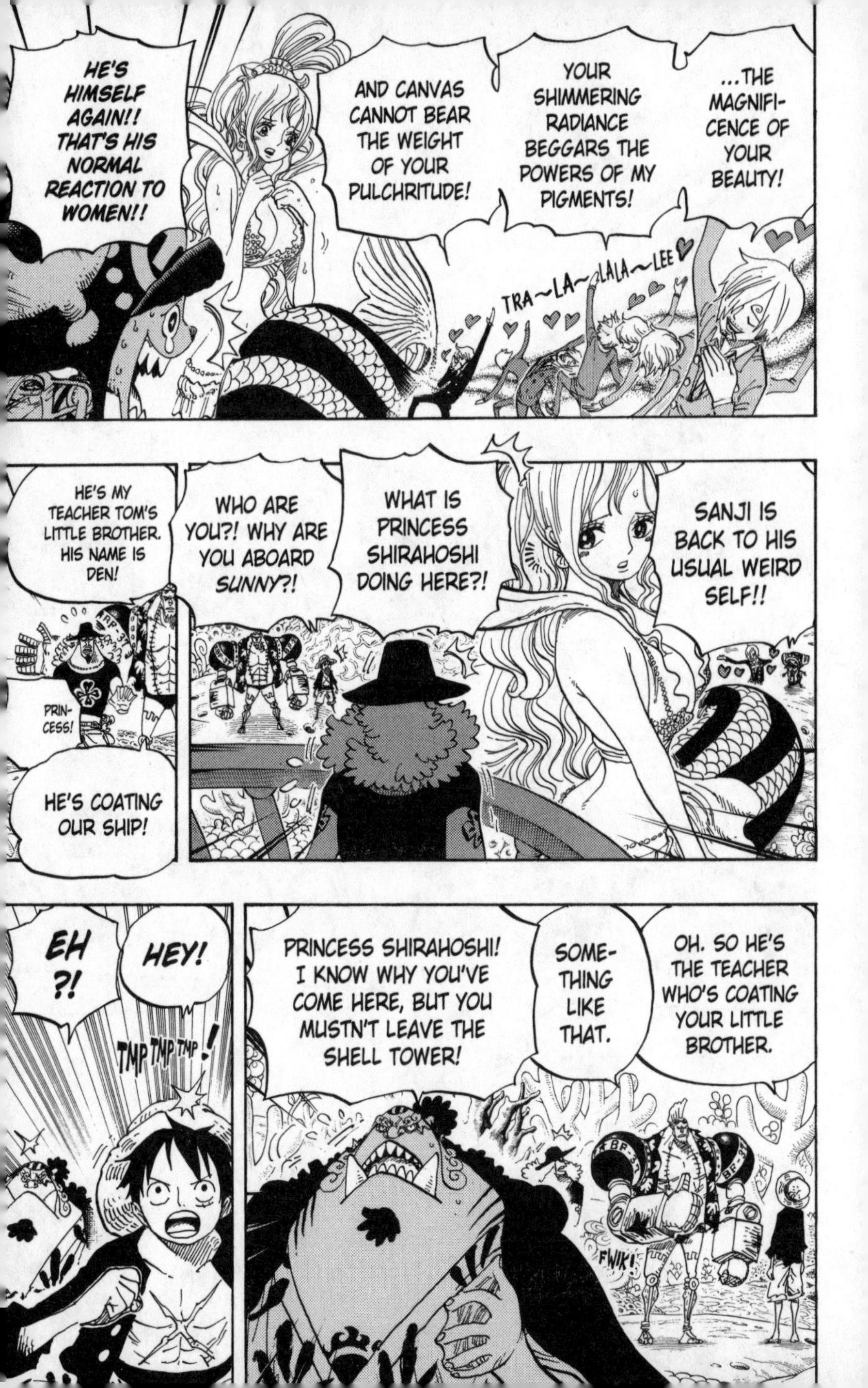
...THE MAGNIFICENCE OF YOUR BEAUTY!
YOUR SHIMMERING RADIANCE BEGGARS THE POWERS OF MY PIGMENTS!
AND CANVAS CANNOT BEAR THE WEIGHT OF YOUR PULCHRITUDE!
TRA~LA~LALA~LEE
HE'S HIMSELF AGAIN!! THAT'S HIS NORMAL REACTION TO WOMEN!!
SANJI IS BACK TO HIS USUAL WEIRD SELF!!
WHAT IS PRINCESS SHIRAHOSHI DOING HERE?!
WHO ARE YOU?! WHY ARE YOU ABOARD SUNNY?!
HE'S MY TEACHER TOM'S LITTLE BROTHER. HIS NAME IS DEN!
PRINCESS!
HE'S COATING OUR SHIP!
OH. SO HE'S THE TEACHER WHO'S COATING YOUR LITTLE BROTHER.
SOMETHING LIKE THAT.
PRINCESS SHIRAHOSHI! I KNOW WHY YOU'VE COME HERE, BUT YOU MUSTN'T LEAVE THE SHELL TOWER!
FWIK!
HEY!
EH ?!
TMP TMP TMP !

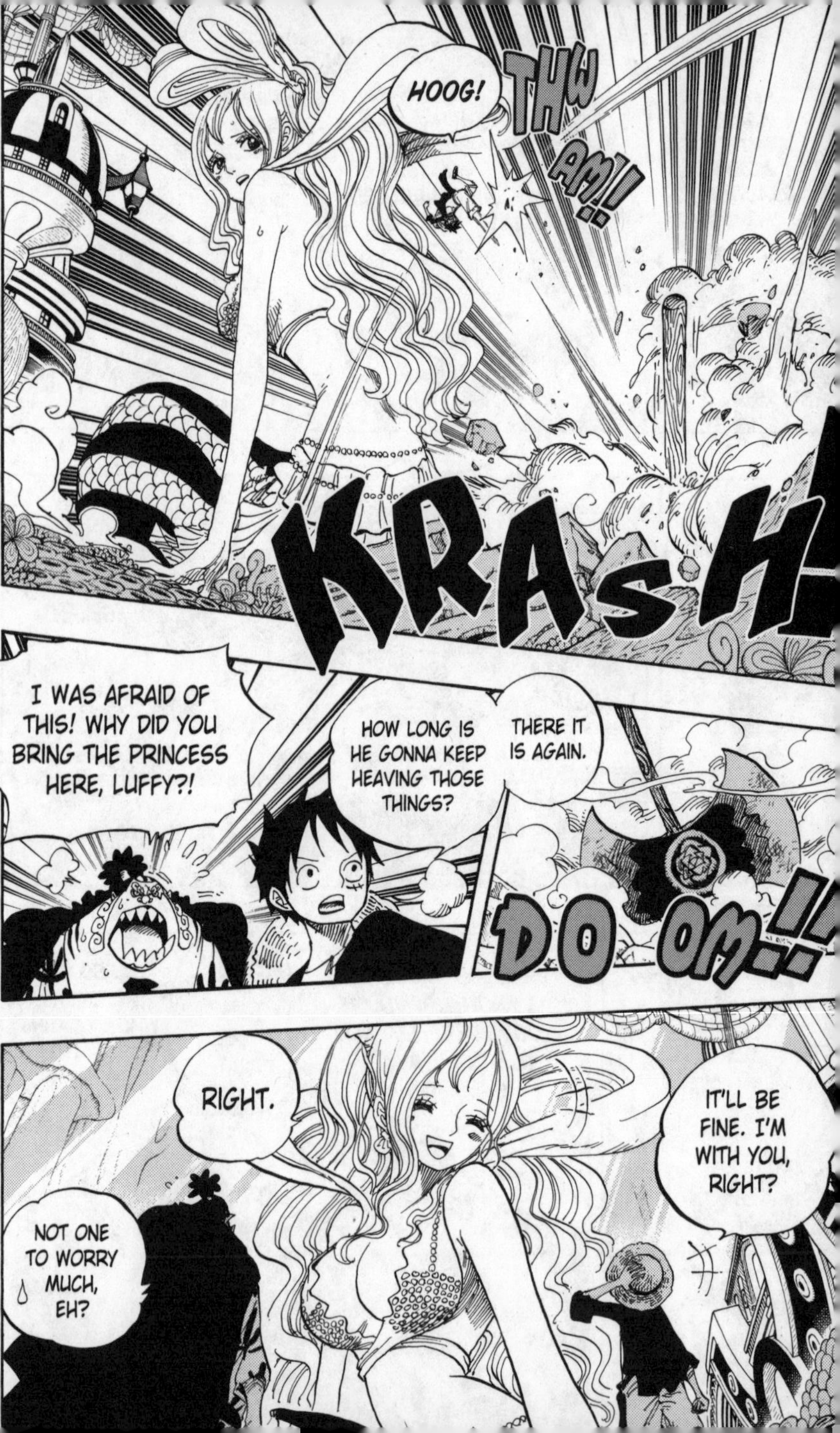
HOOG!
THWAM!!
KRASH!
THERE IT IS AGAIN.
DOOM!!
HOW LONG IS HE GONNA KEEP HEAVING THOSE THINGS?
I WAS AFRAID OF THIS! WHY DID YOU BRING THE PRINCESS HERE, LUFFY?!
IT'LL BE FINE. I'M WITH YOU, RIGHT?
RIGHT.
NOT ONE TO WORRY MUCH, EH?

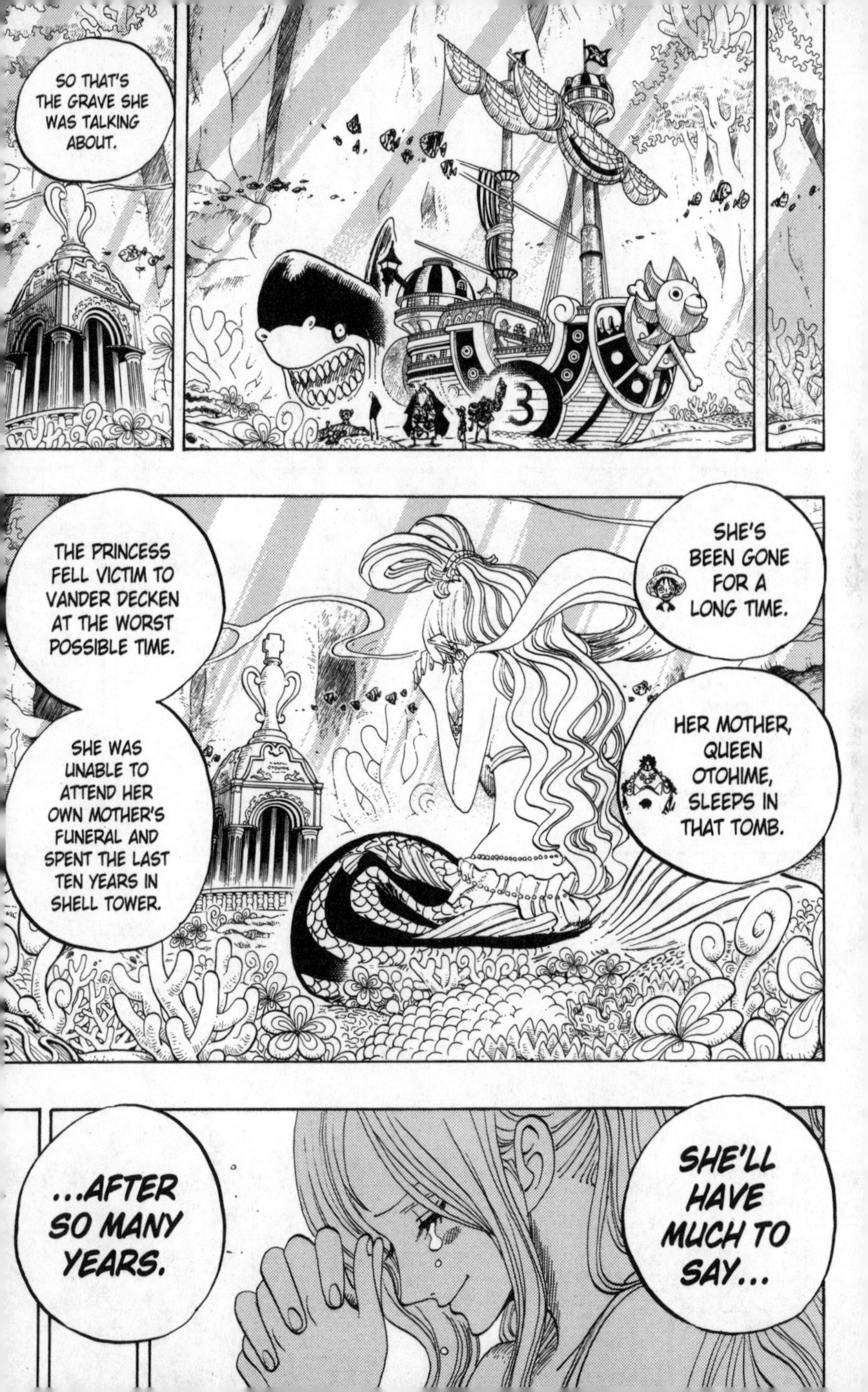
SO THAT'S THE GRAVE SHE WAS TALKING ABOUT.
SHE'S BEEN GONE FOR A LONG TIME.
HER MOTHER, QUEEN OTOHIME, SLEEPS IN THAT TOMB.
THE PRINCESS FELL VICTIM TO VANDER DECKEN AT THE WORST POSSIBLE TIME.
SHE WAS UNABLE TO ATTEND HER OWN MOTHER'S FUNERAL AND SPENT THE LAST TEN YEARS IN SHELL TOWER.
SHE'LL HAVE MUCH TO SAY...
...AFTER SO MANY YEARS.

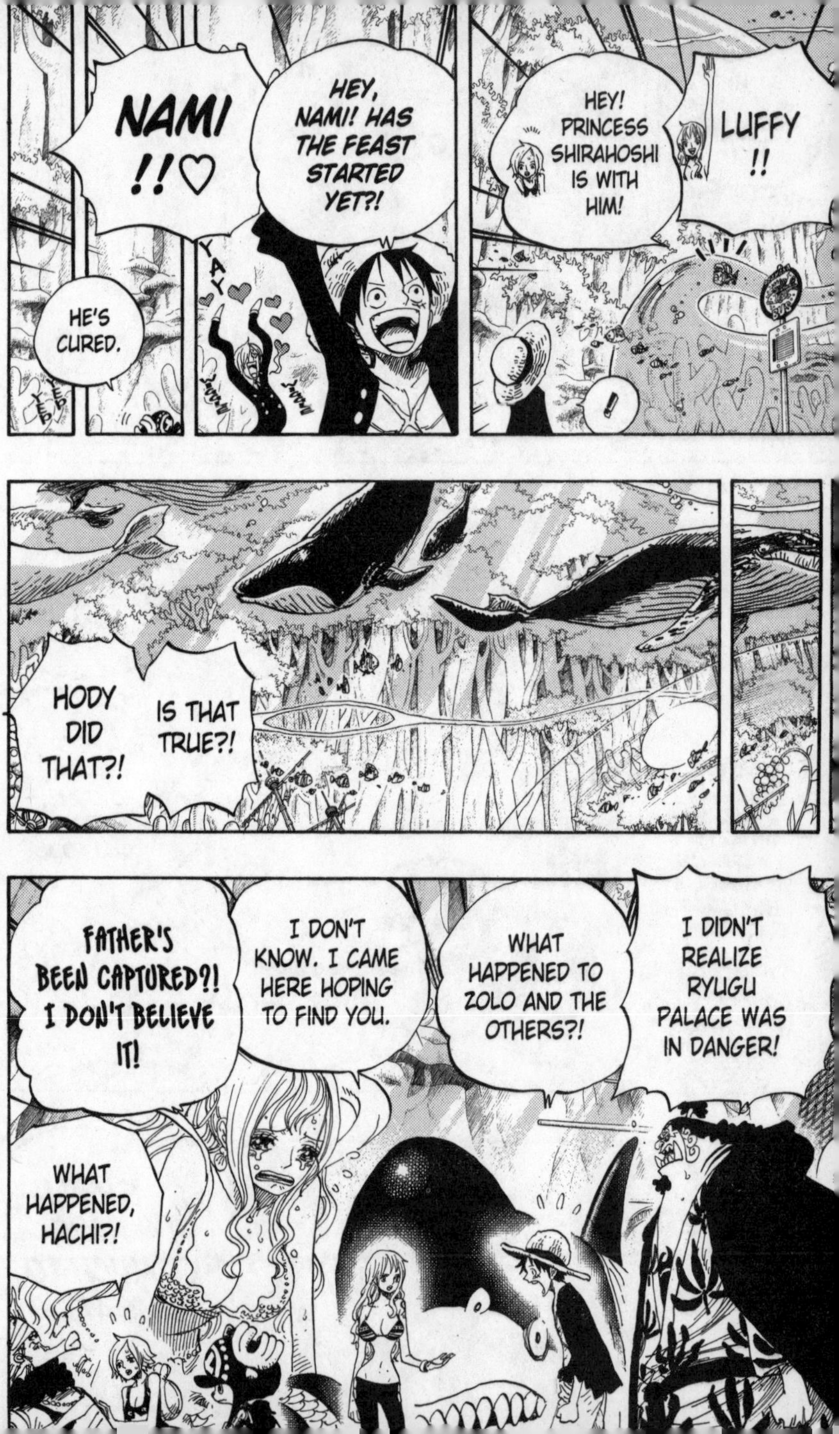
LUFFY !!
HEY! PRINCESS SHIRAHOSHI IS WITH HIM!
!
HEY, NAMI! HAS THE FEAST STARTED YET?!
YAY
NAMI !!♡
HE'S CURED.
IS THAT TRUE?!
HODY DID THAT?!
I DIDN'T REALIZE RYUGU PALACE WAS IN DANGER!
WHAT HAPPENED TO ZOLO AND THE OTHERS?!
I DON'T KNOW. I CAME HERE HOPING TO FIND YOU.
FATHER'S BEEN CAPTURED?! I DON'T BELIEVE IT!
WHAT HAPPENED, HACHI?!

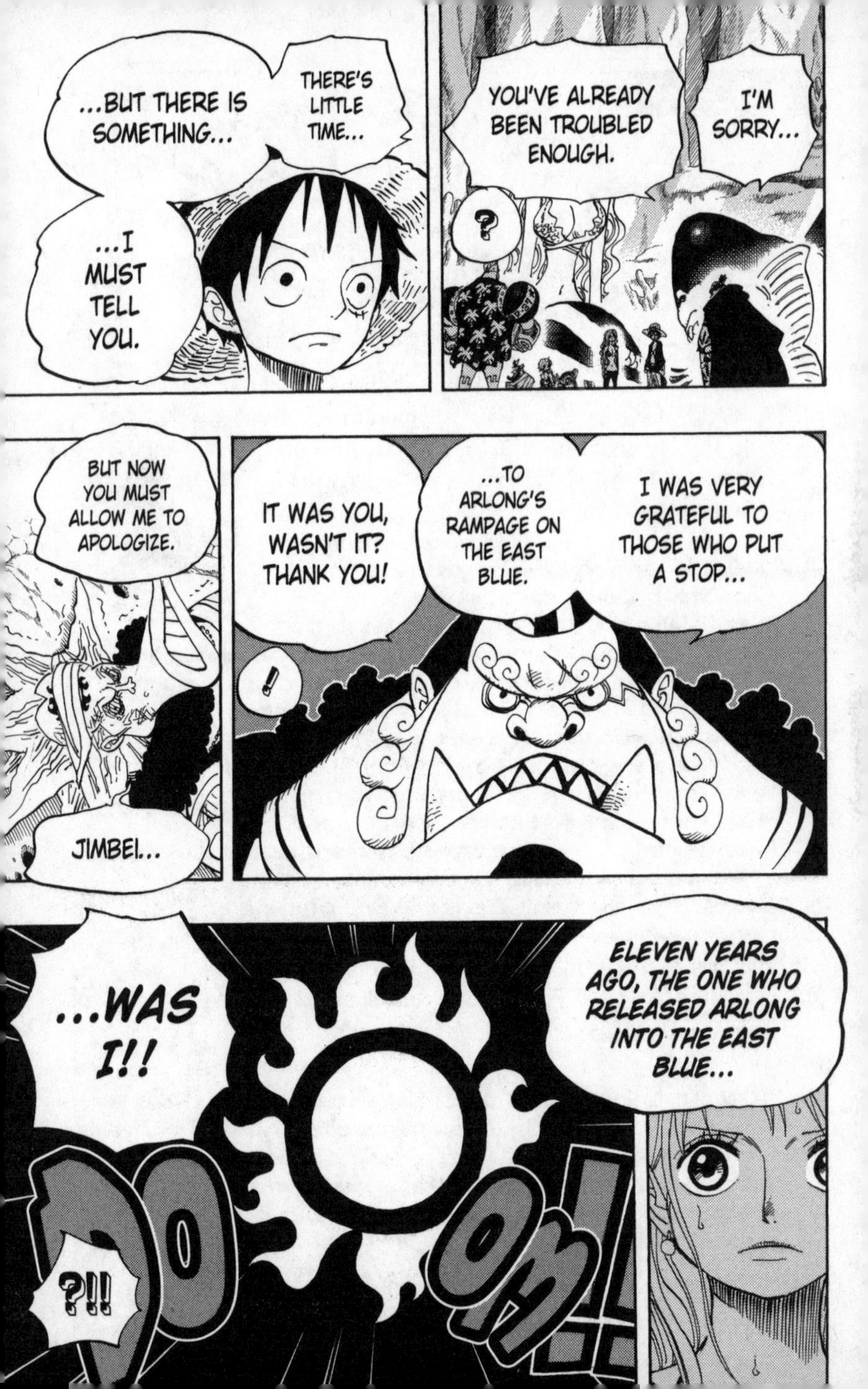
I'M SORRY...
YOU'VE ALREADY BEEN TROUBLED ENOUGH.
?
THERE'S LITTLE TIME...
...BUT THERE IS SOMETHING...
...I MUST TELL YOU.
I WAS VERY GRATEFUL TO THOSE WHO PUT A STOP...
...TO ARLONG'S RAMPAGE ON THE EAST BLUE.
IT WAS YOU, WASN'T IT? THANK YOU!
!
BUT NOW YOU MUST ALLOW ME TO APOLOGIZE.
JIMBEI...
ELEVEN YEARS AGO, THE ONE WHO RELEASED ARLONG INTO THE EAST BLUE...
...WAS I!!
DOOOM!
?!!

質問コーナー
エス ビー エス

(Tomoya Sato, Yamanashi)

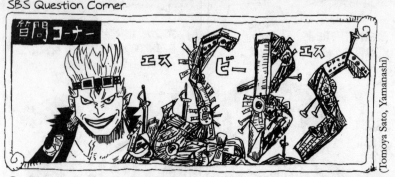

Q: I just realized something huge! If a fish-man's fin splits in two after 30 years old...that means that King Neptune, that "hairy guy," that "Sea Knight," who has only one fin, is in his twenties!! So, if you have any excuses, I'd like to hear them, Odacchi!

--Captain of the Tsuchinoko Gathering Crew

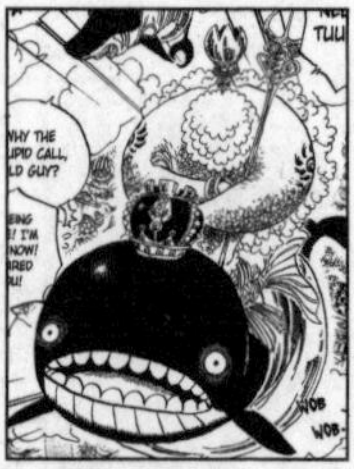

A: Well, this isn't an excuse, I just haven't explained it. Neptune is supposed to be like that. I guess the explanation in the story wasn't very good. It's only the female merfolk whose fins split to allow them to walk on land. If you take a look around Fish-Man Island, you'll see that none of the mermen have fins split in two, even those who are obviously over thirty. The important thing is most mermaids who are in their forties and fifties are living on land! Because I only wanted to draw young and beautiful mermaids in Mermaid Cove! I have my own dream too because I'm a mangaka! This is the kind of thing a man dreams of!

BACK THEN I NEVER THOUGHT...

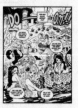

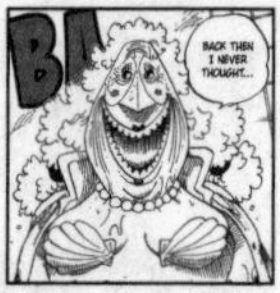

Q: Hey, nice to meet you, Odacchi! I'm 12 years old, and I love Mr. 2 Bon Clay! The mermaids in volume 62 were really cute! Speaking of which, *do mermaids poop?*

--I Love Bakuman

A: You just shut up!! Just think about the way this is going to flow, okay? I just got finished saying that mermaids are what men dream of. I mean, they're living beings, so I guess they do poop. I'd guess that some of their scales flip up, maybe in the back, or maybe in the front.
And then Ahhhhhh!!! PO Stop!!! Huh? Sanji?!

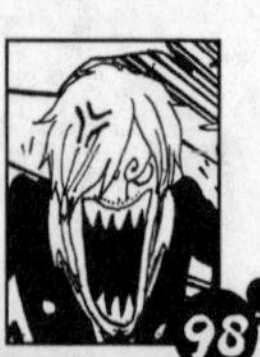

Sanji: **Another word and I'll filet you!!! Mermaids don't crap! You got that?!**

A: Okay... They don't.

Chapter 620:
THE WONDERFUL AMUSEMENT PARK

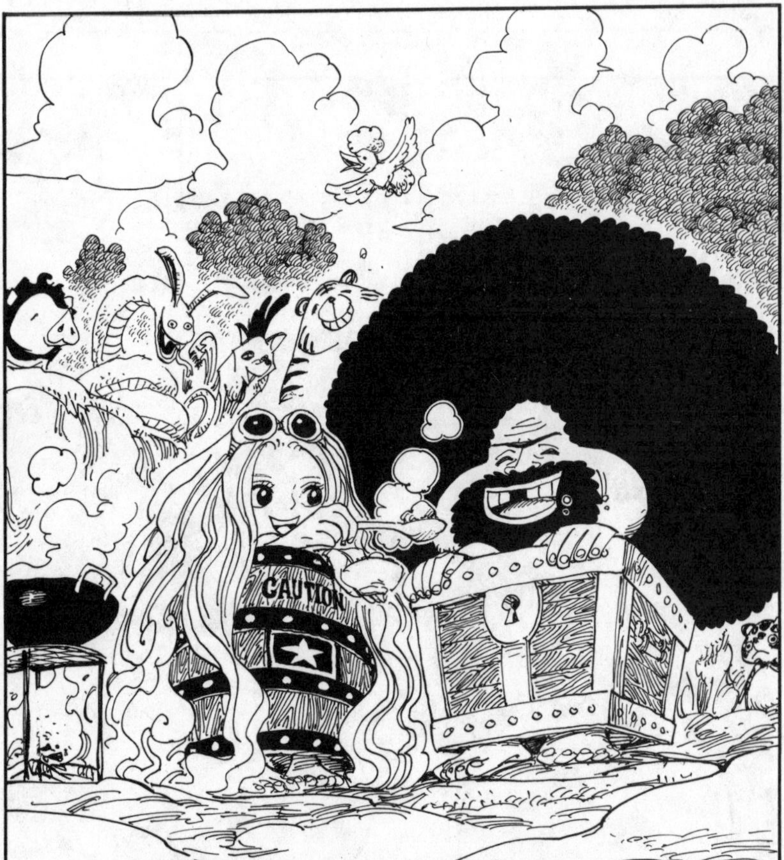
CAUTION

DECKS OF THE WORLD, VOL. 7:
"A NEWCOMER TO THE ISLAND OF RARE ANIMALS—
BARREL WOMAN SARFUNKEL"

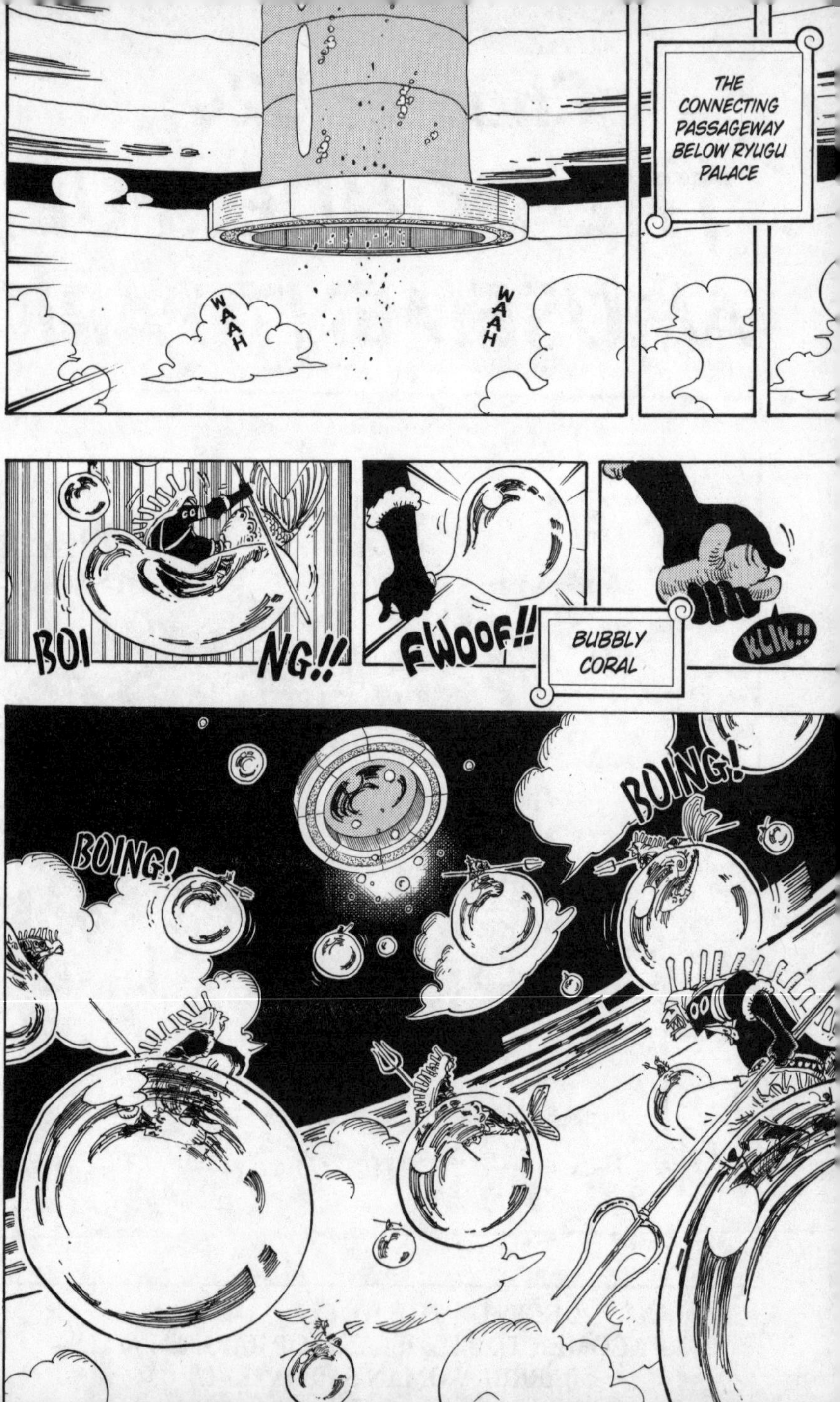
THE CONNECTING PASSAGEWAY BELOW RYUGU PALACE
WAAH
WAAH
KLIK!!
BUBBLY CORAL
FWOOF!!
BOING!!
BOING!
BOING!

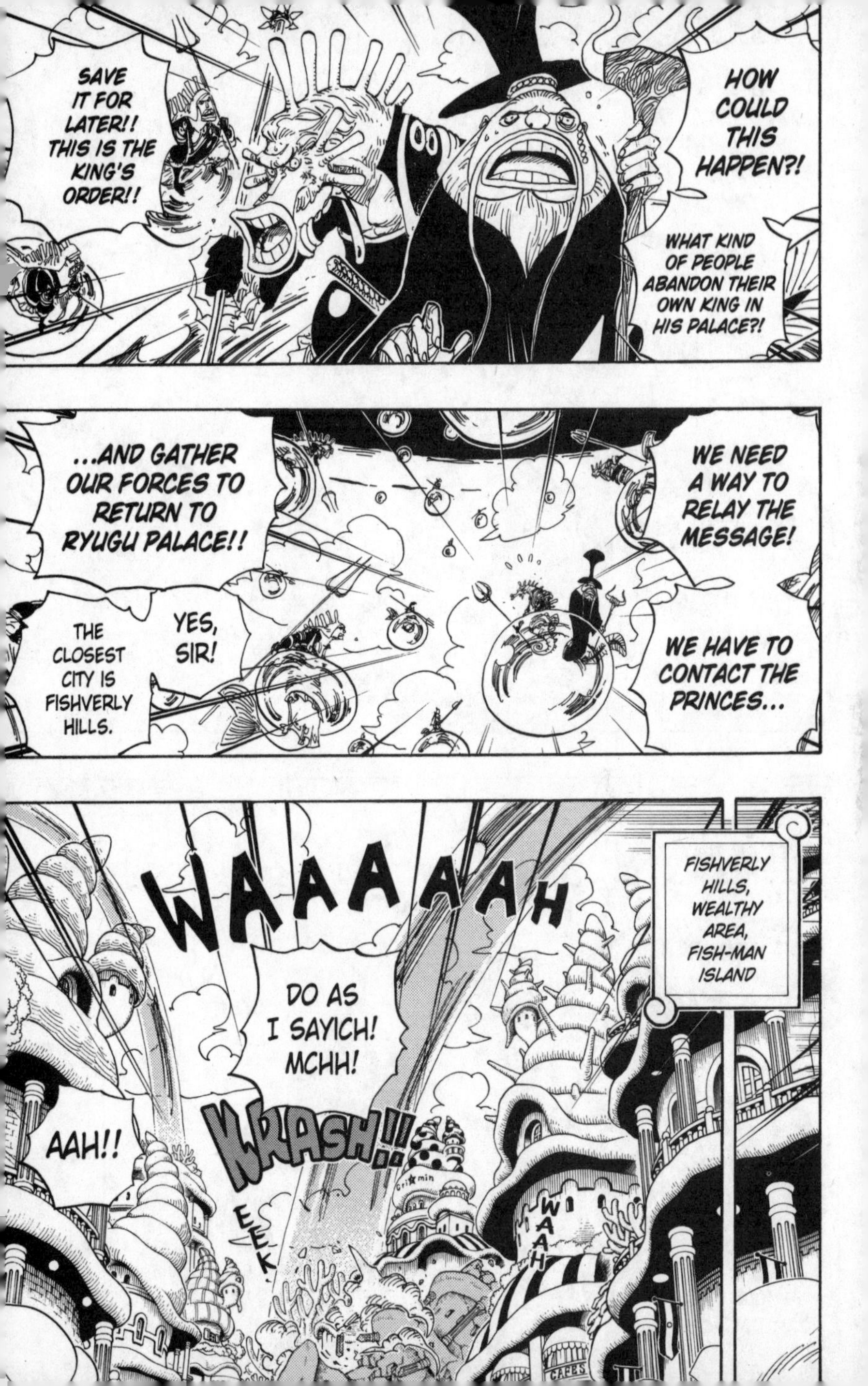
HOW COULD THIS HAPPEN?!
WHAT KIND OF PEOPLE ABANDON THEIR OWN KING IN HIS PALACE?!
SAVE IT FOR LATER!! THIS IS THE KING'S ORDER!!
WE NEED A WAY TO RELAY THE MESSAGE!
WE HAVE TO CONTACT THE PRINCES...
...AND GATHER OUR FORCES TO RETURN TO RYUGU PALACE!!
YES, SIR!
THE CLOSEST CITY IS FISHVERLY HILLS.
FISHVERLY HILLS, WEALTHY AREA, FISH-MAN ISLAND
WAAAAAAH
DO AS I SAYICH! MCHH!
KRASH!!!
WAAAH
EEK
AAH!!

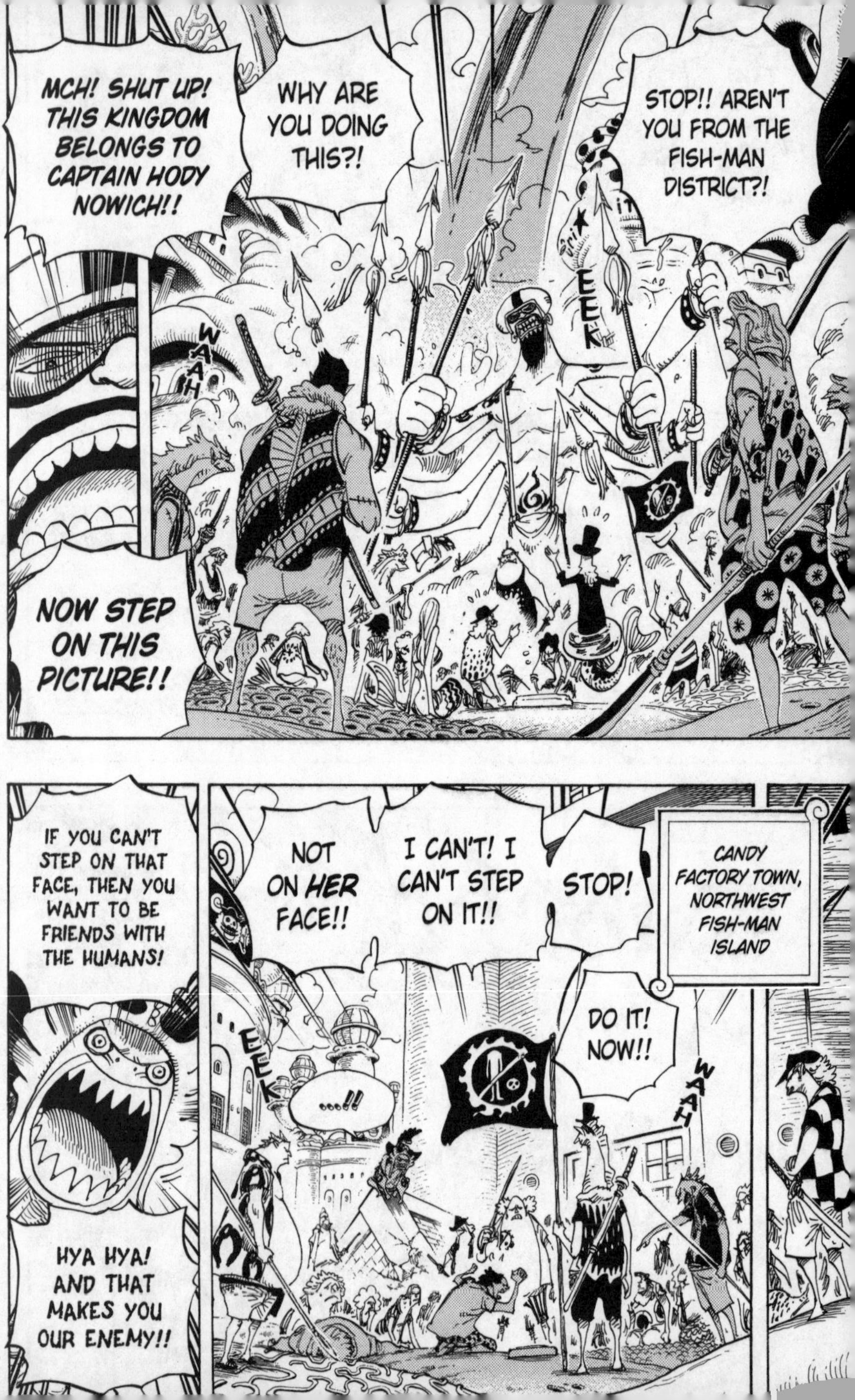
STOP!! AREN'T YOU FROM THE FISH-MAN DISTRICT?!
EEK
WHY ARE YOU DOING THIS?!
MCH! SHUT UP! THIS KINGDOM BELONGS TO CAPTAIN HODY NOWICH!!
WAAH
NOW STEP ON THIS PICTURE!!
CANDY FACTORY TOWN, NORTHWEST FISH-MAN ISLAND
STOP!
I CAN'T! I CAN'T STEP ON IT!!
NOT ON HER FACE!!
DO IT! NOW!!
WAAH
EEK
...!!
IF YOU CAN'T STEP ON THAT FACE, THEN YOU WANT TO BE FRIENDS WITH THE HUMANS!
HYA HYA! AND THAT MAKES YOU OUR ENEMY!!

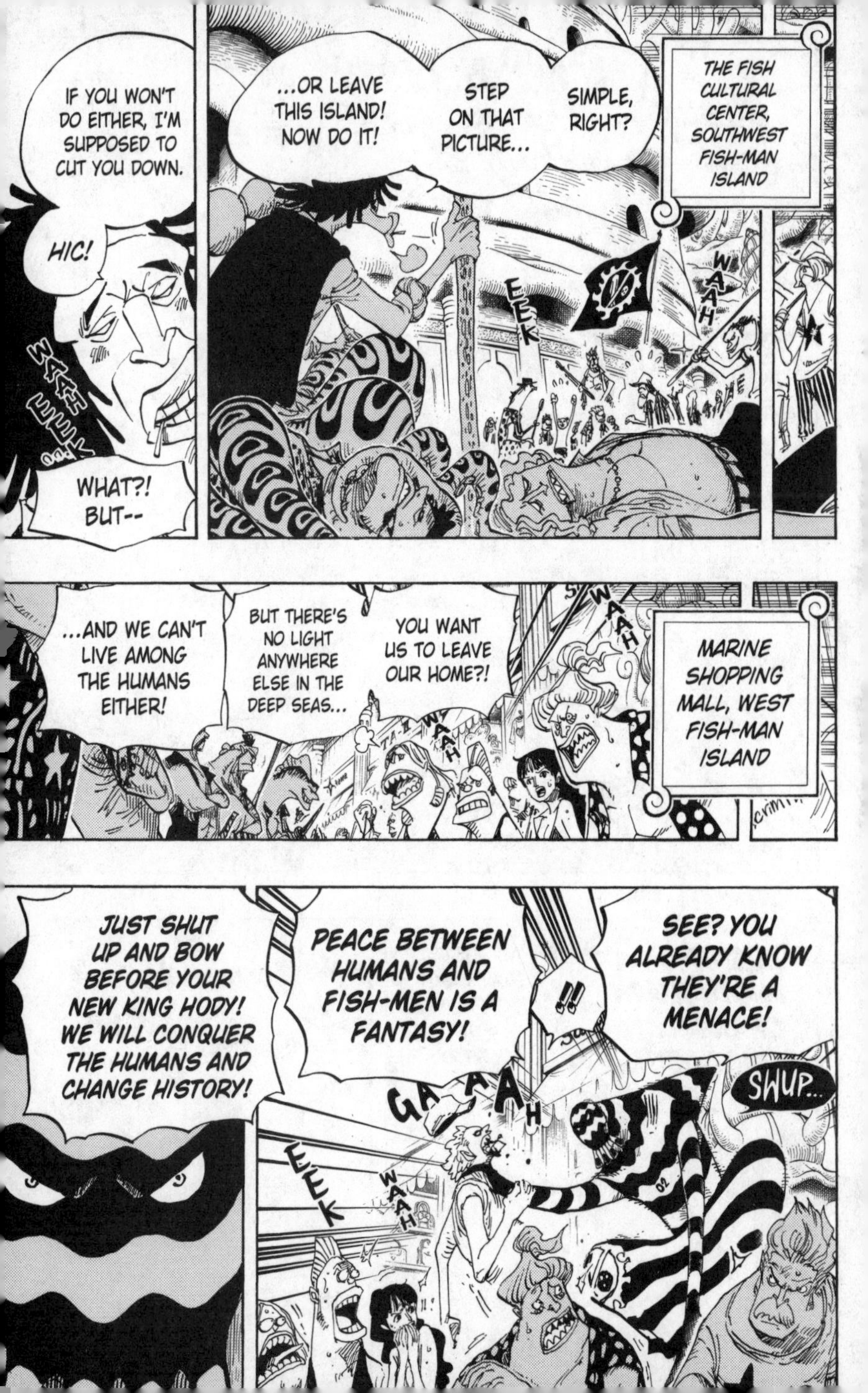
THE FISH CULTURAL CENTER, SOUTHWEST FISH-MAN ISLAND
SIMPLE, RIGHT?
STEP ON THAT PICTURE...
...OR LEAVE THIS ISLAND! NOW DO IT!
WAAH
EEK
IF YOU WON'T DO EITHER, I'M SUPPOSED TO CUT YOU DOWN.
HIC!
WAAH
EEK
WHAT?! BUT--
MARINE SHOPPING MALL, WEST FISH-MAN ISLAND
WAAH
YOU WANT US TO LEAVE OUR HOME?!
BUT THERE'S NO LIGHT ANYWHERE ELSE IN THE DEEP SEAS...
...AND WE CAN'T LIVE AMONG THE HUMANS EITHER!
WAAH
SEE? YOU ALREADY KNOW THEY'RE A MENACE!
SHUP...
!!
GAAAH
PEACE BETWEEN HUMANS AND FISH-MEN IS A FANTASY!
WAAH
EEK
JUST SHUT UP AND BOW BEFORE YOUR NEW KING HODY! WE WILL CONQUER THE HUMANS AND CHANGE HISTORY!

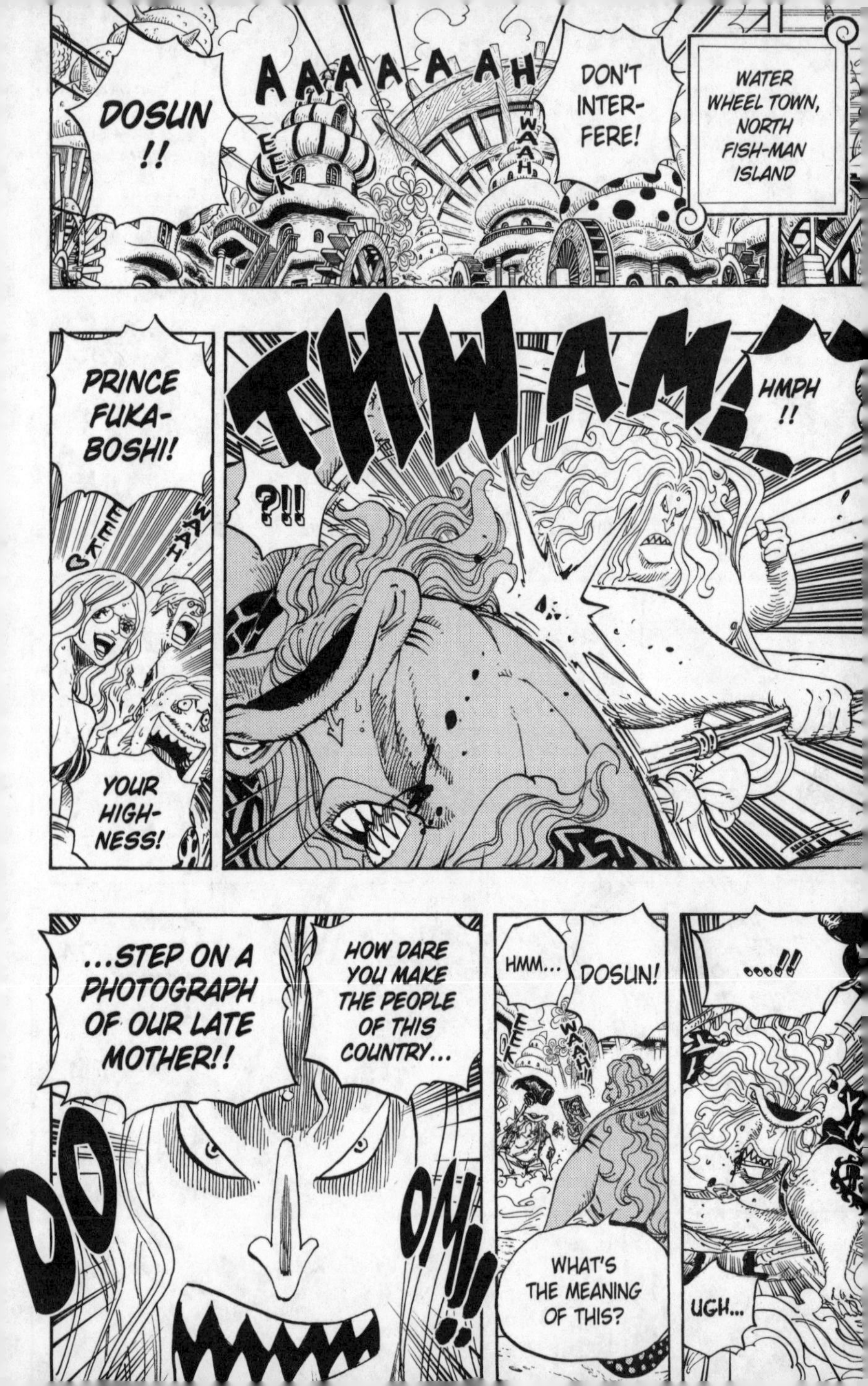
WATER WHEEL TOWN, NORTH FISH-MAN ISLAND
DON'T INTER-FERE!
WAAH
AAAAAAH
EEEK
DOSUN!!
THWAM
HMPH!!
?!!
PRINCE FUKA-BOSHI!
WAAH
EEEK
YOUR HIGH-NESS!
...!!
UGH...
DOSUN!
HMM...
WAAH
EEEK
WHAT'S THE MEANING OF THIS?
HOW DARE YOU MAKE THE PEOPLE OF THIS COUNTRY...
...STEP ON A PHOTOGRAPH OF OUR LATE MOTHER!!
DOOM!!

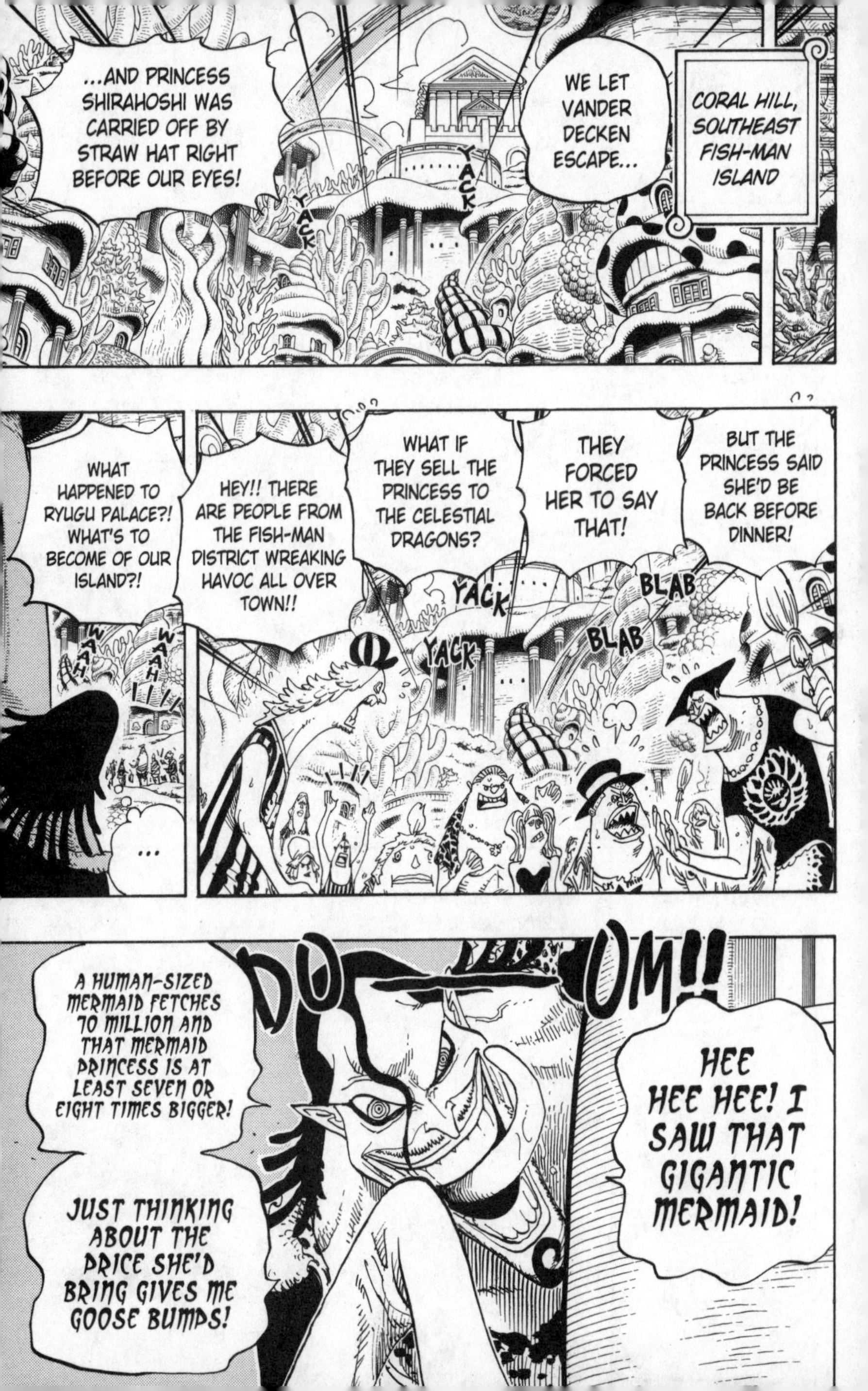
CORAL HILL, SOUTHEAST FISH-MAN ISLAND
WE LET VANDER DECKEN ESCAPE...
YACK
...AND PRINCESS SHIRAHOSHI WAS CARRIED OFF BY STRAW HAT RIGHT BEFORE OUR EYES!
YACK
BUT THE PRINCESS SAID SHE'D BE BACK BEFORE DINNER!
THEY FORCED HER TO SAY THAT!
WHAT IF THEY SELL THE PRINCESS TO THE CELESTIAL DRAGONS?
HEY!! THERE ARE PEOPLE FROM THE FISH-MAN DISTRICT WREAKING HAVOC ALL OVER TOWN!!
BLAB
BLAB
YACK
YACK
WHAT HAPPENED TO RYUGU PALACE?! WHAT'S TO BECOME OF OUR ISLAND?!
WAAH
WAAH
...
DOOM!!
HEE HEE HEE! I SAW THAT GIGANTIC MERMAID!
A HUMAN-SIZED MERMAID FETCHES 70 MILLION AND THAT MERMAID PRINCESS IS AT LEAST SEVEN OR EIGHT TIMES BIGGER!
JUST THINKING ABOUT THE PRICE SHE'D BRING GIVES ME GOOSE BUMPS!

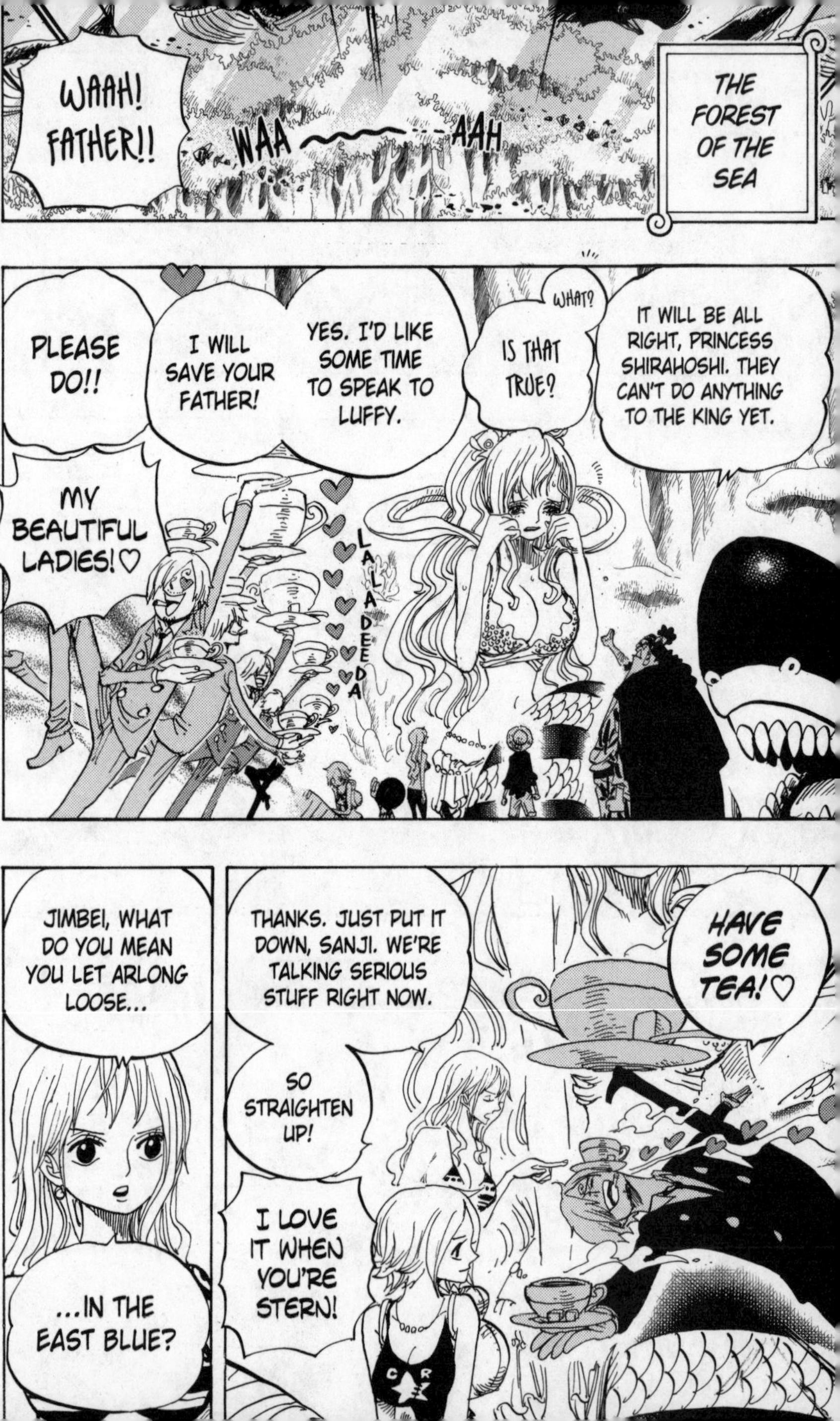
THE FOREST OF THE SEA
WAA~~~AAH
WAAAH! FATHER!!
IT WILL BE ALL RIGHT, PRINCESS SHIRAHOSHI. THEY CAN'T DO ANYTHING TO THE KING YET.
WHAT?
IS THAT TRUE?
YES. I'D LIKE SOME TIME TO SPEAK TO LUFFY.
I WILL SAVE YOUR FATHER!
PLEASE DO!!
MY BEAUTIFUL LADIES! ♡
LA LA DEE DA
HAVE SOME TEA! ♡
THANKS. JUST PUT IT DOWN, SANJI. WE'RE TALKING SERIOUS STUFF RIGHT NOW.
SO STRAIGHTEN UP!
I LOVE IT WHEN YOU'RE STERN!
JIMBEI, WHAT DO YOU MEAN YOU LET ARLONG LOOSE...
...IN THE EAST BLUE?

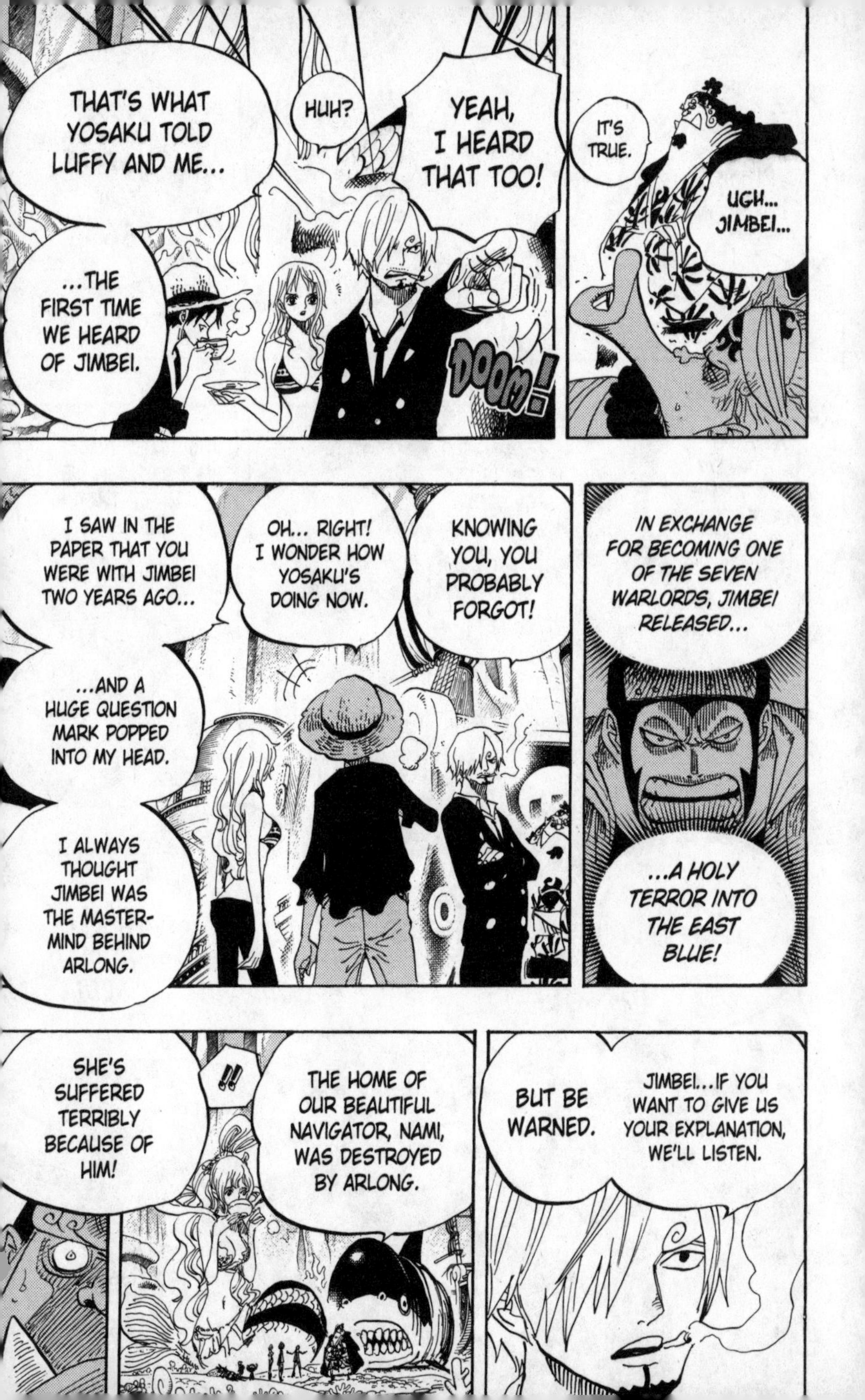
IT'S TRUE.
UGH... JIMBEI...
YEAH, I HEARD THAT TOO!
HUH?
THAT'S WHAT YOSAKU TOLD LUFFY AND ME...
...THE FIRST TIME WE HEARD OF JIMBEI.
DOOM!!
IN EXCHANGE FOR BECOMING ONE OF THE SEVEN WARLORDS, JIMBEI RELEASED...
...A HOLY TERROR INTO THE EAST BLUE!
KNOWING YOU, YOU PROBABLY FORGOT!
OH... RIGHT! I WONDER HOW YOSAKU'S DOING NOW.
I SAW IN THE PAPER THAT YOU WERE WITH JIMBEI TWO YEARS AGO...
...AND A HUGE QUESTION MARK POPPED INTO MY HEAD.
I ALWAYS THOUGHT JIMBEI WAS THE MASTER-MIND BEHIND ARLONG.
JIMBEI...IF YOU WANT TO GIVE US YOUR EXPLANATION, WE'LL LISTEN.
BUT BE WARNED.
THE HOME OF OUR BEAUTIFUL NAVIGATOR, NAMI, WAS DESTROYED BY ARLONG.
!!
SHE'S SUFFERED TERRIBLY BECAUSE OF HIM!

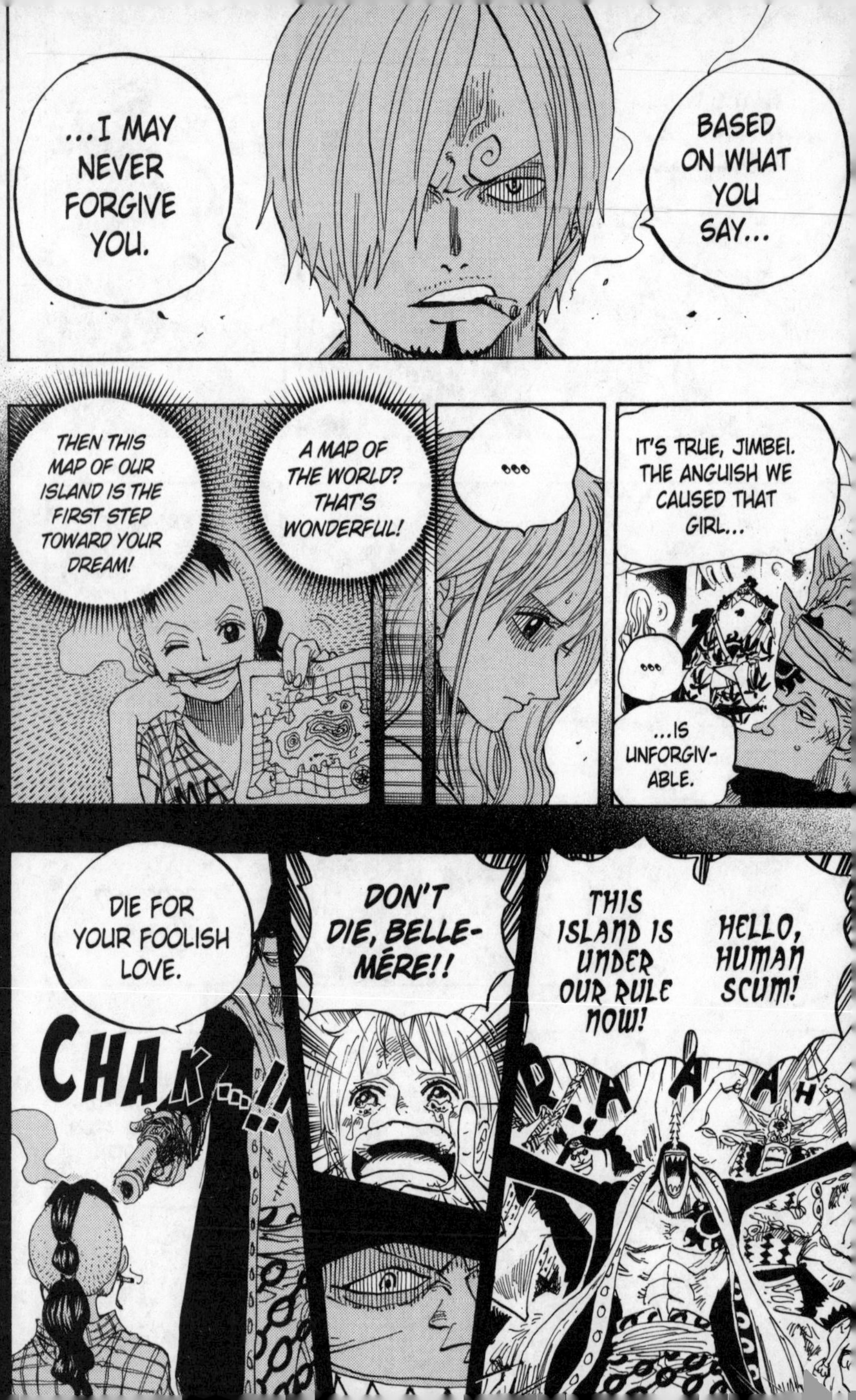
BASED ON WHAT YOU SAY...
...I MAY NEVER FORGIVE YOU.
IT'S TRUE, JIMBEI. THE ANGUISH WE CAUSED THAT GIRL...
...
...IS UNFORGIV-ABLE.
...
A MAP OF THE WORLD? THAT'S WONDERFUL!
THEN THIS MAP OF OUR ISLAND IS THE FIRST STEP TOWARD YOUR DREAM!
HELLO, HUMAN SCUM!
THIS ISLAND IS UNDER OUR RULE NOW!
DON'T DIE, BELLE-MÉRE!!
DIE FOR YOUR FOOLISH LOVE.
CHAK...!!

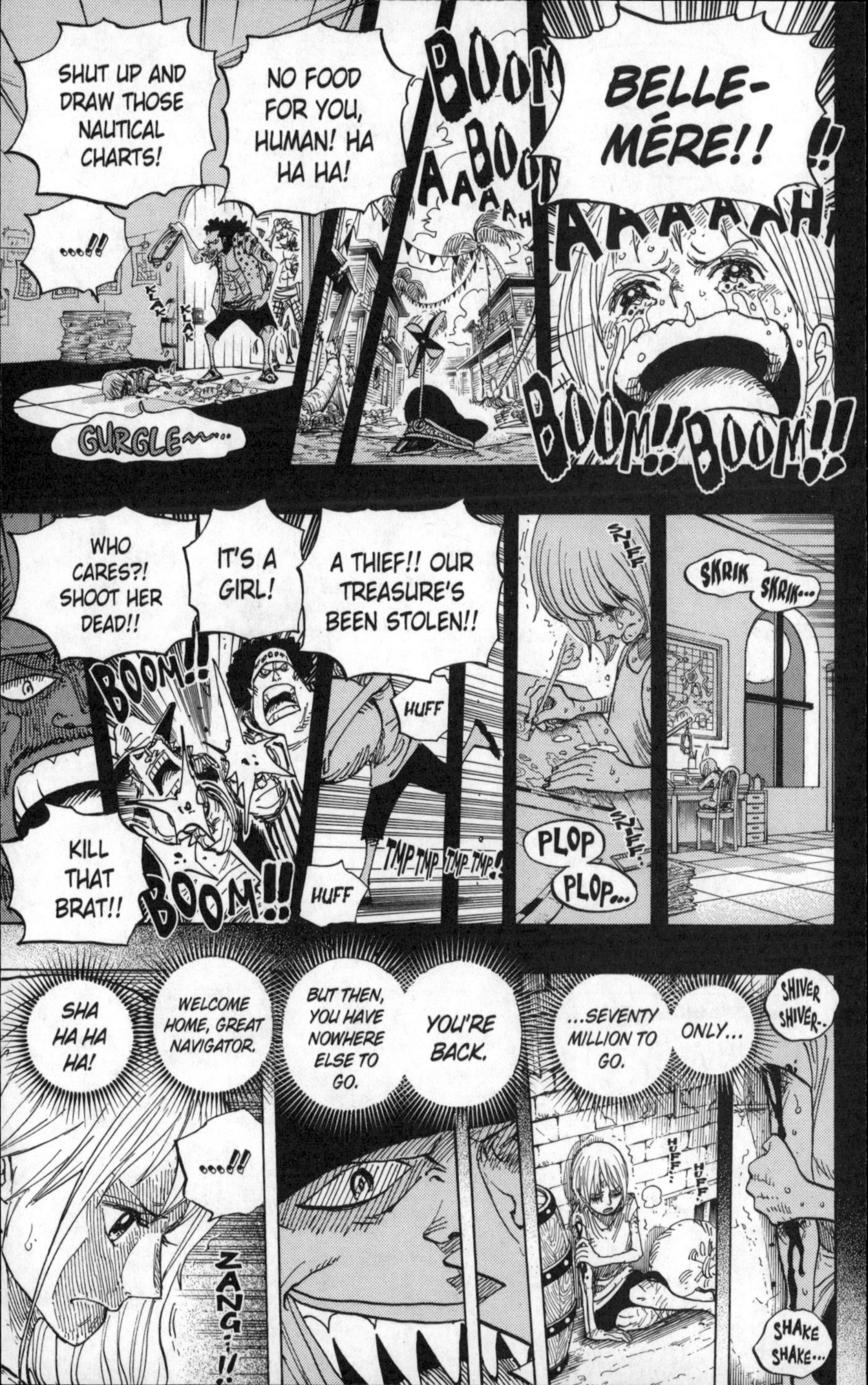
BELLE-MÉRE!!
AAAAAH!!
BOOM!! BOOM!!
BOOM
AABOOM
AAAH
NO FOOD FOR YOU, HUMAN! HA HA HA!
SHUT UP AND DRAW THOSE NAUTICAL CHARTS!
...!!
KLAK
KLAK
GURGLE~~...
SKRIK SKRIK...
SNIFF
SNIFF...
PLOP
PLOP...
A THIEF!! OUR TREASURE'S BEEN STOLEN!!
HUFF
TMP TMP TMP TMP!!
HUFF
IT'S A GIRL!
WHO CARES?! SHOOT HER DEAD!!
BOOM!!
KILL THAT BRAT!!
BOOM!!
SHIVER SHIVER..
ONLY...
...SEVENTY MILLION TO GO.
HUFF...
HUFF...
SHAKE SHAKE...
YOU'RE BACK.
BUT THEN, YOU HAVE NOWHERE ELSE TO GO.
WELCOME HOME, GREAT NAVIGATOR.
SHA HA HA HA!
...!!
ZANG...!!

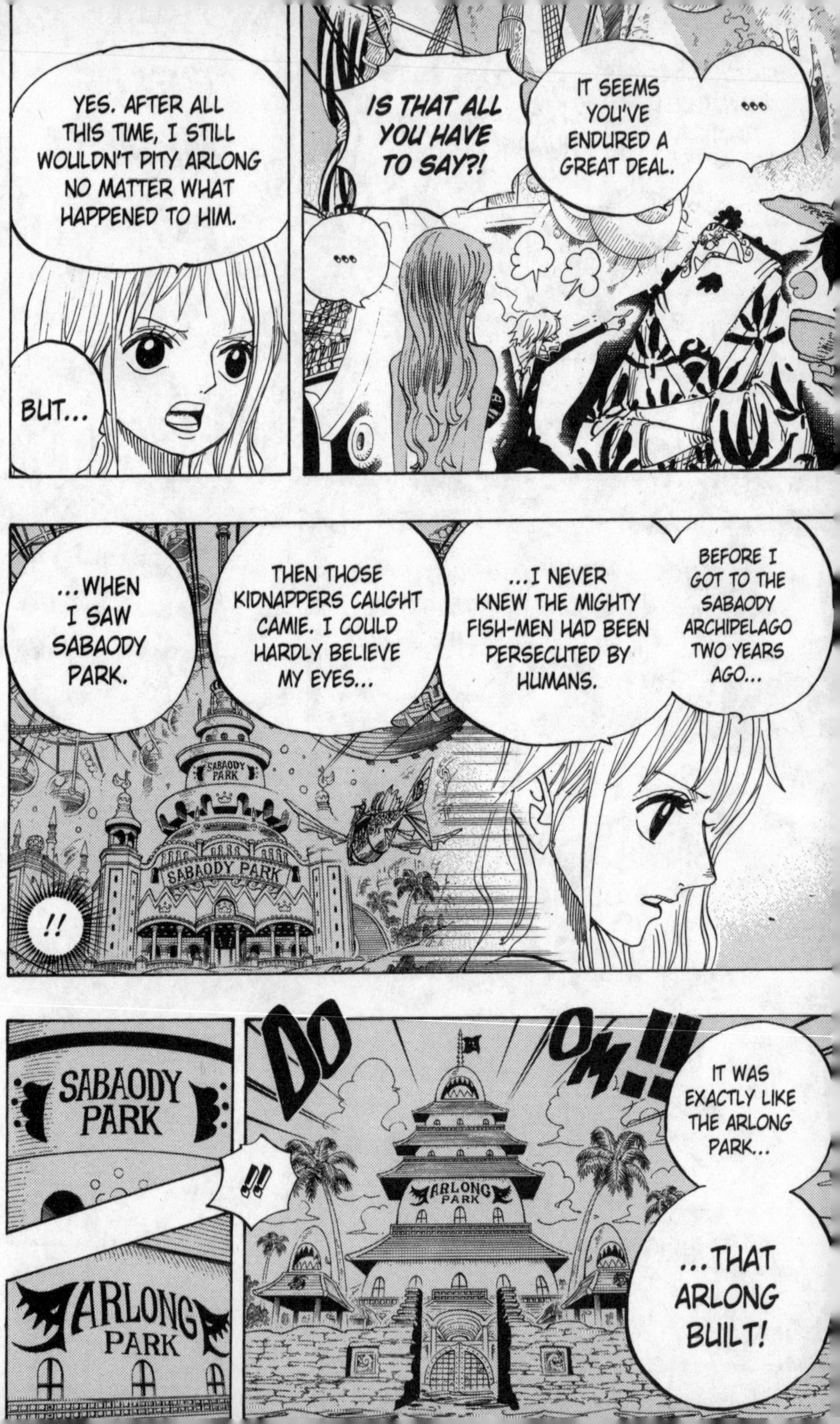
...
IT SEEMS YOU'VE ENDURED A GREAT DEAL.
IS THAT ALL YOU HAVE TO SAY?!
...
YES. AFTER ALL THIS TIME, I STILL WOULDN'T PITY ARLONG NO MATTER WHAT HAPPENED TO HIM.
BUT...
BEFORE I GOT TO THE SABAODY ARCHIPELAGO TWO YEARS AGO...
...I NEVER KNEW THE MIGHTY FISH-MEN HAD BEEN PERSECUTED BY HUMANS.
THEN THOSE KIDNAPPERS CAUGHT CAMIE. I COULD HARDLY BELIEVE MY EYES...
...WHEN I SAW SABAODY PARK.
SABAODY PARK
SABAODY PARK
!!
DO
OM!!
IT WAS EXACTLY LIKE THE ARLONG PARK...
...THAT ARLONG BUILT!
ARLONG PARK
SABAODY PARK
!!
ARLONG PARK

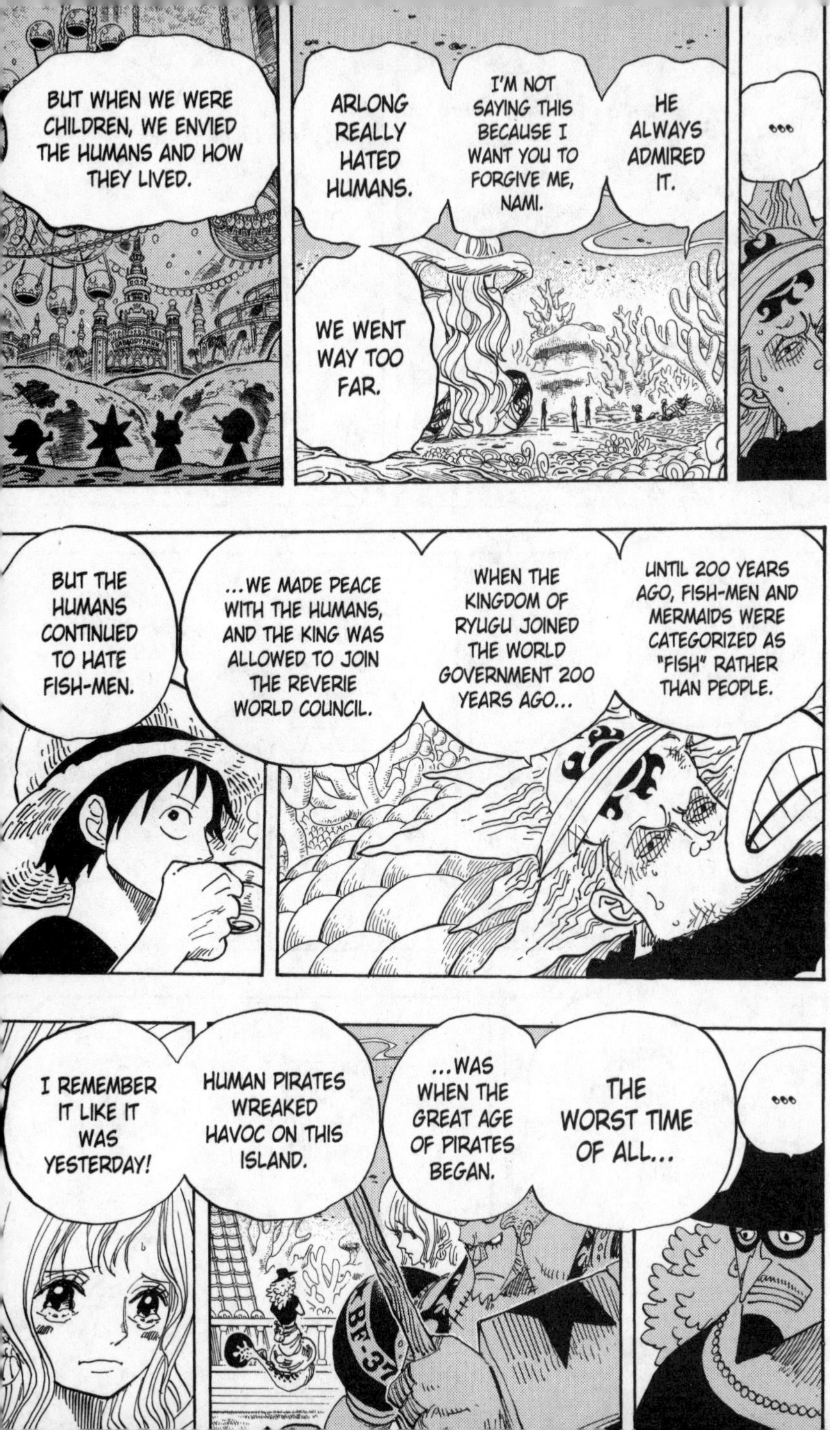
...
HE ALWAYS ADMIRED IT.
I'M NOT SAYING THIS BECAUSE I WANT YOU TO FORGIVE ME, NAMI.
ARLONG REALLY HATED HUMANS.
WE WENT WAY TOO FAR.
BUT WHEN WE WERE CHILDREN, WE ENVIED THE HUMANS AND HOW THEY LIVED.
UNTIL 200 YEARS AGO, FISH-MEN AND MERMAIDS WERE CATEGORIZED AS "FISH" RATHER THAN PEOPLE.
WHEN THE KINGDOM OF RYUGU JOINED THE WORLD GOVERNMENT 200 YEARS AGO...
...WE MADE PEACE WITH THE HUMANS, AND THE KING WAS ALLOWED TO JOIN THE REVERIE WORLD COUNCIL.
BUT THE HUMANS CONTINUED TO HATE FISH-MEN.
...
THE WORST TIME OF ALL...
...WAS WHEN THE GREAT AGE OF PIRATES BEGAN.
HUMAN PIRATES WREAKED HAVOC ON THIS ISLAND.
I REMEMBER IT LIKE IT WAS YESTERDAY!
BF-37

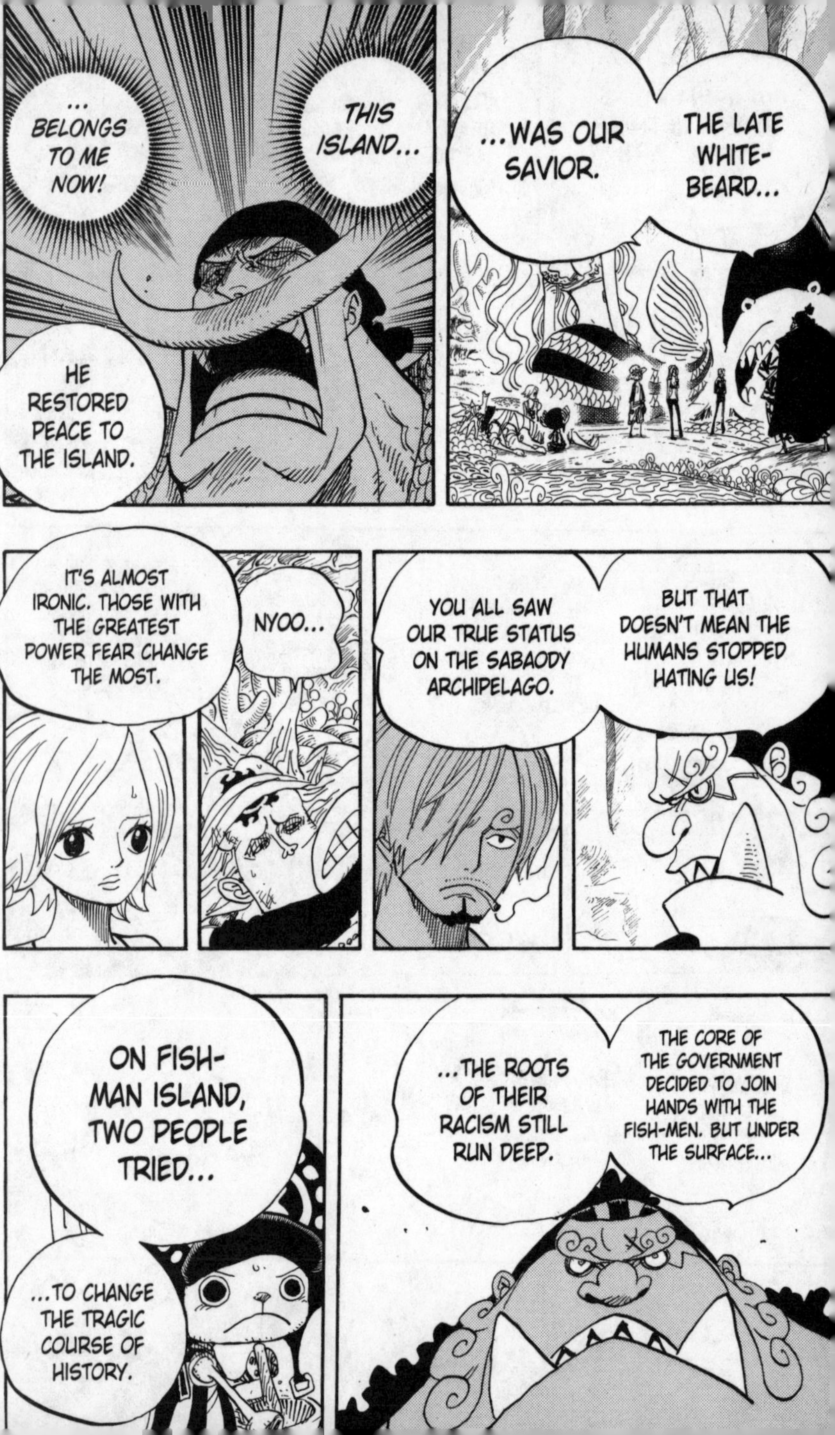

THE LATE WHITE-BEARD...
...WAS OUR SAVIOR.
THIS ISLAND...
... BELONGS TO ME NOW!
HE RESTORED PEACE TO THE ISLAND.
BUT THAT DOESN'T MEAN THE HUMANS STOPPED HATING US!
YOU ALL SAW OUR TRUE STATUS ON THE SABAODY ARCHIPELAGO.
NYOO...
IT'S ALMOST IRONIC. THOSE WITH THE GREATEST POWER FEAR CHANGE THE MOST.
THE CORE OF THE GOVERNMENT DECIDED TO JOIN HANDS WITH THE FISH-MEN. BUT UNDER THE SURFACE...
...THE ROOTS OF THEIR RACISM STILL RUN DEEP.
ON FISH-MAN ISLAND, TWO PEOPLE TRIED...
...TO CHANGE THE TRAGIC COURSE OF HISTORY.

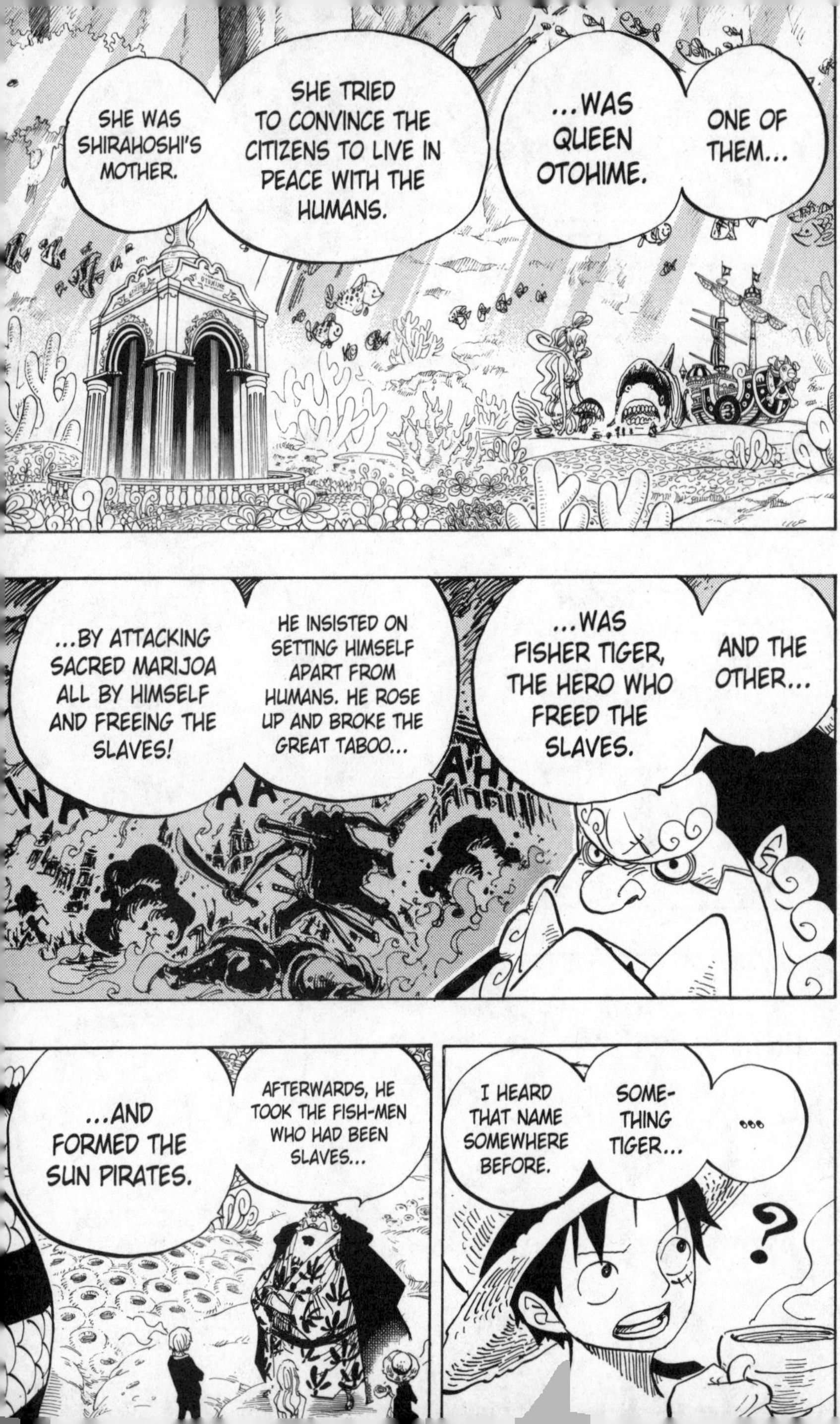
ONE OF THEM...
...WAS QUEEN OTOHIME.
SHE TRIED TO CONVINCE THE CITIZENS TO LIVE IN PEACE WITH THE HUMANS.
SHE WAS SHIRAHOSHI'S MOTHER.
AND THE OTHER...
...WAS FISHER TIGER, THE HERO WHO FREED THE SLAVES.
HE INSISTED ON SETTING HIMSELF APART FROM HUMANS. HE ROSE UP AND BROKE THE GREAT TABOO...
...BY ATTACKING SACRED MARIJOA ALL BY HIMSELF AND FREEING THE SLAVES!
...
SOME-THING TIGER...
I HEARD THAT NAME SOMEWHERE BEFORE.
?
AFTERWARDS, HE TOOK THE FISH-MEN WHO HAD BEEN SLAVES...
...AND FORMED THE SUN PIRATES.

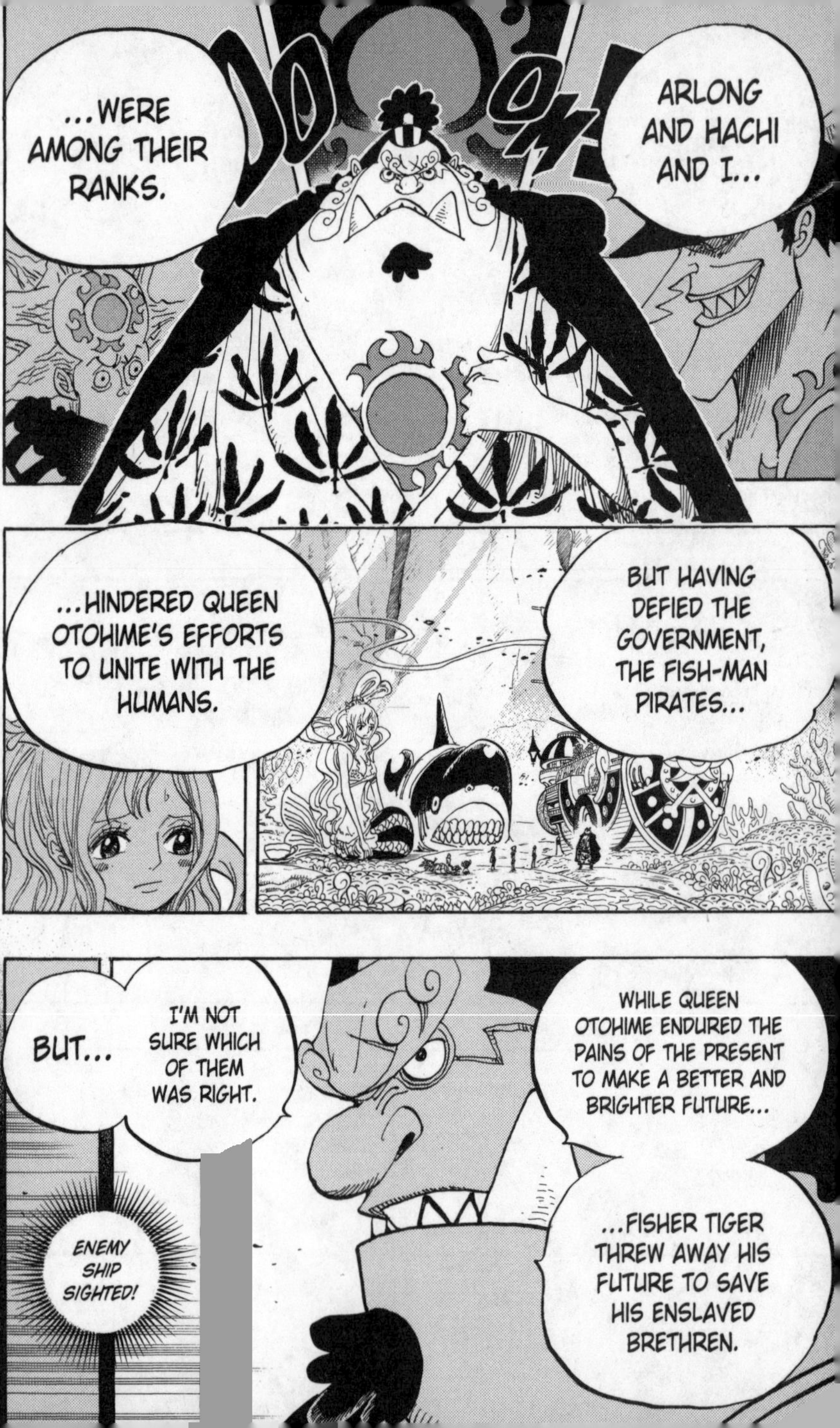
ARLONG AND HACHI AND I...
...WERE AMONG THEIR RANKS.
BUT HAVING DEFIED THE GOVERNMENT, THE FISH-MAN PIRATES...
...HINDERED QUEEN OTOHIME'S EFFORTS TO UNITE WITH THE HUMANS.
WHILE QUEEN OTOHIME ENDURED THE PAINS OF THE PRESENT TO MAKE A BETTER AND BRIGHTER FUTURE...
...FISHER TIGER THREW AWAY HIS FUTURE TO SAVE HIS ENSLAVED BRETHREN.
BUT...
I'M NOT SURE WHICH OF THEM WAS RIGHT.
ENEMY SHIP SIGHTED!

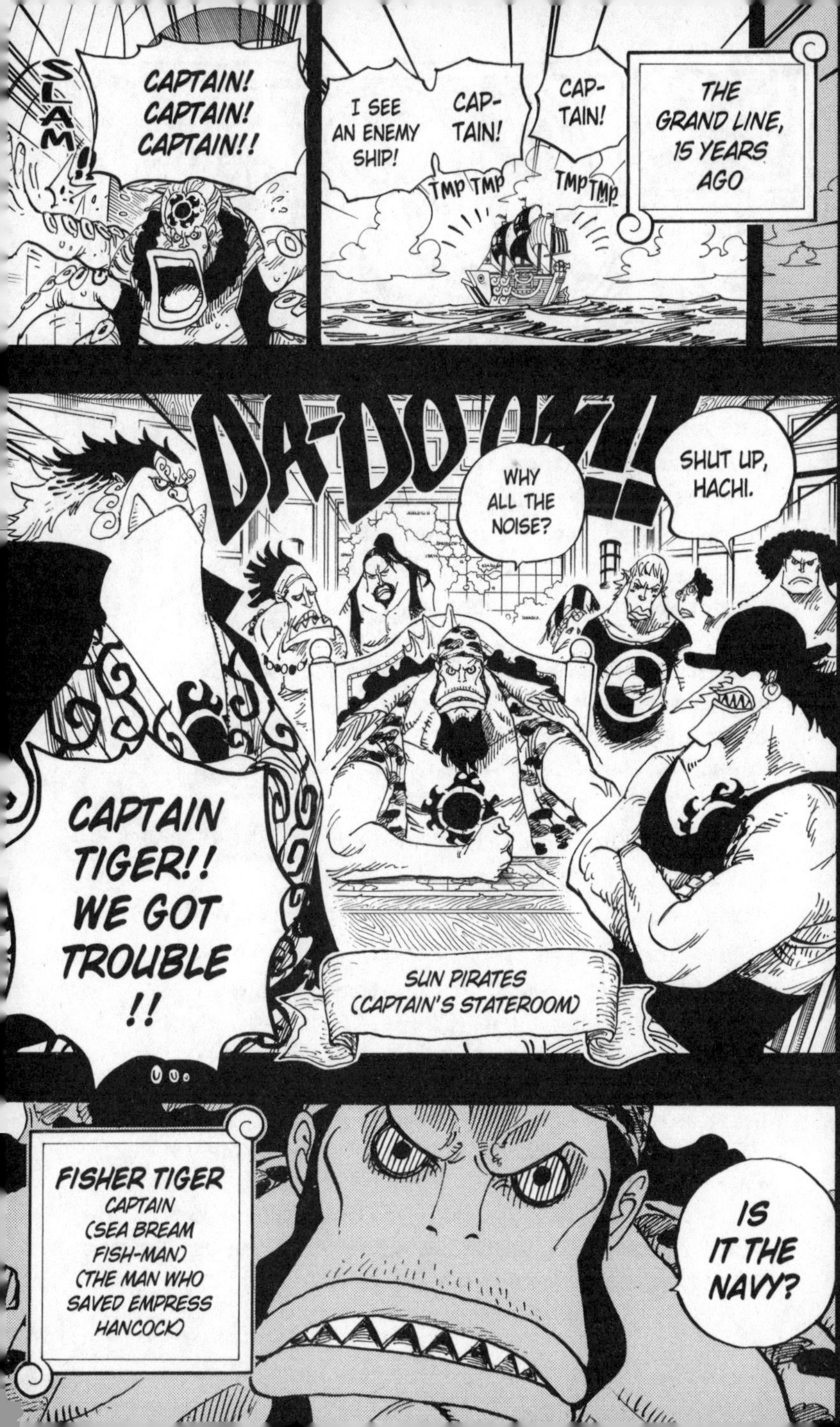
THE GRAND LINE, 15 YEARS AGO
CAP-TAIN!
TMP TMP
CAP-TAIN!
I SEE AN ENEMY SHIP!
TMP TMP
SLAM!!
CAPTAIN! CAPTAIN! CAPTAIN!!
DA-DO
SHUT UP, HACHI.
WHY ALL THE NOISE?
CAPTAIN TIGER!! WE GOT TROUBLE!!
SUN PIRATES (CAPTAIN'S STATEROOM)
IS IT THE NAVY?
FISHER TIGER
CAPTAIN (SEA BREAM FISH-MAN) (THE MAN WHO SAVED EMPRESS HANCOCK)

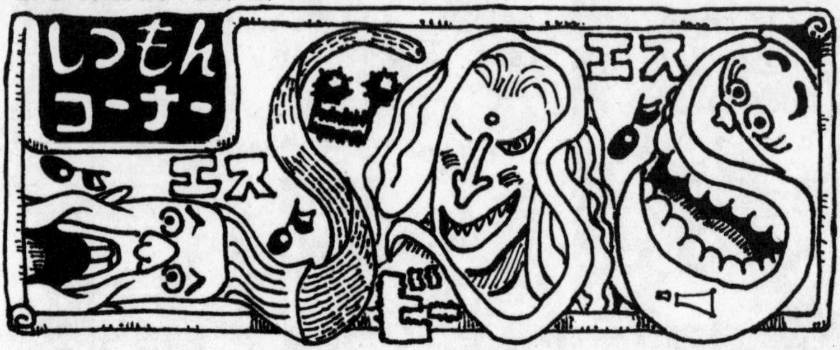
しつもん
コーナー
エス
エス

(Scarlet Barrel Squid Y, Ibaraki)

Q: Odacchi!! Good morning. Can I ask a question? The people running in this picture, are they Hancock and company from the opposite angle?♡ If you answer my question, I'll give you my autograph!♡

--Gonge the Barber

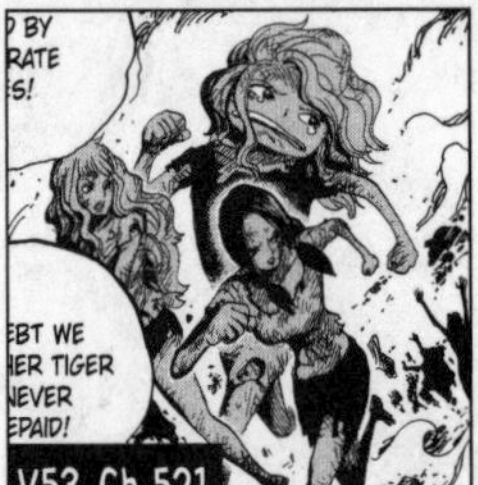

V53, Ch.521

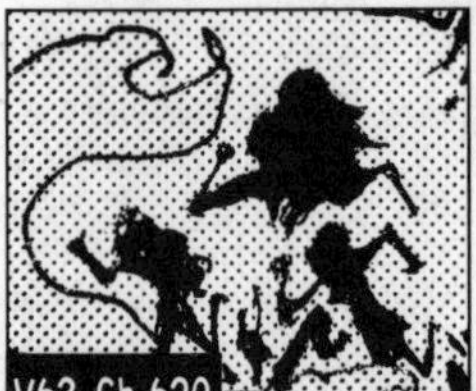

V63, Ch.620

A: I don't want your autograph! But I can only say that was a marvelous deduction! I'm impressed by how hard you look at everything! You're exactly right. The only thing I have to add is that I don't need your autograph.

Q: Sensei, we've got a problem! Apparently you and I are the only ones in the whole world wearing women's underwear on our heads now.

--Mashu

A: What?!? Yo-yo-you've got to be kidding! You're only kidding, right? Huh? Come to think of it, when I was in middle school, everyone just wore school hats. Come to think of it, I get picked up by the police a lot, but only because I'm not wearing clothes, so... Oh well. I've got to look on the bright side! (⬅Positive thinking!) But I'm pretty sure that guy wears underwear on his head. In the next volume Brook's voice actor, Cho, will make his appearance as the last of the voice actors SBS! Look forward to it!

Chapter 621:
OTOHIME AND TIGER

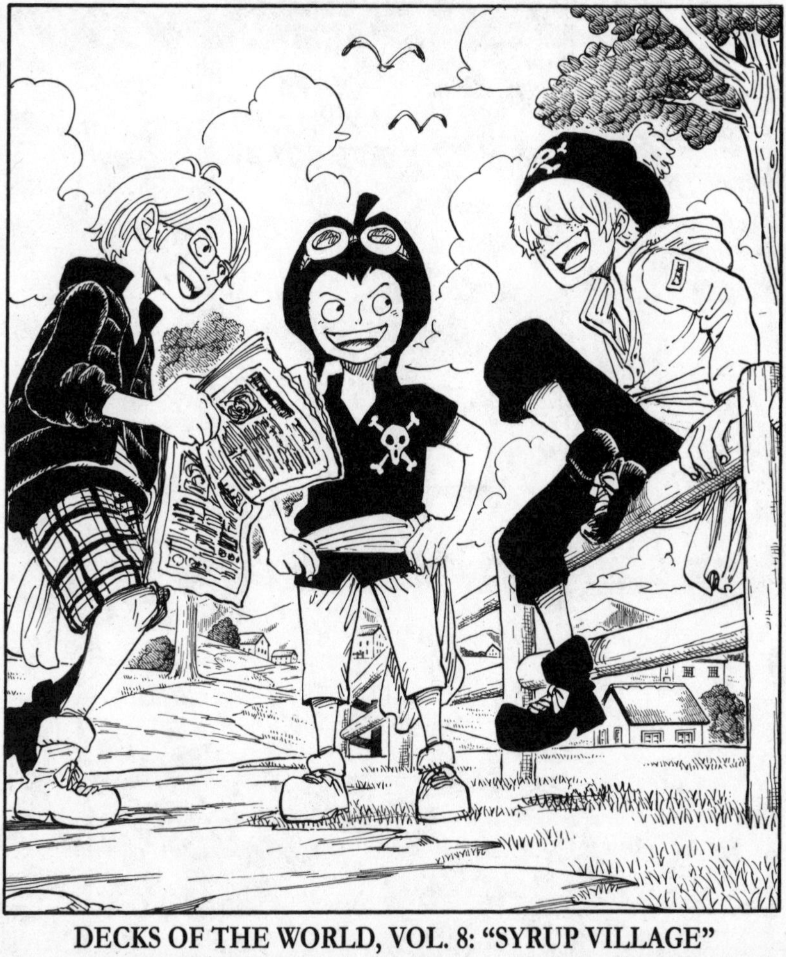

DECKS OF THE WORLD, VOL. 8: "SYRUP VILLAGE"

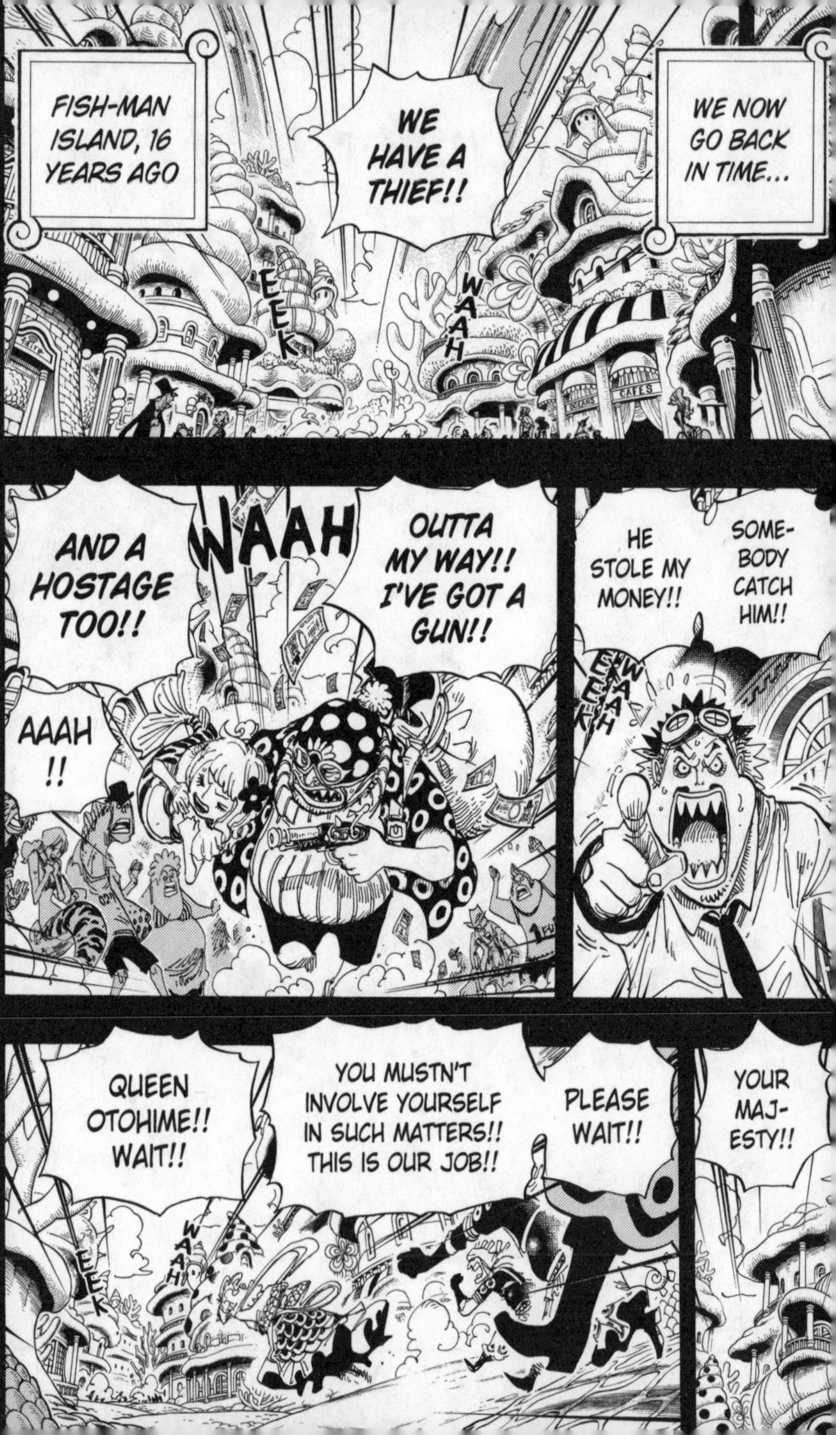
WE NOW GO BACK IN TIME...
WE HAVE A THIEF!!
WAAH
EEK
FISH-MAN ISLAND, 16 YEARS AGO
SOME-BODY CATCH HIM!!
HE STOLE MY MONEY!!
WAAH
EEEK
OUTTA MY WAY!! I'VE GOT A GUN!!
WAAH
AND A HOSTAGE TOO!!
AAAH!!
YOUR MAJ-ESTY!!
PLEASE WAIT!!
YOU MUSTN'T INVOLVE YOURSELF IN SUCH MATTERS!! THIS IS OUR JOB!!
QUEEN OTOHIME!! WAIT!!
WAAH
EEK

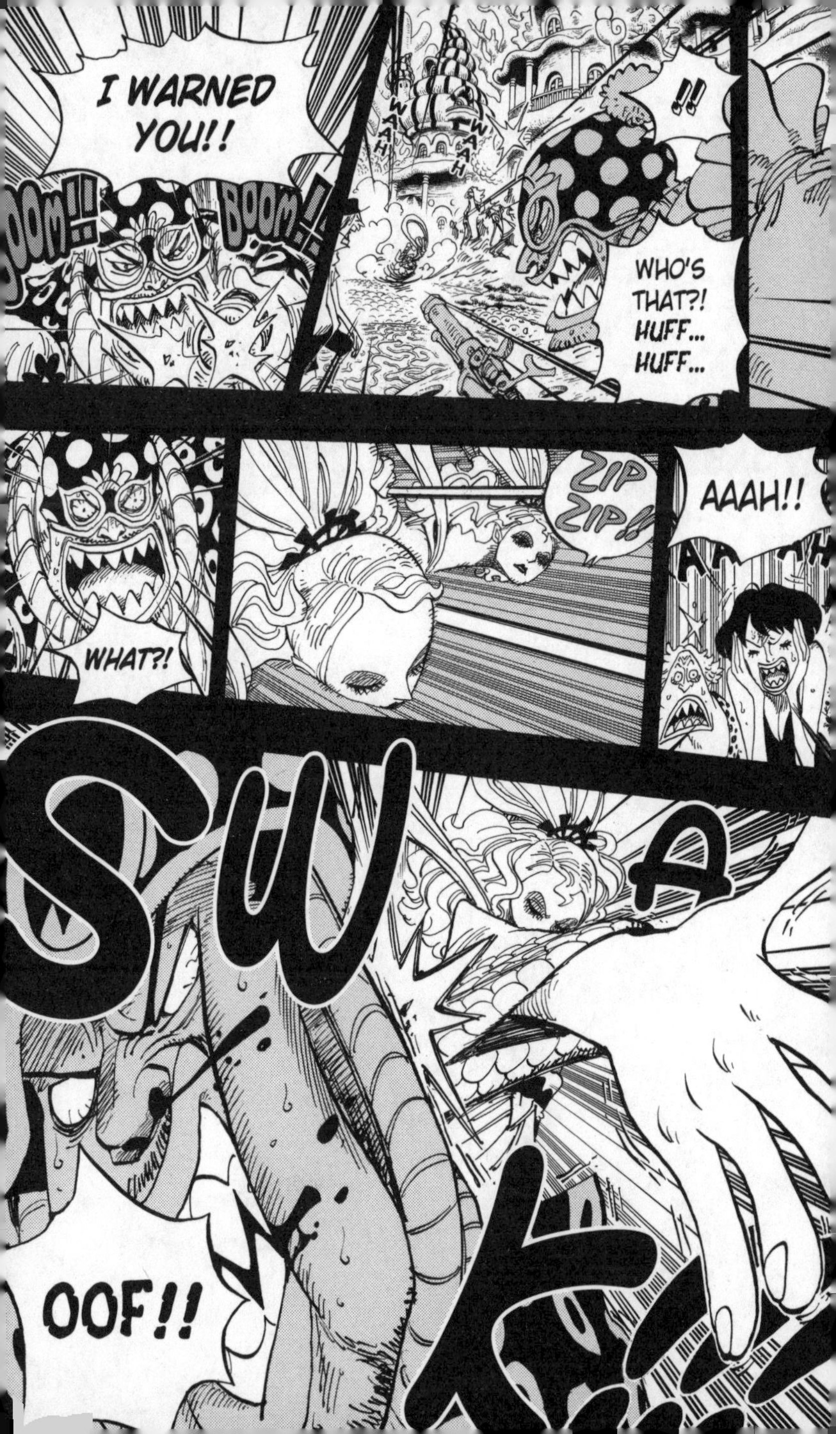
!!
WHO'S THAT?! HUFF... HUFF...
WAAH
WAAH
I WARNED YOU!!
BOOM!!
BOOM!!
AAAH!!
ZIP ZIP!!
WHAT?!
OOF!!

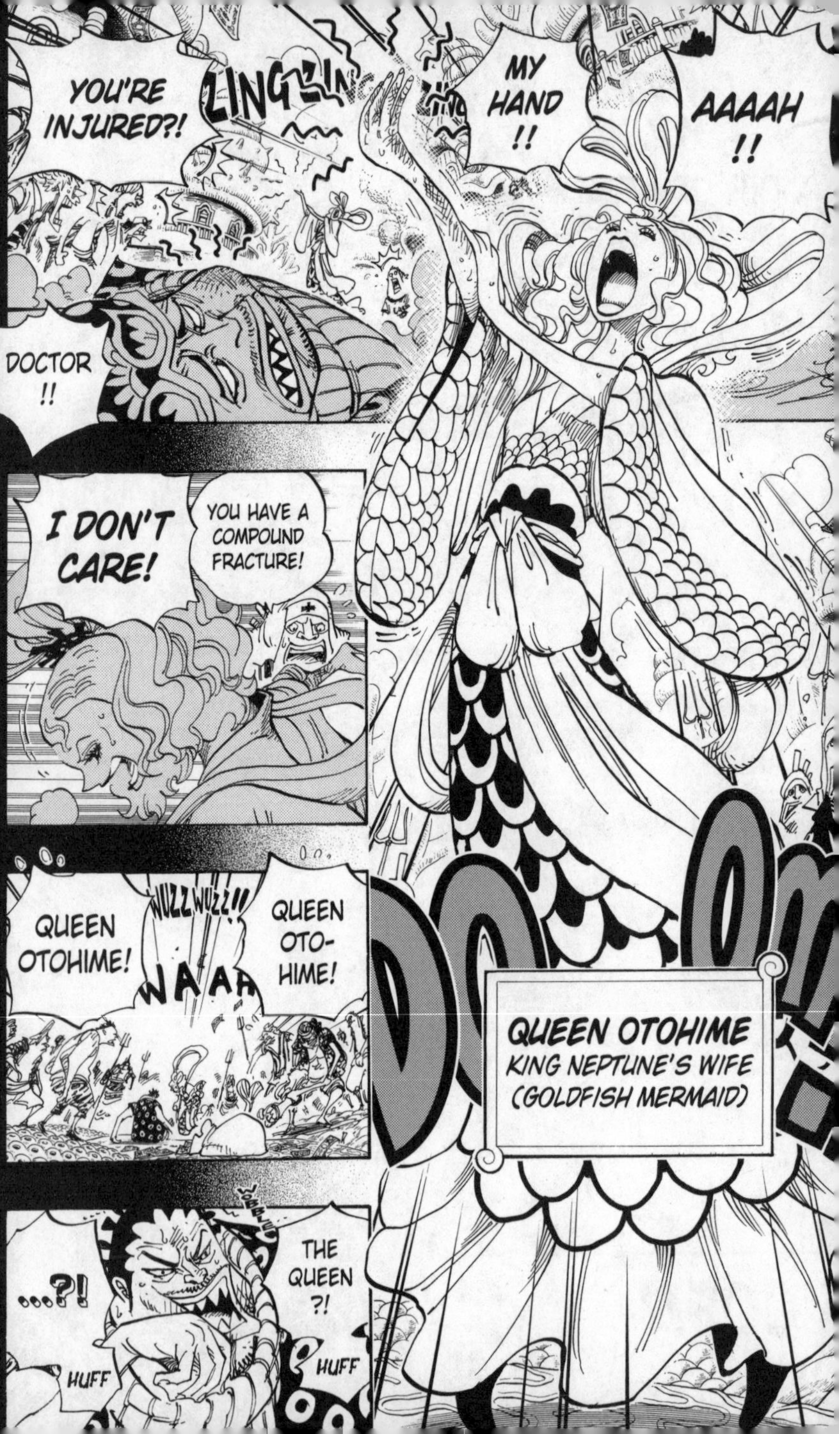
MY HAND!!
AAAAH!!
QUEEN OTOHIME
KING NEPTUNE'S WIFE
(GOLDFISH MERMAID)
LING
ZING
YOU'RE INJURED?!
DOCTOR!!
YOU HAVE A COMPOUND FRACTURE!
I DON'T CARE!
QUEEN OTO-HIME!
WUZZ WUZZ!!
WAAH
QUEEN OTOHIME!
WOBBLE
THE QUEEN?!
...?!
HUFF
HUFF

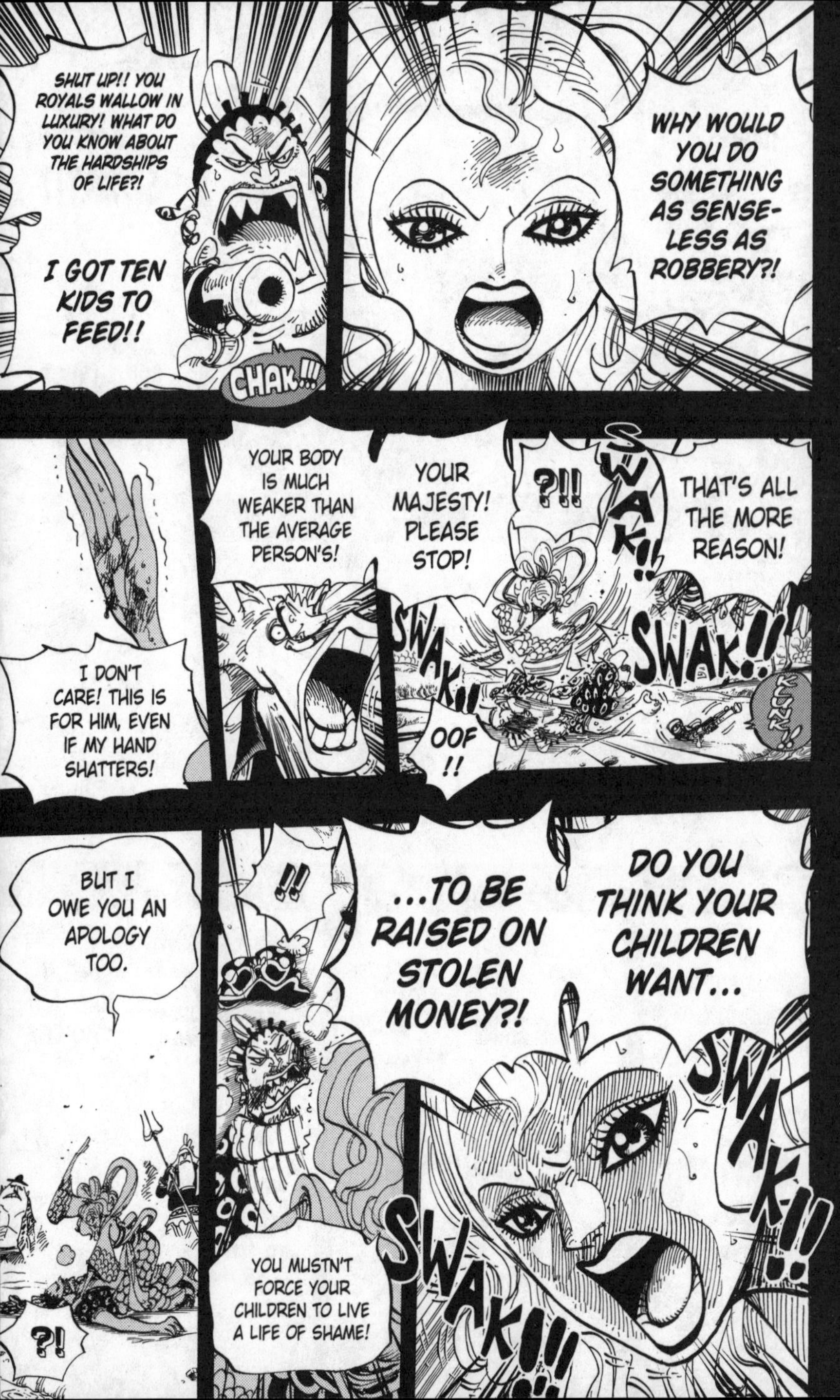
WHY WOULD YOU DO SOMETHING AS SENSE-LESS AS ROBBERY?!
SHUT UP!! YOU ROYALS WALLOW IN LUXURY! WHAT DO YOU KNOW ABOUT THE HARDSHIPS OF LIFE?!
I GOT TEN KIDS TO FEED!!
CHAK!!!
?!!
SWAK!!
THAT'S ALL THE MORE REASON!
SWAK!!
YOUR MAJESTY! PLEASE STOP!
YOUR BODY IS MUCH WEAKER THAN THE AVERAGE PERSON'S!
SWAK!!
OOF!!
I DON'T CARE! THIS IS FOR HIM, EVEN IF MY HAND SHATTERS!
DO YOU THINK YOUR CHILDREN WANT...
...TO BE RAISED ON STOLEN MONEY?!
!!
SWAK!!!
SWAK!!!
YOU MUSTN'T FORCE YOUR CHILDREN TO LIVE A LIFE OF SHAME!
BUT I OWE YOU AN APOLOGY TOO.
?!

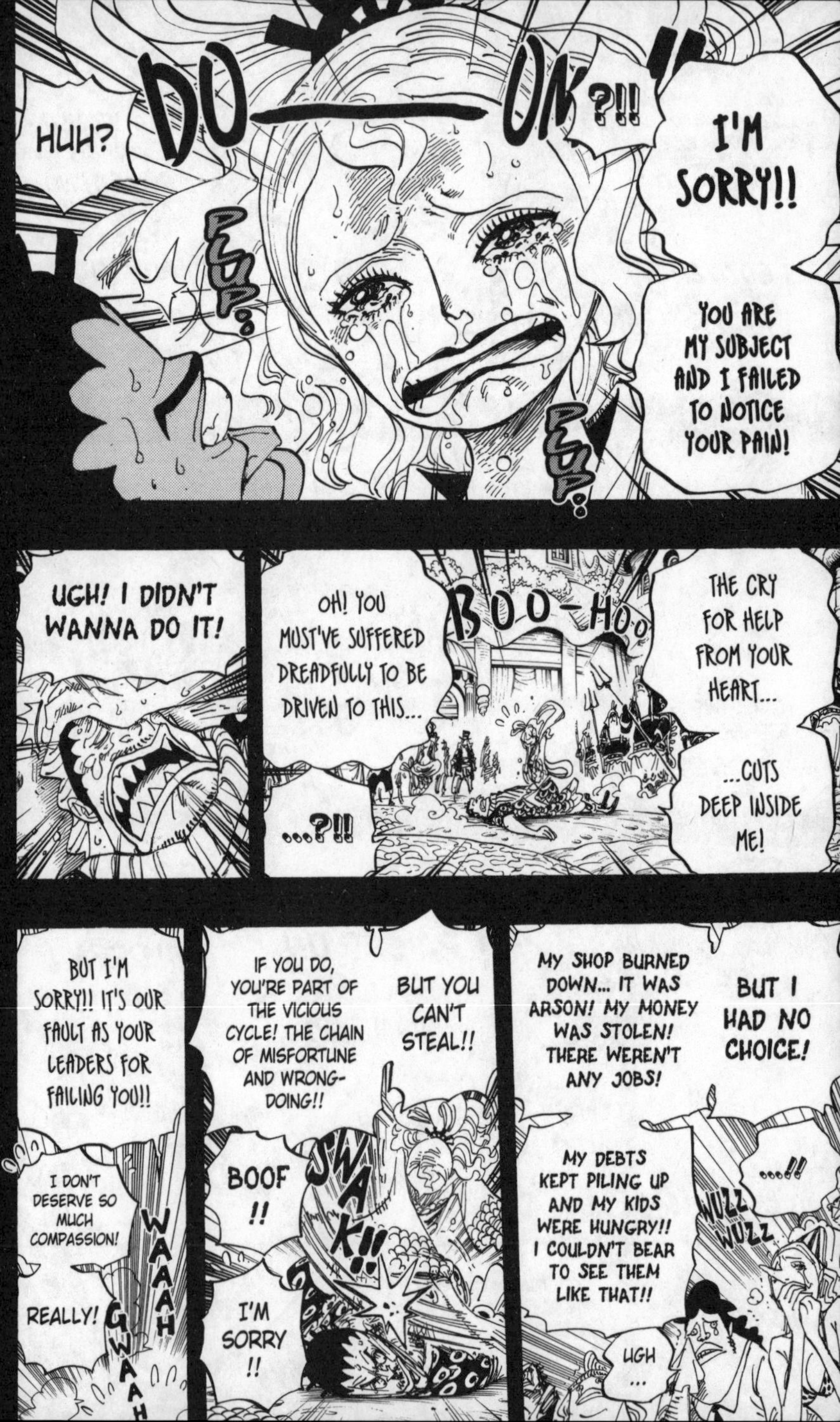
I'M SORRY!!
YOU ARE MY SUBJECT AND I FAILED TO NOTICE YOUR PAIN!
DO——ON?!!
HUH?
THE CRY FOR HELP FROM YOUR HEART...
...CUTS DEEP INSIDE ME!
BOO-HOO
OH! YOU MUST'VE SUFFERED DREADFULLY TO BE DRIVEN TO THIS...
...?!!
UGH! I DIDN'T WANNA DO IT!
BUT I HAD NO CHOICE!
MY SHOP BURNED DOWN... IT WAS ARSON! MY MONEY WAS STOLEN! THERE WEREN'T ANY JOBS!
...!!
WUZZ WUZZ
MY DEBTS KEPT PILING UP AND MY KIDS WERE HUNGRY!! I COULDN'T BEAR TO SEE THEM LIKE THAT!!
UGH ...
BUT YOU CAN'T STEAL!!
IF YOU DO, YOU'RE PART OF THE VICIOUS CYCLE! THE CHAIN OF MISFORTUNE AND WRONG-DOING!!
SWAK!!
BOOF !!
I'M SORRY !!
BUT I'M SORRY!! IT'S OUR FAULT AS YOUR LEADERS FOR FAILING YOU!!
I DON'T DESERVE SO MUCH COMPASSION!
REALLY!
WAAAAH
GWAAAH

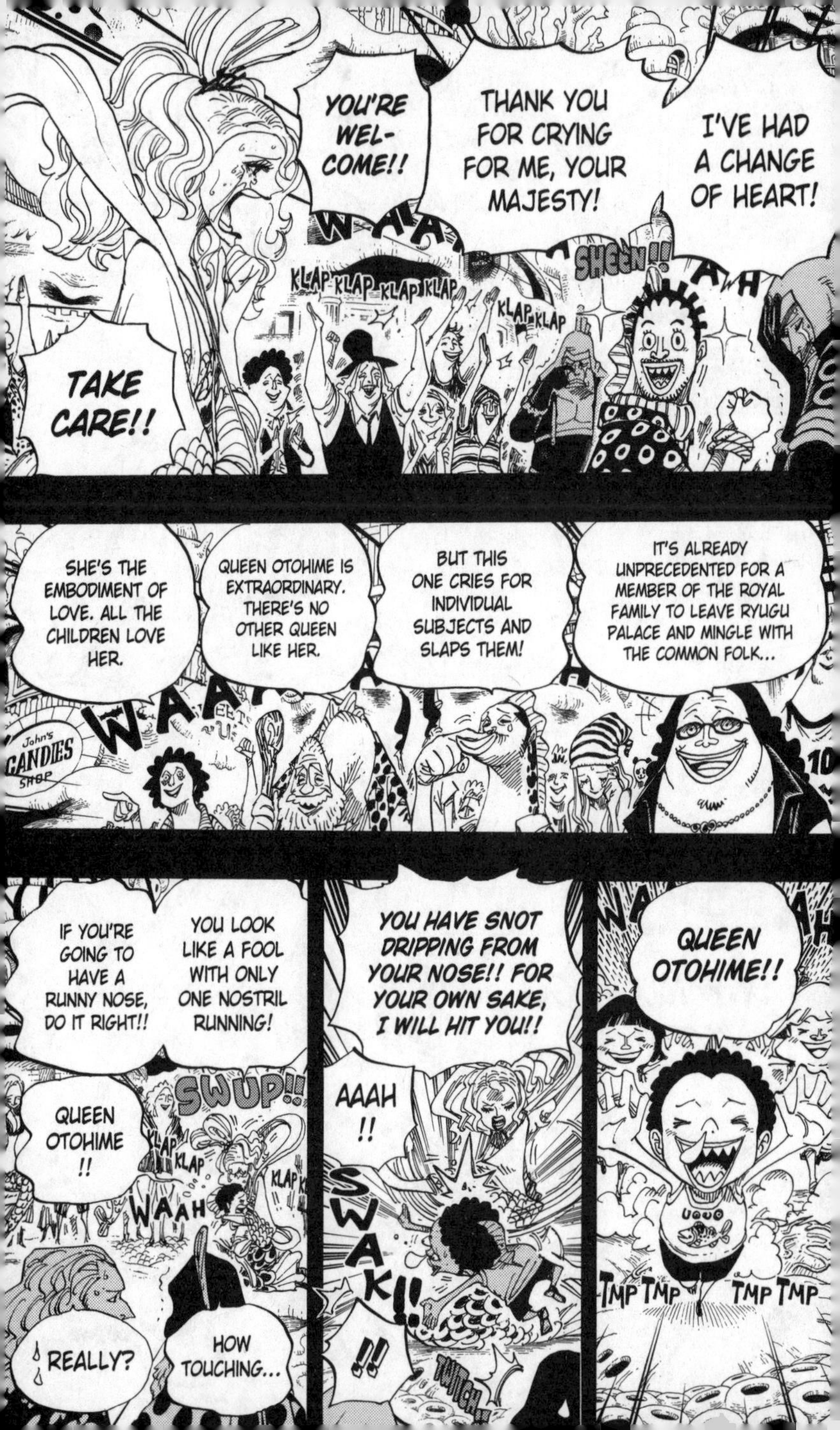
I'VE HAD A CHANGE OF HEART!
THANK YOU FOR CRYING FOR ME, YOUR MAJESTY!
YOU'RE WEL-COME!!
SHEEN!!
AH
WAAAH
KLAP KLAP KLAP KLAP
KLAP KLAP
TAKE CARE!!
IT'S ALREADY UNPRECEDENTED FOR A MEMBER OF THE ROYAL FAMILY TO LEAVE RYUGU PALACE AND MINGLE WITH THE COMMON FOLK...
BUT THIS ONE CRIES FOR INDIVIDUAL SUBJECTS AND SLAPS THEM!
QUEEN OTOHIME IS EXTRAORDINARY. THERE'S NO OTHER QUEEN LIKE HER.
SHE'S THE EMBODIMENT OF LOVE. ALL THE CHILDREN LOVE HER.
WAA
John's CANDIES SHOP
QUEEN OTOHIME!!
TMP TMP
TMP TMP
YOU HAVE SNOT DRIPPING FROM YOUR NOSE!! FOR YOUR OWN SAKE, I WILL HIT YOU!!
AAAH !!
SWAK!!
!!
TWITCH
YOU LOOK LIKE A FOOL WITH ONLY ONE NOSTRIL RUNNING!
IF YOU'RE GOING TO HAVE A RUNNY NOSE, DO IT RIGHT!!
SWUP!!
QUEEN OTOHIME !!
KLAP
KLAP
KLAP
WAAH
HOW TOUCHING...
REALLY?

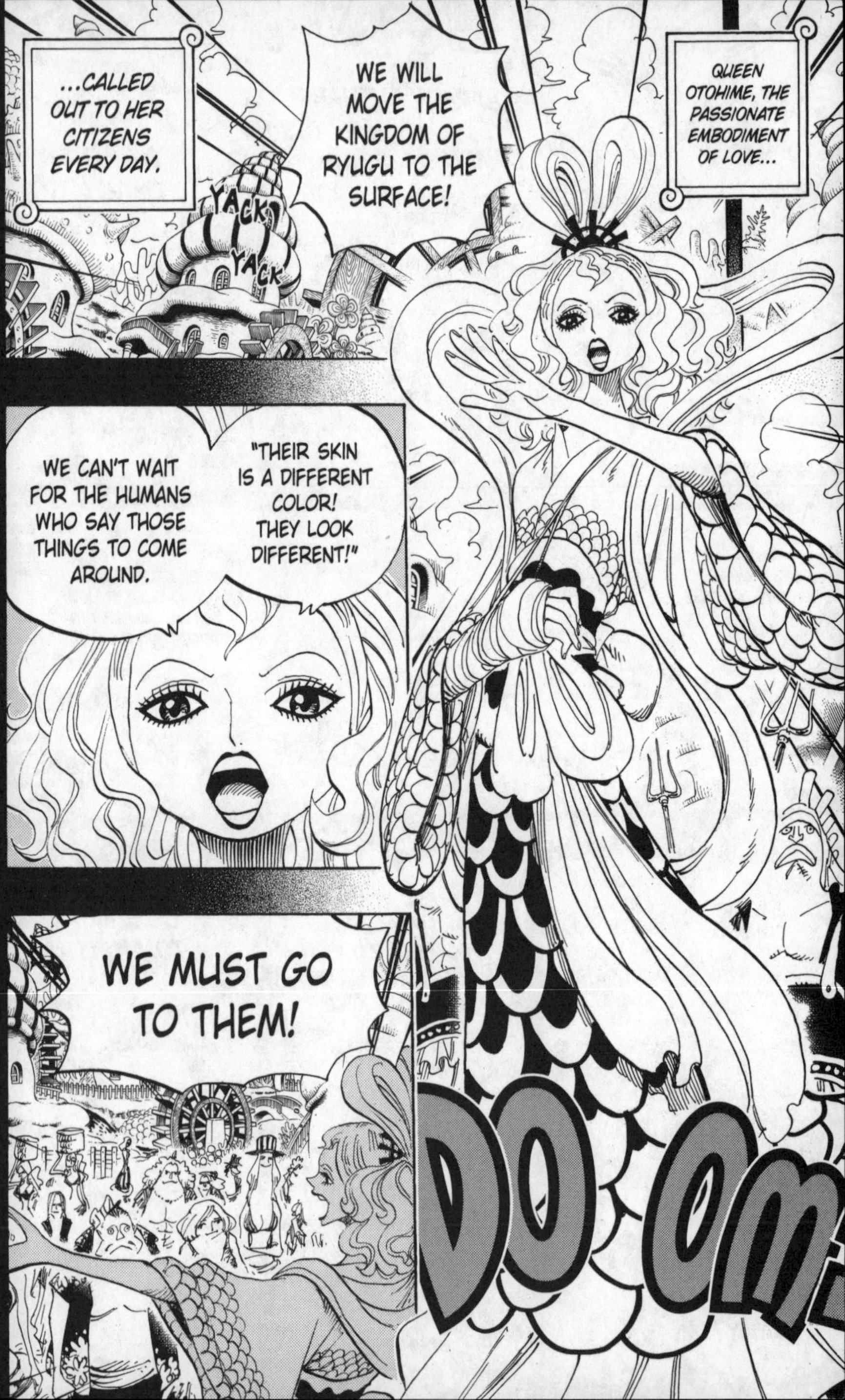
QUEEN OTOHIME, THE PASSIONATE EMBODIMENT OF LOVE...
DO-OM
...CALLED OUT TO HER CITIZENS EVERY DAY.
WE WILL MOVE THE KINGDOM OF RYUGU TO THE SURFACE!
YACK YACK
"THEIR SKIN IS A DIFFERENT COLOR! THEY LOOK DIFFERENT!"
WE CAN'T WAIT FOR THE HUMANS WHO SAY THOSE THINGS TO COME AROUND.
WE MUST GO TO THEM!

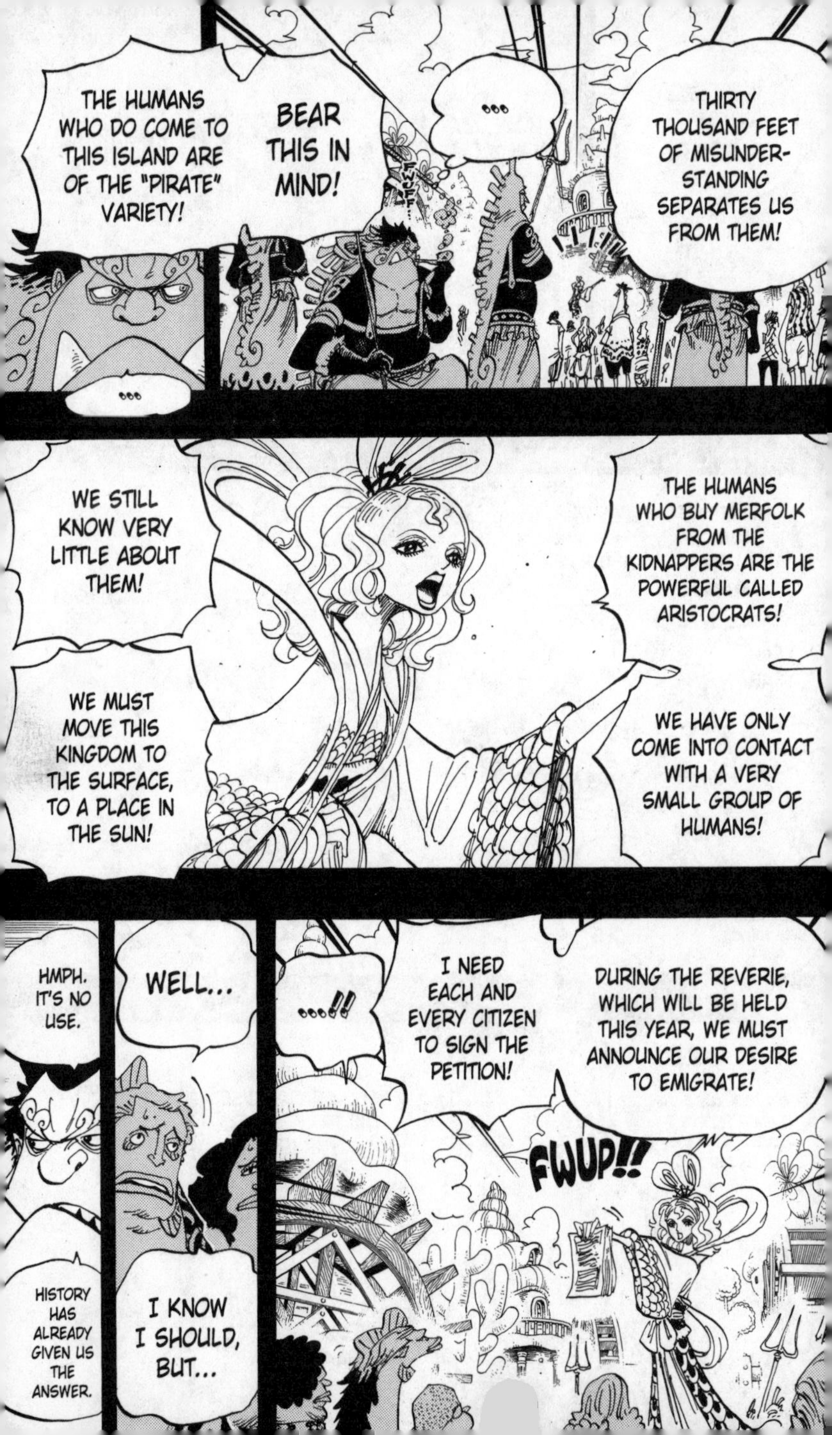
THIRTY THOUSAND FEET OF MISUNDER-STANDING SEPARATES US FROM THEM!
...
FWUFF
BEAR THIS IN MIND!
THE HUMANS WHO DO COME TO THIS ISLAND ARE OF THE "PIRATE" VARIETY!
...
THE HUMANS WHO BUY MERFOLK FROM THE KIDNAPPERS ARE THE POWERFUL CALLED ARISTOCRATS!
WE HAVE ONLY COME INTO CONTACT WITH A VERY SMALL GROUP OF HUMANS!
WE STILL KNOW VERY LITTLE ABOUT THEM!
WE MUST MOVE THIS KINGDOM TO THE SURFACE, TO A PLACE IN THE SUN!
DURING THE REVERIE, WHICH WILL BE HELD THIS YEAR, WE MUST ANNOUNCE OUR DESIRE TO EMIGRATE!
I NEED EACH AND EVERY CITIZEN TO SIGN THE PETITION!
FWUP!!
...!!
WELL...
I KNOW I SHOULD, BUT...
HMPH. IT'S NO USE.
HISTORY HAS ALREADY GIVEN US THE ANSWER.

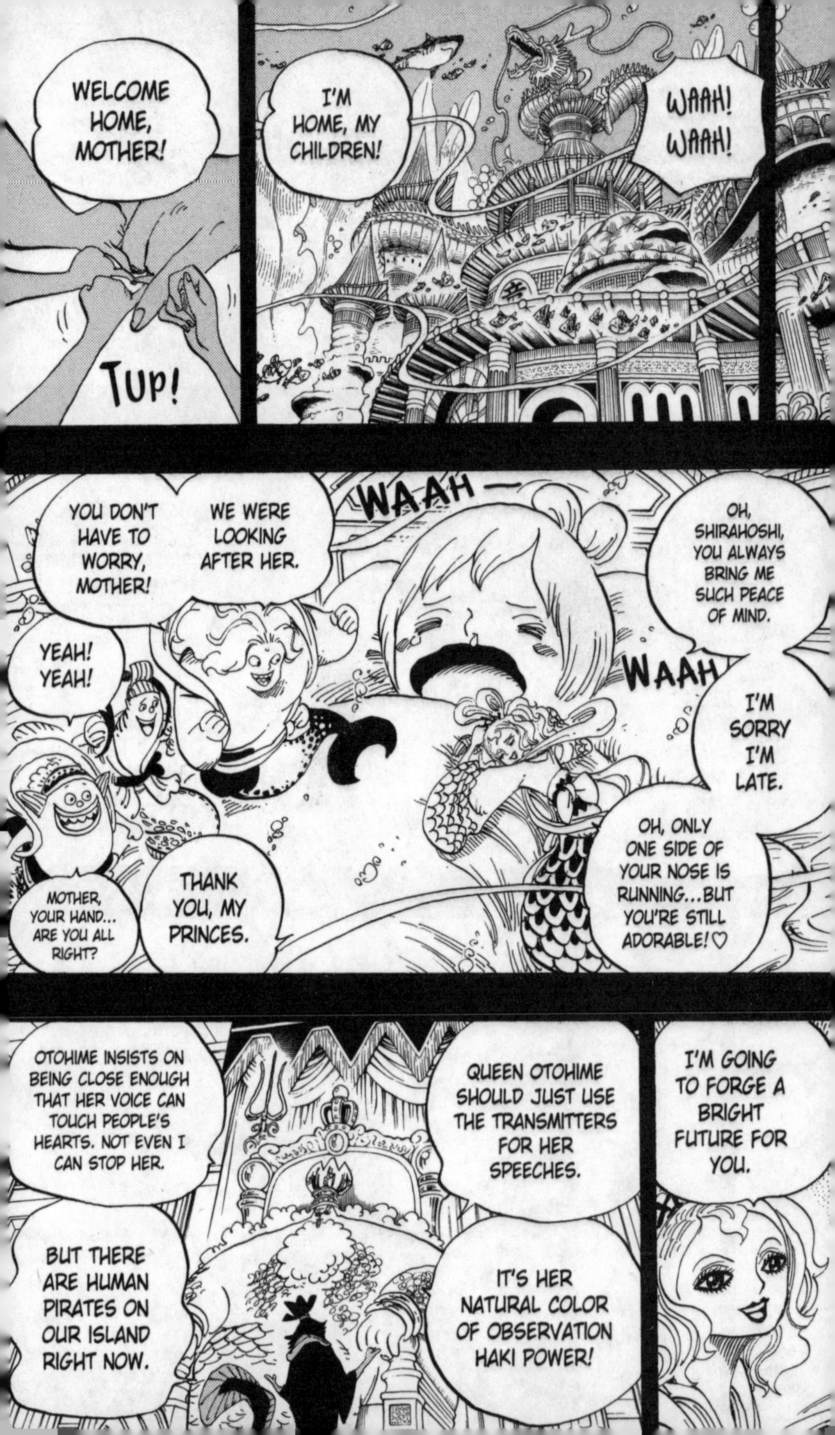
WAAH! WAAH!
I'M HOME, MY CHILDREN!
WELCOME HOME, MOTHER!
TUP!
OH, SHIRAHOSHI, YOU ALWAYS BRING ME SUCH PEACE OF MIND.
WAAH—
WAAH
I'M SORRY I'M LATE.
OH, ONLY ONE SIDE OF YOUR NOSE IS RUNNING...BUT YOU'RE STILL ADORABLE! ♡
WE WERE LOOKING AFTER HER.
YOU DON'T HAVE TO WORRY, MOTHER!
YEAH! YEAH!
THANK YOU, MY PRINCES.
MOTHER, YOUR HAND... ARE YOU ALL RIGHT?
I'M GOING TO FORGE A BRIGHT FUTURE FOR YOU.
QUEEN OTOHIME SHOULD JUST USE THE TRANSMITTERS FOR HER SPEECHES.
OTOHIME INSISTS ON BEING CLOSE ENOUGH THAT HER VOICE CAN TOUCH PEOPLE'S HEARTS. NOT EVEN I CAN STOP HER.
IT'S HER NATURAL COLOR OF OBSERVATION HAKI POWER!
BUT THERE ARE HUMAN PIRATES ON OUR ISLAND RIGHT NOW.

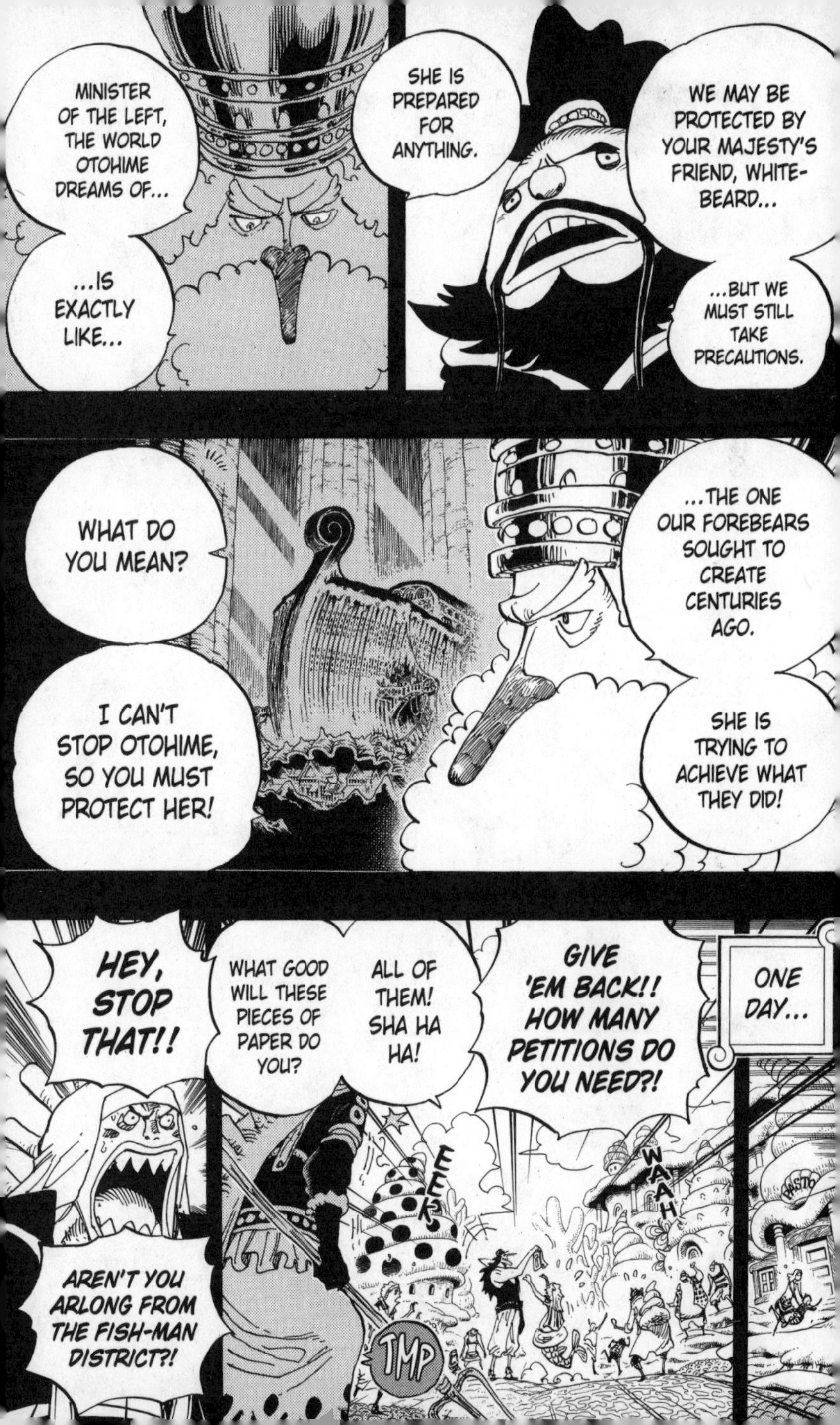

WE MAY BE PROTECTED BY YOUR MAJESTY'S FRIEND, WHITE-BEARD...
...BUT WE MUST STILL TAKE PRECAUTIONS.
SHE IS PREPARED FOR ANYTHING.
MINISTER OF THE LEFT, THE WORLD OTOHIME DREAMS OF...
...IS EXACTLY LIKE...
...THE ONE OUR FOREBEARS SOUGHT TO CREATE CENTURIES AGO.
SHE IS TRYING TO ACHIEVE WHAT THEY DID!
WHAT DO YOU MEAN?
I CAN'T STOP OTOHIME, SO YOU MUST PROTECT HER!
ONE DAY...
GIVE 'EM BACK!! HOW MANY PETITIONS DO YOU NEED?!
ALL OF THEM! SHA HA HA!
WHAT GOOD WILL THESE PIECES OF PAPER DO YOU?
WAAH
EEEK
TMP
HEY, STOP THAT!!
AREN'T YOU ARLONG FROM THE FISH-MAN DISTRICT?!

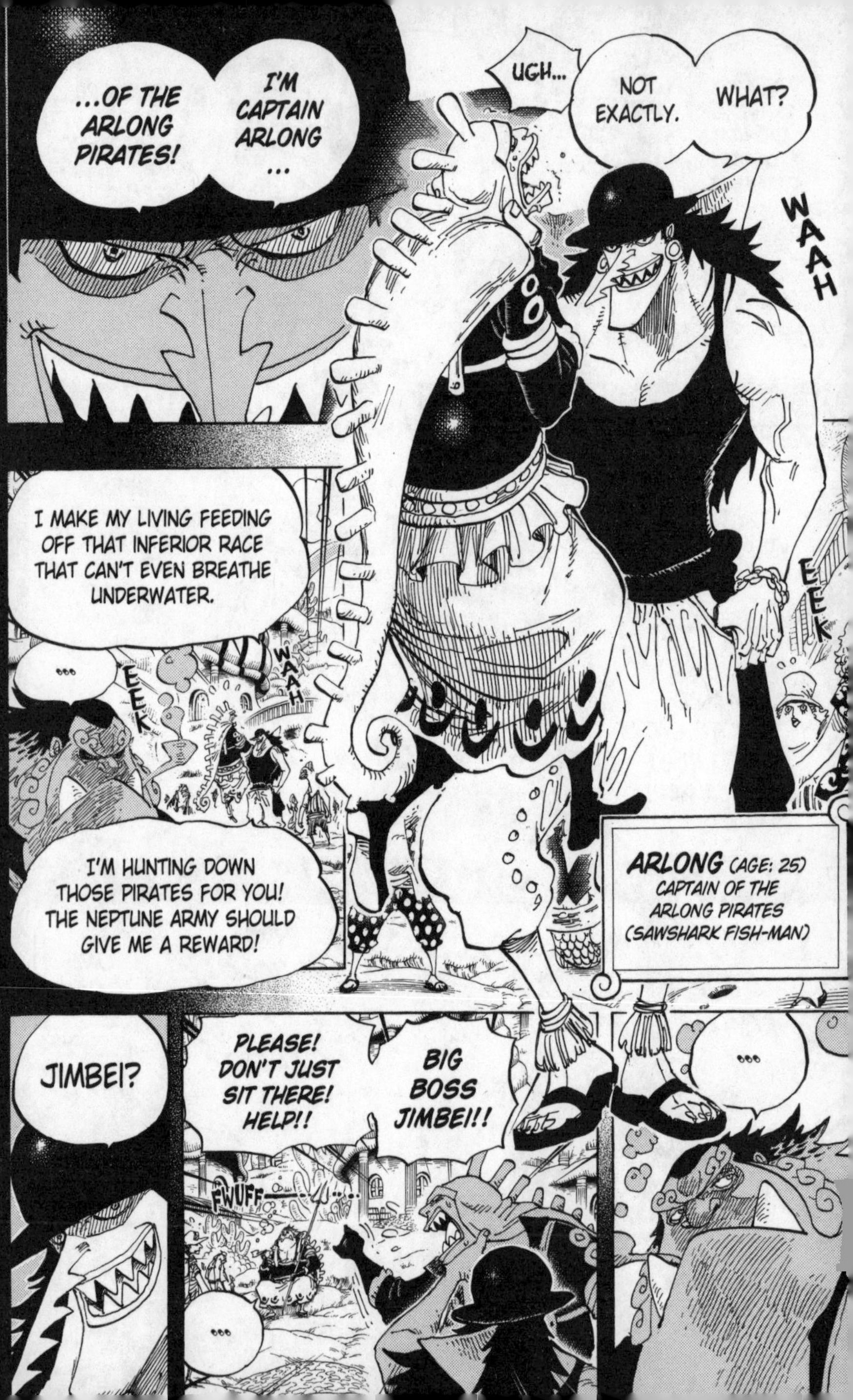
WHAT?
NOT EXACTLY.
UGH...
WAAH
EEK
ARLONG (AGE: 25)
CAPTAIN OF THE ARLONG PIRATES
(SAWSHARK FISH-MAN)
I'M CAPTAIN ARLONG...
...OF THE ARLONG PIRATES!
I MAKE MY LIVING FEEDING OFF THAT INFERIOR RACE THAT CAN'T EVEN BREATHE UNDERWATER.
WAAH
EEK
...
I'M HUNTING DOWN THOSE PIRATES FOR YOU! THE NEPTUNE ARMY SHOULD GIVE ME A REWARD!
...
BIG BOSS JIMBEI!!
PLEASE! DON'T JUST SIT THERE! HELP!!
FWUFF
...
JIMBEI?

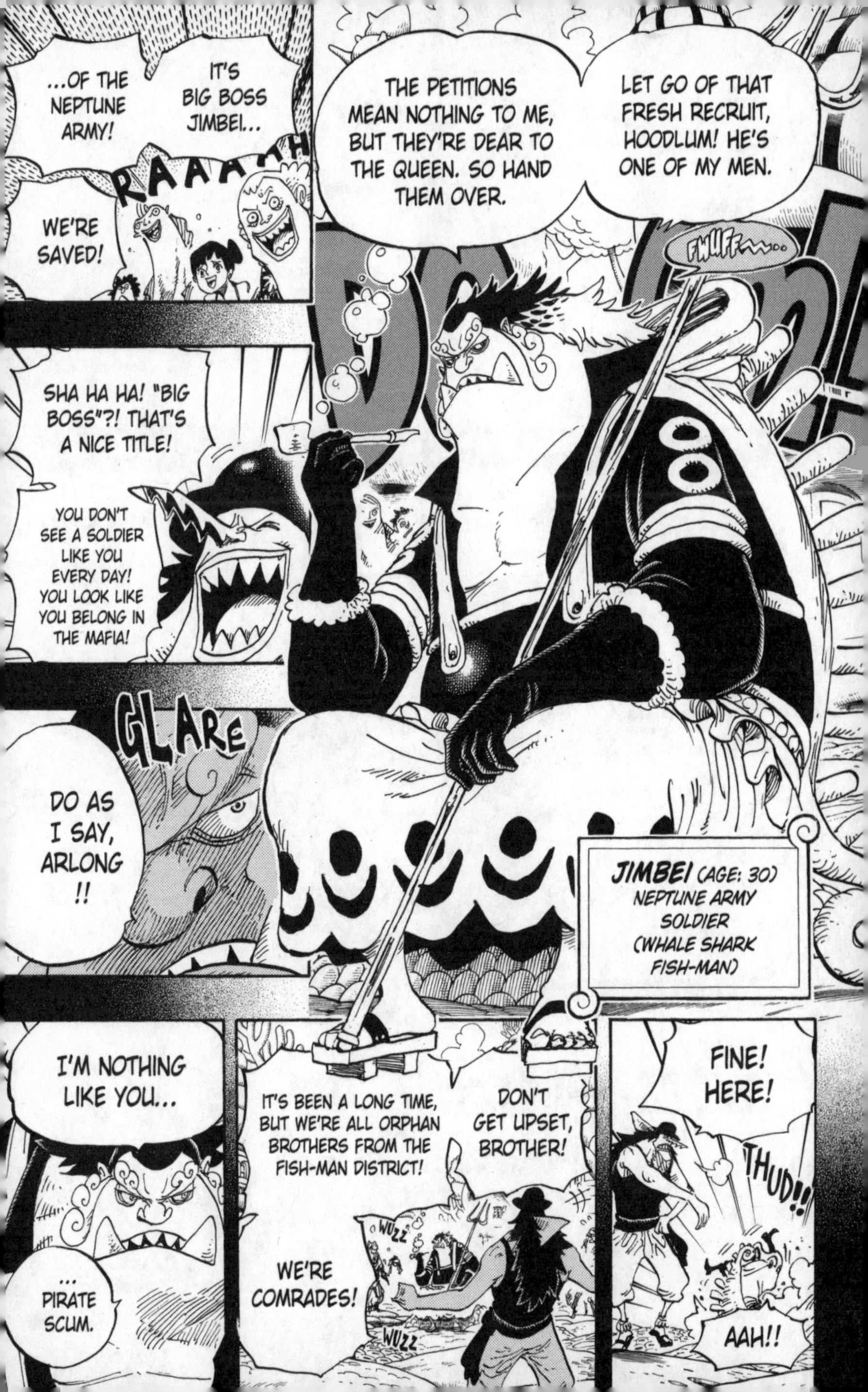
LET GO OF THAT FRESH RECRUIT, HOODLUM! HE'S ONE OF MY MEN.
THE PETITIONS MEAN NOTHING TO ME, BUT THEY'RE DEAR TO THE QUEEN. SO HAND THEM OVER.
FWUFF...
JIMBEI (AGE: 30) NEPTUNE ARMY SOLDIER (WHALE SHARK FISH-MAN)
IT'S BIG BOSS JIMBEI...
...OF THE NEPTUNE ARMY!
RAAAAH
WE'RE SAVED!
SHA HA HA! "BIG BOSS"?! THAT'S A NICE TITLE!
YOU DON'T SEE A SOLDIER LIKE YOU EVERY DAY! YOU LOOK LIKE YOU BELONG IN THE MAFIA!
GLARE
DO AS I SAY, ARLONG !!
FINE! HERE!
THUD!!
AAH!!
DON'T GET UPSET, BROTHER!
IT'S BEEN A LONG TIME, BUT WE'RE ALL ORPHAN BROTHERS FROM THE FISH-MAN DISTRICT!
WUZZ
WE'RE COMRADES!
WUZZ
I'M NOTHING LIKE YOU...
...PIRATE SCUM.

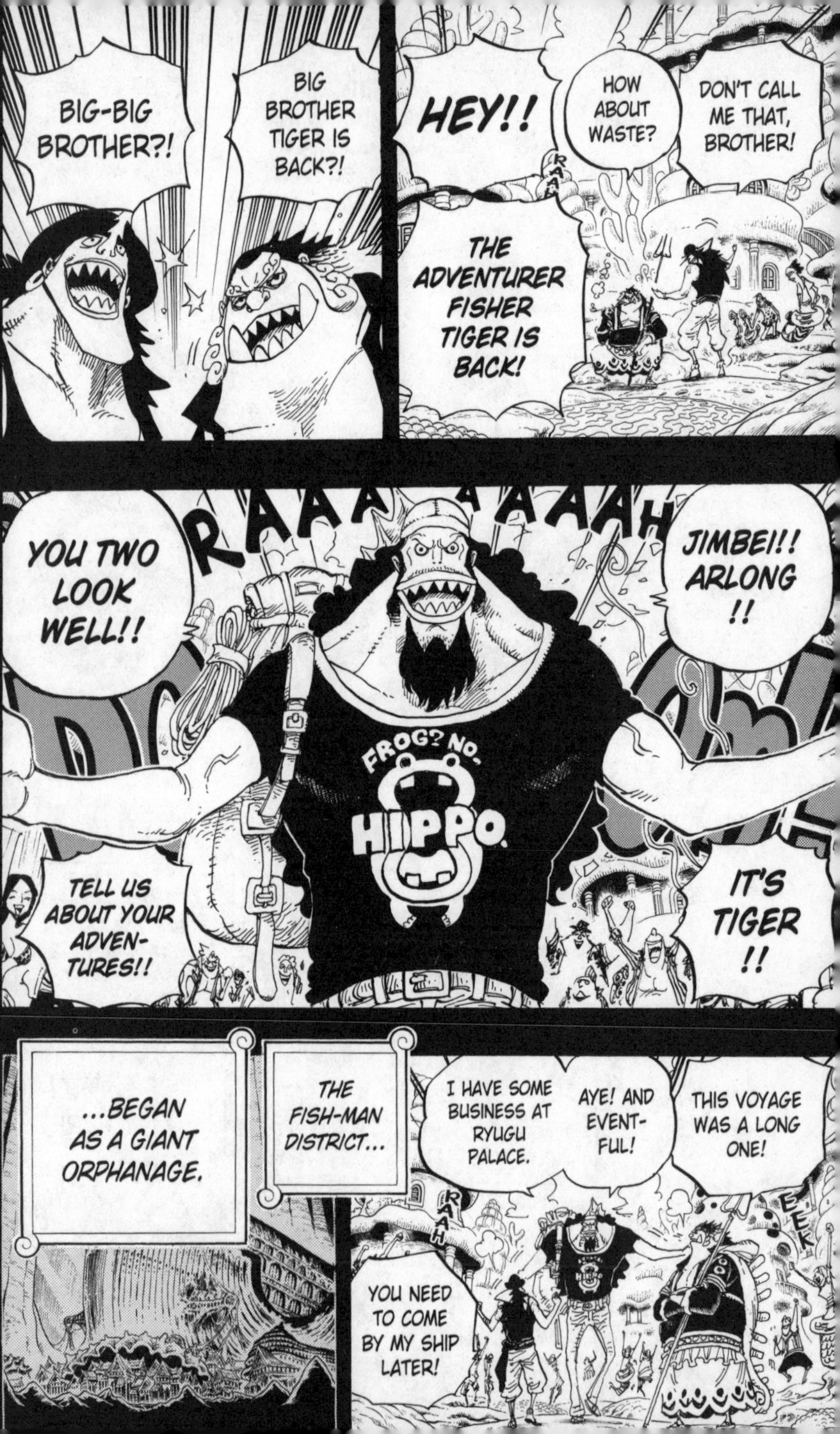
DON'T CALL ME THAT, BROTHER!
HOW ABOUT WASTE?
HEY!!
RAA
THE ADVENTURER FISHER TIGER IS BACK!
BIG BROTHER TIGER IS BACK?!
BIG-BIG BROTHER?!
JIMBEI!! ARLONG !!
RAAAAAAAH
YOU TWO LOOK WELL!!
FROG? NO. HIPPO.
IT'S TIGER !!
TELL US ABOUT YOUR ADVEN-TURES!!
THIS VOYAGE WAS A LONG ONE!
EEK
AYE! AND EVENT-FUL!
I HAVE SOME BUSINESS AT RYUGU PALACE.
RAAH
YOU NEED TO COME BY MY SHIP LATER!
THE FISH-MAN DISTRICT...
...BEGAN AS A GIANT ORPHANAGE.

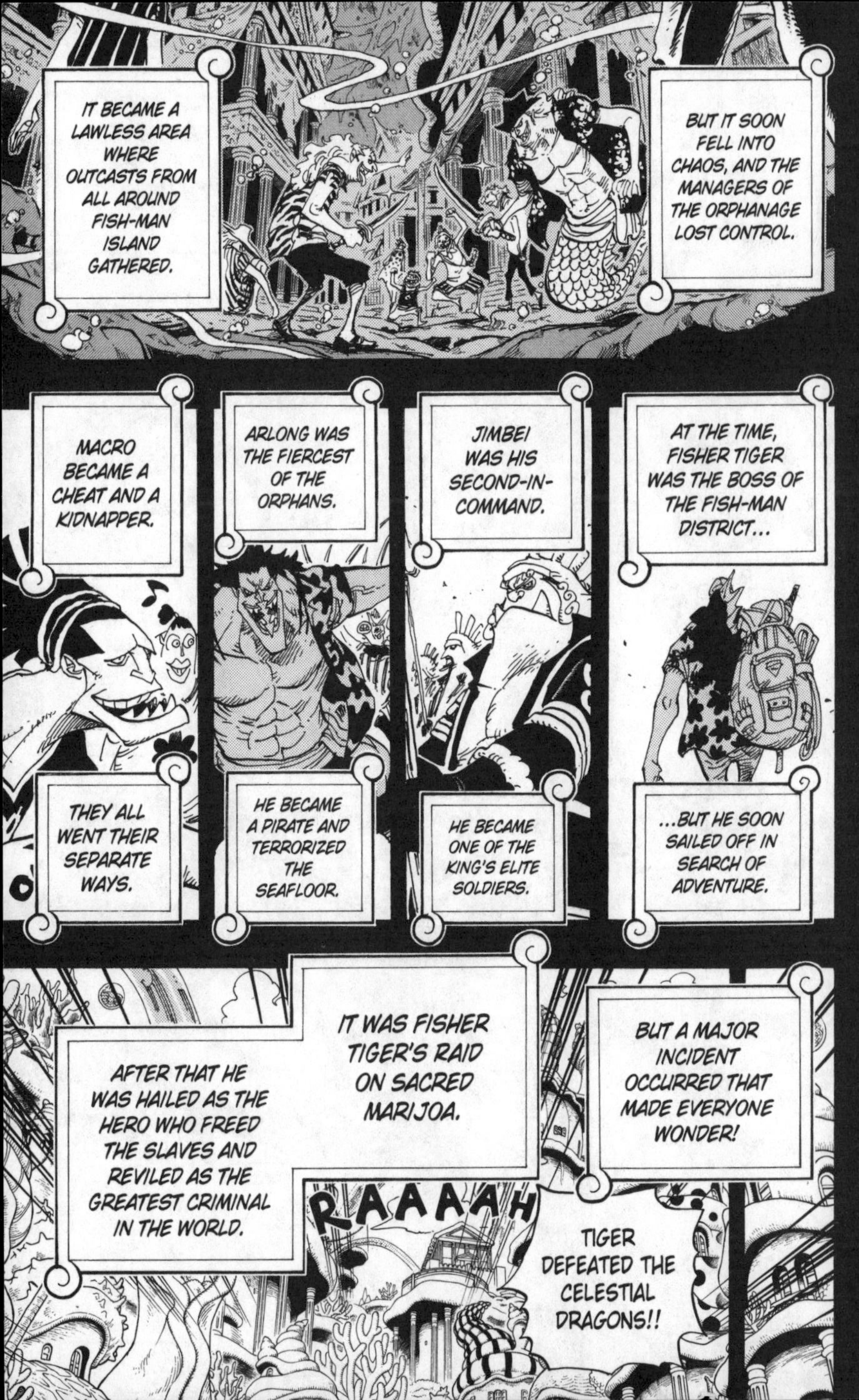

BUT IT SOON FELL INTO CHAOS, AND THE MANAGERS OF THE ORPHANAGE LOST CONTROL.
IT BECAME A LAWLESS AREA WHERE OUTCASTS FROM ALL AROUND FISH-MAN ISLAND GATHERED.
AT THE TIME, FISHER TIGER WAS THE BOSS OF THE FISH-MAN DISTRICT...
...BUT HE SOON SAILED OFF IN SEARCH OF ADVENTURE.
JIMBEI WAS HIS SECOND-IN-COMMAND.
HE BECAME ONE OF THE KING'S ELITE SOLDIERS.
ARLONG WAS THE FIERCEST OF THE ORPHANS.
HE BECAME A PIRATE AND TERRORIZED THE SEAFLOOR.
MACRO BECAME A CHEAT AND A KIDNAPPER.
THEY ALL WENT THEIR SEPARATE WAYS.
BUT A MAJOR INCIDENT OCCURRED THAT MADE EVERYONE WONDER!
IT WAS FISHER TIGER'S RAID ON SACRED MARIJOA.
RAAAAH
TIGER DEFEATED THE CELESTIAL DRAGONS!!
AFTER THAT HE WAS HAILED AS THE HERO WHO FREED THE SLAVES AND REVILED AS THE GREATEST CRIMINAL IN THE WORLD.

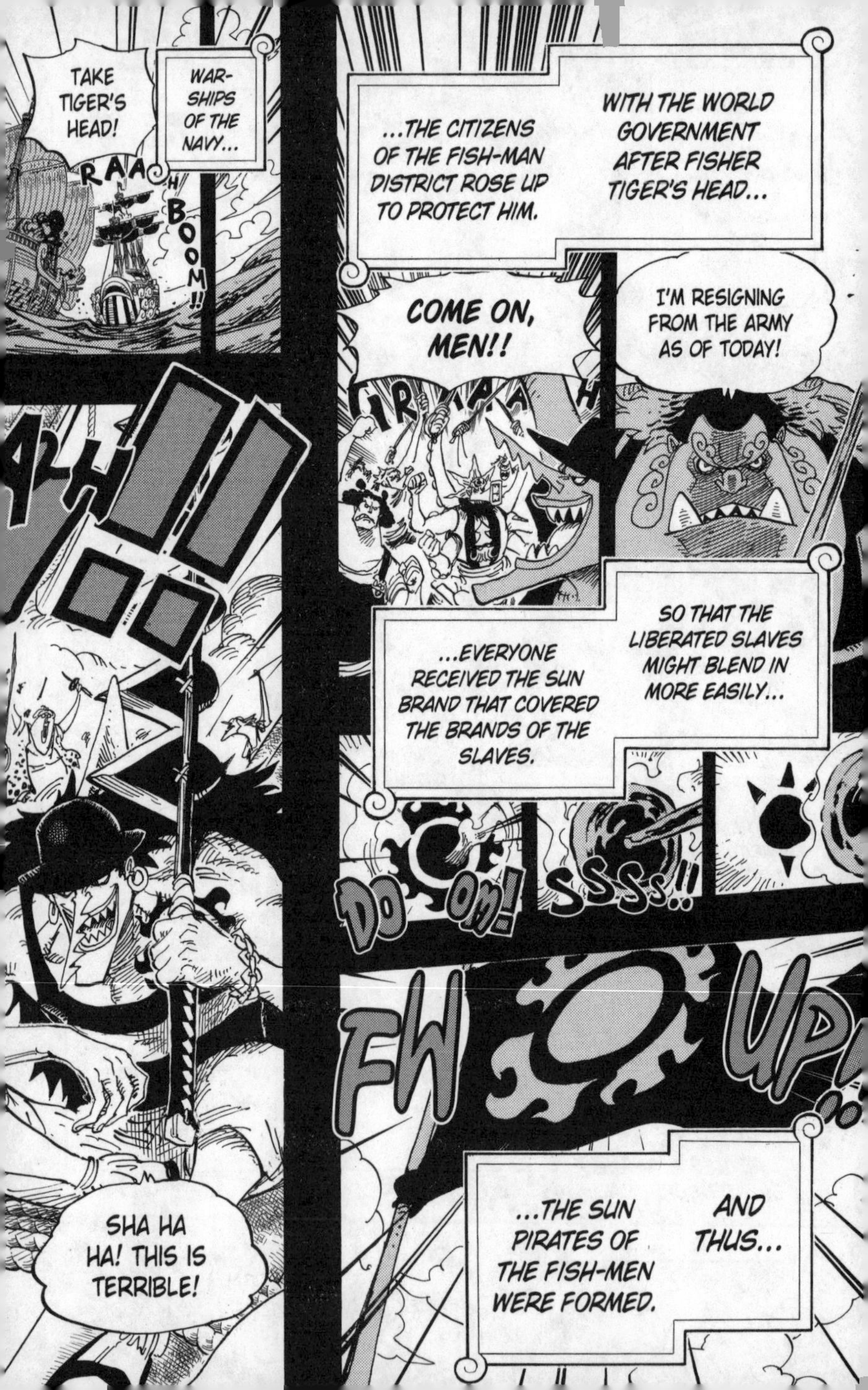
WITH THE WORLD GOVERNMENT AFTER FISHER TIGER'S HEAD...
...THE CITIZENS OF THE FISH-MAN DISTRICT ROSE UP TO PROTECT HIM.
I'M RESIGNING FROM THE ARMY AS OF TODAY!
COME ON, MEN!!
RAAAAH
SO THAT THE LIBERATED SLAVES MIGHT BLEND IN MORE EASILY...
...EVERYONE RECEIVED THE SUN BRAND THAT COVERED THE BRANDS OF THE SLAVES.
SSSS!!
DOOM!
FWUP!!
AND THUS...
...THE SUN PIRATES OF THE FISH-MEN WERE FORMED.
WAR-SHIPS OF THE NAVY...
TAKE TIGER'S HEAD!
RAAAH
BOOM!!
SHA HA HA! THIS IS TERRIBLE!

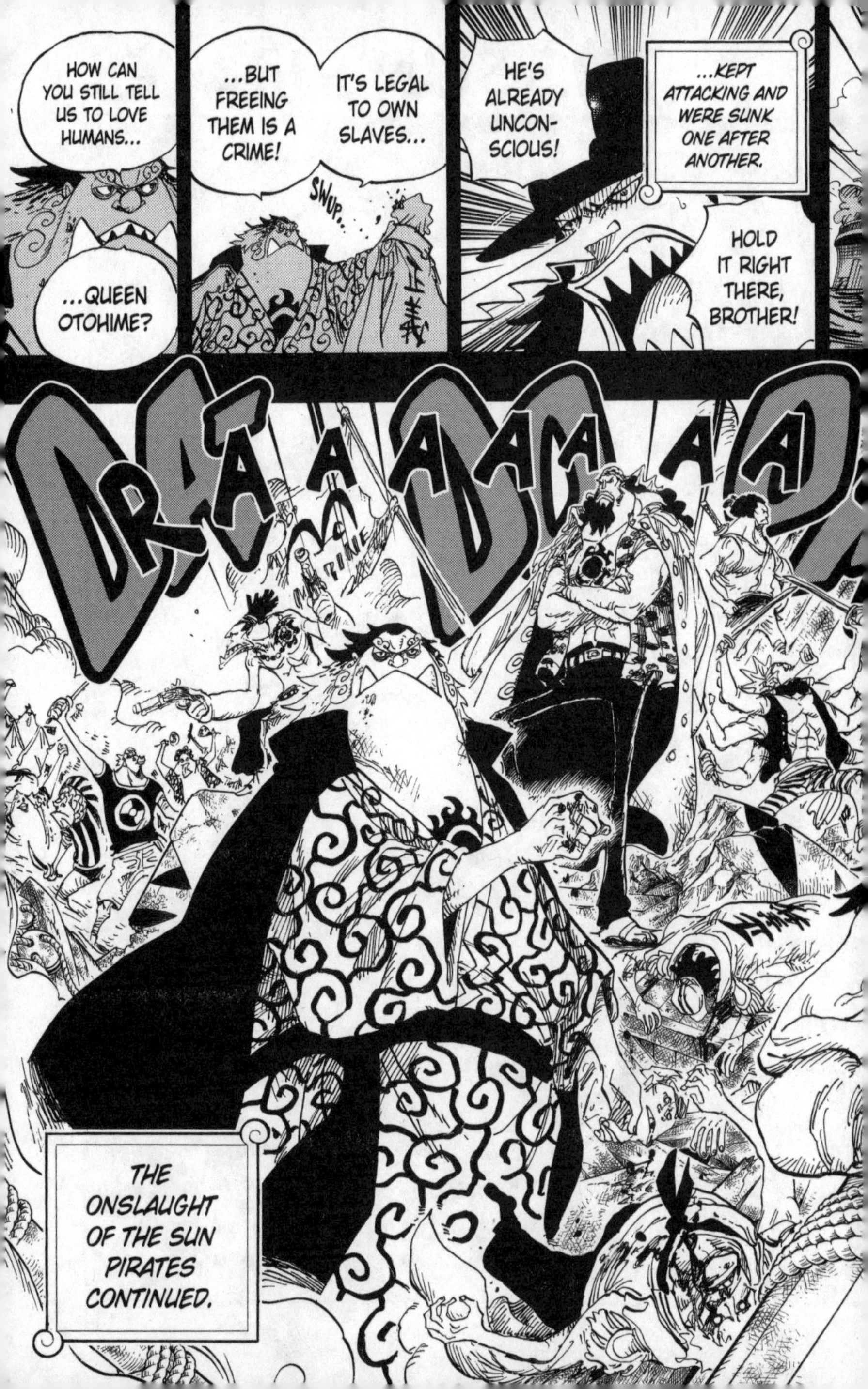
...KEPT ATTACKING AND WERE SUNK ONE AFTER ANOTHER.
HOLD IT RIGHT THERE, BROTHER!
HE'S ALREADY UNCONSCIOUS!
IT'S LEGAL TO OWN SLAVES...
...BUT FREEING THEM IS A CRIME!
SWUP...
HOW CAN YOU STILL TELL US TO LOVE HUMANS...
...QUEEN OTOHIME?
THE ONSLAUGHT OF THE SUN PIRATES CONTINUED.

THE SUN PIRATES

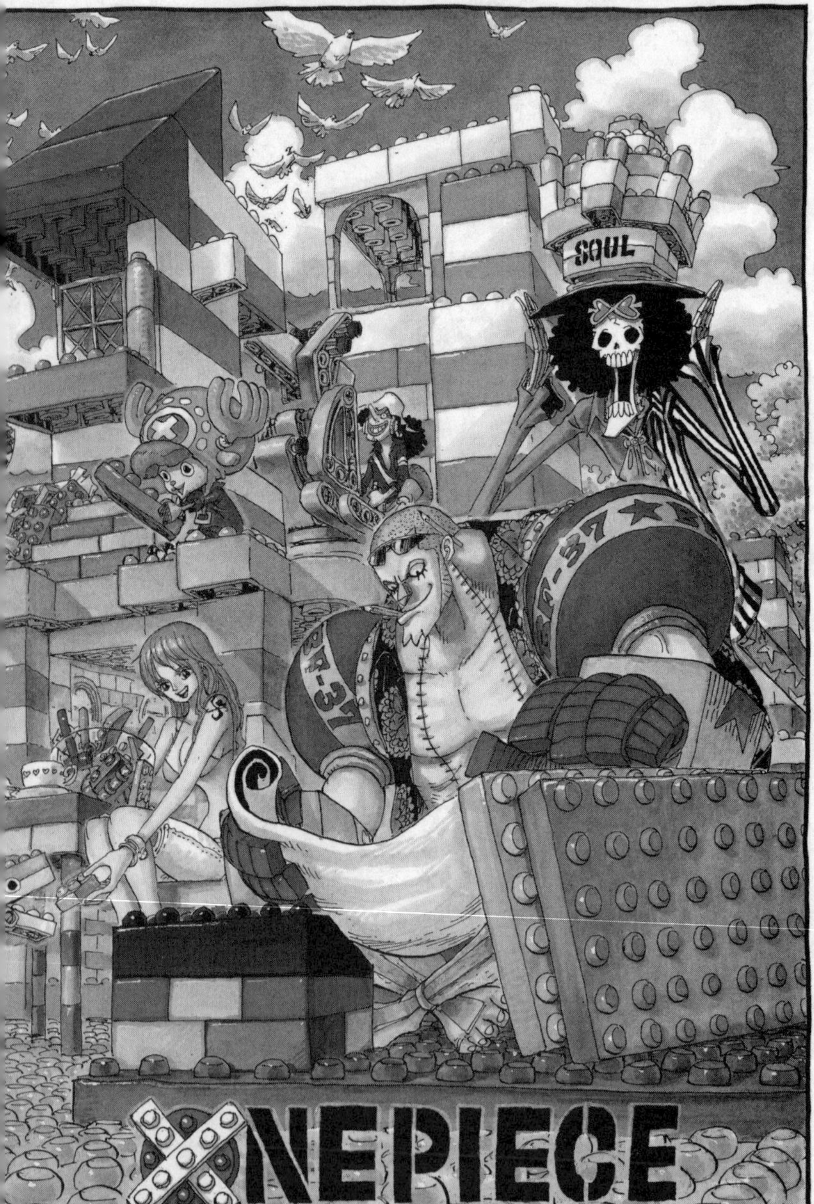
SOUL
SF-37
SF-37
ONEPIECE

Chapter 622:

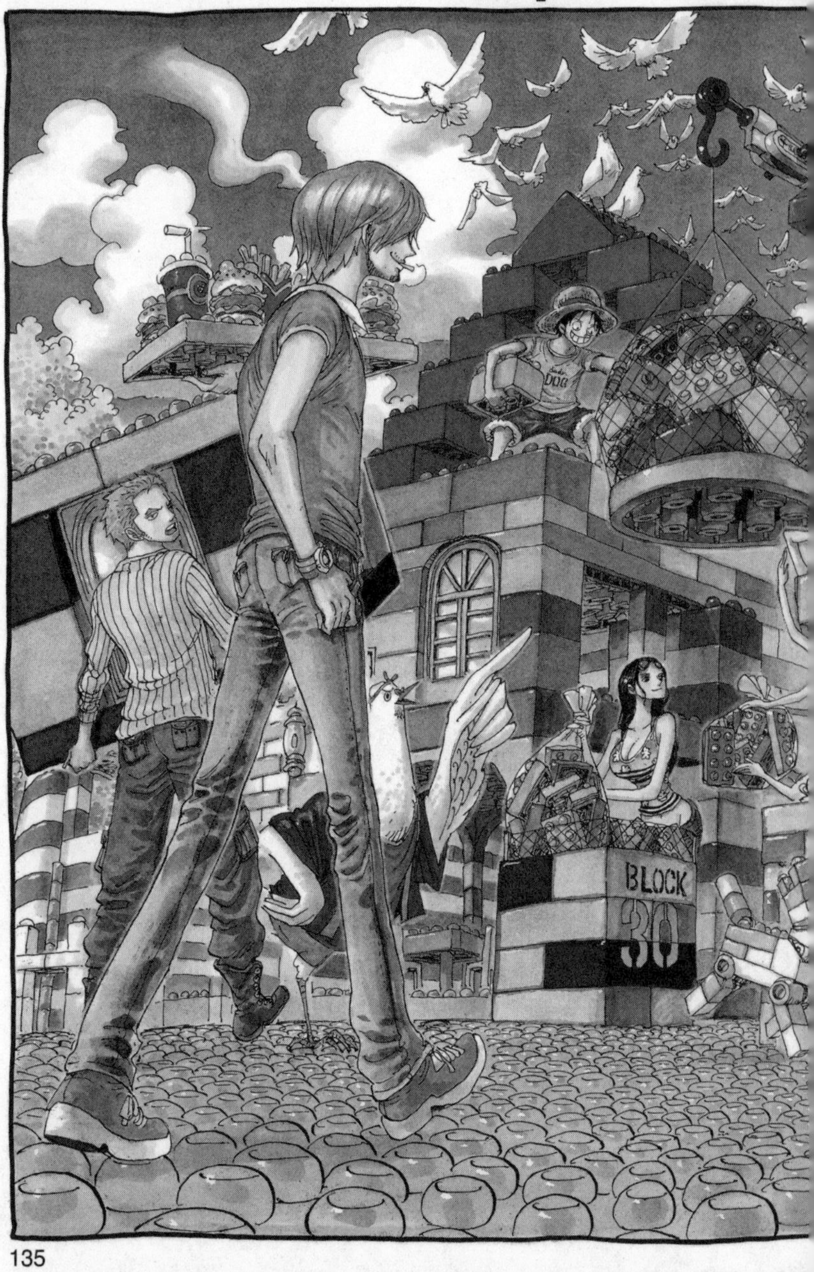
DOG
BLOCK
30

vol.63
ONE PIECE

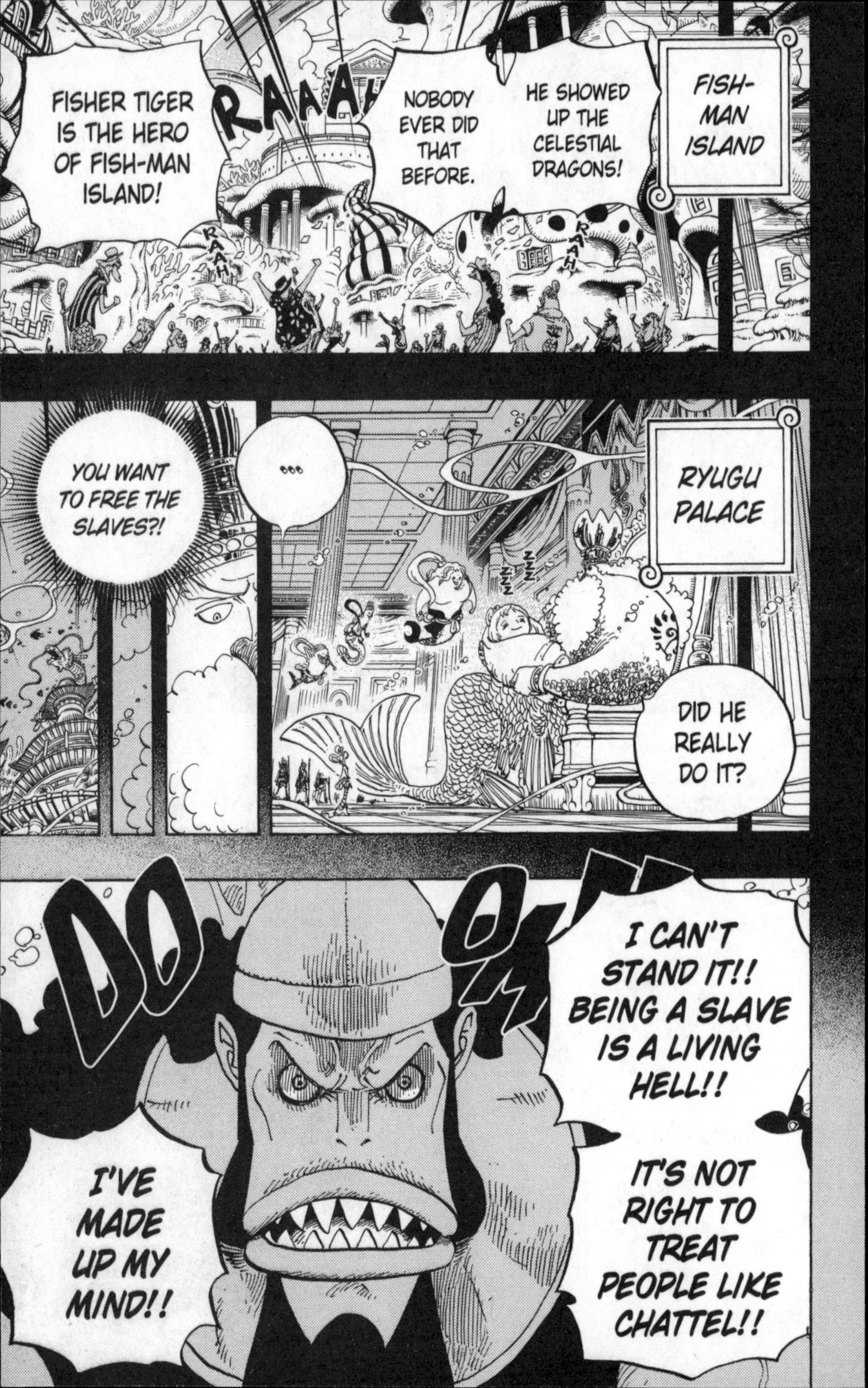
FISH-MAN ISLAND
HE SHOWED UP THE CELESTIAL DRAGONS!
NOBODY EVER DID THAT BEFORE.
RAAA
FISHER TIGER IS THE HERO OF FISH-MAN ISLAND!
RAAH
RAAH
RYUGU PALACE
DID HE REALLY DO IT?
ZZZ
...
YOU WANT TO FREE THE SLAVES?!
I CAN'T STAND IT!! BEING A SLAVE IS A LIVING HELL!!
IT'S NOT RIGHT TO TREAT PEOPLE LIKE CHATTEL!!
DOOM
I'VE MADE UP MY MIND!!

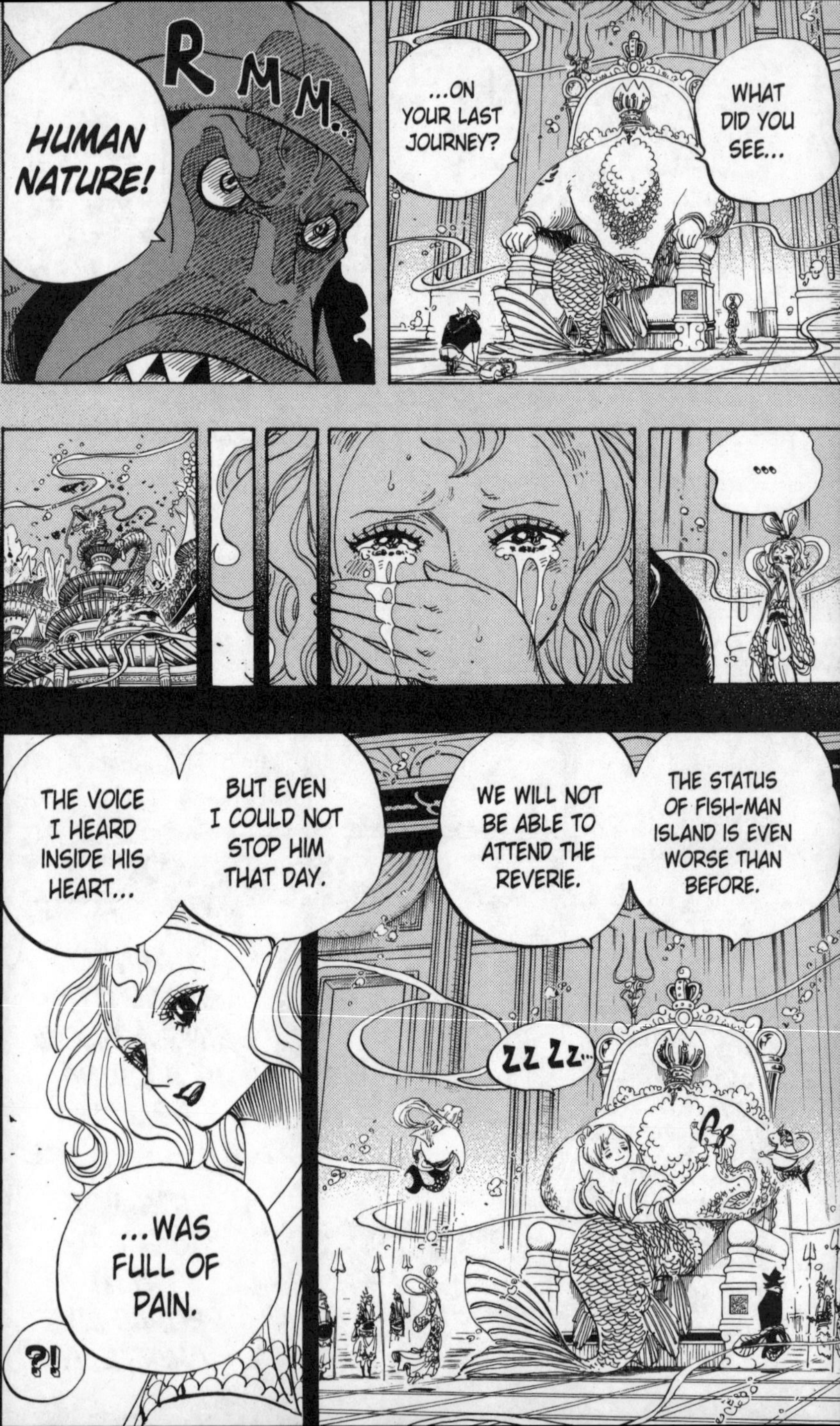
WHAT DID YOU SEE...
...ON YOUR LAST JOURNEY?
RMM...
HUMAN NATURE!
...
THE STATUS OF FISH-MAN ISLAND IS EVEN WORSE THAN BEFORE.
WE WILL NOT BE ABLE TO ATTEND THE REVERIE.
ZZ ZZ...
BUT EVEN I COULD NOT STOP HIM THAT DAY.
THE VOICE I HEARD INSIDE HIS HEART...
...WAS FULL OF PAIN.
?!

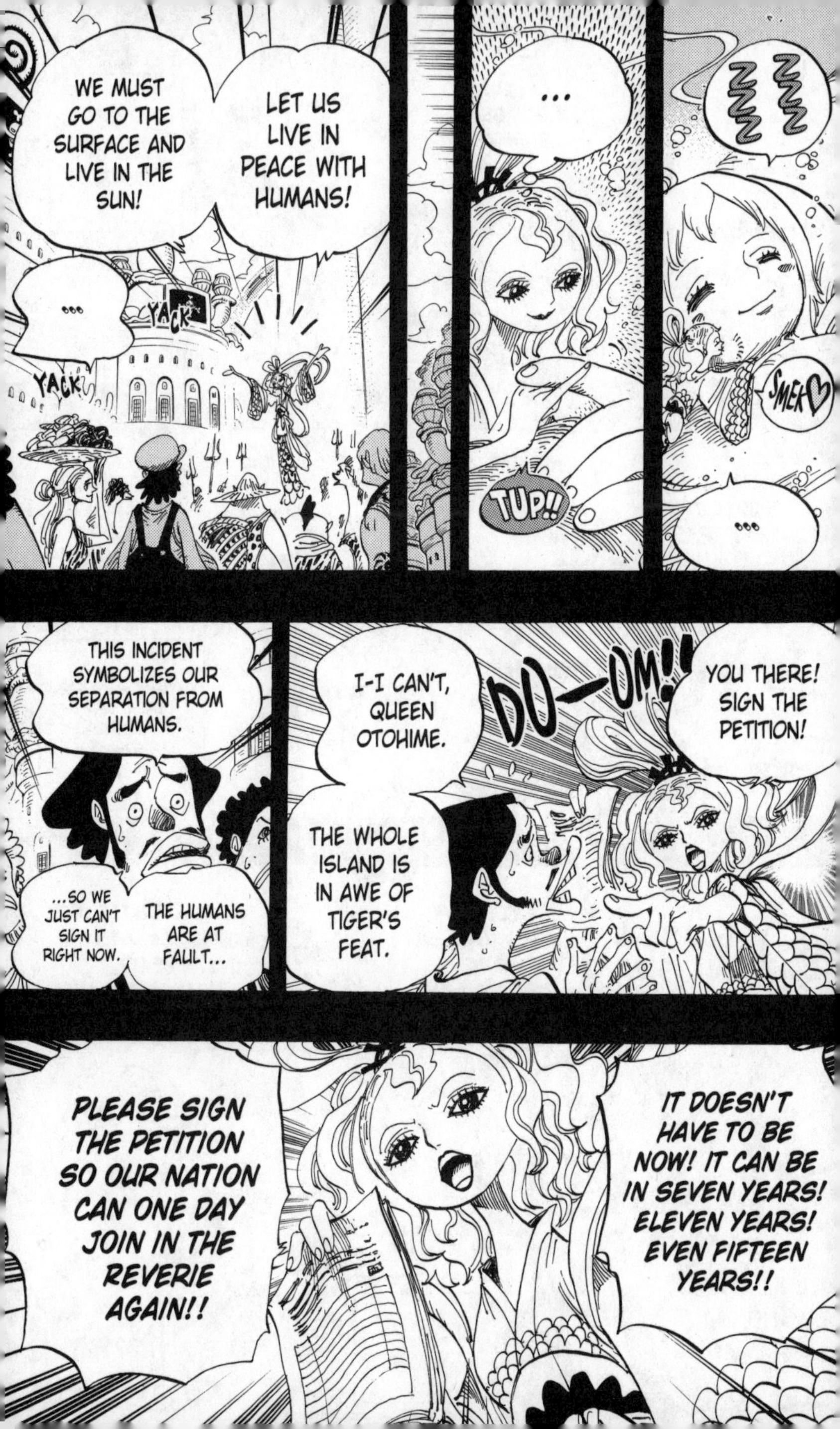
ZZZ
SMEK♡
...
...
TUP!!
LET US LIVE IN PEACE WITH HUMANS!
WE MUST GO TO THE SURFACE AND LIVE IN THE SUN!
YACK
...
YACK
YOU THERE! SIGN THE PETITION!
DO-OM!!
I-I CAN'T, QUEEN OTOHIME.
THE WHOLE ISLAND IS IN AWE OF TIGER'S FEAT.
THIS INCIDENT SYMBOLIZES OUR SEPARATION FROM HUMANS.
THE HUMANS ARE AT FAULT...
...SO WE JUST CAN'T SIGN IT RIGHT NOW.
IT DOESN'T HAVE TO BE NOW! IT CAN BE IN SEVEN YEARS! ELEVEN YEARS! EVEN FIFTEEN YEARS!!
PLEASE SIGN THE PETITION SO OUR NATION CAN ONE DAY JOIN IN THE REVERIE AGAIN!!

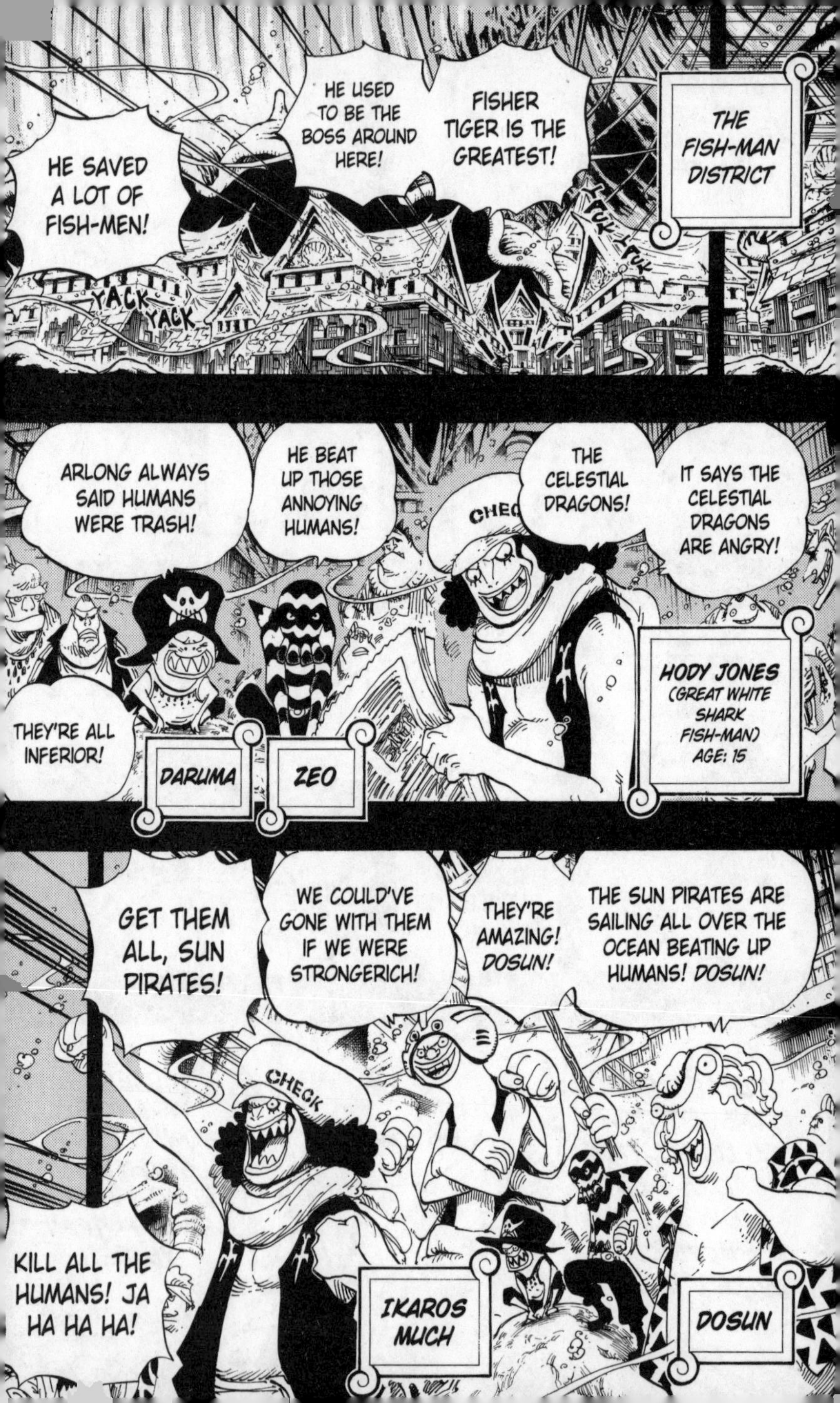
THE FISH-MAN DISTRICT
FISHER TIGER IS THE GREATEST!
HE USED TO BE THE BOSS AROUND HERE!
HE SAVED A LOT OF FISH-MEN!
YUK YUK
YACK YACK
IT SAYS THE CELESTIAL DRAGONS ARE ANGRY!
THE CELESTIAL DRAGONS!
HE BEAT UP THOSE ANNOYING HUMANS!
ARLONG ALWAYS SAID HUMANS WERE TRASH!
HODY JONES (GREAT WHITE SHARK FISH-MAN) AGE: 15
ZEO
DARUMA
THEY'RE ALL INFERIOR!
THE SUN PIRATES ARE SAILING ALL OVER THE OCEAN BEATING UP HUMANS! DOSUN!
THEY'RE AMAZING! DOSUN!
WE COULD'VE GONE WITH THEM IF WE WERE STRONGERICH!
GET THEM ALL, SUN PIRATES!
CHECK
DOSUN
IKAROS MUCH
KILL ALL THE HUMANS! JA HA HA HA!

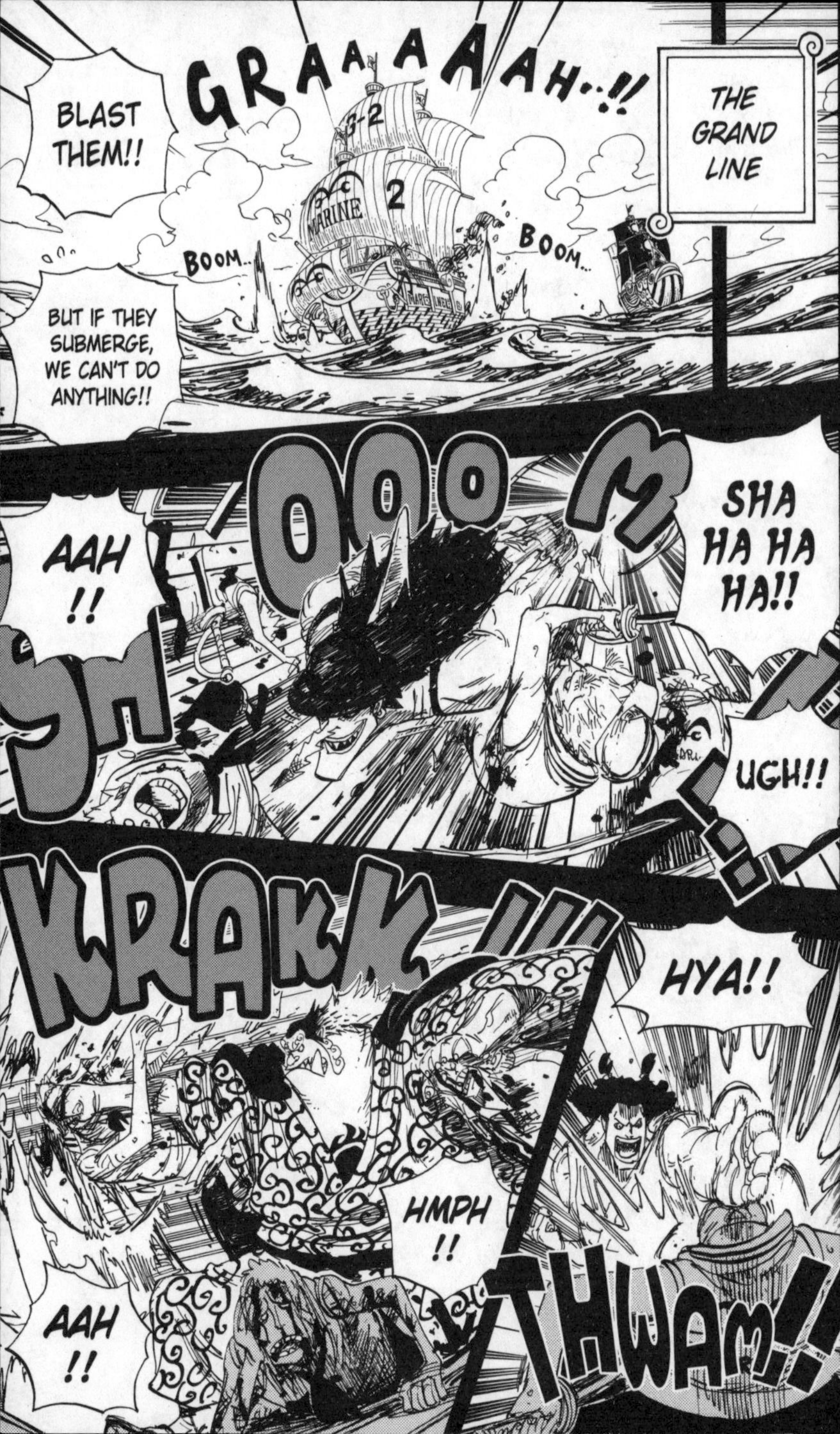
THE GRAND LINE
GRAAAAAAH..!!
BOOM..
MARINE
2
BOOM..
BLAST THEM!!
BUT IF THEY SUBMERGE, WE CAN'T DO ANYTHING!!
SHA HA HA HA!!
UGH!!
SHOOOOM
AAH !!
HYA!!
THWAM!!
KRAKK!!!
HMPH !!
AAH !!

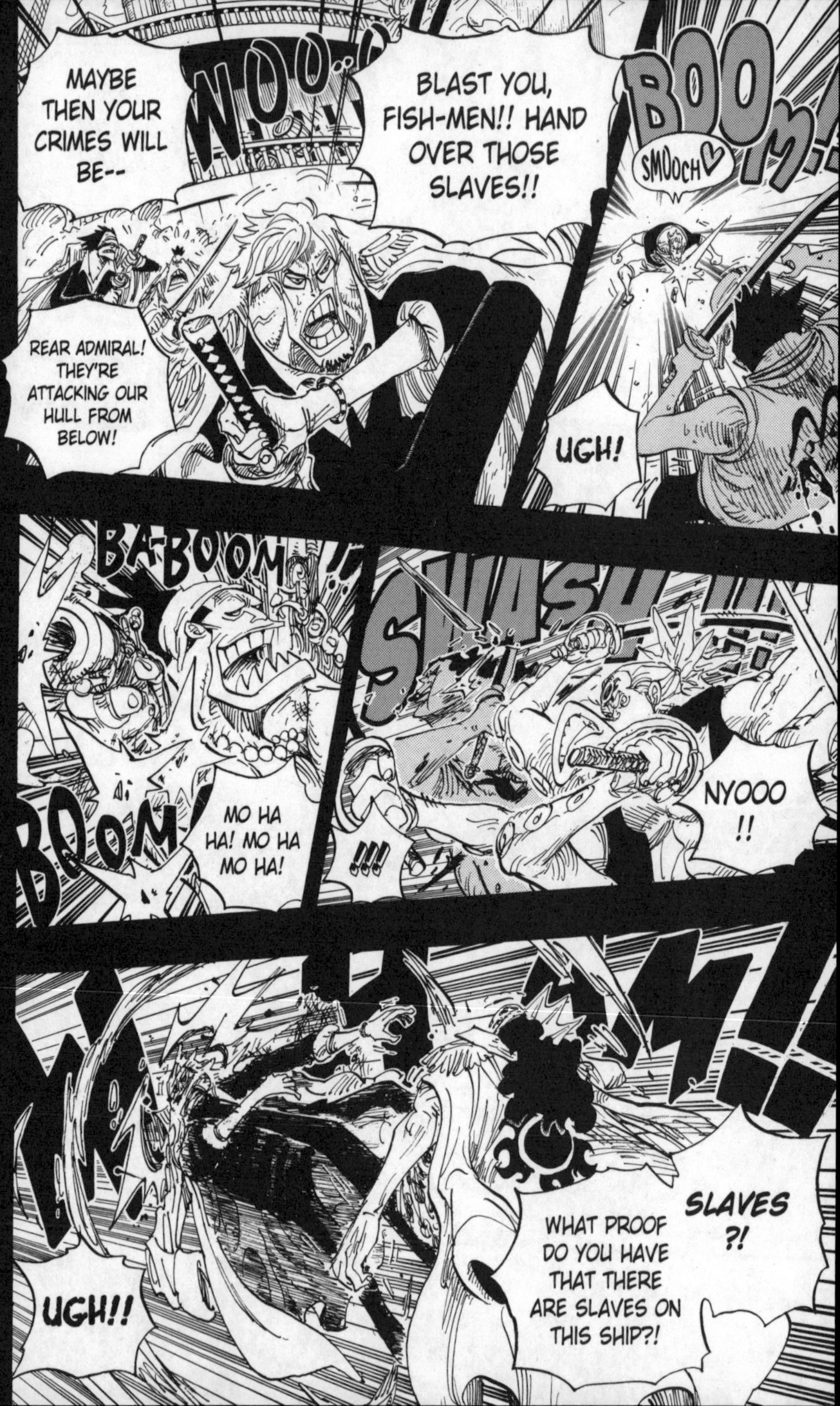
BOOM!!
SMOOCH♡
UGH!
BLAST YOU, FISH-MEN!! HAND OVER THOSE SLAVES!!
WOOO!!
MAYBE THEN YOUR CRIMES WILL BE--
REAR ADMIRAL! THEY'RE ATTACKING OUR HULL FROM BELOW!
SWASH!!!
NYOOO !!
!!!
BABOOM!!
BOOM
MO HA HA! MO HA MO HA!
SLAVES ?!
WHAT PROOF DO YOU HAVE THAT THERE ARE SLAVES ON THIS SHIP?!
UGH!!

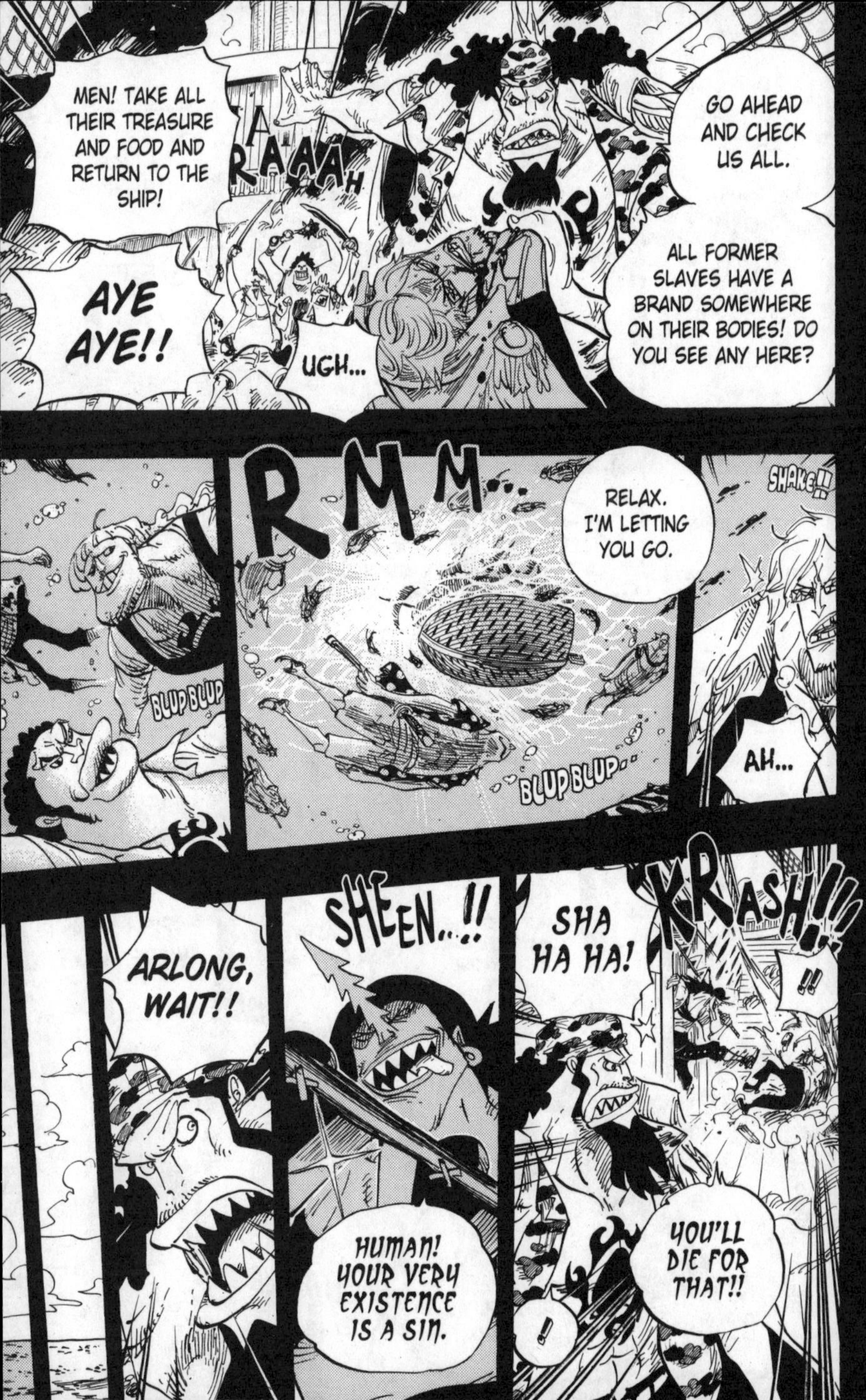
GO AHEAD AND CHECK US ALL.
ALL FORMER SLAVES HAVE A BRAND SOMEWHERE ON THEIR BODIES! DO YOU SEE ANY HERE?
UGH...
RAAAAH
MEN! TAKE ALL THEIR TREASURE AND FOOD AND RETURN TO THE SHIP!
AYE AYE!!
SHAKE!!
AH...
RMM
RELAX. I'M LETTING YOU GO.
BLUP BLUP
BLUP BLUP
KRASH!!!
SHA HA HA!
!!
YOU'LL DIE FOR THAT!!
!
SHEEN..!!
HUMAN! YOUR VERY EXISTENCE IS A SIN.
ARLONG, WAIT!!

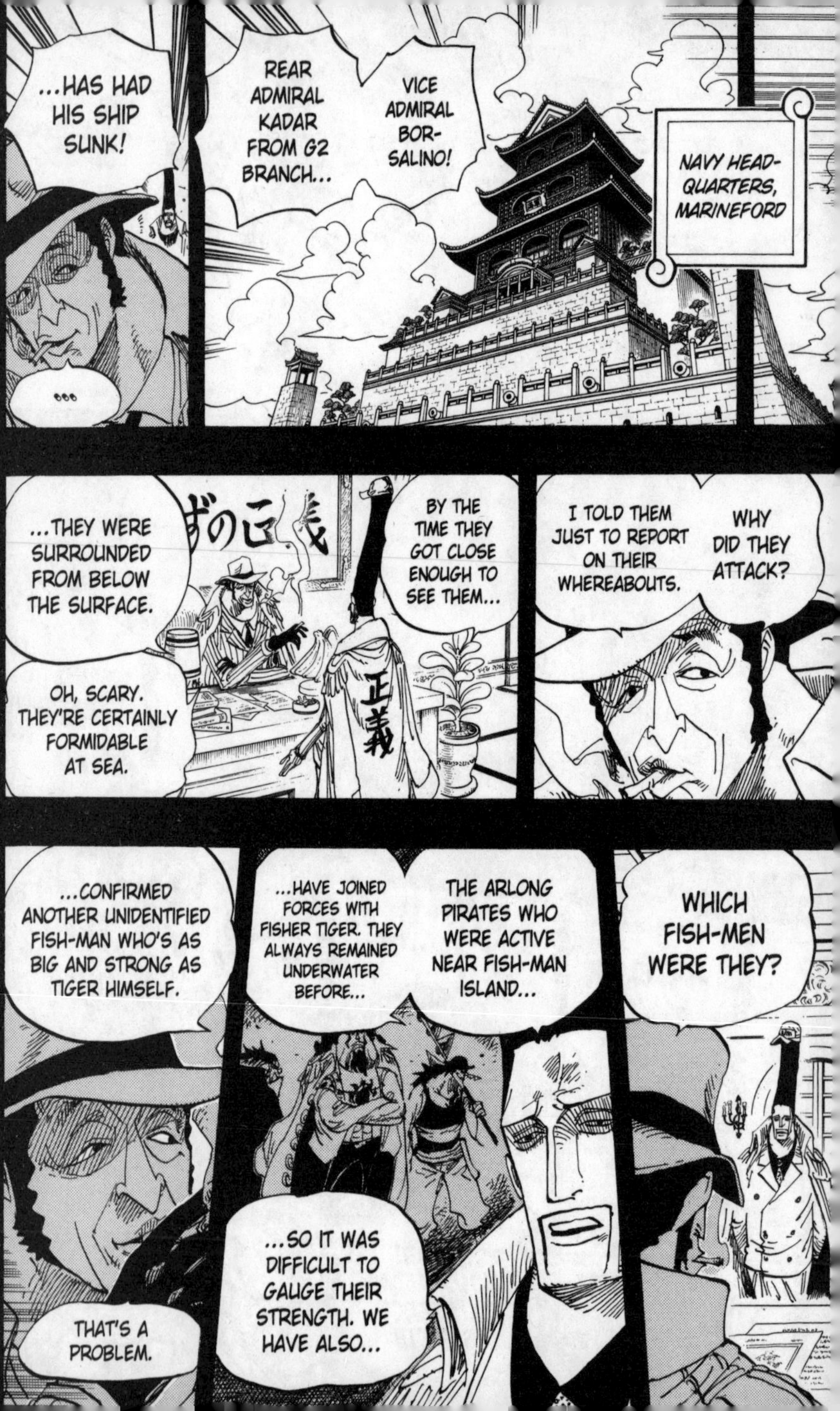
NAVY HEAD-QUARTERS, MARINEFORD
VICE ADMIRAL BOR-SALINO!
REAR ADMIRAL KADAR FROM G2 BRANCH...
...HAS HAD HIS SHIP SUNK!
...
WHY DID THEY ATTACK?
I TOLD THEM JUST TO REPORT ON THEIR WHEREABOUTS.
BY THE TIME THEY GOT CLOSE ENOUGH TO SEE THEM...
...THEY WERE SURROUNDED FROM BELOW THE SURFACE.
OH, SCARY. THEY'RE CERTAINLY FORMIDABLE AT SEA.
WHICH FISH-MEN WERE THEY?
THE ARLONG PIRATES WHO WERE ACTIVE NEAR FISH-MAN ISLAND...
...HAVE JOINED FORCES WITH FISHER TIGER. THEY ALWAYS REMAINED UNDERWATER BEFORE...
...SO IT WAS DIFFICULT TO GAUGE THEIR STRENGTH. WE HAVE ALSO...
...CONFIRMED ANOTHER UNIDENTIFIED FISH-MAN WHO'S AS BIG AND STRONG AS TIGER HIMSELF.
THAT'S A PROBLEM.

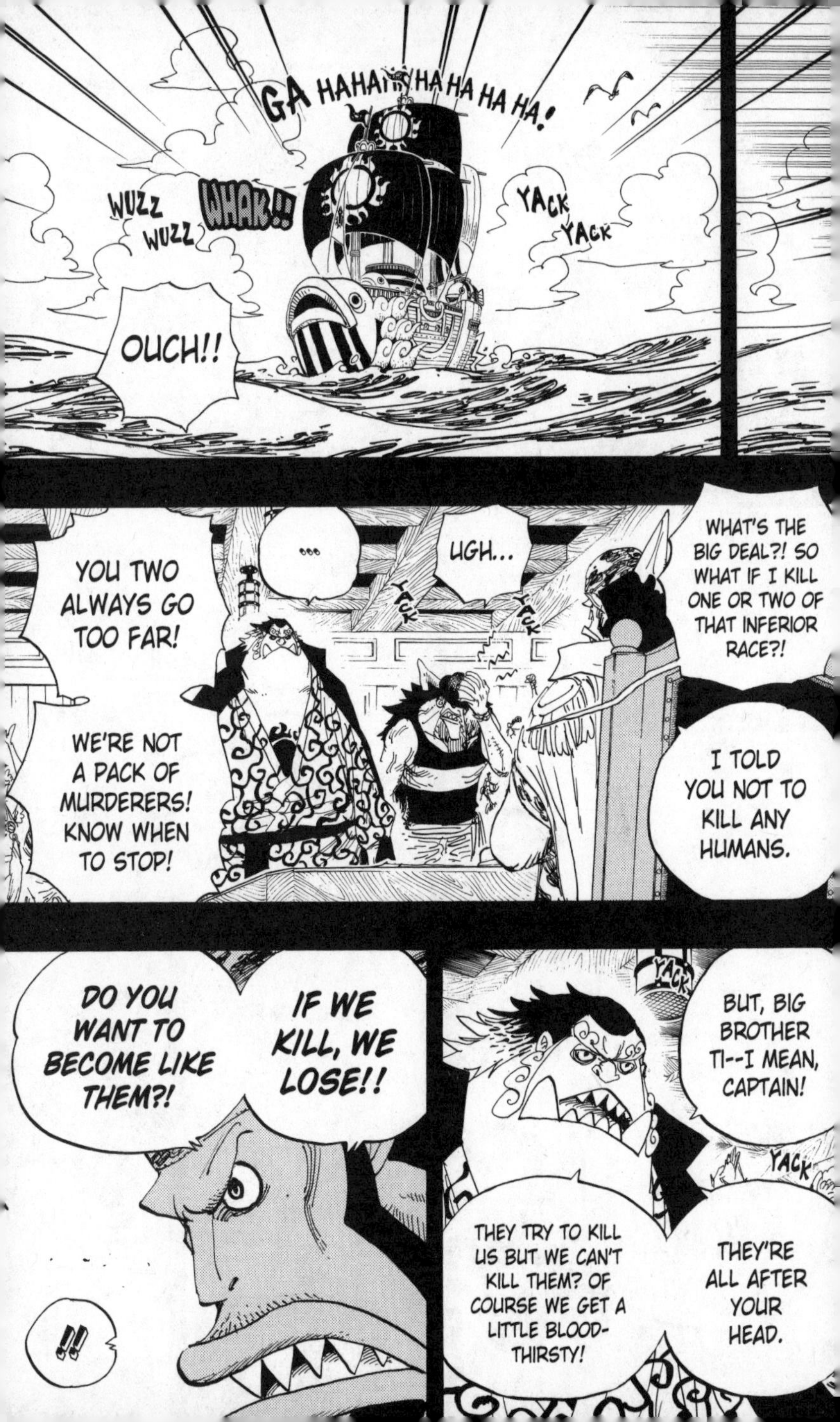
GA HAHAHA HA HA HA!
YACK YACK
WHAK!!
WUZZ WUZZ
OUCH!!
WHAT'S THE BIG DEAL?! SO WHAT IF I KILL ONE OR TWO OF THAT INFERIOR RACE?!
UGH...
YACK
YACK
...
YOU TWO ALWAYS GO TOO FAR!
I TOLD YOU NOT TO KILL ANY HUMANS.
WE'RE NOT A PACK OF MURDERERS! KNOW WHEN TO STOP!
YACK
BUT, BIG BROTHER TI--I MEAN, CAPTAIN!
YACK
THEY'RE ALL AFTER YOUR HEAD.
THEY TRY TO KILL US BUT WE CAN'T KILL THEM? OF COURSE WE GET A LITTLE BLOOD-THIRSTY!
IF WE KILL, WE LOSE!!
DO YOU WANT TO BECOME LIKE THEM?!
!!

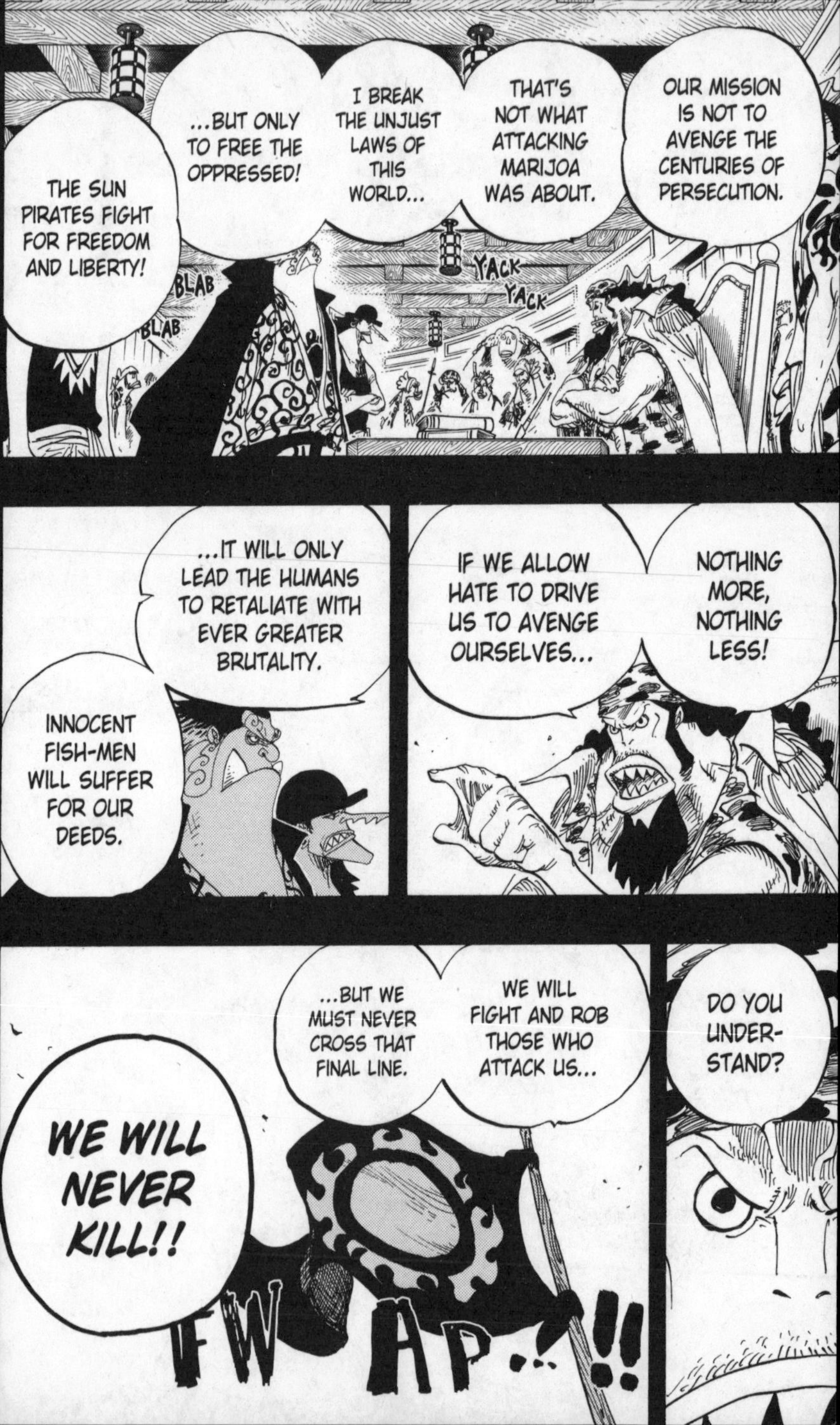
OUR MISSION IS NOT TO AVENGE THE CENTURIES OF PERSECUTION.
THAT'S NOT WHAT ATTACKING MARIJOA WAS ABOUT.
I BREAK THE UNJUST LAWS OF THIS WORLD...
...BUT ONLY TO FREE THE OPPRESSED!
THE SUN PIRATES FIGHT FOR FREEDOM AND LIBERTY!
YACK
YACK
BLAB
BLAB
NOTHING MORE, NOTHING LESS!
IF WE ALLOW HATE TO DRIVE US TO AVENGE OURSELVES...
...IT WILL ONLY LEAD THE HUMANS TO RETALIATE WITH EVER GREATER BRUTALITY.
INNOCENT FISH-MEN WILL SUFFER FOR OUR DEEDS.
DO YOU UNDER-STAND?
WE WILL FIGHT AND ROB THOSE WHO ATTACK US...
...BUT WE MUST NEVER CROSS THAT FINAL LINE.
WE WILL NEVER KILL!!
FWAP..!!

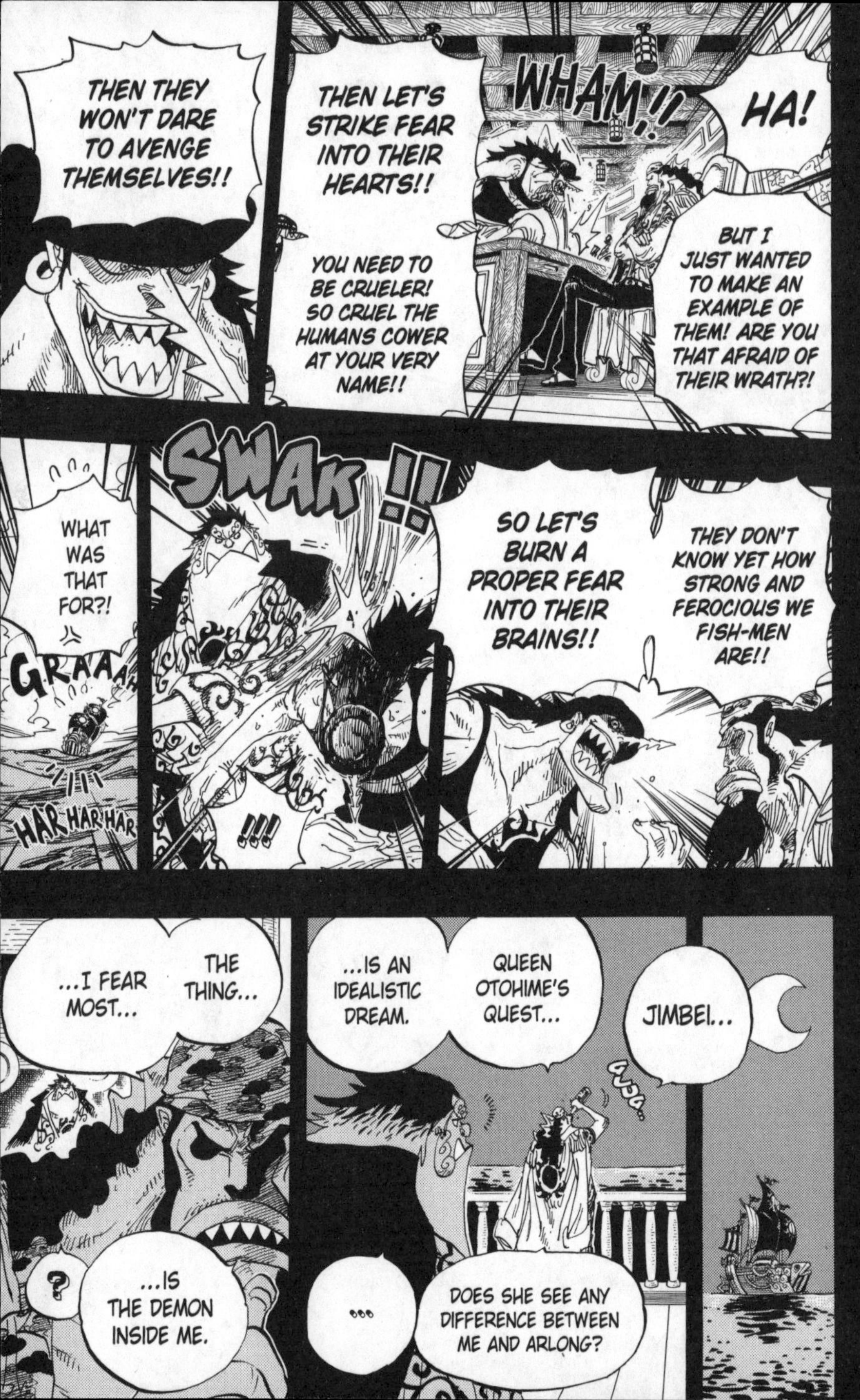
HA!
WHAM!!
BUT I JUST WANTED TO MAKE AN EXAMPLE OF THEM! ARE YOU THAT AFRAID OF THEIR WRATH?!
THEN LET'S STRIKE FEAR INTO THEIR HEARTS!!
YOU NEED TO BE CRUELER! SO CRUEL THE HUMANS COWER AT YOUR VERY NAME!!
THEN THEY WON'T DARE TO AVENGE THEMSELVES!!
THEY DON'T KNOW YET HOW STRONG AND FEROCIOUS WE FISH-MEN ARE!!
SO LET'S BURN A PROPER FEAR INTO THEIR BRAINS!!
SWAK!!
!!!
WHAT WAS THAT FOR?!
GRAAAAH
HAR HAR HAR
JIMBEI...
QUEEN OTOHIME'S QUEST...
...IS AN IDEALISTIC DREAM.
DOES SHE SEE ANY DIFFERENCE BETWEEN ME AND ARLONG?
...
THE THING...
...I FEAR MOST...
?
...IS THE DEMON INSIDE ME.

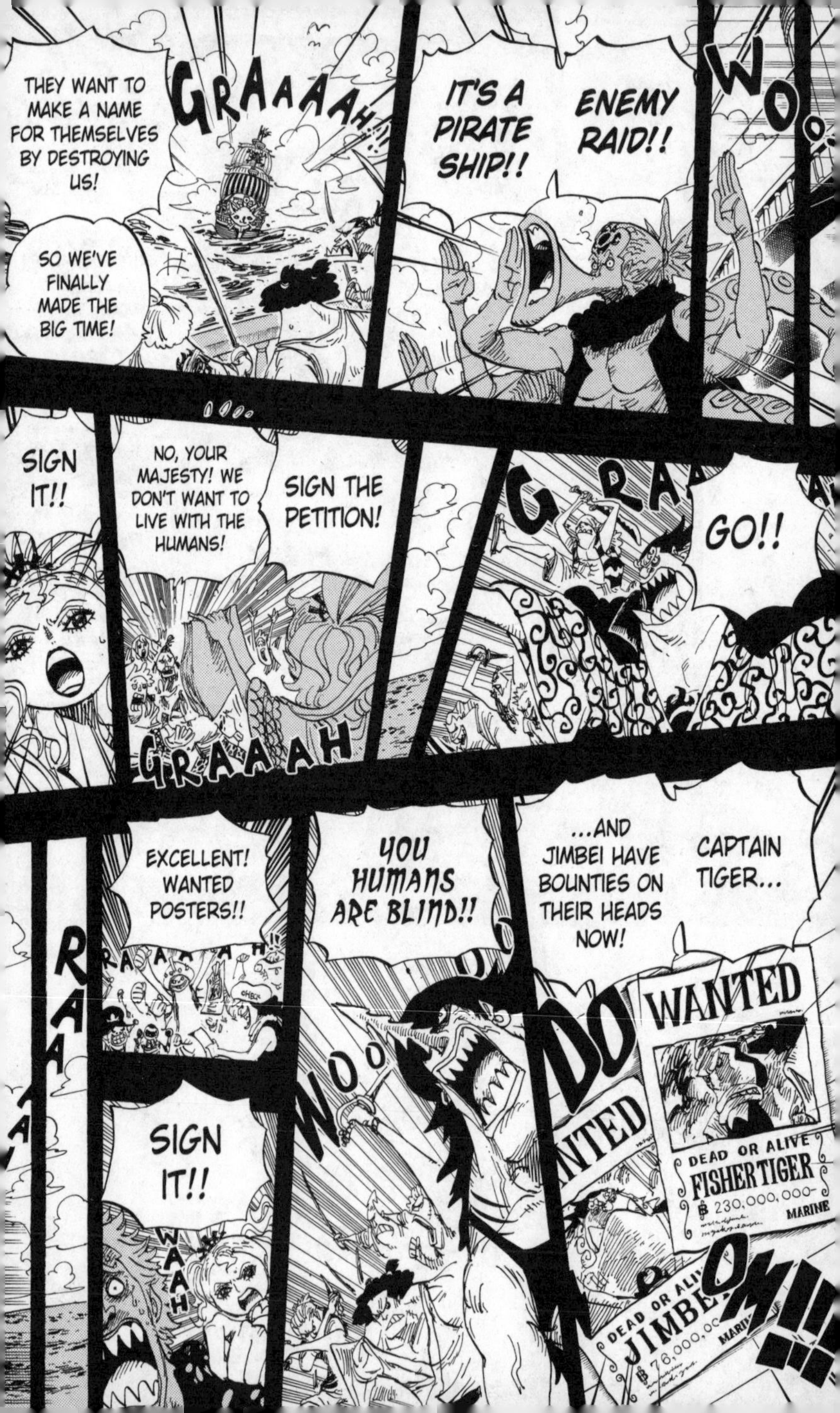
WOO...
ENEMY RAID!!
IT'S A PIRATE SHIP!!
GRAAAAH!!
THEY WANT TO MAKE A NAME FOR THEMSELVES BY DESTROYING US!
SO WE'VE FINALLY MADE THE BIG TIME!
GO!!
SIGN THE PETITION!
NO, YOUR MAJESTY! WE DON'T WANT TO LIVE WITH THE HUMANS!
GRAAAH
SIGN IT!!
CAPTAIN TIGER...
...AND JIMBEI HAVE BOUNTIES ON THEIR HEADS NOW!
WANTED
DEAD OR ALIVE
FISHER TIGER
฿230,000,000-
MARINE
DEAD OR ALIVE
DO
OM!!!
YOU HUMANS ARE BLIND!!
WOO
EXCELLENT! WANTED POSTERS!!
RAAAAH!!
SIGN IT!!
WAAH
RAAA

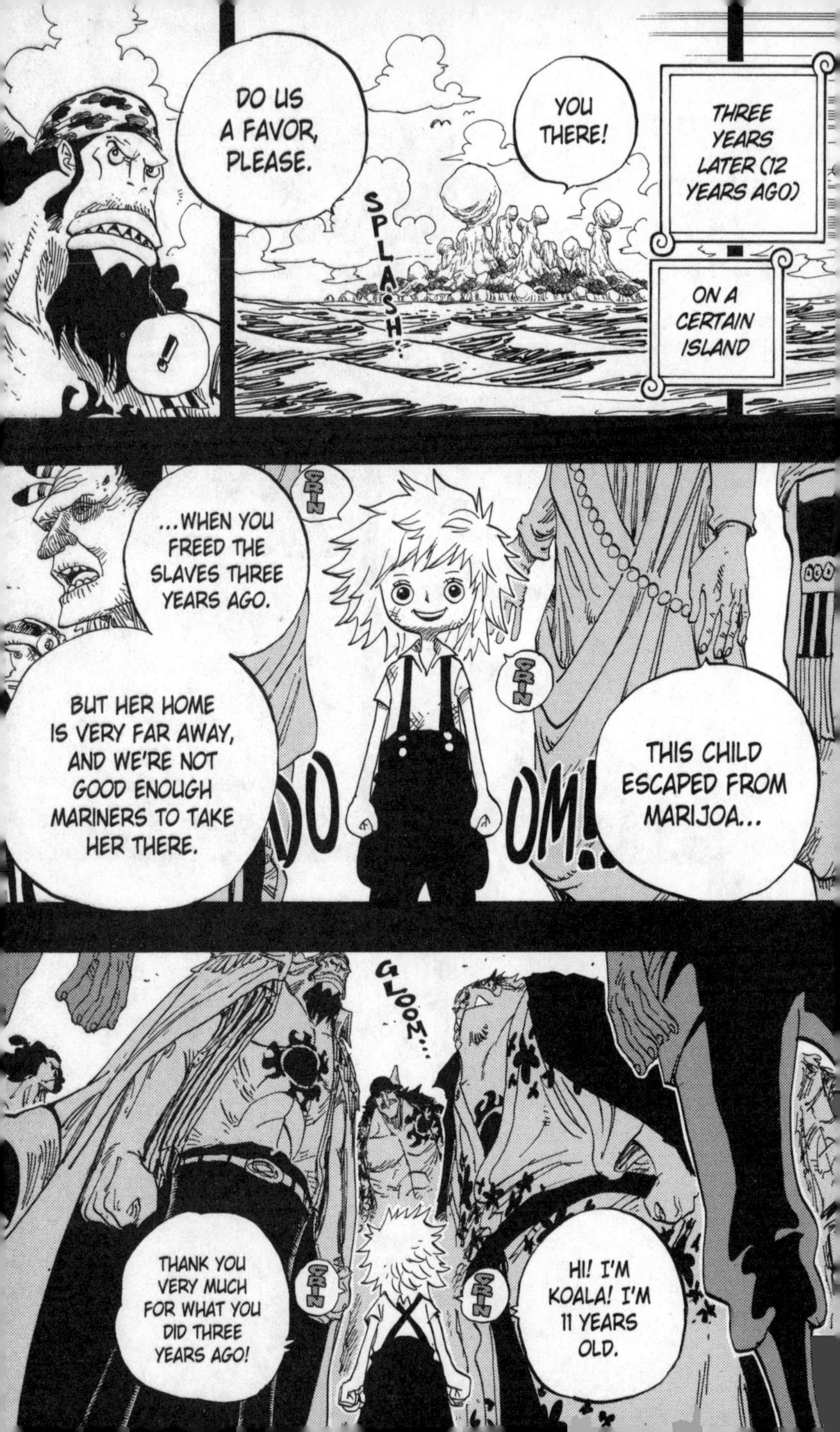
THREE YEARS LATER (12 YEARS AGO)
ON A CERTAIN ISLAND
YOU THERE!
SPLASH!
DO US A FAVOR, PLEASE.
!
GRIN
THIS CHILD ESCAPED FROM MARIJOA...
DOOM!!
...WHEN YOU FREED THE SLAVES THREE YEARS AGO.
BUT HER HOME IS VERY FAR AWAY, AND WE'RE NOT GOOD ENOUGH MARINERS TO TAKE HER THERE.
GRIN
GLOOM...
HI! I'M KOALA! I'M 11 YEARS OLD.
GRIN
THANK YOU VERY MUCH FOR WHAT YOU DID THREE YEARS AGO!

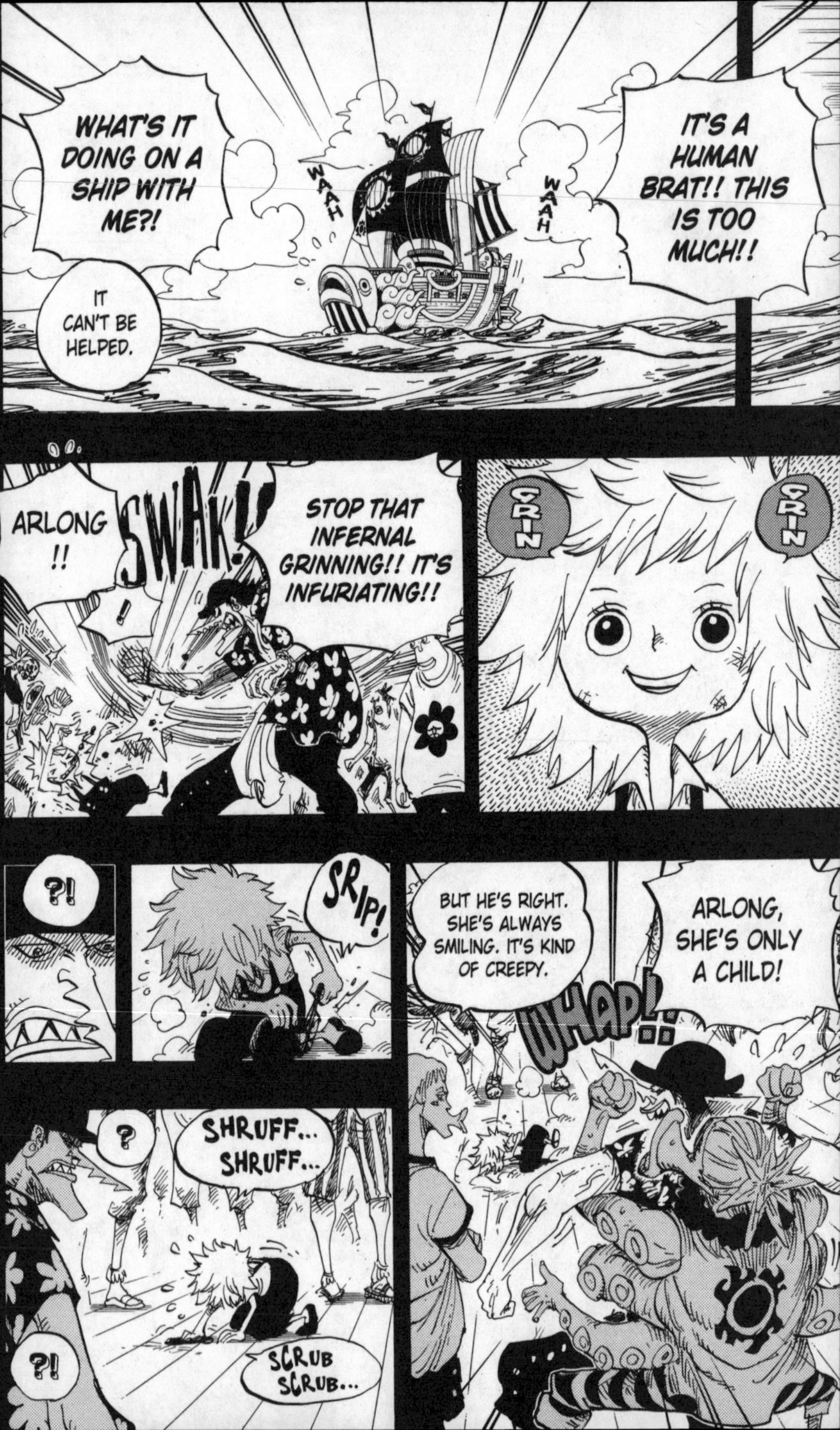
IT'S A HUMAN BRAT!! THIS IS TOO MUCH!!
WAAH
WAAH
WHAT'S IT DOING ON A SHIP WITH ME?!
IT CAN'T BE HELPED.
GRIN
GRIN
STOP THAT INFERNAL GRINNING!! IT'S INFURIATING!!
SWAK!
ARLONG !!
!
ARLONG, SHE'S ONLY A CHILD!
BUT HE'S RIGHT. SHE'S ALWAYS SMILING. IT'S KIND OF CREEPY.
WHAP!!
SRIP!
?!
SHRUFF... SHRUFF...
?
SCRUB SCRUB...
?!

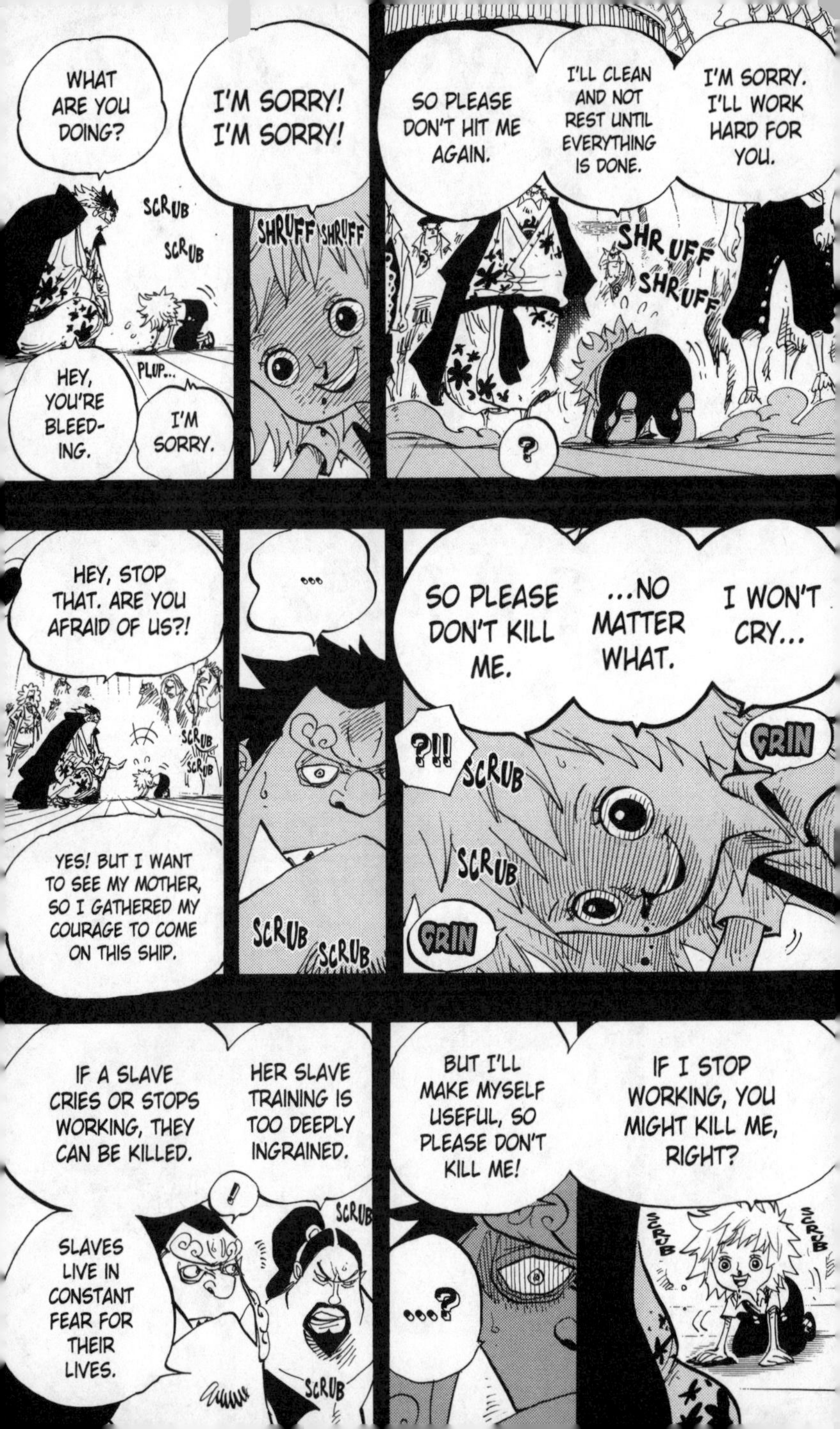

I'M SORRY. I'LL WORK HARD FOR YOU.
I'LL CLEAN AND NOT REST UNTIL EVERYTHING IS DONE.
SO PLEASE DON'T HIT ME AGAIN.
SHRUFF
SHRUFF
?
I'M SORRY! I'M SORRY!
SHRUFF SHRUFF
WHAT ARE YOU DOING?
SCRUB
SCRUB
PLUP...
I'M SORRY.
HEY, YOU'RE BLEEDING.
I WON'T CRY...
...NO MATTER WHAT.
SO PLEASE DON'T KILL ME.
GRIN
?!!
SCRUB
SCRUB
GRIN
...
SCRUB
SCRUB
HEY, STOP THAT. ARE YOU AFRAID OF US?!
SCRUB
SCRUB
YES! BUT I WANT TO SEE MY MOTHER, SO I GATHERED MY COURAGE TO COME ON THIS SHIP.
IF I STOP WORKING, YOU MIGHT KILL ME, RIGHT?
BUT I'LL MAKE MYSELF USEFUL, SO PLEASE DON'T KILL ME!
SCRUB
SCRUB
...?
HER SLAVE TRAINING IS TOO DEEPLY INGRAINED.
IF A SLAVE CRIES OR STOPS WORKING, THEY CAN BE KILLED.
SCRUB
!
SLAVES LIVE IN CONSTANT FEAR FOR THEIR LIVES.
SCRUB

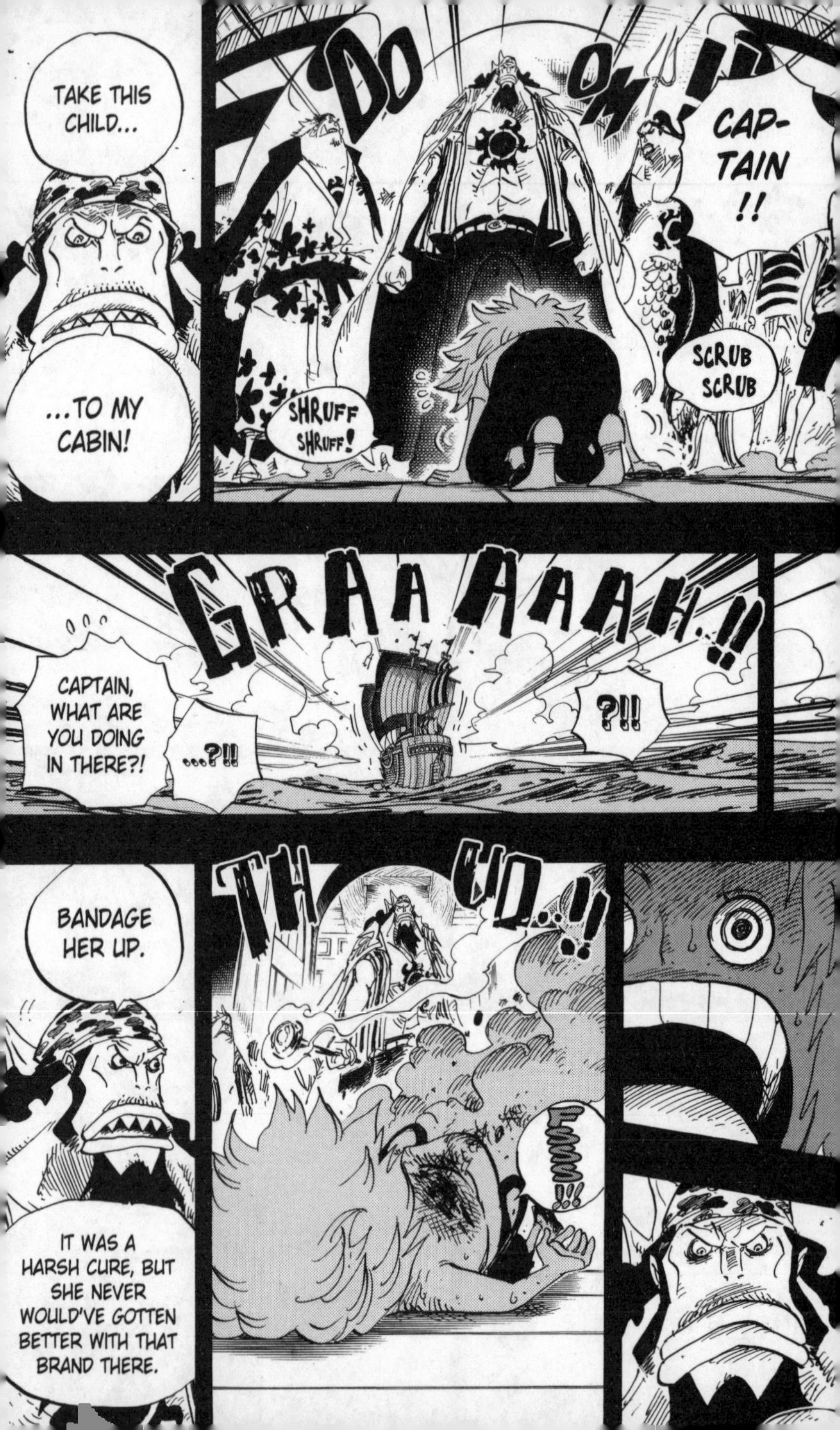
DOOM!!
CAP-TAIN!!
SCRUB SCRUB
SHRUFF SHRUFF!
TAKE THIS CHILD...
...TO MY CABIN!
GRAAAAAH..!!
?!!
...?!!
CAPTAIN, WHAT ARE YOU DOING IN THERE?!
THUD..!!
FSSS!!!
BANDAGE HER UP.
IT WAS A HARSH CURE, BUT SHE NEVER WOULD'VE GOTTEN BETTER WITH THAT BRAND THERE.

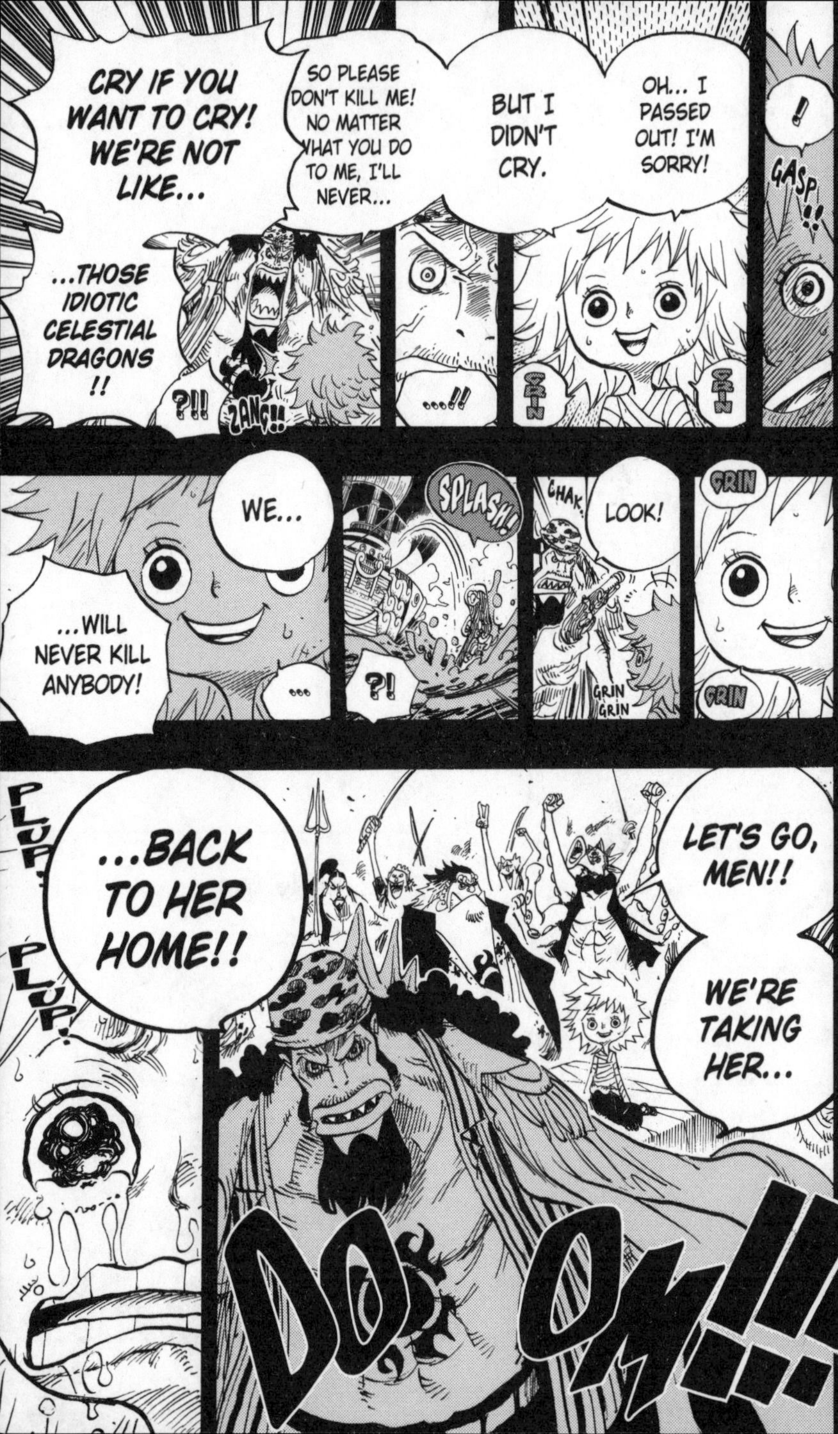
!
GASP!!
OH... I PASSED OUT! I'M SORRY!
GRIN
GRIN
BUT I DIDN'T CRY.
...!!
SO PLEASE DON'T KILL ME! NO MATTER WHAT YOU DO TO ME, I'LL NEVER...
CRY IF YOU WANT TO CRY! WE'RE NOT LIKE...
...THOSE IDIOTIC CELESTIAL DRAGONS!!
?!!
ZANG!!
GRIN
GRIN
CHAK
LOOK!
GRIN GRIN
SPLASH!!
?!
WE...
...WILL NEVER KILL ANYBODY!
...
LET'S GO, MEN!!
WE'RE TAKING HER...
...BACK TO HER HOME!!
DOOM!!!
PLUP!
PLUP!

Chapter 623:

FISHER TIGER THE PIRATE

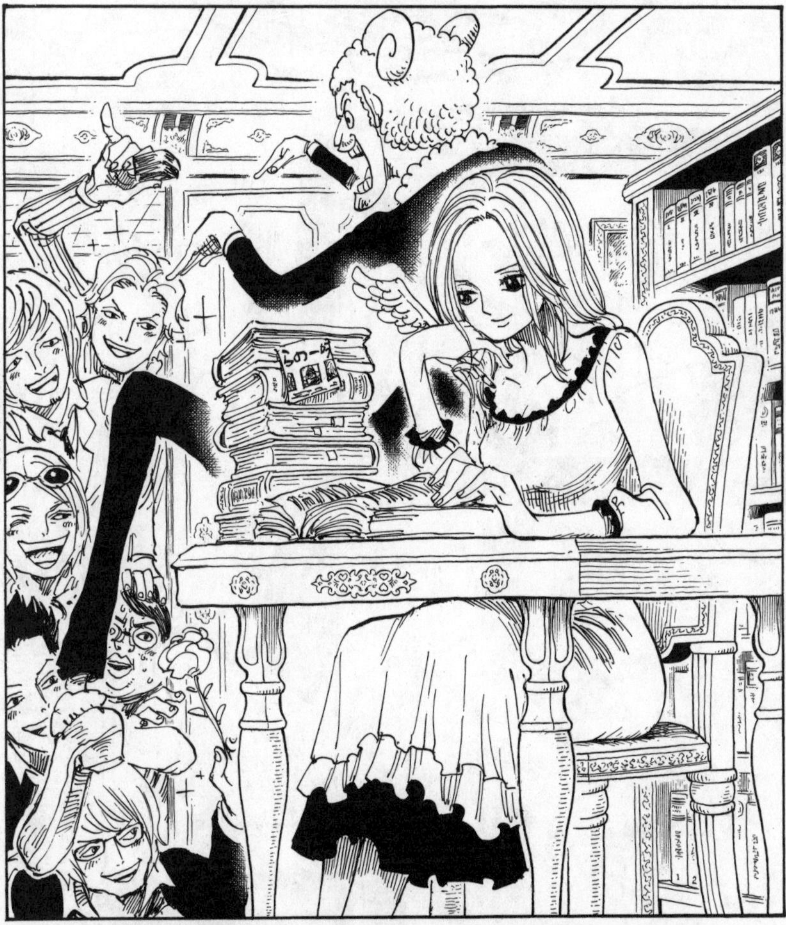

*STRAW HAT

DECKS OF THE WORLD, VOL. 9: "SYRUP VILLAGE, KAYA THE MEDICAL STUDENT"

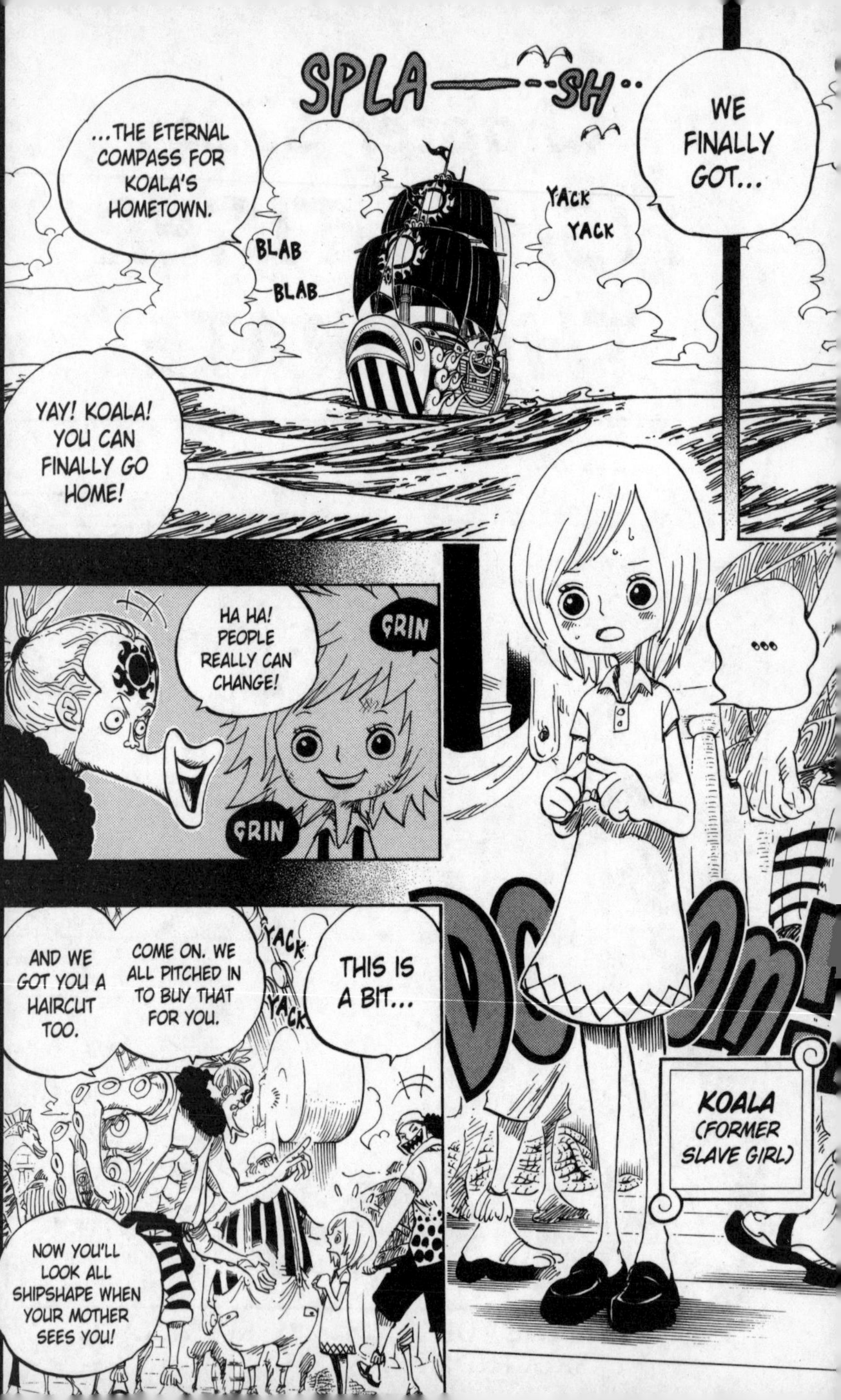
WE FINALLY GOT...
SPLA——SH
...THE ETERNAL COMPASS FOR KOALA'S HOMETOWN.
YACK YACK
BLAB BLAB
YAY! KOALA! YOU CAN FINALLY GO HOME!
...
DOOM
KOALA (FORMER SLAVE GIRL)
HA HA! PEOPLE REALLY CAN CHANGE!
GRIN
GRIN
THIS IS A BIT...
YACK YACK
COME ON. WE ALL PITCHED IN TO BUY THAT FOR YOU.
AND WE GOT YOU A HAIRCUT TOO.
NOW YOU'LL LOOK ALL SHIPSHAPE WHEN YOUR MOTHER SEES YOU!

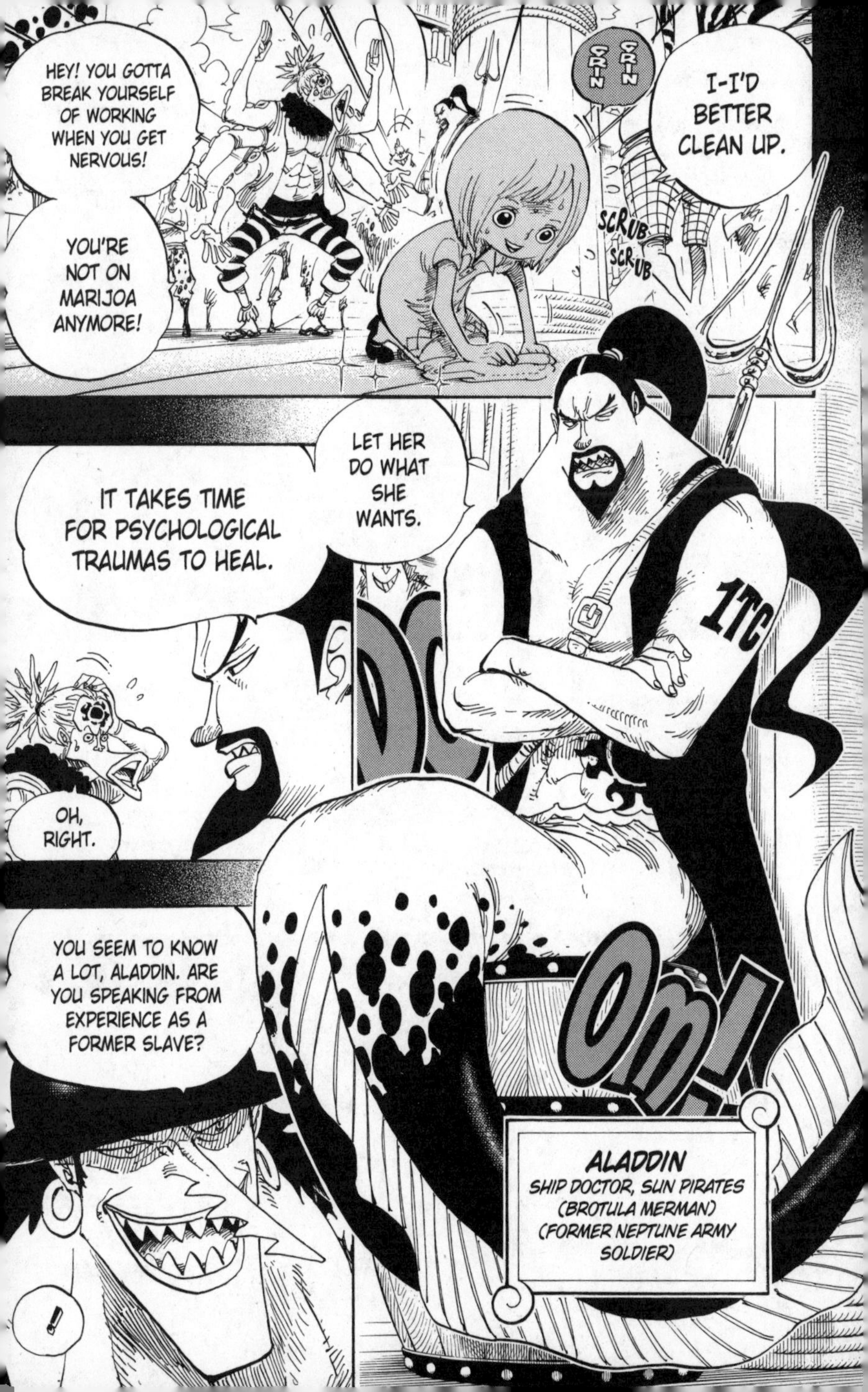

GRIN GRIN
I-I'D BETTER CLEAN UP.
SCRUB SCRUB
HEY! YOU GOTTA BREAK YOURSELF OF WORKING WHEN YOU GET NERVOUS!
YOU'RE NOT ON MARIJOA ANYMORE!
LET HER DO WHAT SHE WANTS.
IT TAKES TIME FOR PSYCHOLOGICAL TRAUMAS TO HEAL.
OH, RIGHT.
DOOM!
ALADDIN
SHIP DOCTOR, SUN PIRATES
(BROTULA MERMAN)
(FORMER NEPTUNE ARMY SOLDIER)
YOU SEEM TO KNOW A LOT, ALADDIN. ARE YOU SPEAKING FROM EXPERIENCE AS A FORMER SLAVE?
!

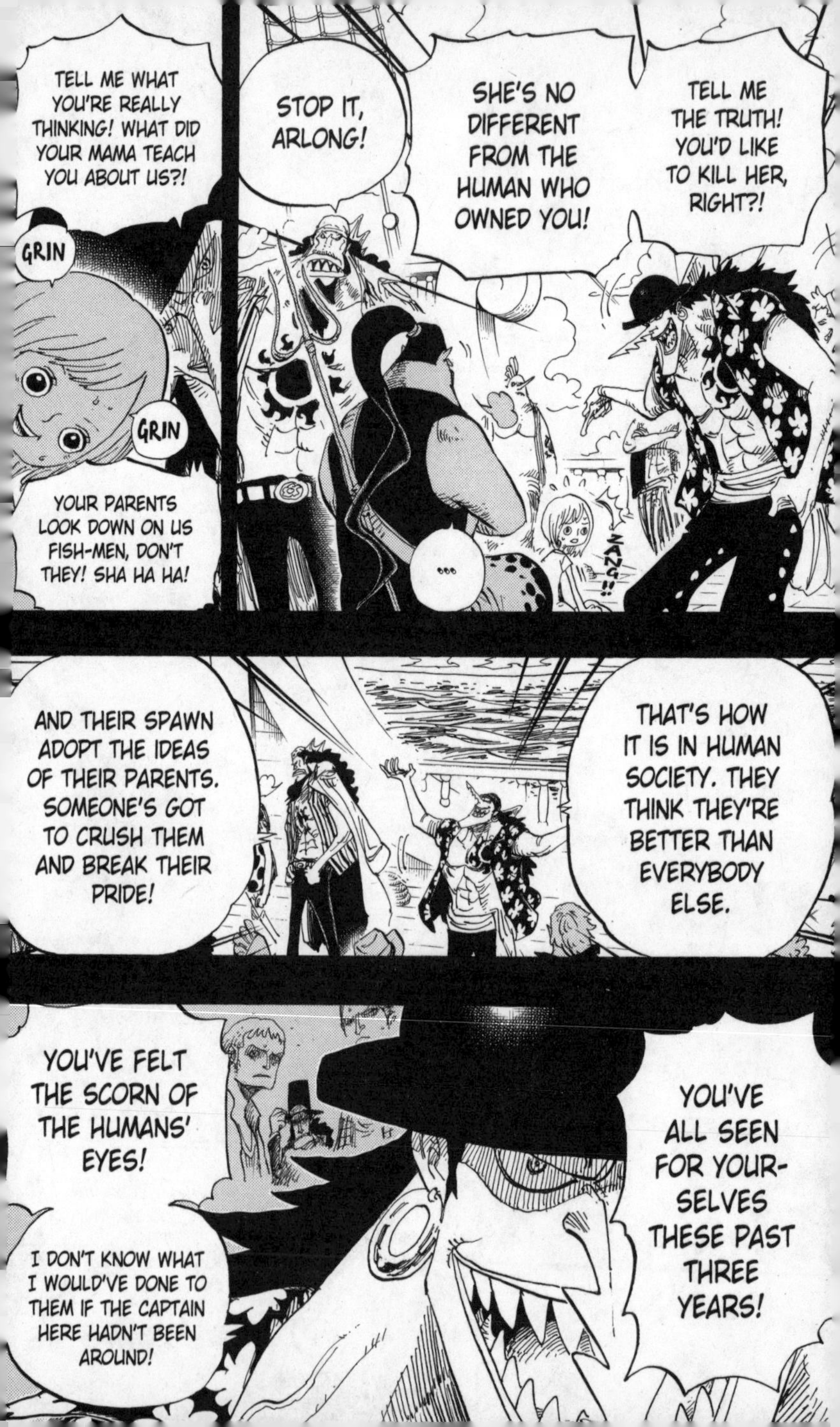
TELL ME THE TRUTH! YOU'D LIKE TO KILL HER, RIGHT?!
SHE'S NO DIFFERENT FROM THE HUMAN WHO OWNED YOU!
STOP IT, ARLONG!
ZANG!!
...
TELL ME WHAT YOU'RE REALLY THINKING! WHAT DID YOUR MAMA TEACH YOU ABOUT US?!
GRIN
GRIN
YOUR PARENTS LOOK DOWN ON US FISH-MEN, DON'T THEY! SHA HA HA!
THAT'S HOW IT IS IN HUMAN SOCIETY. THEY THINK THEY'RE BETTER THAN EVERYBODY ELSE.
AND THEIR SPAWN ADOPT THE IDEAS OF THEIR PARENTS. SOMEONE'S GOT TO CRUSH THEM AND BREAK THEIR PRIDE!
YOU'VE ALL SEEN FOR YOUR-SELVES THESE PAST THREE YEARS!
YOU'VE FELT THE SCORN OF THE HUMANS' EYES!
I DON'T KNOW WHAT I WOULD'VE DONE TO THEM IF THE CAPTAIN HERE HADN'T BEEN AROUND!

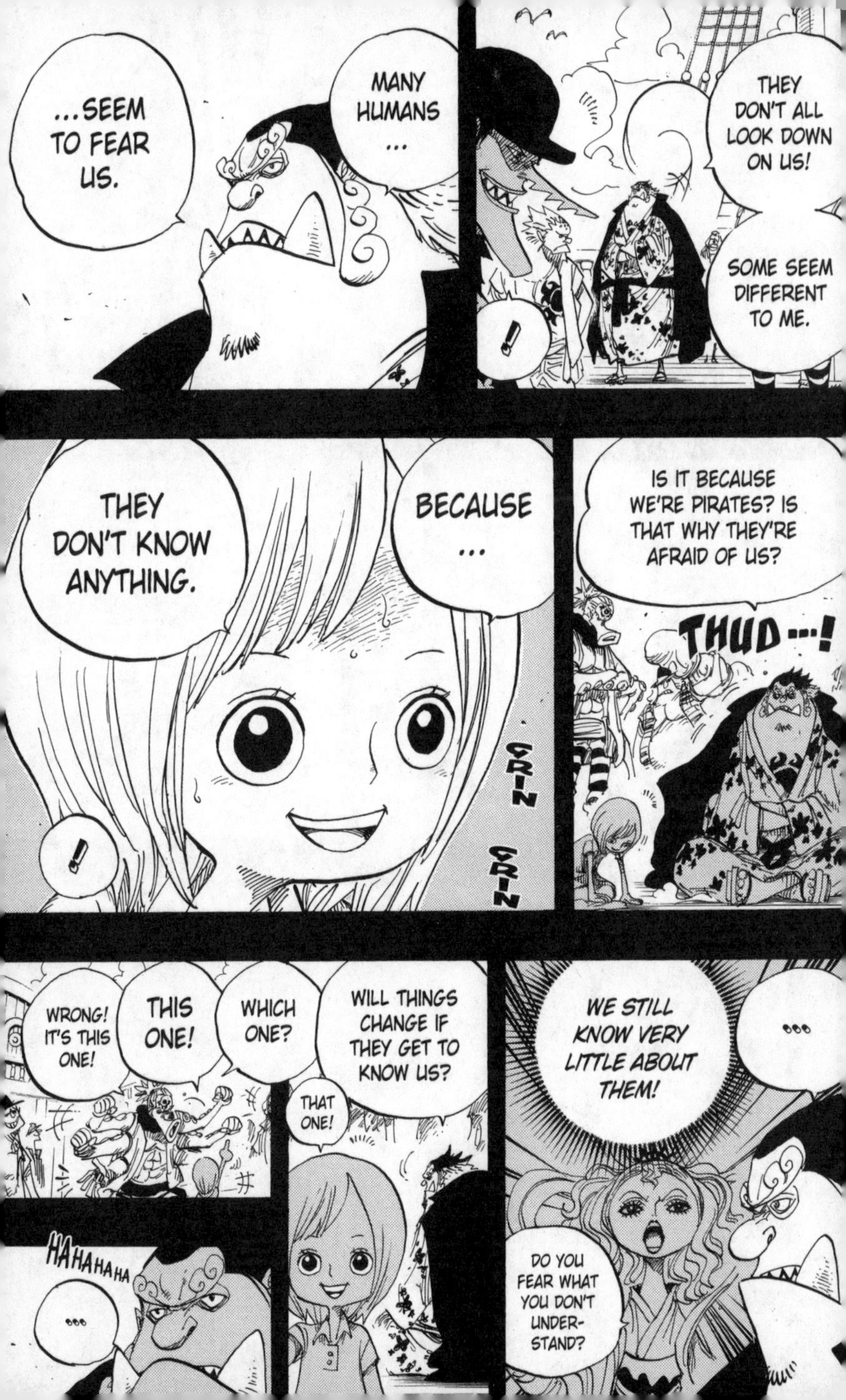
THEY DON'T ALL LOOK DOWN ON US!
SOME SEEM DIFFERENT TO ME.
!
MANY HUMANS ...
...SEEM TO FEAR US.
IS IT BECAUSE WE'RE PIRATES? IS THAT WHY THEY'RE AFRAID OF US?
THUD...!
BECAUSE ...
THEY DON'T KNOW ANYTHING.
!
GRIN
GRIN
...
WE STILL KNOW VERY LITTLE ABOUT THEM!
DO YOU FEAR WHAT YOU DON'T UNDER-STAND?
WILL THINGS CHANGE IF THEY GET TO KNOW US?
THAT ONE!
WHICH ONE?
THIS ONE!
WRONG! IT'S THIS ONE!
HAHAHAHA
...

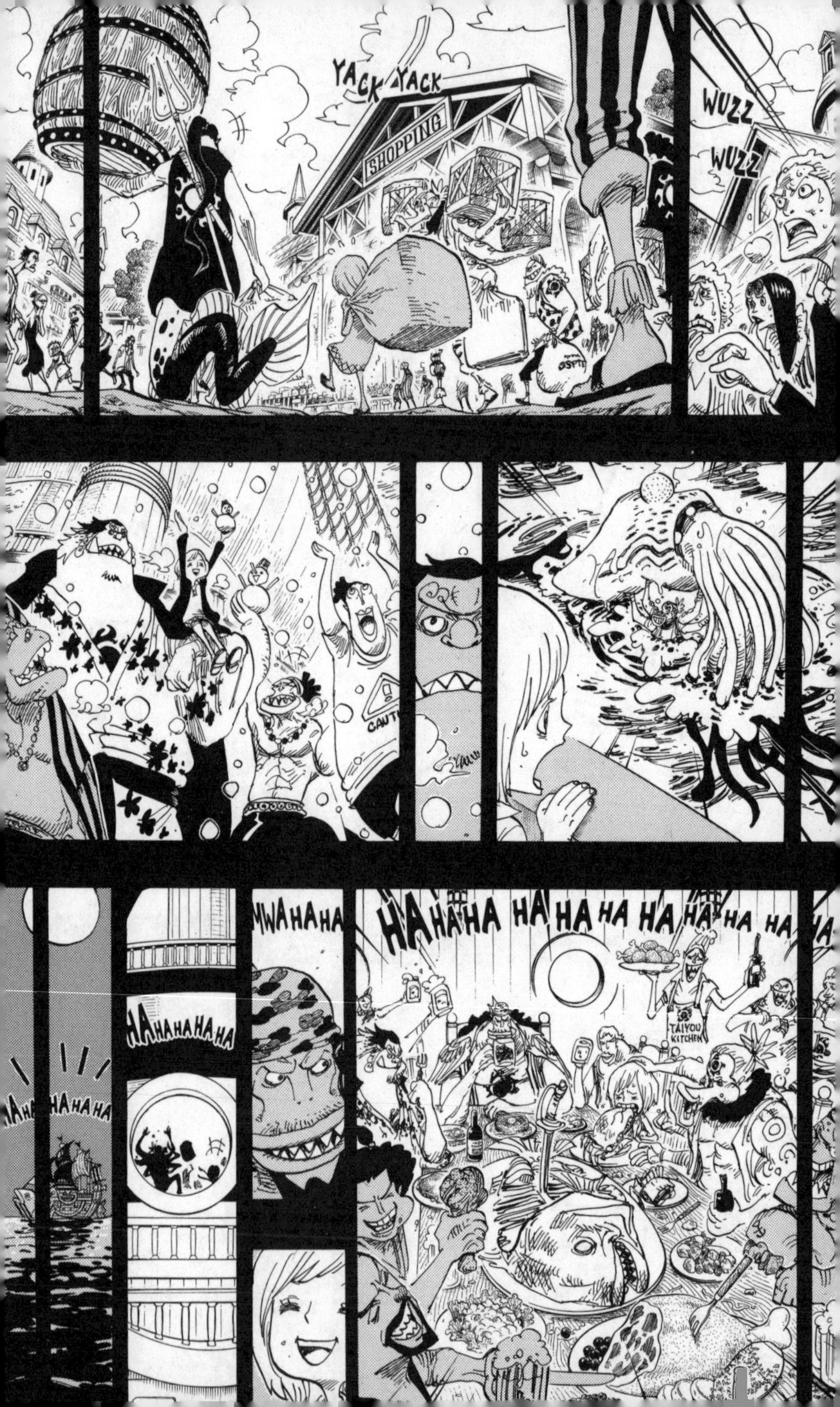

WUZZ
WUZZ
YACK YACK
SHOPPING
HA HA HA HA HA HA HA HA HA HA HA HA
TAIYOU KITCHEN
MWAHAHA
HAHAHAHAHA
AHAHAHAHA

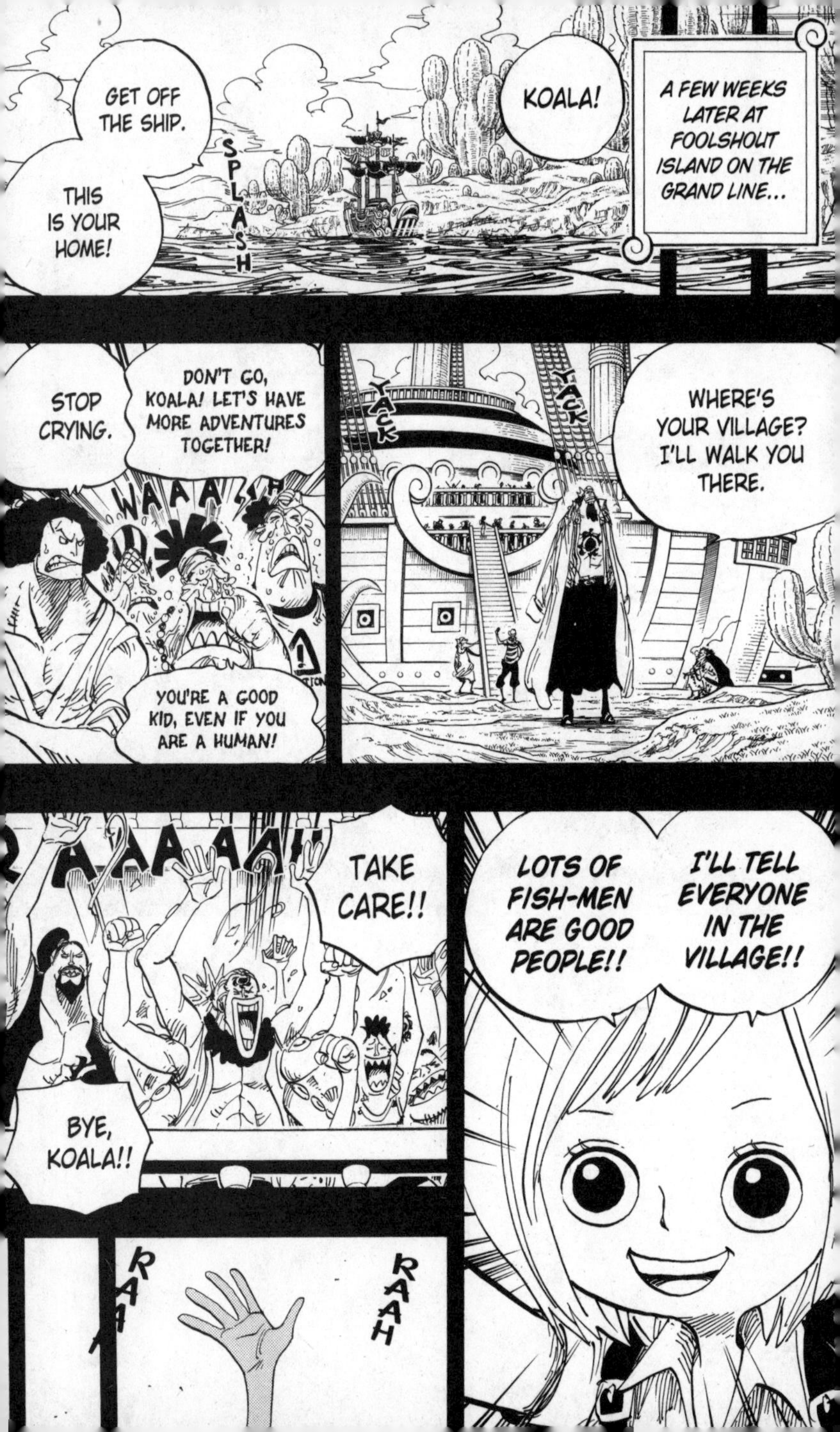

A FEW WEEKS LATER AT FOOLSHOUT ISLAND ON THE GRAND LINE...
KOALA!
SPLASH
GET OFF THE SHIP.
THIS IS YOUR HOME!
YACK
YACK
WHERE'S YOUR VILLAGE? I'LL WALK YOU THERE.
DON'T GO, KOALA! LET'S HAVE MORE ADVENTURES TOGETHER!
STOP CRYING.
YOU'RE A GOOD KID, EVEN IF YOU ARE A HUMAN!
I'LL TELL EVERYONE IN THE VILLAGE!!
LOTS OF FISH-MEN ARE GOOD PEOPLE!!
TAKE CARE!!
BYE, KOALA!!
RAAH
RAAH

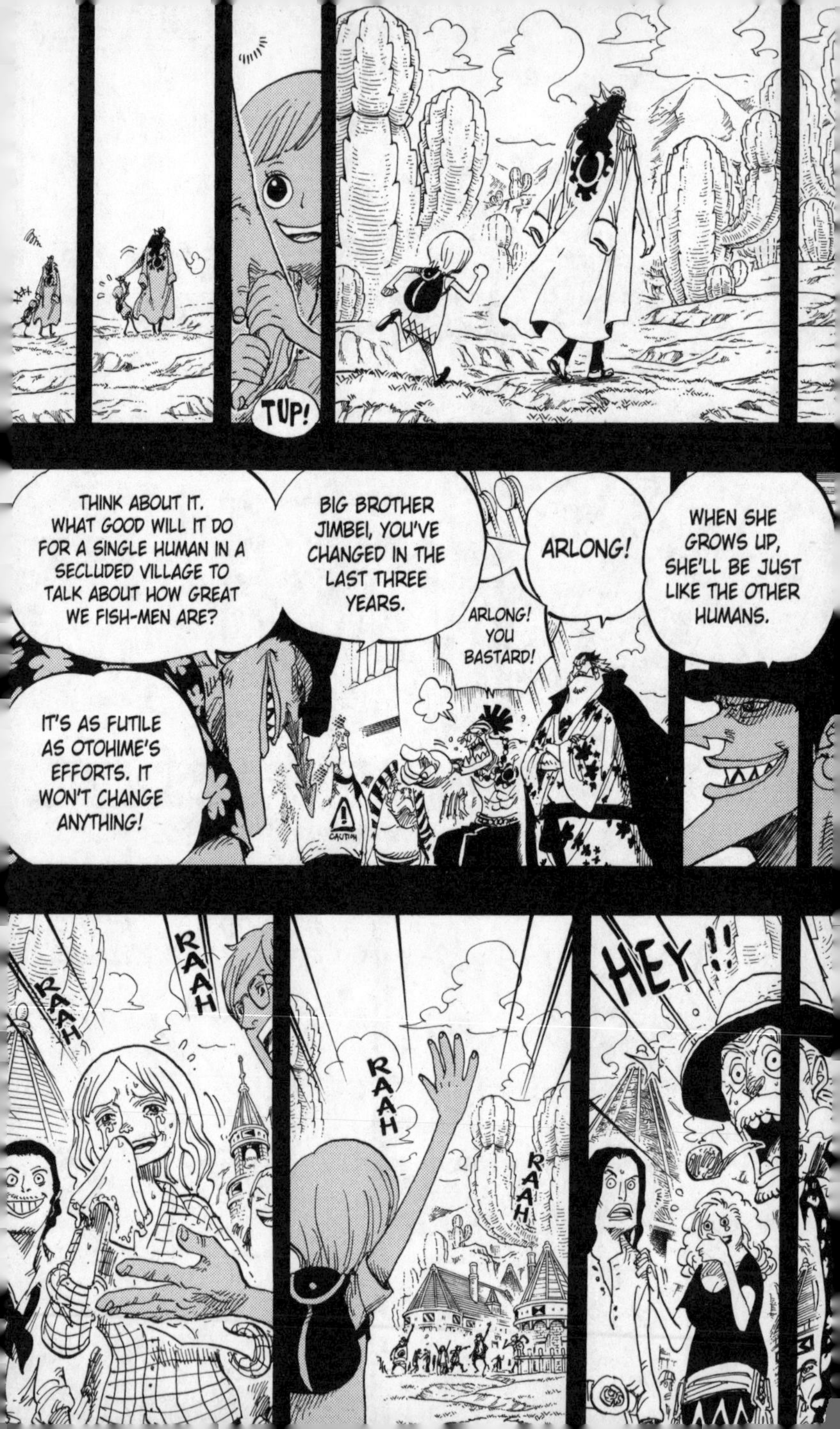
TUP!
WHEN SHE GROWS UP, SHE'LL BE JUST LIKE THE OTHER HUMANS.
ARLONG!
BIG BROTHER JIMBEI, YOU'VE CHANGED IN THE LAST THREE YEARS.
ARLONG! YOU BASTARD!
THINK ABOUT IT. WHAT GOOD WILL IT DO FOR A SINGLE HUMAN IN A SECLUDED VILLAGE TO TALK ABOUT HOW GREAT WE FISH-MEN ARE?
IT'S AS FUTILE AS OTOHIME'S EFFORTS. IT WON'T CHANGE ANYTHING!
HEY!!
RAAH
RAAH
RAAH
RAAH

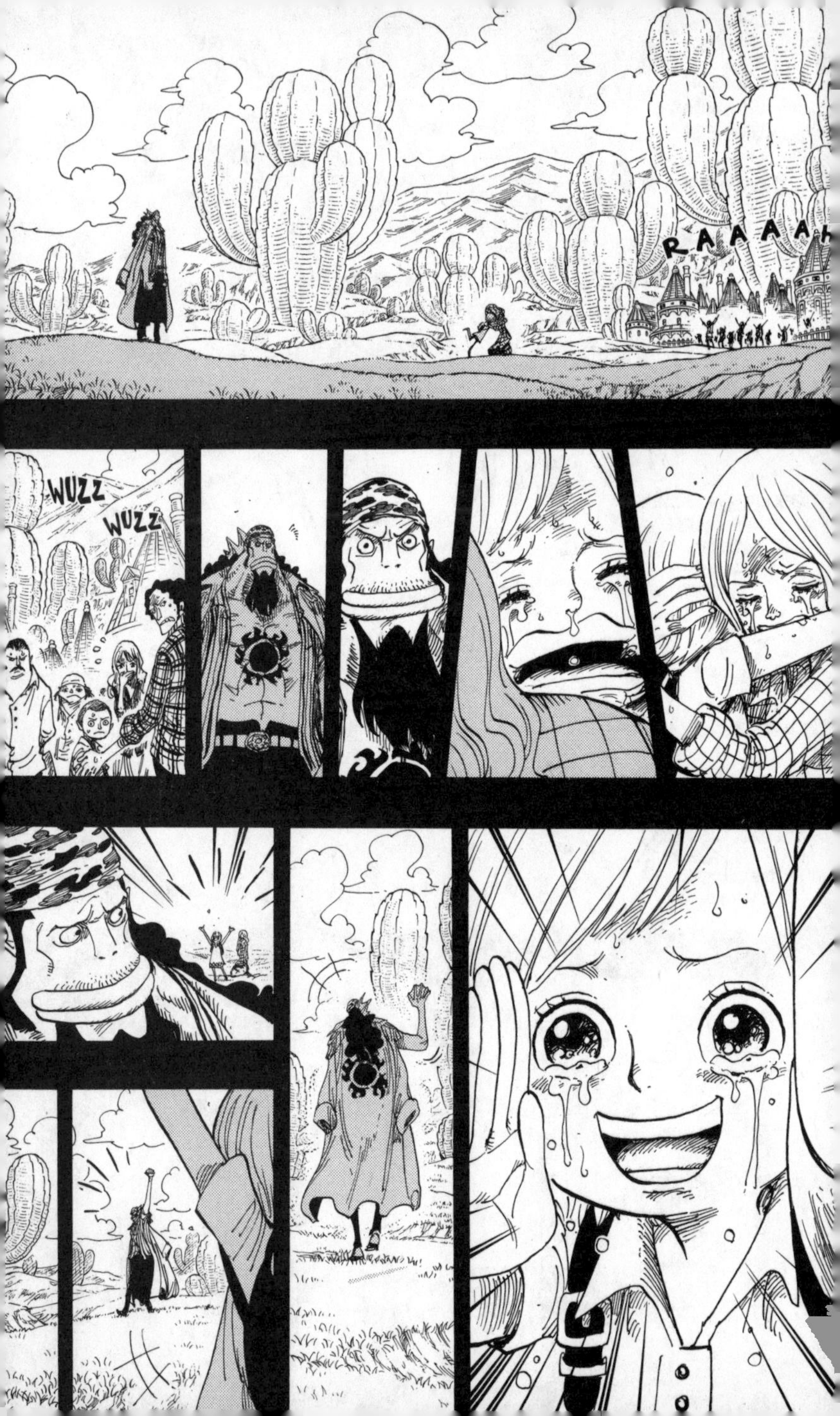
RAAAAH
WUZZ
WUZZ

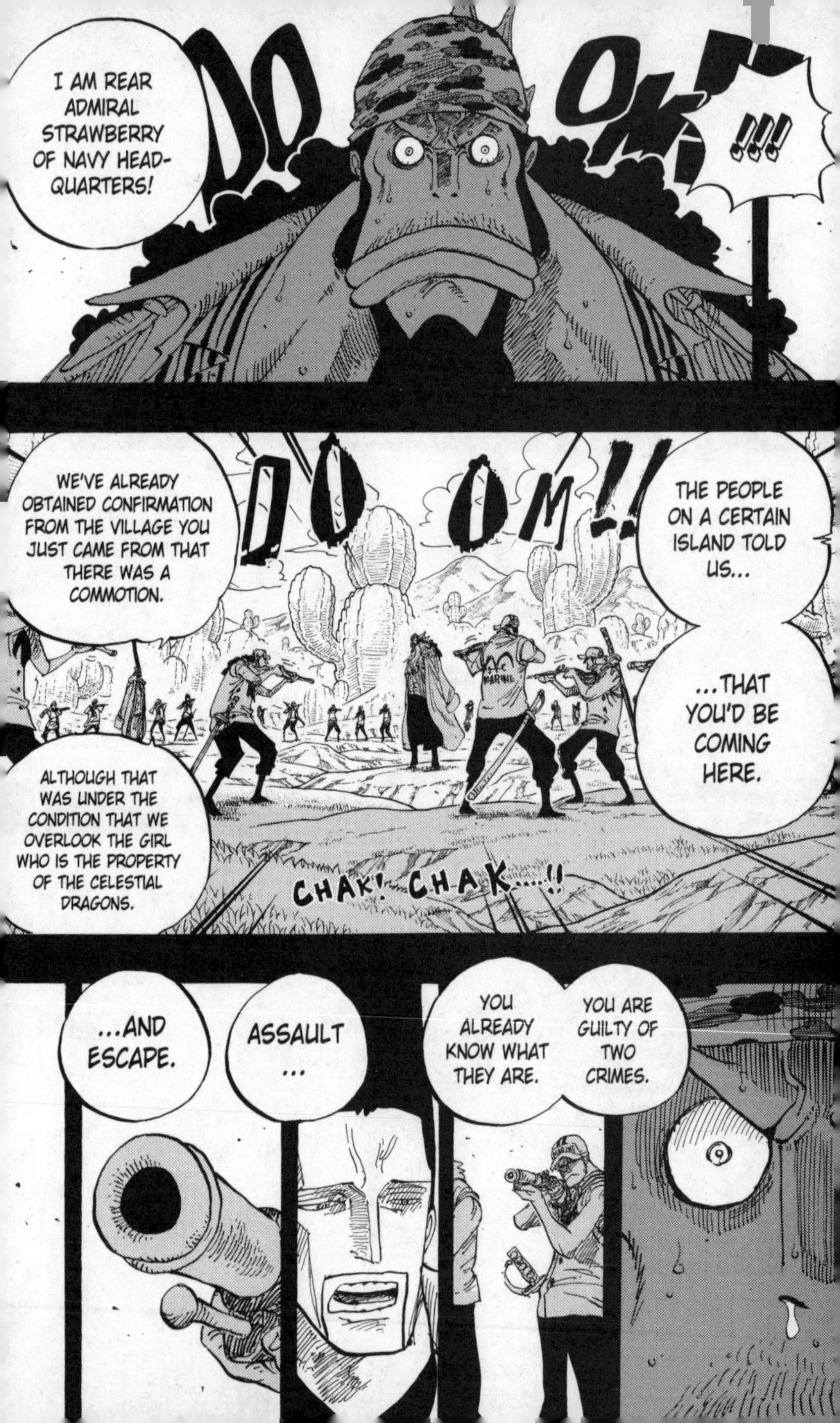
DOOK!!!
I AM REAR ADMIRAL STRAWBERRY OF NAVY HEAD-QUARTERS!
DOOM!!
THE PEOPLE ON A CERTAIN ISLAND TOLD US...
...THAT YOU'D BE COMING HERE.
WE'VE ALREADY OBTAINED CONFIRMATION FROM THE VILLAGE YOU JUST CAME FROM THAT THERE WAS A COMMOTION.
ALTHOUGH THAT WAS UNDER THE CONDITION THAT WE OVERLOOK THE GIRL WHO IS THE PROPERTY OF THE CELESTIAL DRAGONS.
CHAK! CHAK...!!
YOU ARE GUILTY OF TWO CRIMES.
YOU ALREADY KNOW WHAT THEY ARE.
ASSAULT...
...AND ESCAPE.

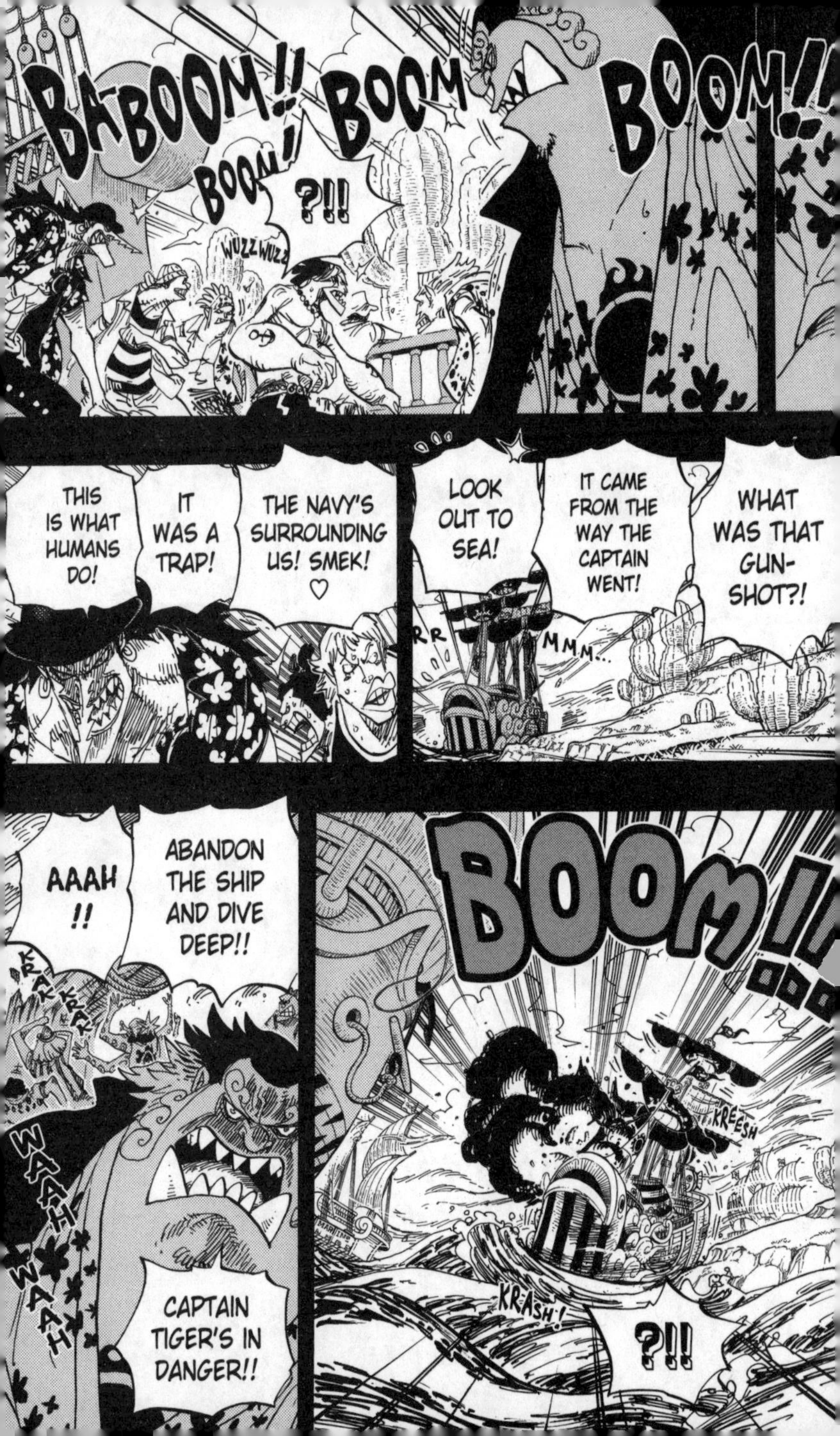
BOOM!!
BOOM
BA-BOOM!!
BOOM!!
?!!
WUZZWUZZ
WHAT WAS THAT GUN-SHOT?!
IT CAME FROM THE WAY THE CAPTAIN WENT!
LOOK OUT TO SEA!
RR
MMM...
THE NAVY'S SURROUNDING US! SMEK! ♡
IT WAS A TRAP!
THIS IS WHAT HUMANS DO!
BOOM!!
KREESH
KRASH!
?!!
ABANDON THE SHIP AND DIVE DEEP!!
AAAH!!
KRAK
KRAK
WAAAH
WAAAH
CAPTAIN TIGER'S IN DANGER!!

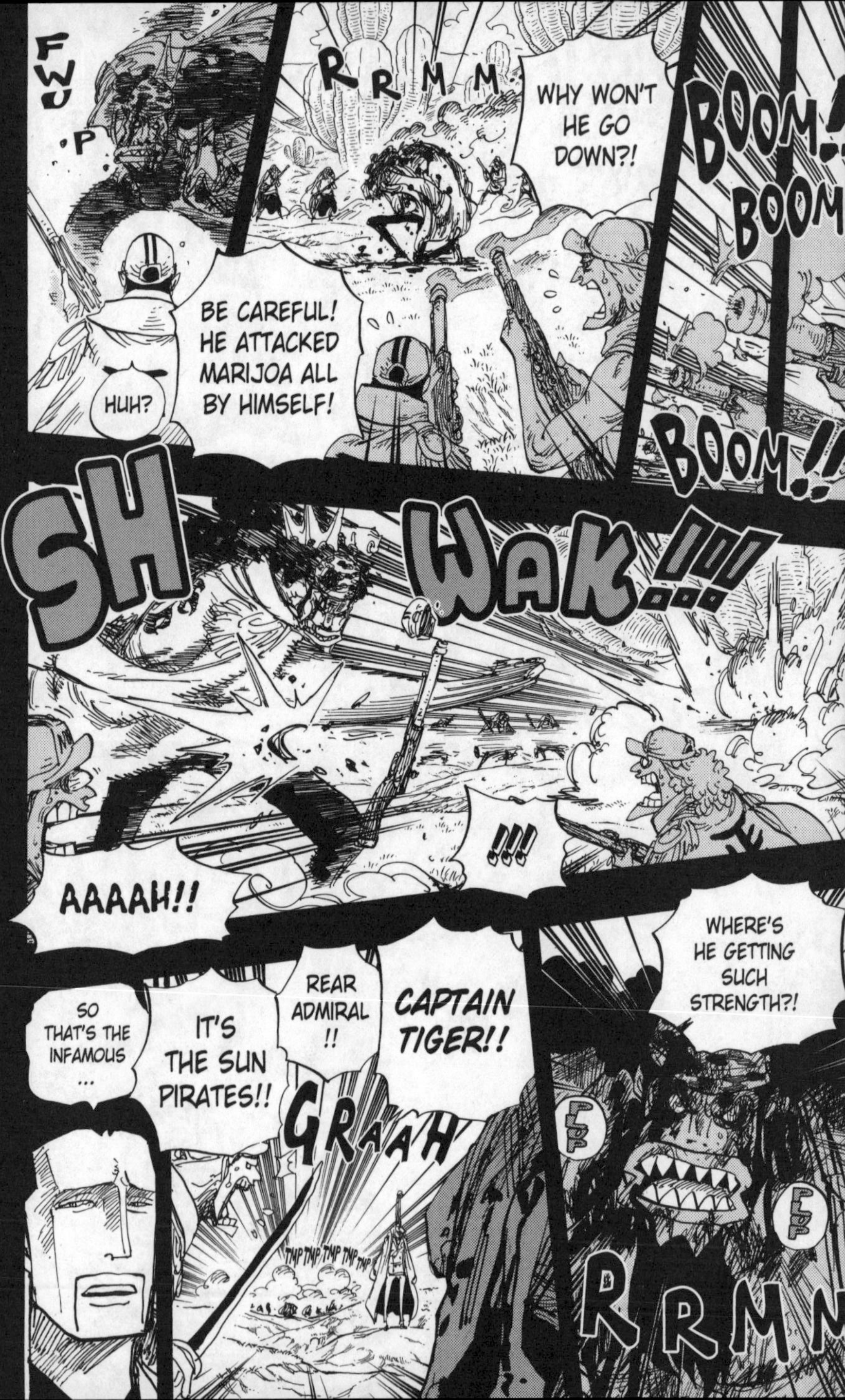
BOOM!!
BOOM
BOOM!!
RRMM
WHY WON'T HE GO DOWN?!
BE CAREFUL! HE ATTACKED MARIJOA ALL BY HIMSELF!
FWUP
HUH?
SHWAK!!!
!!!
AAAAH!!
WHERE'S HE GETTING SUCH STRENGTH?!
RRM
CAPTAIN TIGER!!
REAR ADMIRAL!!
IT'S THE SUN PIRATES!!
SO THAT'S THE INFAMOUS...
GRAAH
TMP TMP TMP TMP TMP

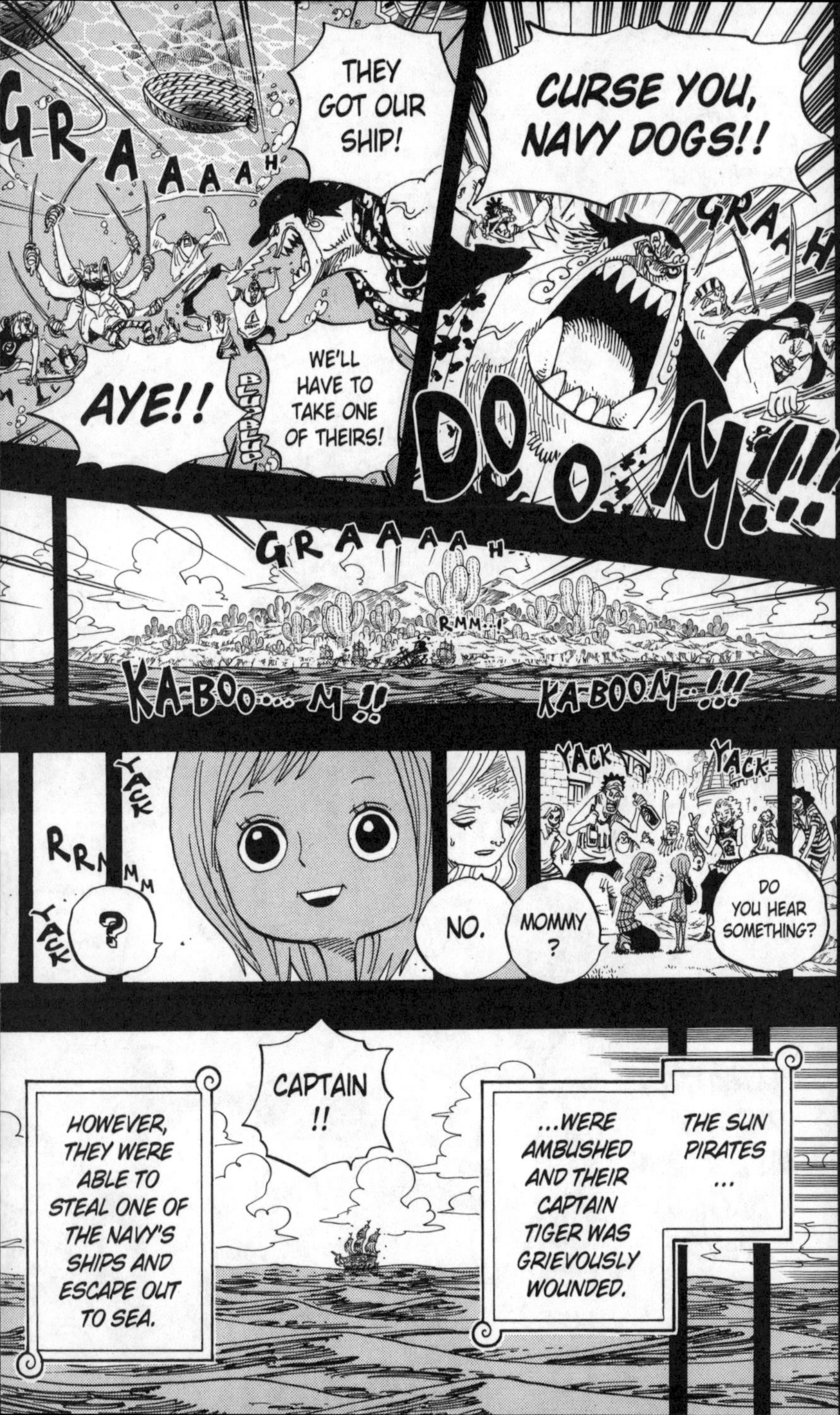
CURSE YOU, NAVY DOGS!!
GRAAH
DOOM!!!
THEY GOT OUR SHIP!
GRAAAAH
WE'LL HAVE TO TAKE ONE OF THEIRS!
AYE!!
GRAAAAAH..
RMM..!
KA-BOOM..!!!
KA-BOO... M!!
YACK
YACK
DO YOU HEAR SOMETHING?
MOMMY ?
NO.
YACK
RRMMM
?
YACK
THE SUN PIRATES ...
...WERE AMBUSHED AND THEIR CAPTAIN TIGER WAS GRIEVOUSLY WOUNDED.
CAPTAIN !!
HOWEVER, THEY WERE ABLE TO STEAL ONE OF THE NAVY'S SHIPS AND ESCAPE OUT TO SEA.

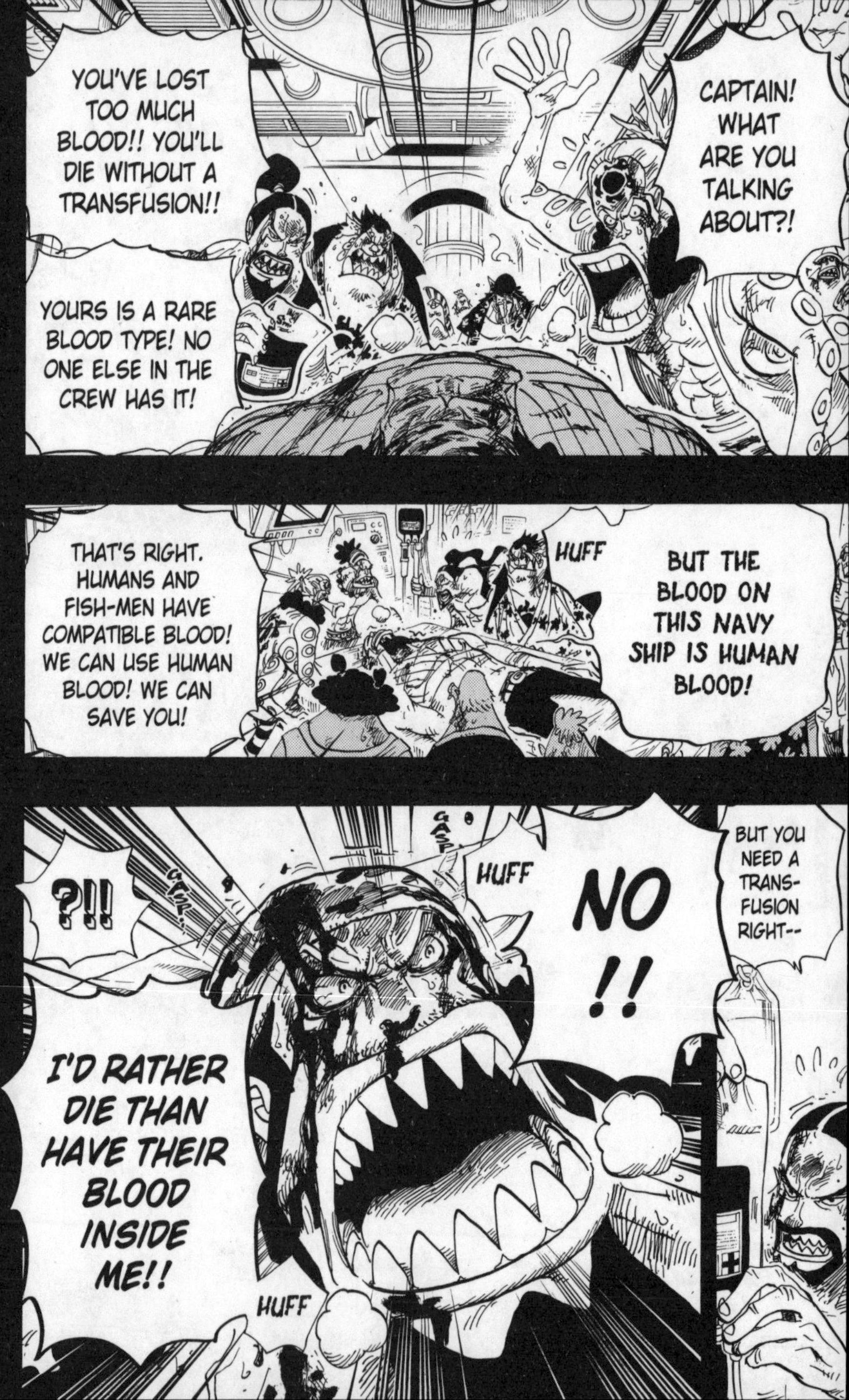
CAPTAIN! WHAT ARE YOU TALKING ABOUT?!
YOU'VE LOST TOO MUCH BLOOD!! YOU'LL DIE WITHOUT A TRANSFUSION!!
YOURS IS A RARE BLOOD TYPE! NO ONE ELSE IN THE CREW HAS IT!
BUT THE BLOOD ON THIS NAVY SHIP IS HUMAN BLOOD!
HUFF
THAT'S RIGHT. HUMANS AND FISH-MEN HAVE COMPATIBLE BLOOD! WE CAN USE HUMAN BLOOD! WE CAN SAVE YOU!
BUT YOU NEED A TRANS-FUSION RIGHT--
NO !!
HUFF
GASP
?!!
I'D RATHER DIE THAN HAVE THEIR BLOOD INSIDE ME!!
HUFF

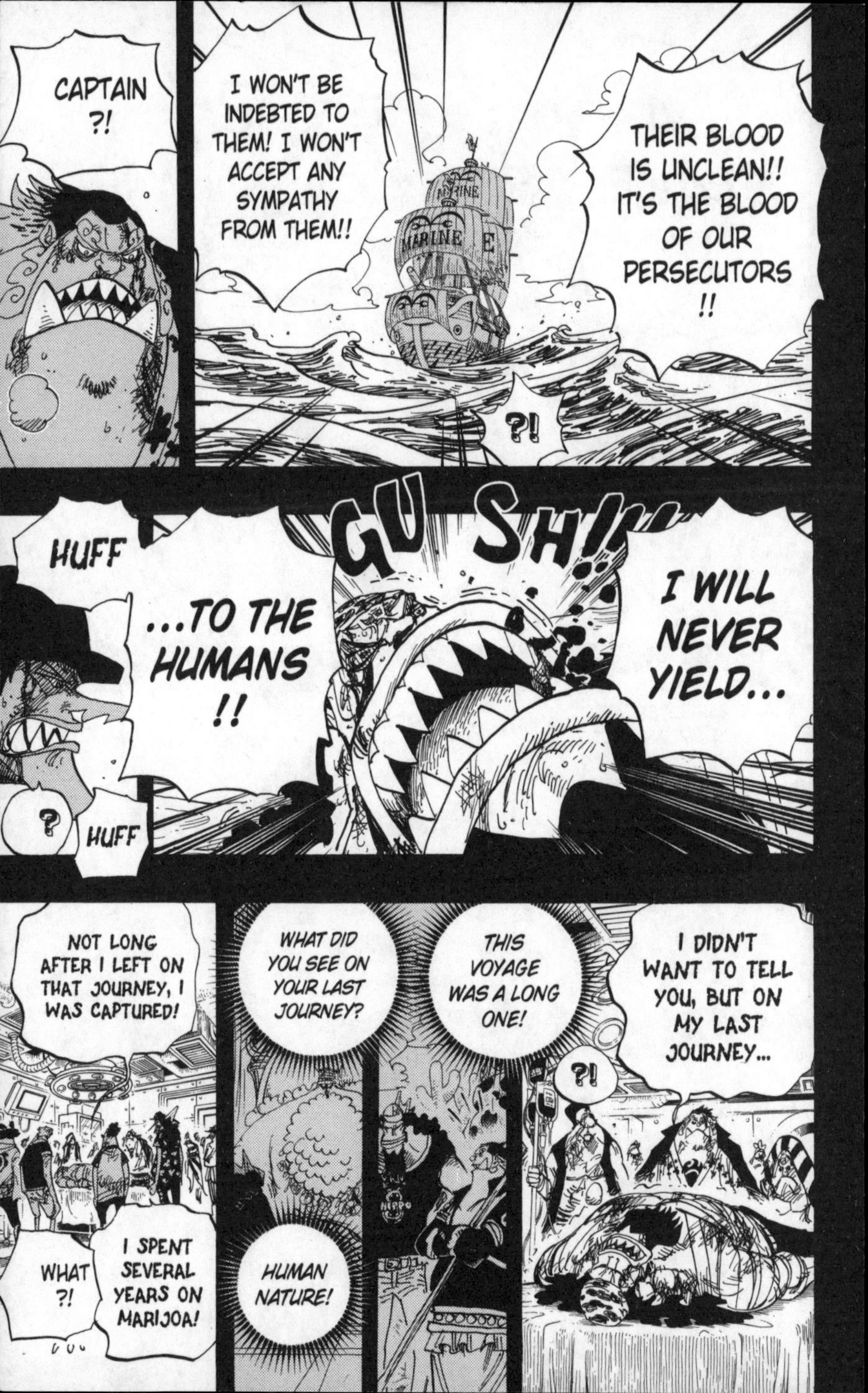
THEIR BLOOD IS UNCLEAN!! IT'S THE BLOOD OF OUR PERSECUTORS!!
I WON'T BE INDEBTED TO THEM! I WON'T ACCEPT ANY SYMPATHY FROM THEM!!
?!
CAPTAIN ?!
GUSH!!
I WILL NEVER YIELD...
...TO THE HUMANS!!
HUFF
?
HUFF
I DIDN'T WANT TO TELL YOU, BUT ON MY LAST JOURNEY...
?!
THIS VOYAGE WAS A LONG ONE!
WHAT DID YOU SEE ON YOUR LAST JOURNEY?
HUMAN NATURE!
NOT LONG AFTER I LEFT ON THAT JOURNEY, I WAS CAPTURED!
I SPENT SEVERAL YEARS ON MARIJOA!
WHAT ?!

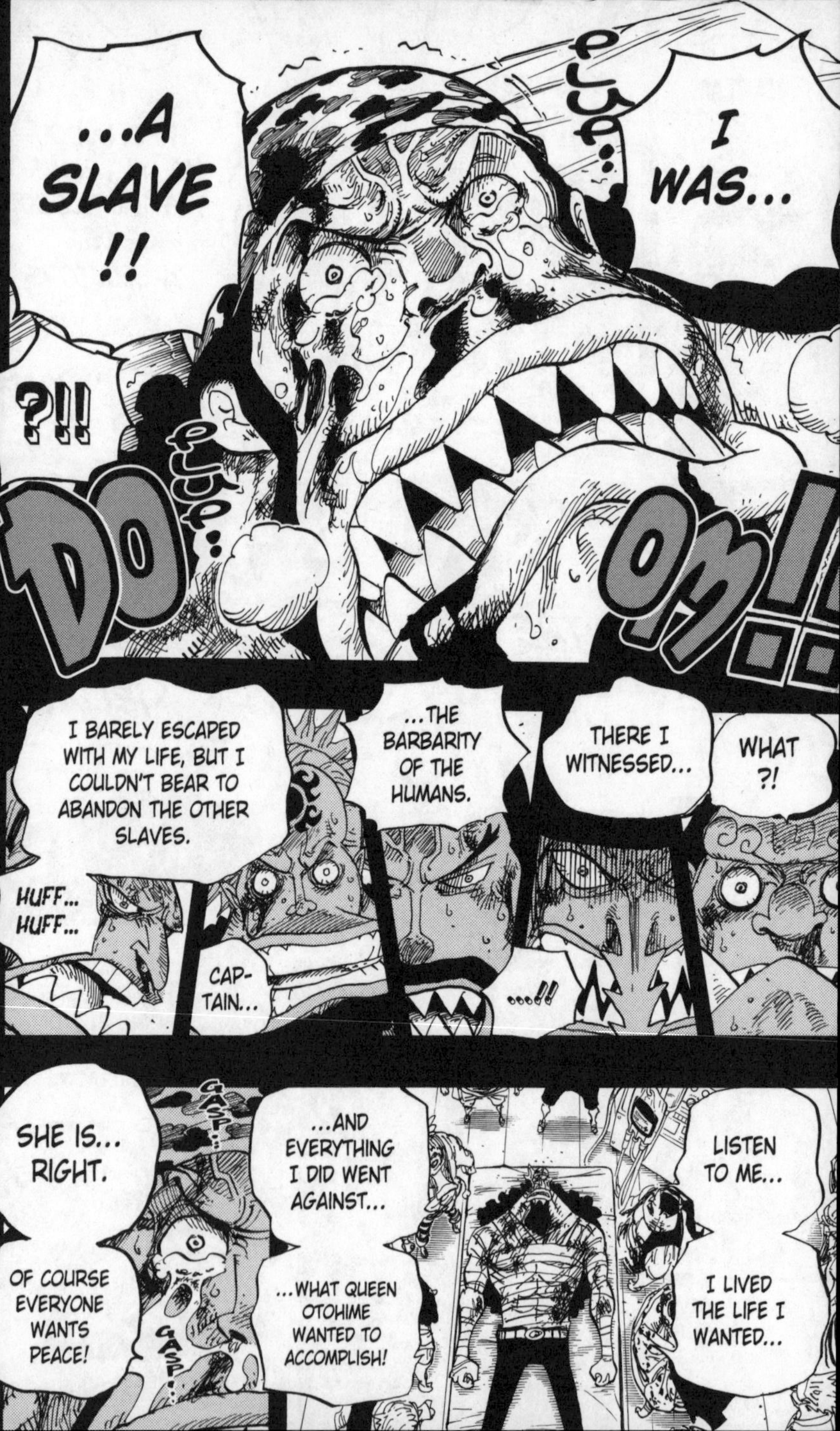
I WAS...
ELUP...
...A SLAVE!!
?!!
ELUP..
DOOM!!
WHAT ?!
THERE I WITNESSED...
....!!
...THE BARBARITY OF THE HUMANS.
CAP-TAIN...
I BARELY ESCAPED WITH MY LIFE, BUT I COULDN'T BEAR TO ABANDON THE OTHER SLAVES.
HUFF... HUFF...
LISTEN TO ME...
I LIVED THE LIFE I WANTED...
...AND EVERYTHING I DID WENT AGAINST...
...WHAT QUEEN OTOHIME WANTED TO ACCOMPLISH!
GASP..
SHE IS... RIGHT.
OF COURSE EVERYONE WANTS PEACE!
GASP..

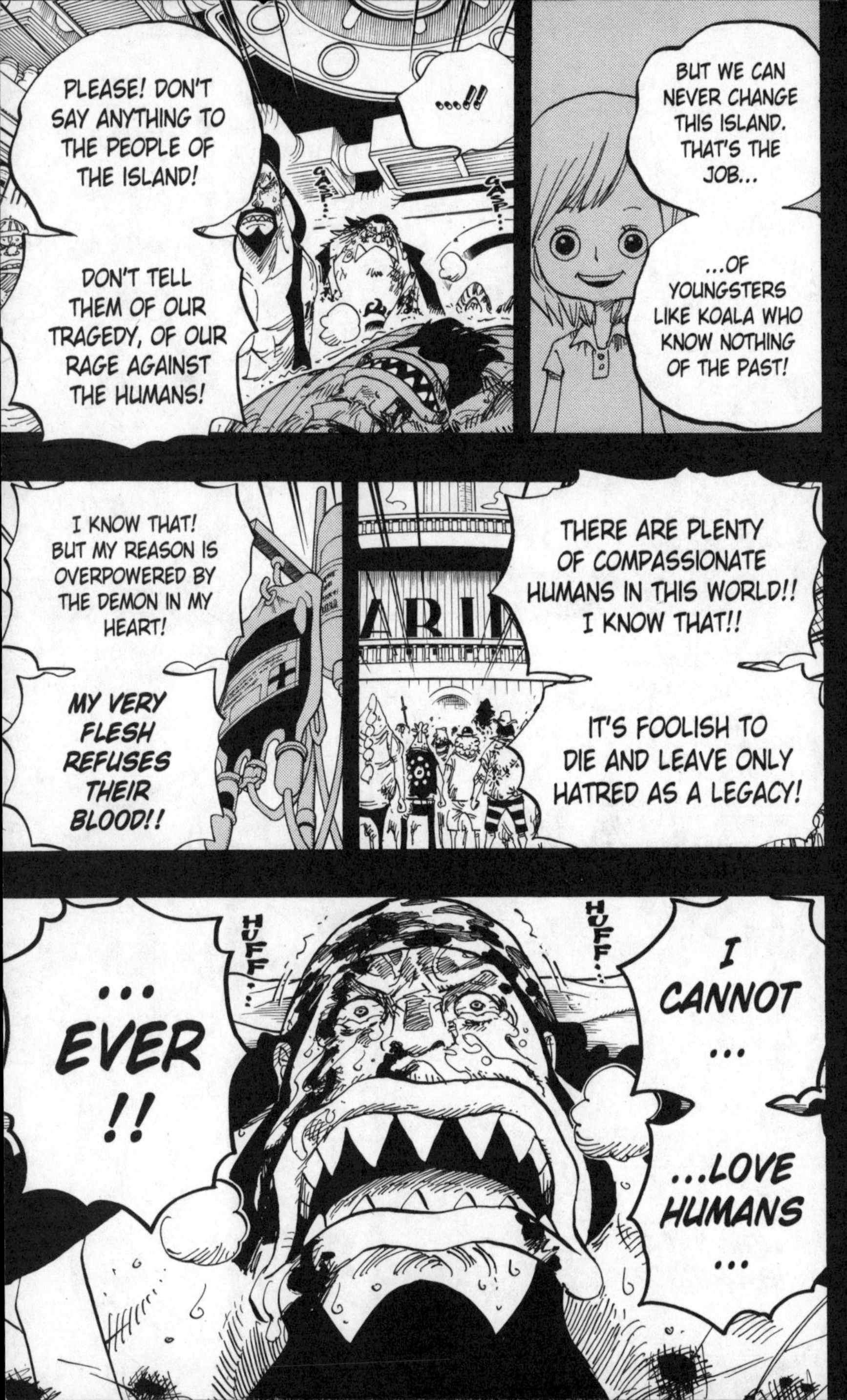
BUT WE CAN NEVER CHANGE THIS ISLAND. THAT'S THE JOB...
...OF YOUNGSTERS LIKE KOALA WHO KNOW NOTHING OF THE PAST!
....!!
GASP...
GASP...
PLEASE! DON'T SAY ANYTHING TO THE PEOPLE OF THE ISLAND!
DON'T TELL THEM OF OUR TRAGEDY, OF OUR RAGE AGAINST THE HUMANS!
THERE ARE PLENTY OF COMPASSIONATE HUMANS IN THIS WORLD!! I KNOW THAT!!
IT'S FOOLISH TO DIE AND LEAVE ONLY HATRED AS A LEGACY!
I KNOW THAT! BUT MY REASON IS OVERPOWERED BY THE DEMON IN MY HEART!
MY VERY FLESH REFUSES THEIR BLOOD!!
I CANNOT ... ...LOVE HUMANS ...
HUFF...
HUFF...
... EVER !!

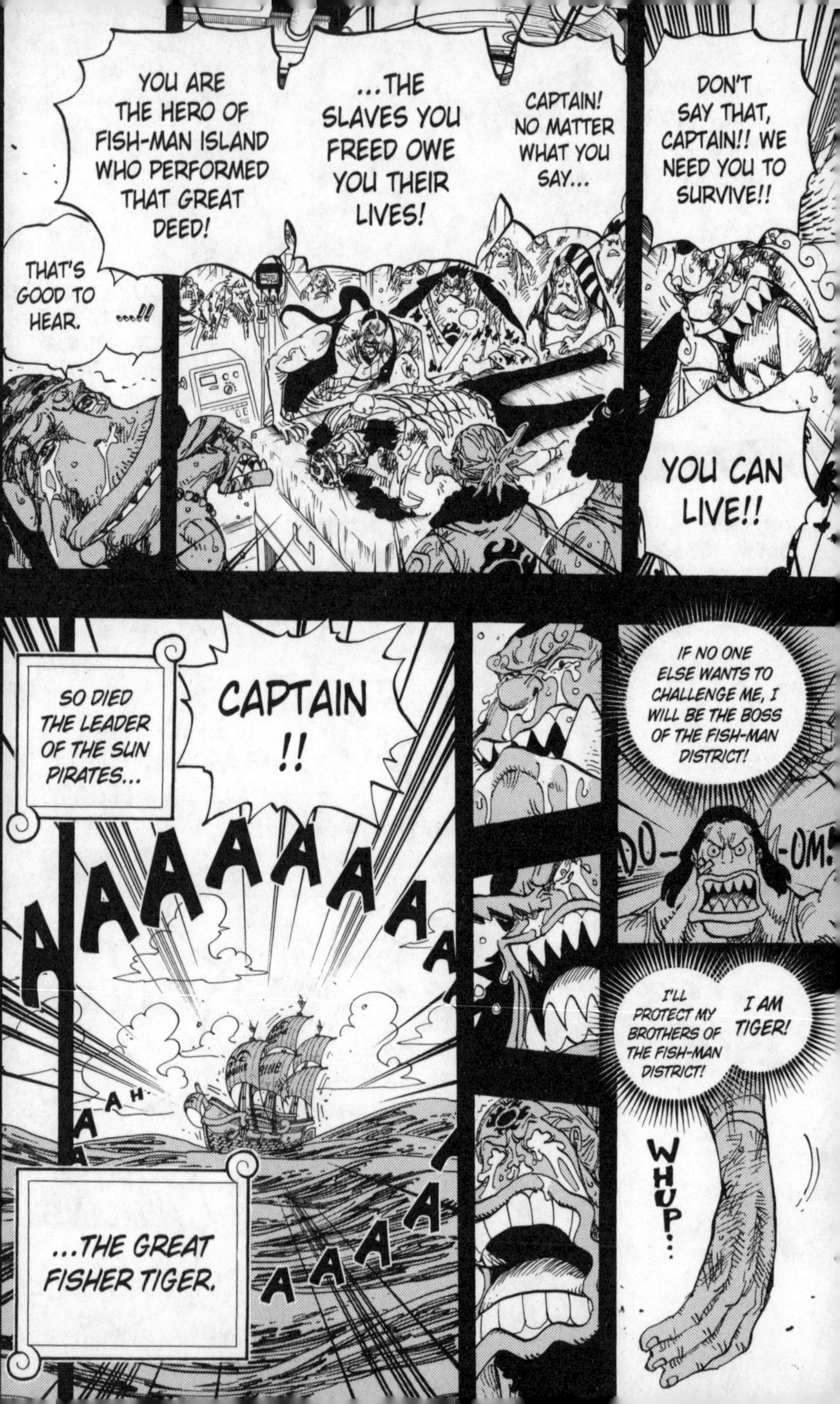
DON'T SAY THAT, CAPTAIN!! WE NEED YOU TO SURVIVE!!
YOU CAN LIVE!!
CAPTAIN! NO MATTER WHAT YOU SAY...
...THE SLAVES YOU FREED OWE YOU THEIR LIVES!
YOU ARE THE HERO OF FISH-MAN ISLAND WHO PERFORMED THAT GREAT DEED!
...!!
THAT'S GOOD TO HEAR.
IF NO ONE ELSE WANTS TO CHALLENGE ME, I WILL BE THE BOSS OF THE FISH-MAN DISTRICT!
DO- -OM!
I AM TIGER!
I'LL PROTECT MY BROTHERS OF THE FISH-MAN DISTRICT!
WHUP...
SO DIED THE LEADER OF THE SUN PIRATES...
CAPTAIN!!
AAAAAAAAA
AAH
AAAAAA
...THE GREAT FISHER TIGER.

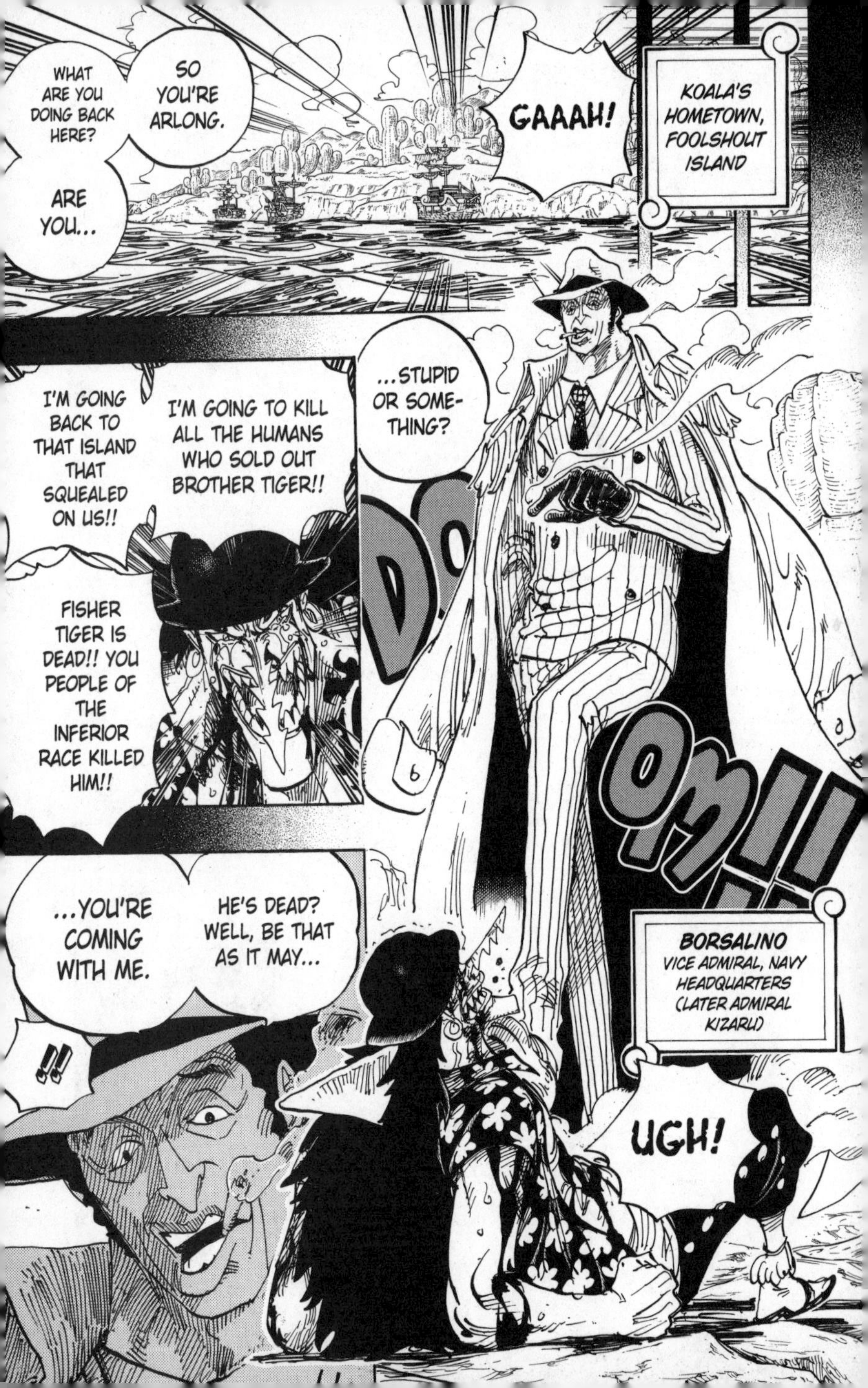
KOALA'S HOMETOWN, FOOLSHOUT ISLAND
GAAAH!
SO YOU'RE ARLONG.
WHAT ARE YOU DOING BACK HERE?
ARE YOU...
...STUPID OR SOME-THING?
DOOM!!
BORSALINO VICE ADMIRAL, NAVY HEADQUARTERS (LATER ADMIRAL KIZARU)
UGH!
I'M GOING TO KILL ALL THE HUMANS WHO SOLD OUT BROTHER TIGER!!
I'M GOING BACK TO THAT ISLAND THAT SQUEALED ON US!!
FISHER TIGER IS DEAD!! YOU PEOPLE OF THE INFERIOR RACE KILLED HIM!!
HE'S DEAD? WELL, BE THAT AS IT MAY...
...YOU'RE COMING WITH ME.
!!

Chapter 624:
QUEEN OTOHIME

*BROTHERS OF COCO VILLAGE PORT *GREAT CATCH *OCEAN

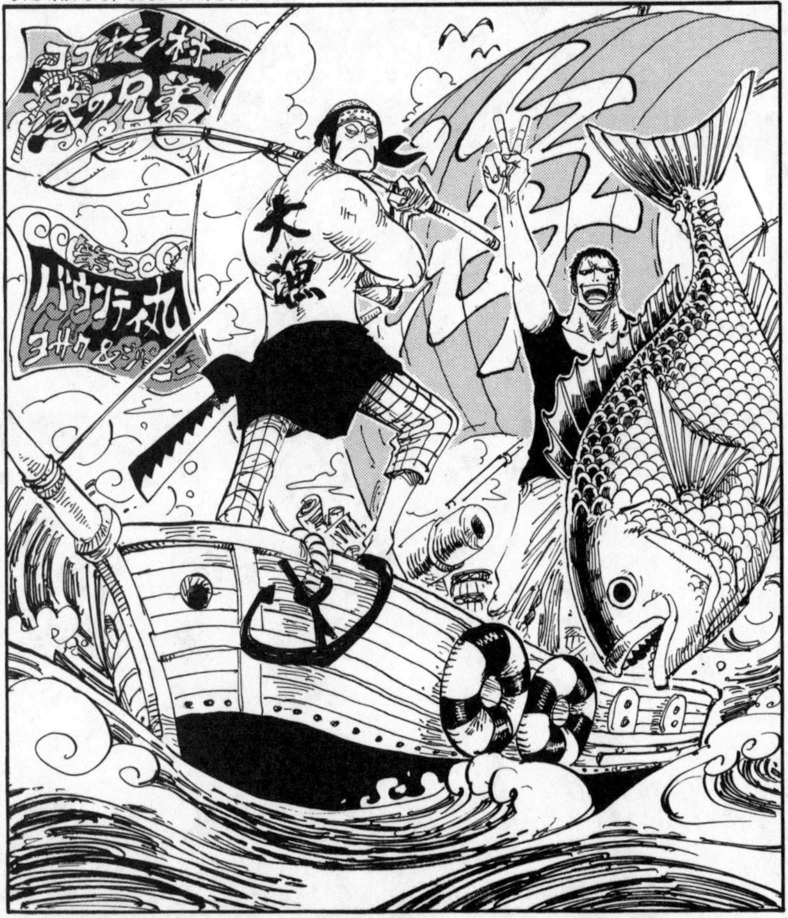

#2 / BOUNTY SHIP / YOSAKU & JOHNNY

DECKS OF THE WORLD, VOL. 10: "COCO VILLAGE—
THE SHIP OF BROTHERS YOSAKU & JOHNNY"

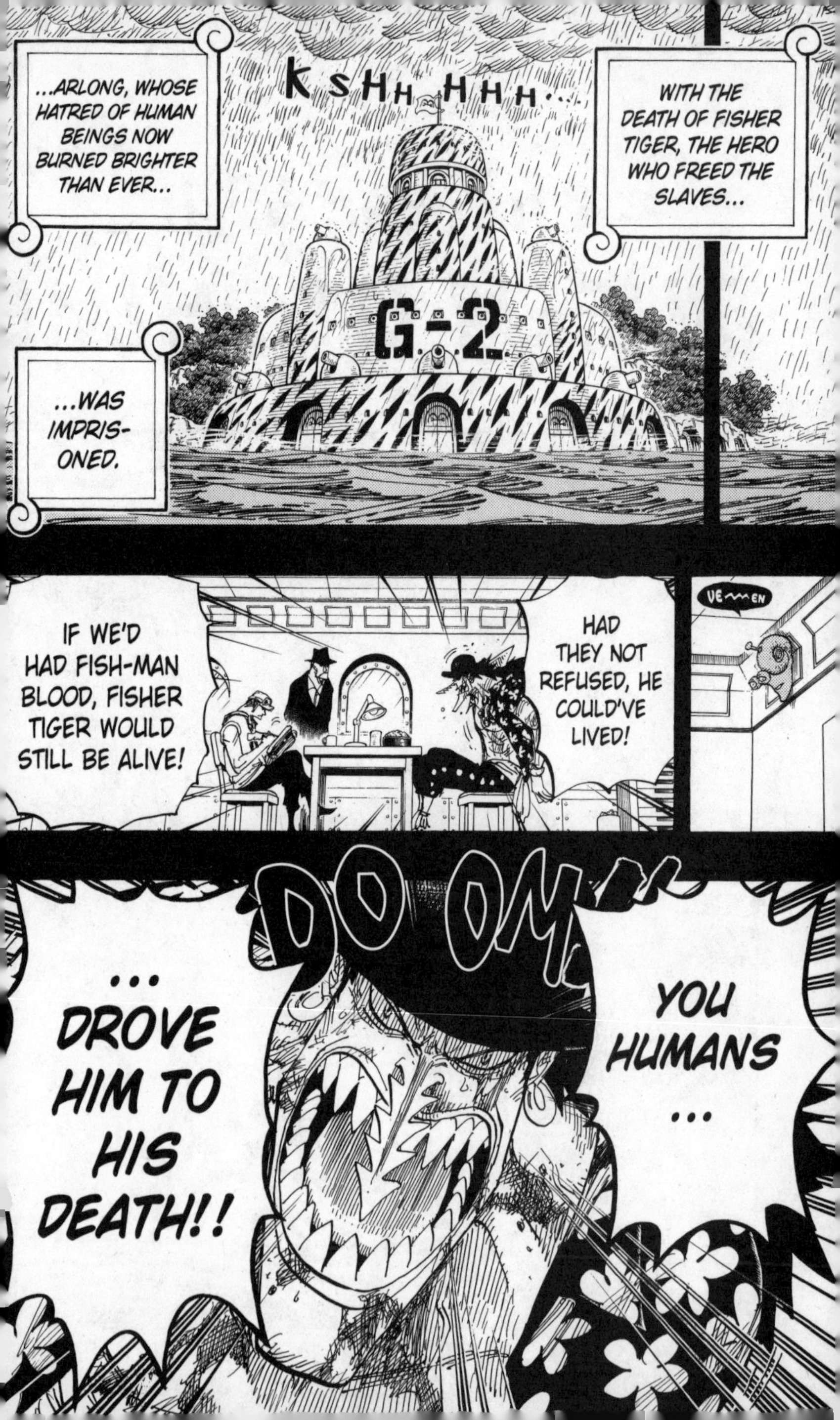

WITH THE DEATH OF FISHER TIGER, THE HERO WHO FREED THE SLAVES...
KSHHHHHH...
...ARLONG, WHOSE HATRED OF HUMAN BEINGS NOW BURNED BRIGHTER THAN EVER...
...WAS IMPRIS-ONED.
VE~EN
HAD THEY NOT REFUSED, HE COULD'VE LIVED!
IF WE'D HAD FISH-MAN BLOOD, FISHER TIGER WOULD STILL BE ALIVE!
DOOM
YOU HUMANS...
...DROVE HIM TO HIS DEATH!!

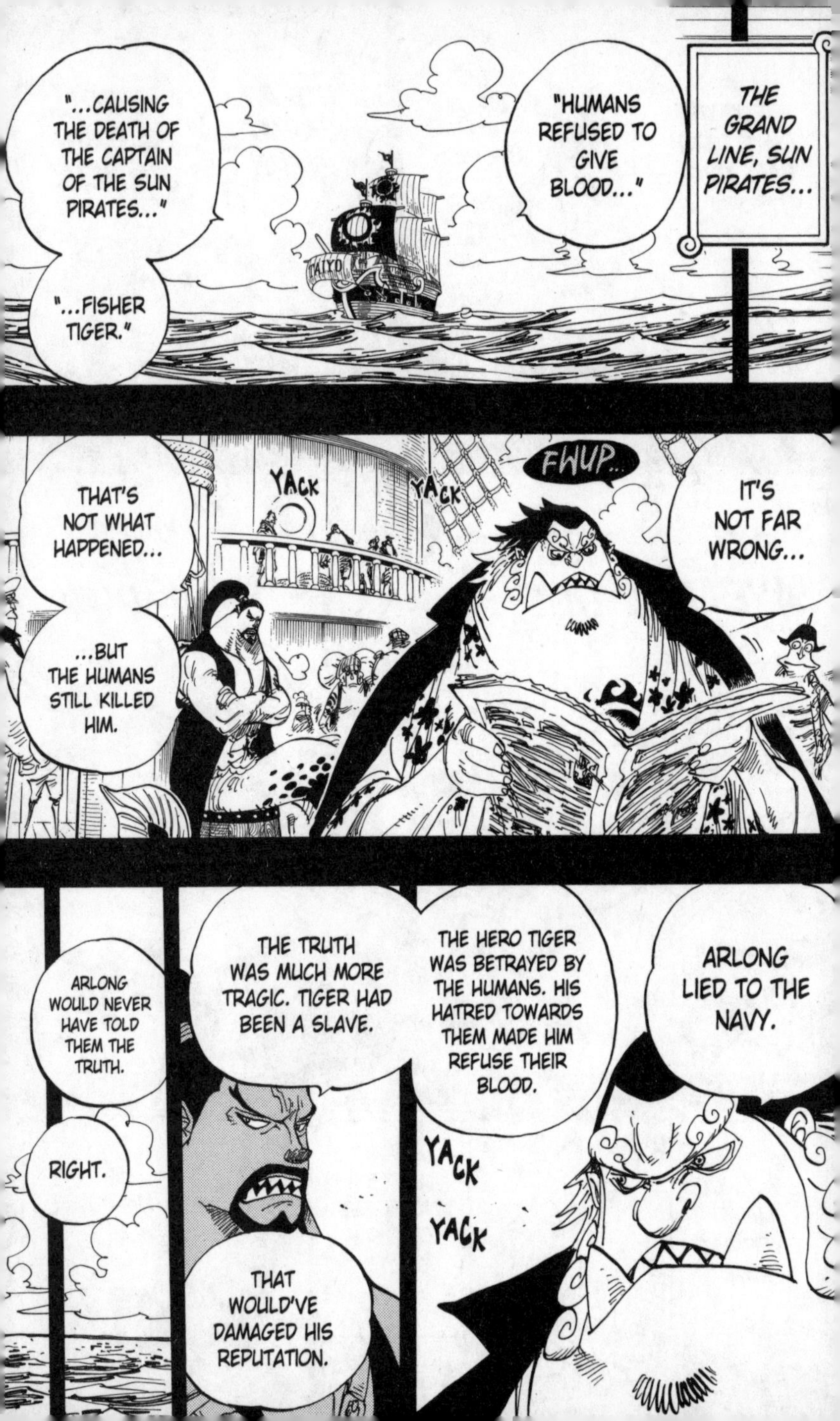
THE GRAND LINE, SUN PIRATES...
"HUMANS REFUSED TO GIVE BLOOD..."
"...CAUSING THE DEATH OF THE CAPTAIN OF THE SUN PIRATES..."
"...FISHER TIGER."
FWUP..
IT'S NOT FAR WRONG...
YACK
YACK
THAT'S NOT WHAT HAPPENED...
...BUT THE HUMANS STILL KILLED HIM.
ARLONG LIED TO THE NAVY.
THE HERO TIGER WAS BETRAYED BY THE HUMANS. HIS HATRED TOWARDS THEM MADE HIM REFUSE THEIR BLOOD.
THE TRUTH WAS MUCH MORE TRAGIC. TIGER HAD BEEN A SLAVE.
YACK
YACK
THAT WOULD'VE DAMAGED HIS REPUTATION.
ARLONG WOULD NEVER HAVE TOLD THEM THE TRUTH.
RIGHT.

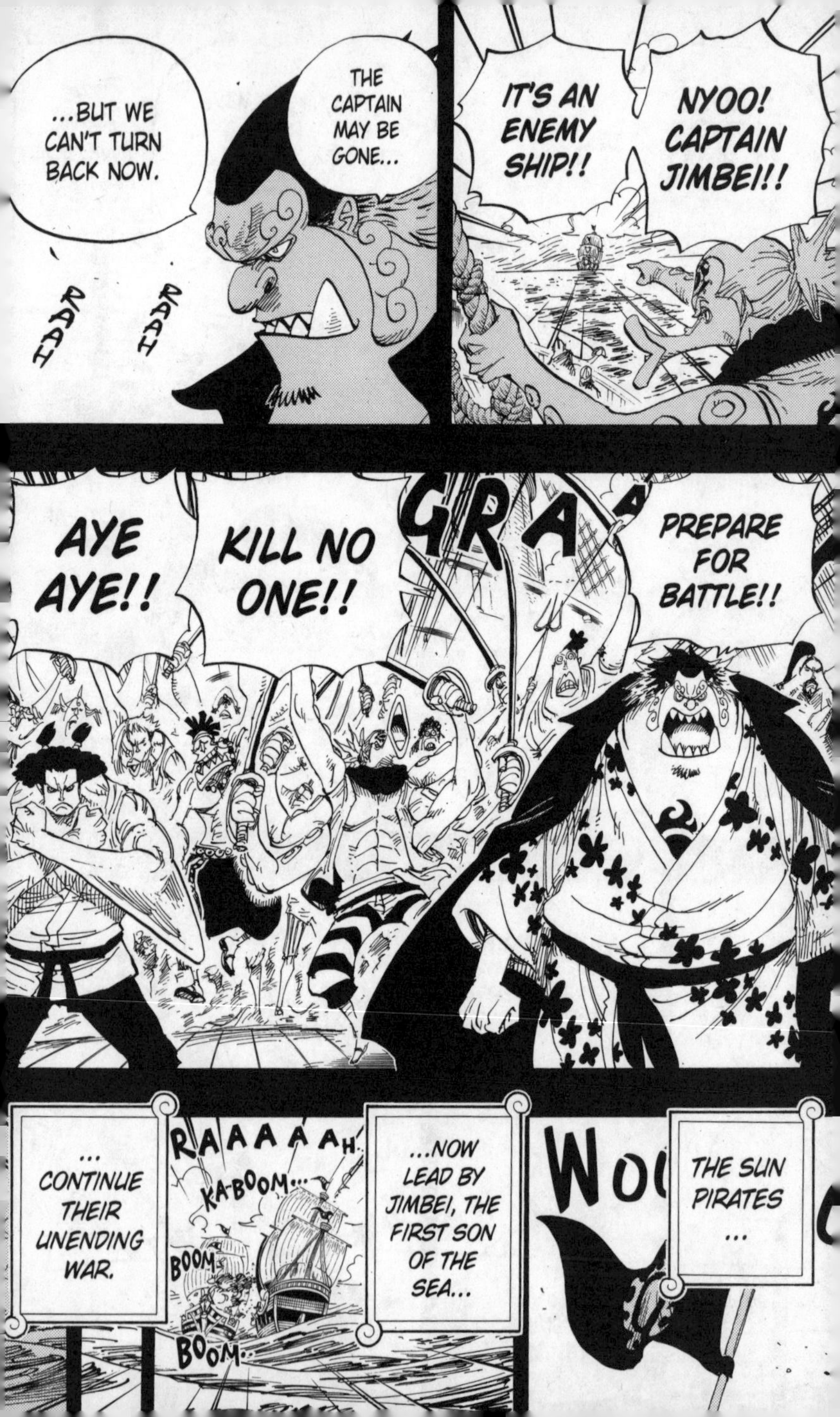
NYOO! CAPTAIN JIMBEI!!
IT'S AN ENEMY SHIP!!
THE CAPTAIN MAY BE GONE...
...BUT WE CAN'T TURN BACK NOW.
RAAAH
RAAAH
PREPARE FOR BATTLE!!
GRAA
KILL NO ONE!!
AYE AYE!!
THE SUN PIRATES ...
...NOW LEAD BY JIMBEI, THE FIRST SON OF THE SEA...
RAAAAAH
KA-BOOM...
BOOM
BOOM
... CONTINUE THEIR UNENDING WAR.

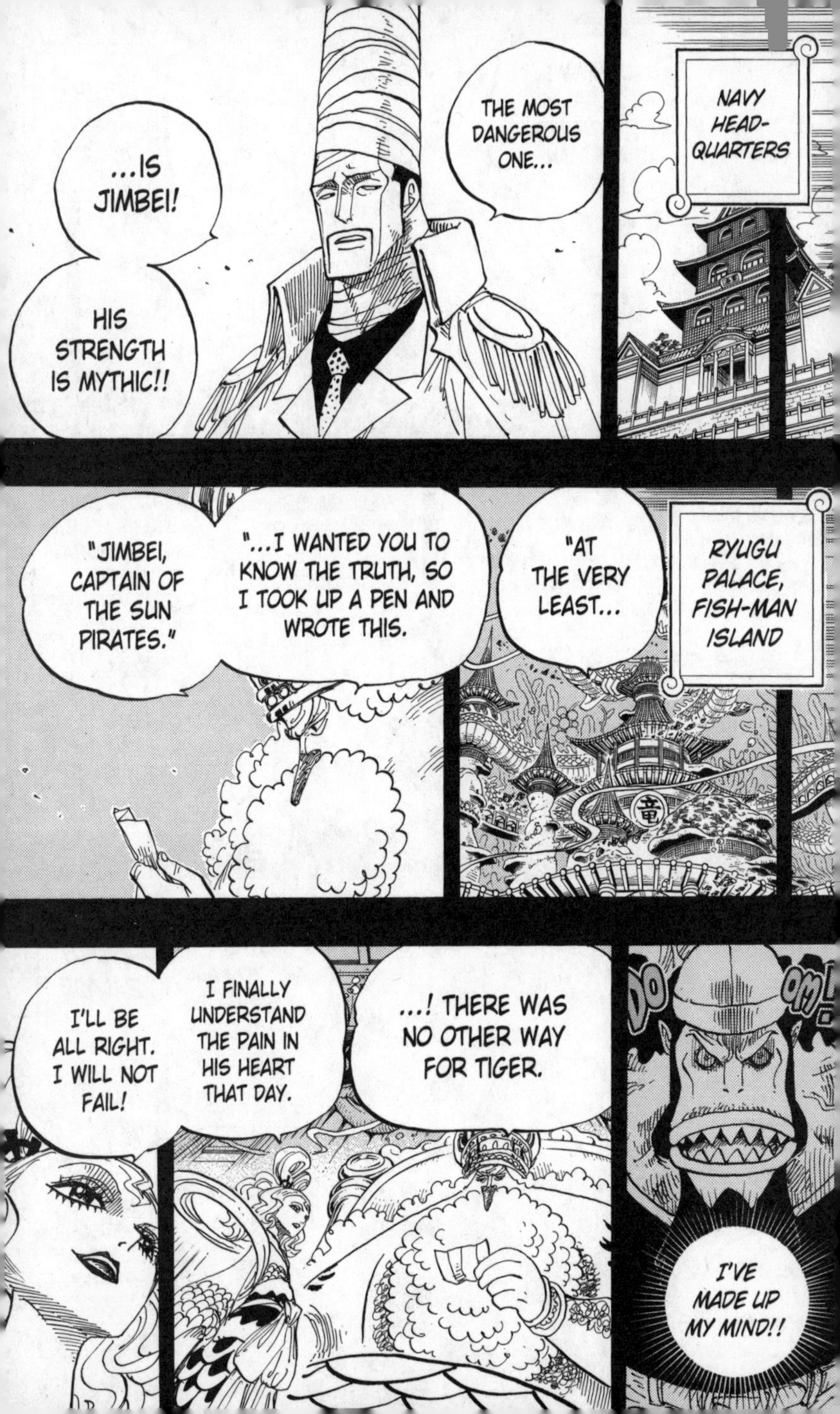
NAVY HEAD-QUARTERS
THE MOST DANGEROUS ONE...
...IS JIMBEI!
HIS STRENGTH IS MYTHIC!!
RYUGU PALACE, FISH-MAN ISLAND
"AT THE VERY LEAST...
"...I WANTED YOU TO KNOW THE TRUTH, SO I TOOK UP A PEN AND WROTE THIS.
"JIMBEI, CAPTAIN OF THE SUN PIRATES."
I'VE MADE UP MY MIND!!
...! THERE WAS NO OTHER WAY FOR TIGER.
I FINALLY UNDERSTAND THE PAIN IN HIS HEART THAT DAY.
I'LL BE ALL RIGHT. I WILL NOT FAIL!

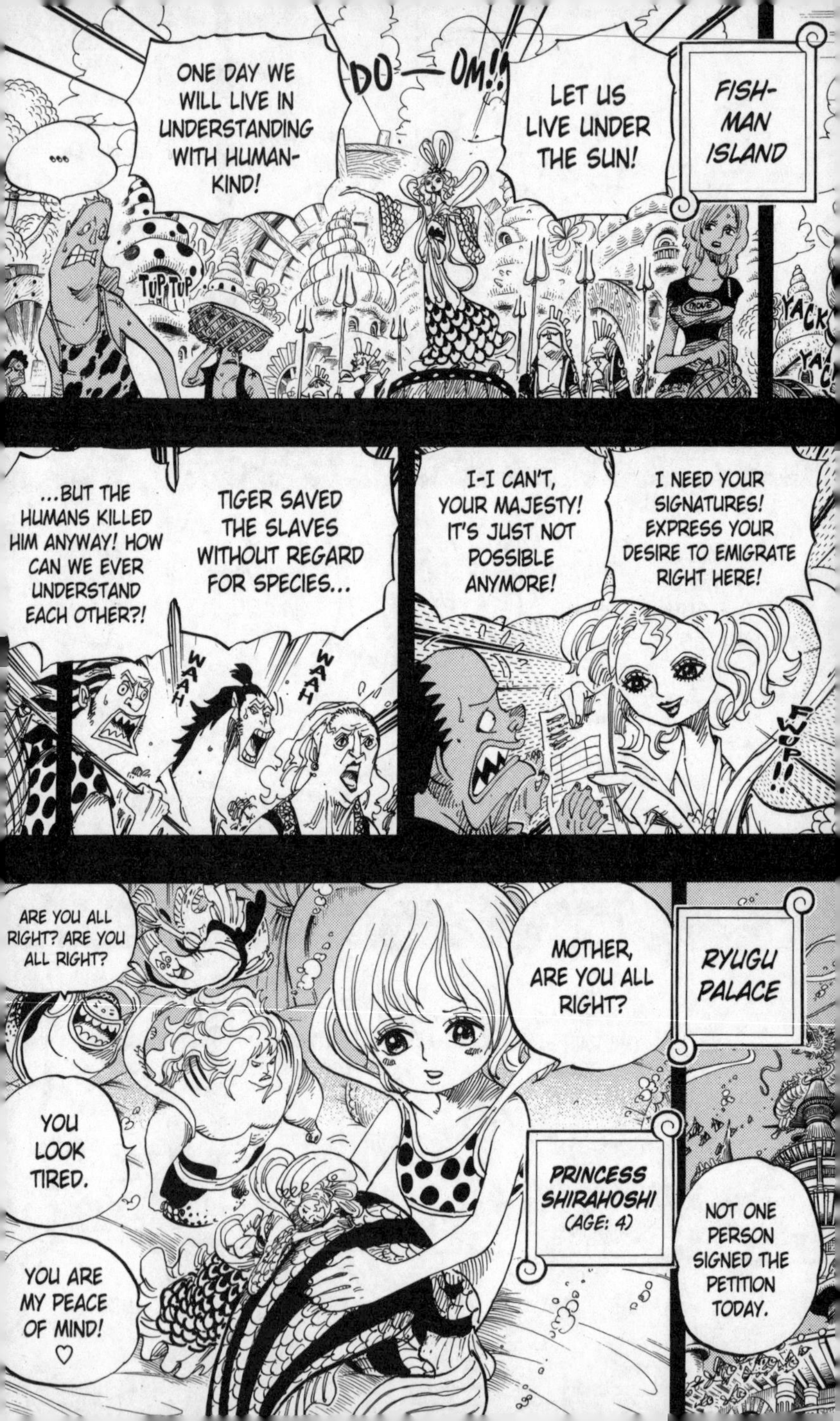
FISH-MAN ISLAND
LET US LIVE UNDER THE SUN!
DO—OM!!
ONE DAY WE WILL LIVE IN UNDERSTANDING WITH HUMAN-KIND!
...
TUP TUP
YACK
YACK
I NEED YOUR SIGNATURES! EXPRESS YOUR DESIRE TO EMIGRATE RIGHT HERE!
I-I CAN'T, YOUR MAJESTY! IT'S JUST NOT POSSIBLE ANYMORE!
FWUP!!
TIGER SAVED THE SLAVES WITHOUT REGARD FOR SPECIES...
...BUT THE HUMANS KILLED HIM ANYWAY! HOW CAN WE EVER UNDERSTAND EACH OTHER?!
WAAH
WAAH
RYUGU PALACE
MOTHER, ARE YOU ALL RIGHT?
PRINCESS SHIRAHOSHI (AGE: 4)
NOT ONE PERSON SIGNED THE PETITION TODAY.
ARE YOU ALL RIGHT? ARE YOU ALL RIGHT?
YOU LOOK TIRED.
YOU ARE MY PEACE OF MIND! ♡

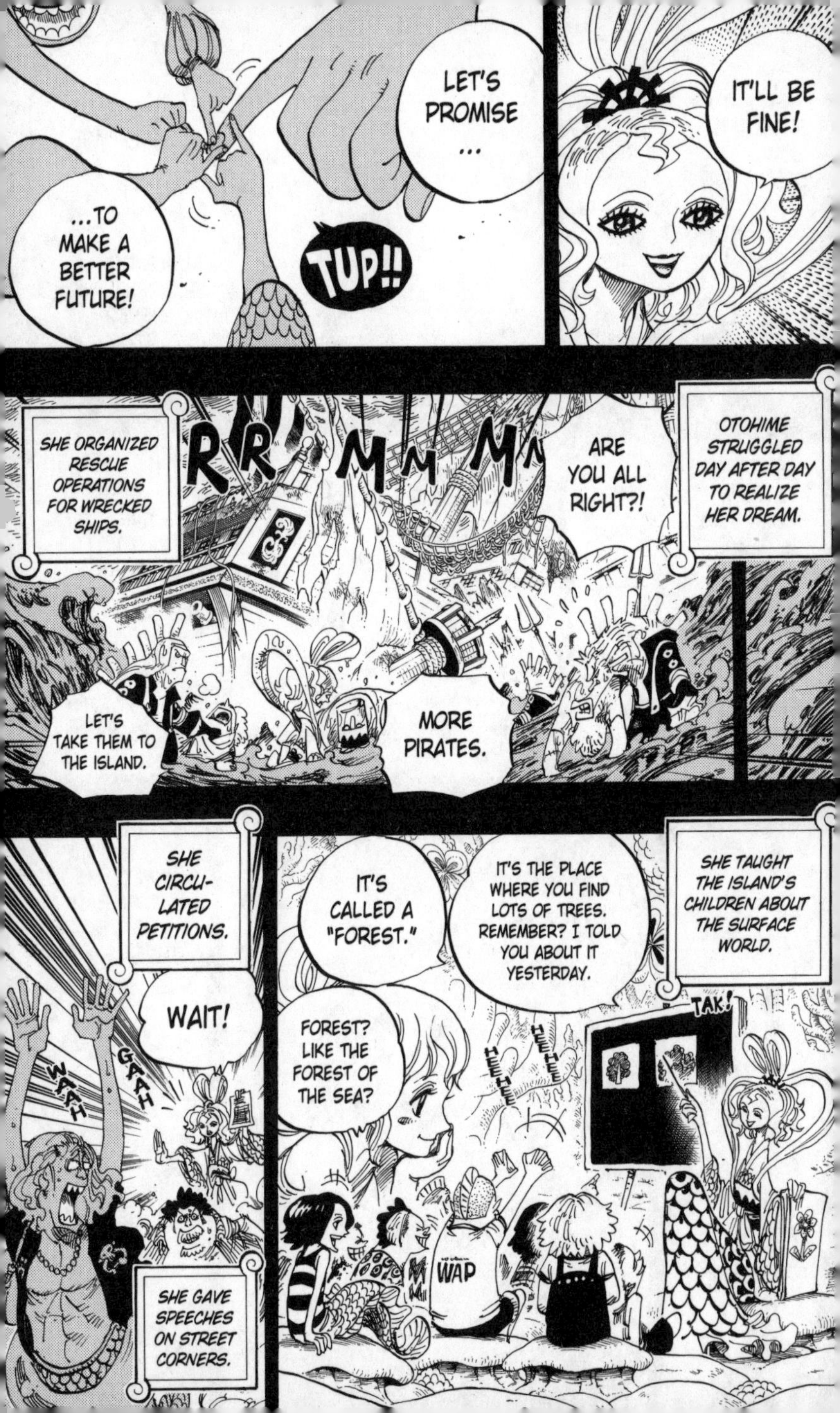
IT'LL BE FINE!
LET'S PROMISE ...
TUP!!
...TO MAKE A BETTER FUTURE!
OTOHIME STRUGGLED DAY AFTER DAY TO REALIZE HER DREAM.
ARE YOU ALL RIGHT?!
RRMMMM
SHE ORGANIZED RESCUE OPERATIONS FOR WRECKED SHIPS.
MORE PIRATES.
LET'S TAKE THEM TO THE ISLAND.
SHE TAUGHT THE ISLAND'S CHILDREN ABOUT THE SURFACE WORLD.
TAK!
IT'S THE PLACE WHERE YOU FIND LOTS OF TREES. REMEMBER? I TOLD YOU ABOUT IT YESTERDAY.
IT'S CALLED A "FOREST."
HEE HEE
HEE HEE
FOREST? LIKE THE FOREST OF THE SEA?
WAP
SHE CIRCULATED PETITIONS.
WAIT!
GAAH
WAAH
SHE GAVE SPEECHES ON STREET CORNERS.

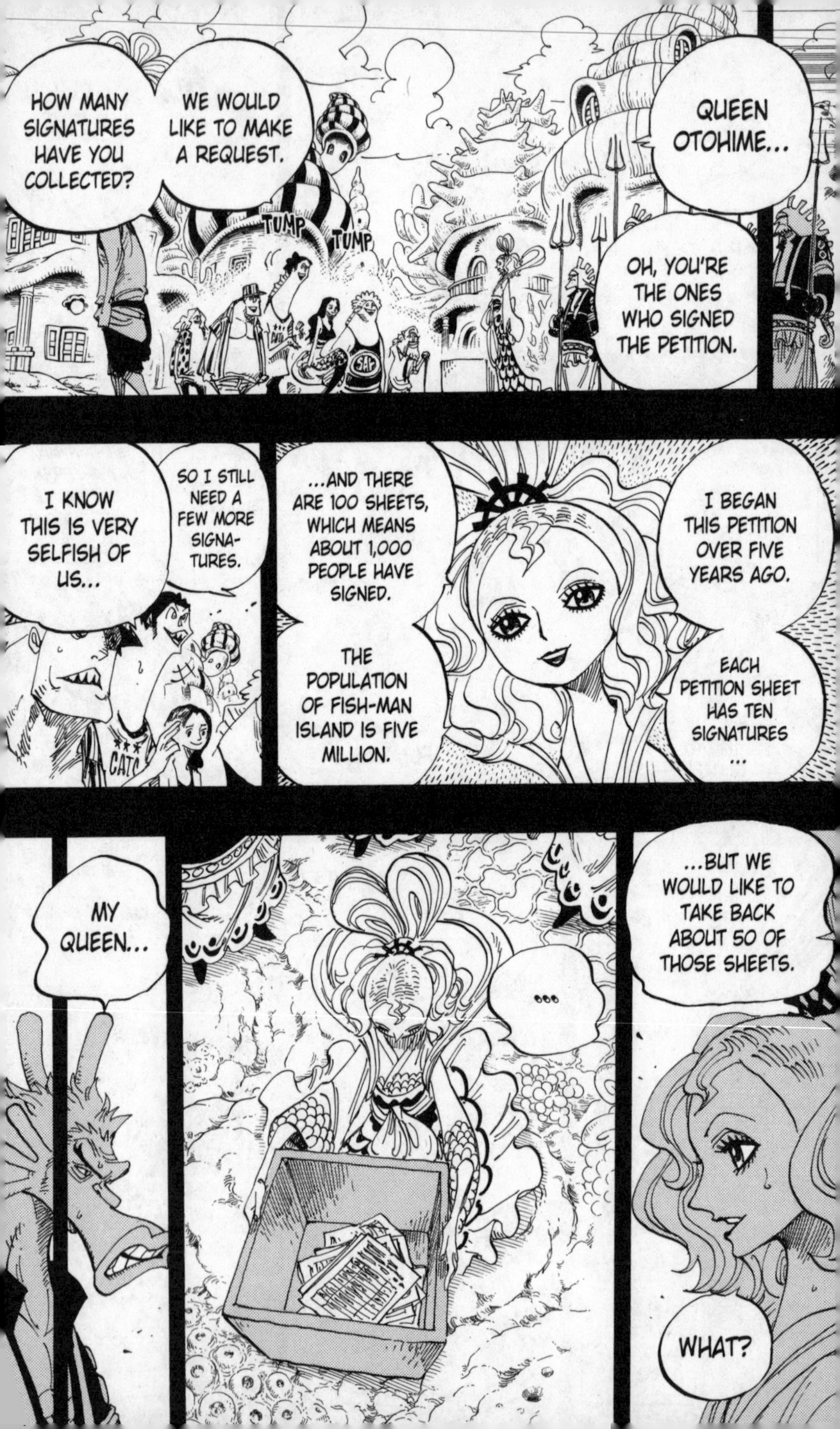
QUEEN OTOHIME...
OH, YOU'RE THE ONES WHO SIGNED THE PETITION.
WE WOULD LIKE TO MAKE A REQUEST.
HOW MANY SIGNATURES HAVE YOU COLLECTED?
TUMP
TUMP
I BEGAN THIS PETITION OVER FIVE YEARS AGO.
EACH PETITION SHEET HAS TEN SIGNATURES ...
...AND THERE ARE 100 SHEETS, WHICH MEANS ABOUT 1,000 PEOPLE HAVE SIGNED.
THE POPULATION OF FISH-MAN ISLAND IS FIVE MILLION.
SO I STILL NEED A FEW MORE SIGNA-TURES.
I KNOW THIS IS VERY SELFISH OF US...
...BUT WE WOULD LIKE TO TAKE BACK ABOUT 50 OF THOSE SHEETS.
WHAT?
...
MY QUEEN...

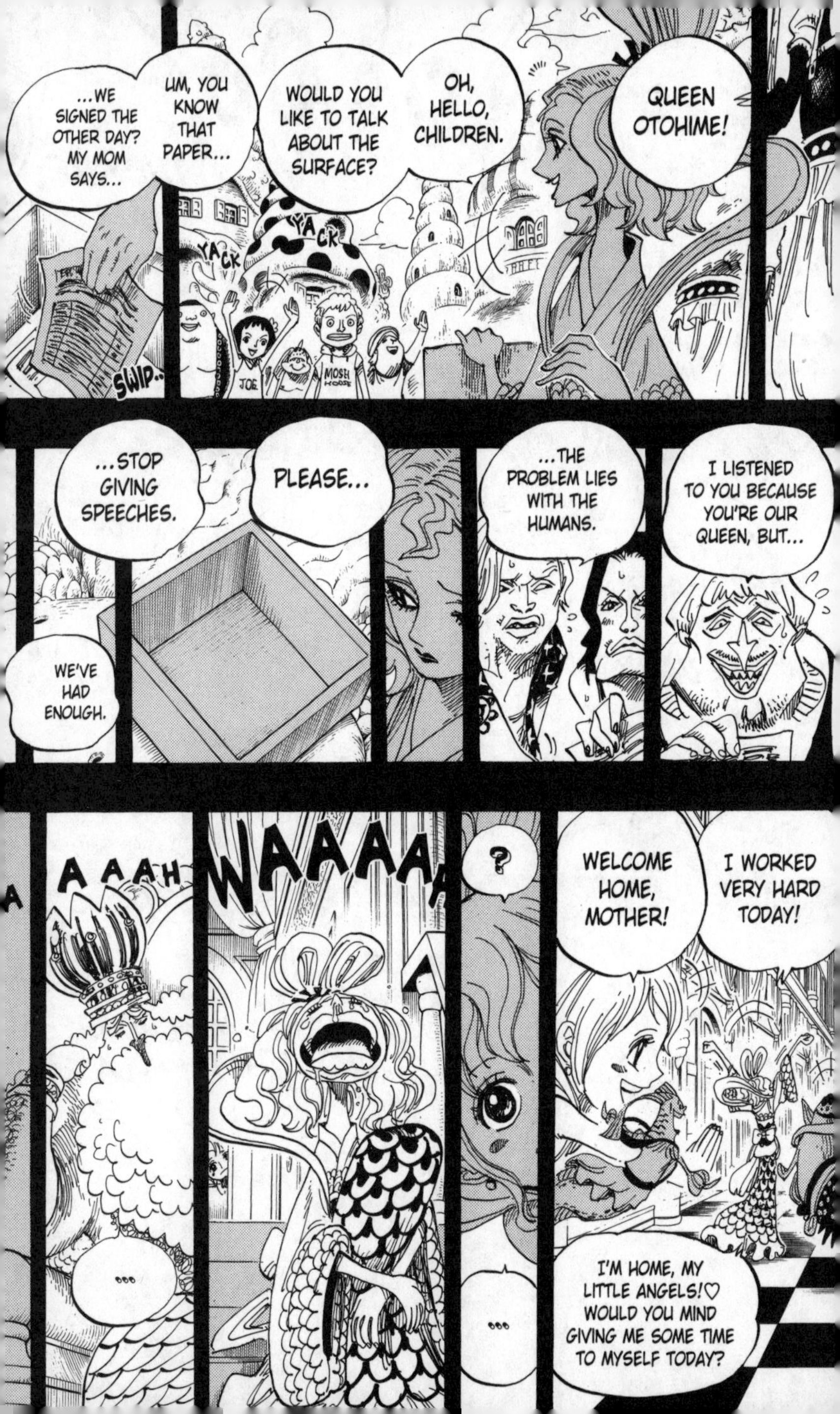
QUEEN OTOHIME!
OH, HELLO, CHILDREN.
WOULD YOU LIKE TO TALK ABOUT THE SURFACE?
YACK
YACK
UM, YOU KNOW THAT PAPER...
...WE SIGNED THE OTHER DAY? MY MOM SAYS...
SWIP..
I LISTENED TO YOU BECAUSE YOU'RE OUR QUEEN, BUT...
...THE PROBLEM LIES WITH THE HUMANS.
PLEASE...
...STOP GIVING SPEECHES.
WE'VE HAD ENOUGH.
I WORKED VERY HARD TODAY!
WELCOME HOME, MOTHER!
I'M HOME, MY LITTLE ANGELS!♡ WOULD YOU MIND GIVING ME SOME TIME TO MYSELF TODAY?
?
...
WAAAAA
A
A AAAH
A
...

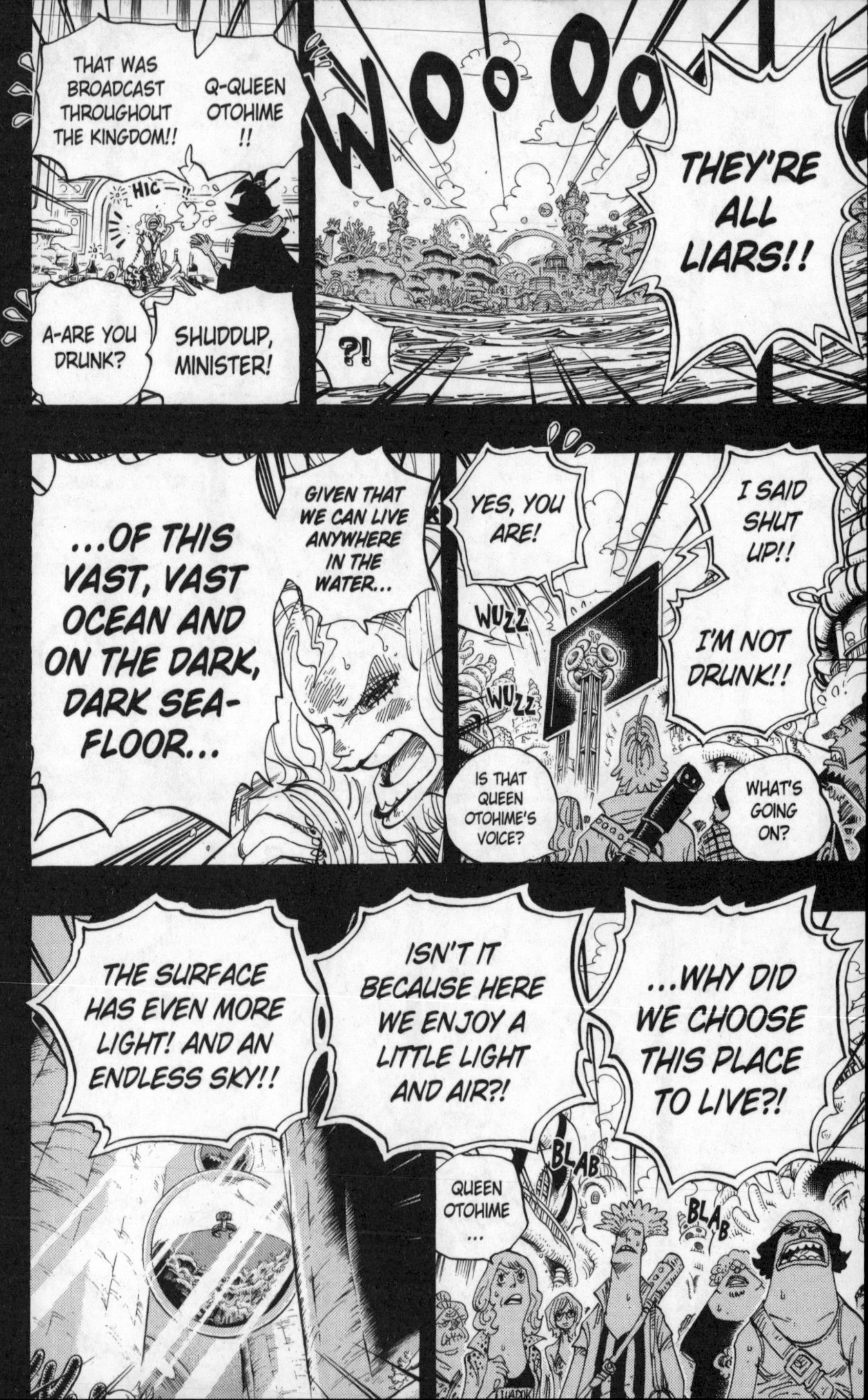
WOOOOO
THEY'RE ALL LIARS!!
?!
Q-QUEEN OTOHIME!!
THAT WAS BROADCAST THROUGHOUT THE KINGDOM!!
HIC
SHUDDUP, MINISTER!
A-ARE YOU DRUNK?
I SAID SHUT UP!!
I'M NOT DRUNK!!
YES, YOU ARE!
WUZZ
WUZZ
WHAT'S GOING ON?
IS THAT QUEEN OTOHIME'S VOICE?
GIVEN THAT WE CAN LIVE ANYWHERE IN THE WATER...
...OF THIS VAST, VAST OCEAN AND ON THE DARK, DARK SEA-FLOOR...
...WHY DID WE CHOOSE THIS PLACE TO LIVE?!
ISN'T IT BECAUSE HERE WE ENJOY A LITTLE LIGHT AND AIR?!
BLAB
BLAB
QUEEN OTOHIME...
THE SURFACE HAS EVEN MORE LIGHT! AND AN ENDLESS SKY!!

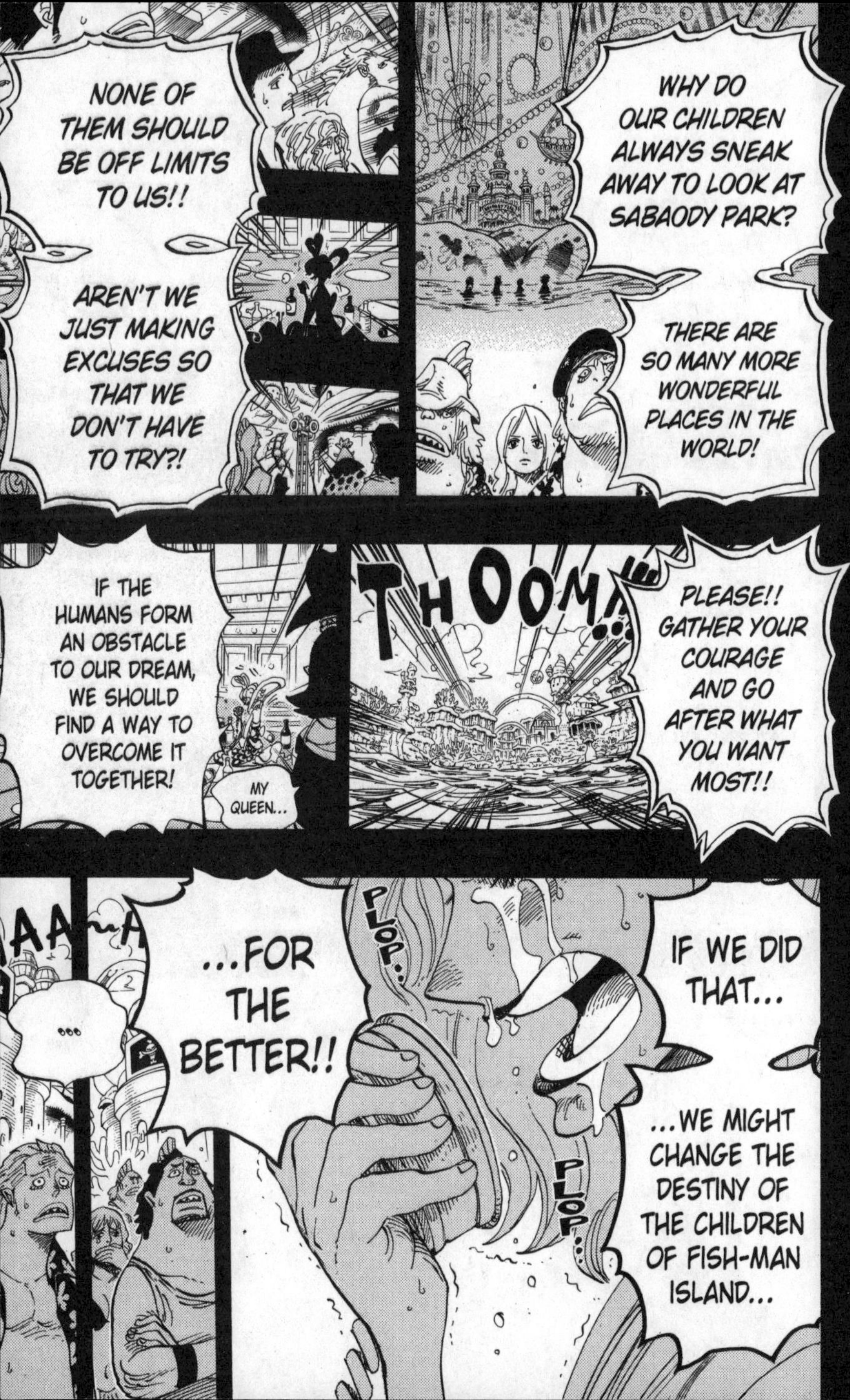
WHY DO OUR CHILDREN ALWAYS SNEAK AWAY TO LOOK AT SABAODY PARK?
THERE ARE SO MANY MORE WONDERFUL PLACES IN THE WORLD!
NONE OF THEM SHOULD BE OFF LIMITS TO US!!
AREN'T WE JUST MAKING EXCUSES SO THAT WE DON'T HAVE TO TRY?!
PLEASE!! GATHER YOUR COURAGE AND GO AFTER WHAT YOU WANT MOST!!
THOOM...
MY QUEEN...
IF THE HUMANS FORM AN OBSTACLE TO OUR DREAM, WE SHOULD FIND A WAY TO OVERCOME IT TOGETHER!
IF WE DID THAT...
PLOP...
...WE MIGHT CHANGE THE DESTINY OF THE CHILDREN OF FISH-MAN ISLAND...
PLOP...
...FOR THE BETTER!!
...

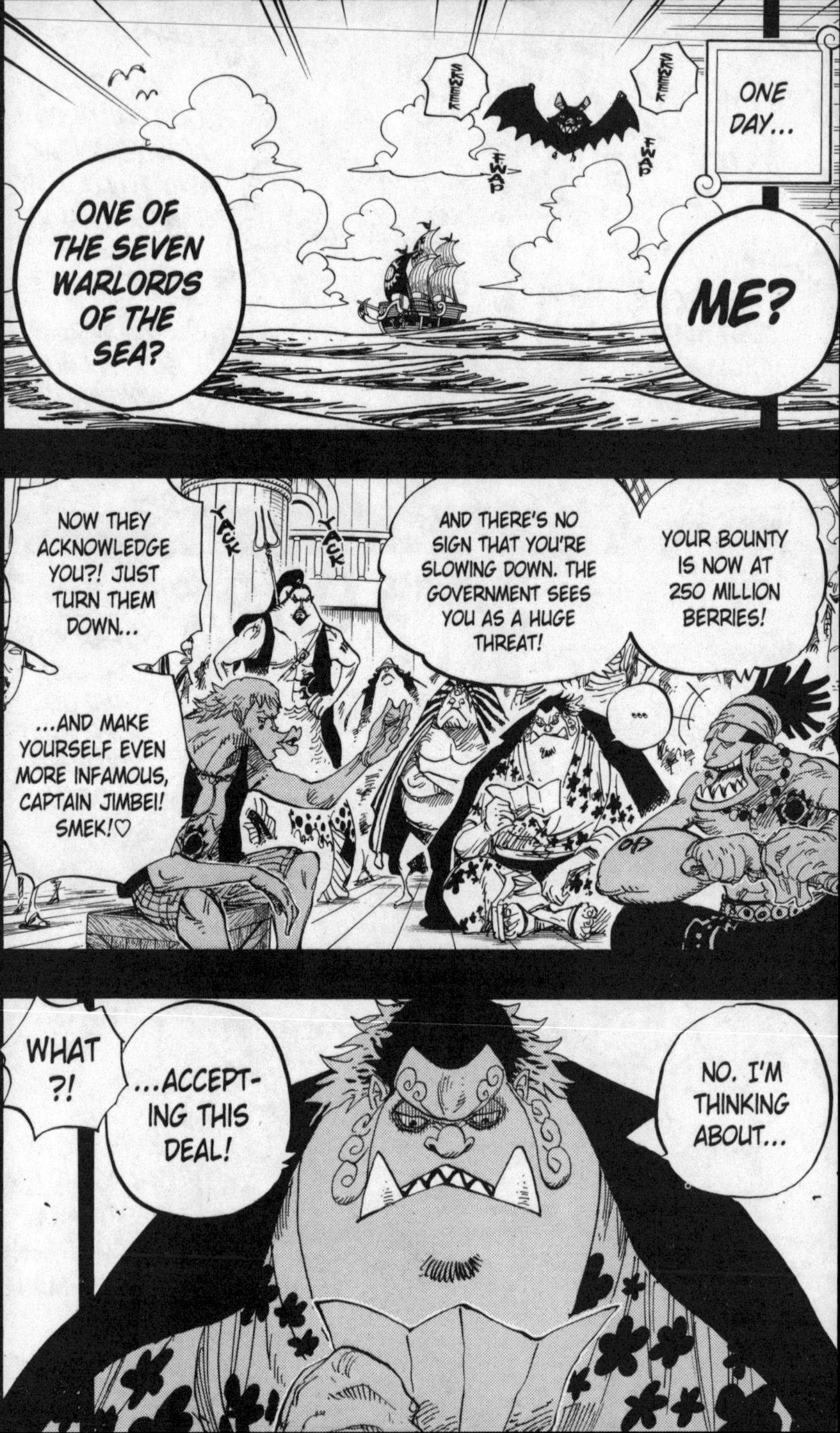
ONE DAY...
SKWEEK
SKWEEK
FWAP
FWAP
ONE OF THE SEVEN WARLORDS OF THE SEA?
ME?
YOUR BOUNTY IS NOW AT 250 MILLION BERRIES!
AND THERE'S NO SIGN THAT YOU'RE SLOWING DOWN. THE GOVERNMENT SEES YOU AS A HUGE THREAT!
...
YACK
YACK
NOW THEY ACKNOWLEDGE YOU?! JUST TURN THEM DOWN...
...AND MAKE YOURSELF EVEN MORE INFAMOUS, CAPTAIN JIMBEI! SMEK!♡
NO. I'M THINKING ABOUT...
...ACCEPT-ING THIS DEAL!
WHAT ?!

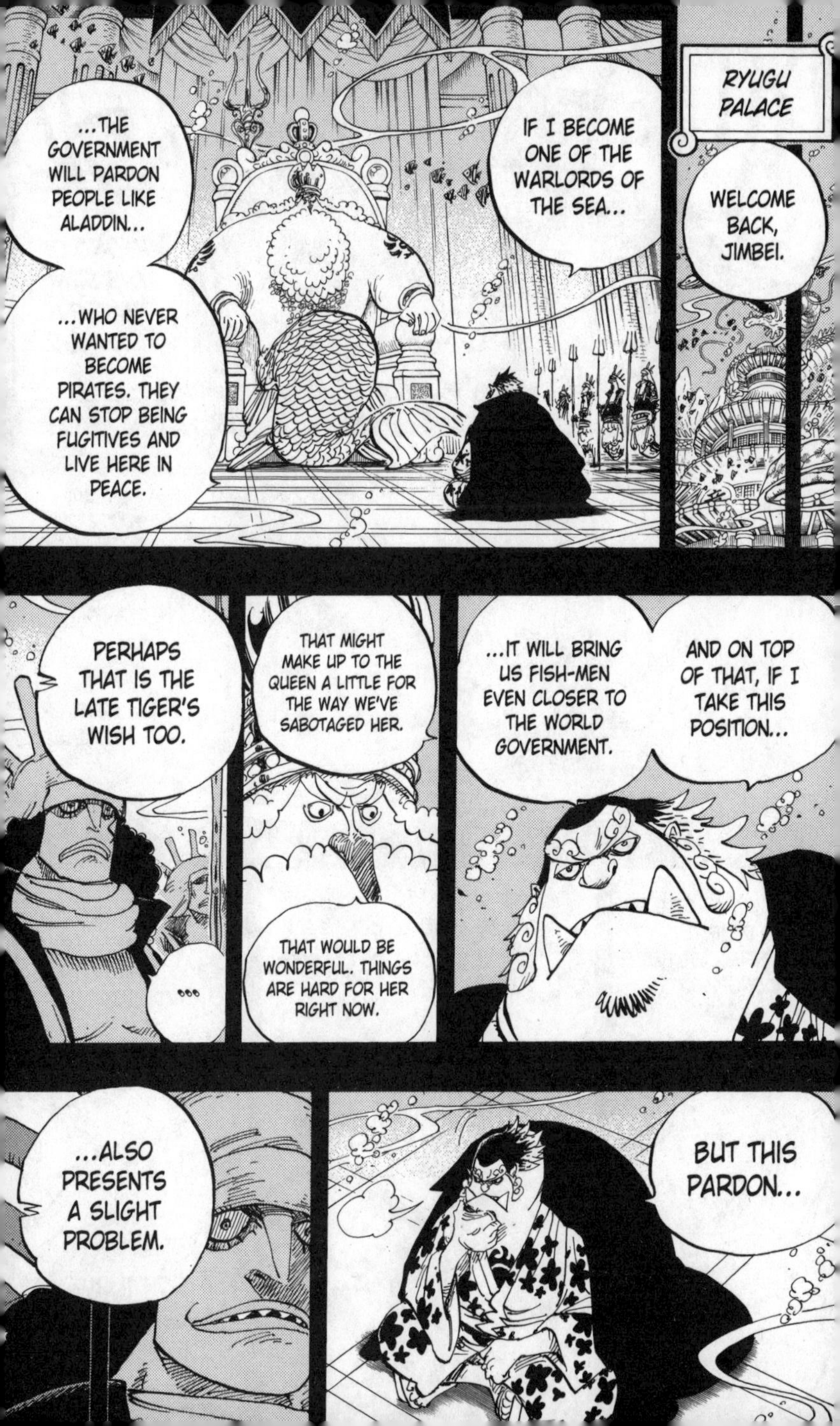
RYUGU PALACE
WELCOME BACK, JIMBEI.
IF I BECOME ONE OF THE WARLORDS OF THE SEA...
...THE GOVERNMENT WILL PARDON PEOPLE LIKE ALADDIN...
...WHO NEVER WANTED TO BECOME PIRATES. THEY CAN STOP BEING FUGITIVES AND LIVE HERE IN PEACE.
AND ON TOP OF THAT, IF I TAKE THIS POSITION...
...IT WILL BRING US FISH-MEN EVEN CLOSER TO THE WORLD GOVERNMENT.
THAT MIGHT MAKE UP TO THE QUEEN A LITTLE FOR THE WAY WE'VE SABOTAGED HER.
THAT WOULD BE WONDERFUL. THINGS ARE HARD FOR HER RIGHT NOW.
PERHAPS THAT IS THE LATE TIGER'S WISH TOO.
...
BUT THIS PARDON...
...ALSO PRESENTS A SLIGHT PROBLEM.

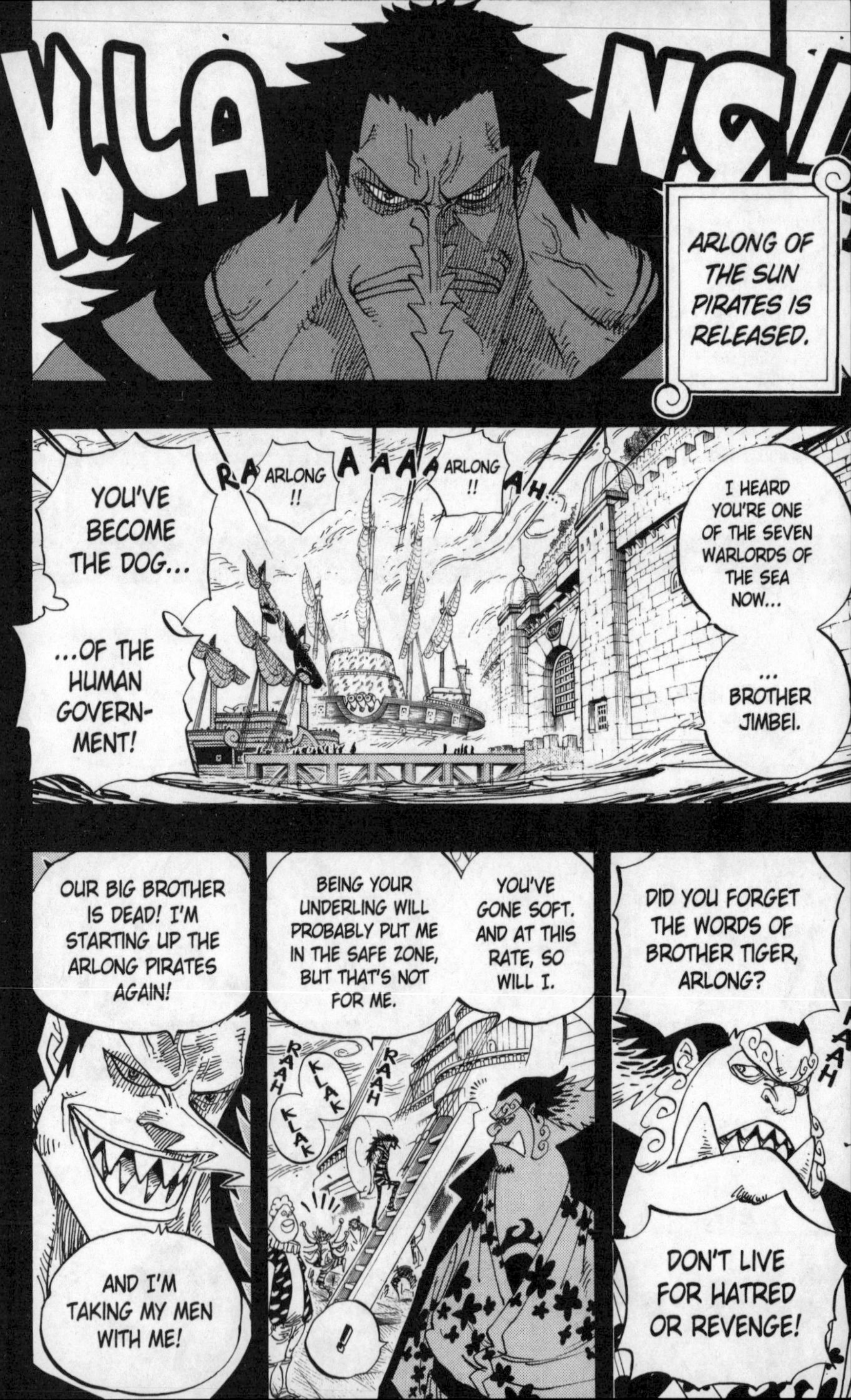
KLANG
ARLONG OF THE SUN PIRATES IS RELEASED.
I HEARD YOU'RE ONE OF THE SEVEN WARLORDS OF THE SEA NOW...
...BROTHER JIMBEI.
RAAAAAH...
ARLONG!!
ARLONG!!
YOU'VE BECOME THE DOG...
...OF THE HUMAN GOVERNMENT!
DID YOU FORGET THE WORDS OF BROTHER TIGER, ARLONG?
RAAH
DON'T LIVE FOR HATRED OR REVENGE!
YOU'VE GONE SOFT. AND AT THIS RATE, SO WILL I.
BEING YOUR UNDERLING WILL PROBABLY PUT ME IN THE SAFE ZONE, BUT THAT'S NOT FOR ME.
RAAAH
KLAK
KLAK
KLAK
RAAAH
!
OUR BIG BROTHER IS DEAD! I'M STARTING UP THE ARLONG PIRATES AGAIN!
AND I'M TAKING MY MEN WITH ME!

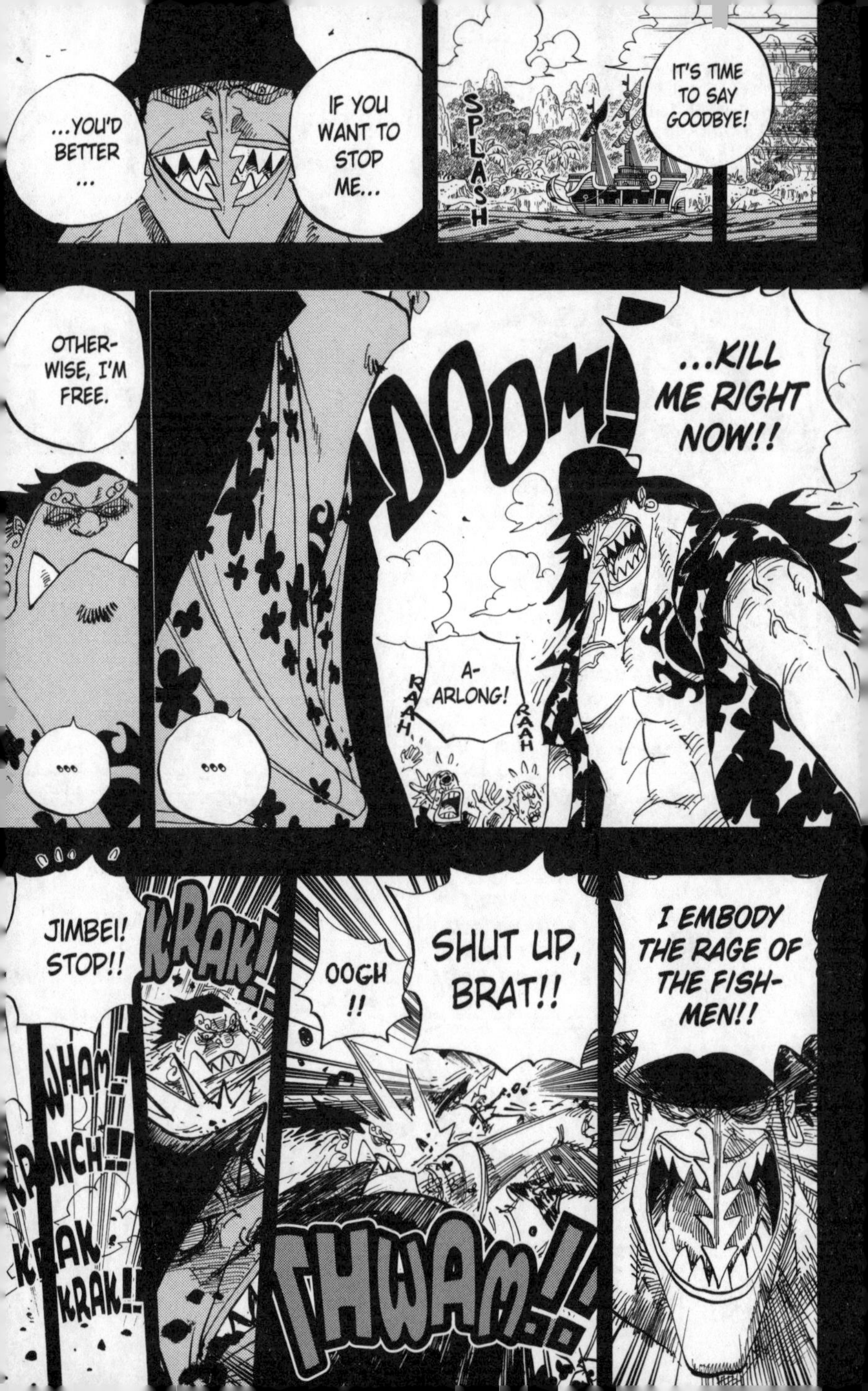
IT'S TIME TO SAY GOODBYE!
SPLASH
IF YOU WANT TO STOP ME...
...YOU'D BETTER ...
...KILL ME RIGHT NOW!!
DOOM!!
A- ARLONG!
RAAH
RAAH
...
OTHER-WISE, I'M FREE.
...
I EMBODY THE RAGE OF THE FISH-MEN!!
SHUT UP, BRAT!!
OOGH !!
THWAM!!
KRAK!!
JIMBEI! STOP!!
WHAM!!
KRUNCH!!
KRAK
KRAK!!

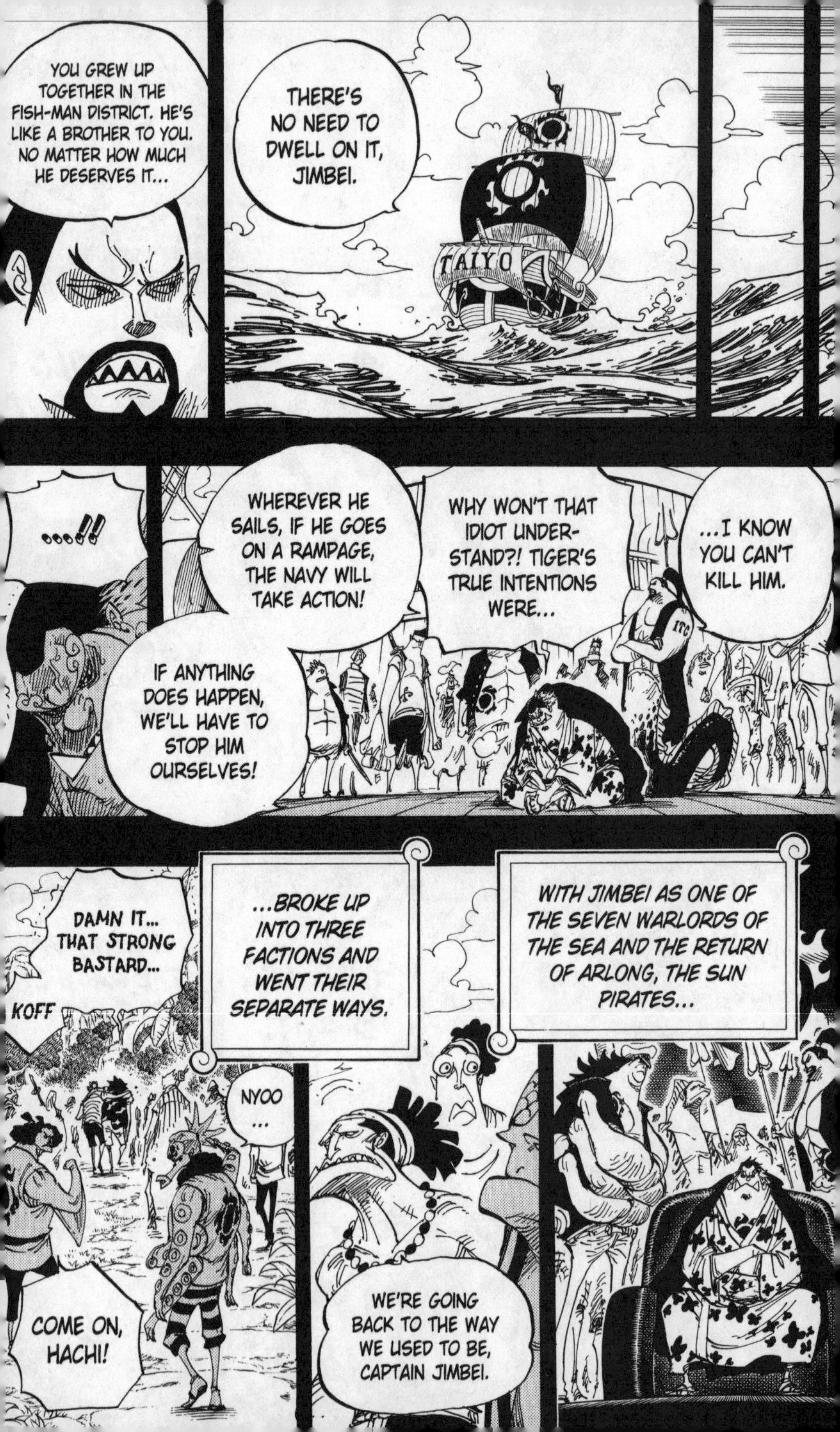
THERE'S NO NEED TO DWELL ON IT, JIMBEI.
YOU GREW UP TOGETHER IN THE FISH-MAN DISTRICT. HE'S LIKE A BROTHER TO YOU. NO MATTER HOW MUCH HE DESERVES IT...
...I KNOW YOU CAN'T KILL HIM.
WHY WON'T THAT IDIOT UNDER-STAND?! TIGER'S TRUE INTENTIONS WERE...
WHEREVER HE SAILS, IF HE GOES ON A RAMPAGE, THE NAVY WILL TAKE ACTION!
IF ANYTHING DOES HAPPEN, WE'LL HAVE TO STOP HIM OURSELVES!
...!!
WITH JIMBEI AS ONE OF THE SEVEN WARLORDS OF THE SEA AND THE RETURN OF ARLONG, THE SUN PIRATES...
...BROKE UP INTO THREE FACTIONS AND WENT THEIR SEPARATE WAYS.
WE'RE GOING BACK TO THE WAY WE USED TO BE, CAPTAIN JIMBEI.
DAMN IT... THAT STRONG BASTARD...
KOFF
NYOO ...
COME ON, HACHI!

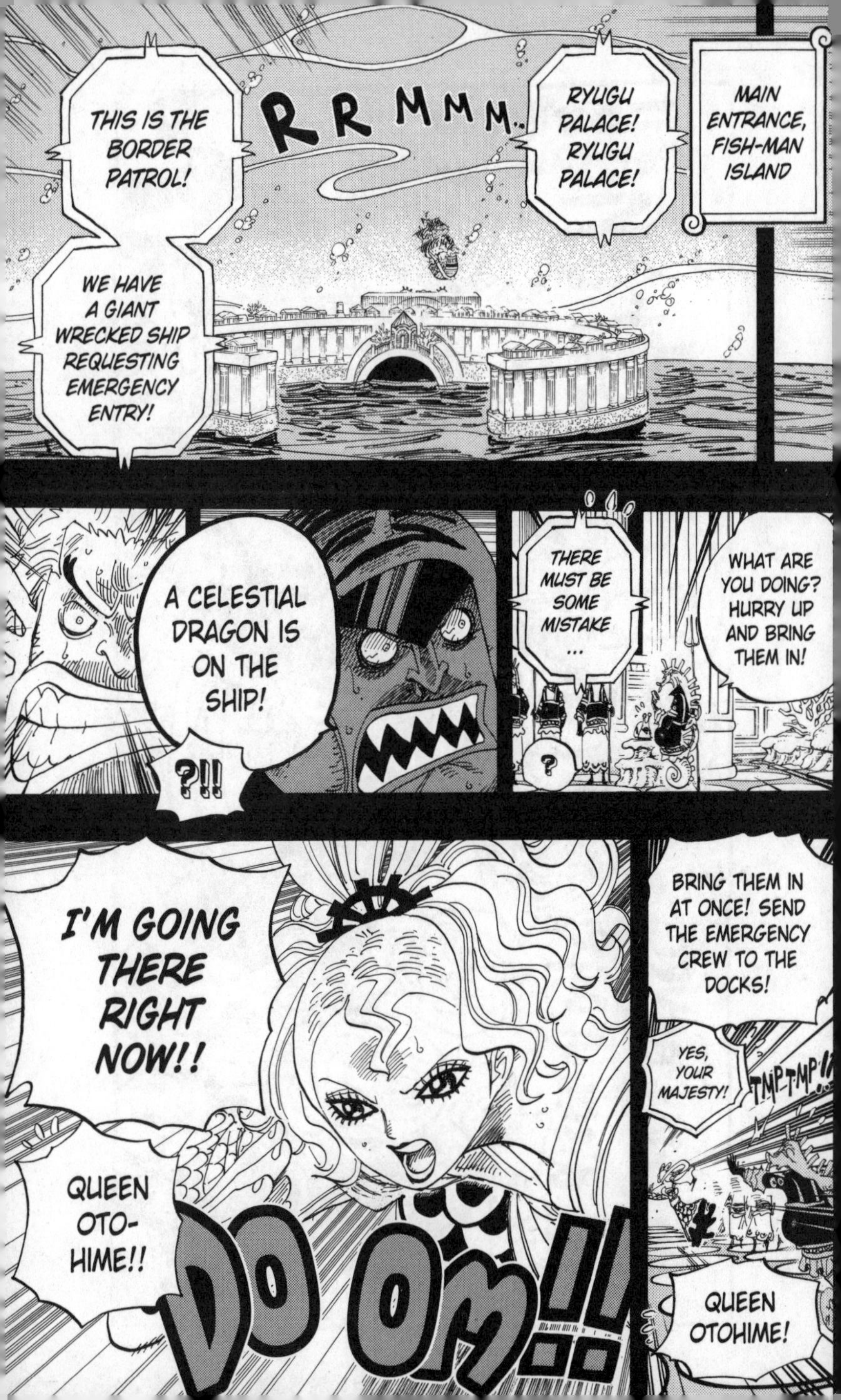
MAIN ENTRANCE, FISH-MAN ISLAND
RYUGU PALACE! RYUGU PALACE!
RRMMM..
THIS IS THE BORDER PATROL!
WE HAVE A GIANT WRECKED SHIP REQUESTING EMERGENCY ENTRY!
WHAT ARE YOU DOING? HURRY UP AND BRING THEM IN!
THERE MUST BE SOME MISTAKE ...
?
A CELESTIAL DRAGON IS ON THE SHIP!
?!!
BRING THEM IN AT ONCE! SEND THE EMERGENCY CREW TO THE DOCKS!
YES, YOUR MAJESTY!
TMP-TMP!!
QUEEN OTOHIME!
I'M GOING THERE RIGHT NOW!!
QUEEN OTO-HIME!!
DOOM!!

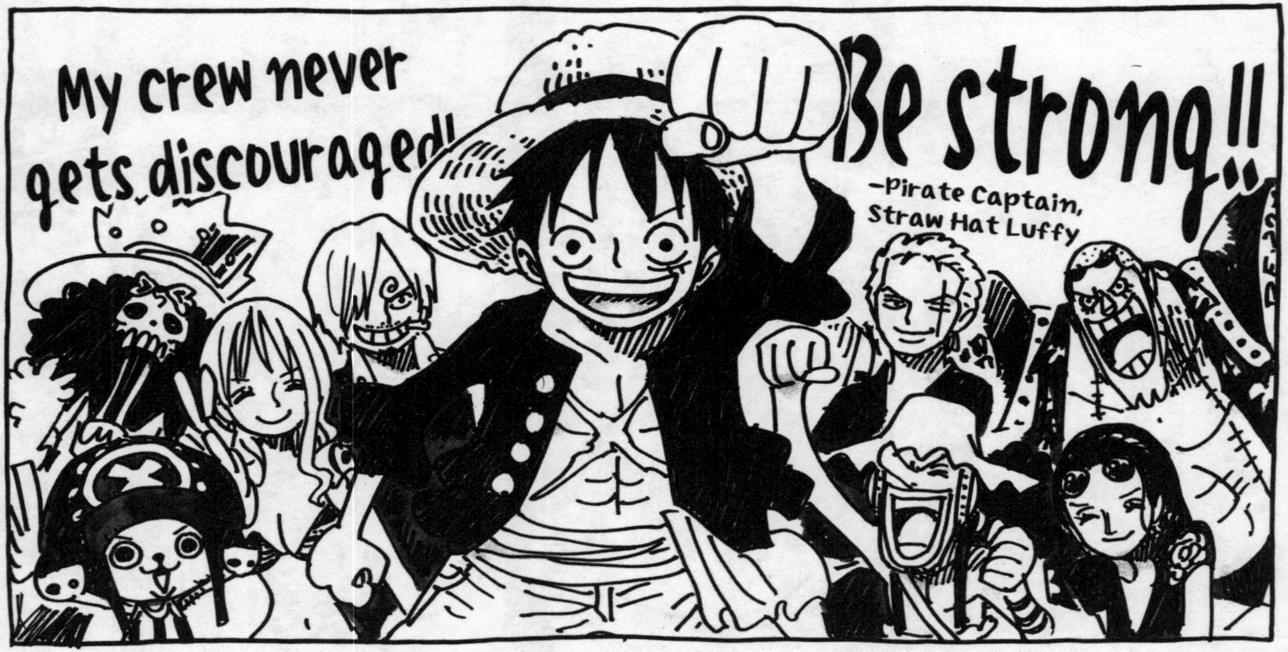
My crew never gets discouraged!!
Be strong!!
—Pirate Captain, Straw Hat Luffy

Chapter 625:
UNINHERITED WILL

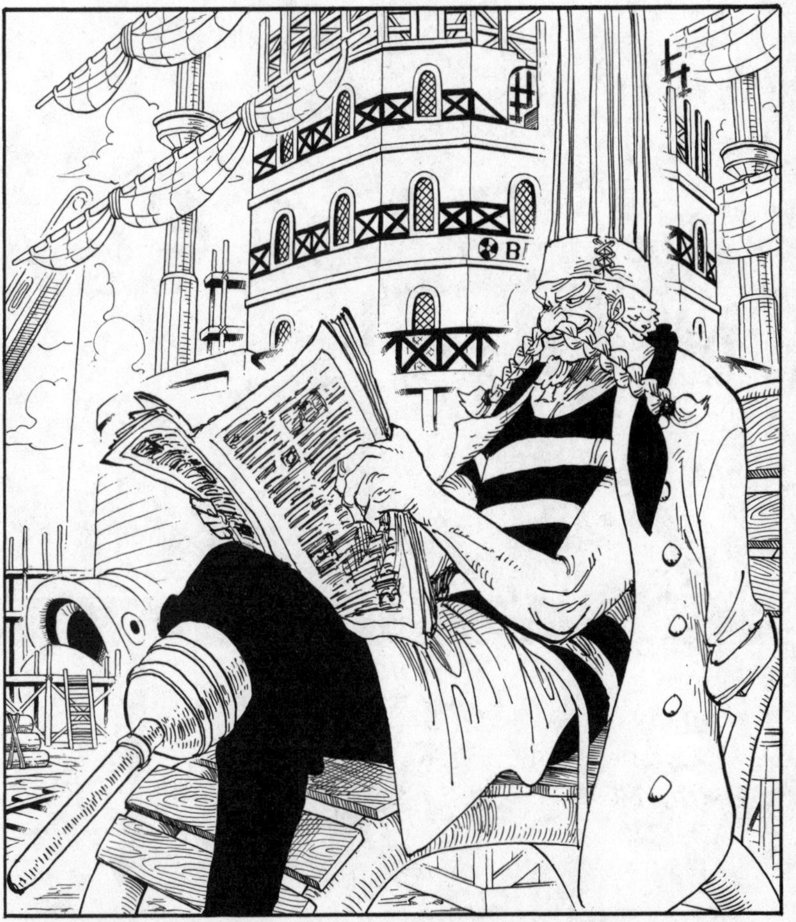

DECKS OF THE WORLD, VOL. 11: "BARATIE REMODELING"

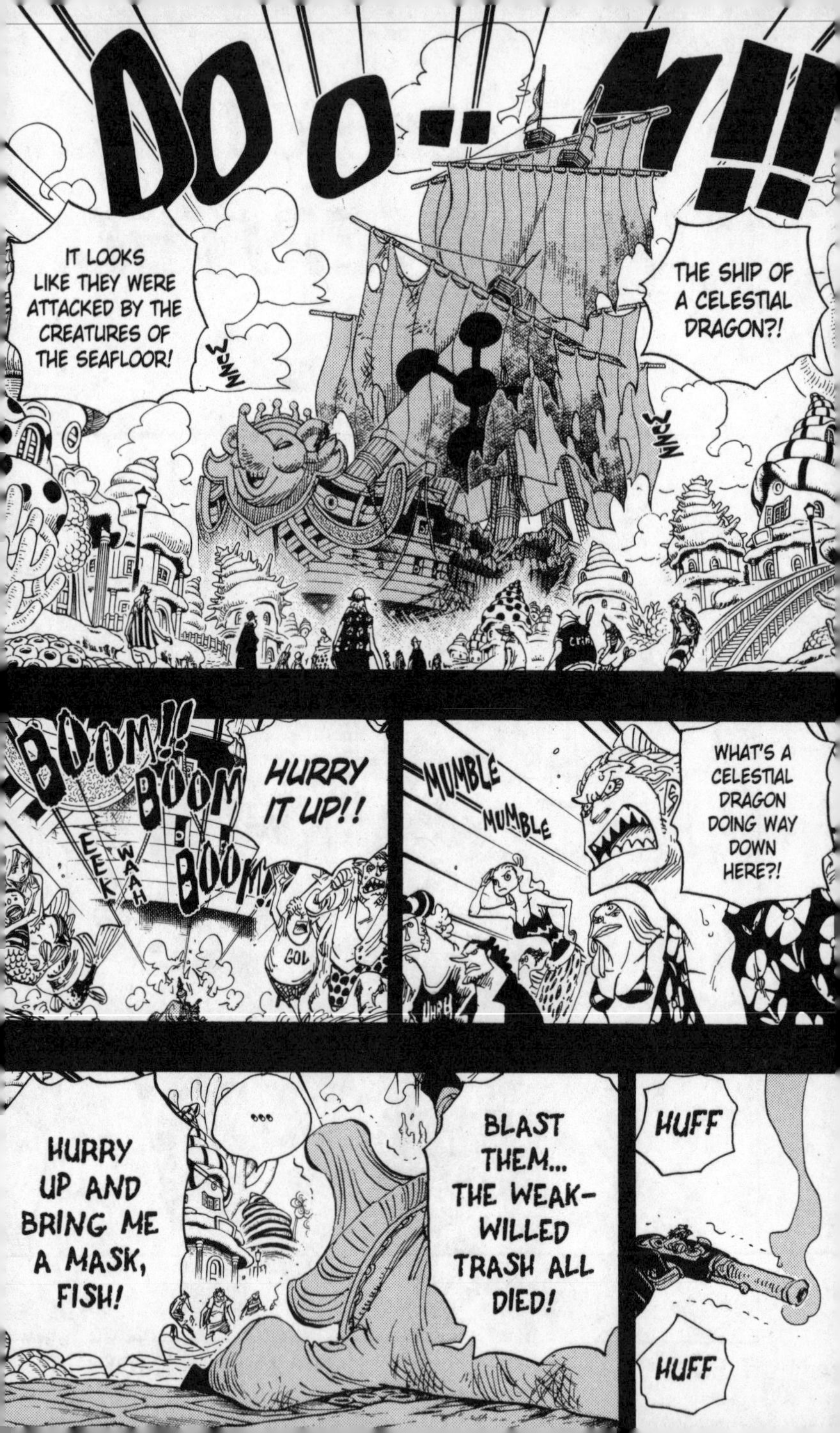
DOO...M!!
THE SHIP OF A CELESTIAL DRAGON?!
IT LOOKS LIKE THEY WERE ATTACKED BY THE CREATURES OF THE SEAFLOOR!
WUNN
WUNN
WHAT'S A CELESTIAL DRAGON DOING WAY DOWN HERE?!
MUMBLE
MUMBLE
HURRY IT UP!!
BOOM!!
BOOM
BOOM!!
WAAH
EEK
HUFF
HUFF
...
BLAST THEM... THE WEAK-WILLED TRASH ALL DIED!
HURRY UP AND BRING ME A MASK, FISH!

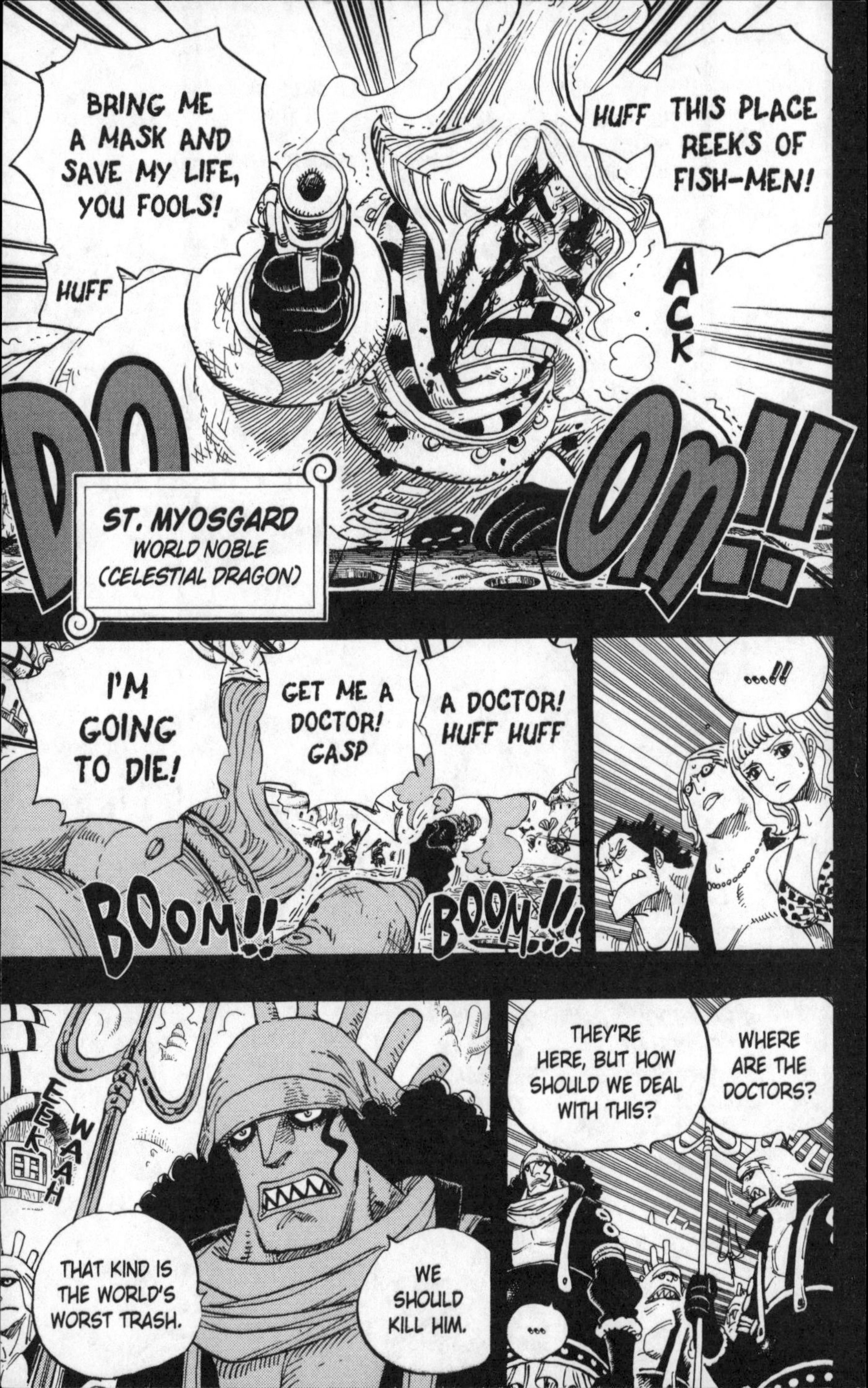
HUFF THIS PLACE REEKS OF FISH-MEN!
ACK
BRING ME A MASK AND SAVE MY LIFE, YOU FOOLS!
HUFF
DOOM!!
ST. MYOSGARD WORLD NOBLE (CELESTIAL DRAGON)
...!!
A DOCTOR! HUFF HUFF
GET ME A DOCTOR! GASP
I'M GOING TO DIE!
BOOM!!!
BOOM!!
WHERE ARE THE DOCTORS?
THEY'RE HERE, BUT HOW SHOULD WE DEAL WITH THIS?
...
WAAAH
EEEK
WE SHOULD KILL HIM.
THAT KIND IS THE WORLD'S WORST TRASH.

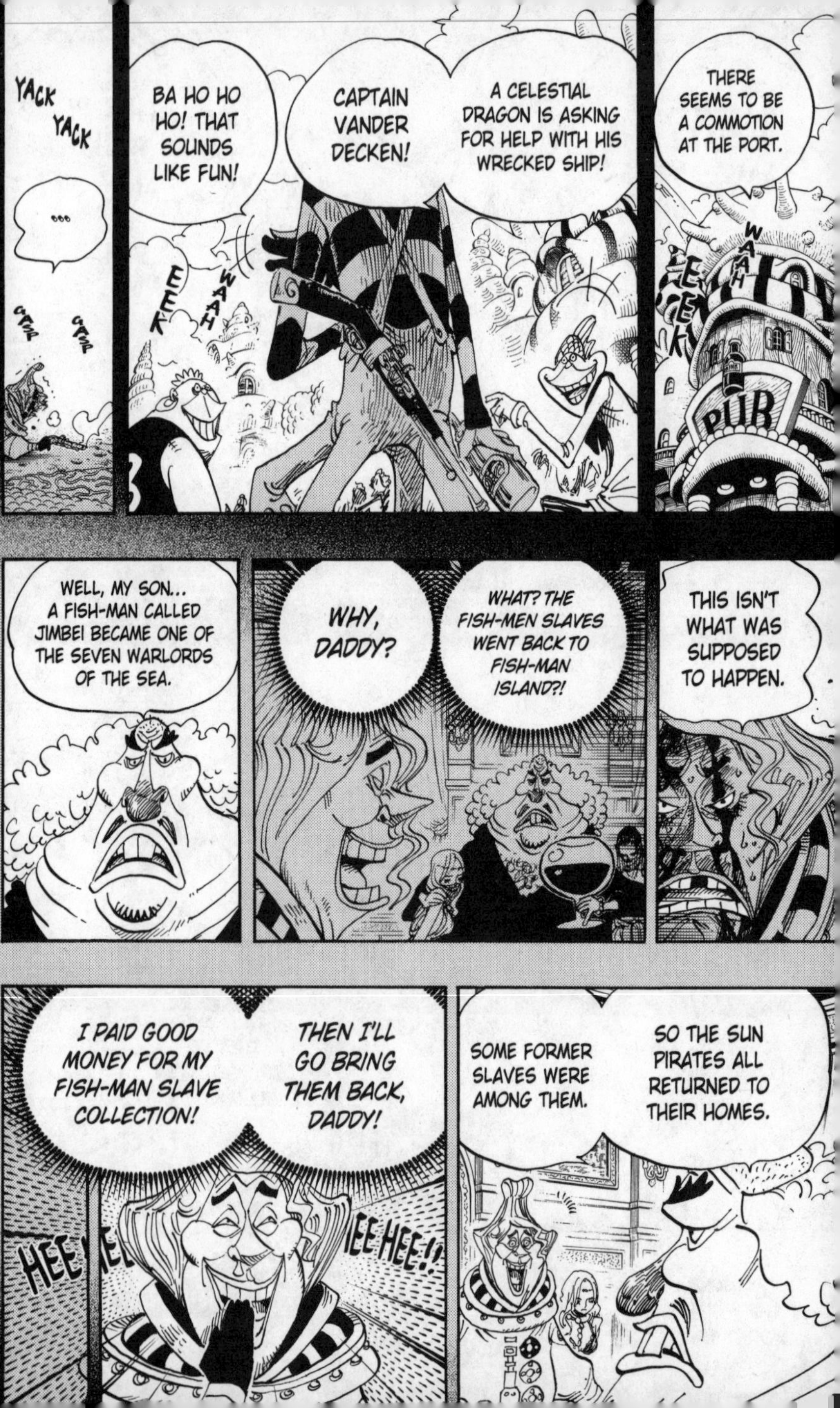
THERE SEEMS TO BE A COMMOTION AT THE PORT.
WAAH
EEK
PUB
A CELESTIAL DRAGON IS ASKING FOR HELP WITH HIS WRECKED SHIP!
CAPTAIN VANDER DECKEN!
BA HO HO HO! THAT SOUNDS LIKE FUN!
WAAH
EEK
YACK YACK
...
GASP GASP
THIS ISN'T WHAT WAS SUPPOSED TO HAPPEN.
WHAT? THE FISH-MEN SLAVES WENT BACK TO FISH-MAN ISLAND?!
WHY, DADDY?
WELL, MY SON... A FISH-MAN CALLED JIMBEI BECAME ONE OF THE SEVEN WARLORDS OF THE SEA.
SO THE SUN PIRATES ALL RETURNED TO THEIR HOMES.
SOME FORMER SLAVES WERE AMONG THEM.
THEN I'LL GO BRING THEM BACK, DADDY!
I PAID GOOD MONEY FOR MY FISH-MAN SLAVE COLLECTION!
HEE HEE!!
HEE

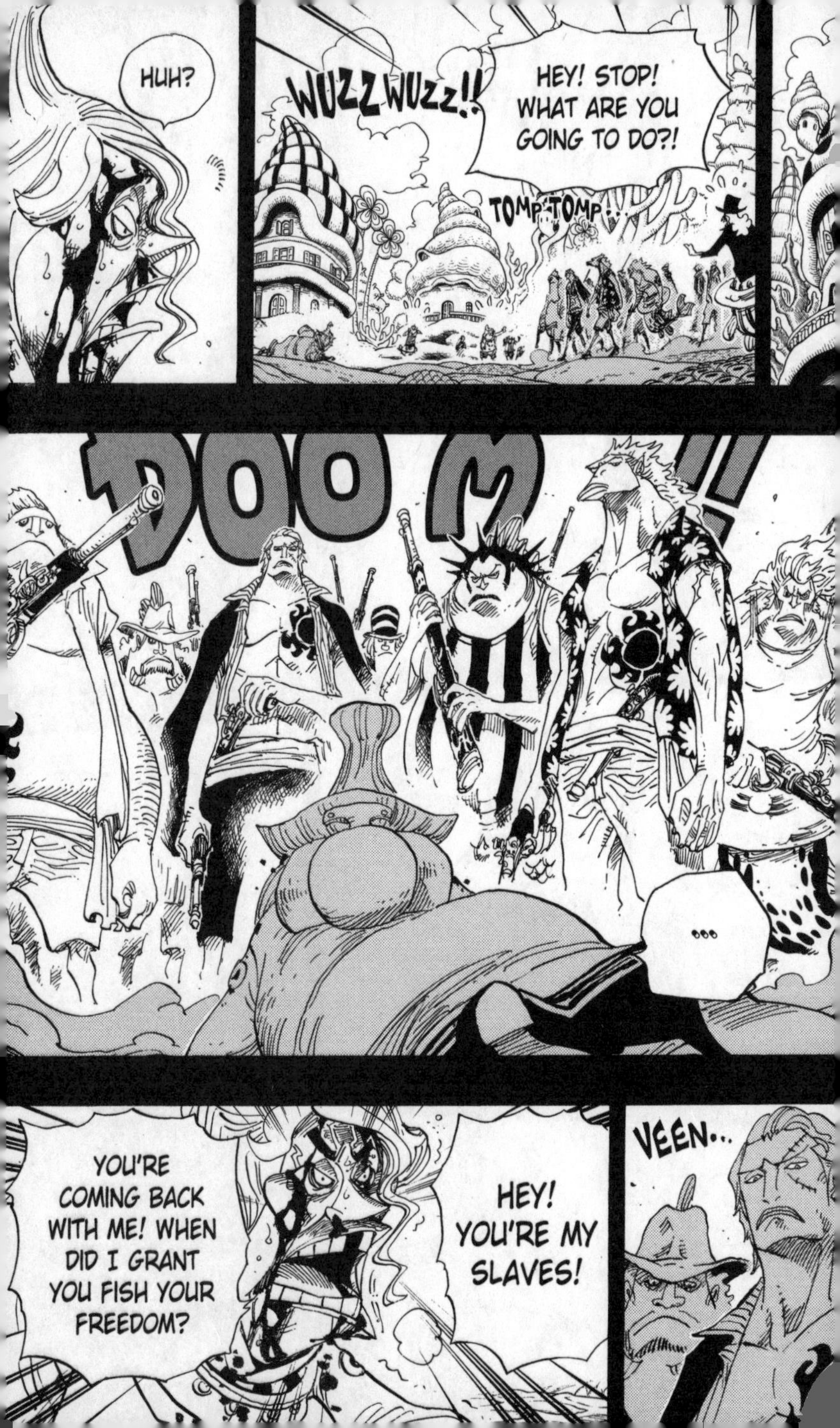
HEY! STOP! WHAT ARE YOU GOING TO DO?!
WUZZ WUZZ!!
TOMP TOMP...
HUH?
DOOM!!
...
VEEN...
HEY! YOU'RE MY SLAVES!
YOU'RE COMING BACK WITH ME! WHEN DID I GRANT YOU FISH YOUR FREEDOM?

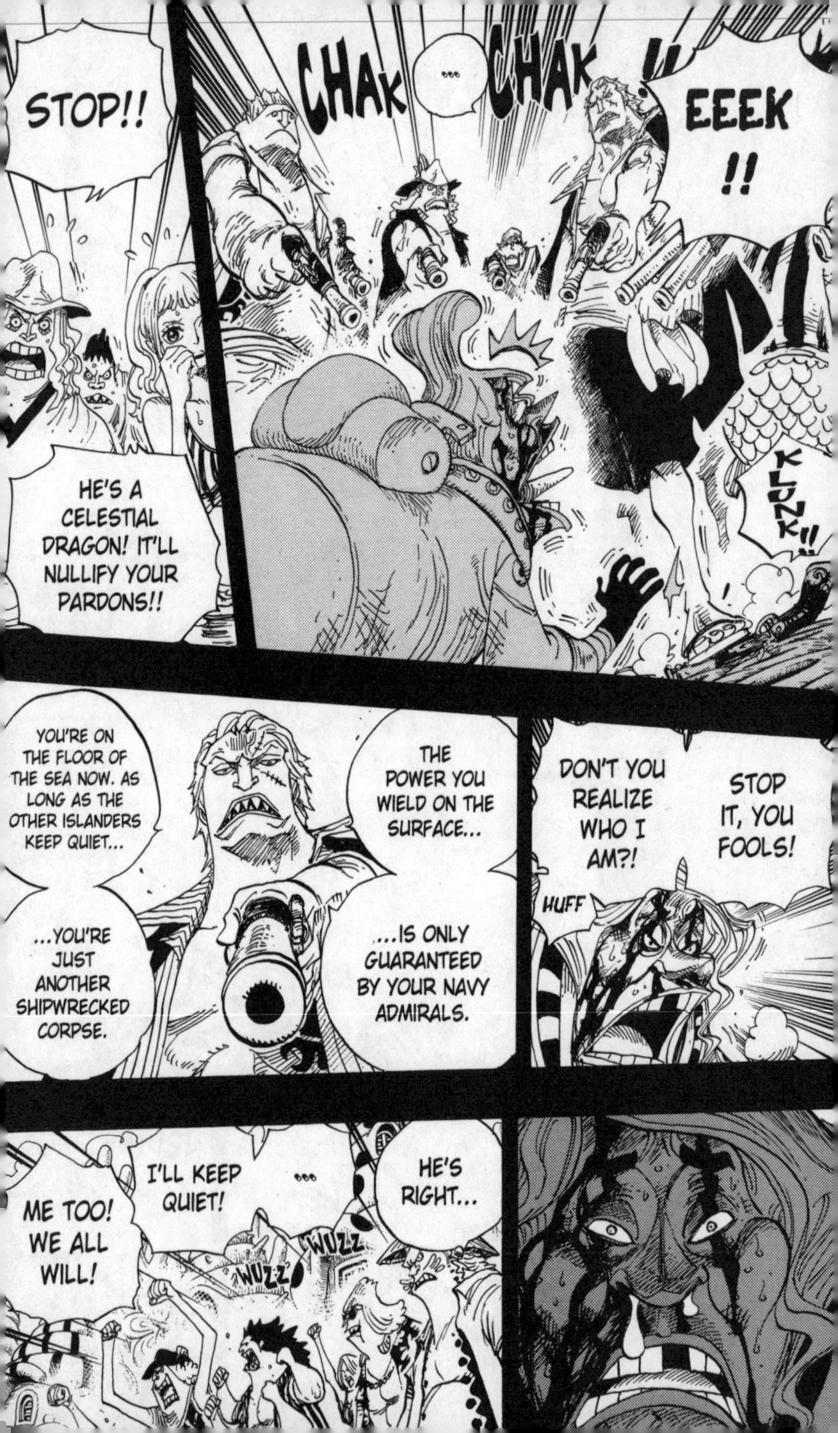
EEEK!!
CHAK
...
CHAK!!
KLUNK!!
STOP!!
HE'S A CELESTIAL DRAGON! IT'LL NULLIFY YOUR PARDONS!!
STOP IT, YOU FOOLS!
DON'T YOU REALIZE WHO I AM?!
HUFF
THE POWER YOU WIELD ON THE SURFACE...
....IS ONLY GUARANTEED BY YOUR NAVY ADMIRALS.
YOU'RE ON THE FLOOR OF THE SEA NOW. AS LONG AS THE OTHER ISLANDERS KEEP QUIET...
...YOU'RE JUST ANOTHER SHIPWRECKED CORPSE.
HE'S RIGHT...
...
I'LL KEEP QUIET!
WUZZ
WUZZ
ME TOO! WE ALL WILL!

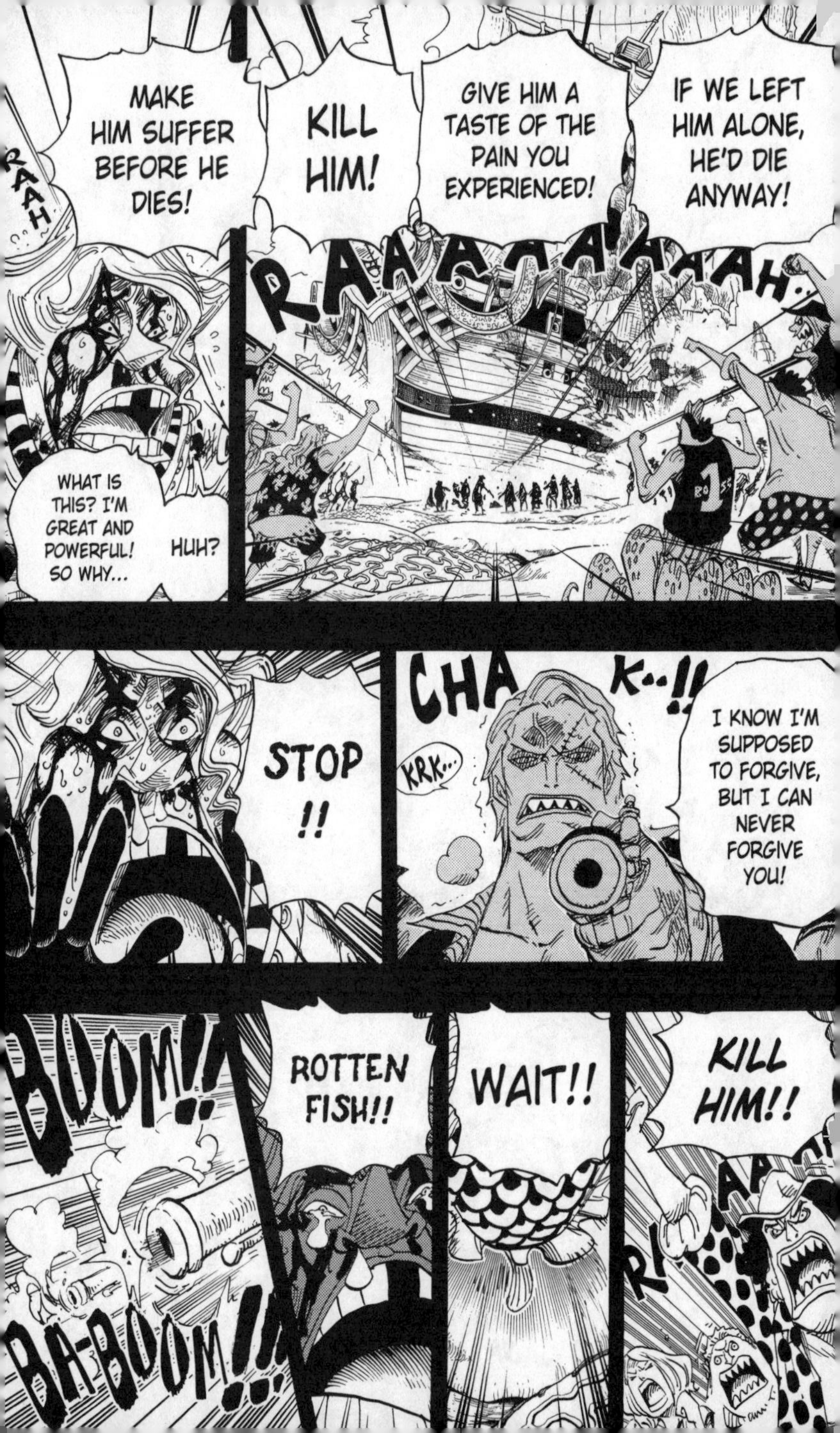
IF WE LEFT HIM ALONE, HE'D DIE ANYWAY!
GIVE HIM A TASTE OF THE PAIN YOU EXPERIENCED!
KILL HIM!
MAKE HIM SUFFER BEFORE HE DIES!
RAAAAAAAAAH
RAAAH
HUH?
WHAT IS THIS? I'M GREAT AND POWERFUL! SO WHY...
CHAK..!!
KRK...
I KNOW I'M SUPPOSED TO FORGIVE, BUT I CAN NEVER FORGIVE YOU!
STOP!!
KILL HIM!!
WAIT!!
ROTTEN FISH!!
BOOM!!
BA-BOOM!!

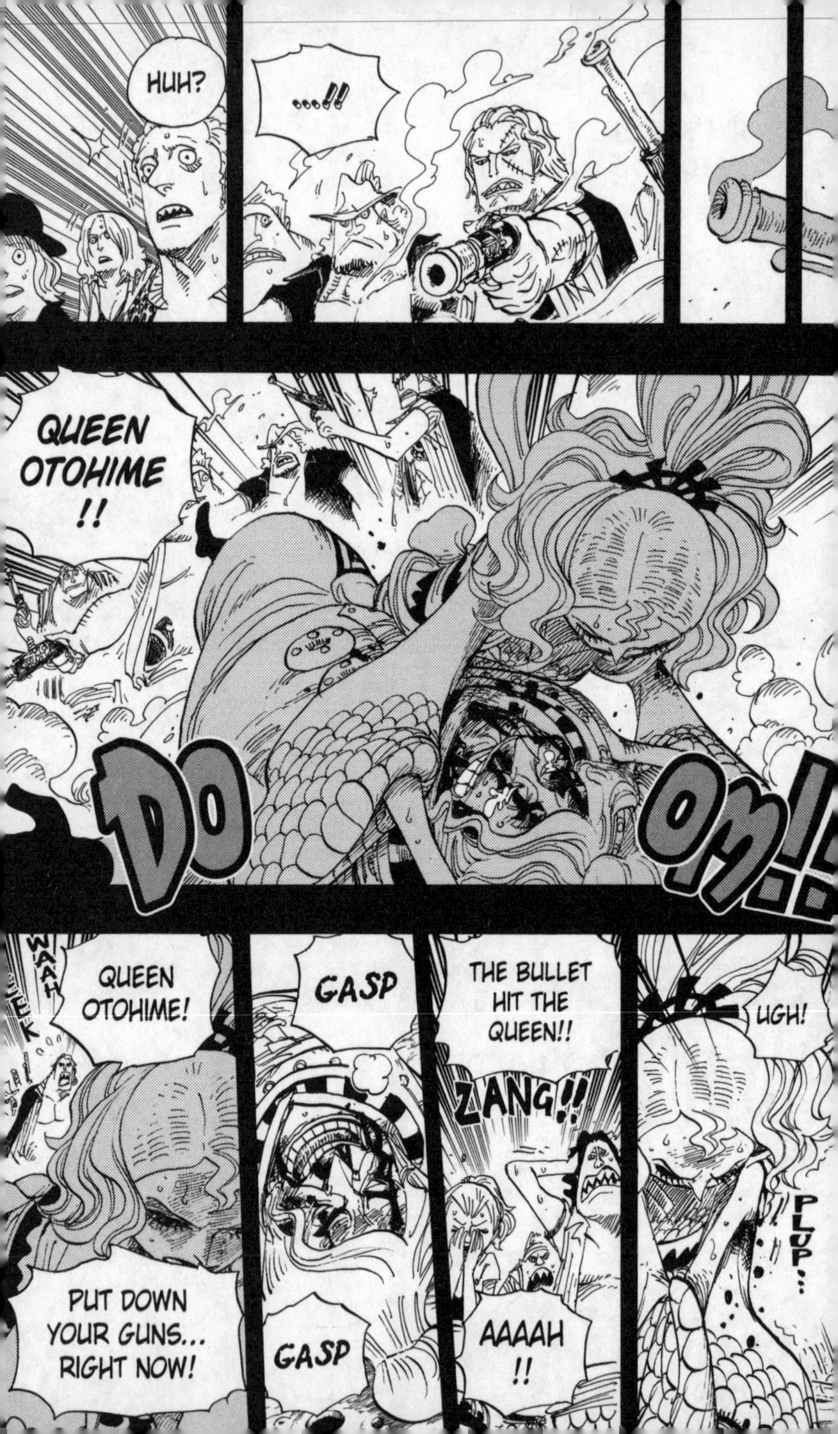
...!!
HUH?
QUEEN OTOHIME !!
DOOM!!
UGH!
PLUP...
THE BULLET HIT THE QUEEN!!
ZANG!!
AAAAH !!
GASP
GASP
QUEEN OTOHIME!
WAAAH
EEK
PUT DOWN YOUR GUNS... RIGHT NOW!

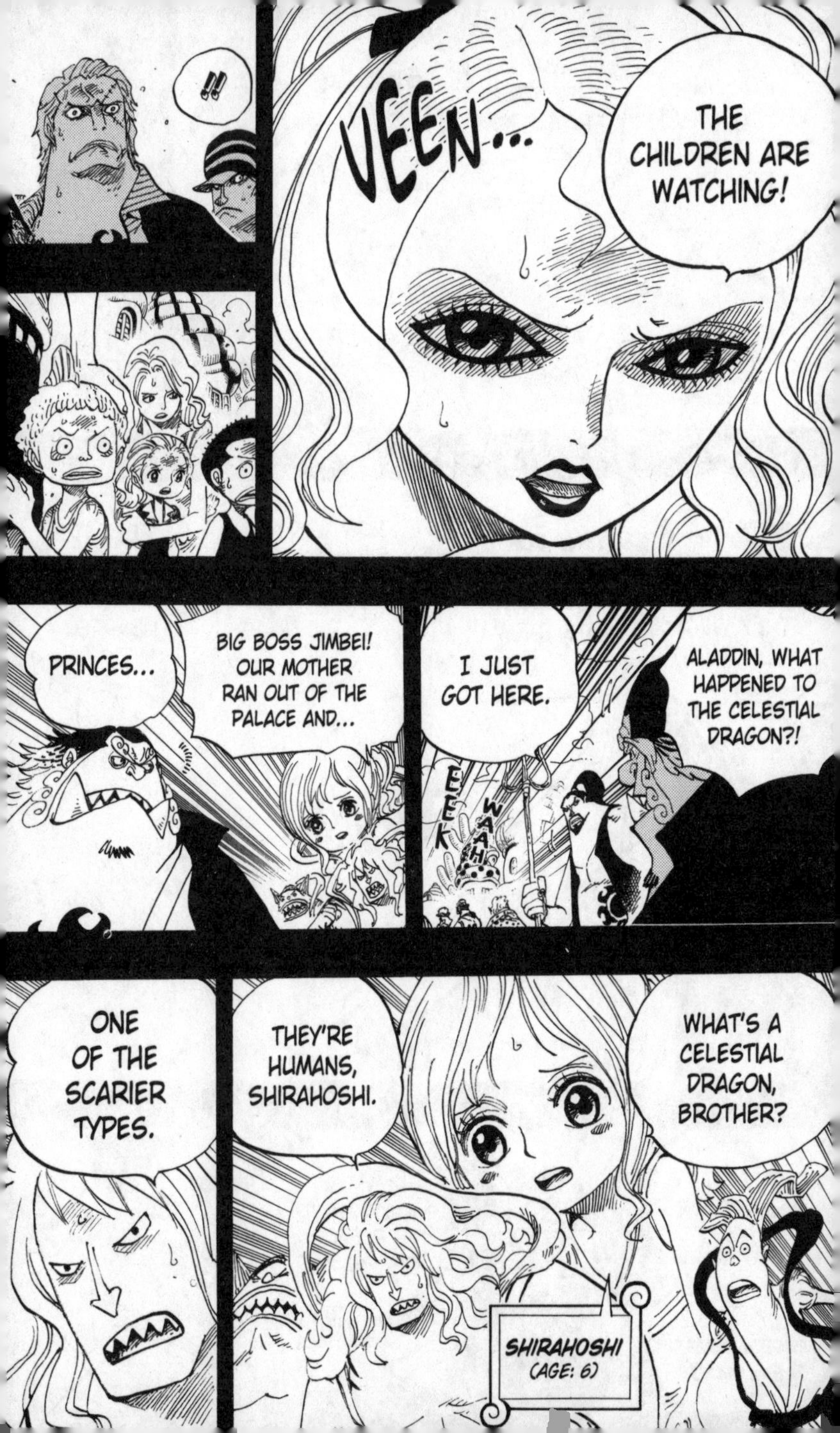
VEEN...
THE CHILDREN ARE WATCHING!
!!
ALADDIN, WHAT HAPPENED TO THE CELESTIAL DRAGON?!
I JUST GOT HERE.
EEK
WAAH
BIG BOSS JIMBEI! OUR MOTHER RAN OUT OF THE PALACE AND...
PRINCES...
WHAT'S A CELESTIAL DRAGON, BROTHER?
SHIRAHOSHI (AGE: 6)
THEY'RE HUMANS, SHIRAHOSHI.
ONE OF THE SCARIER TYPES.

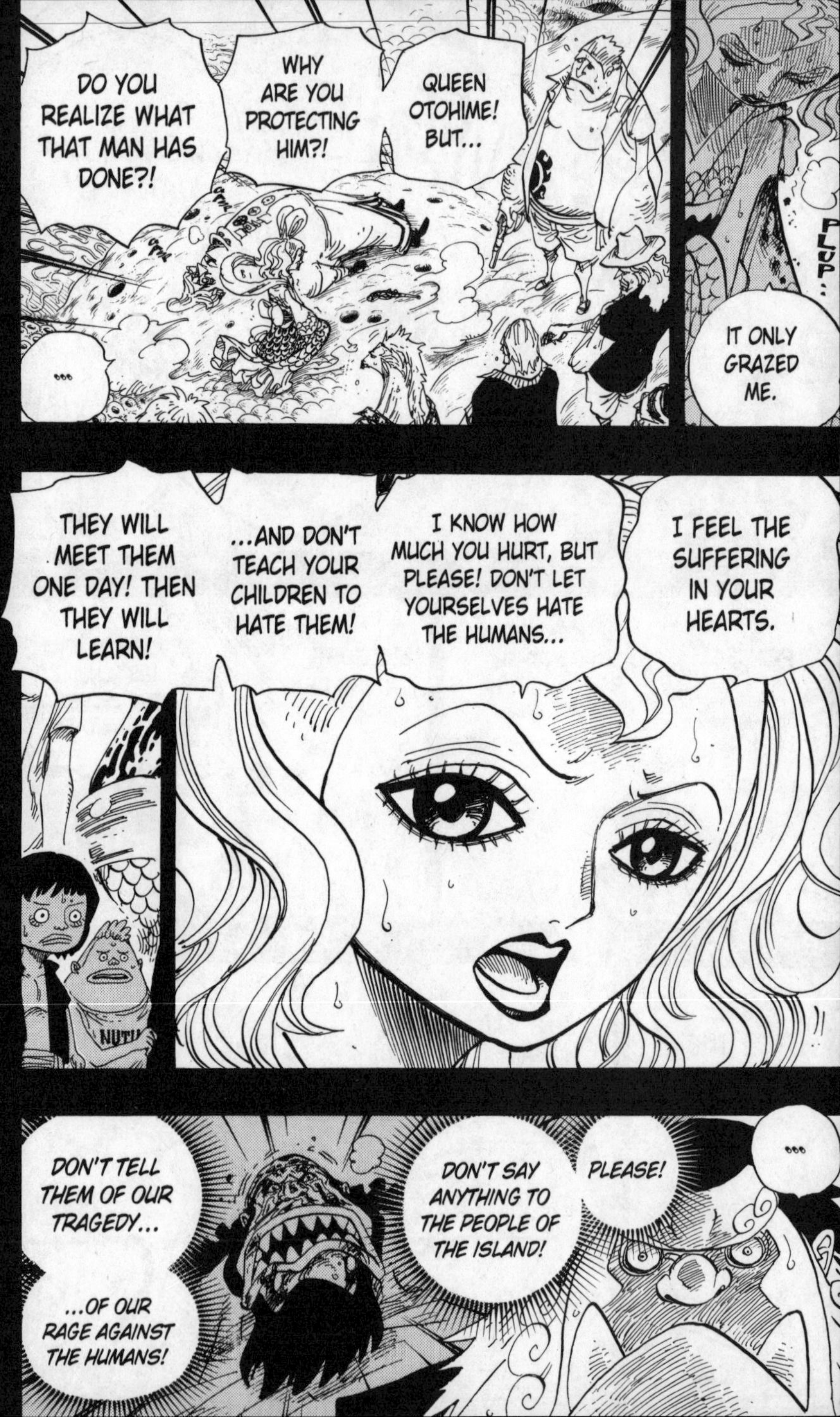
PLUP...
IT ONLY GRAZED ME.
QUEEN OTOHIME! BUT...
WHY ARE YOU PROTECTING HIM?!
DO YOU REALIZE WHAT THAT MAN HAS DONE?!
...
I FEEL THE SUFFERING IN YOUR HEARTS.
I KNOW HOW MUCH YOU HURT, BUT PLEASE! DON'T LET YOURSELVES HATE THE HUMANS...
...AND DON'T TEACH YOUR CHILDREN TO HATE THEM!
THEY WILL MEET THEM ONE DAY! THEN THEY WILL LEARN!
...
PLEASE!
DON'T SAY ANYTHING TO THE PEOPLE OF THE ISLAND!
DON'T TELL THEM OF OUR TRAGEDY...
...OF OUR RAGE AGAINST THE HUMANS!

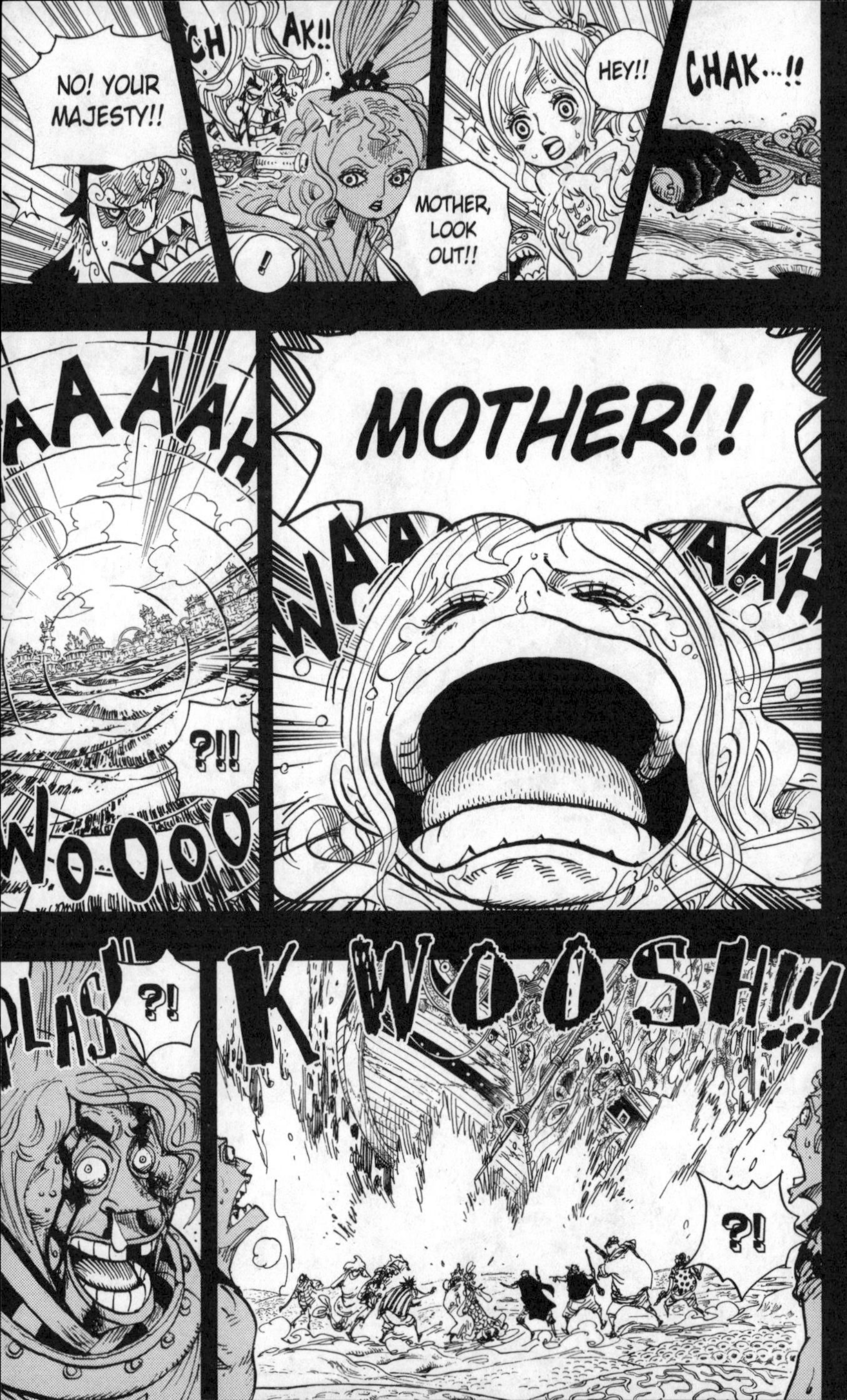
CHAK...!!
HEY!!
CH
AK!!
MOTHER, LOOK OUT!!
!
NO! YOUR MAJESTY!!
MOTHER!!
AAH
WAA
AAAAH
?!!
WOOO
KWOOSH!!!
?!
?!
PLAS

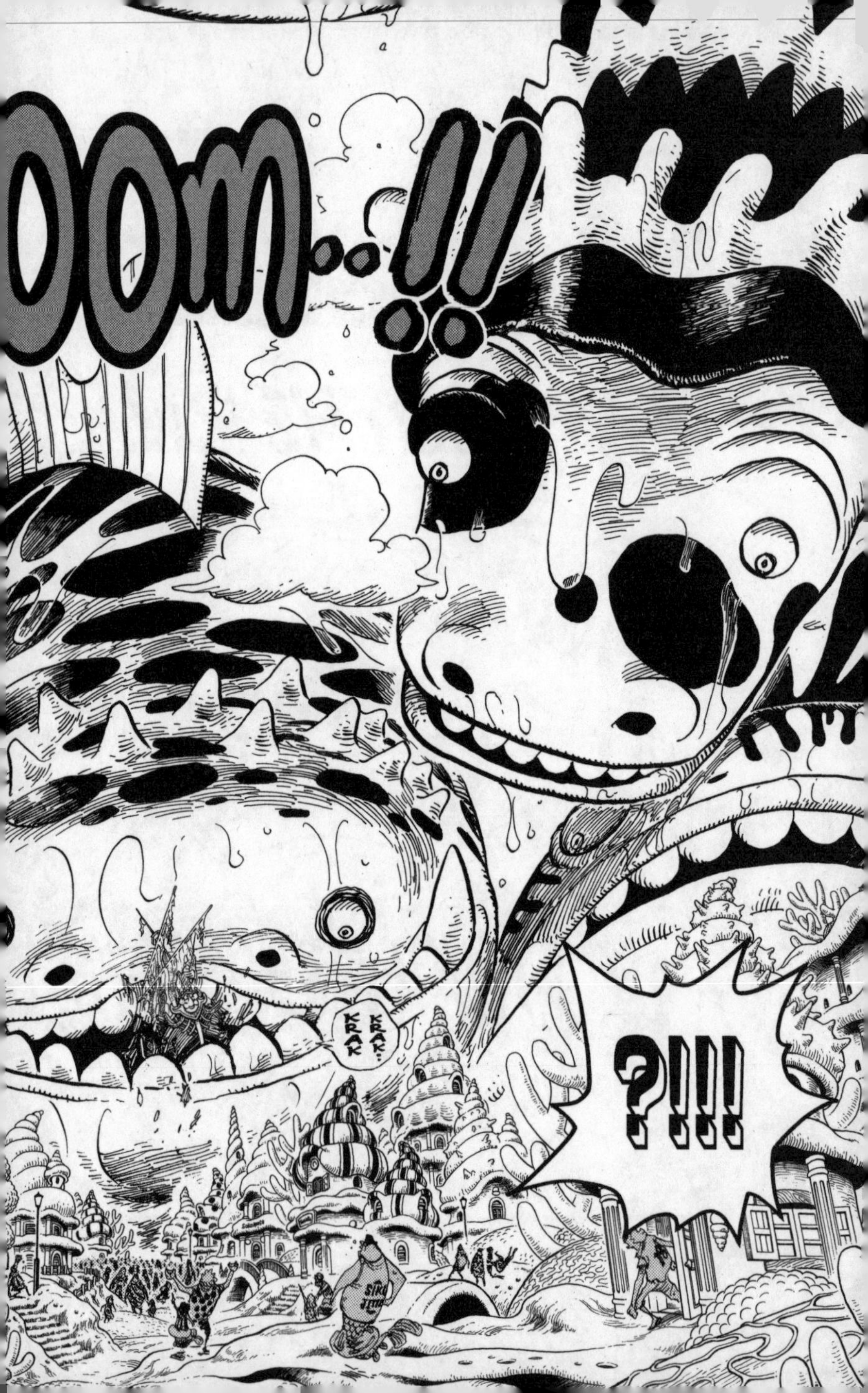
OOM..!!
KRAK KRAK
?!!!
SIKU JITTE

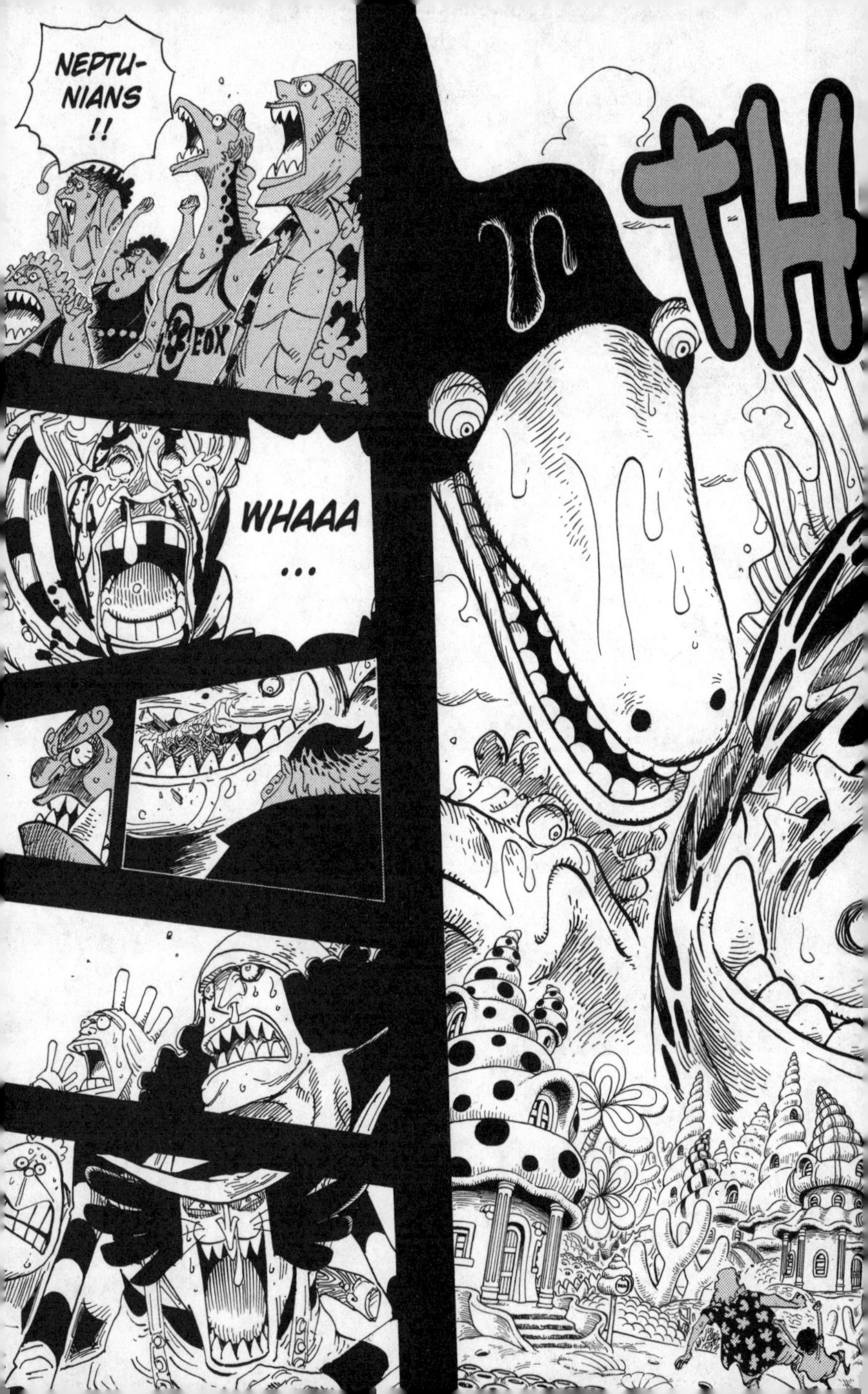
TH
NEPTU-
NIANS
!!
WHAAA
...

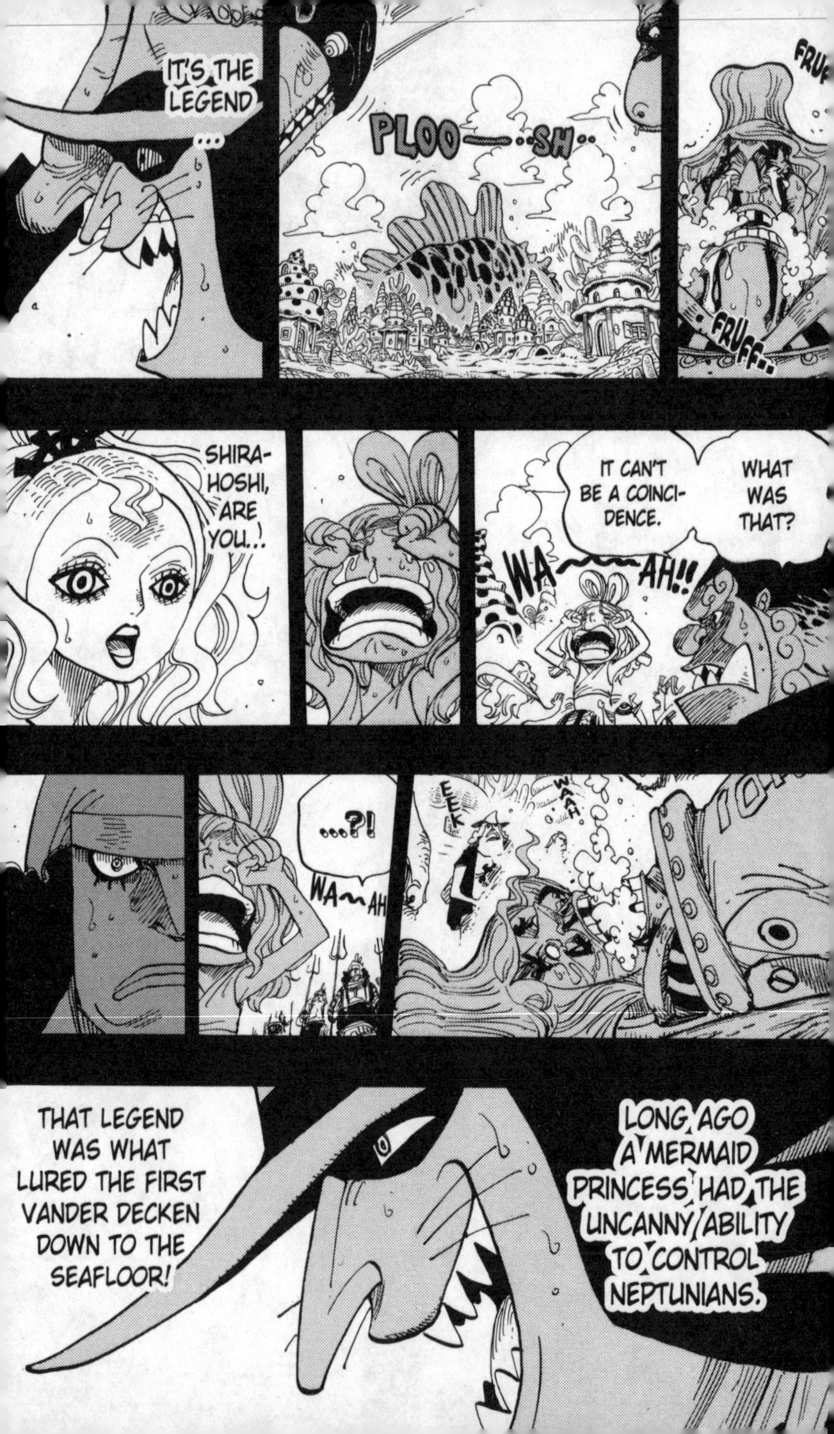
FRUF
FRUFF..
PLOO——SH..
IT'S THE LEGEND ...
WHAT WAS THAT?
IT CAN'T BE A COINCI-DENCE.
WA~~AH!!
SHIRA-HOSHI, ARE YOU...
WAAH
EEK
...?!
WA~AH
LONG AGO A MERMAID PRINCESS HAD THE UNCANNY ABILITY TO CONTROL NEPTUNIANS.
THAT LEGEND WAS WHAT LURED THE FIRST VANDER DECKEN DOWN TO THE SEAFLOOR!

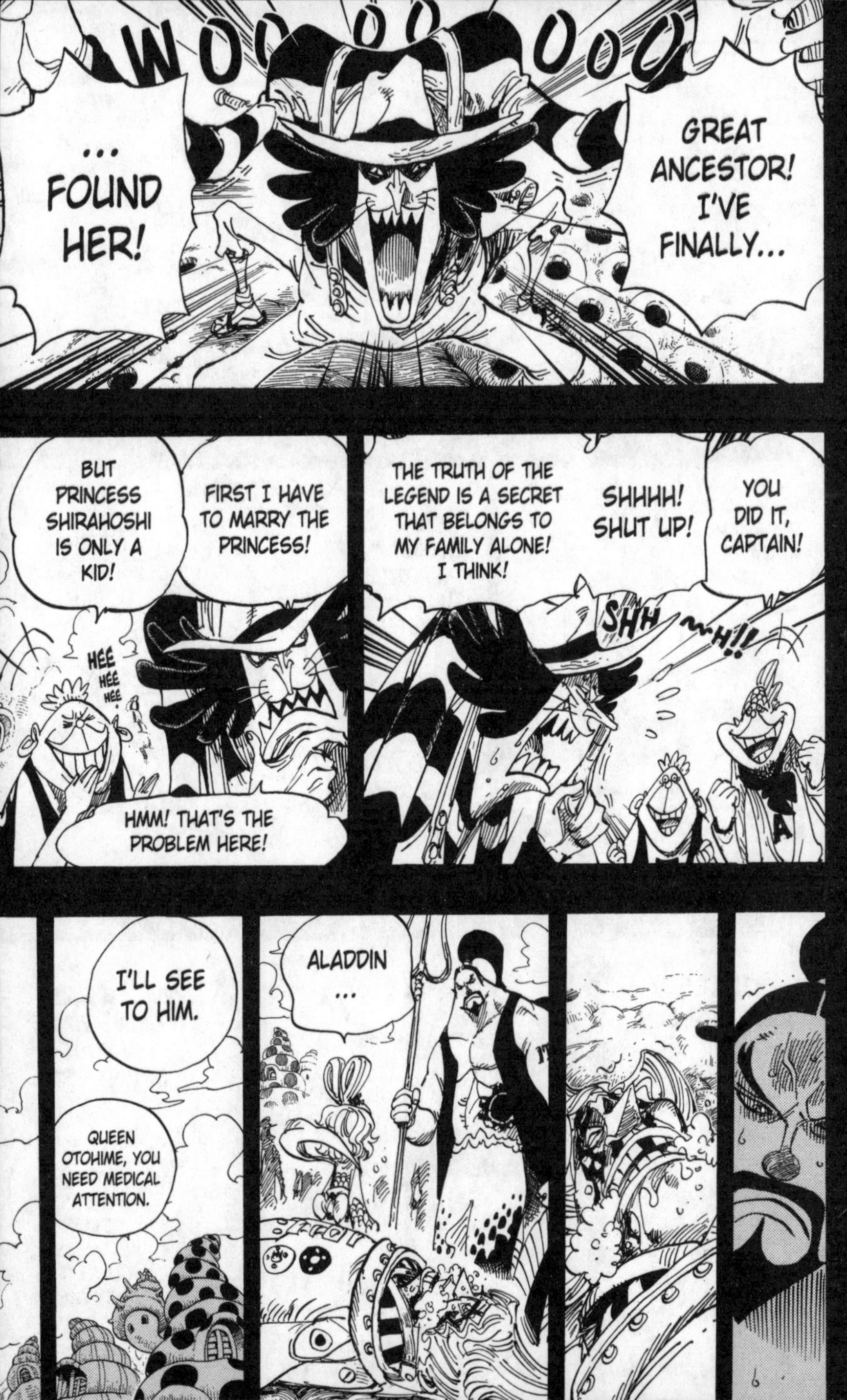
WOOOOOOO
GREAT ANCESTOR! I'VE FINALLY...
... FOUND HER!
YOU DID IT, CAPTAIN!
SHHHH! SHUT UP!
THE TRUTH OF THE LEGEND IS A SECRET THAT BELONGS TO MY FAMILY ALONE! I THINK!
SHHH~H!!
FIRST I HAVE TO MARRY THE PRINCESS!
BUT PRINCESS SHIRAHOSHI IS ONLY A KID!
HEE HEE HEE
HMM! THAT'S THE PROBLEM HERE!
ALADDIN ...
I'LL SEE TO HIM.
QUEEN OTOHIME, YOU NEED MEDICAL ATTENTION.

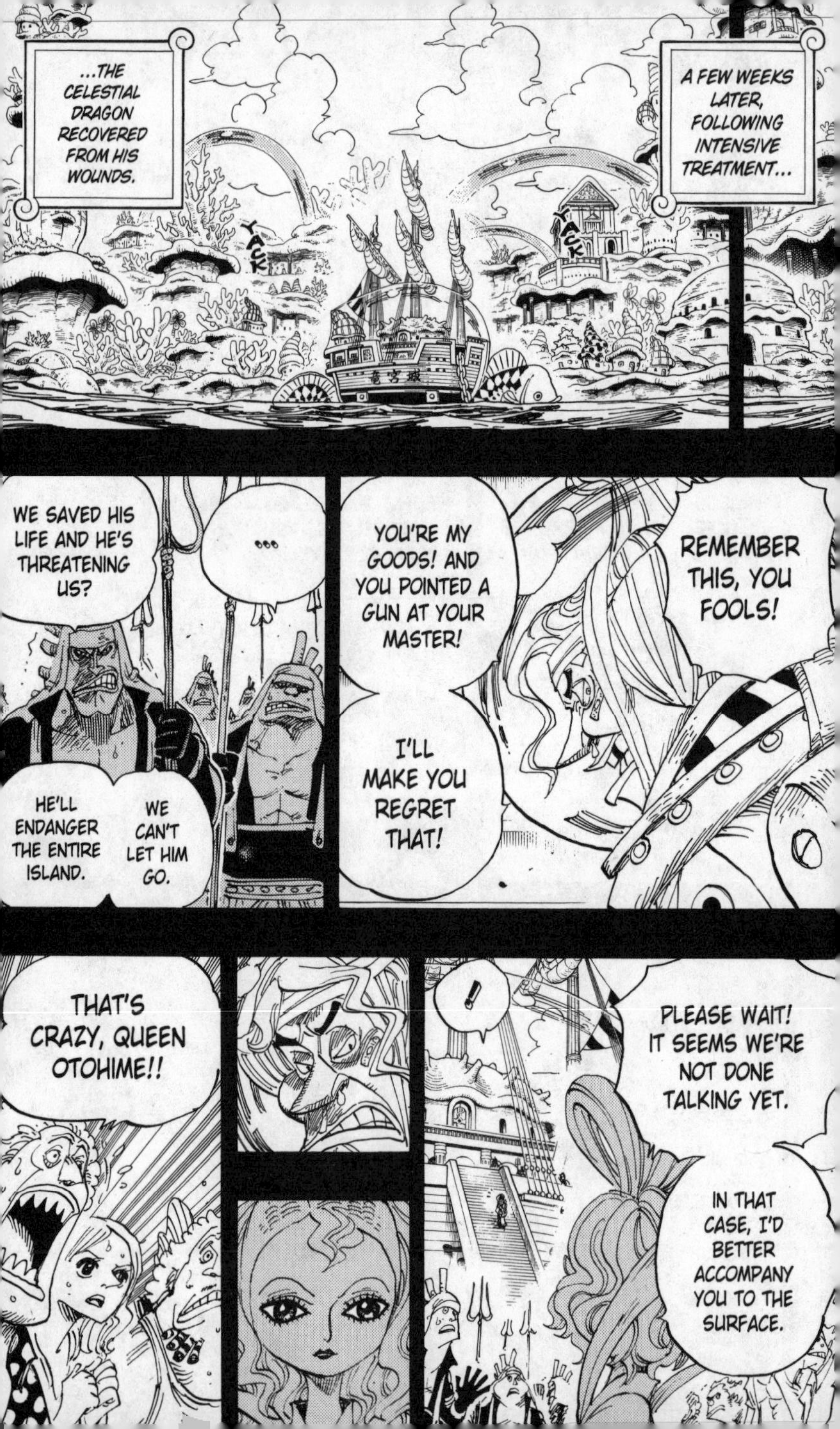
A FEW WEEKS LATER, FOLLOWING INTENSIVE TREATMENT...
...THE CELESTIAL DRAGON RECOVERED FROM HIS WOUNDS.
YACK
YACK
REMEMBER THIS, YOU FOOLS!
YOU'RE MY GOODS! AND YOU POINTED A GUN AT YOUR MASTER!
I'LL MAKE YOU REGRET THAT!
...
WE SAVED HIS LIFE AND HE'S THREATENING US?
WE CAN'T LET HIM GO.
HE'LL ENDANGER THE ENTIRE ISLAND.
!
PLEASE WAIT! IT SEEMS WE'RE NOT DONE TALKING YET.
IN THAT CASE, I'D BETTER ACCOMPANY YOU TO THE SURFACE.
THAT'S CRAZY, QUEEN OTOHIME!!

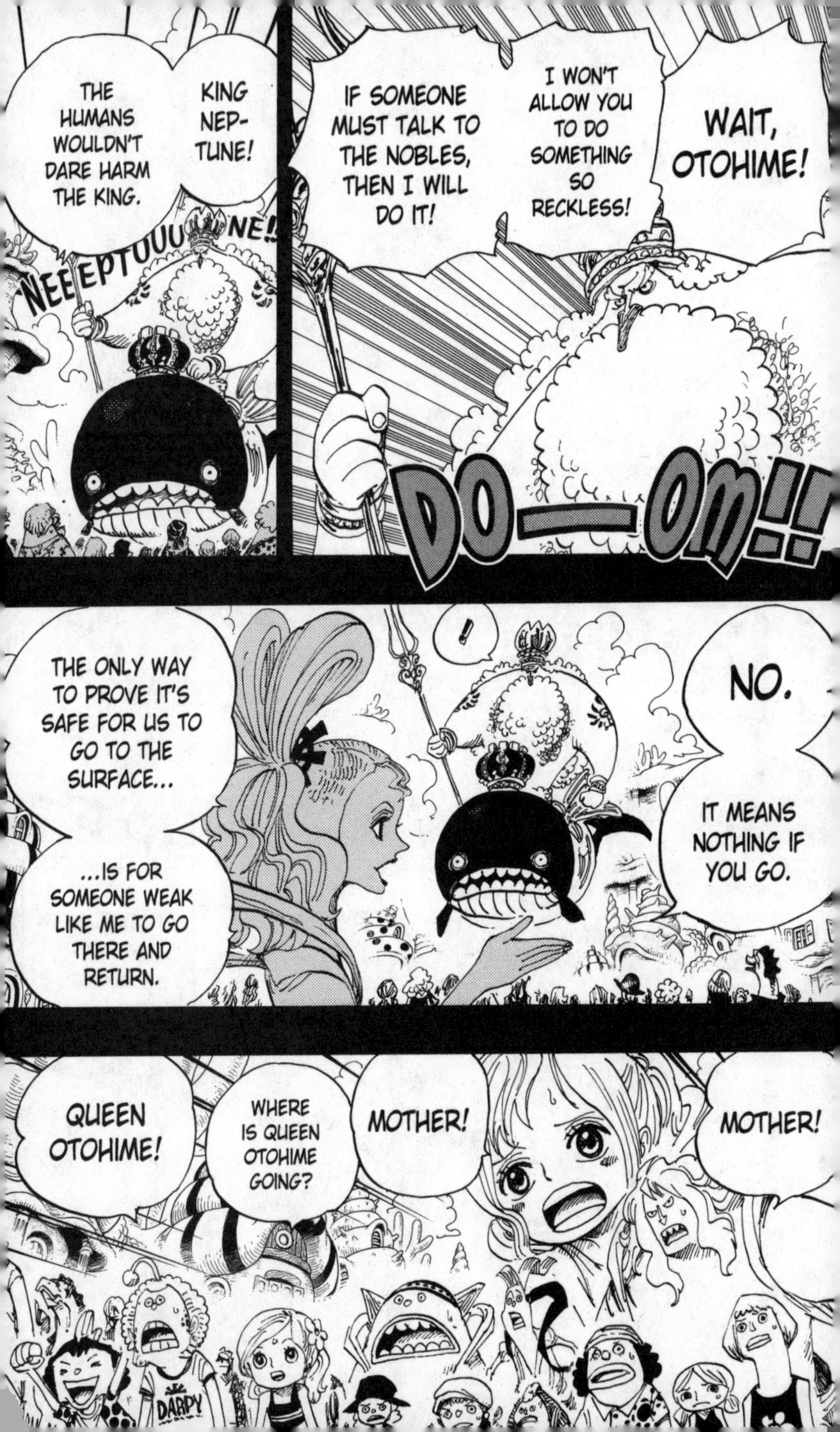
WAIT, OTOHIME!
I WON'T ALLOW YOU TO DO SOMETHING SO RECKLESS!
IF SOMEONE MUST TALK TO THE NOBLES, THEN I WILL DO IT!
DO—OM!!
KING NEPTUNE!
THE HUMANS WOULDN'T DARE HARM THE KING.
NEEEPTOUUUNE!!
NO.
!
IT MEANS NOTHING IF YOU GO.
THE ONLY WAY TO PROVE IT'S SAFE FOR US TO GO TO THE SURFACE...
...IS FOR SOMEONE WEAK LIKE ME TO GO THERE AND RETURN.
MOTHER!
MOTHER!
WHERE IS QUEEN OTOHIME GOING?
QUEEN OTOHIME!
DARPY

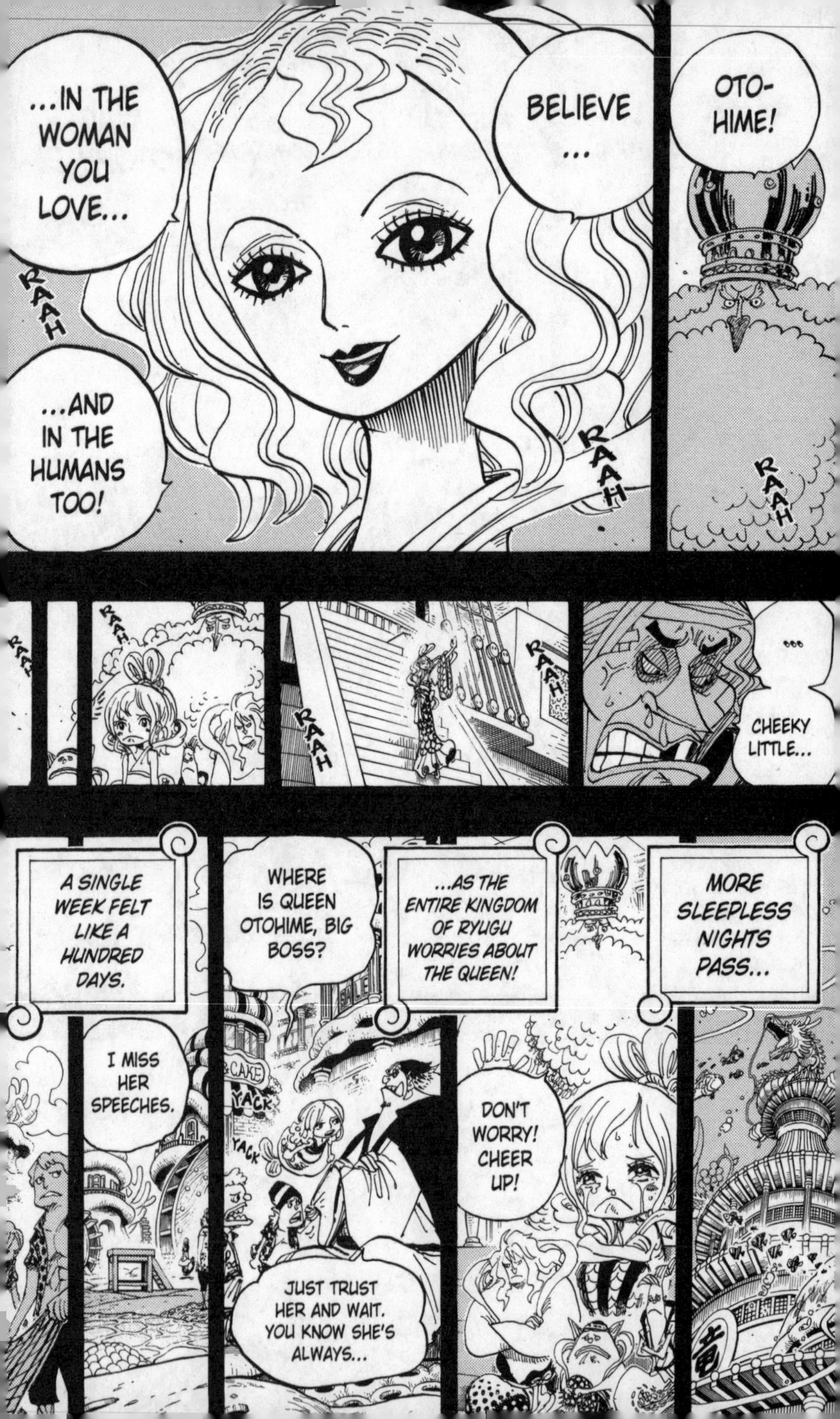
OTO-HIME!
RAAH
BELIEVE ...
...IN THE WOMAN YOU LOVE...
...AND IN THE HUMANS TOO!
RAAH
RAAH
...
CHEEKY LITTLE...
RAAH
RAAH
RAAH
RAAH
MORE SLEEPLESS NIGHTS PASS...
...AS THE ENTIRE KINGDOM OF RYUGU WORRIES ABOUT THE QUEEN!
DON'T WORRY! CHEER UP!
WHERE IS QUEEN OTOHIME, BIG BOSS?
JUST TRUST HER AND WAIT. YOU KNOW SHE'S ALWAYS...
YACK
YACK
&CAKE
SALE
A SINGLE WEEK FELT LIKE A HUNDRED DAYS.
I MISS HER SPEECHES.

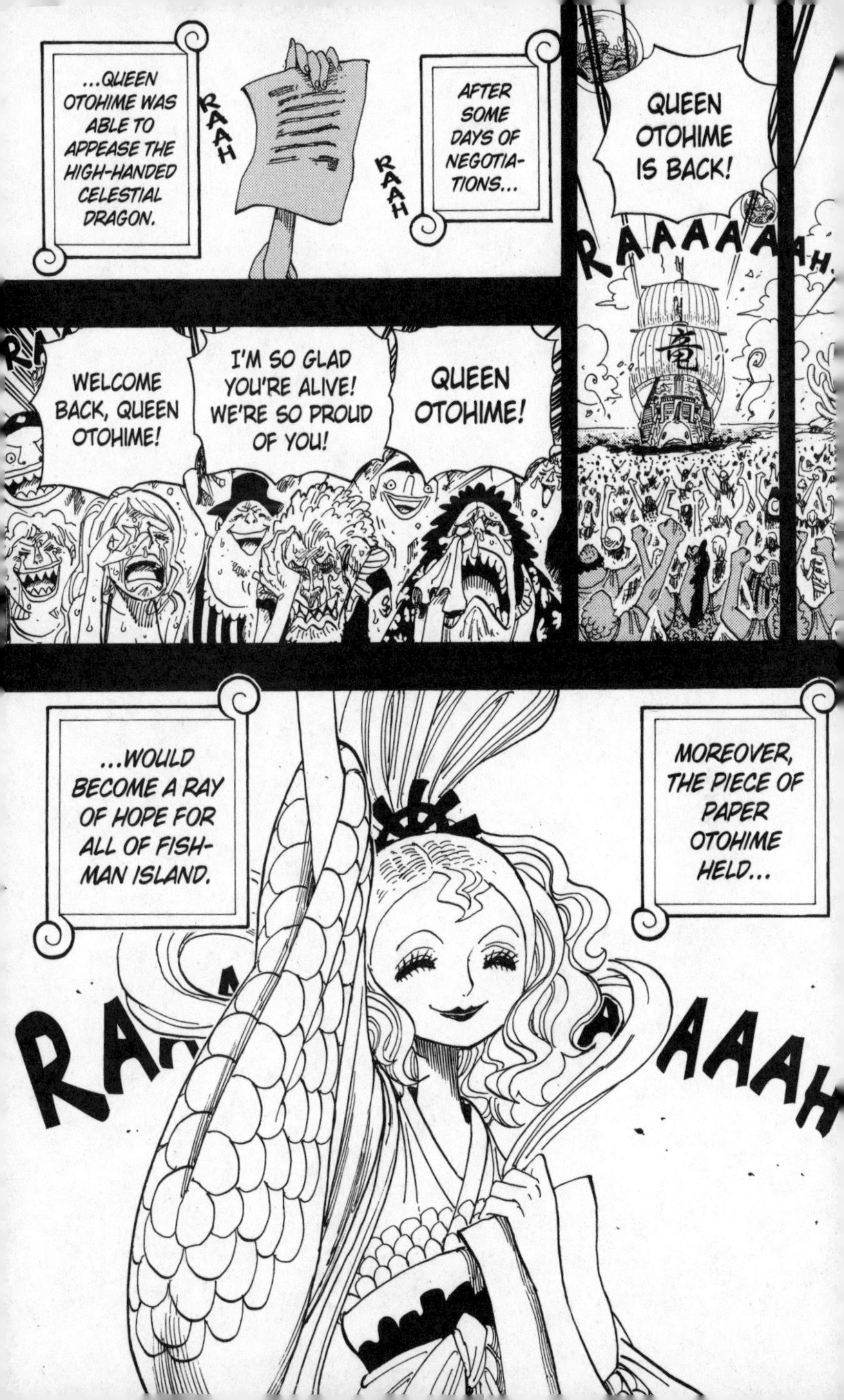
QUEEN OTOHIME IS BACK!
RAAAAAAAH.
AFTER SOME DAYS OF NEGOTIA-TIONS...
RAAH
RAAH
...QUEEN OTOHIME WAS ABLE TO APPEASE THE HIGH-HANDED CELESTIAL DRAGON.
QUEEN OTOHIME!
I'M SO GLAD YOU'RE ALIVE! WE'RE SO PROUD OF YOU!
WELCOME BACK, QUEEN OTOHIME!
MOREOVER, THE PIECE OF PAPER OTOHIME HELD...
AAAH
...WOULD BECOME A RAY OF HOPE FOR ALL OF FISH-MAN ISLAND.

vol.63
ONE PIECE

Chapter 626:
NEPTUNE BROTHERS

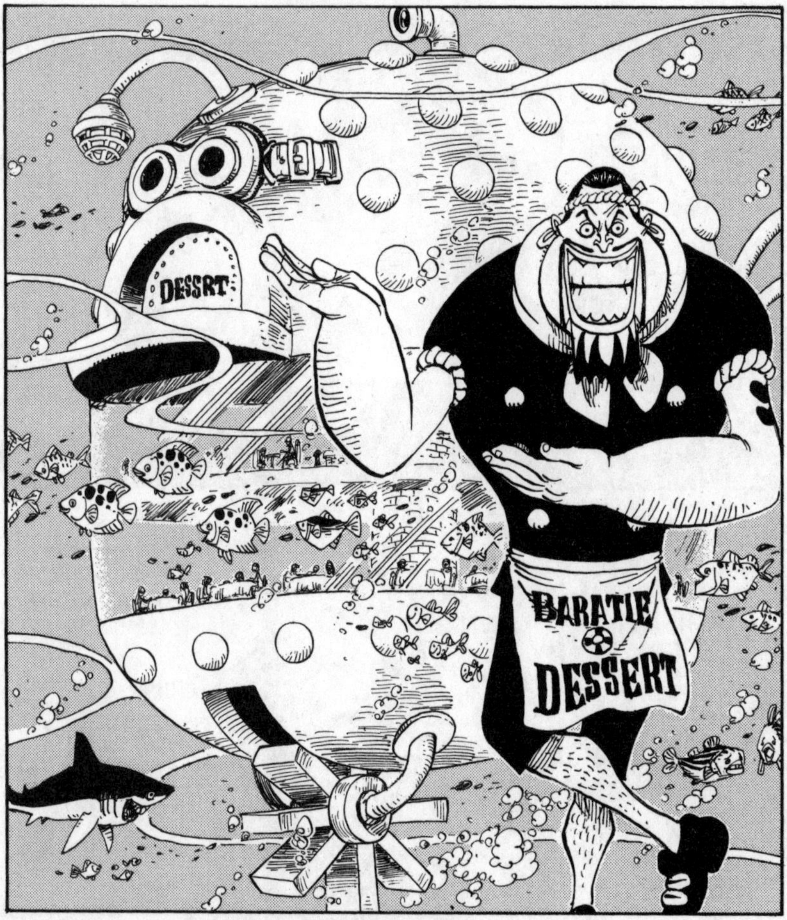

DESSRT
BARATIE
DESSERT

DECKS OF THE WORLD, VOL. 12:
"BARATIE—JOINT DESSERT SHIP: SISTER MONKFISH"

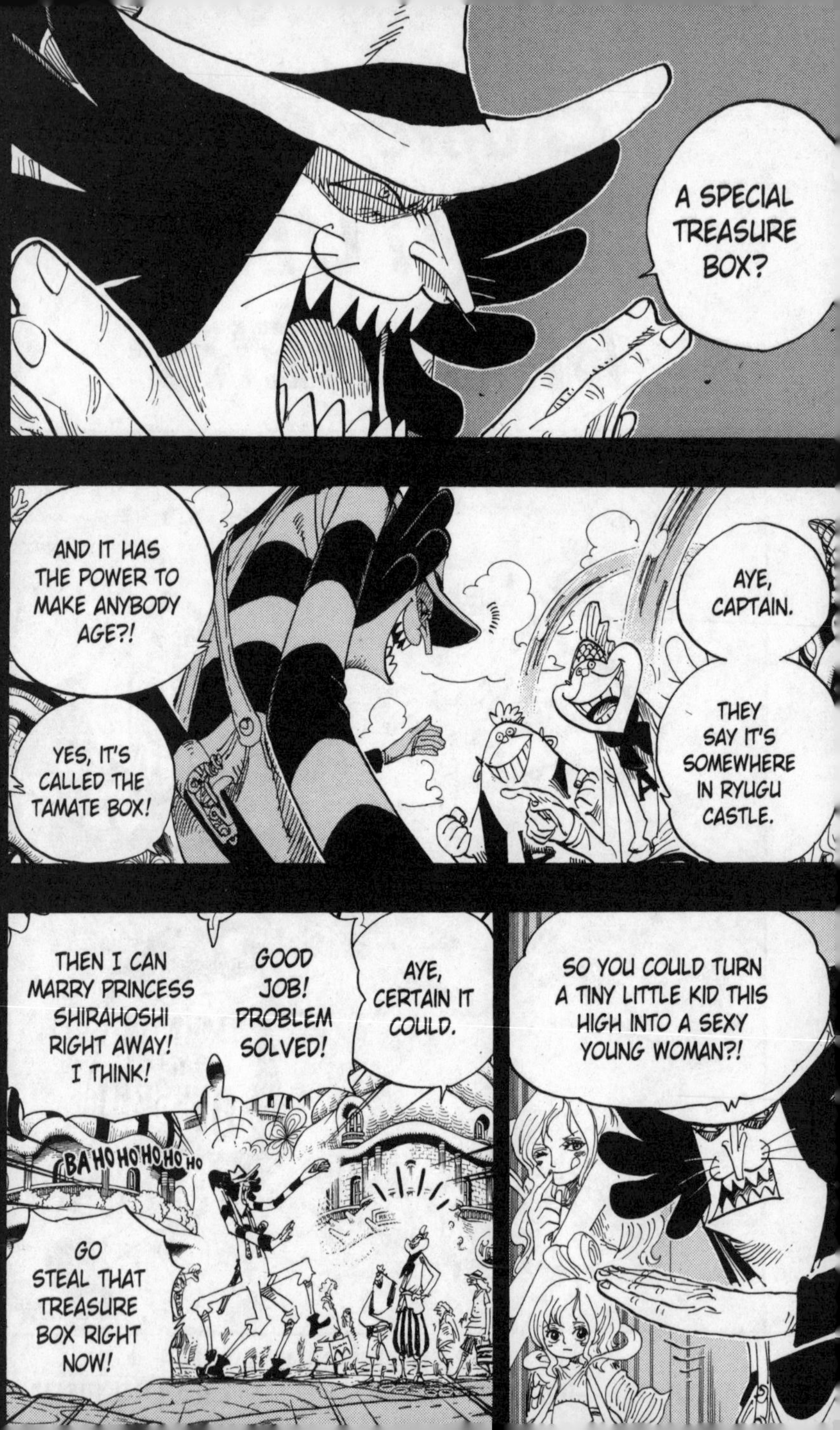
A SPECIAL TREASURE BOX?
AYE, CAPTAIN.
THEY SAY IT'S SOMEWHERE IN RYUGU CASTLE.
AND IT HAS THE POWER TO MAKE ANYBODY AGE?!
YES, IT'S CALLED THE TAMATE BOX!
SO YOU COULD TURN A TINY LITTLE KID THIS HIGH INTO A SEXY YOUNG WOMAN?!
AYE, CERTAIN IT COULD.
GOOD JOB! PROBLEM SOLVED!
THEN I CAN MARRY PRINCESS SHIRAHOSHI RIGHT AWAY! I THINK!
BAHOHOHOHOHOHO
GO STEAL THAT TREASURE BOX RIGHT NOW!

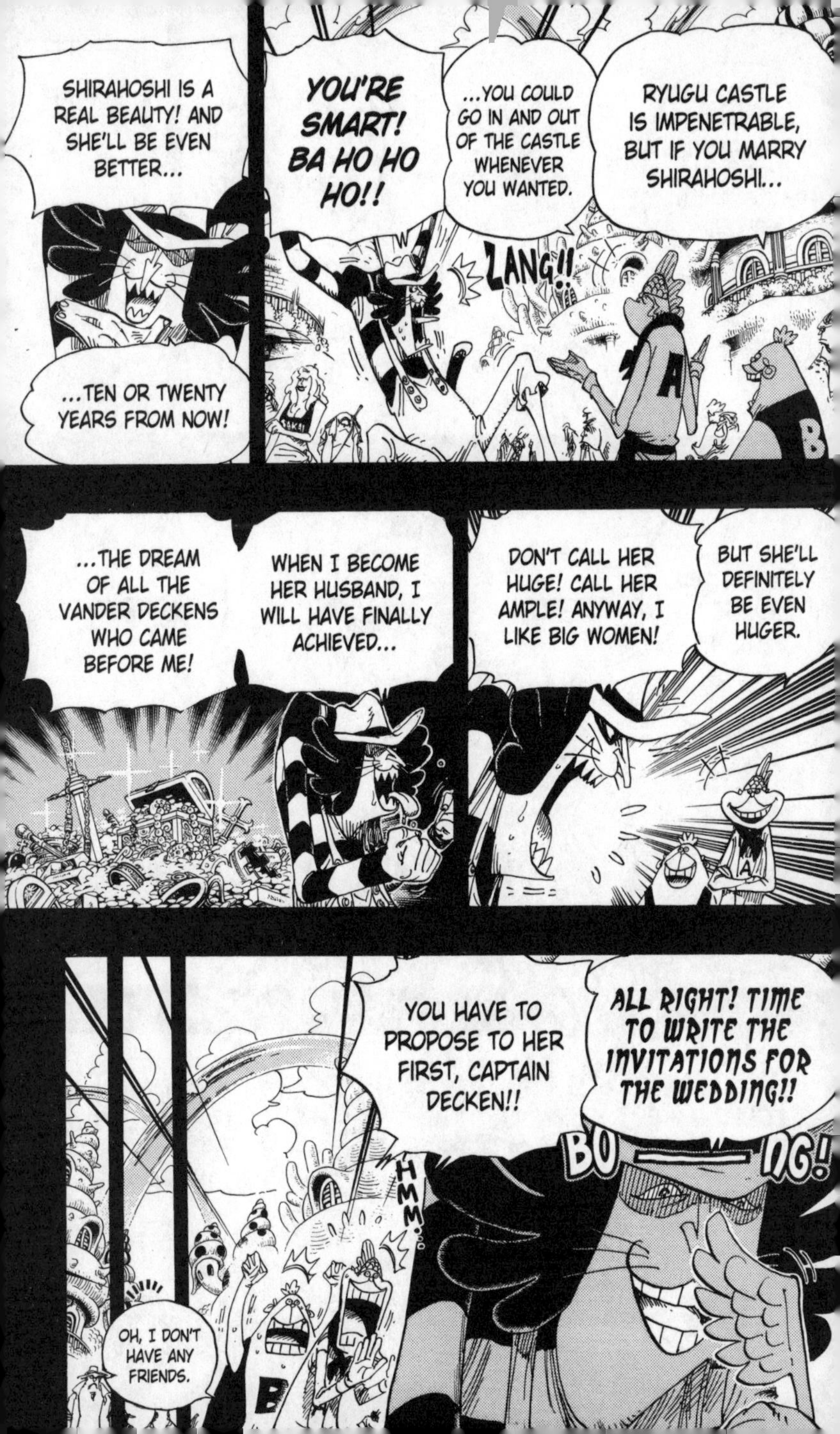
RYUGU CASTLE IS IMPENETRABLE, BUT IF YOU MARRY SHIRAHOSHI...
...YOU COULD GO IN AND OUT OF THE CASTLE WHENEVER YOU WANTED.
YOU'RE SMART! BA HO HO HO!!
ZANG!!
SHIRAHOSHI IS A REAL BEAUTY! AND SHE'LL BE EVEN BETTER...
...TEN OR TWENTY YEARS FROM NOW!
BUT SHE'LL DEFINITELY BE EVEN HUGER.
DON'T CALL HER HUGE! CALL HER AMPLE! ANYWAY, I LIKE BIG WOMEN!
WHEN I BECOME HER HUSBAND, I WILL HAVE FINALLY ACHIEVED...
...THE DREAM OF ALL THE VANDER DECKENS WHO CAME BEFORE ME!
ALL RIGHT! TIME TO WRITE THE INVITATIONS FOR THE WEDDING!!
YOU HAVE TO PROPOSE TO HER FIRST, CAPTAIN DECKEN!!
BO——NG!
HMM...
OH, I DON'T HAVE ANY FRIENDS.

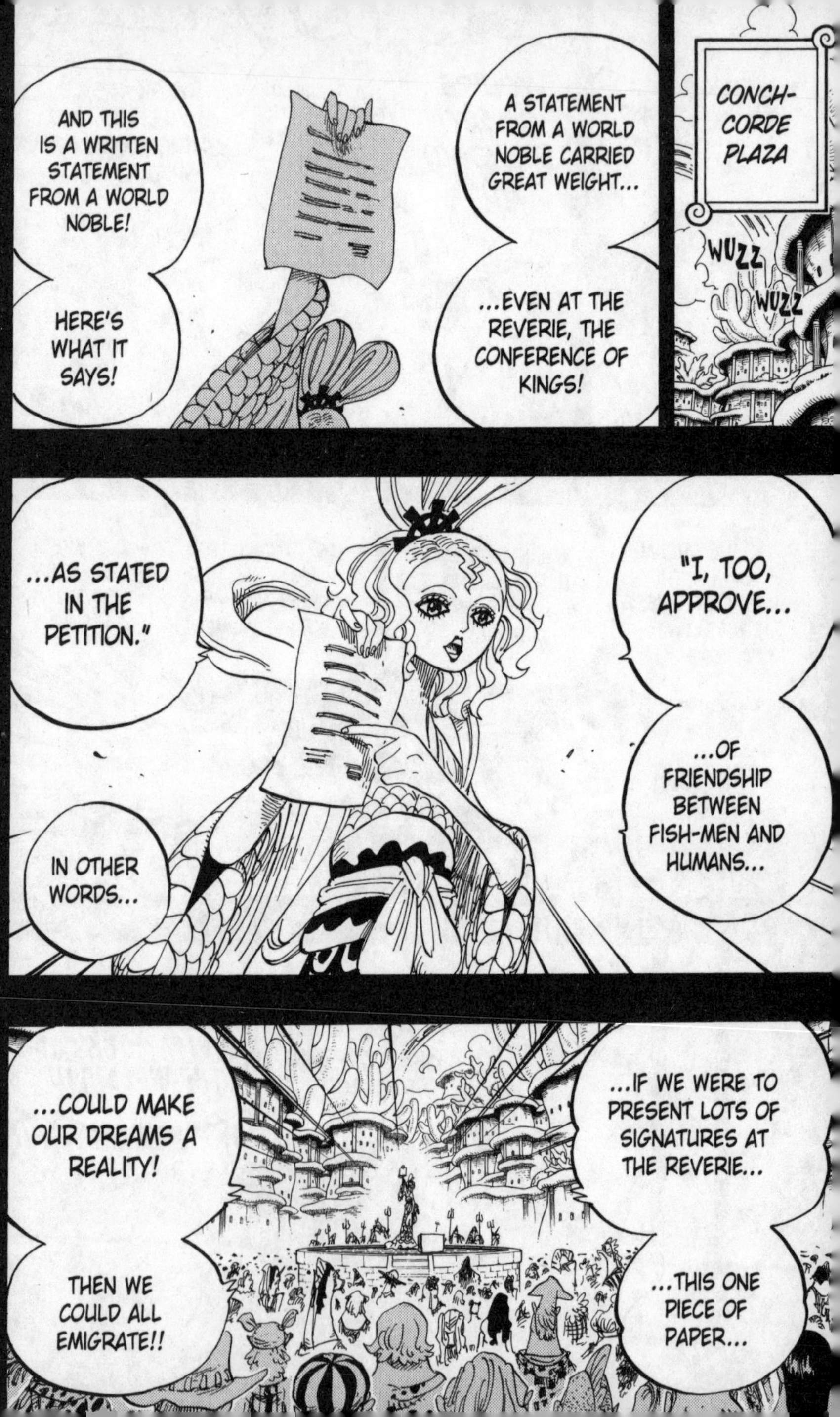
CONCH-CORDE PLAZA
WUZZ
WUZZ
A STATEMENT FROM A WORLD NOBLE CARRIED GREAT WEIGHT...
...EVEN AT THE REVERIE, THE CONFERENCE OF KINGS!
AND THIS IS A WRITTEN STATEMENT FROM A WORLD NOBLE!
HERE'S WHAT IT SAYS!
"I, TOO, APPROVE...
...OF FRIENDSHIP BETWEEN FISH-MEN AND HUMANS...
...AS STATED IN THE PETITION."
IN OTHER WORDS...
...IF WE WERE TO PRESENT LOTS OF SIGNATURES AT THE REVERIE...
...THIS ONE PIECE OF PAPER...
...COULD MAKE OUR DREAMS A REALITY!
THEN WE COULD ALL EMIGRATE!!

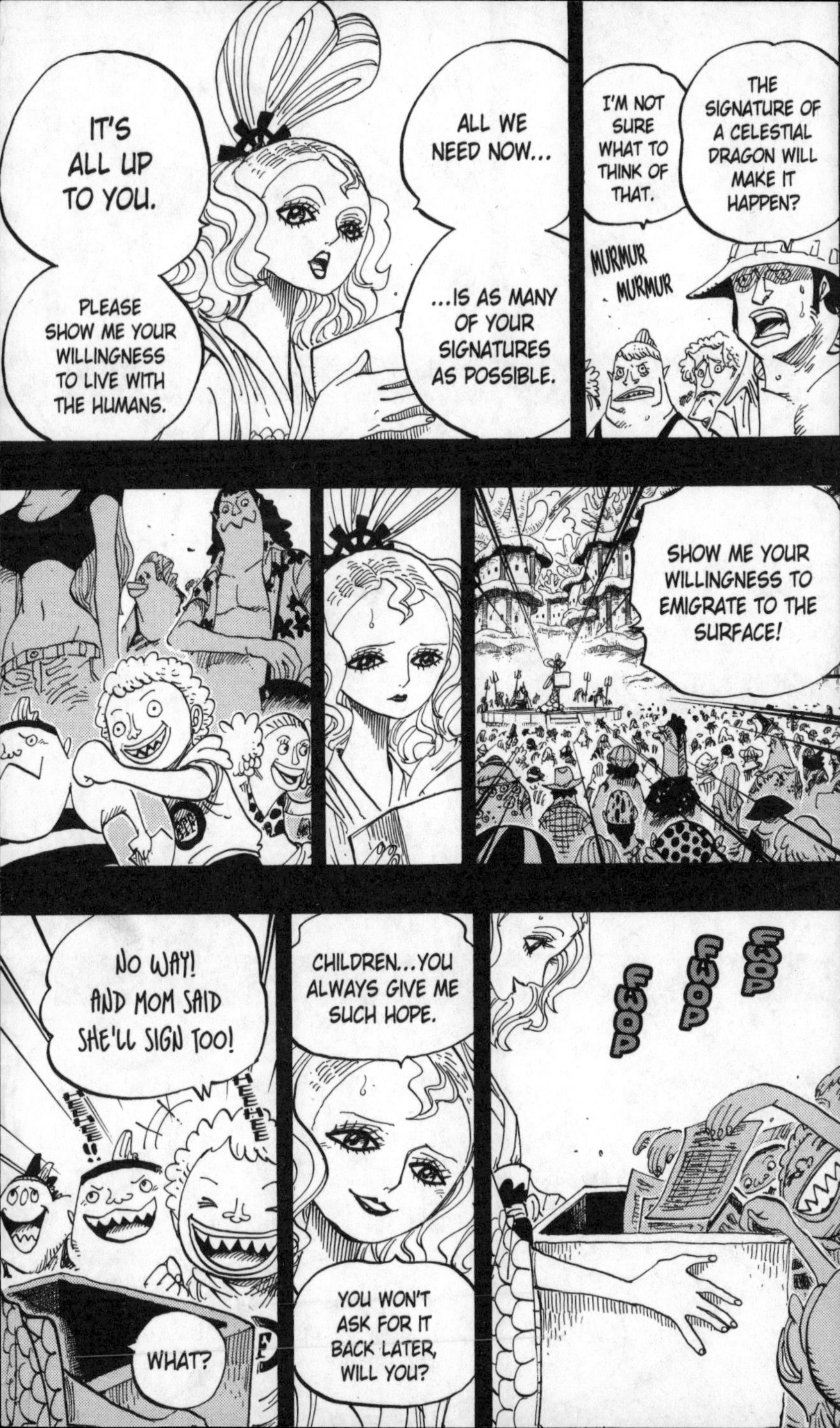
THE SIGNATURE OF A CELESTIAL DRAGON WILL MAKE IT HAPPEN?
I'M NOT SURE WHAT TO THINK OF THAT.
MURMUR MURMUR
ALL WE NEED NOW...
...IS AS MANY OF YOUR SIGNATURES AS POSSIBLE.
IT'S ALL UP TO YOU.
PLEASE SHOW ME YOUR WILLINGNESS TO LIVE WITH THE HUMANS.
SHOW ME YOUR WILLINGNESS TO EMIGRATE TO THE SURFACE!
FWOP FWOP FWOP
CHILDREN...YOU ALWAYS GIVE ME SUCH HOPE.
YOU WON'T ASK FOR IT BACK LATER, WILL YOU?
NO WAY! AND MOM SAID SHE'LL SIGN TOO!
HEEHEE
HEEHEE!!
WHAT?

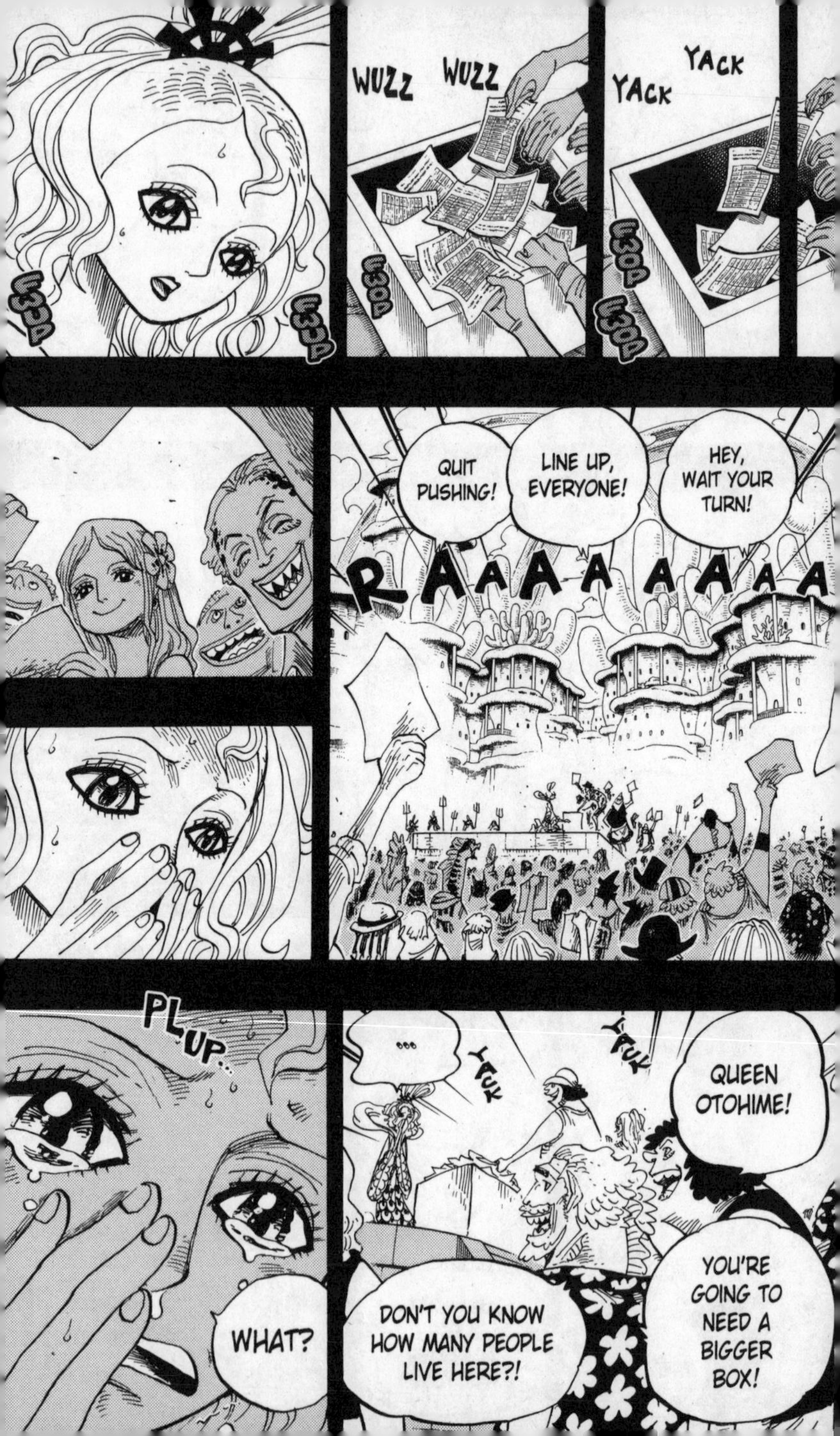
YACK
YACK
FWOP
FWOP
WUZZ
WUZZ
FWOP
FWUP
FWUP
HEY, WAIT YOUR TURN!
LINE UP, EVERYONE!
QUIT PUSHING!
RAAAAAAAA
QUEEN OTOHIME!
...
YOU'RE GOING TO NEED A BIGGER BOX!
DON'T YOU KNOW HOW MANY PEOPLE LIVE HERE?!
PLUP...
WHAT?

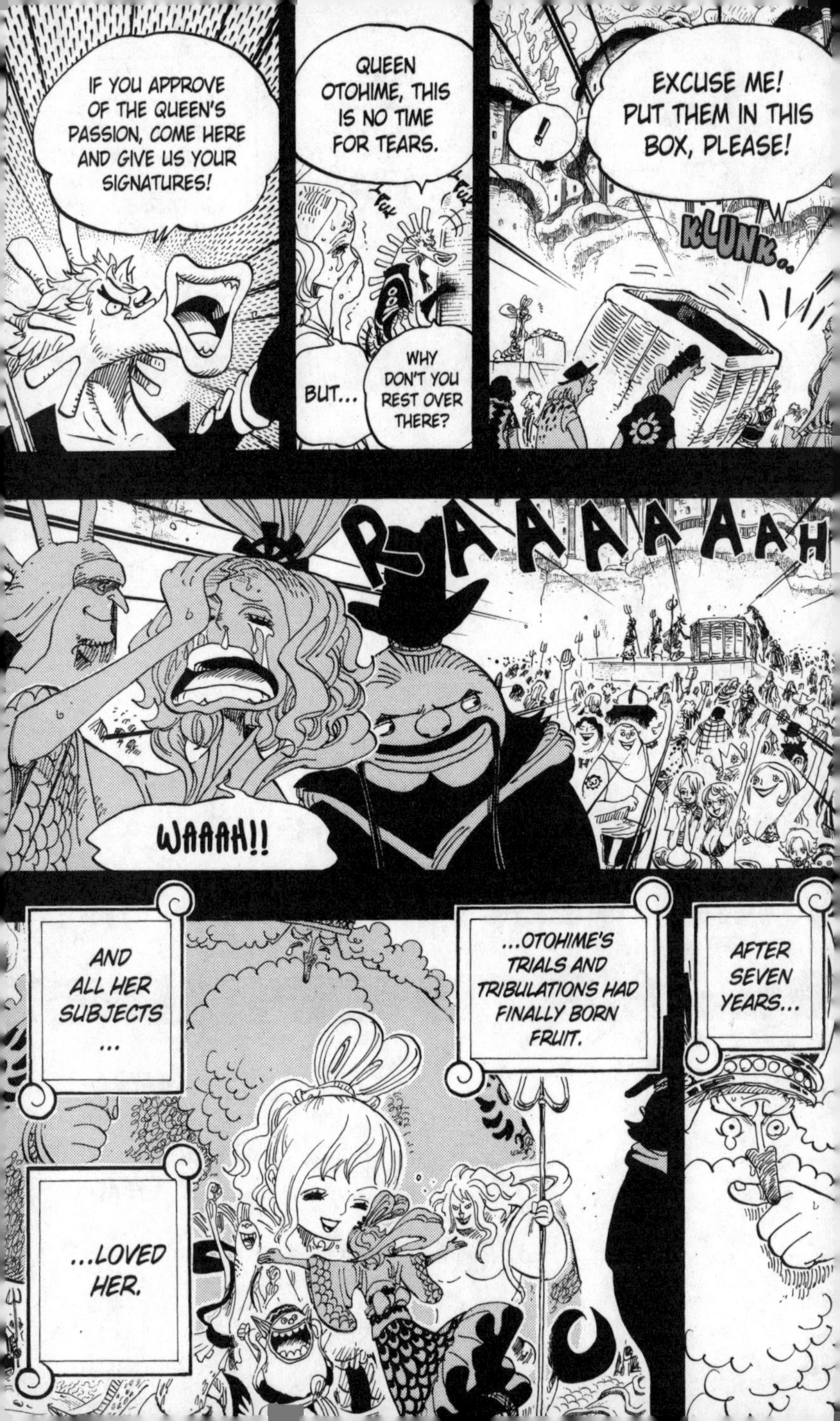
!
EXCUSE ME! PUT THEM IN THIS BOX, PLEASE!
KLUNK..
QUEEN OTOHIME, THIS IS NO TIME FOR TEARS.
WHY DON'T YOU REST OVER THERE?
BUT...
IF YOU APPROVE OF THE QUEEN'S PASSION, COME HERE AND GIVE US YOUR SIGNATURES!
RAAAAAAH
WAAAH!!
AFTER SEVEN YEARS...
...OTOHIME'S TRIALS AND TRIBULATIONS HAD FINALLY BORN FRUIT.
AND ALL HER SUBJECTS ...
...LOVED HER.

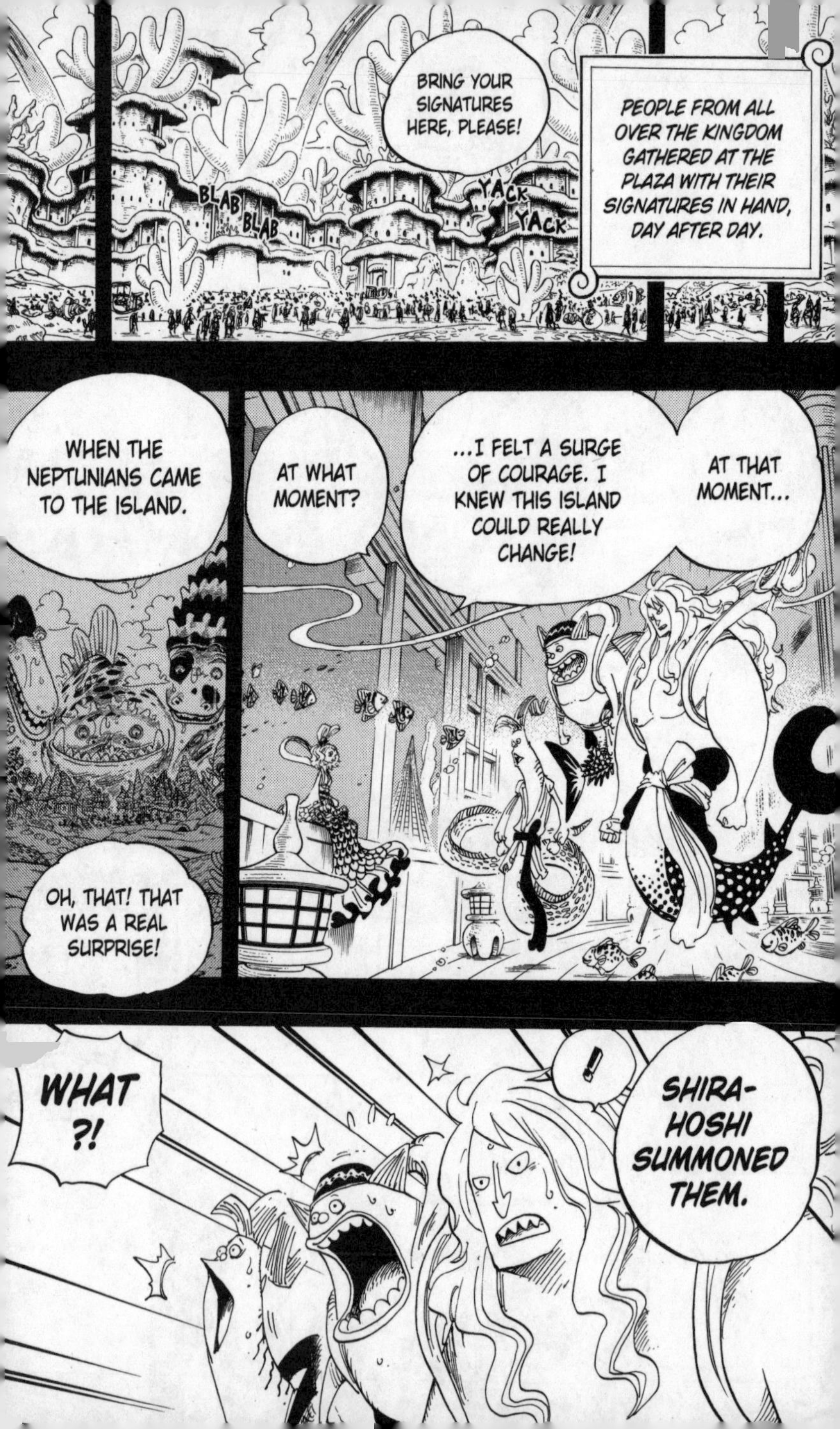

PEOPLE FROM ALL OVER THE KINGDOM GATHERED AT THE PLAZA WITH THEIR SIGNATURES IN HAND, DAY AFTER DAY.
BRING YOUR SIGNATURES HERE, PLEASE!
YACK YACK
BLAB BLAB
AT THAT MOMENT...
...I FELT A SURGE OF COURAGE. I KNEW THIS ISLAND COULD REALLY CHANGE!
AT WHAT MOMENT?
WHEN THE NEPTUNIANS CAME TO THE ISLAND.
OH, THAT! THAT WAS A REAL SURPRISE!
SHIRA-HOSHI SUMMONED THEM.
!
WHAT?!

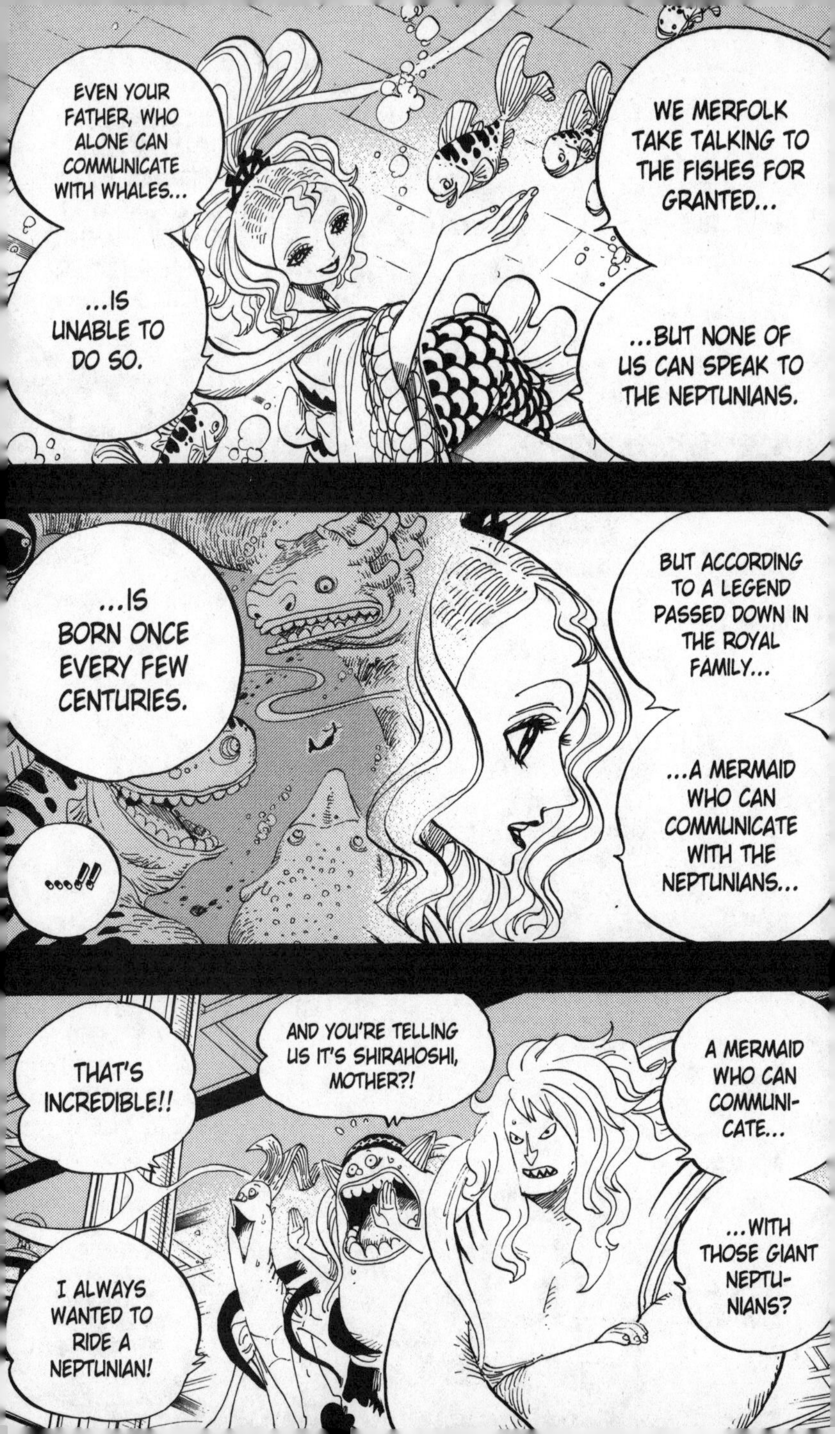
WE MERFOLK TAKE TALKING TO THE FISHES FOR GRANTED...
...BUT NONE OF US CAN SPEAK TO THE NEPTUNIANS.
EVEN YOUR FATHER, WHO ALONE CAN COMMUNICATE WITH WHALES...
...IS UNABLE TO DO SO.
BUT ACCORDING TO A LEGEND PASSED DOWN IN THE ROYAL FAMILY...
...A MERMAID WHO CAN COMMUNICATE WITH THE NEPTUNIANS...
...IS BORN ONCE EVERY FEW CENTURIES.
...!!
A MERMAID WHO CAN COMMUNI-CATE...
...WITH THOSE GIANT NEPTU-NIANS?
AND YOU'RE TELLING US IT'S SHIRAHOSHI, MOTHER?!
THAT'S INCREDIBLE!!
I ALWAYS WANTED TO RIDE A NEPTUNIAN!

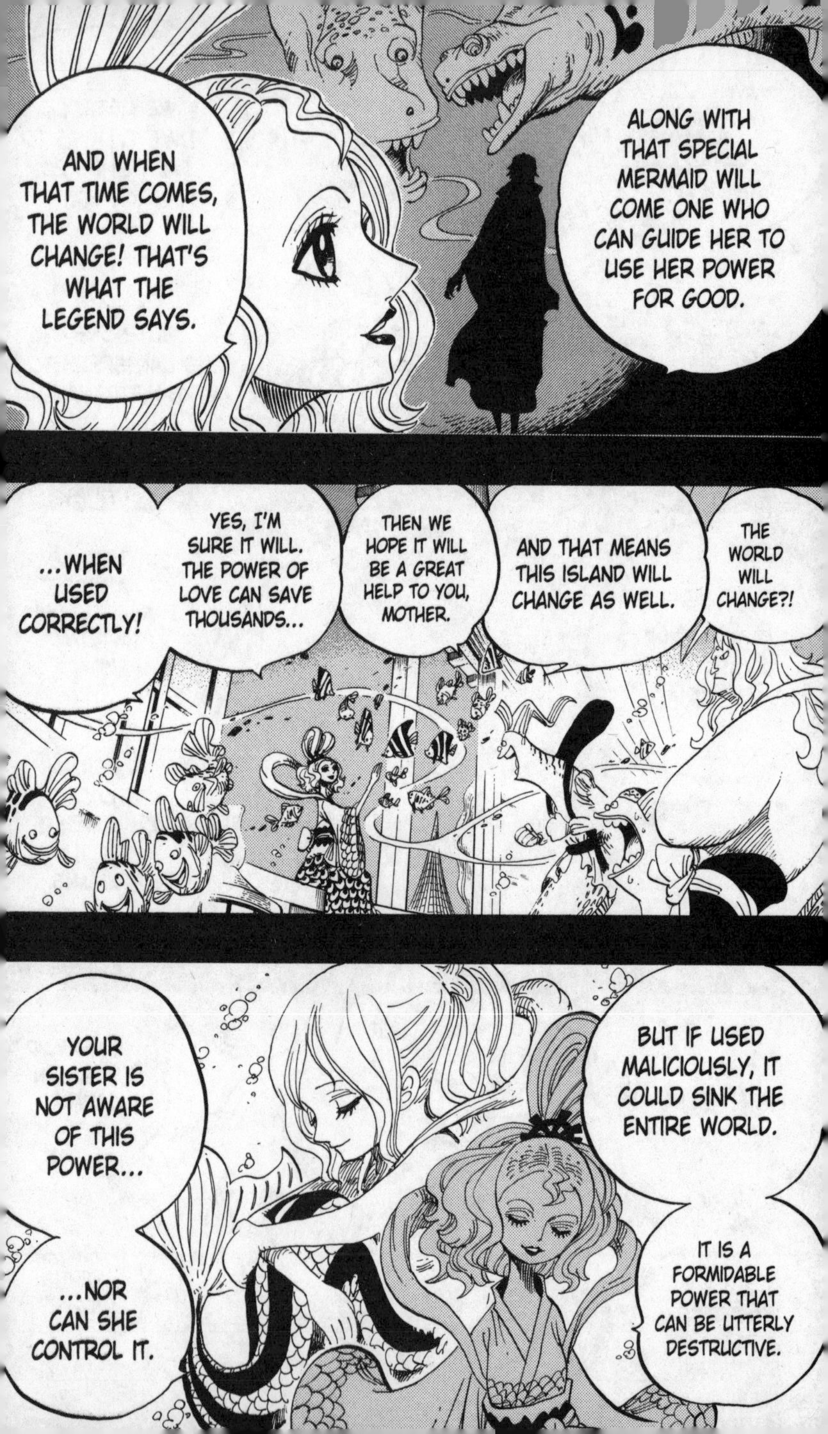
ALONG WITH THAT SPECIAL MERMAID WILL COME ONE WHO CAN GUIDE HER TO USE HER POWER FOR GOOD.
AND WHEN THAT TIME COMES, THE WORLD WILL CHANGE! THAT'S WHAT THE LEGEND SAYS.
THE WORLD WILL CHANGE?!
AND THAT MEANS THIS ISLAND WILL CHANGE AS WELL.
THEN WE HOPE IT WILL BE A GREAT HELP TO YOU, MOTHER.
YES, I'M SURE IT WILL. THE POWER OF LOVE CAN SAVE THOUSANDS...
...WHEN USED CORRECTLY!
BUT IF USED MALICIOUSLY, IT COULD SINK THE ENTIRE WORLD.
IT IS A FORMIDABLE POWER THAT CAN BE UTTERLY DESTRUCTIVE.
YOUR SISTER IS NOT AWARE OF THIS POWER...
...NOR CAN SHE CONTROL IT.

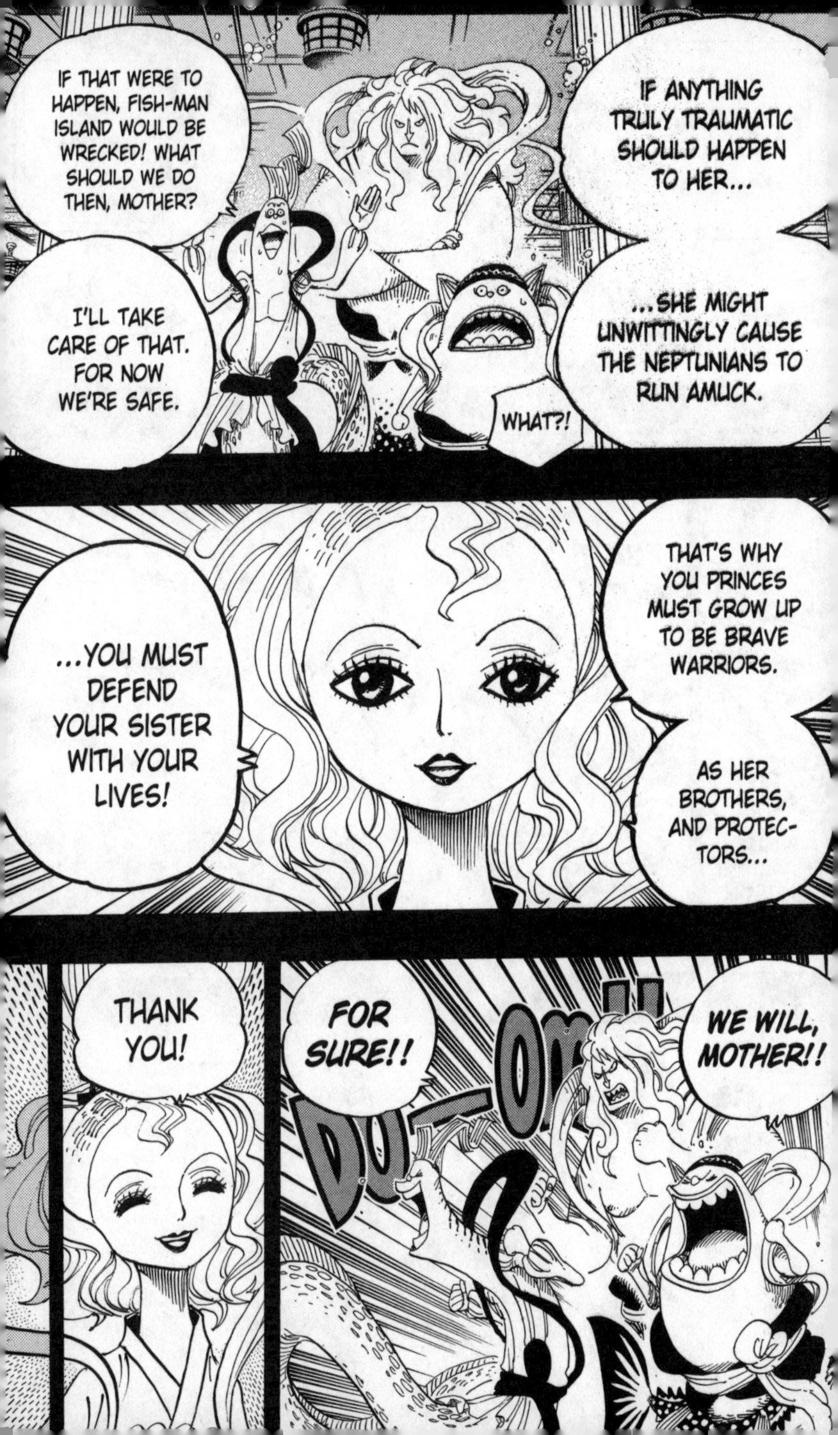
IF ANYTHING TRULY TRAUMATIC SHOULD HAPPEN TO HER...
...SHE MIGHT UNWITTINGLY CAUSE THE NEPTUNIANS TO RUN AMUCK.
WHAT?!
IF THAT WERE TO HAPPEN, FISH-MAN ISLAND WOULD BE WRECKED! WHAT SHOULD WE DO THEN, MOTHER?
I'LL TAKE CARE OF THAT. FOR NOW WE'RE SAFE.
THAT'S WHY YOU PRINCES MUST GROW UP TO BE BRAVE WARRIORS.
AS HER BROTHERS, AND PROTECTORS...
...YOU MUST DEFEND YOUR SISTER WITH YOUR LIVES!
WE WILL, MOTHER!!
FOR SURE!!
DO-OM!!
THANK YOU!

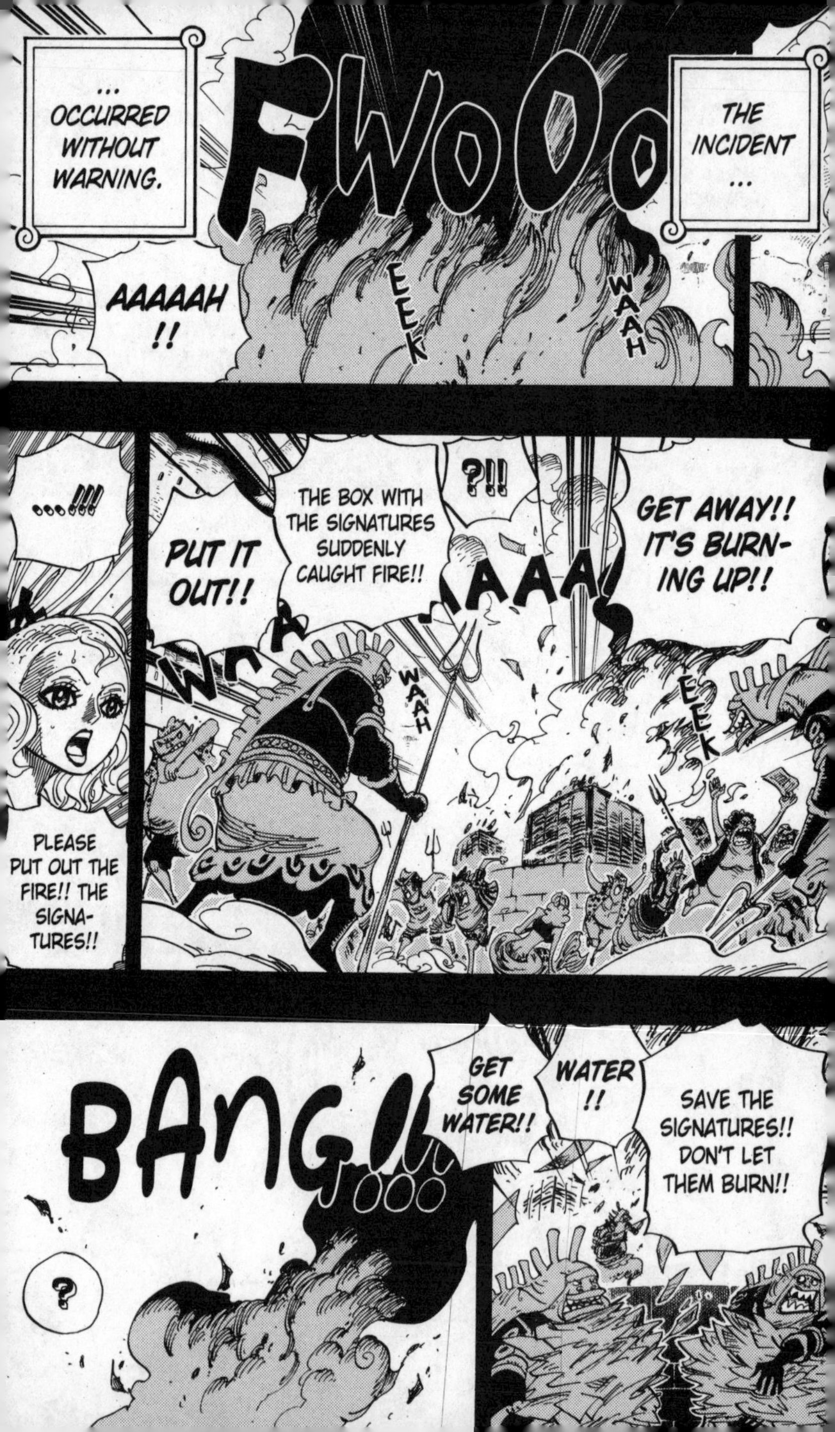
THE INCIDENT ...
... OCCURRED WITHOUT WARNING.
FWOOO
WAAH
EEK
AAAAAH!!
GET AWAY!! IT'S BURNING UP!!
?!!
THE BOX WITH THE SIGNATURES SUDDENLY CAUGHT FIRE!!
AAAA
PUT IT OUT!!
WAAH
EEK
...!!!
PLEASE PUT OUT THE FIRE!! THE SIGNATURES!!
SAVE THE SIGNATURES!! DON'T LET THEM BURN!!
WATER!!
GET SOME WATER!!
BANG!!
?

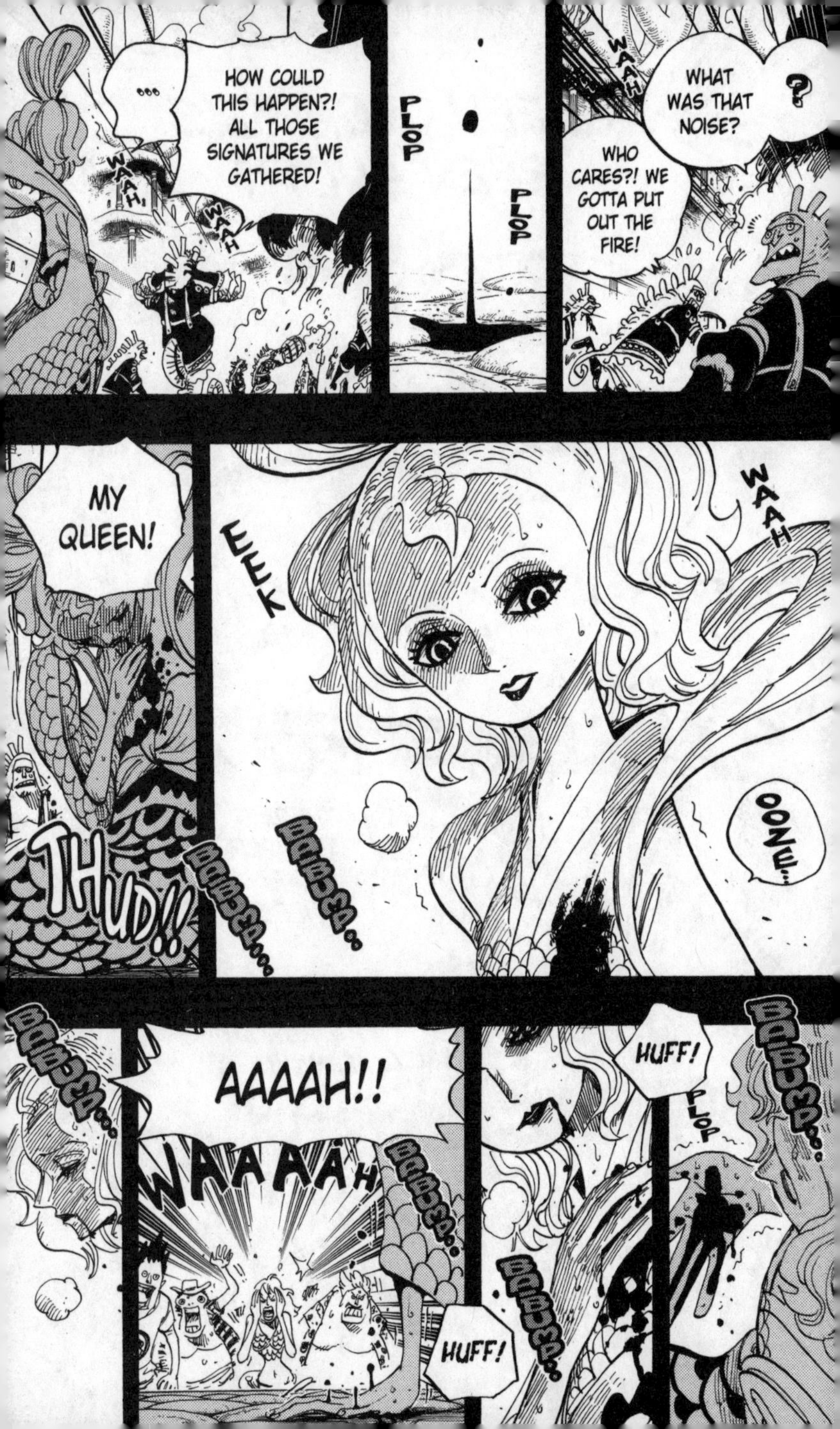
WAAH
WHAT WAS THAT NOISE?
?
WHO CARES?! WE GOTTA PUT OUT THE FIRE!
PLOP
PLOP
...
HOW COULD THIS HAPPEN?! ALL THOSE SIGNATURES WE GATHERED!
WAAH,
WAAH
WAAH
EEK
OOZE...
BABUMP...
MY QUEEN!
THUD!!
BABUMP...
BABUMP...
HUFF!
PLOP
BABUMP...
BABUMP...
HUFF!
AAAAH!!
WAAAAAH
BABUMP...

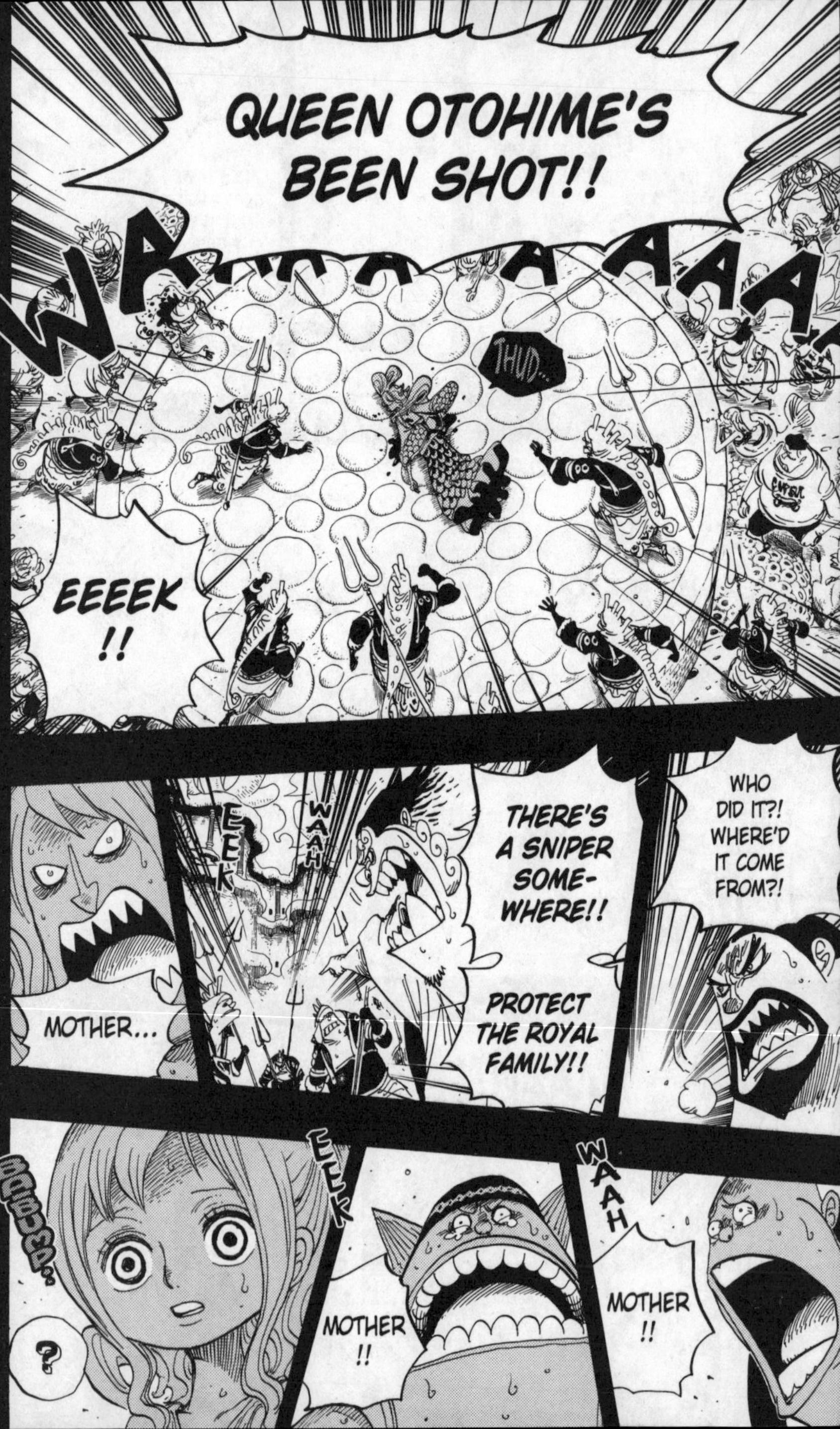

QUEEN OTOHIME'S BEEN SHOT!!
WAAAAAAAA
THUD...
EEEEK !!
WHO DID IT?! WHERE'D IT COME FROM?!
THERE'S A SNIPER SOME-WHERE!!
PROTECT THE ROYAL FAMILY!!
WAAH
EEK
MOTHER...
WAAH
MOTHER !!
EEEK
MOTHER !!
BABUMP
?

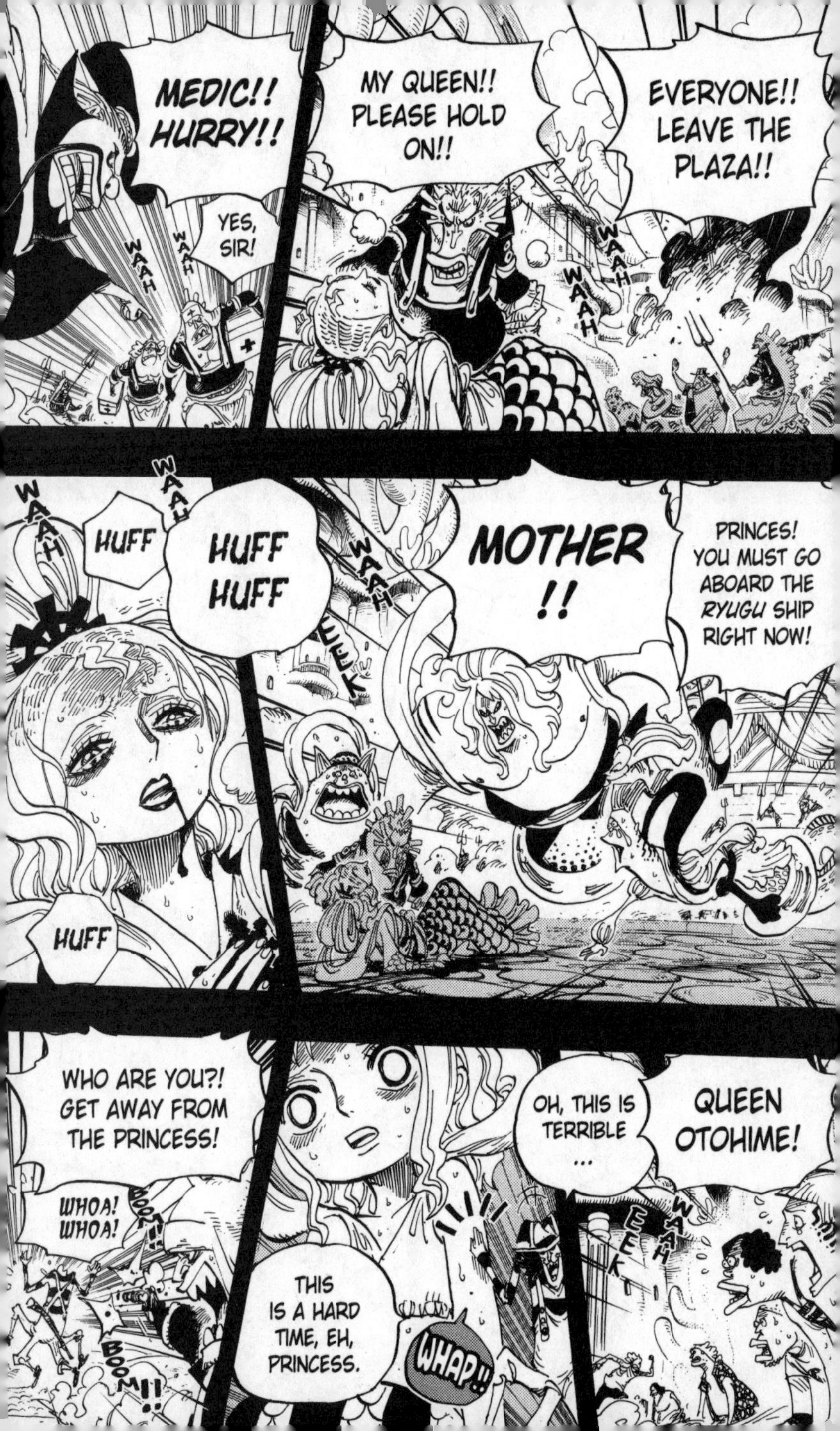
EVERYONE!! LEAVE THE PLAZA!!
MY QUEEN!! PLEASE HOLD ON!!
WAAH
WAAH
MEDIC!! HURRY!!
YES, SIR!
WAAH
WAAH
PRINCES! YOU MUST GO ABOARD THE *RYUGU* SHIP RIGHT NOW!
MOTHER !!
WAAH
EEEK
HUFF HUFF
HUFF
WAAH
WAAH
HUFF
QUEEN OTOHIME!
OH, THIS IS TERRIBLE ...
WAAH
EEEK
THIS IS A HARD TIME, EH, PRINCESS.
WHAP!!
WHO ARE YOU?! GET AWAY FROM THE PRINCESS!
WHOA! WHOA!
BOOM!!
BOOM!!

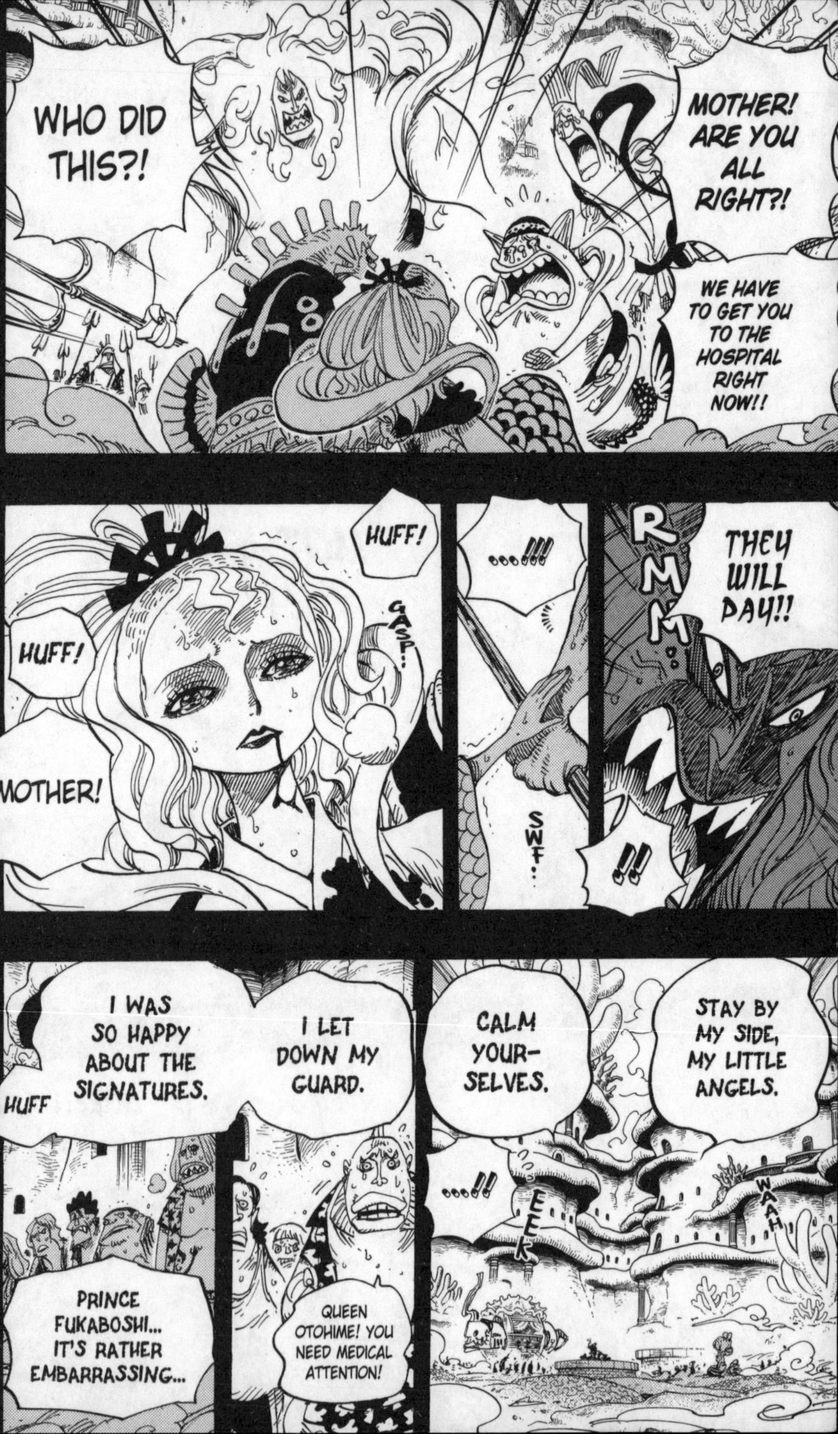
MOTHER! ARE YOU ALL RIGHT?!
WE HAVE TO GET YOU TO THE HOSPITAL RIGHT NOW!!
WHO DID THIS?!
RMM
THEY WILL PAY!!
!!
...!!!
SWF..
HUFF!
GASP!
HUFF!
MOTHER!
STAY BY MY SIDE, MY LITTLE ANGELS.
CALM YOUR-SELVES.
WAAH
EEEK
...!!
I LET DOWN MY GUARD.
QUEEN OTOHIME! YOU NEED MEDICAL ATTENTION!
I WAS SO HAPPY ABOUT THE SIGNATURES.
HUFF
PRINCE FUKABOSHI... IT'S RATHER EMBARRASSING...

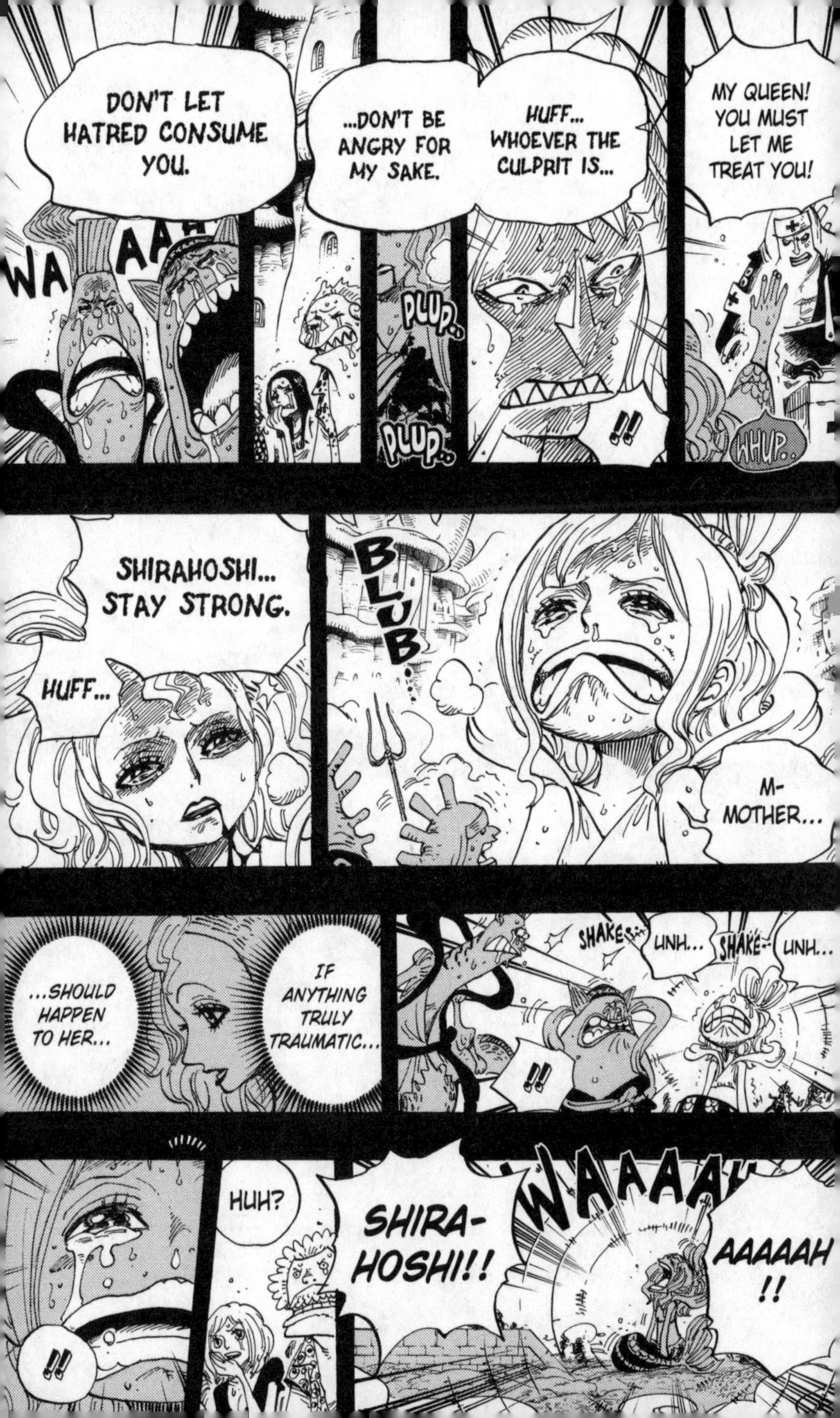
MY QUEEN! YOU MUST LET ME TREAT YOU!
WHUP..
HUFF... WHOEVER THE CULPRIT IS...
!!
...DON'T BE ANGRY FOR MY SAKE.
PLUP..
PLUP..
DON'T LET HATRED CONSUME YOU.
WAAA
BLUB...
M-MOTHER...
SHIRAHOSHI... STAY STRONG.
HUFF...
SHAKE
UNH...
SHAKE
UNH...
!!
IF ANYTHING TRULY TRAUMATIC...
...SHOULD HAPPEN TO HER...
WAAAA
AAAAAH!!
SHIRA-HOSHI!!
HUH?
!!

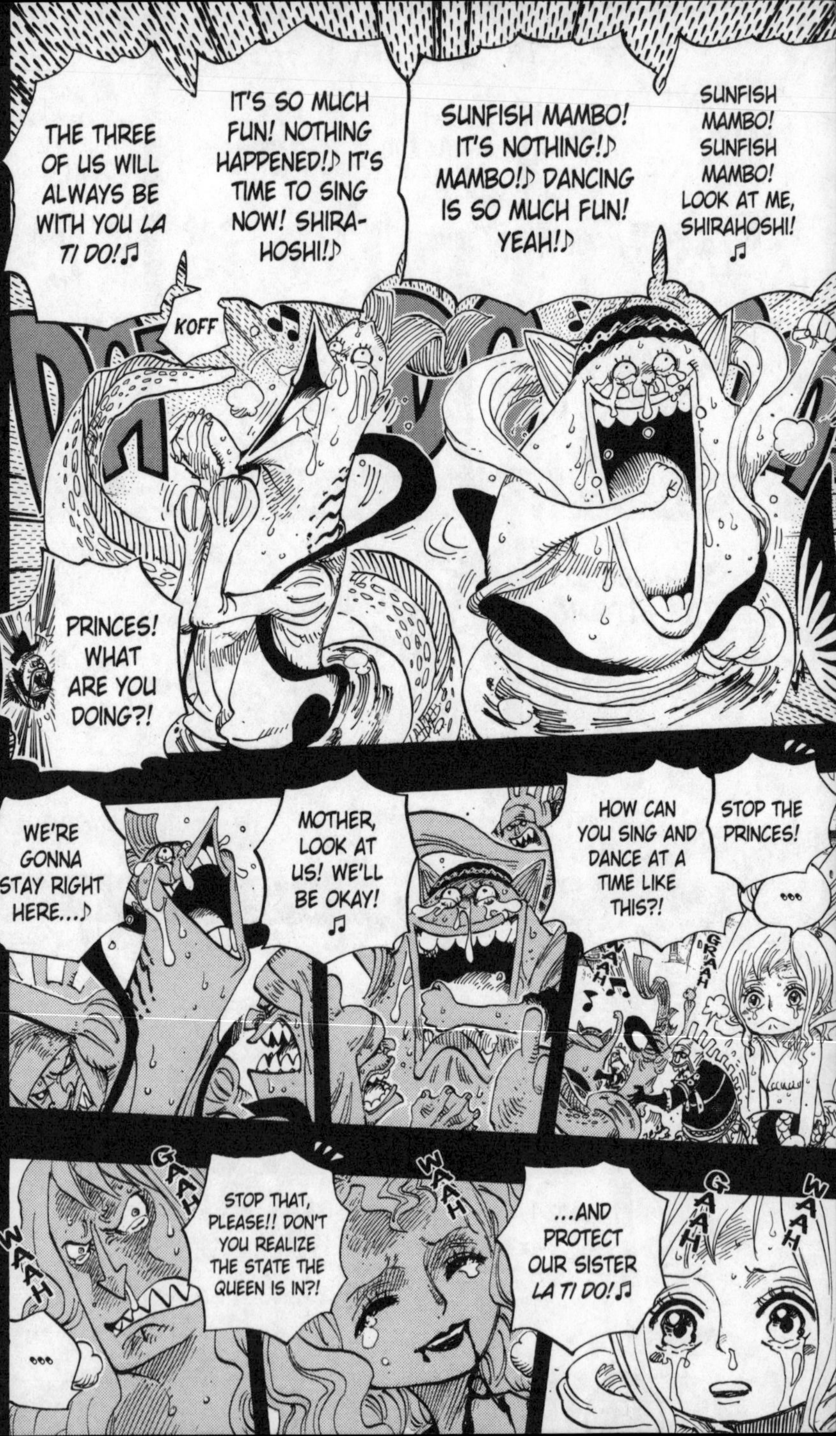
SUNFISH MAMBO! SUNFISH MAMBO! LOOK AT ME, SHIRAHOSHI! ♫
SUNFISH MAMBO! IT'S NOTHING!♪ MAMBO!♪ DANCING IS SO MUCH FUN! YEAH!♪
IT'S SO MUCH FUN! NOTHING HAPPENED!♪ IT'S TIME TO SING NOW! SHIRA-HOSHI!♪
THE THREE OF US WILL ALWAYS BE WITH YOU *LA TI DO!*♫
KOFF
PRINCES! WHAT ARE YOU DOING?!
STOP THE PRINCES!
HOW CAN YOU SING AND DANCE AT A TIME LIKE THIS?!
...
GRAAH
WAAH
MOTHER, LOOK AT US! WE'LL BE OKAY! ♫
WE'RE GONNA STAY RIGHT HERE...♪
WAAH
GAAAH
...AND PROTECT OUR SISTER *LA TI DO!*♫
WAAH
STOP THAT, PLEASE!! DON'T YOU REALIZE THE STATE THE QUEEN IS IN?!
GAAH
WAAH
...

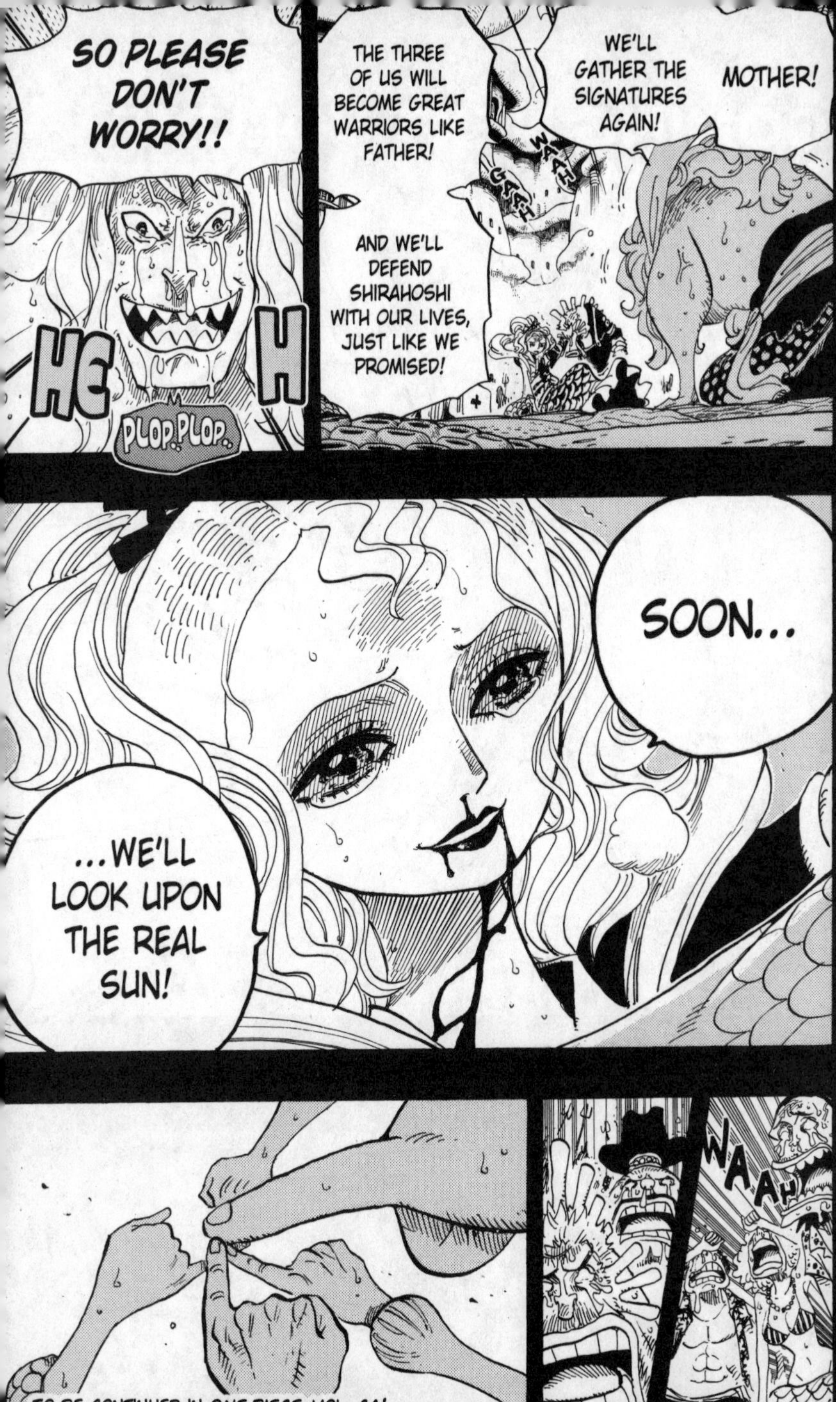
MOTHER!
WE'LL GATHER THE SIGNATURES AGAIN!
THE THREE OF US WILL BECOME GREAT WARRIORS LIKE FATHER!
WAAH
GAAH
AND WE'LL DEFEND SHIRAHOSHI WITH OUR LIVES, JUST LIKE WE PROMISED!
SO PLEASE DON'T WORRY!!
HEH
PLOP.. PLOP..
SOON...
...WE'LL LOOK UPON THE REAL SUN!
WAAAH
TO BE CONTINUED IN ONE PIECE, VOL. 64!

COMING NEXT VOLUME:

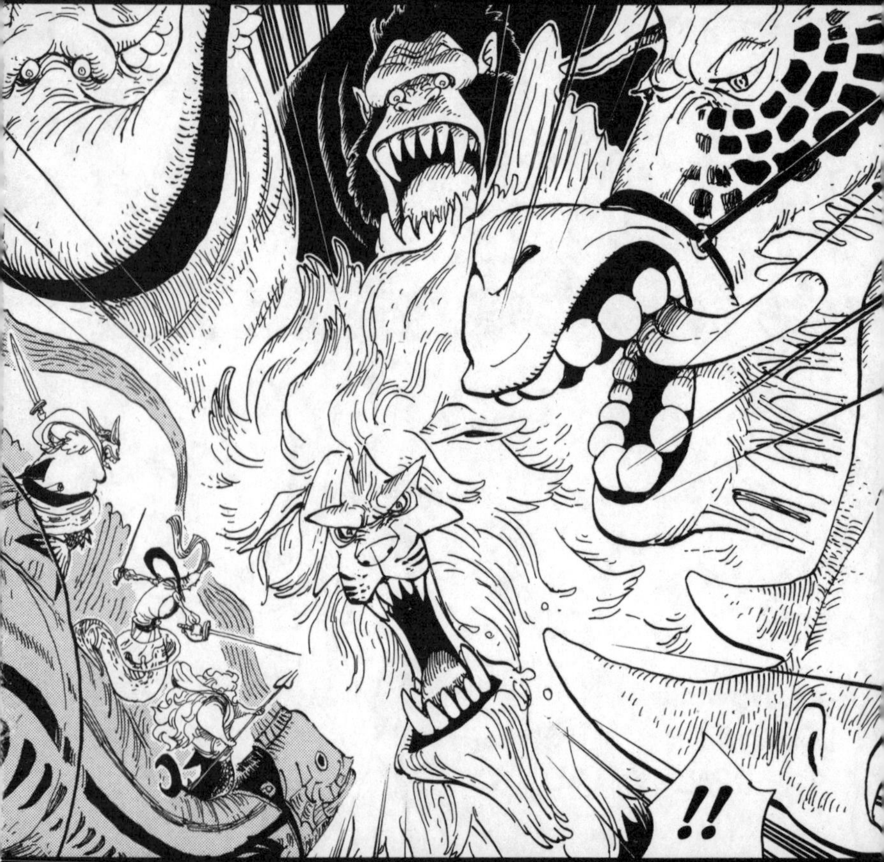
!!

Fish-Man Island is rocked by the death of their beloved queen, but who was behind the assassination? And back in the present time, Hody Jones announces himself as the new king, replacing the captured Neptune. Luffy heads in to save the people of Fish-Man Island, but a surprising person will stand in his way!

ON SALE NOW!